*Missed Opportunities*

# *Missed*

# *Opportunities*

## The Story of Canada's Broadcasting Policy

MARC RABOY

McGill-Queen's University Press
Montreal & Kingston • London • Buffalo

Printed in Canada on acid-free paper
Reprinted on paper 1992

---

**Canadian Cataloguing in Publication Data**
Raboy, Marc, 1948–
    Missed opportunities

    Includes bibliographical references.
    ISBN 0-7735-0743-4 (bound)
    ISBN 0-7735-0775-2 (pbk.)

    1. Broadcasting policy – Canada – History. I. Title.
PN1990.6.C3R32 1990      384.54'0971      C89-090415-4

---

*In memory of Sam Raboy 1912–1982*

*who taught me to*
*think critically and*
*appreciate irony*

# *Contents*

# Preface

This is not the first attempt to write about the history of Canadian broadcasting. It is, however, based on a conceptual approach and a cross-fertilization of documentary sources not present in previous studies. It is, to my knowledge, the first policy study to cover the entire period from the Royal Commission on Radio Broadcasting of 1928 up to the debate over a proposed new Broadcasting Act in 1988. It is also the first general study influenced by a perspective rooted in Quebec. Consequently, it highlights particular contradictions of Canadian broadcasting policy and brings to light information which either eluded or was inaccessible to other scholars.[1]

The emphasis here is unequivocally and almost exclusively on the evolution of Canadian broadcasting *policy*. The reader should not expect a thorough account of the development of broadcast programming or extensive biographical information on the various personalities involved. Similarly, the general sociopolitical context in which broadcasting policy has been made in Canada is only subject to allusion, on the assumption that anyone picking up such a weighty tome as this is already reasonably familiar with the broader context or has the interest and the means to seek it out. Wherever it seemed useful, appropriate secondary references have been indicated.

The book presents an openly *critical* perspective on its subject. In this sense, it is situated in an international current of communication studies that has become increasingly widespread and well-rooted in the past fifteen years or so. This current emphasizes the importance of broad social and economic forces, such as capital and state power, on the relationship that ensues between the structures, practices, and products of mass media institutions, and the audiences, communities, and active publics that make up the society in which the media operate.[2]

Increasingly, communications policy constitutes the interface between media and the public and debates over media policy frame and situate the public politics of communication. In modern society, media are the central

institutions of the public sphere – a battleground in which conflicting interpretations of reality compete with each other for the right to be taken as
representative of public opinion and the public interest. The debates surrounding media – and in the framework of contemporary Western political
culture these debates focus on policy – are thus crucial to the democratic
quality of public life.

Although limited to only one aspect of this general field – broadcasting
policy in Canada – the book is, in my view, far from narrow in scope. The
ideology, organization, and practices of broadcasting vary considerably from
country to country in Western society. But nowhere has broadcasting been
more prominent in political struggles than in Canada. In this respect, the
evolution of Canadian broadcasting can be read as a model for understanding
mass communication in twentieth-century industrial societies, just as it can
be seen as a microcosm for understanding Canadian society.

From its earliest days, broadcasting in Canada has been one of the privileged arenas of struggle over conflicting and competing notions of Canadian
society, the Canadian nation, and the Canadian public. In Canada, broadcasting has meant different things to different people at different times, from
a vehicle for the social aspirations of voluntary associations to an instrument
for nation building – not to mention a good way to make a buck. The
evolution of Canadian broadcasting has been marked by intense political
struggle and debate in which the claim to speak on behalf of a particularly
constituted public has often been a powerful weapon. Divergent and often
opposing conceptions of broadcasting and the public have varied according
to the conflicting interests of the federal government, Quebec nationalists,
private broadcasters, adult educationists, television producers, CBC executives, community activists, and other social groups.

The Canadian broadcasting system is the result of the interaction of popular
social pressure for public service broadcasting, pressure from financial interests to keep broadcasting in the commercial sector and provide favourable
conditions in which to do broadcasting business, and the political project
of maintaining "Canada" as an entity distinct from the United States of
America and united against the periodic threat of disintegration posed by
Quebec. In this sense, broadcasting has been more than a traditional means
of communication in the Canadian experience; rather, through broadcasting,
the Canadian experience has become an experience *in* communication.

The underlying theme running through the book is that the story of Canadian broadcasting illustrates the need to distinguish "national" from "public" interests – and that the tendency to confuse the two ends up turning
broadcasting into an instrument of *state* policy with all that this implies.
Thus, broadcasting policy in Canada has been made to serve the broader
political agenda of the state as its priorities change from time to time – one
day the need for national unity in the face of perceived threats of external

or internal adversity, the next day the promotion of economic development of local capitalist industry, the following day dealing with social pressures and demands for a more equitable distribution of wealth and resources.

In the process of building the Canadian system, social and cultural aspects have been consistently subordinated to economic and political interests as the public dimension has steadily diminished, stripping broadcasting of its democratic potential. At the same time, however, the Canadian experience has given rise to some potent alternatives to dominant broadcasting models which stand as real and potential examples of the role of broadcasting in social change and cultural resistance.

A dominant subtheme of the book is the pivotal role of Quebec as Ottawa's alter ego. On the one hand, Canadian broadcasting policy has often been determined by the need to contain the pressure towards national fragmentation emanating from Quebec. On the other hand, efforts to use the Quebec state to promote alternatives have mirrored Ottawa's official policy stance vis-à-vis the United States. But, as we shall see, the Quebec experience raises many of the same critical questions of political control, commercial imperative, and public exclusion as the Canadian experience.

This leads us to wonder whether the problem lies not in the way the state exercises its authority in broadcasting but in the very nature of state power itself. A good deal of care is necessary here: it is certainly not our intention to suggest a preference for the free market over regulatory mechanisms or private enterprise over public institutions. But if the Canadian broadcasting experience demonstrates anything at all, it is the need to build new, interdependent relationships between creators and publics which minimize their present mutual reliance on the centralizing and dominating tendencies of both capital and the state.

With these elements forming its conceptual framework, the book will review, in some detail, the emergence of the Canadian broadcasting system over a period of sixty years. First, Canadian broadcasting will be situated in an international context and with respect to the principal ideas around which broadcasting has developed in the Western world. Then, the evolution of Canadian broadcasting will be traced as it passes through seven more or less distinct historical phases, from 1928 to the present. Finally, the conclusions to be drawn from the Canadian experience will be utilized in an attempt to examine some alternatives.

As its title implies, the book not only presents a critique but emphasizes the "missed opportunities" that have characterized the history of Canada's broadcasting policy. This is not only a story of what might have been, because opportunities missed need not necessarily be lost. The struggles around Canadian broadcasting have left behind a wealthy store of unrealized democratic potential. Separately, each missed opportunity can be seen as an alternative path that could have been taken at a particular historical moment. Taken together they can form the starting point for considering the possibility of recreating the public dimension of broadcasting and putting it to work in the interest of democratic social life.

# Acknowledgments

This book has been published with the help of a grant from the Social Science Federation of Canada, using funds provided by the Social Sciences and Humanities Research Council of Canada. Preparation of the manuscript was assisted by a Canadian Studies Writing Award, provided by the Association for Canadian Studies through funds made available by the Canadian Studies Directorate of the Department of the Secretary of State of Canada. In an earlier incarnation, the book was a doctoral dissertation in Communications at McGill University; research for that work was facilitated by a fellowship from the Social Sciences and Humanities Research Council of Canada.

The first reader was my exceptional thesis supervisor, Yvan Lamonde, who one day plucked two words from the 850-page text and suggested that if it were ever published, I should call it *Missed Opportunities*. The project to turn it into a book was encouraged by Geegee Robinson of McGill, and Florian Sauvageau of l'Université Laval, who both supplied enthusiastic recommendations to the attention of the Association for Canadian Studies. In a more general sense, colleagues and associates in the Graduate Program in Communications at McGill, the Journalism Program of Concordia University, and the Département d'information et de communication at Laval helped provide a climate and working conditions in which such a task could be accomplished.

During the six years since I began the research that has now resulted in this book, I enjoyed various occasions to speak and to publish as the work and my reflections on it evolved. Papers based on this material have been presented at the Robarts Centre for Canadian Studies at York University, the International Conference on the Evolution of Broadcasting at Concordia University, the International Television Studies Conference at the University of London UK, the Beyond The Printed Word conference at the National Archives of Canada, and at meetings of the International Association for

Mass Communication Research, the Association of Canadian Studies in Australia and New Zealand, the Association for Canadian Studies, and the Canadian Communication Association. Publications have appeared in the *Canadian Journal of Communication*, *Canadian Issues/Thèmes canadiens*, the *Studies in Communication and Information Technology* series of Queen's University, the anthology *Television in Transition* published by the British Film Institute, *Border/lines* and *Possibles* magazines, and *Le Devoir*.

My perspective on the questions addressed in the book has been greatly enriched by participation since 1985 in the communications working group of l'Institut canadien d'éducation des adultes, under the dedicated leadership of Lina Trudel. This experience has shown me that political and scholarly agendas can coincide – happily, as for this scholar at least, they must coincide. It's easy to say this, as others have preceded me, notably three individuals who had no direct connection to my project but whose pioneering work inspired it: Frank Peers, Dallas Smythe, and the late Graham Spry.

As is often the case, the final product has benefited from the detailed comments of anonymous readers recruited by the different institutions which have had to pass judgment on the project as it migrated from university to publisher to granting agency. It is also far more fit and coherent thanks to the editorial surgery of Tessa McWatt who attacked the manuscript with rigour and brio.

Finally, Sheilagh, Paul, and Sean, I can come out of my room now.

*Missed Opportunities*

*"If the cells of Canadian broadcasting now run wild and are producing a technological cancer, the disease has its origin in our own weakness, and in the weaknesses, the compromises, the inadvertence of governments, and in the conflict between high national interests and private business operations ... Over all these years each opportunity, one after another presented to us, we have failed to seize, we have failed to use."*
*Graham Spry testifying at the CRTC hearings on CBC licence renewals, 19 February 1974.*

# Introduction

Broadcasting historians in the Republic of Ireland claim that the world's first radio broadcast was made from Dublin during the anticolonial uprising of 1916. Using a ship's transmitter, republican insurgents sent out messages aimed not at any particular receiver but "broadcast" at large, in the hope of telling their story to the world.[1]

In another outpost of the British Empire, Canada, broadcasting had a less auspicious start, but makes no less grand a claim. In 1919, the Canadian Marconi Co. launched what has been said to be the world's first commercial broadcasting station, XWA (later CFCF) in Montreal.

By the mid-1920s, Irish, Canadian, and no doubt other experiences had been flung to the periphery of broadcasting development as mighty interests in Great Britain and the United States of America, having recognized the economic and political potential of the new technology, struggled to define its shape and form.[2] Radio would not be left to develop in the hands of rebels and upstarts from the hinterland.

Once it was realized that people would spend large portions of their leisure time "listening in," broadcasting became a social issue. Commercial interests claimed a natural right to develop an industry based, first, on the sale of receiving sets and, later, on "air time." But an assortment of other interests – educators, patrons of the arts, politicians – argued that broadcasting should be made to serve a "public" function.

It is not unfair to say that the early conceptions of public broadcasting were as varied and unclear as some of the sounds that came through the air on a stormy night. The idea of the public was in a state of flux and was itself a topic of public discussion in the 1920s. In 1922, the American journalist Walter Lippmann published a controversial and widely circulated treatise, *Public Opinion*, which made a case for expert management of public affairs on behalf of a populace incapacitated by the complex demands of modern life.[3]

While Lippmann discussed at length the role of the press and its limitations as a catalyst of democratic public life, he did not address the new electronic media. Ironically, while public broadcasting was fought for as a chance to achieve what Lippmann said the press had failed to do, the institutions of public broadcasting have developed along the lines that he proposed as a general model for social organization. Lippmann was a prophet, and public broadcasting a major vehicle, of the technocratic ascendancy that James Burnham described some twenty years later as "the managerial revolution."[4]

This was not evident to the proponents of public broadcasting in the 1920s. The definition of a new medium was at stake and the alternative forms that it could take were seen as a question of ownership and control. The main issue in broadcasting in the 1920s was enterprise, public or private, and the main organizational alternatives appeared to be corporate capital or some variation of the corporate state.

In Britain, a broadcasting committee chaired by Sir Frederick Sykes stated in August 1923 "that the control of such a potential power over public opinion and the life of the nation ought to remain with the State, and that the operation of so important a national service ought not to be allowed to become an unrestricted commercial monopoly." But then it added: "When once the principle of public control is established, it is evident that considerable latitude is possible in deciding by whom broadcasting should be operated."[5]

The Sykes committee report led to the disbanding of the British Broadcasting Company, a consortium of receiving set manufacturers set up in 1922, and its replacement by the publicly owned British Broadcasting Corporation (BBC) in 1926. The BBC was strongly shaped by the conception of public service brought to the task by its first director, John Reith, who saw the public as an audience capable of growth and development. But Reith's approach – give the public what we think it needs, not what it seems to want – incorporated a cultural élitism that was to be the Achilles heel of the BBC.[6]

In the United States, meanwhile, broadcasting was developing as an industry, but one which would clearly need to be regulated. In November 1925, US Secretary of Commerce Herbert Hoover told the Fourth National Radio Conference that radio was not to be considered "merely as a business carried on for private gain, for private advertisement, or for the entertainment of the curious. It is to be considered as a public concern, impressed with a public trust, and to be considered primarily from the standpoint of public interest."[7]

The US Radio Act of 1927 consequently provided for government control over channels, licensed for limited periods, and deemed the guiding standard for licensing to be "public interest, convenience and necessity." But "public interest" could mean any number of things, and representatives of the broadcasting industry would protect themselves ideologically by claiming, as CBS executive Frank Stanton did in 1960, that "a program in which a large part of the audience is interested is by that very fact ... in the public interest."[8]

This tautological approach to conceptualizing the public interest in broadcasting as the sum of individual interests in specific programs was greatly strengthened by the industry-supported development of the field of "audience research" in the US in the 1930s and 1940s.[9] One sees in this type of statement an important displacement from debate over the nature of the public to attempts to co-opt the concept itself into legitimating a particular position, in this case broadcasting for the lowest common denominator.

There is a common thread that unites such phenomena as the ratings system in broadcasting, public opinion measurement in politics, and the use of public relations by élite groups in general. The idea of "public opinion" was used for political legitimation as early as 1828 to justify the rise to power of the English bourgeoisie,[10] while in the early twentieth century in the United States a whole new industry – "public relations" – appeared with the sole purpose of creating marketable images favourable to the interests of particularly socially positioned clients.[11] Broadcasting policy emerged and has evolved in this context of curiously articulated notions of "the public" and "its" role in democracy.[12]

In the 1920s and 1930s, national governments in every Western country played a central role in the evolution of broadcasting, either through ownership and operation of broadcasting systems as in Europe, or through regulation as in the United States. In Canada, a Royal Commission on Radio Broadcasting[13] found the British system, based on a state corporation, far more appropriate for Canada than the American one, which was based on a regulated privately owned industry. But the Aird commission also infused broadcasting with a *national* purpose, thus establishing one of the central distinguishing characteristics of Canadian broadcasting. Canadian broadcasting policy would be a national policy and the system it directed would have a clearly national vocation.

The ideas of "public" and "nationhood" thus became fused in the broadcasting policy implied by the Aird commission's report, and would remain that way. But the system proposed by Aird pushed public enterprise a long way and implied an unorthodox view of the country as well. Canada was, after all, not a unitary state like Great Britain. It was more like Germany where, the commission had learned, each state had a broadcasting company responsible for programs broadcast in its territory.[14] The Aird commission therefore proposed a combination of the British and German systems: "That broadcasting should be placed on a basis of public service and that the stations providing a service of this kind should be owned and operated by one national company; that provincial authorities should have full control over the programs of the station or stations in their respective areas."[15]

This proposal had an unhappy destiny and, in fact, Canadian broadcasting policy went on to promote a centralized vision of Canada in which the provinces were only the most evident symbols of potential counterauthority. The "national" purpose of broadcasting policy was to be double-edged. On the one hand, it would be the main cultural component of the federal strategy for maintaining a political entity distinct from the US, a strategy requiring constant and vigilant state involvement in the cultural sphere, and particularly in broadcasting, as the Royal Commission on National Development in the Arts, Letters and Sciences (Massey commission) confirmed in 1951.[16] On the other hand, broadcasting was to serve as a strategic instrument against the *internal* threat to Canada's national integrity posed by cultural resistance among French Canadians in Quebec – which in its most extreme form was articulated as a demand for political independence. In the 1960s this came to be perceived as the more urgent priority and Canada's cultural policy after 1963 was explicitly directed towards promoting national unity. The central element of that policy was declared to be the public broadcasting institution, the CBC.[17]

Thus, one of the major lessons of the Canadian experience would be this: that regardless of the positive value of a "national broadcasting policy" with respect to a nation's cultural sovereignty, a policy that equates the "nation" with the "public," and that is based on activities carried out under the auspices of the state, is likely to end up conscripted to serve the narrowest interests or even the repressive apparatus of the state. In this sense, the history of Canadian broadcasting policy demonstrates what Québécoise sociologist Nicole Laurin-Frenette meant when she wrote that nationalism is *le discours de l'Etat sur lui-même.*[18]

Even in Great Britain, where the BBC had a monopoly on broadcasting content, it did not enjoy hegemony, as the Ullswater committee noted in 1936 when it recommended public takeover of the manufacture and sale of receiving sets as well. In a public service, it said, "the public interest should predominate throughout the whole range. If private profit is allowed a loophole, a proportion of the advantages of the system will be lost to the community."[19]

The recommendation was not heeded, although its supporters argued that consistently applying the public service logic to all aspects of broadcasting would have provided, among other things, an interesting solution to the perennial problem of financing by bringing lucrative areas like set manufacturing into the public sector. Instead, "the public good" in Great Britain would be served by programming alone.

In Canada there was a more significant weak spot. Today, with deregulation and privatization in vogue, the Canadian system, with its combination of "public" and "private" elements, is considered an interesting model as a "mixed" system. In fact, the question of ownership and control has been the subject of unending debate and has never really been resolved. Broadcasting in Canada was intended, in theory at least, to be a "single system" after 1932, when legislation created the Canadian Radio Broadcasting Commission and gave it the power to establish a broadcasting monopoly.[20] This power was continued with the new legislation of 1936 that replaced the CRBC with the Canadian Broadcasting Corporation.[21] But it was never used, and by the 1940s there was no question of eliminating privately owned broadcasters.

The power and importance of "private" broadcasters in Canada have grown steadily and without interruption, but the role of the "public" element of the system has ebbed and flowed. While policy has been directed towards the overall system, its execution has interfered precious little with the economic progress of the private sector but has hindered the social development of the public sector. The public sector has depended on the particular importance attached to broadcasting by the party in power in its attempt to master the political context, while the private sector has grown with just a little help from its friends. The pronouncements of policy notwithstanding, no Canadian government has ever taken concrete steps to contain the profitability of private broadcasting.

In Italy, shortly after a constitutional court ruling in 1976 opened the door to private broadcasting, Franco Iseppi described the stakes at play like this:

> The way in which the relationship between the public and private presence is handled will determine in one sense or another the final structure of the public broadcasting system. In other words if the normalization of the relationship between public and private comes about through the recognition of a "mixed" economy, that is one of competition, there will not be many ways for a public corporation (which still wants to maintain its basic character as a public service) to survive.[22]

He must have had Canada in mind for, in sum, this was a good description of the economics of the Canadian problem. Politically, however, the "mixed" Canadian system can appear attractive to foreign observers when it is placed next to the experience of European public broadcasting monopolies. Often what emerged in those situations was based on the combined self-interests of governments and broadcasting institutions, a product which did not necessarily correspond to anything a public would identify as in its own interest.[23]

The problem of overlapping state and broadcasting/institutional interests is not limited to its effect on programming decisions but is seen in the actual operational structures of public broadcasting. In France, for example, broadcasting was explicitly organized as a state institution following World War II. The Radio-télévision française (RTF) was placed directly under ministerial authority in November 1945, and remained there until 1964, during which time broadcasting was considered a legitimate agency of government information. Even after creation of the formally autonomous Office de la radio-télévision française (ORTF) in 1964, the French Cabinet took an active daily role in programming television news. The government could use the air as it wished, while opposition politicians were not entitled to access at all, even during a presidential election campaign. [24]

The Canadian Broadcasting Corporation evolved within a more liberal, pluralistic framework. But while the system in France may have been the paradigm of broadcasting as an extension of the government of the day, Canada's system is an even more interesting example of broadcasting as an instrument of national policy. Development of a strong, bureaucratic institution, a process aided tremendously by World War II, during which the public broadcaster was closely integrated to the Canadian government's war effort, was the key to creating the CBC as a model for what can be termed "administrative broadcasting," or broadcasting in the interest of the state.

Using the CBC as a case study to examine the problem of "integrating administration and politics in the public interest, through the device of an independent government corporation," J.E. Hodgetts wrote in 1946: "It must be recognized at once that the 'public interest' is merely a convenient political hypothesis which will provide a sanction for state intervention and which will, at the same time, presumably create a standard against which government policy can be measured." [25]

Hodgetts argued that, on the technical side, the CBC had unquestionably fostered the public interest by building a communications infrastructure that only a government corporation could have achieved. In the hazier area of content, however, the CBC "builds its programs *in its own image* of the public interest" persuading itself "that apathy shown towards its offerings is due to the listeners' bad taste rather than its own poor judgment" [26]: "Having delegated both 'administration' and 'politics' to an independent corporation, we are faced with the problem of keeping the agency responsible for its defining and interpreting of the public interest." [27]

Hodgetts suggested a system of controls "to prevent both hardening of the administrative arteries and overzealous pursuit of professionally conceived (and possibly narrow) views of the public interest." [28] None was ever designed, although by 1946 there had been some serious, well-formulated proposals for alternative models of public broadcasting. The provinces, too, were interested in getting involved in broadcasting by 1946, but the government responded with an edict prohibiting the CBC from licensing provincial broadcasting agencies. This was precisely the type of question for which an "independent" mechanism for determining the public interest was necessary.

The postwar CBC was then a powerful institution operating in the national interest in the name of a public that was excluded from its decision-making process. This was clearly driven home, for example, to a coalition of public interest groups that the CBC blocked from acquiring a radio station in Alberta in 1946, because it needed the frequency to complete its national network.

In contrast, consider the German situation that evolved in the effective absence of a central state authority. Before Hitler, each German state, or *Land*, had its own broadcasting company governed by a board responsible for programs broadcast in its territory. After World War II, the allies oversaw reconstruction of a system based on independent *Land* broadcasters. As there was no central state and no economic power strong enough to support a commercial system before 1948, a decentralized system "independent from the state, politics and the economy" emerged. [29]

Early West German broadcasting "played a major part in the construction of West German democracy," according to H.G. Falkenberg, who goes so far as to say that it had an "emancipatory tendency" as broadcasters learned from "the dreadful experiences of German fascism and bas[ed] their programs on a philosophy that was humanitarian, tolerant and pacifist. At the same time, they saw 'public broadcasting' as a meaningful way of replacing bourgeois patronage." [30] Between 1945 and 1955, the climate of West German broadcasting was "extraordinarily liberal and almost progressive ... There could have been no greater contrast to the restorationist, reactionary political atmosphere of the time." [31]

In comparison, the CBC appears to be a model in which the public interest often ends up being poorly served in exchange for the interests of the state, the government of the day, or the institution itself. This is what we mean by "administrative broadcasting."

The structure of state power in Canadian broadcasting underwent a major change in 1958, with the split of the CBC's regulatory and operating functions and the assignment of the former to a new public agency, the Board of Broadcast Governors. [32] While there were cogent arguments showing such a move to be in the public interest (not least of which concerned the dangers of continued concentration of power in an institution that had acquired its own vested interest), this is not why it was done. The separate regulatory board was a long-standing demand of the private interests in broadcasting, and the BBG was structured and staffed in such a way as to ensure that these interests would, at last, be served by a public agency.

From 1958 to 1968 the profits and power of commercial broadcasting rose with breathtaking speed until national concerns imposed a new broadcasting policy, a new mandate for the CBC, and a new regulatory agency. [33] But by 1968 there was a plethora of alternatives in the air, illustrating what Liora Salter has called "the dialectic of public and mass media." [34]

Canada was not alone in this respect. In Europe, state broadcasting monopolies came under attack in the wave of youth and student rebellion that generated new forms of autonomous media.[35] Even in the United States, an alternative to the dominant commercial model was established and called public broadcasting.[36]

Often unconsciously, these alternatives were couched in a new perspective on the place of media in a process of radical social change. In the 1960s and 1970s, new developments occurred in the ways in which critical intellectuals thought about both the media and the public. While much of the intellectual critique of the European and North American new Left simply reduced media to an ideological apparatus of the state,[37] some important new notions emerged which integrated a practice-oriented critique of media to the movements struggling for a restructuring of social life. The most lasting were those associated with the West German theorist Jürgen Habermas and his students.[38]

In Canada, the spirit of the 1960s meant that the CBC was no longer seen by proponents of a *social* role for media as the only model for public broadcasting. But because the idea of "public" media was so ineluctably associated with the centralized, state-owned, hierarchical model, the new approaches were often labelled in other terms, such as "alternative" or "community" media.

As early as 1966, the dominant model was faced with alternatives that surged up from within the CBC in the form of challenges to basic policy assumptions and corporate wisdom about the appropriate role of the public broadcaster. The conception of "public affairs" programming held by the producers of the television magazine "This Hour Has Seven Days" was both irreverent *and* popular, making it all the more subversive at the point where it linked up with the critique of traditional public broadcasting being formulated outside.

Meanwhile, in the news and information services of Radio-Canada, creative and junior-to-middle management personnel interpreted the corporation's public mission with respect to the national question in a way that shocked senior CBC officials and convinced government back-benchers from Quebec that something must be done. The role of Radio-Canada became an important issue in the developing constitutional crisis, and the federal government's insistence that the public broadcaster promote *its* version of Canada once again underscored the repressive aspect of public broadcasting in the national interest, while sharpening the Quebec government's resolve to demand a new division of power and jurisdiction over broadcasting.

In Quebec, the attempts to use state power for the promotion of cultural sovereignty was an ironic replication on a smaller scale of Canadian policy with respect to the United States. In the 1970s, Quebec put forward and sustained several important alternatives that have broadened the scope of public broadcasting, notably the provincial "educational" broadcasting agencies and provincially supported local noncommercial, or "community" broadcasting media. But these initiatives often led into the same blind alleys as the pan-Canadian CBC.[39]

The explosion of new communications technologies in the late 1960s introduced a whole new set of criteria on which broadcasting, and the question of the public in broadcasting, had to be considered. The Canadian government marked the new context with a series of interventions: creation of a Department of Communications in 1969 (Quebec following suit a few months later); establishment of a new "public/private" corporation, Telesat Canada, to develop domestic satellite communications; establishment of a mandate for the new regulatory agency, the Canadian Radio-Television Commission, to develop policy on cable or "broadcasting-receiving" undertakings.

The CRTC was most successful in its trusteeship over the public interest with respect to the CBC, which it repeatedly sought to keep on the path of public service,[40] while protecting it from the more outrageously partisan government demands.[41] With respect to the private sector, however, the CRTC quickly fell into the classical Canadian muddle of seeking an elusive pivot on which to balance the required mixture of private enterprise and public service. From its early policy statements on cable[42] to the 1987 decision on specialized television services,[43] the CRTC has followed the path of diminishing attention to public interest in favour of increasing regard to market considerations. In the process, it has contributed to redefining "the public" in consumer terms.

Internationally, when the state reached a point of crisis in the mid-1970s, broadcasting was one of the areas of the "public sector" that came under attack. The inflation spiral and restrictions on public spending eroded the traditional financial base of public broadcasting. At the same time, the introduction to the marketplace of new media designed for commercial uses stimulated private industry to new heights of aggressive promotion of its interests, while creating a consumer demand based on new modes of consumption. By the 1970s, the major public broadcasting institutions – creatures of an earlier technological and sociopolitical context – were also suffering an identity crisis as they became less and less able to satisfy their publics, increasingly fragmented and self-identified by interest group rather than national collectivity. Finally, the technical impossibility for governments to maintain their monopolies undermined the political usefulness of the media in their eyes, combining with the other factors to favour a shift towards privatization.[44]

The definite turning point in the ideological winds can be marked by the election of the Thatcher government in Great Britain in 1979. Britain thus became the first major Western country with a government actually *com-*

*mitted* to rolling back the boundaries of the state, rather than doing so with rhetorical reluctance in the face of fiscal crisis. Thatcher's Britain has been the model for privatization of nationally owned companies, the best example being the selling off of the commercially successful British Telecom. It has also led the way in transforming the remaining public sector as well, scrapping the notion of public service in favour of "criteria of profitability and market success."[45]

The "political trafficking in new public doctrines and technical systems" received its second boost with the election of Ronald Reagan in the us in 1980.[46] With deregulation of its communications industries, the us created a free market model in which new technologies and traditional broadcasting are blended and made available "to direct audience transactions, something which has in the past been either technically or juridically impossible, or both."[47]

In Italy, Iseppi's fears came true and by 1979 Italy had some 450 private television stations, organized in 150 networks. Introduced into an unregulated free market, capital concentration and dog-eat-dog became the order of the day. By 1981 Italy was the world's greatest importer of television programs from the us, Japan, and Brazil, and the price of imported products to the Italian market had risen 1,000 percent since 1976. By 1982, four networks controlled 80 percent of the total audience of private television (or about 39 percent of the gross total) and an equivalent 80 percent of advertising revenue.[48]

As Anthony Smith notes, the new climate is not only international and intercontinental, but crosses ideological boundaries too.[49] Thus, in France – which in the 1970s was the setting for some of the most innovative and radical experiences in self-appropriation of media – a socialist government dismantled the state broadcasting monopoly and, with no clear program for its replacement, the issue was thrown into the marketplace. In France, as elsewhere, the real political *issues* in broadcasting were no longer in the sphere of programming but in the policy area. These issues – concerning cable, satellite, pay-television, and commercial broadcasting – were played out in the offices of the ministry of communications, where, socialism notwithstanding, the first criterion for policy has been the need to acquire a leading position for French interests (private and public) in the global communications economy. In 1986, France became the first Western nation to sell off a major part of its public broadcasting service.[50]

The Canadian situation in the 1980s fit neatly into this logic. The evolution of Canadian policy clearly placed economic considerations in priority over cultural questions, and the election of a Conservative government in 1984 put people in power who appeared prepared to carry that policy forward, or backward, as the case may be.

The idea of broadcasting as a public service was thus at a low point, both in Canada and internationally, in an increasingly interconnected global system where conservative economic policies antithetical to a democratic public life were in command. Nevertheless, examples abound of concrete attempts to constitute new public spaces in which media could be used otherwise than to serve state-bureaucratic or corporate-capitalist interests, and in spite of the rise of an ideological Right and disillusionment with orthodox and authoritarian state-based alternatives, new approaches to conceptualizing public broadcasting began to reappear in the critical literature in the mid-1980s.[51] In Canada, anxiety about the Conservative government's intentions led to significantly broadened public debate and a wholesale examination of public priorities and expectations with respect to broadcasting.[52] This was a development of major importance, coming at a time when broadcasting policy was high on the national agendas of most Western countries, including Canada, and the role of the public in communications was of international concern.

# CHAPTER ONE

# The National Purpose of Public Broadcasting (1928–32)

## INTRODUCTION

The link between government and private commercial interests in Canada has its origins in economic and political strategies worked out in the nineteenth century.[1] The creation of a "public enterprise culture," as Herschel Hardin has aptly named it,[2] had substantial benefit for the private sector, as the infrastructure for commercial prosperity was laid at public expense while the involvement of the young Canadian state guaranteed protection against the pressures of a continental economy. Conversely, the Canadian state saw involvement in economic life as the only way to establish its own autonomy. As Hardin comments with irony, the Canadian nation itself was an enterprise: "We did not choose public enterprise freely. It was forced on us by American expansion."[3]

Sometimes, as in the case of the federally chartered banks, the structure was set up exclusively on the basis of a regulated national enterprise – although the banking system eloquently illustrates that a "national" system does not necessarily mean one designed with "the public" in mind. In other cases, particularly transportation, the strategy was initially to have the state build the infrastructure needed for trade and commerce (roads, canals), then to have the infrastructure itself become part of the commercial sector (railways). The experience of the railways – where the government had to intervene to save the system from the effects of commercial fraud and bankruptcy – had federal politicians resigned to this strategy by the 1920s.

Thus, the political climate permitted the idea of public broadcasting to be placed on the agenda of the Canadian government when the question of organizing a broadcasting "system" arose. But the fact that it made good long-term economic sense was not in itself enough to overcome the natural advantage of free (that is, "private") enterprise ideology in ruling circles. Broadcasting also had to be recognized as essential to the survival of Canada, as a political entity, as a single market autonomous of the American economy to the south, and as an idea.

We tend, today, to remember the early history of broadcasting in this country as a struggle between the promoters of a nationalist public sector and frontierless private enterprisers. And so it was. But it was also a struggle involving different conceptions of Canada. In the 1920s, the dominant vision of Canada was that of an emerging nation struggling to find its place between a British colonial past and the American dream of the future, anxious to preserve the trappings of the former without denying itself the promised pleasures of the latter. Canadian nationalism of this era spawned a cornucopia of associations with names like the Native Sons of Canada, the Canadian League, and the Association of Canadian Clubs.

Members of the nationalist associations ranged from intellectuals to business people, but they tended to share a common perception of their role, seeking "to 'mould public opinion' in the direction of a national consciousness ... to formulate social goals, to give direction to the national will, and thus to give cohesion to Canadian society."[4]

In itself, the nationalist idea could perhaps have gained a consensus, but it was tied to a political and social structure based on multiple inequalities of class, region, and national group and consequently excluded the aspirations of too many people. Canadian nationalism was dominated by urban, English-speaking, central Canadians. French Canadians, rural Canadians, those in outlying regions, labour, women, and farmers were at best marginal to its concerns, except insofar as their support was needed. In general, the organizations trying to mould public opinion to nationalist ends did so on the basis of a conception of public opinion "derived from class and leadership assumptions which gave ordinary Canadians little role to play except as the consumers of nationalist propaganda."[5]

But ordinary Canadians, too, were beginning to organize and put forward an idea of Canada as a society based on egalitarian relations and rooted in communities defined by common interest. By the mid-1920s, rural and agrarian social movements had developed all across English-speaking Canada, particularly in the west where their radical populism was mixed with a mistrust of urban, eastern institutions. These movements of farmers, women, and, in the cities, workers were interested in building alternative enterprises based on cooperative ownership and collectivist values. On an issue like broadcasting, their interests happened to coincide with those of the traditional urban elite whose concern for the American threat had led to the appearance of the nationalist organizations of the 1920s. The differences between the two types of groups were blurred by the ideological use each made of certain value-laden terms, such as "education."[6] While the political goals of the various organizations varied and were even at odds with each other over the uses to which broadcasting could be put, a consensus was possible among groups as different as the Canadian Legion and the United Farmers of Alberta.

Nationhood was relatively unimportant to the social movements of the 1920s, who were more concerned with democratic values and new forms of social organization. To these movements, Canada was essentially the particular place where one happened to be engaged in social struggle. On either side of the fence, there was nothing uniquely Canadian about it. The natural constituency for this idea included many groups still absent from the public discourse in the 1920s: native peoples, youth, cultural minorities of various sorts. These groups later provided the spark that would rekindle the spirit of the 1920s in the 1960s.

The political context of the 1920s also indicates why it was so important that radio be used to transmit values such as national unity. While the radical political and social movements, such as the United Farmers, were developing mass membership bases with strong regional roots, the traditional élite, through its "voluntary associations," sought to maintain its hegemony through a national communication network.[7]

With the crystallization of class conflict and the emergence of ideologically based national political alternatives like the Co-operative Commonwealth Federation (CCF) and Social Credit in the 1930s, "national unity" became identified as a class slogan in English Canada.

Quebec, on the other hand, offered a third conception of Canada. Once one sliced through the rhetoric, the dominant vision of Canada was an anglo-centric one, in which French Canadians were a benignly tolerated minority. Members of the minority could deal with this in one of two ways: either by demanding full equality as a condition for the continued existence of Canada, or by defining Canada as "the other" and constructing an alternative conception of nationhood in which the homeland was Quebec. Polite Canadian society viewed the demand for equality as an ideal, unfortunately blocked by a vociferous (anglo-Protestant) rabble's refusal to accept it. The demands of Quebec, on the other hand, were threatening, even possibly subversive. The unanswered claims of Quebec undermined and made untenable the dominant vision of Canada as a struggling nation, because, to Quebec, Canada was the oppressor.

The First World War had been the occasion of a major confrontation between Canada's two nationalisms, as the French-speaking population of Quebec massively opposed what it saw as Canadian participation on the shirt-tails of the British imperial parent. The anti-imperialist nationalism of French-Canadian leaders like Henri Bourassa, who sought independence from British policy, was often perceived by English Canadians, mindful of the imperial link, as narrow provincialism. The thrust towards provincial autonomy pursued by successive governments in Quebec was seen as petty, chauvinistic, and especially counterproductive in the struggle to build a pan-

Canadian alternative to the US cultural model. This attitude contained an unfortunate blindspot. It prevented those with it from seeing that the French Canadians were engaged in an even more difficult struggle for cultural and political autonomy in which the dominant majority was English Canada, politically represented by the federal (then Dominion) government in Ottawa. The two nationalisms would now clash again over the question of broadcasting.

Quebec's conservative nationalism in the 1920s favoured private enterprise and provincial autonomy, and thus the idea of public broadcasting did not mean the same thing in Quebec as it did in English Canada. Where public broadcasting found support was among that segment of Quebec opinion which was pan-Canadian in outlook – the group which would always be marginal to Quebec nationalism and secondary to the English-Canadian élites in the Canadian nationalist organizations.

Although Quebec nationalists did not at first mount an organized response to radio, the medium's importance was recognized.[8] Early in its development, however, broadcasting in Quebec was associated with education – an association with different implications than in English Canada. Constitutionally, as education, broadcasting was arguably in the provincial sphere, an important consideration for Quebec nationalists seeking to assert their autonomy through their own institutions: the church and, especially later, the provincial state.

When the Liberal government of Mackenzie King created the Royal Commission on Radio Broadcasting in 1928, it was looking for a solution to a crisis felt especially by English-Canadian nationalists. But in the debate that ensued, the conflicting visions of Canada came into play. The notion of "public" broadcasting that emerged was diversely interpreted. In official circles, where "public" and "national" were interchangeable, public broadcasting was baldly presented as the solution to the problem broadcasting posed to the dominant conception of Canada. Seen this way, the opponents of that conception in Quebec could hardly do otherwise than oppose public broadcasting as well. An important degree of nuance and subtlety came into play in the progressive movement, which was not primarily concerned with the national question but which saw public broadcasting as an important vehicle for its *social* vision.

The progressive movement and the Canadian state would argue about the nature of broadcasting (and later, "communications") down through the years, while Ottawa and Quebec and their respective supporters would use broadcasting as one of the focal points of their continuing argument about the nature of Canada. At the same time, representatives of private capitalist interests in broadcasting and their friends inside the state apparatus would maintain a continuous and increasingly successful campaign to have broadcasting take its natural place in the free market order of things.

The debate has been passed down to us, and continues in much the same guise today.

## CANADIAN BROADCASTING IN THE 1920S [9]

The Canadian government's first intervention in the field of radio broadcasting dates from the Wireless Telegraph Act of 1905,[10] which actually preceded the introduction of over-the-air broadcasting by fourteen years. The act required anyone conducting wireless telegraphy to obtain a licence from the minister of the Department of Marine and Fisheries, who, at the same time, was given full regulatory authority. The Radiotelegraph Act of 1913[11] encompassed voice transmission and anticipated the coming innovation of sound broadcasting, reiterating the requirements of the earlier act. In the "Brief History of Broadcasting in Canada" appended to its report, the 1957 Royal Commission on Broadcasting stated: "From this it is evident that the Parliament of Canada asserted firmly its jurisdiction over the new medium of communication at an early date, and has continued to do so ever since."[12]

The history of Canadian commercial broadcasting begins with the licence granted in 1919 to the Marconi Wireless Telegraph Company for its operations in Montreal. In 1922–23, the Department of Marine and Fisheries issued thirty-four licences for private commercial broadcasting stations, most of them in large metropolitan centres. By 1927 their number had grown to seventy-five and reached into every province. In addition to stations operated for commercial gain, a number of religious organizations held broadcasting licences in the 1920s. One province, Manitoba, actually operated two radio stations of its own, the first "public" broadcasting undertakings in Canada. In 1927, the University of Alberta began operating an educational radio station, financed by a grant from the provincial government. The Crown-owned Canadian National Railways, meanwhile, began broadcasting its own programs to its passenger trains as early as 1923 and had created Canada's first national radio network by 1928.

Beginning in 1922, owners of radio receiving sets were required to pay an annual licence fee of one dollar, and between 1922 and 1930 the number of licences issued grew from under ten thousand to more than five hundred thousand. The number of licences tells only part of the story, however, as licence fee evasion soon became a common practice among as many as 25 per cent of radio users.[13]

Radio was clearly a popular phenomenon and by 1928 had given rise to a number of concerns. One problem, poor reception due to interference from powerful stations in the United States and Mexico, required international negotiations. Another, the lack of facilities in less populated, outlying parts of the country, required a national infrastructure. The problem of program content, disappointing and irritating to a large proportion of "listeners-in," was more subtle, and the solutions less clear. Even at this early date, the economics of broadcasting made production of original, "quality" material difficult, or at best uninviting, for entrepreneurs whose interest in the medium was essentially financial. An alarming proportion of the program material broadcast was imported from the United States.

Canadian authorities had paid little attention to broadcasting up to this point, unlike authorities in the United States and Great Britain, where it was already a public issue. But by 1928, there was an emerging consensus that only some kind of government involvement could deal with all of these problems.

Radio broadcasting licences in Canada were subject to annual renewal. In March 1928, a public controversy arose when the Department of Marine and Fisheries declined to renew a number of stations with ties to the International Bible Students Association. Questioned in the House of Commons on 12 April, the minister responsible, P.J.A. Cardin, indicated that the government was dissatisfied with this *ad hoc* approach to broadcasting. It was therefore considering "whether or not it would be generally advantageous to adopt a policy of national broadcasting along the lines adopted in this respect by the British government." [14]

The issue resurfaced in Parliament on 31 May, during debate on the department's spending estimates. Here, Independent Labour Party MP J.S. Woodsworth indicated for the first time what the purpose of such a policy could be and a precise form that broadcasting could take: "Our forefathers won to a considerable extent freedom of speech, freedom of the press, freedom of assembly; surely it is strange that a Liberal government should seek to deny people freedom of the air. Strange indeed ... The present difficulty would not be without its value if it would lead to public ownership and control of this new industry." [15]

The following day Cardin announced that the government had decided "that a change must be made in the broadcasting situation in Canada," and on 2 June, Parliament designated $25,000 for a commission of inquiry. [16] Then, on 6 December 1928, an order in council established the Royal Commission on Radio Broadcasting, "to examine into the broadcasting situation in the Dominion of Canada and to make recommendations to the Government as to the future administration, management, control and financing thereof." [17]

## THE AIRD COMMISSION, 1928–29

### Representations

The Royal Commission on Radio Broadcasting was made up of Sir John Aird, president of the Canadian Bank of Commerce, Augustin Frigon, one of Canada's leading technical experts in radio, and Charles Bowman, editor of the Ottawa *Citizen*.

Of the three, Bowman was the only one who came to the task with a clear position on the question at hand. He had accompanied Prime Minister Mackenzie King to London for the Imperial Conference of 1926, and the two had visited the BBC together. Soon after their return, Bowman became one of the early advocates of public broadcasting in Canada, publishing numerous articles and editorials on the subject in the *Citizen*.[18]

Sir John Aird, on the other hand, was known as "a strong defender of the private enterprise system,"[19] while Frigon was primarily concerned about the special needs of the province of Quebec. "Both took cautious views on the question of national broadcasting," Bowman later wrote in his memoirs.[20]

The commissioners began their work by studying the US and British systems first hand. In New York they visited the National Broadcasting Company and learned of its plan to "cover" Canada as "part of the North American radio orbit."[21] This shocked both Aird and Frigon and they were further moved when New York Governor Franklin D. Roosevelt told them he hoped they would "make radio government controlled and operated."[22]

In London, Sir John Reith of the BBC spoke to the commissioners of his concept of broadcasting as public service. They also travelled on the European continent, meeting broadcasting officials and gathering material which they later summarized in an appendix to their report.[23]

Back home, the commission asked the nine provincial governments for their opinions on broadcasting. Seven of them submitted an essentially identical resolution stating their willingness to negotiate with Ottawa and the other provinces with a view to the organization of radio broadcasting on a basis of public service, by some method "that may be mutually agreed upon by the said governments."[24]

New Brunswick and Quebec expressed reservations based on the constitutional jurisdiction over broadcasting, which both considered in the provincial sphere.[25] In fact, Quebec had already enacted its own broadcasting legislation while the Aird commission was still sitting. In February 1929, the government of Louis-Alexandre Taschereau presented a bill authorizing it to erect and operate its own radio station, as well as produce programs for broadcast via existing private stations.

Defending the bill in the Quebec Legislative Assembly, Quebec's minister for lands and forests, Honoré Mercier, described radio broadcasting as the most important of modern inventions. The number of radio sets in use in Quebec was rising rapidly, but the government was not pleased about what these sets were receiving: essentially American programs. Consequently, Quebec felt it should have its own broadcasting station.[26]

The bill was hotly debated in the Quebec legislature, with the opposition led by Maurice Duplessis fearing that civil liberties would be threatened by the government using broadcasting for its own purposes. But the provincial secretary, Athanase David, said Quebec broadcasting would be made to serve educational ends.[27]

Quebec's Broadcasting Act[28] took effect in April 1929, but Quebec never went so far as to set up its own station. The Taschereau government did, however, try to give itself an official radio voice through "L'Heure provinciale," a weekly program broadcast during time purchased from private stations.[29] The Aird commissioners were wined and dined by Honoré Mercier when they came to Quebec City, but he made them wait until 29 August, when they were in the final stages of preparing their report, before letting them know Quebec's position.

The Aird commission held public sessions in twenty-five Canadian cities, hearing 164 verbal submissions. In addition, it received 124 written statements. Unfortunately, records of the statements and hearings are not complete, but those which are available in the National Archives of Canada[30] indicate the flavour of the debate.

The order in council appointing the commission had proposed three possibilities for consideration:

(a) the establishment of one or more groups of stations operated by private enterprise in receipt of a subsidy from the government;
(b) the establishment and operation of stations by a Government-owned and financed company;
(c) the establishment and operation of stations by provincial governments.[31]

The commission asked the groups and individuals coming before it to indicate a preference, and this appeal yielded three types of response: organizations involved in broadcasting or other private business activities called for maintaining the values of private enterprise; educators and nationalists called for a public service approach; and French-Canadian groups called for recognizing their special cultural needs.

The Canadian Manufacturers' Association, for example, called for maintaining private ownership, submitting that the producers of goods used by radio listeners were particularly well suited to represent the latter's views.[32]

The Montreal newspaper *La Presse* – an important private broadcaster in its own right via radio station CKAC – said broadcasting should be left to private enterprise, adding without further qualification "especially in the province of Quebec." In a letter dated 29 May 1929, *La Presse* radio director J.A. Dupont opposed state ownership because of the danger that it would lead to political interference and government propaganda (Interestingly, this was the same argument that Maurice Duplessis had raised to Quebec's broadcasting act only two months earlier[33]). Dupont suggested that radio licences be limited to a few locally controlled, high-power stations – a clearly self-interested proposal.[34]

The idea of local control was raised by several spokesmen, especially small businessmen interested in using radio for advertising local products. The Sherbrooke (Quebec) Board of Trade suggested stations be subsidized by the government but controlled by the municipalities in which they were situated. [35]

Even the private broadcasters couched their submissions in a discourse of public interest – "paramount to all other considerations," according to the Canadian Association of Broadcasters, [36] a station owners group formed in 1926 to deal with the demands of radio performers.

Apparently interested in the possibility of government subsidies to privately owned stations, the CAB called for "a permanent non-political, non-partisan" commission to regulate broadcasting, which would remain in private hands – a system along the lines of the one created in the United States by the Radio Act of 1927.

Numerous submissions dealt with the question of "public interest." Groups such as the Royal Society of Canada, the Universities Conference, and the Professional Institute were all in favour of an educationally oriented system under some sort of joint federal-provincial control. [37] Organized labour, in particular, strongly supported the principle of public ownership. The Trades and Labour Congress of Canada stated that "control of the air should remain in the hands of the people" and proposed a federal government-owned and financed company along the lines of the CNR. [38]

The All-Canadian Congress of Labour, Canada's largest labour organization, said broadcasting was "an important means of public instruction, as well as entertainment, and a growing branch of industry that will in time provide a livelihood for many workers in Canada." It denounced the existing system as "gratuitous and voluntary" and unable to "protect the public from undue influence and subtle propaganda by private interests." [39]

It called for setting up a federal commission that would own, control, and operate all broadcasting stations, and a representative advisory council "to assist the commission in the selection of educational and other broadcasting material, and to ensure freedom of speech on questions of public interest." [40]

This submission prompted a sharp exchange between Sir John Aird and the labour spokesman, W.T. Burford:

> Chairman: Has labour formed any opinion as to what a system would cost presuming it was decided for the Government to take control of the whole system. To compensate the present owners of broadcasting stations and what it would cost to convert them.
>
> Mr. Burford: We would not consider the compensation of the present owners of broadcasting stations.
>
> Chairman: Labour wishes to be fairly treated, they should treat capital right ...

Mr. Burford: Why should the public of Canada be called upon to compensate for having established an advertising medium?[41]

Associations representing French-Canadian communities outside Quebec insisted on the need to provide for French programming and wanted guarantees, regardless of the structure of the system.[42]

While the commission was in Sherbrooke, Sir John Aird made an important statement indicating the commission's attitude towards the language question:

> We realize that Quebec is 90% French, loyal citizens of Canada, and the question of the dual language comes up and this question brings educational questions and for that reason it will be necessary for the Governments to get together so that the large population of the Province of Quebec will have a system which will enable them to get in touch not only with their own people, but with the people who live in British Columbia and the West ... I cannot conceive of anything more interesting in the West where there are a great many French people, hearing from their own people in Quebec.[43]

The chairman's diplomacy was well-chosen, for in considering national radio at all, Canada had to deal not only with the resistance of English Canadians to French but also with the desire to protect the indigenous culture of French Quebec.

### Deliberations

By July 1929 the commissioners had completed their investigation. Sir John Aird said he would sign anything the other two agreed on.[44] He had been convinced by the educationists and the nationalists of the need for a national, publicly owned system. Frigon was willing to endorse this, on condition that attention was paid to the special needs of Quebec. Bowman insisted on a strong, centrally controlled system that was not diluted by the provinces.

Bowman and Frigon each went off to write a draft report,[45] and commission secretary Donald Manson revised Bowman's draft, which became the basic framework of the final report. But the details of the provincial role remained in question. On the typewritten version of the revised draft in Bowman's papers in the National Archives of Canada, next to the proposal that a provincial director should have "full control of the programs broadcast" in each province, there is a hand-written marginal note asking: "What does control of programs mean?"[46]

By the end of August, only two things held up the report: the awaited resolution from the government of Quebec and a decision on the issue of provincial involvement. Bowman and Frigon haggled over the nature of provincial representation on the board or commission that their report would recommend to be in charge of broadcasting in Canada. Bowman wanted full control to remain with Ottawa and proposed a system by which provincial governments would nominate representatives but the governor-general would appoint them. Frigon wrote to Bowman on 19 August that "this would be contrary to the principle of cooperation which we have adopted as it would give to the Federal Government a definite control of the whole board and would not sufficiently protect the provinces."

> After all, by giving each province the right to appoint one director we only give to each one of them one twelfth of the votes in the control of the company. In this organization the Federal Government should be considered as being one of the partners ... It is not likely that enough provinces could get together in such a way that they would control the situation against the Federal and the other provinces acting together. If this was to happen it could very well mean that their action would be in the interest of the general public.
>
> ... the provinces should feel that they are fully represented in the direction of our national broadcasting.[47]

Bowman said he could agree only if the provinces assumed an equivalent share of financial obligation. On 20 August, he wrote to Aird that he was willing "to allow the provinces to control their own broadcasting to the fullest possible extent, but cannot bring myself to the point of asking the Dominion authorities to find all the money but to hand over seventy-five per cent of the control to the provinces."[48]

The two could not agree. Finally, on 30 August, Frigon wrote to Bowman that he still considered the Dominion government "one party out of ten" and suggested that their report refer the method of appointment of provincial directors to a Dominion-provincial conference.[49]

The royal commission's report, in fact, remained mute on the method of appointment.

### Recommendations

The Royal Commission on Radio Broadcasting submitted its report on 11 September 1929. On one fundamental question it had found unanimity: "Canadian radio listeners want Canadian broadcasting."[50]

The large majority of organizations that had submitted positions favoured "the placing of broadcasting on a basis of public service," the commission reported.[51] This was consistent with what it had found in Europe, where governments everywhere were in the process of organizing national broadcasting systems "in the public interest."[52] The commission had been especially impressed with the organization of broadcasting in Great Britain and Germany, where publicly owned and controlled systems were in operation.

In Canada, the report said, the existing structure was responsible for some of the system's problems. The need for revenue obliged private enterprise to force too much advertising on the listener and tended to crowd stations into large urban centres. The report mentioned the potential of broadcasting as an instrument of education "in the broad sense, not only as it is conducted in the schools and colleges, but in providing entertainment and of informing the public on questions of national interest."[53] Consequently, "in the interests of the listening public and of the nation," it concluded the need for "some form of public ownership, operation and control behind which is the national power and prestige of the whole public of the Dominion of Canada."[54]

Starting from this fundamental principle of operation on the basis of public service, the report recommended establishing a national company, to produce and acquire "programs of high standard." The company would be governed by a twelve-member board made up of three Dominion representatives and one representative of each of the provinces. In each province, a provincial radio broadcasting director, assisted by a provincial advisory council on radio broadcasting, would have full control of programs.

The commission recommended erecting a series of high-power stations across Canada and expropriating, with compensation, all existing stations and their apparatus, either integrating them into the new system or closing them down.

Operation and maintenance of the service would be financed by the revenue from receiver licence fees (to be increased from one dollar to three dollars), the sale of "indirect" advertising, and government subsidy. Aside from the start-up costs (placed at $3.2 million plus the cost of compensation to the private station owners), the commission estimated the system would require an annual subsidy of $1 million. But it insisted that the money would be well spent, considering the importance of broadcasting "in promoting the unity of the nation."[55]

The Royal Commission on Radio Broadcasting summarized its principal recommendation as follows: "That broadcasting should be placed on a basis of public service and that the stations providing a service of this kind should be owned and operated by one national company; that provincial authorities should have full control over the programs of the station or stations in their respective areas."[56]

It may not be an exaggeration to say that all subsequent debate on broadcasting in Canada has centred on one or another part of this brief phrase. Years later, Charles Bowman would write in his memoirs that "the principle had to be established that the radio realm is a natural monopoly: no private interest, or combination of private interests, could be safely left free to monopolize it."[57]

The Aird commission established that principle, but could not ensure that it would be put into effect.

## SETTING THE STAGE, 1929–32

### Reactions and the Foundations of Conflict

The late 1920s was a time of strong nationalist sentiment in English Canada, and the Aird report confirmed what most thoughtful Canadians apparently felt: that the only viable alternative to American domination of the Canadian airwaves was a national public enterprise. But the powerful lobby mounted by the private broadcasters and their supporters was a force to be reckoned with, and the stock market crash that followed the report by only a month dampened immediate enthusiasm for a project which some felt to be economically dubious, even if culturally and politically beneficial. The question of constitutional jurisdiction also had to be resolved before a national broadcasting project could proceed.

Press comment from newspapers without radio interests was swift and favourable.[58] But soon, a lobby was forming in opposition. On 13 December 1929, the Montreal *Gazette* reported a spokesman for the Chambre de commerce saying: "We are probably going to see a lining up of the forces of private ownership against the forces of public ownership."[59]

And there was also the question of Quebec. "Quebec is certain to resist all attempts to establish a public ownership monopoly of radio," wrote the Quebec City *Chronicle Telegraph* on 14 September.[60]

A major salvo in the offensive combined both the private interest position and Quebec opposition. Soon after publication of the Aird report, *La Presse* issued a bilingual pamphlet opposing what it called the élitist nature of the plan by drawing attention to aspects like the proposed increase in the receiver licence fee and the presumably highbrow programming a public company would produce. Radio belonged in the commercial domain, and the commercial effects of the plan would be disastrous, *La Presse* warned a population still traumatized by the recent stock market collapse: "The question to decide is this: Shall private ownership or State ownership – also called State Socialism – dominate in our land?"[61]

The *La Presse* pamphlet prompted a response by Charles Bowman in the Ottawa *Citizen* in January 1930. Bowman referred to the pamphlet as "a class appeal," as opposed to the Aird commission's recommendations which had been made "in the interests of Canadian listeners and in the national interests of Canada." The recommendations did not threaten the Canadian radio industry but would promote it and protect it from US competition, Bowman wrote. Besides, there was a broader position to consider, "that radio broadcasting must be controlled in the public interest," and this position was the basis of radio policy "in virtually every country where there is any policy ... On the surface, the issue may seem to be whether the radio service in Canada is to be under state ownership or privately owned. It is, however, a far bigger question. The Canadian people have to decide whether Canada is to have an independent Canadian broadcasting system worthy of Canada or to become dependent upon US sources for radio service."[62]

While the debate in the press focused largely on the question of public versus private ownership, the aspect of how a public system would be organized remained in view. Augustin Frigon, in his public interventions, typically emphasized the question of provincial involvement. The multiplicity of interests represented by Dominion and provincial authorities, he said, ensured that public service radio would be run in "a healthy spirit of competition ... free of political influence."[63] But the question of provincial involvement, begrudgingly included in the Aird commission's report, would be the first aspect of its recommendations to fall away.

In spite of the economic crisis, a coming federal election, and the controversy in the private sector, the Department of Marine and Fisheries went ahead and prepared a draft bill based on the Aird recommendations. On 15 February 1930, Donald Manson wrote to a department superintendent in British Columbia stating: "The Bill is already prepared and simply awaits final approval by the Minister himself before it is printed for the Cabinet."[64]

But nothing ever came of this bill. In view of the business community's agitation against the Aird proposals, and with federal elections approaching, the government let the matter fall, in spite of having announced in its speech from the throne that it would bring the Aird report before the House.[65]

The Liberals were defeated in the general elections of 28 July 1930. The new Conservative government took no immediate action on broadcasting. However, the National Archives of Canada files on the Aird commission contain a document of "explanatory remarks" referring to the draft legislation that is significant in light of later developments. Based on these remarks, the proposed bill would have closely followed the Aird recommendations, with one important departure: provincial representatives would be "*nominated* by the Lieutenant Governor of the province, but *appointed* by the Governor in Council," in light of Ottawa's preponderant role in financing the operations.[66]

In short, the draft bill followed Charles Bowman's position in his argument with Augustin Frigon and put aside the Aird commission's compromise. However, the author of the "explanatory remarks" pointed out that if Quebec and New Brunswick were constitutionally correct in claiming that broadcasting licensing was a provincial prerogative, the provinces could well argue that they were indeed participating in financing through their residents' licence fees.

At the end of 1930, then, a constitutional dispute was imminent. But meanwhile, the question of ownership was in the forefront of public debate.

## Mobilizing the Private and Public Lobbies

During the hiatus on the Aird report, supporters of both "public" and "private" ownership began to mobilize formidable lobbies. The most important of these was the Canadian Radio League.

A number of writers have described in great detail the origins of the league.[67] It was created in Ottawa in October 1930, shortly after the federal elections, on the initiative of two individuals, Alan Plaunt and Graham Spry. The league's objective was to promote the general principle of the Aird report – broadcasting as public service – in order to create a model of educational and public purpose broadcasting distinct from the US model and separate from the US system. Regarding some specific recommendations, the league was a good deal less radical than Aird had been. For example, it would have allowed low-power local stations to remain privately owned. The league realized that the nationalist argument was the key to moulding opinion in favour of public broadcasting; thus, its first slogan was "Canadian radio for Canadians." But the league had a very particular idea of what "Canadian" would mean. National unity, for the Canadian Radio League, was a way of organizing the free public discussion on which the democratic political process was based.

The league has been called "a superb example of the extent and efficiency of the nationalist network of contacts which was developed among men of affairs and academics in the 1920s."[68] It was set up as a lobby, "to organize Canadian opinion" in favour of the main Aird recommendations.[69] But its nationalism had a strong social thrust. In a letter to Brooke Claxton dated 6 October 1930, the day after the founding of the league, Graham Spry wrote that its purpose was to "protect Canada from a radio system like that of the US."[70] This could only mean one thing: "a radio system like that of the US" would necessarily be a commercial system based on business principles and free enterprise ideology. A "Canadian" system would have to be substantially different.

Spry and Plaunt realized from the start that the league would need to attract support in French Canada to be effective. So they went about recruiting prominent Quebecers like former Aird commissioner Augustin Frigon, the editor of Le Devoir, Georges Pelletier, and the secretary of the University of Montreal, Edouard Montpetit. Next, they turned their attention to the regions,[71] where, with the help of confederates like E.A. Corbett of the University of Alberta, they mobilized support for the Aird report among groups such as the Trades and Labour Congress of Canada, the Canadian Congress of Labour, the National Council of Women, the various provincial organizations of the United Farmers of Canada, and the Independent Labour Party.[72] The lobby was built systematically and across class lines, as Spry and Plaunt recruited bankers, financial leaders, and businessmen as well.

The league apparently approved the intent of the draft legislation to limit the provincial role in the proposed new company. In a letter to Fred Mackelcan of the National Trust Company in Toronto, who had expressed fear that Ottawa would not have firm enough control, Spry wrote that he had "definite authoritative knowledge" that the law would give Ottawa "predominant control" and that only specifically educational and provincial broadcasts needed to be left to the provinces. He framed this piece of information as an "inside tip," noting that it would be unfortunate if Quebec, Ontario, and New Brunswick learned of it since they were determined to gain provincial control of broadcasting.[73]

The question of federal versus provincial control of programs was raised by Georges Pelletier, a strong league supporter in Quebec, in a letter to Spry at the end of 1930. Spry replied that the issue seemed to be the main stumbling block raised by opponents of the plan on both sides who used this to cover up their basic opposition to the more substantive issue of public versus private ownership. In his letter to Pelletier on 21 January 1931, Spry noted that the Toronto *Telegram* said the proposals would mean English Canadians would be forced to listen to French on the air, while *La Presse* said it would mean English domination of the airwaves in Quebec. At this point, the question threatened to divide the league: "These are rough waters and there are dangerous reefs for the Radio League on both shores. It is a typical Canadian situation. Economic interests playing upon race fears, and legitimate but different conceptions of federal authority appearing."[74]

Spry said he was personally "generally favourable to increased Dominion control in most questions, recognizing to the utmost, however, the special position of Quebec." He proposed to Pelletier the interesting solution that the league should stick to the deliberate vagueness of the Aird report and let anglophone and francophone spokesmen offer their own, if necessarily differing, interpretations. On the same day, however, he wrote to Brooke Claxton, the league's principal anglophone Quebecer: "Isn't this a typical Canadian situation? No wonder we are a nation of hypocrites, incapable for the most part of mental honesty."[75]

Meanwhile, the private sector was far from idle. Its lobby was led by one of the most powerful companies in the country, the Canadian Pacific Railways, and the Canadian Association of Broadcasters, the station owners group that was to become "one of the most powerful and influential factors on the Canadian broadcasting scene."[76]

By 1931, the main proposal emanating from the private sector called for the creation of two networks: one government-sponsored and programming educational and culturally "uplifting" programs, the other based on commercial sponsorship and the corporate leadership of the CPR. The public ownership lobby criticized this proposal for making the public bear the cost while the private interests stood to reap the profits of broadcasting.[77]

The private broadcasters – like the public interest groups – couched their position in a discourse of public service. R.W. Ashcroft, a leading lobbyist and head of an organization called Trans-Canada Broadcasting Company, wrote in a January 1931 pamphlet, "Whatever we do with radio in Canada, let our motto be: 'The public be pleased'."[78]

The title of Ashcroft's pamphlet – "Government vs. Private Ownership of Canadian Radio" – indicated the way semantics entered the debate. Ashcroft posed the ownership question as a choice between "government" and "private" ownership. The object of ownership, in either case, was something known as "Canadian" radio, and Ashcroft argued that only "private" ownership was in the public interest. The public lobby, on the other hand, argued that government involvement would make possible a "public" system, holding out the only hope for "Canadian" radio to exist.

It was an ideological debate.

### Nationhood and the Federal-Provincial Dispute

The Aird commission notwithstanding, the provincial authorities in Quebec continued to strengthen their legislative position with respect to broadcasting. In January 1931, Quebec introduced some minor amendments to its 1929 broadcasting act.[79] A month later, Quebec introduced a new Radio Act dealing with the licensing of transmitters and receivers.[80] A third piece of legislation was introduced in Quebec at this time, concerning civil responsibility for broadcast material.[81] Clearly, the Taschereau government was seeking to stake out a position in the field.

In contrast, the other provinces were rallying around the Aird position. On 2 February 1931, the Alberta legislature adopted a resolution "that the best interests of Canada will be served by the adoption of the policy of national ownership of radio broadcasting" and recommended early federal legislation.[82]

An internal memo dated April 1931, and deposited in the files of the Department of Marine and Fisheries in the National Archives of Canada, indicated the federal point of view at this time. The existing system of private ownership, it said, "is very unsatisfactory. Licences are held by those fitted and unfitted to use this great instrument of potential culture to project such programs as they themselves decide, into the sacredness of the home of the broadcast listener." Subsidies to private stations, according to this memo, would be equally unsatisfactory, "putting the interests of the community in the hands of a body whose interests are in principle selfish."[83]

The memo went on to discuss Ottawa's perception of the federal-provincial aspect of the question and appeared concerned about Manitoba, where the government was in fact operating two broadcasting stations and enjoying a provincial monopoly. In general, however, the author felt there was no widespread interest in provinces actually controlling the system.

But in order to act on this definite policy orientation, the government needed to resolve the constitutional question. On 18 February 1931, Ottawa asked the Supreme Court whether the Parliament of Canada had jurisdiction to regulate and control radio communication, and, if not, to what extent its jurisdiction was limited. Arguments were filed with the court in April.[84]

The reference case was provoked by Quebec's new Radio Act, which in effect challenged the jurisdiction in Quebec of the federal Radiotelegraph Act of 1913. In addition to the prior existence of its own legislation, Ottawa had signed the International Radio-Telegraph Convention of 1927, indicating an international (and, therefore, federal) dimension to the question as well.

Quebec, supported by Ontario and New Brunswick (Manitoba, Saskatchewan, and Alberta were represented by counsel but did not take active part in the case), argued that broadcasting was "property and civil rights" and thus fell within the residual jurisdiction of the provinces. Ottawa argued that broadcasting was an "extraprovincial" matter, analogous to transport.

It is important to note the role of the Canadian Radio League in the constitutional debate. Some leading members of the league had an ulterior motive for their interest in the case – as Canadian nationalists, they saw a chance to strengthen Dominion authority against provincial encroachment.[85] Furthermore, the granting of its request to be heard by the Supreme Court meant recognition of the league as "a highly patriotic, nationalistic organization duly qualified to represent 'the public'."[86]

The league's factum, written by Brooke Claxton, unreservedly supported the federal position, embellishing the constitutional argument with an appreciation of the social importance of radio:

Broadcasting, by reason of its very nature, is inevitably interprovincial, and not intraprovincial. The instant a sound is broadcast, the waves that issue are perceptible in every province ...

Broadcasting is the most powerful instrument ever devised for the development of public opinion and public taste. The possibility of dumping advertising matter and releasing propaganda requires that there be safeguards against it as adequate as the tariff or the defence force. Broadcasting can become "a menace to the national life of Canada" not only justifying but requiring action for the whole country by the Dominion ...

Radio is a work and undertaking of the same class as lines of steam and other ships, railways, canals, and telegraphs; it connects the provinces with other provinces and necessarily extends beyond the limits of a province.[87]

The Supreme Court ruled three to two for Ottawa on 30 June 1931, holding that Dominion jurisdiction could be found in section 92(10)a of the British

North America Act which gave the Dominion power to control undertakings that connect provinces or extend beyond provincial boundaries, such as telegraph lines.[88] "The decision is unquestionably a great victory for the Dominion," Brooke Claxton wrote in the us-based *Air Law Review* in November 1931.[89]

Quebec appealed to the Judicial Committee of the Privy Council in London, and the struggle took on the allure of a holy conflict over the very nature of Confederation. Brooke Claxton was determined to go all the way against the provinces, which he described, in a letter to Spry, as "the forces of disintegration."[90]

Anxious about the implications of the league's constitutional stand for its support among French Canadians, Spry consulted Pelletier and Louis St. Laurent, another key supporter in Quebec. Both advised the league to go ahead.[91]

The Judicial Committee of the Privy Council heard the appeal in December 1931. Quebec was supported by the province of Ontario, and the Dominion was supported by the Canadian Radio League.[92] On 9 February 1932, London dismissed the appeal, ruling in favour of the Dominion, on the basis of its residual powers to legislate "for the peace, order and good government of Canada" when an area was not explicitly mentioned in the BNA Act, as in the case of broadcasting. It confirmed the Parliament of Canada's exclusive legislative power to regulate and control radio communication in Canada.[93]

The way was now clear for Ottawa and, seven days later, Prime Minister R.B. Bennett convened a special parliamentary committee to study broadcasting problems and make recommendations.

While it appeared to resolve things, London's decision placed communications at the centre of controversy over the nature of Canadian dualism, where it remains. Analysts of that day and since have seen the issue as more than the question of radio and as a turning point in the shift in Canadian federalism towards Ottawa and away from the provinces (which had enjoyed the support of court decisions for the previous fifty years).

Indeed, broadcasting became a major area of federal government assertiveness as its role expanded. The court decision of 1932 was a key step in the process by which Canada was to become increasingly what constitutional scholar Gil Rémillard has called "a decentralized unitary state," to the detriment of the provinces, regionalism, and the idea of two nations – a process that would accelerate as Ottawa intervened in social policy during the economic crisis of the 1930s, then through the war effort, and, more recently, in natural resources and communications.[94]

Because of its cultural implications, the question of jurisdiction over communications is more than a constitutional issue. Here, the two major conceptions of Canadian dualism conflict: the idea of Canada as one nation comprised of two peoples versus the idea of Quebec as a national homeland for one of those peoples. But, as Rémillard has written, while a state can not exist without a nation, a nation can exist without a state and the national question would continue to be one of the major focal points of the broadcasting system in spite of the constitutional ruling of 1932.

In retrospect, it can be said that the constitutional argument was misplaced, both sides basing their arguments on the technical aspects of radio transmission. Quebec might have done well, for example, to argue on the basis of culture and education. Only the Canadian Radio League, in its factum to the Supreme Court, had dealt with the social dimension of broadcasting, although it had done so within the framework of a centralist conception of Canada that would later be used for repressive ends in times of crisis.

In this important episode, which gave broadcasting jurisdiction in Canada to the central government, the conflicting and competing conceptions of the Canadian public and the Canadian nation were exposed. The league's role in the constitutional challenge was an important turning point in the evolution of this historic conflict over broadcasting in Canada.

The English-Canadian founders of the league had sought the support of French Quebec. However, their contacts there tended to be among the pan-Canadian federalist sector of opinion rather than among French-Canadian nationalists and provincial autonomists. So when the constitutional question arose, the league was advised that it would be prudent to support the Dominion position, which it then proceeded to do. But the Radio League itself reflected the tensions and ambiguities of the two conceptions of the public in Canada in the early 1930s – the democratic and the technocratic – and while a young lawyer and future Liberal cabinet minister like Brooke Claxton had leapt on the constitutional case with gusto, a democratic socialist like Graham Spry was torn over the implications of alienating Quebec.

### A Social Conception of Broadcasting

The idea of a national pressure group of English- and French-speaking Canadians, crossing class lines, originated with Graham Spry.[95] Spry viewed the issue of broadcasting as a question of freedom: "Let the air remain as the prerogative of commercial interests and subject to commercial control, and how free will be the voice, the heart of democracy. The maintenance, the enlargement of freedom, the progress, the purity of education, require the responsibility of broadcasting to the popular will. There can be no liberty complete, no democracy supreme, if the commercial interests dominate the vast, majestic resource of broadcasting."[96]

In a 1931 article aimed at the arguments of the private sector lobby, Spry made this interesting analogy: "Broadcasting ... is no more a business than a public school system is a business ... Broadcasting, primarily, is an instrument of education in its widest significance, ranging from play to learning, from recreation to the cultivation of public opinion, and it concerns and influences not any single element in the community, but the community as a whole."[97]

This conception of broadcasting as a public resource belonging to the community, rather than a commercial vehicle, attracted all but that sector of private enterprise which was directly interested in broadcasting industries (station owners, receiving set manufacturers, advertisers). But a centralized, coordinated, adequately financed *national* system represented a particular hope: "A national radio system, intelligently directed, would give Canada many of the stimuli her national life requires ... It would enable different sections of Canada to speak their hopes and problems unto the others."[98]

Nearly thirty-five years later, Spry reexamined the climate in which the struggle for public broadcasting had taken place:

> It was a period not of "nationalism" in any narrow sense but of "nationhood" ... there was simply the emotion and conviction to carry forward in every field the concept of Canada and of Confederation, not in opposition to or separation from others but in the realization of a national self ... The activists of plus or minus thirty years who ran the Canadian Radio League were not thinking of broadcasting only for its own sake; they were thinking of it very deliberately and consciously as an instrument of communication which could contribute to the easing of the problem of Canadian nationhood.[99]

This was Spry looking backwards from 1965, but in the 1930s he repeatedly emphasized aspects of broadcasting far removed from such primarily national considerations. One of his most outspoken interventions was at the Conference on Canadian-American Affairs held at St Lawrence University, Canton, New York, in June 1935, where he took a rather different approach.

There, he spoke of the role of broadcasting in "the inevitable and incalculable social revolutions which are in process of being born" and of the probability that capitalism and nationalism would not survive much longer in their existing forms. Frontiers were changing, class power was being transformed, and freedom of expression was essential to change taking place peacefully. Only some form of public ownership of media could guarantee that freedom of expression: "If, for example, either class in the social struggle of the times is silenced by the greatest medium for change and cultivating public opinion, then ... there can be no peace."[100]

The movement for public ownership and control had two driving motives, Spry said: to use broadcasting for developing Canadian national unity, and "the hope that new movements of opinion, as represented by socialist groups, trade unions and farm associations, would be able to develop their support by the use of radio." The government was mainly concerned about US influences and, consequently, the first of these driving motives. But the Canadian Radio League combined the two.[101]

Personally, Spry felt the most important objective of a publicly owned broadcasting system was "freedom of the air." The motivation of many of the groups involved in the league was a fear "that so long as private interests owned and operated broadcasting, minority – especially radical minority – opinions would be excluded from the air".[102] In this context, the league's anti-Americanism was really anti-monopoly-capitalism. In a time of capitalist depression and class-divided public opinion, the press was no longer free, but was a repressive representative of narrow nationalism and capitalism:

> The question I raise is this, shall radio broadcasting, still in its infancy particularly in short-wave and television, become the repressive instrument of one or other of the classes into which society is now dividing? In Canada and in the United States, whatever cautious tolerance may now be exercised, this majestic power for influencing public opinion is mainly owned and controlled and used for the purposes of that class which is challenged by those who feel themselves exploited and who demand fundamental changes in ownership and objective.[103]

It has been suggested that Spry's Canton speech, which was widely reported in Canada and the US, was a strategic attempt to intervene in the debate that, in 1935, focused on the failure of the first Canadian effort at national public broadcasting, the Canadian Radio Broadcasting Commission, and would soon lead to creation of the Canadian Broadcasting Corporation.[104] But what we should remember about Graham Spry is not his considerable talents as a publicist and organizer but his vision of Canada, politics, and the public. His was undoubtedly the clearest, most comprehensive, and most consistent social conception of broadcasting to appear in Canada, and recognized the democratic potential of broadcasting organized around the idea of the public.

### A PUBLIC DEBATE, 1932

#### *The Parliamentary Committee*

On 16 February 1932, Prime Minister R.B. Bennett brought the debate on Canadian broadcasting to the floor of the House of Commons. His statement announcing a parliamentary Special Committee on Radio Broadcasting would be cited dozens of times down through the years, usually by politicians of other parties responding to Conservative critics. This statement, the first policy pronouncement on broadcasting by a Canadian prime minister, stands as a major ideological position:

It must be agreed that the present system of radio broadcasting is unsatisfactory. Canadians have the right to a system of broadcasting from Canadian sources equal in all respects to that of any other country ... The enormous benefits of an adequate scheme of radio broadcasting controlled and operated by Canadians is abundantly plain. Properly employed, the radio can be made a most effective instrument in nation building, with an educational value difficult to estimate. [105]

Bennett's statement was an indictment of the existing system. The alternative he envisaged would have to be Canadian, an instrument in nation building, and of educational value. He went on to propose "further inquiry" to build on the "very helpful information" contained in the report of the Aird commission. The House committee would be required to prepare "a complete technical scheme of radio broadcasting for Canada" and to propose "the most satisfactory agency for carrying out such a scheme." So as not to prejudice the work of the committee, Bennett added that it would hear both representatives of private interests and advocates of public ownership. The committee hearings that began on 11 March 1932, turned into a major ideological and political battleground, and Parliament and its various committees would continue to play such a role for the next thirty-five years and more.

The first major witness at the 1932 hearings was Graham Spry. The problem of radio broadcasting, he said, was "a public question": "The position of the Canadian Radio League is that so powerful and useful an agency of communication should be used for the broadest national purposes, that it should be owned and operated by the people, that it should not primarily be adapted to narrow advertising and propagandist purposes by irresponsible companies subject to no popular regulation or control." [106]

The league favoured the general principles of the Aird report with some modification. But it pointed to a sense of urgency in which the national interest was at stake: a new international radio convention was scheduled to be negotiated in Madrid in September 1932, and Canada's interests had to be protected. [107]

Canada, Spry told the committee, was considered part of their territory by the giant American groups like the Radio Corporation of America, RCA. What would Canada's position be, "wedged as she is between a fiercely competitive group of European nations and a dominant American group? Without a program, without a policy, how can Canada claim her share of the air, either at Madrid or at Washington?" [108]

Canada needed a program of broadcast development if it were to argue credibly for a just share of the broadcast spectrum. According to Spry, "a policy of public ownership and operation of radio broadcasting stations in Canada alone will utterly assure Canadian ownership and make possible a system which will justify Canada's claims for more channels." [109]

The choice before the committee was clear: "it is a choice between commercial interests and the people's interests. It is a choice between the State and the United States." [110] Spry was above all a skilful polemicist. These words, concluding a powerful argument of national and state interest, could not fail to shake the politicians of the committee out of their potential sympathies for the collection of businessmen, large and small, who would later follow with arguments in favour of their own clearly vested interests.

The next major witnesses were former royal commissioners Bowman and Frigon. Frigon reiterated his insistence on provincial control of programs, in spite of the constitutional ruling which, as he pointed out, gave the federal government the right to do as it pleased but did not preclude it from using its power intelligently. Frigon also warned of the danger of expecting a system made up of both public and private sectors to serve the national interest: "you cannot mix up the interests of the man who wants to make money out of the equipment and the man who wants to render service to his country." [111] It was a powerful point, coming from one known to have no commitment to public ownership as a general principle.

Later in the hearings, Sir John Aird appeared and said he still endorsed his commission's report. Aird had become a strong supporter of the view that broadcasting should be primarily a means of education and not of commercial exploitation. He stated that private enterprise was too weak to sustain the necessary service in Canada. For the advocates of a public system, this dovetailed nicely with Frigon's earlier testimony.

Further support for a public system came from E.A. Corbett, director of the extension branch of the University of Alberta, which had been involved in educational broadcasting since 1924. A provincial government grant had enabled the university to build a radio station, CKUA, in 1926, and the government had been a financial supporter of the project ever since. Corbett, the western representative of the Canadian Radio League and later a founder of the Canadian Association for Adult Education, was to be one of the leading figures in the public broadcasting movement in Canada. He told the committee that government control was the only way to support education by radio.

Wilfred Bovey, of McGill University's department of extramural relations, echoed this view. In a memo to the committee, Bovey proposed placing the educational vocation of radio ahead of other considerations, and structuring the system accordingly. In Bovey's view, the questions of ownership and control were clearly separated for the first time, with the emphasis placed on control. Whether the infrastructure was owned by the government or by businessmen, there was a need for independent "public" involvement.

The emphasis on education, the fact that some provinces were already involved in broadcasting, and the special interests of Quebec kept the question of a provincial role on the agenda. The Manitoba Telephone System, which operated two provincially supported stations, said it supported the Aird report except for the question of Dominion ownership and operation. Manitoba had a provincial radio policy since 1923, when it had asked Ottawa for complete control. The telephone company proposed a scheme of separate chartered companies in each province, along the lines of the telephone system.

The government of Quebec, meanwhile, sent one of the province's most distinguished attorneys, Aimé Geoffrion, to represent it in a joint appearance with *La Presse* and CKAC. As Graham Spry had feared, the commercial interests of one of the most important private broadcasters in Canada and the regional interests of a provincial government coalesced around a strong argument based on the special needs of the French-speaking population of Quebec. Premier Taschereau, in a telegram to Geoffrion, had given him a precise mandate: "oppose government ownership and if regulation accepted it should be under a commission composed of some members appointed by provinces."[112] The Quebec government saw itself as a countervailing force,[113] but not all provinces shared this view. The government of Nova Scotia, for example, considered the public interest best served by a system of private ownership and federal control, "as is now the case."[114]

Not surprisingly, the most important support for private ownership came from the so-called private sector. In some instances this was a soft position, as in the case of the Canadian Manufacturers' Association which distinguished the interests of radio listeners from those of the firms engaged in the manufacture of sets and supplies. The CMA brief had the merit of attempting to define "good programs" – which in the final analysis was the only issue for disinterested parties and individuals across the land. The first aim of a national policy, it said, should be "programs that provide inspiration, education, information and entertainment; that eliminate that which is offensive to good taste or subversive to morals; that prefer Canadian numbers without entirely excluding the best productions of other countries; and that will satisfy the great majority of reasonable people who like to listen to the radio."[115]

The Association of Radio Manufacturers, which had a very precise interest to protect, took no position on ownership but called for a national regulatory commission that would include representatives of broadcasters, advertisers, and radio manufacturers, as well as the provinces.

The Canadian Association of Broadcasters appeared concerned about the state of the Canadian economy in its call for preserving the status quo. Its brief began: "We believe that this is no time for any Government to invest public funds in broadcasting equipment."[116]

Individual stations, such as CHRC (Quebec City), feared "the community angle of broadcasting" would suffer if private ownership were to disappear.[117] It was ironic to see large national organizations of farmers and labour unions calling for a national, centralized, "public" system while small capitalists called for local, "community" broadcasting.

The one serious private sector alternative to a public system was proposed by CPR president E.W. Beatty, who framed the problem in terms of a need to serve the public interest while taking full advantage of the commercial possibilities of radio. Beatty's scheme was to create a national company in which the railways and other interests would be joint participants through stock ownership. The company would acquire the existing private stations in Canada in exchange for stock in the new company. It would own and operate the stations, subject to regulation by a federal commission, thus combining "private administration and operation, political non-interference and government control."[118]

The fundamental difference between Beatty's plan and the Aird report was that Beatty's company would be owned by the railways and the radio interests while Aird's would be owned by the Crown. To Aird's "public" monopoly, Beatty opposed a "private" monopoly, but both were monopolies nonetheless. In both cases, the public would contribute financially by means of the licence fee and its interest would be served to the extent that the company operated in a public spirit. While the public broadcasting lobby was arguing that a commercial company could never place the public interest above its commercial interests, the private lobby argued that a government-controlled company would also have its own "private" interests to serve. This was a unique confrontation between corporate and state conceptions of the public interest, and, as we know, the state won out. Beatty's plan did not get past the committee, but we owe him this unique formulation: his plan would have meant "a private public service corporation, as against a Government corporation."[119]

The widest range of opinion expressed before the committee favoured some form of public ownership and control. Labour and farm groups, particularly, saw a national broadcasting system as important to providing a platform for their particular interests. Among the labour organizations that either appeared, sent written submissions, or made representations through the Canadian Radio League[120] were: the All-Canadian Congress of Labour, the Trades and Labour Congress of Canada, the Canadian Brotherhood of Railway Employees, the Allied Trades and Labour Association, the Independent Labour Party of Saskatchewan, the Alberta Federation of Labour, and local labour councils from Lethbridge, Hamilton, Prince Rupert, Victoria, Winnipeg, Toronto, and Moncton. Only one labour organization, the Union typographique Jacques-Cartier, intervened against public ownership. Farmer support for public broadcasting came from the United Farmers of Alberta, the United Farmers of Canada, and the United Farmers of Manitoba, as well as the UFA-controlled Alberta legislature. Support for government ownership and control was also filed by the Canadian Legion, the Native Sons of Canada, the New Brunswick Federation of Women, the National Council of Women, the Imperial Order of the Daughters of the Empire, the Catholic Women's League of Canada, the Federated Women's Institutes of Canada, the Canadian Federation of University Women, the Canadian Chamber of Commerce, and various local boards of trade. The National Broadcasting Company of New York declined an invitation to appear.

A month into the parliamentary hearings, Graham Spry appeared a second time and explained the nature of the Canadian Radio League: "We think that it is a somewhat unique organization and can fairly claim to represent the public. What other organization is there that combines bankers and financiers with labour unions and united farmers, Daughters of the Empire and Native Sons of Canada, east and west, Catholic and Protestant, French and English?" [121]

The league's memorandum cited broadcasting as "the most powerful of all human agencies of communication ... so majestic in its potentialities, so capable of both good and ill ... that no other agency than the State should ultimately be responsible for its operation and control." Democracy, the league said, was by definition a system of government by public opinion, and broadcasting was "palpably the most potent and significant agency for the formation of public opinion." [122]

The league was careful not to advocate public ownership as a general principle. Its position was based on the view that radio was a natural monopoly rather than a competitive business and that only the Canadian government could prevent the undue influence being exercised by commercial groups in the United States. To Spry, the issue was a North American one between "powerful electrical monopolies and the peoples of the two nations." [123] According to the Canadian Radio League, the parliamentary committee held in its hands the fate of the shape and character of public opinion in Canada. Indeed, Spry was saying, it was an issue that transcended nationalism.

The league's proposal for "public ownership of stations, private enterprise and competition in programs" included some major differences from Aird's. Rather than a public monopoly, the league favoured a network of publicly owned stations, a national system owned and operated by a national company, and a series of low-powered local stations owned and operated by local organizations, subject to regulation by the national system. [124]

While recommending a consultative role for the provinces and recognition of "the special position of the Province of Quebec," the league's position on Quebec was vague enough to provoke an exchange with committee members. MP Onésime Gagnon pointed out that some members of Parliament were opposed to public ownership on the grounds that it would mean the necessary broadcast of French to western Canada. Spry said, indeed, such broadcasts should be given consideration. Discussion continued:

> Mr. Garland: As a matter of fact, Mr. Spry, don't you think it is far more likely that those interests will get fairer consideration under public ownership than they could ever expect under private ownership?
>
> Witness: Under our institutions, French Canadian people exert a greater influence under democratic organizations where their votes have an influence than under commercial organizations, where their votes have no influence. [125]

The following day, CKAC director Arthur Dupont made an important intervention in opposition to the league plan. Dupont had already appeared on behalf of CKAC, along with Aimé Geoffrion, at which time he called for continuing the policy of private ownership under federal government supervision, increased wattage to stations who wanted it, subsidized transmission lines, and cooperation between station owners and provincial authorities on matters of national interest and education – a real pot-pourri that only the major private station in Quebec could have concocted. This time, however, Dupont spoke as a "Canadian of French extraction," arguing that the league plan would deprive French Canadians of French-language stations, as "national" programs would inevitably be in English:

> Mr. Chairman and gentlemen, forget for a moment that I am appearing before you as Director of CKAC ... Under Government ownership when you tax the French-speaking people of Canada for their entertainment you must be prepared to give them the same amount of entertainment as you accord our English-speaking compatriots. This, gentlemen, entails two chains, not one ... Is it not better to lay our cards on the table and in a friendly manner discuss these issues rather than rush through National ownership without provision for such issues, which might cause strife and bitter feeling between two great races? Gentlemen, one can easily see how broadcasting, instead of bringing our two great races together in bonds of harmony, could through immaterial judgment work incalculable harm. [126]

Read in the context of Graham Spry's 1931 letter to Georges Pelletier, this can be seen as a skilful emotional appeal against public ownership. Indeed, Spry immediately intervened to call Dupont "totally erroneous" because of the provision in the league plan for provincial control of programs. However, Dupont definitely touched a raw nerve in this early formulation of an argument that would return to haunt the architects of public broadcasting in Canada again and again, and would also determine Canadian broadcasting's basic structure and, ultimately, its history.

The Special Committee on Radio Broadcasting reported to the House of Commons on 9 May 1932. Its three-page report was an articulate statement of national needs, with no direct mention of the public. It emphasized "the national importance and international character of radio broadcasting ... as a medium of education, thought-provoking development, and fostering of Canadian ideals and culture, entertainment, news service and publicity of this country and its products, and as an auxiliary to religious and educational teaching, also as one of the most efficient mediums for developing a greater National and Empire consciousness within the Dominion and the British Commonwealth of Nations." It concluded that "the present system, excellent as it is in certain respects, does not meet the requirements in quality and scope of broadcasting to ensure its maximum benefits."[127]

The report recommended a chain of nationally owned high-power stations, supplemented by low-power stations to serve outlying areas as second stations, for educational purposes, experimental work, and local broadcasting of community interest. The system was to be self-sustaining, and financially based on a licence fee and advertising income. It would be run by a three-member commission, with an assistant commissioner for each province. The commission would have the power to regulate and control all broadcasting in Canada, including programs and advertising. It could own, build, and operate stations, acquire existing ones, originate or acquire programs, determine stations, issue broadcasting licences, prohibit private chains, and in the final analysis, "subject to the approval of the Parliament of Canada, ... take over all broadcasting in Canada." It was extremely important, the committee said, "that the Board should not assume, or even be suspected of assuming, a political complexion."[128]

As several writers have noted, the proposed commission was a departure from the main recommendation of both the Aird report and the Canadian Radio League, which had each called for a "public" corporation or company that would be independent of government control by definition.[129] The House of Commons adopted the committee's report on 11 May 1932.

### The Radio Broadcasting Act (1932)

On 16 May 1932, the government introduced legislation along the lines of the parliamentary committee's report, but with some additional administrative restrictions. On 18 May, moving second reading of the bill, Prime Minister Bennett made another historic statement emphasizing its "national" aspects:

> First of all, this country must be assured of complete Canadian control of broadcasting from Canadian sources, free from foreign interference or influence. Without such control radio broadcasting can never become a great agency for the communication of matters of national concern and for the diffusion of national thought and ideals, and without such control it can never be the agency by which

national consciousness may be fostered and sustained and national unity still further strengthened ...

Secondly, no other scheme than that of public ownership can ensure to the people of this country, without regard to class or place, equal enjoyment of the benefits and pleasures of radio broadcasting. Private ownership must necessarily discriminate between densely and sparsely populated areas. This is not a correctable fault in private ownership. It is an inescapable and inherent demerit of that system. [130]

The plan, Bennett said, would assure "equality of service" via the chain of high-power stations, and "the particular requirements of any community" by low-power stations for local broadcasting. At the same time, he announced, an arrangement made with the United States would free up new channels as required for Canadian use: "Then there is a third reason ... The use of the air, or the air itself ... that lies over the soil or land of Canada is a natural resource over which we have complete jurisdiction under the recent decision of the privy council ... I cannot think that any government would be warranted in leaving the air to private exploitation and not reserving it for development for the use of the people." [131]

The Liberal spokesman, Ernest Lapointe, endorsed Bennett's views and gave "full accord" to the principle embodied in the bill. Then, Independent Labour Party member J.S. Woodsworth (who had been the first MP to call for public broadcasting back in 1928) congratulated the prime minister for his "admirable statement." Only one MP, E.J. Young of Weyburn, Saskatchewan, opposed the principle of the bill.

Debate on the bill raised no opposition to public ownership, focusing instead on finances, the naming of commissioners, the control of programs, and guarantees against political abuses. As the committee had recommended, the bill proposed a system of three commissioners and nine assistant commissioners representing each province. It also provided for provincial or local advisory committees "so that from the small unit up to the Dominion there is effective democratic control of broadcasting," in Bennett's words.

The bill said the assistant commissioners "may" be appointed by the governor in council, after consultation with each province (as in the 1930 draft legislation's solution to the Aird dilemma). Liberal critic P.J.A. Cardin wanted assurance that the assistant commissioners would, indeed, be named, in light of the lack of obligation implied by the wording. Bennett assured him the provincial commissioners would be named. [132]

On 24 May, the bill was given third reading, and on 26 May, the Canadian Radio Broadcasting Act became law, creating the Canadian Radio Broadcasting Commission, or CRBC. [133] To the pressure groups, it was a victory of public service over private profit. The Canadian Radio League considered it had achieved its goal and became inactive. [134]

But the official discourse was one of "national purpose," not public service, as the texture of the legislation reflected. Graham Spry said R.B. Bennett, the champion of private enterprise, "had a conflict within his soul" when he took up the cause of national broadcasting against his own ideological conviction and some strong opposition within his party. [135] But in fact, Bennett had been convinced of the need for state intervention in broadcasting if there were to be a Canada. Bennett had come up against a typically Canadian problem and he had met it head on. [136]

# CHAPTER TWO

# Administrative Broadcasting (1932–49)

## INTRODUCTION

"The Broadcasting Act of 1932 was a great innovation," Herschel Hardin wrote in *A Nation Unaware*. "Since then we have gone backwards."[1] In the less-charged language of the 1957 Royal Commission on Broadcasting, "the newly created national system did not succeed in providing overnight the broadcasting service which the 1932 legislation envisaged."[2]

Canadian broadcasting had begun to develop on the periphery of the embryonic American radio industry, basically unhampered by public intervention. Then, in the 1920s and 1930s, a broad consensus emerged around the view that only a public broadcasting system could meet the national objectives of Canadian broadcasting. The early objections to public broadcasting came from those who saw broadcasting as an industry and those who had a different, in effect, "non-national" view of Canada. The consensus for public broadcasting was shared by men as politically disparate as R.B. Bennett and Mackenzie King on one side, and E.A. Corbett and Graham Spry on the other. These men had different conceptions of the public but shared the common view that their particular conceptions could be advanced by a national public broadcasting system.

Broadcasting, along with the ambivalent political and cultural needs of the Canadian élites of the 1930s, evolved as a hybrid of the British and American public service and commercial models. The agency created to oversee all broadcasting activity in Canada, the Canadian Radio Broadcasting Commission, demonstrated the Canadian dilemma: behind an official rhetoric of public service and national pluralism, the CRBC ran up against the ideology of private enterprise and the politics of anglo-centric domination. The brief CRBC experience left a double legacy: it established the reality of public-private competition in broadcasting as overriding the policy objective of public supremacy and it demonstrated the impossibility of reconciling Canada's two national interests within a single broadcasting service.

Between these two great paradoxes stood the proponents of broadcasting as an essentially progressive tool for education and social action. Voluntary associations, trade unions, and educators generally saw the state as the appropriate vehicle of sponsorship for socially committed broadcasting, but were unsatisfied with the CRBC.[3]

In 1935, in the midst of an economic depression that saw one Canadian worker in three without a job, Mackenzie King and the Liberals were returned to power in Ottawa. Convinced that the country was on the brink of chaos, King became obsessed with the need to create and maintain a sense of national unity.[4] In this context, he was particularly susceptible to a renewed campaign by the Canadian Radio League in support of new legislation and a new broadcasting agency – the result was the Canadian Broadcasting Act of 1936,[5] which did away with the CRBC and created the Canadian Broadcasting Corporation.

The debate surrounding creation of the CBC marked the ascendancy of a technocratic approach to broadcasting in which "public" and "national" interests were deemed to be equal. The new act appeared to create an autonomous public corporation but it in fact unleashed a process of bureaucratic power-grabbing which would soon be denounced by some of the people closest to the CBC. The legislative and administrative framework created by the act of 1936 was a victory for the managerial view of democracy. It established an important ideological steering mechanism for the state, without preventing the ultimate strengthening of the private sector.

The 1936 act may have been a short-term setback for private broadcasters but, again, over the objections of no less a supporter of private enterprise than the former Conservative prime minister R.B. Bennett, the King government continued to license private radio broadcasters. The campaign that had led to public broadcasting was followed by an eventually far more sustained effort in favour of private, commercial broadcasting which, by virtue of a position intrinsically more consistent with the overall orientation of the Canadian public authority, imposed itself and its interests increasingly over the years.

But from 1936 through to the end of the war, the main development was the consolidation of public broadcasting. In general, the war provided the opportunity for forging strong, technology-based institutions that would transform the nature of power in industrial societies. This was particularly crucial in the case of institutions operating in the sphere of ideas.[6] The CBC quickly acquired the relative autonomy of state bureaucracies that had led some contemporary observers of the political economy of the 1930s and 1940s to refer to the dawning of a new era of "managers."[7]

While managing the public airwaves in the public/national interest in the pre- and immediate postwar periods, the CBC developed a techno-bureaucratic mode of functioning. During this time, the contradictions in the system were underscored by the way the CBC was linked to the Canadian war effort and in the centralized, bureaucratic exercise of dominance by the corporation over attempts to express alternative visions of public broadcasting. At the same time, the CBC nonetheless innovated popular forms of broadcasting involving listeners as citizens.

So, in the 1930s and 1940s, the "state-administrative" view of the public and the "social-participative" view coexisted, often uneasily, within the corporate framework of the CBC. While public broadcasting was a tool of nation building (and, in wartime, of state propaganda), it also played a role in stimulating public discussion and debate on social issues. However, broadcasting could only with great difficulty be used for building a sense of community at any level other than the national one, and in no case could it be used for building an alternative solidarity that could be perceived as threatening to Canadian national unity.

A second historic compromise thus emerged during the period 1936–49, as public broadcasting was consolidated as an extension of the state. Meanwhile, the CBC shared the Canadian airwaves with increasingly numerous and important privately owned radio broadcasters, who, by the late 1940s, had successfully imposed their own conception of the public, defined as an audience of consumers of radio fare. By demonstrating the esteem in which they were held by particular sectors of the audience "market," the private broadcasters won legitimacy for their conception of the public – which, importantly, coincided with the dominant postwar ideology of North America.

## A FALSE START: THE CRBC, 1932–36

### "Fair Play"

The new Canadian Radio Broadcasting Commission was fraught with difficulty. It was underfunded, understaffed, and according to its critics, poorly led. To chair it, the government named Hector Charlesworth, a well-known Toronto journalist and editor of *Saturday Night* magazine. Charlesworth later painted a picture of continuous attempts "to hamstring public broadcasting" by government officials trying to undermine the prime minister, and "covert conspiracies hatched in the lobbies."[8]

In spite of the unanimity of the 1932 legislation, there was a lack of agreement in political circles as to the objectives of broadcasting and the location of responsibility for meeting them. It was especially unclear how "national" objectives could be reconciled with the rights of private station owners.[9]

The CRBC was entirely dependent on the government, but the government did not know what to do with it. Bennett hired as his adviser on broadcasting an expatriate Canadian expert from the BBC, Gladstone Murray, and he wrote to Alan Plaunt at the end of 1932 that the prime minister was "obviously in a muddle" as to how the CRBC should work.[10] Murray recommended a "partnership" of publicly and privately owned stations, working together in a system guided by a philosophy of social responsibility, but the law indicated a public service monopoly while many Conservatives' ideological convictions favoured the independence of private enterprise.

By the fall of 1933, less than a year after beginning operations, the CRBC was a high-profile embarrassment to the government and, also, the source of a political crisis over language. At the end of 1932, the CRBC hired Arthur Dupont to organize its French-language operations. As of May 1933, it began broadcasting nationally for one hour each night. With vice-president Thomas Maher in charge of programs, three or four national hours each week were broadcast in French. Before long, there occurred what Weir has called "the rumpus over programming in French." Despite their quality, the sudden appearance of French programs on the national network in peak listening time "provoked a veritable flood of protests from press and public, from the Maritimes, and particularly from Ontario and Western Canada."[11] According to Weir, who was employed by the commission at the time, the presence of general programming in French on national radio sparked "a queer mixture of prejudice, bigotry and fear."[12]

E.A. Corbett has described the climate this way: "During the summer of 1933, a particularly bitter wave of feeling against the Commission occurred as a result of the preponderance of programs in French, originating in Montreal and broadcast over the Canadian network. A great many people in Ontario and in Western Canada awoke to the fact that Canada is a bilingual country; and led by certain Dominion-wide organizations, vigorous protest was made against what was considered to be an infringement of majority rights."[13]

According to Austin Weir, the trouble came from anti-Catholic organizations like the Orange Order, the Ku Klux Klan, the Royal Black Knights of Ireland, and the Protestant Vigilance Committee. Some groups called for the abolition of the CRBC, and in 1933 there were demonstrations at Massey Hall in Toronto against French on the air.

Feeble attempts to deal with the situation did little to help. For one thing, the provision in the law for provincial commissioners and advisory committees was never put into effect, keeping the onus of the problem on the three-member commission. In May 1933, Charlesworth tried stopping French broadcasts at the Ontario-Manitoba border. Maher objected and reinstituted them.[14] In the summer of 1933, Charlesworth travelled west, knowing he would "face a challenge with regard to French on the air."[15] The language issue was his main subject of discussion from Winnipeg to Vancouver. Charlesworth was called on by representatives of the Ku Klux Klan, then active in Saskatchewan and Alberta, who told him they did not want to hear French on the radio. Charlesworth argued that programs originating in the west came into Quebec in English, but the Klan was not impressed.[16]

The radio experience irritated sentiments in Quebec, where nationalist opinion generally was that the Bennett government was moving away from national conciliation. For example, Bennett had only three French-Canadian cabinet ministers whereas Mackenzie King had employed six out of respect for proportionality.[17] The experience of the CRBC was further evidence of what Frank Peers calls "the disagreement on the meaning of Canadian nationhood ... National radio was one of the most direct ways of reminding English Canadians that they shared their country with French-speaking citizens, and the reminder was not always welcome."[18]

Having created a system on the basis of nationalist feeling, the architects of Canadian public broadcasting thus found themselves unable to reconcile competing and conflicting concepts of the Canadian nation. In 1934, the CRBC split its service in two and began doing separate programming in French for Quebec. Later, the Canadian Broadcasting Corporation would institutionalize this situation by creating separate services for French and English programming.

This is the less than glorious background to the origin of one of the great paradoxes of Canadian public broadcasting: the promotion and sustainment of the French-Canadian, later Québécois, difference by a system set up expressly to promote pan-Canadian national unity. As early as 1934, Canadian public broadcasting served two audiences, two markets, and two publics with one policy, one mandate, and one institution.[19]

In March 1934, a special parliamentary committee began meeting to review the operations of the CRBC. Its deliberations revealed a curious semantic evolution in the discourse on broadcasting. Politicians repeatedly referred to private stations as "private community stations," prompting CRBC chairman Charlesworth to comment at one point: "I do not know what is meant by a community station. That is a very loose definition. We call them privately-owned stations."[20]

Charlesworth's testimony revealed that the CRBC had little hope of establishing itself as the predominant broadcaster in Canada since it had not been provided with the necessary capital to acquire private stations as foreseen in the law. For example, in Montreal, the CRBC's major production centre and one of Canada's major radio markets, the CRBC had to create a new station in competition with the CBS and NBC affiliates, CKAC and CFCF, in order to gain exposure for its programs.

Because the CRBC lacked the means to establish a fully nationalized system, its practical goal was limited to establishing a national network. The private stations, meanwhile, sought to take advantage of the situation. Harry Sedgwick, owner of CFRB (Toronto) proposed that broadcasting operations be left in private hands and that the commission's role be redefined as one of regulation and provision of assistance to private broadcasters.

The Canadian Radio League submitted a written brief to the committee stating that the principle of a public system was "imperilled" by the existing system, and reiterating its 1932 proposals for a national organization "with the powers of a private corporation and the functions of a public utility." An independent public corporation would exercise indirect public control, the league said. The key aspect of this proposal was a nonpartisan, unpaid, broadly representative board of directors, which would act as a buffer between the operating agency and the government of the day, and also between the operating corporation and "community pressure." The general manager would be responsible to the board, not to Parliament. Thus, in the league scheme, the broadcasting agency's board of directors – not the government or the programmers – would represent the public interest in broadcasting.[21]

The All-Canadian Congress of Labour also presented a public interest position, deploring the fact that the CRBC had not achieved a monopoly in broadcasting. W.T. Burford described the private stations' claim to a right to exist as "a peculiarly arrogant vested interest." The congress called for complete removal of radio from the commercial sphere by not renewing private broadcasting licences upon expiry. It claimed to speak for the listener, not labour, pointing out that this measure, and the elimination of advertising, would undoubtedly cost jobs. The congress position was consistent with its general policy for nationalization of all basic industries as public utilities: "But in radio, above all, we believe there is no room for competition if the public is to be served."[22]

An interesting difference can be noticed in the positions of the league and the congress. While the league recognized a role for small-scale private broadcasting at the local or "community" level and addressed itself in this case strictly to the structures and organization of the public component of the system, the labour organization was strongly in favour of a public monopoly. Distinctions of this sort would become increasingly important in the evolution of the system during the next fifteen years.

The language question was another theme of the committee's hearings. Private broadcasting lobbyist R.W. Ashcroft sent a letter stating that the French language was offensive to British-Canadian homes. The radio editor of the Toronto *Telegram* concurred. A spokesman for the Moose Jaw Radio Association tabled a collection of letters from listeners calling for the removal of French from the air. The committee also heard suggestions that separate programs be aimed at English and French audiences, rather than subjecting both audiences to bilingual announcements. A specific area of controversy concerned the broadcasting of bilingual inter-university debates which the CRBC had been doing as a public service.

The secretary of the University of Montreal, Edouard Montpetit, testified that national broadcasting had brought the provinces closer together and bilingualism was a question of "fair play." This view was countered by Regina MP F.W. Turnbull, who saw the use of French on the air in Saskatchewan "as an assertion that Saskatchewan is bilingual, when the people of Saskatchewan say it is not."[23]

The opposing views of Canada evident here were thus thrust into the debate on public broadcasting. Ironically, Turnbull's view of a tolerated minority confined to a clearly defined territory, Quebec, supported the assertions of those who opposed public broadcasting on the basis of Quebec's need for autonomy, while Montpetit's idealistic view of one harmonious nation made up of two equal peoples became one of the most persuasive arguments for a strong, centralized public broadcasting system.

The committee reported to Parliament on 29 June. It basically avoided dealing with the potential controversies that had been laid before it. But without rocking the boat, it noted that a greater commitment of public funds was required in order to achieve the objectives of 1932. In the short term, the committee recommended putting operations of the CRBC under a general manager, simplifying the manner of collecting licence fees as a means of increasing revenue, and a more liberal interpretation of the legal restrictions on advertising. It also indicated the first slight shift in attitude towards the fundamental question of a public monopoly when it proposed that "pending nationalization of all stations, greater co-operation should be established between privately-owned stations and the Commission."[24]

By 1934, then, a pattern was emerging. The system was beginning to be shaped by the need to balance pressures from "public" and "private" interest groups at the same time as it was being used in the struggle to determine the shape of Canada itself.

*A New Act*

In spite of the parliamentary inquiry, problems continued to plague the CRBC – inadequate funds, a cumbersome set-up, lack of independence. With an election coming, the Canadian Radio League began to lobby the Liberals, with the accurate expectation that they were about to return to power.[25] Radio actually became an issue in the 1935 elections when the CRBC allowed a series of clumsy paid political broadcasts in favour of the Conservative Party to go on the air unidentified as such. Using information supplied by Alan Plaunt of the league, the Liberals attacked the CRBC as a partisan organization.[26]

The CRBC provided a national news service via an arrangement with the Canadian Press. It imported major US and British programs but it could not compete with the mass demand for American programs in the continental popular culture which was taking shape. Meanwhile, criticism of the commission's programs and policies was often difficult to separate from opposition to the underlying principles. For example, some segments of French-Canadian opinion saw opposition to the CRBC as opposition to the use of French in Canada. At the same time, the CRBC was seen in certain English-Canadian circles as "an instrument of French domination, or at least as a French-dominated organization."[27] But Quebec nationalists, too, were not happy with the quality of the broadcasts offered by the CRBC.[28]

The editor of *L'Action nationale*, Arthur Laurendeau, in a substantial two-part article on radio about a year later, was critical of the medium in general. Radio, he wrote, was slipping into a state of barbarity: "We can no longer remain indifferent towards radio as a whole, contenting ourselves with the odd hour of refuge before a beautiful symphony. We must be concerned with what is done there the rest of the week, for if there is any further reduction in present standards, we will soon see the day when there is no longer place on the air for a symphony. Art is distinguished by quality as opposed to quantity. But radio survives only by force of quantity. On radio, silence is forbidden."[29]

According to Gladstone Murray, Prime Minister Bennett had planned to create a department of communications to centralize radio, telegraph, and telephone operations.[30] But, in October 1935, a new Liberal government was elected. Prime Minister King wanted an early reorganization of broadcasting and was interested in using Alan Plaunt of the Canadian Radio League as a resource person. Graham Spry, on the other hand, was officially out of the picture now since he had become an organizer with the newly formed Co-operative Commonwealth Federation (CCF).

However, Spry was still a vocal advocate of a social conception of public broadcasting. As we saw earlier, he had developed what we might call a socialist view of the question, as compared with the nationalist view of official policy and the technocratic view that was about to emerge. In his 1935 talk to the conference on Canadian-American affairs he, too, had declared the CRBC a failure: "[It] has become an instrument for subsidizing private enterprise, it has become a creature in some measure of the party in power, and its regulations, though not enforced, are a challenge to the freedom of the air ... The Canadian experiment has failed ... If Canada is to have a Canadian public opinion, then Canada must have a first-class and adequately financed system of national broadcasting ... administered by an independent body, above party or commercial consideration and capable of the broadest tolerance and freedom."[31]

The new minister responsible for broadcasting, C.D. Howe, ordered up two draft bills, one from Brooke Claxton and Alan Plaunt and the other from the director of radio in the Department of Marine and Fisheries, C.P. Edwards. Both proposed replacing the CRBC with a corporation, but there was a major difference: Plaunt and Claxton wanted the new corporation to regulate the private stations (as the CRBC had done), while Edwards wanted regulatory control to revert to the minister.

This involved an important principle: the relationship between the public and private sectors of broadcasting. The main complaint of the private stations had been their resentment at being regulated by the CRBC. The arrangement was justified as a temporary one, since the 1932 legislation foresaw the eventual disappearance of private stations altogether.

At the end of 1935, C.D. Howe told Plaunt "he was being deluged with submissions" from organizations such as the Bell telephone system, the Canadian National Railways, the Canadian Pacific Railways, the Canadian Daily Newspaper Association, the Canadian Press, and the Canadian Association of Broadcasters.[32] The American networks CBS and NBC were also lobbying in Ottawa for a government exodus from broadcasting, which they proposed to run for Canada as a concession. While there was little sympathy for this plan, Howe told Plaunt in January 1936 that he did not like the idea of an "ultimate monopoly" for the public company, but preferred Edwards's proposal of ministerial control. Howe also wanted board members to hold office "at pleasure," rather than for a fixed term. However, he sent Claxton a copy of Edwards's draft for critique and Claxton objected to the fact that the proposal placed the public corporation "on an equal footing with any private person operating stations." This, he said, completely ignored the ultimate objective of a national public monopoly. "I quite see that the day of bringing that about is relatively far off but I do not think that we should give up the principle of ultimate public ownership and immediate public control now," he wrote the minister.[33]

As word of the draft bill got out, similar objections began to issue from other quarters. C.D. Howe put the legislation on hold and convened yet another parliamentary committee on radio broadcasting in March 1936.

By now, there were two views of public broadcasting on the table: C.D. Howe's view of a mixed-ownership system under ministerial control, and the Canadian Radio League's view of a publicly controlled monopoly with limited place in the system for private ownership. The 1936 committee was to be the site of confrontation between the two views and of a victory for the league that the supporters of public broadcasting would prematurely consider final.

The committee's main mandate was to inquire into the operations of the CRBC and its administration of the act and to recommend changes. The first witness was Hector Charlesworth, who complained that the act bore only "a very small resemblance" to the Aird report. He noted that the provincial assistant commissioners had never been appointed and that the government had not acted on the recommendations of the 1934 committee. In defence of the CRBC, he pointed out that the only sustained attack on its activities had come from those opposed to hearing French on the air.[34]

The 1936 committee quickly became the occasion for consideration of the relationship between broadcasting and the formalities of the political process. As a result of the controversies surrounding the CRBC's role in the general elections of 1935, the committee's mandate from Parliament had included the charge of inquiring into the extent to which there had been any abuse of broadcasting privileges for political purposes.[35] During the committee's deliberations, it emerged that the CRBC had no real policy regarding election-time broadcasts, and had actually tried to interfere as little as possible with the parties in 1935. However, according to Charlesworth, it had taken a more directive stance in the Quebec provincial elections of 1936, exercising censorship of election speeches that it considered "inflammatory."[36] These were the first election campaigns in which radio played an important part, and led to the first attempts to formulate regulations on the subject.

The Canadian Radio League appeared before the committee and presented a plan to reorganize the broadcasting system, reiterating the basic principle that the league had argued for in 1932: that of "a single national authority to control ... all broadcasting in Canada, both public and private, and ultimately to own a monopoly of the high-power chain stations."[37]

The Broadcasting Act of 1932 recognized this principle, the league brief stated (the act actually went further, and foresaw a complete monopoly), but the league was disappointed with the performance of the existing structure. It called, instead, (as it had in 1932 and 1934) for "a public corporation, modelled on business lines, with a broadcasting expert as general manager and a representative and non-partisan board of directors or governors."[38] This proposal combined two important notions: political autonomy and technical expertise. In this combination, the idea of public control by technocracy was beginning to emerge.

The league's base of support was the same as it had been in 1932. It submitted statements from the Canadian Legion, the Trades and Labour Congress, the Universities Conference, the United Farmers of Alberta, and the United Farmers of Canada (Saskatchewan). As in the past, it invoked the support of public opinion to back up its campaign. In arguing for the principle of a public system, the league emphasized the "natural monopoly" of radio, and the insufficient revenue base for a Canadian system to survive without submitting to US influence. It named the possible alternatives – subsidized private ownership, commission control without ownership, competing public and private chains, or private monopoly – and rejected each of these as undesirable. A national broadcasting system, the league said, would be "as important to the continued existence of Canada as an independent nation in the twentieth century as transcontinental railways were to its inception in the nineteenth."[39]

In its detailed reorganization plan, the league emphasized that "broadcasting is a special medium not susceptible of ordinary types of public control." It reiterated the "buffer" principle it had introduced in 1934, calling for a board to protect corporate management from "community or partisan pressure." The board would be "the guarantee to the public that broadcasting was being administered in a business-like and non-partisan fashion"; it would be "the trustees of the national interest in broadcasting." But operations would be conducted by a single chief executive, as in "any other business."[40]

In oral summary of the league position, Alan Plaunt stated what was to become the underlying philosophy of national public broadcasting in Canada: "The conditions of successful public service broadcasting are expert management, free from partisan or community interference, together with ultimate parliamentary control over major, as distinct from day-to-day, policy."[41] Thus, the technocratic bent was further emphasized, by equating "partisan" and "community" pressure. At the same time, the public and the national interests were defined as meaning the same thing.

The language of broadcasting was still a question in the minds of some MPs in 1936. Asked how the league would deal with it, Plaunt replied that the key was to set up a board representing the regions, both language groups, and the national interest – "a national board and not ... a board representing sections of Canada."[42]

The league's claim to speak for French as well as English Canada was supported by Father Henri St-Denis of the University of Ottawa. The educational and religious authorities of French Canada were behind the league, he said, because it was the only organization promoting the idea of broadcasting as an instrument of both education and national unity. French-Canadian public opinion saw radio "as a national and educational affair," and considered that "the educational aspect of radio will be best promoted by government control."[43]

The Association of Canadian Advertisers, the Canadian Association of Advertising Agencies, and the Canadian Association of Broadcasters made representations to the committee calling for the separation of regulatory and operating functions along the lines of the government's draft bill. They were prepared to accept government control and supervision but opposed government ownership of stations (they never referred to "public" ownership as such). The role of a government agency would be to produce, acquire, and distribute programs, to supplement the commercial broadcasters, to organize distribution lines, and to ensure the broadcasting of events of national and international importance too costly for private broadcasters or commercial sponsors to bear. It was a candid and interesting perspective of the role of the public sector, and an interesting one to recall in light of later history.[44]

The draft bill appeared, in this context, to be a kind of compromise between the "public" and "private" positions, calling for a public corporation yet recognizing the separateness of the private stations. The Canadian Radio League took strong issue with the government's proposal, which it referred to as a policy of "divided control," in which "the public system becomes simply one of a number of competing systems, invited to capture the field, if it can."[45]

Despite the intense behind-the-scenes efforts of the private lobby and the personal attitude of the minister responsible and some of his closest advisers, the argument for the need for public pre-eminence carried the day. Mackenzie King told committee chairman A.L. Beaubien, "We want the Aird report and this [the league proposals] is the Aird report brought up to date."[46] But Hector Charlesworth's assertion that by 1936 "nationalized radio had become an accepted institution which it would have been folly to oppose"[47] turned out to be rather premature.

The parliamentary committee report, tabled 26 May 1936, closely followed the recommendations of the Canadian Radio League. In general, it reaffirmed the broad principles of the Aird report, the Radio Broadcasting Act, and the parliamentary committees of 1932 and 1934. It called for a new act "which will place the direction of broadcasting in the hands of a corporation," operating through an experienced broadcasting executive as general manager responsible to an honorary board of nine governors representing all parts of Canada. It explicitly reaffirmed the principle of "complete nationalization of radio broadcasting in Canada." Pending the accomplishment of a fully public system, the committee called for "the fullest cooperation" between the corporation and the private stations, and said it would be "a fundamental requirement" for the minister to consult with the corporation before taking any steps to affect the status of any private station (effectively recognizing the corporation as regulatory authority).[48]

On 15 June 1936, the minister of the Department of Marine and Fisheries, C.D. Howe, introduced a bill to create the Canadian Broadcasting Corporation "for the purpose of carrying on a national broadcasting service in Canada."[49] The former prime minister, R.B. Bennett, made a long intervention criticizing the part of the proposal that provided for the continued licensing of private stations: "All you have to do is grant enough licences and you destroy the public character of Canadian broadcasting."[50] Bennett well characterized the problem of the emerging Canadian broadcasting compromise in his assessment of the private interests:

Their idea is that it should be in the hands of private enterprise. The two or three great enterprises across the line have watched with increasing anxiety the operations of this publicly owned facility. They do not desire that their privately owned enterprises should be regarded merely as tentative experiments; they wish to continue as a privately owned enterprise and not be merged in a publicly owned and controlled broadcasting system such as we have in this country.[51]

C.D. Howe rebutted Bennett with the argument that the bill maintained the principles which had been evolving since 1928, and the Canadian Broadcasting Act became law on 23 June 1936. The act created a national public corporation with political autonomy and a clearly privileged position *vis-à-vis* the private stations, including considerable regulatory powers. It prohibited private stations from forming or joining networks without CBC permission and charged the CBC to review annually each station's activity and to recommend licence renewals to the minister. But it did not go as far as the 1932 legislation in providing for an eventual public monopoly; it took no step towards implementing the parliamentary committee's recommendation of nationalization. In this, it followed most closely the proposals of the Canadian Radio League.

The new law seemed to be "better than anything we could have hoped for," Brooke Claxton wrote Plaunt on 19 June while the bill was being debated in Parliament.[52] Having seen its main policies incorporated in legislation, the public broadcasting lobby considered its purpose achieved and went out of existence.[53]

The new arrangement appeared to be a setback for the private broadcasters and, to a lesser degree, for C.D. Howe and the technocrats. But it engaged a process that was to lead, on the one hand, to the sure and steady strengthening of the commercial sector and, on the other hand to the exclusive vesting of public broadcasting in a bureaucratic, supposedly neutral, state institution.

## BUILDING A BUREAUCRACY: THE CBC, 1936-39

The reform of the system introduced after the Liberals returned to power was a beneficial adjustment to the faulty focus of the earlier effort. But from the very beginning, the evolution of the CBC was marked by its relationship with the government. The strong-minded minister, C.D. Howe, worked hard to impose his vision of the role to be played by a public bureaucracy against the resistance of more liberal visionaries like Alan Plaunt (who was named to the first board of governors of the corporation).

Gladstone Murray was named general manager – a positive step as perceived by public broadcasting advocates, since Murray had been a friend of their movement since the early days. But Murray was essentially a technocrat – an "expert" who combined Sir John Reith's conception of public broadcasting as cultural uplift, Walter Lippmann's vision of public opinion as a management problem, and R.B. Bennett's loyalty to the British Empire. Murray proceeded to mould the new institution according to prevailing management techniques and philosophy.

Trusteeship over the system was vested in the CBC board, chaired by Leonard Brockington, a Winnipeg lawyer known for his oratorical skills. Brockington saw the CBC as a podium for politically unfettered free expression and promotion of public debate. So the public service function of the CBC would be carried out in collaboration with groups and organizations interested in the use of radio as a medium for fostering public discussion and, until the war, this appeared to be a satisfactory set-up. Under Brockington, the CBC board of governors would be the main voice in favour of the ideal of public broadcasting.

In 1937, Brockington and C.D. Howe clashed over interpretations of the act and the respective roles of the CBC and the government, especially with respect to the regulation of private broadcasters.[54] But a consensus of sorts was soon reached. Day-to-day operations of the CBC were in the hands of the general manager, who was more ideologically in line with the thinking of the government even though he was responsible to the board.

One of the first problems to surface concerned programming. Was the CBC's purpose to be uniquely Canadian and noncommercial, or was it supposed to compete with the private broadcasters? In 1938, the CBC began to acquire US and commercial programs. The private broadcasters opposed this move, labelling it unfair competition from the state corporation, and their supporters called for the CBC to stick to pure public service radio and leave commercial programming to the private sector.

The dilemma lay in the conception of the audience and its relationship to the public broadcaster. In Canada, a mass audience had been built on American commercial programming. By the time public broadcasting was in a position to create its own, different programs, the audience's taste had been formed. The public broadcaster was thus in the difficult and contradictory position of having to choose whether it was going to produce programs for a discriminating minority or meet the mass audience on its own ground.

The failure to resolve the relationship between public and private sectors aggravated the problem by framing the question of the audience in terms of "mass" and "alternative." Commercial broadcasting, by its nature, sought an undifferentiated mass audience. Uplifting "cultural" or "educational" broadcasting would reach only a minority. The private sector tried to dominate the mass market and relegate public broadcasting to this latter role. But in order to support its long-term goal of a public monopoly, the CBC had to prove that the private sector had no role to play. So instead of defining itself on its own terms, the CBC situated itself in the context that had existed before it began operations. This became a source of perpetual tension within the organization, between market and sociocultural tendencies. At its best, but only rarely, the CBC has been able to function as a service in which some programs were designed for the mass and others designed for different minority audiences.

Another anomaly was that the problem presented itself differently in English and in French. After the initial unpleasant experience of the CRBC, the language question had begun to work itself out in practice through the separation of services, even in the absence of any clear policy. By 1938, French-language service was effectively autonomous. Because of the language barrier, it had to rely more strongly on local resources and could more easily create a distinctive relationship with its audience. Thus, instead of contributing to "national unity" in the coast-to-coast sense, the CBC, in spite of itself, began to foster the feeling of difference that would eventually take the form of radical nationalism in Quebec.

Thus, as the CBC began its operations, certain patterns that would colour the future history of the system began to emerge: competition between politicians and technocrats for control of the system, to the exclusion of the public; confusion as to the place of the public sector in the overall system (monopoly or component?); the view of public service as an alternative to commercial "mass-audience" programming; the insoluble contradiction between autonomy for the groups making up Canada (manifested as linguistic diversity) and "national unity."

However, by early 1938, there was an apparent feeling of satisfaction with the way the CBC was fulfilling its mandate. Asking Parliament to increase the annual radio receiver licence fee (which went to finance the CBC) to $2.50, C.D. Howe (now minister of transport) said the persistent attacks from the private sector against the principle of public ownership "are being made not because the Canadian Broadcasting Corporation is a failure but because it is a success."[55] In keeping with what had now become a tradition, a parliamentary committee was convened to consider and review the policies and operations of the CBC.

The proceedings of the 1938 committee were much less controversial than any of the earlier ones. Gladstone Murray and Leonard Brockington handled themselves with ease and aplomb, to the satisfaction of committee members. Discussion centred mainly on housekeeping aspects like finances and transmission. Not yet two years old, the CBC appeared to be an independent public corporation, free from government interference.

An important refinement of the CBC's function was developing around the issue of national versus community broadcasting and the potential partnership between public stations and community stations. The important approach taking root at this time held that the "public" service was primarily "national" in scope, while "local" or "community" service was in the private sector. The CBC's mandate to establish a "national broadcasting service" was specified in the 1936 act (which never used the word "public" in discussing the corporation), but this had not then been seen as its exclusive role. Yet, the CBC had immediately begun building a "network," in which privately owned affiliates would play a key role as partners in bringing network programming to areas unserved by CBC stations.[56]

At least twenty-five stations had signed affiliation agreements by the time the 1938 committee met. However, most of the major private stations saw the CBC as a competitor, not as a partner. The notion of "partnership" tended to pigeonhole the private sector at the local, "community" level. This was a strategic move, as the CBC was already engaged in competition with private broadcasters for national advertising. The private sector argued strongly that the CBC, as a publicly funded corporation, should not compete for advertising dollars. There was, as yet, no established political principle regarding advertising, and the CBC argued it should be allowed to go aggressively after certain types of advertising. To support this argument, it defined the role of commercial stations in terms of "community" service, a role the stations eventually came to accept since it gave them a distinct function in the overall system. In 1938, the public/private dichotomy thus came to be framed in terms of "public" versus "community," where "public" meant national and publicly owned, and "community" meant local and privately owned.

The 1938 committee proceedings may have marked the high point of public sector dominance in Canadian broadcasting. For the first and last time, private broadcasters were not even heard. The parliamentary investigation came out highly in praise of the CBC, reporting that it had been well constituted and its policies well designed and well executed. The committee approved the CBC's proposed policy of a national system of high-power stations, with the hopeful comment that "the broadcasting system emerging in Canada is, and can increasingly be, an important factor in creating a sense of national unity."[57]

But while the public service idea enjoyed the support of the Liberal majority in Parliament (as well as its traditional base outside), the commercial view was well represented politically by articulate right-wing MPs like H.H. Stevens, who, in the House of Commons, wondered "whether the time has not arrived when we might well consider the abandonment of the actual administration of broadcasting stations by the government of Canada through this corporation and the turning of them back to private ownership."[58] This idea and others based on similar sentiments would be repeated with increasing frequency during the coming years. But, for now, the idea of the public was on a high roll and the technocrats were in command.

Meanwhile, a debate was going on over what came to be known as "controversial" programming. C.D. Howe believed no program should offend any part of the population while the CBC board thought controversy should have a prominent place. In 1937 the CBC had banned abusive comment on racial and religious questions, but this net was broad enough and vague enough to prohibit, for example, any discussion of birth control. Guidelines were eventually laid out in a "white paper" essentially drafted by board member Alan Plaunt in 1939 and still in effect well into the 1960s.[59]

It is important to recall that the CBC was, in those days, not only the public broadcaster but the custodian of all broadcasting in Canada. The scope and extent of its power became evident during an incident that occurred early in 1939, after the CBC refused to sell network time to the publisher of the Toronto *Globe and Mail*, George McCullagh. McCullagh then arranged to have his editorial messages broadcast over a network of private stations – something which had to be approved by the CBC in its capacity as regulator. Individual private stations were allowed to sell time for sponsored broadcasts as long as these did not violate the law of the land. But only the CBC could authorize a hook-up of private stations. The CBC refused to allow Mc-Cullagh's network and issued the following statement: "No individual may purchase any network to broadcast his own opinions and no profit-making corporation may purchase any network to broadcast opinions. Far from being a restraint on free speech, the Corporation's policy is an assurance that liberty of discussion is preserved, that all main points of view are fairly represented, and that the possession of wealth does not confer the right to use network broadcasting to influence opinion."[60]

Here, the CBC was really acting as the public trustee. It had made a policy decision that access to the air could not be bought by private individuals and corporations. This was a particularly strong position considering that the CBC provided free access to organized groups ranging from the Canadian Clubs to the Communist Party (the latter even in Quebec, where giving a platform to the CP was illegal). And the CBC enjoyed full autonomy on such matters. Intervening in the House of Commons on the McCullagh affair, the prime minister said "the CBC is an autonomous public body with which the government does not interfere and has no desire to interfere."[61]

The issue became a question of principle. Before the parliamentary committee, Leonard Brockington read a statement on programming policy that he had first made the previous year. The CBC believed that "censorship is undesirable, and perhaps impossible beyond the limits of decency," but would oppose "any attempt to buy the right on our network for the advancement of personal opinion or propaganda." It went on to state: "If opinion sufficiently informed on the lips of an attractive speaker is available, it will be offered by the CBC without remuneration as a contribution to national enlightenment and provocative discussion. The free interchange of opinion is one of the safeguards of our democracy, and we believe we should be false to our trust as custodians of part of the public domain if we did not resist external control and any attempt to place a free air under the domination of the power of wealth."[62]

McCullagh himself brought the question before the parliamentary committee, laying out a position in which he made an interesting analogy between broadcasting and publishing: "As far as private stations are concerned, as long as this government allows private enterprise to own broadcasting stations ... they have no more right to say whether they join together in a network than they have to say that the Southams or the Siftons or anybody else, cannot buy a chain of newspapers."[63]

No government in Ottawa would ever really resolve the contradictions between the ideology of private enterprise and the principle of public control. But in the months preceding the outbreak of war, the government foresaw the importance of a broadcasting arbiter and, consequently, allowed power to consolidate within the CBC.

Recognizing the context, the private sector adjusted its aim and decided to work quietly with the CBC. In 1939, the parliamentary committee invited the Canadian Association of Broadcasters to appear, but its president, Harry Sedgwick of CFRB, was content to send a letter stating the main issues upon which the CAB had been assured: "Our right to continue is recognized as being inherent in Canadian broadcasting, and ... whatever seems reasonably necessary to enable us to complement the service being given by the corporation and to improve and extend our facilities in the interest of the listening public will be granted to us."[64]

It was suggested for the first time at the 1939 committee, by Liberal MP Paul Martin, that the radio licence fee be replaced by a general parliamentary grant, since "the CBC is intended as a medium for the moulding of national character" and parliamentary support would be "in the interests of strengthening the state control and ownership of radio in this country."[65] The national leader of the CCF, J.S. Woodsworth, favoured maintaining the licence fee as a guarantee that the CBC would not become dependent on the government of the day. Brockington said the licence fee provided a secure form of revenue that was an aid to long-range planning, and the committee voted to maintain it. But the question of how to finance the public system launched yet another debate that remains unresolved.

## BROADCASTING IN WARTIME, 1939–45

### Strengthening the Administrative Model

The first indication of the role that broadcasting was to play in the Canadian war effort came more than fifteen months before the war actually began.

On 10 May 1938, the government introduced legislation replacing the Radiotelegraph Act of 1913, which regulated the technical aspects of radio transmission. While primarily updating the provisions to deal with the new technological context of the 1930s, the new Radio Act introduced an additional power for the governor in council, to "make regulations for the censorship and controlling of radio signals and messages in case of actual or apprehended war, rebellion, riot or other emergency."[66] Patriotic feeling made it impossible to oppose such a stipulation and only one opposition MP raised the fear that the open-ended "other emergency" gave the government too much power.[67]

The question of the wartime potential of radio was raised at the parliamentary committee of 1939. Radio was vastly important "from a nationally patriotic standpoint," said MP A.G. Slaight; in the event of war in Europe, radio "would help determine ... whether or not our country should participate."[68] J.S. Woodsworth took exception to this, and offered a pacifist view of the possibilities of radio:

> We should get the idea of militarization of our young people out of the picture altogether ... There are all sorts of listeners; there are some who are just as strongly opposed to war as there are those who are in favour of war ... Radio is a rather peculiar medium. It goes into the homes of all our people, all classes of people. I believe if we for one generation in Canada could get the military idea out of the minds of our youth we would go a long way towards abolishing war altogether ... Forget the national boundaries and get the international spirit going. That ought to be one of the primary functions of radio.[69]

A year later, with war now a reality, the CCF's T.C. Douglas articulated a vision of how radio could be used in wartime:

> More use could be made of propaganda over the radio – and I am using the word in its best sense as meaning the propagation of an idea. We have not begun to use the radio as it might be used ... people do not want to hear just one class of people over the radio. I should like to hear, for example, a trade unionist say why he has something at stake in the war. I should like to hear a farmer tell over the radio what he has at stake and a socialist tell why he feels he has something at stake in this war. I should like to hear a man who believes in the principle of Christianity tell us of the stake he has in this war. All classes of people in Canada representing different faiths and ideologies ought to be presenting their side of this whole war question, thus reaching others in the community who are like-minded.[70]

The distinction between propaganda and the free expression of ideas was an interesting one, particularly in light of the role radio would eventually play in the Canadian war effort.

The war crystallized the simmering divergences between democratic and technocratic conceptions of public broadcasting. Within the CBC, this took the form of a split between board member Alan Plaunt and general manager Gladstone Murray. Plaunt felt Canada should stay out of the war and urged an objective role towards war news and commentary for the CBC. As soon as war broke out the board was eclipsed in the name of the need for a close day-to-day working relationship between the government and the operating side of the CBC. Murray saw eye to eye with C.D. Howe (now responsible for war production as well as the CBC) on both war and broadcasting, and the two met three or four times a week throughout the duration.[71]

Brockington and Howe disagreed on the CBC's wartime functions. Brockington was a patriot, but he was sensitive to the views of new Canadians and French Canadians. On 13 September 1939, he resigned the chairmanship of the CBC board, writing to the prime minister that he hoped radio would be allowed to function freely during the war and that the board would play a role in presenting a truly national viewpoint on the issue. Brockington recommended Alan Plaunt as his successor, but the government named vice-chairman René Morin, a Montreal businessman and former Liberal MP, instead.

Critics of the government soon began attacking the close relationship developing between the government and the broadcasting service. In January 1940, the CBC suspended paid political and controversial broadcasting on its own and network stations, except for election campaigning. (Individual private stations could still carry such broadcasts, however.) On 30 August 1940, Alan Plaunt resigned from the CBC board of governors, citing a lack of confidence in the internal organization and executive direction of the CBC, in spite of what he called the admirable framework of the Broadcasting Act.[72] On 12 November 1940, the CCF's M.J. Coldwell called for an investigation, citing the CBC's "antidemocratic bias." He read into the parliamentary record part of Plaunt's letter of resignation, which said that "the present conditions seriously hamper the corporation in fulfilling its functions in the war emergency and prejudice its survival as an effective instrument of national unity afterwards."[73] One week later, John Diefenbaker called for an investigation of the CBC, claiming it had become a "party vehicle."[74]

Coldwell kept returning to the subject and his critique was not merely partisan. The CBC, he said, was becoming more and more ideologically and politically alien to the forces that had fought to create it. As an example, Coldwell noted the CBC's policy opposing unionization of its employees[75] and restriction of commentary on the war to government spokesmen.

The Department of National War Services, created in 1940, had authority to "coordinate the existing public information services of the government." Under this legislation, and the War Measures Act, the CBC (along with the newly created National Film Board) was officially attached to the government's war effort as of 11 June 1941. The minister responsible was now Joseph T. Thorson.[76]

### Challenging Conscription

In 1936, the CBC had set an objective to improve French-English relations, and both Brockington and Murray had been attentive to this need. The main concrete measure was the establishment of a separate French network with its own program schedule.[77]

Augustin Frigon, formerly of the Aird commission, had been named assistant general manager of the CBC and was responsible for the technical expansion of the system. With the separation of program services, Frigon became the senior official in charge of French programming as well. But while the French service was separate, it was not equal, and was almost nonexistent outside Quebec. In 1940, French-language service in western Canada, for example, was limited to three hours per week (out of a total 115 hours broadcast) over the CBC's high-power station CBK. News service in French was a full five minutes a day and nothing on the weekend (compared to 160 minutes a day in English).[78] Quebec nationalists pointed to the double standard that forced French-Canadian organizations in the west to campaign incessantly for a few more French programs while, in Quebec, the anglophone minority enjoyed equal status with its own CBC station. Wrote *L'Action nationale* in June 1941: "It is not difficult to understand why certain of our compatriots, pushed to the limit, desire a change of flag."[79]

The war changed both the structures and the sociocultural context of broadcasting. On the one hand, the needs of war coverage and propaganda, particularly among French Canadians, contributed to rapidly building up the French service, especially in Quebec. On the other hand, the one-sided role of the CBC on the conscription question branded it, perhaps irrevocably, as an institution in Ottawa's pocket. So while the war, and conscription particularly, reminded French Canada of its place in Canadian politics, it also enhanced its cultural specificity by giving rise to what would become a major institution, Radio-Canada.

The pressing need for national unity raised by the war gave the French network full autonomy and *de facto* equality with the English.[80] As a result, the French presence was established from coast to coast and a policy of extension of service to French-language communities was adopted – even if it would be decades before anything close to real equality was achieved.[81]

In 1941, the CBC created a national news service with a bilingual bureau in Montreal. Soon, CBC English- and French-language correspondents in Europe were filing daily dispatches from the front. Wartime propaganda needs also led to the development of new types of programs geared to the particular conditions of the receiving publics rather than based on standardized models. Thus, the need for an ideological instrument of war propaganda contributed to the emergence of the *radio-feuilleton*, or Québécois radio serial, which would become a popular, indigenous cultural form.[82]

In both English and French, as a matter of high policy, radio was appropriated for the war effort. This transformed the CBC from a national "public service" into a propaganda vehicle for the interests of state. As we have seen above, however, this transformation did not come about without struggle and resistance by those who saw public service broadcasting as something necessarily independent of the state at all cost. But without the backing of the nationalist supporters of public broadcasting, for whom the war effort came first, there was no contest. The only breach was over the question of conscription.

It may be argued that French-Canadian pacifism emerged as a self-interested form of resistance to British rule following the Conquest of 1759. Nevertheless, the fact is that it has been over two hundred years since French Canadians voluntarily went to war. Beginning on 1 September 1939, street demonstrations in Montreal and parliamentary interventions by Quebec MPs in Ottawa made it clear that French Canadians would not easily be convinced to participate in a Canadian military expedition in Europe. The government, for its part, even in declaring war on Germany, imposing censorship, and introducing emergency war measures making opposition to the war effort illegal, made a solemn commitment that no Canadians would be sent to fight against their will.

The CBC's propaganda efforts had different objectives in English and in French. In English, it was largely a question of maintaining morale in a war that most people supported. But in French, the audience first had to be convinced that it was their war too. On the whole, a major objective of Canadian propaganda was to conciliate two opposing nationalisms, the Québécois and the English-Canadian.[83]

The CBC's propaganda efforts took place in a climate of censorship that outlawed alternative interpretations of the events in Europe. This was another issue that divided Canada along ethno-linguistic lines. In English Canada, censorship primarily affected the Communist press, and English-Canadian opinion generally accepted press censorship as "an unpleasant, but unavoidable necessity."[84] In French Canada, censorship was directed against publications critical of the Canadian war effort, and against coverage of the statements and activities of antiparticipationists like Montreal's mayor Camillien Houde.[85]

Usually the censorship was relatively mild and at least able to draw attention to itself. The September 1939 issue of *L'Action nationale* was delayed for the censor's approval but appeared, nonetheless, with a note stating that "freedom of expression is dead in Canada."[86] In the following issue, editor Arthur Laurendeau felt obliged to advise his readers that the state of censorship was preventing him from expressing himself freely.[87] In fact, Communist critics of Canada's war policy were more severely repressed than the French-Canadian nationalists. The only daily newspaper actually suspended from publication during the war was the Communist *Clarion* out of Toronto,[88] although there were suggestions in 1942 that *Le Devoir* be prosecuted.[89]

The question of censorship struck at the ideology of freedom of expression. In wartime, all but the most extreme libertarians were prepared to accept some curtailment of this freedom. The question of access to the public domain of the airwaves was a different issue.

Although the prime minister had made a solemn commitment that Canada's declaration of war would not mean participation with troops, by 1940 government propaganda was beginning to get people used to the idea of an expeditionary force. The CBC's pioneering news coverage from the front – in both French and English – captured the imagination of hearth-front listeners at home. Then, on 22 January 1942, the government announced it would hold a plebiscite asking the people to free it from its earlier engagement not to resort to conscription as a means of mobilization for military service. The plebiscite was scheduled for 27 April.

Elsewhere, the result of the vote was a foregone conclusion. But in Quebec, the Ligue pour la défense du Canada, a broad common front of French-Canadian political and social leaders opposed to actual Canadian military participation, campaigned vigorously for a "No" vote. The league began making extensive use of commercial radio in its campaign.

As we saw earlier, CBC policy before the war provided for free access to the air for organized groups. Political parties were entitled to use the air at election time. Private individuals and corporations could buy time on private stations but could not form networks. But after January 1940, all paid political and controversial broadcasting was excluded from the CBC, except for election purposes.

On 13 February, André Laurendeau, secretary for the Ligue pour la défense du Canada, wrote to Augustin Frigon asking whether the CBC intended to allow partisans of both sides to use the air during the campaign.[90] Frigon replied on 16 February that in all likelihood the CBC's regulations covering election-time broadcasts would be used in the plebiscite campaign. This meant that only the four political parties represented in the House of Commons – all of which supported conscription – would have access to the air. Frigon recalled that CBC policy did not permit the sale of air time for political or controversial broadcasts, but that the league could buy time on individual private stations. The CBC, because of its "national character," had to remain "neutral in political matters."[91]

Their correspondence continued back and forth, Laurendeau pointing out the absurdity of calling "neutral" a policy in which one side would be represented four times (by each of the parties in the House) and the other not at all. How did Radio-Canada justify excluding one side of a question the government evidently considered legitimate, a side presumably taken by millions of tax-paying Canadians? On 24 February, Frigon wrote urging patience; the CBC was studying the question.[92] Then, on 8 April, Frigon advised Laurendeau of the CBC's decision to grant free time to political parties only. The CBC, he wrote, was "conforming to instructions received from the federal government."[93] According to Laurendeau, CBC governor Adrien Pouliot confirmed a week later that the decision had been made directly by the government.

On 10 April 1942, the government announced that it had asked the CBC to provide eight half-hour time periods, in French and English, for each of the four parties in the House of Commons to discuss the plebiscite. Reporting the news, *Le Devoir* noted that the announcement had come from the minister's office and not from the CBC, "an agency that is supposed to be impartial and to belong to the public."[94]

The same day, Laurendeau published his correspondence with Frigon in *Le Devoir* and the CBC's role became an issue in the remaining days of the campaign. Quebec newspapers denounced the CBC policy and in the legislative assembly the opposition Union Nationale presented an unsuccessful motion calling on Ottawa to provide equal access to the "No" side. Maurice Duplessis, then leader of the opposition, said the issue was freedom of speech and claimed that he knew what it meant to suffer at the hands of Radio-Canada, referring to the 1939 provincial election campaign when his refusal to submit his speeches to the CBC censor resulted in his exclusion from the air.[95]

The "No" side in the conscription plebiscite was thus restricted to buying advertising on individual "private" stations – which the latter were only too happy to accept. On 27 April 1942, the people of Canada voted 63.7 percent in favour of the government's proposal and conscription soon followed. But in Quebec, 71.2 percent of the people voted "No," and in some regions, like the Beauce, "No" support was as high as 97 percent.

The role of the CBC in the conscription plebiscite could not but further alienate French Quebec from any feeling of solidarity with the "public" broadcaster. The experience cost the idea of public broadcasting dearly in Quebec, where it became associated not only with the government of the day, but with the domination of the Canadian state.

This must have been evident even to the decision makers, whose 1942 position appears to have been taken with only the short term in view. In 1946, during a parliamentary committee exchange over political broadcasts, Augustin Frigon, by then general manager of the CBC, was asked why the "No" side had been refused air time in 1942. He replied: "That was in 1942, four years ago. We have changed our policy somewhat since then and I can say that, perhaps, we made a mistake in 1942. That is all I can tell you."[96] It was thus in Quebec in 1942 that Canadian broadcasting first came to be associated with the repressive apparatus of the state, and that "public" broadcasting first appeared, concretely, to be more appropriately labelled "state" broadcasting.

## Further Consolidation

The pressures of war did not inhibit the government from setting up the parliamentary committee on radio broadcasting once again in 1942. This was the first public discussion of broadcasting since the outbreak of war and the first since the departures of Brockington and Plaunt from the CBC board. The committee convened on 13 May, only days after the conscription plebiscite.

Plaunt had passed away on 12 September 1941, but his influence was still felt. A letter he had written to board chairman René Morin in August 1940, reiterated his indictment of the CBC's executive management and specifically deplored the wartime changes in CBC policy. "I do not think democratic rights should be thrown away, even in wartime, without apparent necessity," he had written. He also maintained the corporation was being too friendly towards some of the powerful private stations and had compromised the public interest in news broadcasting by allowing the private stations input into its news policy. Plaunt measured the CBC's performance against the ideal of public broadcasting he had helped developed since the days of the Canadian Radio League and found it wanting.

An important issue raised at the 1942 committee was the resignation of the CBC's supervisor of public affairs programs, Donald Buchanan, who had quit in November 1940, criticizing Gladstone Murray's authoritarian practices. Buchanan said the general manager had let the government's wartime information officers take the place of the CBC's own staff. He accused Murray of deliberately undermining board policy and of a "disturbing" and "illiberal" attitude towards broadcasting in wartime. Caprice had replaced public policy at the CBC, he charged. According to Buchanan, it was the general manager who encouraged the close relationship between the CBC and the government as a way of circumventing the board.

Although it was Murray who was under attack and not the board, René Morin stated the board's position that wartime was not the occasion to engage in controversial programming – public opinion had to be united behind the effort to win the war. However, the attention drawn to the general manager by Plaunt and Buchanan was accentuated by some unaccountable expenses and the committee recommended Murray's removal. Murray resigned soon thereafter and was temporarily replaced by a member of the board, Dr J.S. Thomson.

The 1942 committee was also the setting for more discussion of the language question in broadcasting – although not a word was spoken about the recent plebiscite crisis. Frigon, who emerged clearly as the man in charge of French-language programming, referred to "the so-called French network," which he said was really treated as a regional division within the CBC. Program planning was done "on a national basis" out of Toronto, "with proper consideration given to the possibility of exchange of programs between the national network and the Quebec network. All programs broadcast on the national network which may have appeal for the province of Quebec are carried on the French network. The same applies the other way around."[97]

Conservative MP Gordon Graydon wanted to know the distinction between the "French network" and the "national network." Frigon replied that "the French network group is regarded as a separate entity within the programs division."[98] The national network consisted of five regions: British Columbia, the Prairies, Ontario, the Maritimes, and English Quebec; the French network group dealt with French Quebec.

The tone of the discussion indicated the degree of concern of some MPs, as well as the justification for the CBC's policy:

Q: Is there growing up within the Canadian Broadcasting Corporation two definitions of the term "Canadian," do you suggest that?

A [Frigon]: No. If you want to reach the French Canadians with these war programs, if you want to speak to them, you must have them as listeners; and to have them as listeners you must give them the programs they like to listen to. Therefore we must have a background of sustaining programs which are designed to meet the tastes of the French population so that we will have listeners, who will be there, when we want to speak to them on anything; otherwise you will have nobody listening to you.

Q: I think that is all right as long as we do not get into the position of getting two different definitions of what a Canadian is.

A: Not at all. I am strictly speaking on the matter of program taste. I am not saying that we tell something to one part and something else to another part.[99]

Renewed interest in the possibilities of broadcasting as a tool for the enhancement of democracy surfaced at the 1942 committee. MPs M.J. Coldwell (CCF), Brooke Claxton (Liberal) and Gordon Graydon (Conservative) tossed around ideas with Gladstone Murray about a series of programs that would promote the values of parliamentary democracy, combining broadcasting with group discussions.[100] While Coldwell insisted that democracy had to be practised rather than taught, Claxton saw broadcasting being used "to modernize the old corner-store discussions around the stove."[101] Murray thought this was a fine idea and told the committee he would follow up its suggestions.

By 1942, partisan positions on the central question of ownership and control of the system were hardening. M.J. Coldwell was concerned about the emergence of private broadcasting chains with ties to newspaper groups, such as Thomson. Social Credit's E.G. Hansell spoke against the CBC's regulation of the private sector. Brooke Claxton recalled the first principle of Canadian broadcasting, that "it is to be a publicly-owned system with the private stations allowed to occupy some part of the field that the publicly-owned system does not choose to occupy."[102]

But the private sector held a different view. In his opening statement to the committee, the minister responsible for broadcasting, J.T. Thorson, had refused to make public the CBC's minutes on the grounds that this would give an unfair advantage to its private "competitors." The status of competitor was precisely what the private stations were struggling to achieve, and CAB president and general manager Glen Bannerman took the opportunity to point out that this was the first time that a responsible person had recognized privately owned stations as competitors of the CBC. The broadcasting act's provision for the CBC to regulate its competition was, Bannerman said, an embarrassment at best and a sore point to the privately owned stations and commercial sponsors.[103]

This question would be the focus of debate after 1943 when the CAB would launch a campaign for a "separate regulatory body" and recognition of the "dual system" – a campaign it would pursue through the 1940s and 1950s, ultimately with success.

The parliamentary committee tabled a highly critical but constructive report on 25 July 1942. Along the lines of Alan Plaunt's critique, it expressed confidence in the broadcasting framework but disappointment in execution. It reaffirmed the key principles of Canadian broadcasting, notably that of a "single national authority to control all broadcasting in the public interest," and formulated a new one: "that public broadcasting is a great instrument of education and national unity as well as of entertainment. In war, broadcasting can play a major part in mobilizing the resources of the nation and the will of our people to defend our country and defeat the enemy."[104]

The report was not unanimous.

## The "Forum" Programs

While the war was making special demands of the public broadcaster in the national interest, the dynamic possibilities for radio revealed by war-effort programming created a thirst for new programs in the listening public. At the same time as the CBC's wartime responsibilities multiplied, there was increased demand for national programs in general. Entire new departments were set up to do farm, school, and children's broadcasts, in French and English. In 1941, over the cries of unfair competition from the private sector, the CBC created a second national network in English to provide an "alternative" program choice.[105]

The demand for increased "public service" broadcasts was articulated and backed with concrete proposals by the five-year-old Canadian Association for Adult Education, which was comprised of a broad base among populist, rural social movements and the voluntary associations of the urban élite.[106] The CAAE's founding director was E.A. Corbett, who had been, as we saw earlier, a pioneer of educational broadcasting in Canada and an active organizer for the Canadian Radio League.

During the war, the CAAE formed a bridge between the CBC and mass-membership organizations, developing two major program series based on the principle of organized listener groups. The first, "Farm Forum," was directed to English Canada's farm population and was planned in conjunction with the Canadian Federation of Agriculture. The programs would deal specifically with "the economic, social and educational problems" of farm people, and would address such interests as the development of producers and consumers cooperatives and credit unions "as media for the improvement of general living standards in rural areas."[107]

Corbett later recalled that when the farm broadcasts began in winter 1939, "they awakened a certain amount of resentment among the champions of free enterprise."[108] The series was abruptly removed from the air as a result of businessmen's objections, but was restored after a press campaign attacking interference with a public utility.

By 1941, the broadcasts had evolved into a program intended to act as the starting point for weekly discussions by listener groups. Through the 1940s and 1950s, "Farm Forum" reached an *organized* listening audience of about thirty thousand, meeting weekly in groups of ten to twenty. The approach was later adopted by several Third World countries and was adapted to local conditions, especially after UNESCO published a book, *Canada's Farm Radio Forum*, about it in 1954.[109]

In 1957, Corbett wrote about the National Farm Radio Forum:

Within the communities involved it has created a new sense of neighbourhood and hence of social responsibility. It has provided a medium through which farm people by studying, talking and planning together have arrived at a sharper understanding of local and national problems. It has strengthened farm organizations by creating a greater sense of the dignity and human values in farming as an occupation. Through action projects (which are the lifeblood of any organization) the Forums in hundreds of Canadian districts have discovered that by working together in tolerance and good-will it is possible to revitalize the social and economic life of a community with higher standards of public health, improved methods of agriculture and a new sense of community responsibility.[110]

In 1943, the CAAE identified a number of major problems Canada would have to face after the war, such as the need for "democratic planning," the need to overcome the bitterness between English and French Canadians engendered by the war, and the need to rekindle a spirit of active participation in public life.[111] The CAAE proposed to use radio to promote public discussion of these and other controversial reconstruction issues, in a series modelled along the lines of "Farm Forum," but this time directed to urban Canadians. Again working jointly with the CBC, a plan was developed for a national weekly program to be known as "Citizens' Forum."

The plans for the broadcasts were worked out at a CAAE-sponsored conference in St Anne de Bellevue, Quebec, in September 1943, attended by 135 delegates from across Canada. The conference also created provincial committees whose job was to set up and coordinate the activities of the listening groups.

As the project neared airtime in November 1943, government discomfort with the idea of public discussion of controversial topics surfaced. According to Corbett, the trouble started when the National Committee for Citizens' Forum (made up of representatives of organizations behind the project, ranging from the Canadian Congress of Labour to the YMCA), showed government officials a proposed list of participants: "violent exception was taken by two prominent Liberal members to several of the speakers from the opposition parties whose names were on the list. The feeling in the matter became so violent that one member of the Mackenzie King Cabinet announced that the CBC would not be permitted to proceed with the program."[112]

Ironically, the government attack on the project was led by Brooke Claxton, former central figure of the Canadian Radio League and now parliamentary assistant to the prime minister and chairman of the Liberal Party policy committee.[113] On 16 November 1943, the story of the controversy broke in the Winnipeg *Free Press* and soon afterwards the CBC announced that the series would go ahead as planned. It went on the air on 23 November.

The incident showed, on the one hand, the strength of the coalition of liberal sentiment in favour of CBC independence and social activists determined to use it for social goals and, on the other hand, the increasing consciousness in the corridors of power that public broadcasting was a political instrument that would have to be controlled.

The "Citizens' Forum" series went ahead, subject to wartime censorship. It quickly developed a national audience and was reluctantly tolerated by the government, offering a left-of-centre political orientation reflecting the position of social movements in English Canada in the 1940s.[114] The people involved in the programs ranged from social activists to professionals nurtured on the CBC tradition of "free and balanced discussion of controversial issues."

The audience for the "Citizens' Forum" reached as high as half a million people, but it was not as successful at organizing listening groups as the "Farm Forum." About twelve hundred listener groups were organized in 1943–44, but the number dropped after that, stabilizing at about four hundred in the late 1940s, and then three hundred in the early 1950s.[115]

The "Forum" programs, from their introduction to the arrival of television a decade later, were among the most popular Canadian public affairs programs. They were clearly important as unique experiences in using radio for promoting the ideals of "two-way" communication and participatory democracy. But the exercise remained somewhat abstract. According to Faris: "Theoretically, a communication system capable of sustaining a social movement was established; yet no such movement developed around the forums. It was clear that there were forces operating both within and upon the CAAE – forces which, while occasionally encouraging the growth of social movement aspects, tended to militate against such growth."[116]

The end of the war and the accompanying climate of optimism and economic prosperity marked the decline of the social movements which had developed before and during the depression. At the same time, it marked the emergence of a strengthened, relatively autonomous CBC. The notion of social action broadcasting fostered by the CAAE and expressed in the "Forum" projects was absorbed by the CBC and transformed into institutional public affairs programming. Public interest groups would never again be directly involved in programming, except in a strictly advisory capacity.[117] Meanwhile, the "Forum" programs continued into the 1950s and were adapted for the French network as well.

### Integrating the Commercial Sector

Following the 1942 parliamentary committee report, some reforms had taken place at the CBC – most notably the removal of the general manager and the revamping of the corporation's bylaws. But opposition MPs demanded another chance to review the CBC's activities and, on 7 May 1943, Parliament again convened a special committee.

The main source of controversy at the 1943 committee concerned the relationship between the CBC and the private radio stations. Challenged by E.G. Hansell of Social Credit, a declared opponent of CBC control of all broadcasting, the CBC's interim general manager J.S. Thomson insisted that, contrary to what was frequently alleged, "There is no competition between the CBC and the private stations. There is co-operation."[118]

Expanding on the different roles of the public and private broadcasters, Thomson gave an interesting indication of the evolution of these ideas: "The real distinction between the CBC and the private stations is that the CBC is a national institution providing programs for the whole of the Canadian people on a national basis. The private stations are local stations, providing what is a highly important and very essential service for the Canadian people, namely that of a local broadcasting station. There is no competition between these two services. I should say they are supplementary. They represent two very important interests in anything that affects the Canadian people."[119] Thomson also warned that a separate authority to deal with private stations would depart from the ideal of a national system and detract from the CBC as a symbol of Canadian unity.

The Canadian Association of Broadcasters was represented at the committee hearings by its lawyer, Joseph Sedgwick. After reaffirming the CAB's position of the previous year, Sedgwick said private stations had managed to survive in spite of the fact that "their extinction was at one time threatened."[120] He pointed out that the Canadian system had evolved a long way since the proposals of the Aird report and suggested that private stations needed some security of licence tenure "if they are best to serve the public interest." Finally, regarding the tendency to designate private stations as "local," or "community" stations, Sedgwick said that there was no argument to justify limiting their transmission power. As he put it, Montreal is a community, and Chilliwack is a community, and you cannot arbitrarily limit the power of a station which is to serve a community. The CAB brief referred to its members as the "independent stations."

The parliamentary committee report, tabled 22 July, again reaffirmed the basic principles governing Canadian broadcasting. It quoted the new Minister of National War Services L.R. Laflèche's affirmation that the CBC was not a department of government. It commended the CBC on its efforts to improve its internal problems, on its programming innovations (notably the "Forum" approach), and on its extension of French network services both in Quebec and the rest of Canada.

Regarding the private broadcasters' position, the committee limited itself to noting the existence of good relations between the CBC and the private sector, recognizing that private stations serve a useful function, and recommending that the CBC exercise its control with fairness. But while emphasizing that radio was a public service and a public utility, the committee also made some general comments that revealed the evolution of official thinking about broadcasting brought on by the war:

> The advent of the present war has altered the slowly evolving perspectives of the Canadian Broadcasting Corporation ... The radio is the newest instrument of modern warfare and its influence is being felt more keenly each day. Radio in

the present war serves not only as an instrument of entertainment and general education but it is the most vital morale builder at a nation's command. In addition, the radio has become one of the most subtle intelligence instruments of modern warfare. In short, radio has become one of the major instruments of the state and the responsibility is great for him who would abuse its function by taking only a segmental view of its importance. [121]

The call for reorganizing the fundamental structure of the broadcasting system had by now become a regular feature of parliamentary discussion. In 1944, John Diefenbaker became a leading spokesman for the need for a "new type of national authority to control broadcasting." [122] Diefenbaker accepted the principle of a national public service, but argued that the increasingly commercial nature of the CBC's activities made it unfair for the CBC to regulate its competition. He called for limiting advertising on the CBC and creating a semi-judicial regulatory body to oversee cooperation between the national and private sectors. This view would eventually be reflected in the Broadcasting Act of 1958.

For now, debate ranged from the CCF recalling that R.B. Bennett had intended the public sector to take over all broadcasting in Canada in 1932, to the Social Credit's call for state withdrawal from the field. The government view in 1944, expressed by the minister responsible for broadcasting, L.R. Laflèche, was that Canada had a "dual system," halfway between those of the United Kingdom and the United States.

At the 1944 parliamentary committee, under strong partisan opposition questioning led by Diefenbaker, Laflèche went a long way towards recognizing the legitimacy of the private sector's interests. The CAB, through Joseph Sedgwick, said that its interest was to give better broadcasting service to Canadians. The CAB recognized that public broadcasting was here to stay, but not as a monopoly. Sedgwick was content to agree with Laflèche that Canada had a dual system, but objected to the existing regulatory method. [123]

Here, one begins to see the process of slow but steady erosion of the first principle of Canadian broadcasting, through ministerial interpretation, opposition aggressiveness, and private sector insistence on recognition of its privileged position. While CBC board chairman René Morin said the CBC did not view the private stations as competitors, the CBC tended to be aloof towards the question of the overall broadcasting system, preferring to concentrate on consolidating a secure position for itself.

Augustin Frigon, who had been named acting general manager of the CBC in September 1943, argued against creating a separate regulatory commission or a private network. But his dismissal of the argument that the CBC represented a state monopoly was based on conceding that private local stations, especially in small communities, could serve the public interest. Frigon recognized the legitimacy of the commercial aspirations of private broadcasters: "Under the present system, there is plenty of room in Canada for private broadcasting to develop, to render good service to the population and to make plenty of money." [124]

Television entered the discussion for the first time in 1944, when the CAB complained that its members had been denied the right to experiment with the new technology. In the US, the commercial possibilities of television were already being explored, and John Diefenbaker denounced Canada's lagging behind as a perfect example of why regulation should be removed from the CBC's hands. But M.J. Coldwell of the CCF pointed out that a separate regulatory authority would place the CBC and the private stations on equal ground, thus undermining the intention of Canada's traditional policy that the nationally owned system be dominant and not merely one among equals. The issue of regulation thus pivoted on the question of whether private broadcasters existed in Canada by right or by privilege.

Another new wrinkle that appeared in 1944 was the charge that the CBC was harbouring Communists. Social Credit's E.G. Hansell launched an attack on the CBC's Richard S. Lambert, chairman of the Writers', Artists', Broadcasters' and Musicians' Council (later, supervisor of educational broadcasting). Lambert denied he was a Communist, admitting that he was active in the Canadian Association for Adult Education and the Civil Liberties Association. The affair went nowhere, but right-wing accusation of the CBC as a hotbed of communism continued through the 1940s and 1950s until it was eclipsed in the 1960s and 1970s by the charges that Radio-Canada was a haven for separatists.

The 1944 committee saw a revival of involvement by socially active groups in the question of public broadcasting. The Canadian Federation of Agriculture, the Canadian Congress of Labour, and the Canadian Association for Adult Education each made strong interventions before the committee. H.H. Hannam, president of the CFA, reaffirmed the principle of public broadcasting and said the key issue was not ownership but control. The policy of a public utility responsible to Parliament was fundamentally sound, he said, as were the constitution and organization of the CBC, which "provides an important safeguard for freedom of speech." Hannam cited the CBC's role in developing citizen participation through its "Forum" programs. The CAAE, through its vice-president W.H. Brittain, also emphasized the importance of "two-way" types of programming that encouraged participation. [125]

The Canadian Congress of Labour deposited a brief, reiterating its support for the principle of public ownership and reframing it in the context of the current debate: "The radio belongs and ought to belong to the people of Canada; it is far too important a means of information and education to be allowed to fall under the domination of private interests." [126] The CBC should be supported and strengthened, the CCL said, because: "Freedom of discussion is far greater and far more secure on the publicly-controlled radio than in the privately-controlled press."[127] While praising the CBC's "important contribution to the democratic way of life" through its "Forum" programs, the labour organization made a number of specific proposals; one such proposal was that the CBC accept collective bargaining with its employees. By 1944, there was thus an alignment of positions on broadcasting in Canada involving public organizations and the CCF on the left, the CBC and the Liberal government in the centre, and the conservative parties and the private broadcasters on the right.

Taking its role as arbiter seriously, the parliamentary committee reaffirmed the principles of Canadian broadcasting that previous committees had included in their reports and rejected the private sector's contentions. The CAB had "very evidently forgotten that private broadcasting stations have no vested interest in the radio frequencies they are allowed to use," the committee said, adding unequivocally that "nothing would be gained for the public" by changing the existing regulatory arrangements.[128]

There was little further controversy until the end of the war. As far as the CBC's status was concerned, the protective stance of the parliamentary committee and its popular support kept the wolves at bay. Towards the end of the war, J.J. McCann, who had been chairman of the parliamentary committee, replaced Laflèche as minister of national war services and thus as minister responsible for the CBC.

## POWER AND PROSPERITY, 1945–49

### Centralization and "the Public"

In February 1945 there was a new challenge to the system when the Quebec government of Maurice Duplessis, re-elected in 1944, introduced an act "to authorize the creation of a provincial broadcasting service." The legislation referred to broadcasting as "a powerful medium of publicity and intellectual and moral training," and claimed that Quebec had the constitutional authority to create a broadcasting organization.[129]

Duplessis had repealed Taschereau's 1931 legislation when he first became premier in 1936, but he had also promised to set up a provincial radio network in three election campaigns and considered that he had a clear mandate. Even the Liberal opposition supported the principle (although opposing the proposed centralization of power in the premier's office).[130]

During debate in the Legislative Assembly, André Laurendeau (now leader of the Bloc populaire) said the law was extremely important because of the power of radio as a means of propaganda and a tool of education, capable of transforming one's way of thinking. It was all the more important for Quebec, where an entire culture was at stake. Such a law was long overdue, Laurendeau said, because Radio-Canada had failed to serve Quebec. Particularly since the beginning of the war, he said, Ottawa had been using radio towards imperialist ends; Radio-Canada was being used to promote an artificial sense of national unity, and, in order to do so systematically, had banned an entire school of thought from the air.[131]

The act was adopted on 20 April 1945. It created a corporation called the Quebec Radio Bureau, to be run by a three-member administrative body named by the lieutenant-governor. The object of the corporation was "to establish, possess and operate a broadcasting system to be called Radio-Québec."[132]

Around the same time, provincial governments in Alberta (Social Credit) and Saskatchewan (CCF) were interested in acquiring radio stations but found their efforts blocked by Ottawa. Not coincidentally, each of the three provinces was then governed by a regional party ideologically and politically opposed to the framework of centralized decision making that characterized the Canadian political system. But neither Saskatchewan nor Alberta went so far as to adopt legislation.

On 3 May 1946, C.D. Howe announced in the House of Commons, in response to a question from John Diefenbaker: "The government has decided that, since broadcasting is the sole responsibility of the Dominion government, broadcasting licences shall not be issued to other governments or corporations owned by other governments."[133]

At the same time, Howe announced that discussions were taking place with the government of Manitoba with respect to the sale of the two stations operated by the Manitoba telephone utility since 1923. Under the circumstances, Quebec did not try to put its law into effect and Alberta's and Saskatchewan's hopes were dashed as well. Within two years, Manitoba had divested its interests in Canada's oldest public broadcasting stations. Ottawa had taken absolute exclusivity in public broadcasting and would keep this policy in place until the provinces, again led by Quebec, extracted control over "educational" broadcasting in the 1970s.[134]

Meanwhile, the CBC's internal troubles prompted Parliament to amend the Broadcasting Act in 1944, making the position of chairman of the board a full-time job. The first person appointed to the post, in 1946, was Davidson Dunton.

Dunton held a strong view of the CBC's autonomy, which he spelled out in a statement to the parliamentary committee in June 1946: "We are not part of the government. The government is responsible for the appointment of members of the board and for exercising certain specific powers of approval as laid down in the Act. But the corporation is not subject to government control and is not answerable to the government. The board is responsible for the policies of the corporation and for all its acts. We are responsible for our policies and acts to the supreme authority of Parliament. And we are glad to report to Parliament on our stewardship." [135]

This position was, for better and for worse, to become the working definition of the CBC's relationship to political authority. The CBC came out of the war as a strong and reliable agency that could be counted on to act in the interests of the state with no need for direct control by the government of the day. Augustin Frigon, now CBC general manager, told the committee: "So far as I am concerned we have only one authority, and that is the Radio Broadcasting Act. We do not even have to follow government policy." [136] From 1946 to 1958, the CBC would be the only institutional power in Canadian broadcasting.

The CBC at this point was still relatively autonomous financially. The annual radio licence fee – proceeds from which were turned over to the CBC by the government – and advertising revenue enabled the CBC to show annual operating surpluses until 1945, when it recorded a deficit for the first time. [137] Between 1947 and 1953, CBC financing was a subject of heated debate and various formulas were tried until the staggering costs of television made an outright annual grant from treasury the only viable method. Thereafter, the CBC's claim to autonomy was somewhat hollow, as it was indeed dependent on the government which, in turn, would always be under pressure to get its money's worth.

But in 1946, there was only one aspect of broadcasting service that was considered a direct agency of the state: the CBC's international service, consisting of short-wave broadcasts initiated towards the end of the war and beamed at selected overseas audiences. The international service was, from the beginning, financed by a direct appropriation from Parliament and was designed and deemed to be in the service of Canada's external affairs policy. Originally part of the war effort, the international service was pressed into action in the ideological cold war of the late 1940s and later became a kind of international public relations agency for Canada under the auspices of the Department of External Affairs.

Canada's internal propaganda needs also continued after the war, and radio continued using many of the structures set up during the war. For example, the Wartime Information Board continued to oversee the orientation of the popular soap operas developed during the war, adapting them to the political and ideological needs of the new context. Soap opera plots were used first to support the war effort, then to ease the aches and pains of reconstruction, and later to promote the ideology of anticommunism and support the policies it demanded, such as the need to maintain a mobilized armed forces and to welcome refugees from eastern Europe. [138]

The private sector had yet to launch its strongest offensive, but the parliamentary committee of 1946 was the scene of important debate on the relative place of public and private broadcasting in Canada and some important evidence of the implications of the CBC's consolidation of the "national" system.

The Canadian Association of Broadcasters presented the same basic position it had held since the early 1940s, with some semantic refinements. It now described its membership as a system of "independently-owned community stations." By posing as a system, the private broadcasters constituted themselves as an equal to the CBC; they claimed to be independently owned, as opposed to government-owned – not privately owned as opposed to publicly owned. The CAB claimed a social vocation for private broadcasting by placing it under the sign of "community": community stations would serve local needs, stimulate the national system through competition, and protect "the democratic elements of freedom of speech."[139]

As it had done in 1943, the CAB defined community in terms broad enough to justify the demand of some stations for high-power transmission capacity, which the CBC was trying to reserve for itself.[140] Under the terms of the North American Regional Broadcasting Agreement drafted in Havana in 1937, Canada was entitled to six "clear" (high-power) channels, thirty-three "regional" channels, and six "local" channels.[141] In 1946, the CBC was trying to complete its national network by occupying all six of the clear channels available to Canada. The CBC maintained that the spirit of the law intended high-power stations to be publicly owned and community stations to be kept at low power. But in 1946, two of Canada's clear channels were occupied by private licensees, using only ten kilowatts of power but hoping to increase their power to the fifty kilowatts permitted by the Havana agreement.

In the struggle to claim these two frequencies, the CBC became embroiled in two very different controversies which it faced with a single approach in the name of the national interest. One case involved a classical power struggle with a private interest, but the second pitted the CBC against a competing public interest. In asserting its strength in both cases, the CBC actually emerged diminished, in the one case mobilizing the private interest lobby against it, and in the second discouraging an important part of the public interest coalition that was its traditional base of support.

The first case involved Toronto radio CFRB, one of the most established, most lucrative private broadcasters in Canada. The CBC proposed that CFRB move to another frequency, but CFRB objected on the grounds that it would lose its audience and argued that it had an acquired right. The CBC argued that there was no such thing as acquired rights of private broadcasters, whose right to use a particular frequency was limited to the duration of their licences. The CBC position was firmly based in law – and provided powerful ammunition for the private broadcasting lobby's argument that the law had to be changed. In this straightforward power struggle, the CBC won the battle but would eventually lose the war.

The second case involved Calgary radio CFCN, the oldest station on the prairies, broadcasting since 1922. Here, too, the CBC wanted CFCN's frequency for its national network. However, in this case, it had to face down not only a private station owner but a move to set up a "people's" station which would have been owned by the farm organizations and small shareholders. At the same time that the CBC was preparing to take over CFCN's frequency, the station was considering a buy-out proposal from a joint venture intending to run the station as a cooperative.

At the parliamentary committee of 1946, CFCN owner Herbert G. Love appeared along with representatives of the United Farmers of Alberta, the Alberta Federation of Agriculture, and the Alberta Wheat Pool. Their appearance was supported by telegrams from the Western Stockgrowers' Association, the Alberta Farmers' Union, and the Alberta Association of Municipal Districts. Spokesman for CFCN and the groups, lawyer Marsh M. Porter, made a passionate argument for local ownership and local operation and spelled out the mechanics of this alternative to "national" radio.

The groups made the important distinction between "public" and "government" ownership. They proposed to form a corporation which would be required by law to have a minimum of ten to fifteen thousand shareholders, none of whom would be allowed to hold more than a nominal number of shares: "We would have public ownership of radio which, remote as we are from the seat of authority in Ottawa, is a vastly different thing from government ownership of any project ... we would have a listener ownership representative of the interests of the people who are using these facilities." [142]

The company would be structured so that no organization could dominate it. Instead, it would be organized according to principles of representative democracy. The province would be divided into roughly fifty geographic areas. Once a year, shareholders living in each area would send a delegate to a meeting which would select a board of directors "responsible to that group for their conduct." The concept was not particularly radical – the existing farm organizations were already being run in a similar way. The structure was not only intended to be democratic, but would have an important feedback function with respect to programming. It was also seen as an important check on the concentration of ownership and a guarantee of free expression:

We are coming to the time when the radio in Alberta is going to belong to two people. Radio is going to belong to corporate-owned newspapers, probably chain-owned; and as they become chain-owned, they become less capable of resisting major advertising pressure; and radio is going to be owned by the CBC whose function was never to serve our local needs.

... we talk about freedom of speech a good deal and we think of it as belonging to the speaker. Freedom of speech belongs to the listener. Freedom of speech belongs to the reader. Freedom of speech is of no value to anybody if the opportunity to speak is not freely available. [143]

This was the first attempt to create a nongovernmental "public" alternative to "national" broadcasting, but it was dismissed patronizingly by the CBC. Dunton said the CBC found the idea interesting, "but our Board must view the particular suggestion made in relation to the structure of radio in Canada." Besides, he said, "as a result of CBC plans, Alberta will gain greatly in radio service." [144]

CFRB and CFCN both eventually gave up their fights and moved to new frequencies in 1948. (The CBC compensated CFRB by allowing it to transmit at fifty kilowatts on a regional frequency, making it the most powerful and most lucrative private radio station in the country.) In addition, the CBC acquired the clear channel occupied by the Manitoba telephone system's station CKY and completed its national chain.

This experience, along with the government order prohibiting provincial broadcasting, made the direction of national policy in 1946 only too clear. The CBC alone was now entitled to speak for the public interest with respect to broadcasting in Canada. [145] By 1946, national broadcasting had its own agenda and it was not necessarily concordant with public concerns.

### Regulation and Authority

The 1946 parliamentary committee confirmed the legality of the CBC's frequency takeovers. But it also went a long way towards legitimating the position that the private broadcasters had collectively staked out. Its report, tabled 16 August, recognized "a place for, and a definite need for private community stations supplementary to the national system ... They have and we believe they should have good opportunity for service and for business. A national broadcasting system is for one purpose and community stations are for another purpose ... it is in the public interest that the distinction of purpose between the two should be stated ... Network broadcasting and nation wide coverage ... are the functions of the national system. Service to community areas is the function of the private system." [146]

The parliamentary committee thereby opened a door through which the Conservative opposition would proceed to drive a tank. On 23 August 1946, during debate on a minor amendment to the Broadcasting Act, Conservative critic Donald Fleming brought the question of the relationship between the CBC and the private stations into the House of Commons. Pointing out that Conservative and Social Credit members of the parliamentary committee had not endorsed the recent report, he denounced the "absorption of two major wave lengths now held by private companies in this country." The climate had evolved, he said, from the spirit of the Aird commission and the Broadcasting Act to one of increased sympathy for private broadcasting.

It was time "a separate public board" were set up to regulate broadcasting, a board that would ensure the public interest by navigating between the CBC and the private interests.[147] From that moment on, the Conservatives in Parliament and the private broadcasters outside maintained that position until it became the very basis for the Canadian approach to broadcasting.

Pressure from private broadcasters reached its peak in 1947 when the question of the CBC's regulatory role became a major issue at the parliamentary committee. The CAB presented the committee with a comprehensive brief, proposing for the first time an alternative plan for radio. The brief, entitled "Control of Radio: An Urgent Canadian Problem," was heavily couched in terms of freedom of expression. It called for a "Radio Bill of Rights," that would "establish and guarantee for radio, the constitutional freedoms and safeguards which should prevail in a democratic country."[148]

The CAB argued that broadcasting in Canada was under government control and referred repeatedly to "the government's CBC." Its position was based on three arguments: "There is no legal right to freedom of speech on the air in Canada ... Any government-of-the-day can exercise arbitrary power over the operation of all radio stations in Canada ... Present legislation results in ... 'subsidized competition' with power and control of regulation in the hands of one of the 'competitors'."[149] The CAB's proposed solution was to recognize freedom of speech on the air as "a matter of right," and safeguard this freedom of speech by placing licensing and regulation of broadcasting in the hands of an independent authority responsible directly to Parliament.

In fact, the only difference between the CAB demand and the *status quo* was that the CAB wanted to separate the operating and regulatory aspects of CBC activity. Otherwise, it is difficult to see how the proposed system would have been any further removed from possible government interference. But the strong civil-liberties language of the CAB position certainly made it appear as though it was proposing a radical change in state involvement in the broadcasting field.

The CAB submission to the committee was supported by an extensive advertising campaign in more than seventy Canadian daily newspapers, as well as on its member stations (the CAB at this point represented 89 of the country's 103 private stations). CBC chairman Davidson Dunton described the CAB campaign as "probably the most intensive publicity campaign ever waged by a group of interests for fundamental changes in certain laws of Canada."[150] The committee also received letters supporting the existing system and opposing the CAB proposal from six major farmers' and cooperative organizations as well as from the Canadian Congress of Labour. The latter group said that while labour was still unsatisfactorily represented on the CBC, it was much better treated there than on the "community" stations.

In its report, tabled 8 July, the committee reiterated its support of private broadcasters but refused to recommend any change in the regulatory process.

It noted that "[private] radio broadcasting is in most cases a quite lucrative form of private business."[151] Again, the conservative opposition parties did not support the report.

The government, meanwhile, stood fast to the traditional policy in place since the 1930s. Speaking in the House on 14 July, the minister responsible for the CBC, J.J. McCann (now minister of national revenue), said: "It is generally known and understood that radio in this country and elsewhere is one of the big prizes in the current struggle for power by reactionary private enterprise ... [Private broadcasters are seeking] more freedom to make profit and to exploit the public through channels which they have been allowed to use."[152] The government's resolve was significant in view of important policy decisions then being formulated with regard to television – or possibly, it was the desire to keep television under its control that determined the government's resolve.

### Technology versus Policy

Between September 1947 and January 1949, the CBC board of governors issued a series of statements which became, in effect, Canada's initial policy regarding television. On 17 May 1948, the CBC proposed development of television along the basic lines that had been adopted with respect to radio. The board felt that television could be "of great benefit to Canada," and if "properly directed, has wide possibilities in the cultural and broad educational fields." It expected that, after initial capital investment, television could be financed from a receiving set licence fee and some commercial revenue.[153]

The CBC said it would exercise "great care" regarding the licensing of television broadcasting stations for private companies or individuals. The necessary channels should first be reserved for the national system and, in any case, must not be granted to non-Canadians. Network television "should be developed in the national interest ... it would not be in the general Canadian public interest for individual private television stations to become outlets in Canada for non-Canadian television systems. Therefore, [the CBC] will follow a policy of not granting permission for individual private Canadian television stations to become outlets for non-Canadian systems."[154]

The board of governors issued another statement on television on 3 November 1948.[155] No progress had been made since May because the government had not acted on the CBC's financing proposals. But the board was now faced with six pending applications by private groups, four for Toronto and two for Montreal channels. It noted "the apparent uncertainty ... of most of the applicants with regard to the quality and kind of service they will be able to broadcast," and was concerned about their capacity to sustain it. [156] The only strong proposal came from the Famous Players Canadian Corporation, a group controlled by US motion-picture interests.

At the public hearing on the applications, representation had been made against granting licences to any of the applicants "and in favour of initial co-operative development in which private broadcasting interests would participate with the national system." [157] The board felt private broadcasters would be interested in such a plan because it would enable them to participate without committing very large resources, while supplying necessary capital that the public treasury might not be willing or able to provide.

It thus recommended deferring the private applications, pending consideration of such "initial co-operative development." But it injected a new sense of urgency to the question: television, if soundly developed, would become an important social force and "care should be taken at the present in establishing monopoly positions that will likely be of great importance in the future." [158]

The private sector was anxious about the delay. In the US, radio entrepreneurs were multiplying their rates of profit by parlaying their expertise and their markets into television. In Canada, the CBC was studying the situation and the government appeared to be waiting. Despite opposition calls, the government declined to convene the parliamentary committee in 1948 and 1949, breaking the long-established pattern of having it meet at least every second session.

On 20 January 1949, the CBC board produced, but did not make public, a confidential memorandum the CBC later described as "the most complete statement of what the board believes are the vital considerations for Canada in matters of television." [159] The memorandum began with the words: "We believe that the main question is whether or not television broadcasting is to be developed so as to benefit the national life of Canada." [160] It went on to describe the importance of television – "the most vital and effective means of mass communication yet devised" – as a social and psychological force:

The basis of its development will determine whether that force is for the public good – or detriment.

We believe that if soundly developed in line with Canadian needs and conditions television broadcasting can greatly stimulate and enrich the national life of Canada; if developed otherwise it will have a negative value, probably a harmful effect, and be almost entirely a means of intimately projecting non-Canadian ideas and material into Canadian homes in a very forceful way ...

Because of greater impact on the minds of the public, we believe it even more essential in television than in sound broadcasting that national plans be made and a public operation established.

... We believe that in the years ahead television, developed in the public interest, can become a potent force for the growth of our national life and for creating understanding and unity of feeling among Canadians.[161]

Basic decisions had to be made in advance of any development and development should not be delayed, the board said. There were two arguments against delay. The first was public pressure. Canadians were becoming more and more exposed to reports about television in the US and UK and television broadcasts from the US were beginning to spill over into southern Ontario. Second, television would greatly stimulate the Canadian electronics industry whose manufacturers might otherwise have to severely curtail their operations. Television would thus have economic benefits and could even be vital "to our defense potential."[162]

The memorandum warned that private development of television would lead to the same situation the Aird commission had found in 1929: that radio was "chiefly a means of pumping American material into Canadian homes." Advertising would dominate and private commercial television would be impossible to control. Therefore, the CBC had to be the main motor for the development of television.

The memorandum then laid out the CBC plan: to begin by establishing stations in Montreal and Toronto and later expand into other areas, building "a service of wide coverage step by step" (the Montreal stations would broadcast in English and French). The financial basis would be a ten dollar licence fee and commercial revenue. A licence fee would mean "only those people with television sets benefitting from the service would contribute to it. The general taxpayer would not be contributing to public television."[163] To begin operations, the CBC would need a $5.5 million loan.

Finally, the CBC reiterated the possibility of "initial co-operative development" between the public system and private interests – if the government decided that private interests were to play a part – "with the prospect of division into separate public and private operations later when the television public had grown."[164] But the CBC wanted assurance that it would be in the leadership position.

Thus, from the very beginning, the Canadian government had a clear picture of the sociocultural, economic, and political issues at stake in television. It also had a blueprint for action. But the discourse in which its policy was framed was a long way from that of 1932.

Two months after the CBC's confidential memorandum, on 28 March 1949, Minister of National Revenue J.J. McCann made the first official statement of government policy regarding television.[165] McCann said the government had for some time been considering "how television broadcasting could be developed in Canada in a way that would best serve the national interest." While other countries were doing the difficult and costly developing of television, "it seemed wise to delay the introduction of television in Canada." Now, television was to be one of the subjects of inquiry of a royal commission that was about to be established:

> In the meantime, however ... the government has decided that the development of a Canadian television system on an interim basis should be undertaken. By entering the field now, Canada will benefit substantially from the experience of others in the establishment of proper facilities and operating methods. A further advantage ... will arise from the large new outlet which will be provided for the electronics industry. Television will help to maintain and materially increase the contribution of this important industry to our national life ... This new medium can be of great benefit to the national life of Canada if properly developed. On the other hand, it could have a negative or even detrimental effect on our national life if it grew in a haphazard and unco-ordinated manner. [166]

The government was concerned to provide "that Canadians in various parts of Canada will have the opportunity to receive Canadian programs." Consequently, it was prepared to support the establishment of facilities in Canada "that will meet the desire of the Canadian people to have a television system of their own." Linking Canada's sparse population would require special efforts:

> For these reasons, it is clear that a large measure of public participation in television will be necessary. It is not the intention, however, to exclude private operations from the field of television. The development of radio broadcasting in Canada through a combination of public and private enterprise, in a manner which a vast majority of disinterested Canadians approve and support, has shown the feasibility of this method of procedure ... This procedure will be adopted, with suitable adjustments, for the development of television. The public operation of television will be established, to be supported by those who benefit from the system. At the same time private stations which will share in the development of television will be licensed. The government believes that in this way television will become a means of encouraging Canadian talent, of expressing Canadian ideals, of serving the needs of the country as a whole, and of stimulating and strengthening our national life and consciousness. [167]

The government's "interim plan" entrusted "the general direction of television broadcasting in Canada" to the CBC. The CBC was to establish national production centres and transmitting stations in Montreal and Toronto, providing broadcast services for its own as well as for licensed private stations to be set up. Only one licence would be granted in any city or area in Canada.

While the policy clearly revolved around the role of the CBC, the statement sought to play down the extent of public involvement. It mentioned the expectation that television operations would become self-supporting from licence fees and commercial revenues within a few years. The emphasis was on programming benefits – the national plan would make possible "a core of Canadian television broadcasting," although it was not intended to exclude non-Canadian material: "the public will wish Canadian stations, both public and private, to carry some good programs from other countries." [168]

Finally, while minimizing the government role, the policy statement highlighted the potential benefits that would accrue to private interests. The plan called for a minimum of public support and coordination while providing conditions under which private organizations could participate in the system.

On 8 April 1949, the government of Prime Minister Louis St. Laurent (who had succeeded Mackenzie King as Liberal Party leader in November 1948) announced the creation of the Royal Commission on National Development in the Arts, Letters and Sciences. The first specific aspect of its mandate was to make recommendations regarding "the principles upon which the policy of Canada should be based, in the fields of radio and television broadcasting." [169] While it sat, the CBC refused to recommend any licensing of private television stations.

# CHAPTER THREE

# The Private Appropriation of the Public Sphere (1949–58)

## INTRODUCTION

"In 1945, as peace came, it was possible to discern an explosive set of circumstances," writes US television historian Erik Barnouw. "Electronic assembly lines, freed from production of electronic war matériel, were ready to turn out picture tubes and television sets. Consumers, long confronted by wartime shortages and rationing, had accumulated savings and were ready to buy. Manufacturers of many kinds, ready to switch from armaments back to consumer goods were eager to advertise. The situation awaited a catalyst, a signal."[1]

The signal came in the form of a Federal Communications Commission decision to begin licensing commercial television (only a handful of "experimental" stations were in operation prior to 1945). By July 1946, the FCC had issued twenty-four licences and "television fever" was on its way.[2] The implications for Canada were enormous, as history appeared ready to repeat itself.

Having established broadcasting as a cultural and political instrument, the federal government was uncertain how to deal with the postwar industrial demand for the introduction of television, which it seemed to view somewhat as a threat from foreign (US) technology that would resurrect all the difficulties the system had been carefully constructed to prevent. By 1948, as the federal government began to develop a policy for television, it realized – as an earlier federal government had twenty years earlier – that a full-dress airing of the question was necessary. The need for a national policy with respect to television was one of the specific incitements for the creation in 1949 of the first full-scale inquiry into cultural questions in Canada, the Royal Commission on National Development in the Arts, Letters and Sciences chaired by Vincent Massey.

The Massey commission was the setting for the most extensive public discussion of communications in Canada up to that time. Its report[3] eventually reaffirmed the need for broadcasting to remain firmly planted in the public sector, rejecting the demands of the private broadcasters. But it did so in a way that recognized their acquired status and amplified the "national" dimension of public broadcasting. It opened the door for an increased role for the state in cultural policy generally and in broadcasting in particular, emphasizing especially the importance that television be developed in the public interest under the auspices of the CBC. But on the crucial question of technical standards, it acquiesced to the Department of Transport's proposal to adopt the American system – and the flood of programming that crossed the border along with it.[4] A truly independent Canadian policy position on this question at this time could have obviated the next forty years of lament.

As in the period of the Aird commission, private enterprise reacted furiously to the implication that only "the government" could be said to serve the public interest. This time, it was supported by a minority report, an increasingly aggressive Conservative opposition, and a political climate sympathetic to private economic initiative and suspicious of the "socialistic" connotations of public enterprise. The Massey commission notwithstanding, the development of television would see the private appropriation of broadcasting away from the public sphere.

Well into the 1950s, the formal status of the private broadcasters within the Canadian "single system" remained unclear and their own descriptions of themselves went through repeated ideological and semantic transformations, as they characterized their activity variously as "local," "community," "free enterprise," and "nongovernment," as well as "private" broadcasting.

While the distinction between "public" and "private" was continually at play during these years, the deemed purpose of broadcasting underwent its own interesting evolution. The typically Canadian ambivalence towards resolving the contradiction between public and private enterprise was well characterized in a 1953 article by historian A.R.M. Lower:

> Our Canadian pattern in these public matters seems to be fairly consistent ... First we get into a muddle. Then we have a Royal Commission which recommends a public agency. Having set up the public agency, we let it get into another muddle. This brings on the infuriated attacks of the private enterprise people, all made with the holiest of motives. We then have another Royal Commission. This time we compromise, maintaining the public agency but allowing private enterprise to come into the picture too. Eventually some sort of balance gets worked out ... this is our Canadian pattern, now quite well-marked and distinctive enough to be unique.[5]

As if on cue, the government instituted a Royal Commission on Broadcasting, chaired by Robert Fowler, in 1955. The most substantial examination yet of Canadian broadcasting, the Fowler commission's report put a new edge on the basic assumptions that guided the development of broadcasting in Canada. The royal commissions of 1929 and 1951 had stated the purpose of broadcasting as threefold: "to inform, to educate and to entertain." To these, the royal commission of 1957 added a fourth purpose: "to sell goods," and added significantly: "Any broadcaster who performs only one of these functions and none of the others, or even too much of one and too little of the others, is not a good broadcaster."[6] (In 1965, an advisory committee chaired by the same Robert Fowler would drop "to sell goods" and replace it with "to promote national unity." These semantic migrations illustrate the importance of language in the struggles surrounding broadcasting in Canada, especially in legitimating the placing of economic or political objectives over sociocultural ones.)

Thus, in the 1950s, the basic principles that had guided the first thirty years of Canadian broadcasting were rewritten as the underlying practices were reworked. By the time the Conservative Party returned to power in 1957, the stage was set for these changes to be codified in law.

## THE MASSEY COMMISSION, 1949-51

### Representations

If Canada has an aristocracy, Vincent Massey was a scion of one of its leading families. A former ambassador to the US and high commissioner to the Court of St James, he had also been a privileged adviser to the organizers of the Canadian Radio League in its early years and would become Canada's first native-born governor-general in 1952. The royal commission he now chaired had as its other members Norman MacKenzie, president of the University of British Columbia, Hilda Neatby, a distinguished historian, author, and educator, Arthur Surveyer, a civil engineer, and Father Georges-Henri Lévesque, the Dominican founder and Dean of the Faculty of Social Sciences at Laval University. Lévesque, still active forty years later, is recognized as one of the intellectual precursors of Quebec's Quiet Revolution; his stature is such that the royal commission of 1949–51 is often referred to as the "Massey-Lévesque" commission, although he did not actually share the chair.

Between August 1949 and July 1950, the Massey commission held public hearings across Canada, receiving some four hundred submissions from groups and individuals. The Canadian Broadcasting Corporation and the Canadian Association of Broadcasters each appeared before it several times, at the beginning and the end of the commission's investigations. As in the case of the Aird commission in 1928–29, dozens of public interest groups appeared as well. The transcripts and briefs[7] provide an exhaustive portrait of opinion with regard to broadcasting and, especially, prospective views on television in Canada halfway through the twentieth century.

Counsel to the commission Peter Wright set the tone on the first day of public meetings with an elegant introductory statement placing broadcasting in a Canadian historical perspective. "The concepts of Canada and of radio were born and have grown together," Wright said.[8] As in the case of rail, road, and air transport, Canada had decided "to pay the price for the national asset of an all-Canadian trans-continental system binding us all together as Canadians. That horizontal solution of our nation-wide communications problems in Canada has become typical."[9] Although the Aird report had recommended national radio broadcasting, Wright noted, "private radio broadcasting has flourished with the years so that today a different situation faces you than faced the Aird Commission in 1929."[10] As Wright put it, every parliamentary committee since 1932 had supported a "nationally-owned radio system and full and complete national control over all broadcasting in Canada." But, "commencing in 1946 they began to recognize the position of the private station in serving the particular needs of community areas."

Thus, the CBC and the private broadcasters became the major actors before the Massey commission in 1949. But in the course of the commission's work and the ensuing political debate, different alignments of interests emerged.

As we saw in the last chapter, the CBC and the government shared certain mutual interests at this point. The government's main concern was to maintain a national system close to the apparatus of the state, to use as needed, whether to promote overall policy or in time of crisis. This meant a strong, central agency like the CBC. The CBC, meanwhile, had developed its own bureaucratic survival instinct, which did not necessarily contribute to its public service mission. Seen this way, there were really three sets of positions: the public interest position on the political left, the state/national interest represented by the CBC and the government in the centre, and a kind of libertarian right grouped around the private broadcasters.

The forces for public broadcasting were basically the same as in the 1930s, except that in the place of the coalition of groups that led the way in the original campaign, there was now an established public broadcaster. As far as private broadcasting was concerned, the argument that had finally turned the Conservative government of 1932 against it was no longer valid. R.B. Bennett had believed the private sector was too weak to sustain a "Canadian" national system, but private broadcasting had proven to be tremendously lucrative.

The summary of the CBC's position before the Massey commission was a good synthesis of the basic principles on which Canadian broadcasting had been built.[11] The CBC position combined the established principle that the air is a public asset – the principle established by the Aird commission and the original Radio Broadcasting Act of 1932 – with the pragmatic recognition that private stations had a role to play. Its strategy was to define this role as "ancillary" to the "national system," and necessarily under its control. On this basis, the CBC could then argue against the proposal to remove its regulatory powers: the needs of the national system must be "paramount," and "In any question between private or local interests and national interests, the national interest must prevail."[12]

This was a particularly interesting and self-interested formulation. In principle, the CBC said, all broadcasting decisions must be made in the public interest. In practice, however, the CBC recognized that a certain form of private ownership was in the public interest – although it was cautious to maintain a critical stance in this regard.

As we saw earlier, the CBC plan called for applying these principles to television. Television would be developed and its operations would be overseen by the national system while, as in radio, private enterprise would have opportunities to use the public air. It was evidently too costly to develop the system on the strict basis of publicly owned stations, and the private sector would have to be involved.

The main distinction made between publicly and privately owned sectors was that the private sector was "local" while the public sector was "national." CBC board chairman Davidson Dunton told the commission on its first day of public hearings that the CBC did not accept the view that it was in competition with private stations: "because our field is in national network broadcasting, whereas their field is local community broadcasting."[13]

CBC dominance, then, depended on defining the national interest as superior to local interests. It was a tactical position in a power struggle with the private interests and their supporters, but it had far-reaching political implications. As the public sector, the CBC could have framed its argument in terms of private, or capitalist, interests, versus public, or community, interests. Instead, it conceded local community interests to the private sector and equated the public interest with the national interest – or, more precisely, with the interest of the national system. The conflict between the centre and the periphery – or regions – would become a leitmotif of Canadian broadcasting.

In light of the private broadcasters' strong campaign, the CBC had toughened its stand by the end of the Massey commission's main round of hearings in April 1950. At the final session on 13 April, Dunton argued strongly for privileged CBC access to clear channels, control of network broadcasting, and regulation of programming in the public interest – all of which denied the demand for a separate regulatory body. Yet even Dunton accepted the legitimacy of the private broadcasters' basic position: "The system is based on the concept that the over-all public interest should be served, yet there is lots of opportunity for private initiative and private enterprise."[14]

There were, in 1949, "two different concepts of radio in Canada," the one laid down by Parliament ("the concept of public service in broadcasting and the responsibility of any broadcasting organization to the public, who own the limited number of air channels which there are"[15]), and the other being promoted by the private sector ("the allotting of portions of the public domain, the air channels, for the use of those privileged to use them in the way that is most advantageous to them commercially"[16]).

While the first concept still had a rhetorical advantage that would be reinforced by the Massey commission's report, the second concept was becoming more and more strongly anchored in Canada's broadcasting reality and would, with the development of television, completely transform the nature of Canadian broadcasting.

The main representation on behalf of private broadcasting was made by the Canadian Association of Broadcasters. Like the CBC, the CAB was asked to appear at the beginning and the end of the Massey hearings and its intervention took various forms.

The royal commission evidently felt the need to treat the CAB on a somewhat equal footing with the CBC, but approached it warily. The CAB's September 1949 brief,[17] was based on the notions of freedom to broadcast and rights of broadcasters. Distributing copies to the commission members, secretary Archibald Day enclosed a confidential memorandum in which he wrote: "The conclusion I come to is that financial considerations are more important than the theory of freedom, so far as the development of radio is concerned, and so far as the elimination of present monopoly factors are concerned."[18]

The CAB's economic theory was made clear in a document replying to a series of questions posed by the commission: "The relation of profit to broadcasting is precisely the same as the relation of profit to any other business ... We do not believe that the making of profit by broadcasters is any concern of the regulatory body ... We see no reason why the profits and statements of broadcasting stations should be made public while this is not done by other businesses."[19]

The CBC's powers were "undemocratic and dangerous," said the CAB; there should be no restrictions on economic development and expansion of private broadcasting, the CBC should be financed by a statutory parliamentary grant and it should abandon advertising. The CAB opposed the notion of "advisory or citizen bodies" that public interest groups were circulating, on the grounds that such bodies would end up in the hands of "cranks at best or subversive influences at worst."

CAB chairman William Guild, of radio CJOC (Lethbridge), told the commission of the prevailing threat to individual freedom and enterprise in the world, and of the importance of diversified ownership in preserving democracy. Private enterprise had created broadcasting, he said, the national system should not be allowed to supplant or destroy it. Guild put forward the idea that the marketplace, not Parliament, should decide the nature of the broadcasting system: "While the CBC is responsible to Parliament, the private stations are, and a privately-operated network would be, responsible to the people ... a privately-operated network would find its sole source of revenue in its commercial activities, and consequently, to be successful would have to be popular with the people." [20] Guild thus provided an ideological alternative to the political conception of the public prevailing since Aird: the notion of the economic public, the public as market.

In a supplementary brief filed at the end of the Massey hearings, the CAB responded directly to the public interest argument. The term "public interest," it contended, "means that which concerns, affects or pertains to the convenience, needs, benefits, advantages or profit of the people as a whole by insuring to them that there shall be in the broadcasting transmission of ideas and information of every lawful character such freedom of speech, freedom of economic competition and freedom from unnecessary interference as would protect the democratic way of life of Canadians." [21]

For the first time, the CAB called not only for a "separate, impartial and unbiased" regulatory body, but for clear demarcation of two systems of broadcasting in Canada: a publicly funded, noncommercial national system, and a competing free enterprise, wholly commercial system.

In this vision – which strongly resembled the shape that Canadian broadcasting would soon take – it is noteworthy that the private broadcasters no longer referred to themselves as "community" or "independent," or even "private" stations, but as "free enterprise broadcasting stations." When this was pointed out in questioning, William Guild said they had chosen this designation as a way of distinguishing themselves clearly.

According to the CAB, the public sector should concentrate on "cementing the unification of Canada," developing Canadian talent, and doing "finer types of broadcasting." Allowed to form networks, permanently licensed, subject only to the law of the land, and freed from competing with the CBC for advertising dollars, the private sector would do commercial programming.

By now, the public sector had no monopoly on nationalist rhetoric. The CAB plan, it said, would "provide the citizens of Canada with better service from its radio broadcasting stations and provide the radio broadcasting industry with a proper opportunity to expand, develop and play an even greater role in the unification of Canada, in its commercial development and in the fostering of ... Canadianism." [22]

The Massey commission also heard from dozens of groups and organizations interested in the broadcasting issue, among them organizations which had been consistently present in the struggle for public broadcasting from the beginning. The Canadian Congress of Labour reiterated its call for an

entirely publicly owned system, in accordance with the original Aird recommendations. The plea for an independent regulatory body, it said, went
against public policy of the past twenty years and threatened the CBC; the
private broadcasters wanted a privately owned system with ancillary public
stations, rather than the opposite as at present.

The CCL was one of the few participants to engage in debate on the
semantic level. The CAB, it said, was trying to camouflage its commercial
pursuits by equating the public with the audience: "'Public interest' and
'*the* public interest' are not the same thing. The public may be greatly
interested in a program which is not in the public interest."[23] This was a
useful distinction that was only too rarely pursued.

The Canadian Federation of Agriculture, too, supported "the principle of
public ownership and operation of national radio, and ... the system of radio
operation and control as it functions today in Canada."[24] As most of the
public interest groups, the CFA felt private stations were all right as "local
community enterprises," provided they performed a public service.

The CFA also addressed the question of media and democracy: "The issue
of national radio is important not only for itself but as a vital part of the
question of whether we are to develop a progressive, responsible and alert
democracy. It is vital to our prospects for the development of a citizenship
capable of critical analysis and balanced judgment."[25] This position was
echoed by regional farm bodies such as the Alberta Federation of Agriculture,
which pointed out that contrary to charges coming from the opponents of
public broadcasting, CBC projects like the "Farm Forum" study groups were
"most democratic."[26]

The Canadian Association for Adult Education also praised the CBC's
concrete action on the "democratic principle of free discussion" and called
for increased public financial support, with no major change in the structure
of the system. Television held out even more compelling reasons for public
control, it said.[27]

The spirit of democratic radio was best expressed by the "Farm Forum"
project itself, which described itself as a "circle of communication" or
feedback loop. The "Forum" appeared before the royal commission as a
joint CAAE-CBC-CFA project and the CAAE's E.A. Corbett praised the CBC's
"courage to act on the democratic principle of free discussion."[28]

The Federated Women's Institutes of Canada implied that the men who
made the rules and regulations of broadcasting knew nothing about the
problems of women. It called for "more citizen participation in the programs" and, specifically, a citizens' advisory committee on programs for
women.[29]

Among the private interest groups that appeared, the All-Canada Mutually
Operated Radio Stations, representing eleven, primarily western stations,
was to the right of the CAB in its fundamentalist free enterprise thinking.

"Radio broadcasting is a medium of mass communication and is not a public utility," it said, adding that the right to use a broadcast channel should be like the right to use the land.[30] It called for an independent regulatory body, as did the Canadian Chamber of Commerce[31] and the Radio Manufacturers' Association of Canada.[32]

A unique submission was made by a Toronto public opinion research group, Elliott-Haynes Ltd. Elliott-Haynes had been hired during the war by a consortium of fifteen Canadian corporations to survey public opinion on attitudes towards socialism and private enterprise, and on the question of socialization of specific businesses and industries. Elliott-Haynes had pioneered radio audience ratings in Canada in the late 1930s, so it may have been natural for the firm to focus on broadcasting in the second phase of its study. In 1949 the results were updated and company president Walter E. Elliott presented the findings to the Massey commission. In short, the population surveyed was more favourable to private than to government ownership, both in general and specifically regarding radio broadcasting, and more strongly so in 1949 than in 1944. Needless to say, the results of this survey helped the private broadcasters' position.[33]

As usual, a distinct perspective was forthcoming from Quebec. The Confédération des travailleurs catholiques du Canada (CTCC) said it opposed private enterprise domination in broadcasting because of the danger to French-Canadian interests presented by largely American programs that did not consider their ethnic, linguistic, and religious specificity. They pointed to the cinema as a negative example of what private enterprise could achieve.[34]

But the CTCC was also critical of Radio-Canada. During the recent Asbestos strike, the CTCC had been refused the right to reply against attacks launched against it over the public air (in the guise of a regular Union Nationale party political broadcast). As a remedy to antisyndicalism, the CTCC proposed a weekly hour-long program, along the lines of the "Farm Forum," to be run by the unions and addressed to workers on French and English networks. The CTCC also proposed replacing the CBC board of governors with two "consultative committees," one in French and one in English, to advise management on broadcasting policy. This was conceived as a check against centralization. But the system was seen nonetheless as one of "state broadcasting," in the words of CTCC president Gérard Picard.

The Fédération des mouvements de jeunesse du Québec (whose delegation included Pierre Juneau and Claude Ryan) echoed the call for a representative consultative committee. While favouring the independence of the CBC, it called for decentralization of production.[35]

An interesting distinction set off the Société canadienne d'enseignement post-scolaire from the Société d'éducation des adultes du Québec. The former, a national federation with a pan-Canadian outlook, made national unity and strengthening the "two cultures" the key issue. It emphasized extension of Radio-Canada services to francophone centres outside Quebec. The latter, a split-off from the CAAE, emphasized feedback programming and urged the formation of more programs based on organized listening groups.[36]

As in the past, nationalist groups saw the basic questions in fundamentally different terms. Thus, the Union catholique des cultivateurs (UCC) considered Radio-Canada's farm broadcasts "an intrusion by a federal body in an area that should be off-limits to it."[37] The Fédération des sociétés Saint-Jean-Baptiste du Québec said Radio-Canada had to accept competition from private stations in radio and television.[38]

The clearest nationalist position was that of the Ligue d'action nationale, represented by André Laurendeau and François-Albert Angers. It said there were two principles the commission must not forget: that Canada was a federation in which education was exclusively a provincial jurisdiction, and that Canada was a bicultural country in which there could be no unity without diversity.[39]

The league recalled a history few others seemed to remember. Federal authorities, it said, had gone beyond the scope of the court decisions of the 1930s to appropriate the educational and cultural – that is, programming – aspects of broadcasting as well as the technical aspects of transmission and reception. "It would have been far more in line with the spirit of the constitution to stick to the recommendations of the Aird commission," and leave program jurisdiction with the provinces. The league called for a review of this question to bring radio into touch with Canadian reality. It opposed the use of broadcasting as "an instrument of domination, centralisation, and direction of the country's cultural life."[40]

The Massey commission's deliberations stalled, but did not completely stop political discussion on broadcasting. On 31 March 1950, Parliament again set up a committee on broadcasting, providing the occasion for each of the major parties to reiterate its position. John Diefenbaker for the Conservatives said the CBC had held back the development of television and private industry would have to be encouraged if Canada were to catch up with the US. He called again for a "semi-judicial body" to regulate all broadcasting.[41]

For the government, J.J. McCann emphasized the necessary autonomy of the CBC from partisan influence. The CBC was not answerable to the government and the government was not responsible for the CBC, he said. Regarding television, he repeated the national policy goal contained in the CBC's own documents of the previous year: television should be enabled to develop as "a strong social force," in the interests of Canadian nationhood.[42]

M.J. Coldwell of the CCF used the experience of the CBC to justify the supremacy of public over private broadcasting. The CBC enjoyed such hearty support among workers' and farm organizations because it provided "something that we seldom get in any other way, namely, a free and frank discussion of problems that are affecting the people."[43] But Coldwell criticized the CBC for having "played into the hands of powerful broadcasting interests in this country" by allowing some private stations to increase their transmission power bit by bit over the years, to the detriment of local community stations and against the spirit of the broadcasting act. He called for eliminating advertising from CBC radio and levying a high tax on private advertisement revenue to be turned over to the CBC. As for television, it should be kept entirely out of the commercial arena and should be "used as a public educational facility."

These were the major political positions in 1950, while waiting for the Massey commission to report. The main issue before the parliamentary committee that year was the need to find a new financing formula for the CBC, which had close to a $1 million deficit in 1950–51. The committee did not hear from the private sector in 1950, prompting Donald Fleming to charge in the House that it was only considering one side of the story.

### Recommendations

The royal commission tabled its report on 1 June 1951. Regarding broadcasting, it basically recommended the *status quo*, rejecting the private broadcasters' demands. However, one member, Arthur Surveyer, filed a substantial dissenting position supporting the argument for a new, separate regulatory authority. While opposition leader George Drew denounced the CBC's "monopolistic privileges," and Donald Fleming cited the Surveyer dissent, J.J. McCann said the Massey commission had produced "a splendid report" and, for the first time in its history, the government awarded the CBC a small direct grant to meet its costs.[44]

The Massey commission's report recapitulated the orthodox justification of the Canadian broadcasting system, but with a major revision – it recognized the legitimacy of the private stations: "The inclusion of private stations in the national system, although not contemplated when the original principles for broadcasting were established, has in practice proven to be in the national interest."[45] The two main problems now facing the system, it said, were the financial crisis in the public sector and the dissatisfaction of the private sector with its status.

The commission spent some time referring to the comments of the various groups that had appeared before it. It had come away with the impression that "the present national system has succeeded to a remarkable degree in doing exactly what the writers of [the Aird] report wanted it to do." It was Canadian in character, appreciated throughout the country, and had contributed "powerfully, we were told, to a sense of Canadian unity ... We observed indeed a certain alarm at any suggestion of change in the existing system."[46]

The commission took a basically favourable view of the CBC's programming record, citing, among others, the forum programs which "correct in part the passive listening habits encouraged by ordinary broadcasting." These programs were "of great value in making better citizens of us, in that they awaken our critical faculties." In summing up attitudes towards the CBC, the report said: "Canadians ... like what they get, on the whole, but they want more of it, and of even better quality. The statement that the CBC often underestimates public taste appears more than once, and the demand ... that national radio be used as an instrument of education and culture came from every section of the country."[47] It also underlined the expressed need for broader coverage of service, "and, in particular, for a nation-wide French network."

The report was tolerantly critical of the private stations: "Indeed the general program content of the private stations was rather severely criticized."[48] Their "undistinguished programs" could not be justified, but their services to the public justified their continued existence as part of the system. In fact, as many of the groups that appeared before the commission had pointed out, the CBC was partly responsible for the situation because of its laxity in regulating the private broadcasters.

The report was bemusedly understated regarding television: "This remarkable new form of broadcasting has evoked great interest and enthusiasm among the general public, the advertising industry, and in all groups whose interest or duty it may be to inform, entertain or influence the public. This interest and enthusiasm is one important fact about television not open to dispute. Another equally important but perhaps not equally recognized fact is its unpredictability. Its history indicates that we can be certain only of its uncertain future."[49]

The report stated, mildly but firmly, that American television, "essentially a commercial enterprise, an advertising industry," would not serve Canada's "national needs." But it accepted without concern the assumption that Canada would adopt the same technical specifications for television that the US had established. Other systems were being developed in Europe, but US and Canadian television sets would be compatible. Thus, in the border areas where most of the Canadian population lived, it would be possible to pick up signals from the United States as well as Canadian ones. The implications of this would be monumental for the development of television, particularly in English Canada. A different pattern of "lines and frames" would have technically protected the Canadian market for Canadian signals right from the start.[50]

The keynote of the Massey commission's report was that the Canadian state would have to play a greater role in nurturing cultural and intellectual activity if national objectives were to be met. Practically, this meant a greater commitment to funding for cultural purposes.

The proposed public policy for broadcasting rested on the principle that broadcasting, as a monopoly because of the physical nature of the air channels, must be recognized as part of the public domain and thus be subject to state control. The state could either limit its involvement to the issuing of licences to ensure the uncluttered use of channels, as in the United States, or it could treat broadcasting as a public trust.

The commission clearly favoured the latter view. Broadcasting, it said, was "a social influence too potent and too perilous to be ignored by the state which, in modern times, has assumed increasing responsibility for the welfare of its citizens."[51] But it also noted that the "peculiarities" of the Canadian situation (notably, the continued existence within the national system "of 'private', 'commercial' or 'community' stations as they are variously styled"[52] seemed to preclude any ready-made solution.

Most private stations had prospered under the existing system. Between 1946–48 alone, their total revenues increased twice as rapidly as those of the CBC, and in 1948 the combined assets of private investors were three times as great as those of the CBC. This growth in prosperity, the commission said, was perhaps the reason for the private stations' increasing protest about their status. But the commission rejected the private stations' position on the grounds that Canadian broadcasting legislation provided for a single, national system:

> The principal grievance of the private broadcasters is based, it seems to us, on a false assumption that broadcasting in Canada is an industry. Broadcasting in Canada, in our view, is a public service directed and controlled in the public interest by a body responsible to Parliament ...
>
> The only status of private broadcasters is as part of the national broadcasting system. They have no civil right to broadcast or any property rights in broadcasting. They have been granted in the national interest a privilege over their fellow-citizens, and they now base their claim for equality with their "business rivals" on the abundant material rewards which they have been able to reap from this privilege.[53]

The Massey commission rejected the private stations' call for a "separate regulatory body." As divisive, destructive, or at best redundant, "it would alter the present national system and would result in two independent groups of radio broadcasting stations, one public and one private."[54] It then recommended: "That the grant of the privilege of radio broadcasting in Canada continue to be under the control of the National Government; that the control of the national broadcasting system continue to be vested in a single body responsible to Parliament; that the Canadian Broadcasting Corporation as now constituted be that authority and continue to provide directly by its operations and indirectly by its control of the operations of others a national radio broadcasting service free from partisan influence."[55]

The commission opposed the permission of private network broadcasting, but recommended that the CBC abandon local commercial advertising in areas where there were private stations. Thus, it reinforced the notion that public broadcasting was essentially national, while private broadcasting was local in scope.

In sum, the Massey commission reinforced the status of the private stations within the "single system," while resisting their most aggressive demands. The Aird commission had called for an exclusively public system, and the legislation of 1932 and 1936 had provided for eventual nationalization of all broadcasting, but the Massey commission reaffirmed the view that had begun to be expressed by the parliamentary committees of the 1940s (and that was willingly conceded by the CBC), that private stations had an "ancillary" place in the national system. The commission never asked a crucial question however: was the national system the only form of public service that could meet the public interest?

The commission recognized the question of financing the CBC as a major problem. As mentioned earlier, revenue from licence fees and advertising began to be insufficient to meet CBC operating costs after the war. Now, there was a demand for increased coverage of Canada's territory, in both French and English, and recommendations to eliminate local advertising. The commission calculated that in 1948, when the CBC earned $7.5 million (essentially from licence fees and advertising), it would have required $14.2 million to do its job as was now being proposed: "We see no solution to the financial problem of the CBC except in additional support from public funds."[56]

But "public funds" could mean various things. The CBC itself had proposed to increase the annual receiver licence fee to five dollars, but this was generally opposed by the mass organizations which were its strongest supporters. The commission felt a moderate user's fee should be maintained. But this would have to be supplemented from general tax revenue.

The commission drew an important distinction between an "annual grant" from Parliament, and a "statutory grant." An annual grant would make the CBC dependent on the government of the day and opened up the possibility of political influence, while a statutory grant would enable the CBC to make long-range plans with confidence. The commission proposed the latter course and recommended that the CBC's income for radio purposes be set by statute for five years, with Parliament making up any shortfall not met by licence and commercial revenue.

Television, however, would be more dependent on public funds. The Massey commission recommended that this "new and unpredictable force in our society" should be organized as a national system along the lines of what it had proposed for radio. It agreed with the government's interim policy vesting direction and control of the system in the CBC, but went farther than the government in this respect, recommending that no private television stations be licensed until the CBC was ready to proceed with national television programs. Also, all private stations should be required to serve as outlets for national programs. This recommendation would be the focus of even more severe opposition from the private sector through the 1950s.

The Massey commission recommended strict separation of accounting between CBC radio and television, parliamentary grants to cover the capital costs of setting up the national television broadcasting system, and a statutory formula for operational funding similar to the one it proposed for radio (licence fee, commercial revenue, and statutory grants as necessary). Finally, it recommended an independent investigation of television be held within three years of the beginning of regular television broadcasting.

Dissenting commissioner Arthur Surveyer presented twenty-five pages of "reservations and observations" on his colleagues' report,[57] basically supporting the position of the private broadcasters and, specifically, their demand for an "independent regulatory body." Their grievances, he noted, were backed by the country's businessmen while opposed by voluntary associations which did not realize all the implications of the broadcasting act.

Surveyer was basically at odds with the other four members of the commission on the fundamental question of the role of the state. He objected essentially to any government involvement in an area that could be served by private industry. While accepting a national purpose for the CBC, and the need to grant it "whatever amounts are needed to maintain an adequate service," he believed substantial savings could be realized "by entrusting the production of commercial programs to private producers." "This suggestion stems from my conviction that, as a rule, private organizations can produce more economically than governmental agencies ... the State ... should attempt commercial production only when private enterprise is unable or unwilling to venture."[58]

From a similar ideological position, conservatives would consistently oppose the basic policy thrust of state-based "public" enterprise in coming years. First through Liberal complicity and then through explicit steps taken by the Conservatives, the private sector would have most of its main demands met by the early 1960s. But philosophically, the viewpoint of the Massey majority would endure into the 1980s.

Thus, while the Massey commission articulated the traditional public rhetoric behind Canadian broadcasting policy, it contributed to widening the gap between that rhetoric and the actual reality of the system. The complementary role for private broadcasting that Massey recognized for the first time with respect to radio would become a dominant one when transferred to television.[59]

### TELEVISION AND THE NEED FOR A COHERENT POLICY, 1952–55

#### *Chipping Away at First Principles*

On 9 November 1951, the minister reporting to Parliament for the CBC, J.J. McCann, introduced amendments to the broadcasting act, providing the CBC with $6.25 million a year for five years, in line with the principle of the Massey commission's recommendation.[60]

Debate on the amendments was the occasion for further discussion on underlying principles.[61] The government, supported by the CCF, emphasized the importance of broadcasting for nation building. The Conservatives felt it was time to adopt the thinking of the Canadian Association of Broadcasters. If the CBC were no longer to be self-financing, said Donald Fleming, it should leave commercial programming to the private sector.

In the wake of the Massey commission report and the debate on amendments to the act, the parliamentary committee convened and became the scene of yet another strong presentation by the Canadian Association of Broadcasters. Buoyed by the findings of the Elliott-Haynes survey referred to above, the CAB argued that its position was more representative of public opinion than that of the organizations which had opposed the private broadcasters at the Massey commission. The "public majority" preferred private radio programs, the CAB argued.[62]

The CAB argued that broadcasting should be treated as any other business, and stated that all business provided a public service or else did not survive. The Massey commission, the CAB said, had failed to see how the radio industry had responded to public need; it was "biased and misleading," its recommendations "unwise," and not in the public interest. Characterizing the CBC as a government agency and propaganda machine, the CAB stated that radio should not be considered in the public domain (which it defined, citing Webster's dictionary, as "the territory belonging to a state or to a general government"). There should be no policing of program content; only use of wavelengths should be regulated.

Again, however, the parliamentary committee reiterated the orthodox view in its report tabled 15 December: "the national broadcasting service carried on by the CBC is essential in the development of our national life in Canada, and is efficiently performing an extremely valuable and important function."[63] The committee categorically rejected the idea that regulation should be limited to technical matters: "our concepts of freedom can best be served ... when Parliament is in a position to ensure that the principles of freedom are carried out to the greatest extent possible."[64] The Conservative and Social Credit members of the committee did not endorse the report.

The 1951 parliamentary committee was also the occasion for an attack on the CBC from the extreme right, for "startling people with materialism" by broadcasting speakers like Bertrand Russell and Anna Freud, at a time when Canada was "fighting communist materialism forces."[65] The committee expressed no opinion, endorsing the CBC's right to determine such matters for itself, but attacks of this type became more and more frequent during the 1950s. The committee did, however, comment on the important propaganda role of the CBC's International Service which, it said, was performing a valuable function "in spreading an understanding of Canada and Canadian ideas, in helping towards greater mutual understanding among democratic peoples, and in furthering information and understanding of the free world and the cause of freedom by people shut off from ordinary contacts with it."[66]

The political and ideological lines highlighted by the split between public and private broadcasting were now well-drawn, with the government, the CCF, the CBC, and the public interest groups on one side, gathered around the policy enunciations, historic interpretation, and recommendations of the Massey commission, and the conservative opposition parties, the private broadcasters, and the business community riding the tide of the postwar/cold-war climate that would define the 1950s.

Operationally, the two approaches differed in their attitude towards involvement of the state. The private sector lobby often couched its argument in libertarian terms, where "freedom" was seen as inversely proportional to state involvement. On the other hand, as we saw in the discussion of the Massey commission's report, the supporters of the public service approach to broadcasting were heavily tied to the expansion of the welfare-state, and gave little thought at this time to the implications of concentrating "public" media in a single state corporation.

The only place such a question was raised was in Quebec. The Jesuit journal *Relations* commented in an editorial on the Massey commission: "It is regrettable that such a generally praiseworthy piece of work tends concretely towards the takeover by the central State of culture and education in Canada."[67] *Relations* found the Massey report simultaneously satisfying and upsetting; the federal government was proposing to enter the cultural sphere in a substantial way, but was doing so in a framework of Canadian nationalism and a certain sensitivity to Canada's French fact.[68]

André Laurendeau echoed this ambivalence in an editorial in *Le Devoir* entitled "Tant de clairvoyance et tant d'aveuglement" (So clear and yet so blind). The Massey commission, he wrote, recognized the threat to Canada of the American way of life: "What dike can be built to defend against this irresistible tidal wave? Only that of a Canadian national culture – that is to say, a myth, a phantom, the shadow of a shadow. There is not *one* Canadian national culture. There are two: one English and one French."[69]

The effect of Massey's centralizing approach, Laurendeau wrote, would be to undermine Quebec's prerogatives as a provincial state. The Massey approach would defeat its own stated purpose: "From now on, political brigandry will have the look of a cultural crusade ... how could the commissioners opt for cultural centralism? Do they not see that in doing so they are uprooting and upsetting the framework of French Canadians, who are still the best agents of resistance?"[70]

Similar arguments against centralization could have been formulated from the point of view of other regional, cultural, or social communities. But only around the ethnolinguistic, or "national," question were the contradictions sharp enough to attract critical attention in 1951.

### Organizing "the Unpredictable Force"

In 1952, the government was concerned with the early development of television and the pursuit of the consolidation of radio by providing the funds recommended by the Massey commission. In the House of Commons, J.J. McCann announced that the CBC would begin television broadcasting in September in Montreal and Toronto and moved to provide a parliamentary loan. M.J. Coldwell of the CCF meanwhile criticized the CBC for being too soft on offensive advertising and too lenient towards the private stations (two areas of criticism also cited by the Massey report).[71]

During debate on CBC funding, Conservative leader George Drew suggested for the first time that the public and private sectors should be considered equals, with the same rights to set up networks, for example. As for public broadcasting, its role should be concentrated in areas (programming and geographic) that would otherwise go uncovered.[72]

This type of thinking would be repeated with increasing vigour over the next few years. Meanwhile, however, the government was beginning to feel the pressure of the private broadcasters and their friends. In October 1952, the advisory council of the National Liberal Federation called for "development of television in Canada by private enterprise along with the CBC" over the objection of J.J. McCann, and in November the prime minister received a CAB delegation for the first time.[73] Private broadcasting thus added prime ministerial recognition to the imprimatur of the Massey commission, further increasing its legitimacy.

The next session of Parliament, closely following the beginning of Canadian television broadcasts, was the most active yet in terms of debate on broadcasting. The throne speech of 20 November 1952, announced that the CBC would establish stations in Halifax, Winnipeg, and Vancouver, to follow those of Montreal, Toronto, and Ottawa. It also announced that applications would be considered for private stations proposing to serve areas which could not be reached by the six CBC stations. Licences would be granted on a basis of "appropriate cooperation" between the CBC and the private backers.

Heated discussion started during debate on the throne speech, with a remarkable intervention by Conservative MP Henri Courtemanche (representing the riding of Labelle, formerly held by Henri Bourassa). The inauguration of television, he said, was a sad day: "We were glad that at last television had come to our homes ... But, while enjoying this pleasure, we could not but think that the government had just created a new state monopoly; that it had just strengthened bureaucracy by striking a terrible blow to free initiative and enterprise in Canada."[74]

Courtemanche's speech was a masterpiece of knee-jerk antisocialism. The CBC, "a corporation of socialistic inspiration," had "a perfect state monopoly"; "state management" of "state television" was "a giant step ... on the road to socialism." The CBC was a haven for large-L liberalism and "atheistic propaganda."

At the same time, Courtemanche invoked a traditional provincial autonomy position. The "state monopoly or government dictatorship" in television was a natural outgrowth of the Massey commission, which had allowed "the Liberals to launch a new drive for centralization and commit further encroachments upon provincial autonomy."[75] A stream of Quebec Liberal back-benchers took issue with Courtemanche, but the juxtaposition of his position and that of André Laurendeau illustrated the problem of sorting out the various aspects of the basic ideological gap between proponents of public and private broadcasting.

The Conservatives also pursued their more sober attack on government policy. Donald Fleming described the measures announced in the throne speech as "throwing to private enterprise a bone from which all meat and nourishment have been completely removed," and as evidence of a "bureaucratic" and "paternalistic" attitude: "Here is private capital and private enterprise willing to take all the risks involved if this bureaucratic government, with its mania for monopoly and bureaucracy, will not restrain the development of something for which the people of Canada are crying."[76]

However, the government *was* accommodating the needs of capital. J.J. McCann explained that the private sector would be invited in to minimize the amount of public funds needed to help extend national television service, and would be allowed to profit from the system in return. The result would be creation of a string of privately owned CBC "affiliates," which would be a central aspect of Canadian television.

The government had a policy objective "to make national television service available to as many Canadians as possible." To ensure that priority rested with the extension of service, "no two stations will be licensed ... to serve the same area." The "single-station policy" as this came to be known would be a new bone of contention for the private sector.[77]

George Drew responded immediately, reiterating what he had said the previous year: the purpose of the public system was to provide service where it was financially unattractive for private industry, not in the lucrative markets. In a sense, this was compatible with traditional Conservative policy towards public enterprise – in 1932, a national radio system was considered unlikely to be profitable. Now, with television looming, Drew urged review of the basic concept of public ownership in broadcasting.[78]

On 27 January 1953, the House of Commons debated appointment of the Special Committee on Broadcasting, its name streamlined to encompass both radio and television. J.J. McCann said the government intended to follow closely the Massey recommendations; however, there would be "an awful lot of opportunity for private enterprise" in television. But to John Diefenbaker, the government's television policy was "a denial of every right of private enterprise." Donald Fleming said government and CBC policies had never been so unpopular, and criticized what he described as procommunist programs. But R.R. Knight of the CCF said only public control ensured representation of all shades of public opinion, and saw the CBC as a rare case of a public corporation being "given a chance to be a success" instead of taking over where private enterprise had failed.[79]

On 19 February, the government proposed to finance CBC television services with a 15 percent excise tax on television sets and tubes. At the same time it proposed to revoke the licence fee on radio and replace it with a similar measure.[80] Both changes were approved in May, with the opposition objecting to a direct handout to the CBC and arguing for an annual parliamentary review as basic to public control.[81]

On 17 March, Transport Minister Lionel Chevrier made an outstanding statement that summarized the history of Liberal policy on broadcasting:

There would be no Canadian nation at all if our founders had not realized that its creation, as well as its continued existence, required positive policies and careful planning in the fields of transportation and communications ... Coordinated efforts of public and private enterprise ... have been characteristic of the growth of Canada from its earliest history ... In every significant field or stage there have, of course, been struggles between those who put the national interest first and those who had regard primarily for their own personal profits. Fortunately, the national interest has usually won out. The interesting thing is that private enterprise has prospered and succeeded side by side.[82]

The principles laid down by R.B. Bennett in 1932 were still appropriate in 1953, Chevrier said. Frequencies were part of the public domain and should be controlled so as to ensure the "freest possible expression of opinion." There must be a public presence in broadcasting production, "to make sure there is a sufficient Canadian content in the broadcasting to keep Canada Canadian."[83] There was also room for private broadcasters, not as competitors but as a complement to the CBC.

This, Chevrier said, was the traditional policy of the Liberal Party. But the Tories believed in "handing over the exploitation of the public domain to their wealthy political friends." They had abandoned Bennett's "enlightened and patriotic" policy. The policy recently articulated by George Drew would provide "special privileges to a few of its [the opposition's] wealthy supporters," but would also mean no regional or minority programming, such as French-language broadcasts.

The difference between Liberal and Conservative policy at this point was a significant one. The government wanted a system of mixed ownership but public control,[84] while the opposition called for mixed ownership and "impartial" control.[85] The entire debate centred on the special interests of private broadcasters.

On 30 March 1953, McCann clarified government policy. The "single station" principle was to apply only until "an adequate national television system is developed." Its purpose was not to create a monopoly or limit the number of stations indefinitely. In due course second stations would be permitted. This statement recognized the pecuniary rights of private station owners in a way that had never been done with radio. McCann guaranteed that licences granted for private stations in areas where there was no CBC station would specify that the CBC would not establish a competing station without ascertaining that the area could financially support two stations.[86] The government thus established the protection of commercial markets as one of the objectives of regulation. At the parliamentary committee, then in session, Canadian Association of Broadcasters' general manager T.J. Allard commended the government for its 30 March statement.[87]

The parliamentary committee was becoming more and more of a partisan forum, overlapping with debates going on in the House. In 1953, the debate setting up the committee was itself the occasion for controversial and revealing statements on broadcasting. Debate on amendments to the broadcasting or radio acts would characteristically start in the House, be referred to committee, and return to the House, all in a matter of days.

While MPs promoted their partisan positions strongly, the CBC tended to adopt a dry approach in its committee appearances. The CBC was reporting to its patron and would not get involved in passionate posturing. In 1953, the CBC reported no major policy or program changes. It had dropped local radio advertising since getting its parliamentary grant, as Massey had recommended. Its established core programs were still providing satisfactory justification; the "Farm Forum," for example, with thirteen hundred listener groups, was now the largest project of its kind in the world.

The CBC had a new general manager, Alphonse Ouimet, who had succeeded Donald Manson on 1 January 1953. It was a sign of the times: Ouimet was a television engineer, Manson a radio expert. Ouimet was a CBC insider, Manson had come from the Department of Marine and Fisheries (he had also served as secretary to the Aird commission). Ouimet was the first CBC career man to head the corporation's operations. When he succeeded Davidson Dunton as president a few years later, it marked the consolidation of the CBC as a corporate entity able to nurture and draw on its own resources.

An additional outgrowth of the Massey recommendations was the extension of the French radio network to western Canada. The real challenge, however, was in television. At the parliamentary committee, Dunton made special mention of the talent and ability developing in French Canada. In Montreal, television was still broadcasting in both English and French over a single station, but plans were to split the service in two as soon as a second transmitter was functioning.

In contrast to the CBC, the Canadian Association of Broadcasters continued to take an aggressive stance in 1953. Once again, its brief to the committee focused on the demand for a separate regulatory body, and contained statements like: "Broadcasting requires regulation in the public interest," "Regulation is democratic. Control is dictatorial," and "Proper regulation will stimulate growth of both CBC and non-government stations." The issue, the CAB insisted, was freedom of broadcasting, not public versus private ownership.[88]

The CAB position was strongly taken to task by the Canadian Congress of Labour, which basically aligned with Massey, the government, and the parliamentary committees of the previous twenty years. While highly critical of the CBC's labour relations, the CCL supported public broadcasting against the arguments of the CAB:

Broadcasting is publishing. But it is a special form of publishing ... it is also a public utility. As a public utility, it must be subject to public regulations ... Other forms of publishing are not public utilities, and so do not require such public regulation and control.

... the more thoroughly we adopt the policy of free enterprise in radio and television, the more completely these great media of information will fall under the control of commercial interests whose enthusiasm for labour, and for new ideas and policies is, to put it mildly, very moderate. For these people, things as they are have worked out well; it would be asking too much of human nature to expect them to allot much time on their radio or their television to people who want to make changes, at any rate unless those people are prepared to pay through the nose for the privilege, which they won't be able to do.[89]

It is noteworthy that the labour federation was able to place the public interest ahead of the corporate interests of its member CBC technicians whose certification bid was then being strongly opposed by CBC upper management. But the Conservatives were not convinced. Davie Fulton said the CAB "may have overstated the case" for private broadcasting generally, but he still favoured an independent regulatory body.

The committee's report was tabled in the House 9 May 1953. It continued the search for a new consensus that the government's 30 March statement had indicated: the twin objectives of adequate production and nation-wide distribution of Canadian programs could best be met by the development of a national system "in which both the CBC and privately owned stations play their part."[90]

The system for television was envisaged as a "partnership," in which the private stations earned their place by acting as carriers of national programs in areas without CBC service. For the first time, the committee did not reject outright the CAB demands on regulation, which it deemed more reasonable than in the past. It said it had been unable to study the proposal for a separate regulatory body "with the care which it would appear to merit."[91]

For the first time in many years, the committee's report was unanimous. A new compromise was emerging, as the Liberals bartered the historic foundation of Canadian broadcasting against a certain perception of public opinion, and the Conservatives adjusted their free enterprise principles to the operating realities of the system.

When the CBC's budget for 1953–54 came before Parliament less than a week later, Donald Fleming was content to say: "In the successive statements of policy I think there have been improvements."[92] The CBC was awarded $26 million, roughly half for radio and half for television. But the opposition's concern was that private television stations be licensed without any more delay. In the Toronto market, about 76 percent of the television audience was watching Buffalo, and the Conservatives implied that a private station would be able to repatriate it.

Debate continued in this vein in 1953–54. On 25 November 1953, in response to the throne speech, Montreal Conservative MP W.M. Hamilton used the CBC as an example of the "steady movement of the present government toward socialism." The CBC was receiving millions of dollars "from the taxpayers of Canada for performing a service which, under a government less socialistically inclined than the present one, private enterprise would perform for nothing."[93]

A few months later, during debate on the budget in April 1954, a call for licensing second television stations came from the government side for the first time, when Liberal back-bencher Elmore Philpott (a former broadcaster) called for recognizing the proper place of free enterprise by licensing competing stations.[94] The Young Liberals, too, were calling for competition between publicly and privately owned operations.[95]

By June 1954, seven CBC stations were operating or about to begin operations, and Montreal and Toronto had been joined by a direct network connection for over a year. Four private stations were part of the national system, and sixteen more had been authorized. Canadians were buying television sets at such a pace that the excise tax had produced more revenue than expected ($11.7 million in 1953–54), and the CBC had an operating surplus for television of about $5 million. J.J. McCann told Parliament that Canada was developing "one of the most extensive television systems in the world. It represents one of the great developments in the history of our country and it is being built under a scheme of sensible co-operation between public and private interest."[96]

The Conservatives, however, continued to oppose a statutory grant for the CBC or unchecked funding through something like an excise tax. They demanded a thorough annual review before awarding funds for the CBC, competition between publicly and privately owned stations in the profitable markets, and a separate regulatory body. In the public interest, they said, the CBC should be more tightly controlled and controls on the private sector loosened up.

Discordant views continued to come from within the Liberal party as well.[97] In March 1955, the advisory council of the National Liberal Federation recommended an independent regulatory body for radio and television broadcasting.[98] Liberal party positions were beginning to resemble opposition policy more closely than the government's. But the policy makers were still concerned with consolidating the national system as a priority and feared that a separate regulator would weaken it. By now Canada had twenty-five television stations (seven CBC and eighteen private), transmitting "national programs" to 1.25 million receivers. By 1955, Canadians had spent a half billion dollars purchasing television sets. Canada was the second television country in the world in terms of stations, area covered, sets per capita, and overall program production. The government was pleased with the model whereby network programs were carried nationwide without the cost of establishing public stations everywhere; the private broadcasters, meanwhile, received lucrative commercial programs from the CBC for free.[99]

When the parliamentary committee was convened, Davidson Dunton reiterated the objectives of Canadian television: "to produce a substantial amount of Canadian programming done by Canadians for Canadians; secondly, to convey these programs, together with programs imported for the national service, to the greatest possible number of Canadians all across the country ... The system that is trying to reach these objectives ... is one overall system with its public and private components, working as a whole toward these national objectives."[100]

The function of the CBC element of the system was to ensure basic Canadian production and national distribution; private stations were a "means by which the national system reaches the public which they serve." As a whole, the system operated "very much as one," and relations between the private and public elements had been good, Dunton said.

The immediate demand of the private broadcasters' organization (now known as the Canadian Association of Radio and Television Broadcasters, CARTB) was for the permission of "non-government" stations (second stations) in cities where the CBC was currently installed, as well as an independent regulatory board. The CARTB position was supported by the Canadian Chamber of Commerce, which sent a one-paragraph brief that captured the essence of the legitimating argument for the private sector position: "Radio and television offer two of the most influential channels of communication. The chamber believes in the principle that no person or organization in any field should be both competitor and regulator and urges the establishment of a separate regulatory body having minimum essential regulatory powers over radio and television broadcasting in Canada."[101]

Taken on its own merits, the argument was a strong one: If a private sector was a legitimate part of the Canadian broadcasting framework, why should it be regulated by its competitor? The problem was that there was not, in fact, a consensus in Canada on the legitimacy of private broadcasting, and especially on the appropriate relationship between private and public broadcasting. The question of the role of the regulatory body was thus never really debated on its merits, but became instead the battleground between the proponents of a system based on public service and those who placed broadcasting in the sphere of free enterprise. It was the debate of the 1930s all over again.[102]

The conservative position during these years was not only motivated by affinities for private enterprise, but also by displeasure with the liberalism of the CBC. Donald Fleming tried to have the parliamentary committee adopt a motion recommending that the CBC revise its regulations so as to prevent the Labour Progressive Party from obtaining free-time election broadcasts.[103] It was an ironic move to originate in the quarters of the defenders of broadcasting freedom, and even Social Credit did not support the motion, fearing that it could be used against them too.

The committee reported on 17 June. It "took note" of the CARTB brief, but felt that the evidence did not warrant meeting the private broadcasters' demands "at the present time."[104] This time, the report was not unanimous.

## Nationalisms

The Massey commission had recommended that a full-scale inquiry of television be held three years after its inception in Canada. On 2 December 1955, the government announced the creation of a Royal Commission on

Broadcasting under the chairmanship of Robert M. Fowler, president of the Canadian Pulp and Paper Association. Its other two members were James Stewart, president of the Bank of Commerce, and Edmond Turcotte, former editor of *Le Canada* and Canadian ambassador to Colombia.

As the Aird commission before it, the Fowler commission came to its task with strong free enterprise credentials. The central issue it had to deal with was the relationship of the public and private components of the system, and the question of how the system should be controlled. The government's main concern was to assess the likely long-term cost of a television policy for Canada.

The stakes of the issue facing the royal commission had been well summarized in A.R.M. Lower's 1953 article.[105] Lower had noted that, unlike Great Britain and the United States where control of television seemed to be following the same general pattern as radio, "in Canada, the pattern is not yet fully decided." Lower was sceptical about the possible power of "the public" to influence development in the face of the private sector lobby, but noted that broadcasting fit into the Canadian tradition of planning "to make the scattered provinces of British America into the Canadian nation."[106] He laid out a position similar to that of the Canadian Radio League nationalists of the 1930s, making an argument for public broadcasting that was articulated essentially in terms of the national interest. Only the state could prevent the influence of American broadcasting on Canadian life: "The issue of public vs. private control is so vital in Canada that it must necessarily be reflected in politics."[107] It was not a question of "socialism" versus "free enterprise."

Lower's article appeared as pressure was mounting on the Cabinet to turn the tide in favour of private broadcasting. According to one account, Prime Minister St. Laurent (who had been close to the Canadian Radio League in the 1930s) attempted to counteract the pressure by urging Lower, in 1953, to mobilize a counterlobby in favour of public broadcasting.[108] Lower later became one of the key members of the Canadian Radio and Television League when it was founded in 1954.

Meanwhile, the introduction of television was having an unexpected impact in Quebec. The new medium provided a forum for discussion and presentation of ideas and issues hitherto restricted to small intellectual journals or marginal circles. Public affairs television brought Quebec society's major debates into the public arena for the first time, and Radio-Canada became one of the rallying points for the extra-parliamentary opposition in Quebec.[109] Ottawa, with no great sympathy for the Duplessis regime in Quebec City, had no complaint with this, but there was, nonetheless, concern that the tendency to concentrate on "provincial" affairs was an abuse of the service's mandate. The CBC's head office tried to deal with this from Ottawa, and sent memos to Montreal instructing CBFT to deal with federal affairs

more systematically.[110] So, while Radio-Canada became a focus of opposition to the Duplessis government and to clerical conservatism in general,
sensitivity to pan-Canadian "national" concerns also filtered out certain
interpretations of where Quebec was heading.

As the Fowler commission began its work, the basic issues in Canadian
broadcasting were thus the same as they had been at the time of the Aird
commission. Twenty-five years after the initial debates over radio, the battle
between proponents of "public" and "private" television was still taking
place against the backdrop of the national question.

## THE FOWLER COMMISSION, 1955-57

### Representations

The royal commission was given a mandate to recommend a policy for
television, including measures to provide an adequate proportion of Canadian
programs for both public and private broadcasting, licensing and control of
private stations, and the financial and managerial requirements of the CBC.
It was instructed to bear in mind two principles: that the granting of broadcasting channels would continue to be under control of Parliament, and that
the central feature of Canadian broadcasting policy would continue to be
"the broadcasting and distribution of Canadian programs by a public
agency."[111]

The commission began public hearings in Ottawa on 30 April 1956.[112]
Its first interlocutor was the CBC. When the commission was set up, Donald
Fleming had said in the House that he hoped the CBC would not advocate
a policy before it, as its role as a public servant was to carry out policy,
not help make it.[113] The CBC was sensitive to this view, and declined "to
plead for any particular national policy or law in broadcasting; nor for any
specific financial arrangements or amounts."[114] This stoic approach did not
serve the CBC well.

However, in spite of the disclaimer, the CBC actually took an advocacy
stance on most of the key issues. Its brief to the royal commission criticized
the proposal to finance the CBC by means of an annual grant on grounds that
this would expose broadcasting to partisan influence and prevent it from
freely planning its activities. It explained that "second stations" would mean
increased American programming and reduced advertising revenue for CBC,
while diverting energy away from the strengthening of basic service. It
justified continuing to regulate private stations on the grounds that broadcasting was a public trust: "The channels exist in usable form only through
continued action by the state acting on behalf of the public, and can be said
to belong only to the public."[115]

The CBC demonstrated considerable sophistication in its understanding of its own relationship with the public. Discussing CBC program philosophy, the brief said: "The CBC has to face the fact that there is no 'typical Canadian listener', no uniform Canadian 'public', which has one taste ... In trying to serve its national purpose the CBC cannot be guided merely by 'ratings', by the number of people who listen to different types of programs ... It must be its job to see that the more worthwhile things have a reasonable place in television."[116]

A separate document filed with the commission, entitled "National Program Service" was the CBC's most mature statement up to that time, on the role of the public broadcaster:

> The CBC ... is answerable for its operations to Parliament in the first instance and ultimately to public opinion.
>
> Believing that the citizen of a free society is a complex of interests, tastes and capacities for enjoyment, the starting point in the production of CBC programs is the conception of listeners and viewers as individuals, not as a mass ... Within its resources CBC has made the democratic compromise of trying to serve all of the people some of the time rather than some of the people all of the time.
>
> Understanding begets tolerance. As citizens of a nation embracing two cultures and languages, two aboriginal races and many other racial stocks, sectional economic interests and a scattered population, Canadians have need of an extra portion of tolerance and understanding.
>
> One of the tests of a healthy democracy is the tolerance of unpopular minority opinions, of new expressions of art and ideas, either native or imported, which are essential to the nation's development.[117]

The document's eloquence was eclipsed by Davidson Dunton's oral presentation to the commission. Broadcasting channels can only be used when the state takes action, Dunton said. A nation has to "deliberately make up its mind what it is going to do about broadcasting." Canada does not have much good oratory about why it exists as a nation. It has had to take a lot of practical steps, such as creating the CBC: "In all its decisions and its workings the only standard the corporation can offer is that of public interest ... It is the job of the corporation to sort out all the various claims on public interest and to find the overall way to meet the public interest, the national interest, in the best way it can."[118]

Beneath the eloquence, an old theme was being replayed: the equation of the public with the national interest. When Fowler asked him to define what he meant by "public interest," Dunton said: "It stems from the broadcasting act which said that there should be a national service."[119] But for the royal commission, the public interest, or the national interest, was to be found on the bottom line. For Fowler, the financial problem was the commission's central task and this was to direct the main thrust of its work.

The private broadcasters' association, the CARTB, appeared before the Fowler commission on 2 May 1956. Its brief[120] restated the main positions the private broadcasters had been promoting for several years, and focused on two essential proposals: "immediate licensing of non-government television broadcasting stations in all areas of Canada," and "creation by legislation of an independent regulatory board for Canadian broadcasting."

In a supplementary document filed later, the CARTB offered a brief but trenchant critique of the way the CBC used the terms "national service," "national system," and "national programs": "Is the word 'national' supposed to mean that which is heard or seen in all parts of the nation? Does it then mean at one time or different times? Or does it simply mean that which is owned by the State? Or is it intended to mean a specific type of program designed to serve a specific objective of the State?"[121]

The CARTB argued that a national "service" was not the same thing as a national "system." The broadcasting act required the CBC to carry on a national "service." However, said the CARTB, "While there may be a national service in Canada, there is not one national system, but two."[122]

As in previous years, the CARTB reduced its position to a series of succinct slogans, negating the arguments of the public service promoters: "Radio and television broadcasting are publishing"; "Democracy is based on the right to know"; "The broadcasting channel is an intangible"; "Broadcasting is not a natural monopoly"; "Broadcasting is not a public utility"; "Broadcasting is not public domain."[123]

Not to be outdone by the CBC, the CARTB made equally skilful use of the discourse of public service and public interest. T.J. Allard told the commission: "Each of these stations has a very proud record of public service and does service in the public interest to its or to their respective communities."[124] Where the CBC had spoken of the national interest, the CARTB invoked freedom of the press, democracy, and people's right to know. One of the objectives of regulation, Allard said, "ought to be such as to permit a free distribution of news, information and opinions."[125] The CARTB still demanded to be considered a competitor on equal footing with the CBC, and suggested "that the public interest can more accurately and confidently be assessed by a body which either subconsciously or unconsciously is not trying to confuse its own interest with the public interest."[126]

In questioning the potential objectivity of the CBC, the CARTB had indeed found a weak spot, since, by 1956, the CBC was an organization with its own institutional interest. That interest may have been a lot closer to the "national" interest and even to the "public" interest than the private broadcasters', but it was a vested interest nonetheless.

As at earlier similar forums, a wide variety of public interest groups made submissions to the Fowler commission and generally supported the main features of the existing system.[127] The one-million-member Canadian Labour Congress (newly formed by a merger of the Trades and Labour Congress and the Canadian Congress of Labour) supported the general principles of Canadian broadcasting policy, central to which was "the complete control of all broadcasting in Canada by the Parliament of Canada" through the CBC.[128] Traditionally, labour had been in favour of complete nationalization but had come to accept the private stations, provided they performed useful services and did not compete with the CBC: "They must never be allowed to develop into even a semblance of equality with the national system."[129]

The Canadian Association for Adult Education said that only a public network could do programs such as the CBC's "Forum" series. It said the system had "made an immense contribution to Canadian national unity" and called for more stringent enforcement of regulations.[130] The CAAE also called for public funding of communications research, citing the work being done in the US by researchers such as Paul Lazarsfeld.

La Société canadienne d'éducation des adultes (whose brief was presented by its executive committee chairman, Claude Ryan), placed a similar emphasis on public interest and tried to be more specific about what that might mean. Its argument followed a logical progression. Given that broadcasting frequencies were limited, radio and television broadcasting should be considered in the public interest. Given their influence, public interest required that cultural and social values take priority over commercial or entertainment values. Consequently, radio and television should be seen as means of communication in the service of national unity and popular education. The SCEA saw the Canadian government playing an active (but not exclusive) part in production and coordinating the complementary relationship between the state and the private sector.[131]

The only political party to appear, the Labour Progressive Party, took a strong pro-CBC stand. The LPP said broadcasting should serve the national interest, "to help create among Canadians an image of themselves as a democratic, peace-loving people with a proud heritage and a glowing future."[132] The voluntary appearance of an organization like the LPP before a public hearing at the height of the cold war speaks to the importance of broadcasting, and particularly the CBC, in Canada during those days. A joint brief by the Manitoba Provincial Federation of Labour, the Winnipeg and District Trades and Labour Council, the Winnipeg Labour Council, and the Central Council of the One Big Union, spelled it out. They said they were doubtful free expression would be possible without the CBC.[133]

Several groups represented French Canadians in western Canada. The thrust of their presentations underlined the ongoing struggle of French Canadians in the west for a fair share of public broadcasting since 1932, in spite of the CBC's good intentions. From the time of Hector Charlesworth's recognition in principle of the right to French programming, to the Massey commission's recommendation to extend the French network to the west, French-language public radio had been limited to one hour a day. In 1956 western Canada received only two hours a week of television in French. The French-Canadian associations in Manitoba, Saskatchewan, and Alberta had dealt with the radio problem by organizing Radio-Ouest-Française in 1944 and applying for private licences in the three provinces. A French station in St Boniface began broadcasting in 1946, a second one in Alberta in 1949, and two in Saskatchewan in 1951 and 1952. Radio-Ouest-Française had been financed with $750,000 raised by public subscription, but this formula could hardly be followed for television, given the much higher costs. The prairie French-Canadian associations supported the principle of CBC supremacy in the system, and demanded French-language television for the west. [134]

Aside from the educators, only two major Quebec groups made presentations: the Confédération des travailleurs catholiques du Canada (CTCC) and the Société Saint-Jean-Baptiste de Montréal (SSJB). Both agreed that the CBC had performed more democratically than other federal administrative bodies, with important reservations.

The CTCC supported the existing system. Its brief spoke of the educational and cultural importance of television to workers, in some cases their only access to these benefits. It emphasized the importance of "public affairs" programs. The CTCC was thoroughly dissatisfied with the performance of private broadcasters and proposed that the CBC award licences only to recognized public institutions such as universities. It reiterated the recommendations for consultative bodies that it had made to the Massey commission. Both the CTCC and the Parti ouvrier canadien (Quebec wing of the LPP) reported that Montreal radio CFCF had refused to sell them time. [135]

The SSJB felt the public-private mix was a fortuitous one, prompting Fowler to remark that this was the first time anyone had characterized the system in such terms. [136] The SSJB brief was most remarkable, however, for its nationalist perspective on the history of Canadian broadcasting, and especially the role of the CBC. On the whole, it praised the CBC's record regarding French Canada, but emphasized the process of struggle that had led up to it and its serious shortcomings. The brief also drew out the historic ambivalence of the CBC as a vehicle for French Canadians, and argued for a provincial role in broadcasting. [137] This Quebec attitude towards broadcasting would create institutional conflict within the CBC in the 1960s, and would turn into constitutional conflict between Quebec and Ottawa after 1968.

Of course, not all the voices heard by the Fowler commission were favourable to the public system. The Social Credit government of Alberta, for example, called the existing policy "a jumble of socialism and free enterprise with the socialist side having all of the authority." It said private stations should have the opportunity to function without "government interference," and all governments should have the opportunity to operate stations, although with limited control.[138]

The Canadian Chamber of Commerce invoked "freedom of choice" to argue against the existing single-station policy, and the separation of powers principle to support the call for a separate regulatory body.[139]

St. Clair Balfour, of Southam Press Ltd, said the CBC should be an alternative to popular commercial broadcasting. Mass communications media, he said, "are strongly competitive and must live by the free choice of the public which they serve." He spoke against restricting multiple ownership of private outlets, on the grounds that "broadcasting, whether radio or television, is merely an additional and alternative means of mass communication. It is a part of the Press, it is a newer technique, but basically the same business."[140]

The Association of Canadian Advertisers, however, refused to take sides, sticking to an exposition of the importance of broadcasting and advertising for Canadian nationhood. Its brief was presented by Peter Wright, who had been counsel to the Massey commission. As he had done in 1949, Wright recalled the importance of national policy in Canadian history. The primary purpose of Canadian broadcasting "is the maintenance of Canada as a distinct and independent country ... that is to preserve the integrity of Confederation and keep Canada Canadian ... in the broadest sense the real reason for the broadcasting system is a political one ... On the one hand we must have a distinct Canadian system to carry out our national policy, on the other hand we must recognize the influence of American broadcasting and ways of life in the lives of Canadians."[141] Wright argued that the key to Canadian autonomy was its trade and commerce and, consequently, national broadcasting policy had to take account of the importance of advertising.

One of the major indications of the climate at the time of the Fowler commission was the revival of a lobby for public broadcasting. A number of individuals, including adult education activists E.A. Corbett and Roby Kidd, professors A.R.M. Lower and Frank Underhill, and writer Pierre Berton, got together for this purpose as early as June 1953.[142] However, it was only a year later that the initiative bore fruit, when Corbett undertook to organize a new group after discussing with Vincent Massey the idea "that an organization of commercially disinterested citizens was needed to counterbalance the propaganda of the commercial broadcasting lobby."[143] On 11 October 1954, a public statement was issued announcing the formation of the Canadian Radio and Television League: "a new organization roughly equivalent to its famous predecessor ... one that can act as critic, watchdog and defender of Canadian radio and television."[144]

The league was formally launched in January 1955, and published several issues of a newsletter, *Dial*, but it never achieved the notoriety of its ancestor. Its main intervention was a brief to the Fowler commission prepared by Lower and signed by Corbett as president. The league did not appear before the commission, but Lower presented an expanded version of its position in his own name. [145]

The league described itself as "a group of individuals interested in securing the best possible standards of radio and television in Canada." [146] Claiming to have no ulterior purpose and to represent no private interest, its position on the question at hand was simple and unequivocal: "the continuance of radio and television services on their present basis." [147] The league accepted the historical justification for local private broadcasting, but saw a far loftier role for the public sector: the CBC, it said, had "saved this country from something like disintegration." [148]

The league took a pragmatic view of Canadian Confederation, an act that created "a political entity based on the faith that in time this artificial entity would take on reality." In setting up the CPR, the chartered banks, and protective tariffs, "We have never hesitated to invoke the power of the state for national interests." Canada, the league said, was built on "these inter-actions of public and private enterprise" [149]: "The effect of any weakening of our public services would be to throw more power, more control, and more financial resources into hands that sooner or later would come under American control. We must use the power of the state to maintain control of our television and radio ... The only guarantee of continued national existence is the continued nationalization of the key sectors of our national life, of which broadcasting is one." [150]

Thus, as its predecessor had done in 1932, the league in 1956 assumed state intervention to mean a strong *federal* role in broadcasting. But in addition to promoting national unity, it saw public broadcasting as the guarantee of free discussion: "private control would really be a kind of monopoly, whereas the public medium is kept free by public interest and vigilance." [151]

The league submission drew a detailed rebuttal from the private broad-casters. The CARTB described the proposal of continued nationalization of key sectors as "socialism in its most radical form," and astutely identified the league's weak spot: "Their main concern seems to be to increase the power of the federal government." [152] The CARTB attacked the league's idea of national unity as one in which conformity was the key and the CBC the instrument for "enforcing a national pattern of ideas": "The people of Quebec may be somewhat upset to learn that the League wants the CBC to destroy their localism." [153]

Indeed, there was no sign in 1956 that the league sought to reconcile Canada's "other" nationalist sentiment, as the Canadian Radio League had tried to do in 1932. It was no small irony that this omission was left open as a bare target for the private sector to attack.[154]

Meanwhile, the context of the political debate surrounding Canadian broadcasting stimulated the emergence of public discussion on broadcasting in Quebec. In August 1956, the sociopolitical journal *Cité libre* devoted its entire issue to broadcasting. Most of the articles focused on cultural aspects rather than on political questions of structure and control, with the notable exception of an article entitled "La guerre des ondes" (The war of the airwaves) by F.R. Scott, who argued that Quebec had an interest in defending the existing system with its strong public dimension. The surest safeguard of the French language and culture in Canada rests with the development of CBC policy and regulations, Scott wrote.[155]

The importance of television was also recognized by nationalist spokesmen like André Laurendeau. In June 1956, Laurendeau spoke to the Humanities Association of Canada on "Television and Culture in French Canada." Laurendeau emphasized that "French-Canadian television" was something more than simply "television in French." The way of approaching things, he said, was more important than language. The fact that men like Gérard Pelletier and René Lévesque were being seen and heard on the air every week had become "an important sociological phenomenon" in Quebec. Laurendeau was concerned, however, that television would contribute to accenting the idea of Quebec as a "reserve" for Canada's French Canadians, as the refusal of English Canadians to accept bilingual stations confined French broadcasting to Quebec. Television had arrived, he said, at a difficult moment in French-Canadian history. Only Ottawa ("l'Etat central") could deliver French television to French Canadians outside Quebec.[156]

By the late 1950s, broadcasting was firmly on the agenda of social groups in Quebec. Thus, for example, the question of media influence was the theme of the annual Semaines sociales du Canada meetings in 1957,[157] and in 1959 the Institut canadien d'éducation des adultes (ICEA) organized the first of what would become regular public study sessions on the role and evolution of broadcasting media.[158]

### Recommendations

The Fowler commission reported on 15 March 1957. In the introduction to its report, the commission announced the implications of its recommendations:

(1) ... the mixed Canadian system of public and private ownership is here to stay;

(2) ... the state agency may grow, as Canada grows, but its functions are not to be extended to do the whole job of providing radio and television services to Canadians;

(3) ... private stations should individually be required to justify the continued grant of a valuable public franchise and that some may lose their licences because of a shabby performance, but private operations should stop worrying about the bogey of nationalization that has filled them with suspicion and fear in the past;

(4) ... for the foreseeable future, we will continue to have a single broadcasting system in which all Canadian radio and television stations, public and private, present and future, will be integral parts, regulated and controlled by an agency representing the public interest and responsible to Parliament. [159]

The Fowler commission's report thus put all parties in their place, sanctifying the *status quo* rather than the spirit of the legislation, and honoring its terms of reference rather than any one set of demands that had been placed before it. It qualified the Canadian system as "mixed," but "a single system" nonetheless. It reminded the CBC and its supporters that "the state agency" would never gain a monopoly, and warned the private stations that their performance would be individually judged. But it appeared to grant the private broadcasters their main demand for a regulatory body separate from the CBC and, while it insisted that this body's function would be to oversee the integrity of the overall system, for the first time the private and public elements of the system appeared to be on equal ground.

In addition to its specific recommendations, the Fowler report reformulated some of the classical assumptions about broadcasting in Canada. The most important of these concerned the function of broadcasting. The Aird commission had seen this as threefold: "education in the broad sense ... providing entertainment and ... informing the public on questions of national interest." [160] The Massey commission had expressed the function of broadcasting in similar terms: "Radio in any democratic country has three main functions: to inform, to educate and to entertain." [161] Fowler revised this formulation significantly, adding a fourth function: to sell goods. But selling goods was not to be a principal activity of the public sector, whose raison d'être continued to be to furnish "a national broadcasting service." The Fowler report noted, however, that nowhere was it spelled out just what this meant. The CBC's mandate, it said, should be precisely defined.

The Fowler commission was astonished at the number of organizations which had suggested the creation of advisory groups of one kind or another to help the CBC design its programming. In spite of this, the commission did not agree. Such groups, it said, would usurp the function of the CBC's board of governors, which was to represent "the people of Canada."

The commission also revealed some striking statistics. As of 1956, Canadians had spent ten times as much money buying television sets ($850 million) as the combined reported assets of both the CBC ($41 million) and the private broadcasters ($44 million). At the same time, however, the public cost of public broadcasting was accelerating annually and Fowler had to recognize that it would only continue to rise. Parliamentary subsidy to the CBC in 1955–56 was $31 million; in 1954–55 it had been $23.7 million, and in 1953–54, $16.7 million. Roughly 50 percent of Canadian households (2.3 million) had television sets in December 1956.

The Fowler commission's major recommendation was for the creation of a new agency that would, it said, bring the regulatory aspect of Canada's broadcasting legislation up to date with reality. The commission was satisfied that regulation was "a legitimate and proper function of the state" and rejected the CARTB argument that broadcasting was not in the public domain. Ironically, its position was based on acceptance of the essential claims of private broadcasters, that broadcasting could be a business – as long as we had broadcasting, there was a need for public control "to restrain commercial forces from the excesses to which they may go."[162]

The commission recommended a "factual separation of powers" between the two public elements of the system, the operating agency and the regulator. The CBC should continue as operator, while a new board responsible to Parliament should be created "for the direction and supervision" of Canadian broadcasting.[163]

Both the public and the private sectors in broadcasting would be responsible to the proposed Board of Broadcast Governors. The BBG was to "reflect public opinion"; it would be insulated from possible interference by statute. However, the commission emphasized, its recommendation was not identical to that of the private broadcasters, who had called for an "independent" regulatory board, separate from the CBC. The Fowler proposal called for two separate public agencies, the CBC to operate the public service and the BBG to supervise the entire system.

In making this proposal, the commission expressed the hope that it would resolve the question of the nature and basis of the system once and for all, so that future debate could be directed towards operations. The distinction between its proposal and the private sector's demand was clear to the Fowler commission. It would be less clear to the legislators who came to implement the recommendation in 1958.

The Fowler commission took the view that the potential role of the private sector was essentially benign, but it was less than sympathetic towards the way in which the private broadcasters went about defending their stake. The CARTB's "one-sided" and "misleading" representations ("propaganda ... largely unanswered by the CBC") had served "to enroll the Canadian instinct for freedom behind hidden mercenary motives and to foment misunderstanding and confusion among the well-meaning."[164]

Nonetheless, the commission's bottom line was favourable, if cautionary, towards the private broadcasters: "The presence of private elements in our broadcasting system should be clearly accepted as valuable and permanent; but the performance level of private stations should be a high one to justify the grant to them of valuable public rights."[165] To ensure continued Canadian control of the system, Fowler recommended a ceiling of 20 percent be placed on foreign ownership of any private broadcasting station.

The commission clearly appreciated the function of the CBC: "not only a central feature, but a vital and essential feature of our broadcasting system. Without a public agency such as the CBC ... we would have no national broadcasting system at all."[166] Yet throughout its report, a recurring catch phrase summed up the new way of thinking the commission had introduced. After Fowler, Canadian broadcasting would be said to comprise "a single system embracing public and private elements subject to supervision and control by an agency of the state."[167]

Why did the Fowler commission so warmly endorse the ownership mix that had arisen demonstrably out of the failure to execute Canadian broadcasting legislation in the spirit of the law? Why did it follow, for example, that "independent, local" stations must be privately owned commercial ventures? The answer is not to be found in the text of the commission's report, but in the casual way it applied the pervasive ideology of corporate capitalism and interpreted the role of the state therein.

Unlike the Aird commission, which had an open mandate to consider the broadcasting situation and propose a framework for the system, and unlike the Massey commission whose mandate was to propose a national cultural policy, the Fowler commission was instructed not to depart from established policy guidelines – it had to address a number of specific, mostly financial, problems. As stated, its main purpose had been "to determine the nature and scope of activities of the CBC, to estimate how much these activities should cost, and to suggest how this money should be provided."[168]

Thus, for example, where Aird had proposed the elimination of all but a tiny amount of indirect advertising, Fowler called on the CBC to be vigorous in seeking commercial revenue. While Massey had recommended the CBC abandon local radio advertising in the interest of its cultural mandate, Fowler proposed a return to local advertising.

But in spite of its friendliness to private capital, the Fowler commission was sympathetic to the CBC as well. On the crucial financial question, it brought the Aird commission's famous comment up to date: "Canadians want Canadian broadcasting and they expect to have to pay for it."[169] Parliament should approve the CBC's capital budget annually, thus keeping control over policy decisions. Operations – or the execution of policy – however, should be protected from the government of the day, and should be assured for a number of years by statutory provision. (Fowler suggested five years.)

The basis of Fowler's financial recommendations was that if the CBC's mandate were clarified, the politicians would have no need to question its day-to-day moves. The Fowler commission estimated the CBC's financial needs to March 1963 at $468 million – $353 million for operations and $115 million for capital expenses. Needless to say, the politicians were not so quick to relinquish control.

The Fowler commission's report contained a separate chapter on French-language broadcasting. It tended to view the situation through rose-coloured glasses, praising the CBC's French programming efforts and claiming to have found a general degree of satisfaction with the system among representative organizations of French Canadians. To the extent that this was so, it was no doubt due in large measure to the powerful cultural place taken by indigenous French-Canadian broadcasting. However, many parts of Canada still had no broadcasting service in French. There was progress to report in "reciprocal tolerance and mutual understanding," but: "It remains a moot question ... whether Canada has yet reached the stage of complete national maturity where the introduction of French on the airwaves ... would not be regarded by a substantial majority as an intolerable intrusion rather than the cultural complement that in truth it would be."[170]

If English Canadians would not tolerate bilingual stations, and coercing the private sector was out of the question, the only remaining alternative was the costly one of extending full French-language CBC service to all parts of the country. The commission suggested the investment would be worthwhile: "The result may well be the building of the best possible instrument to achieve complete spiritual harmony and indissoluble national unity in Canada within the life of this generation."[171]

Meanwhile, the commission had disappointing news to report regarding the extension of French television to the west – consisting at the time of two hours a week out of Winnipeg. The Canadian public, the report said, was averse to bilingual stations. But limited "duality" should not be ruled out where it was the only way to deliver "national public service." Indeed, judging from the sentiments being expressed in Quebec by people like André Laurendeau, such a measure was even politically essential.

In the commission's portrait of the situation of French-language broadcasting in Canada in 1956, one remarkable situation stood out: the case of the four nonprofit, listener-backed French-language stations in the prairie provinces. These stations, "although privately owned," were "not commercial ventures but public service stations in the true sense of the word."[172] In French, on the prairies, private, noncommercial ownership was providing a politically sensitive service that neither public nor commercial ownership could meet.

## THE BROADCASTING ACT, 1958

### Political Transition

The Fowler commission's deliberations dominated debate on broadcasting in 1956–57, but a number of Conservative parliamentary interventions during this time foreshadowed things to come. During the annual discussion of CBC budget estimates in July 1956, Donald Fleming reasserted the need for an independent regulatory tribunal, deplored the "single-station" policy, and insisted that the CBC continue to come before Parliament each year for its operating grant. During the same debate, John Diefenbaker said: "I find it difficult to understand why the CBC, having available to it the best outlets in Canada, is continually in the red ... Private stations make money ... [The CBC] should make profit ... I am one of those who believes that the time has come to put a stop to this trend." [173]

While the Fowler commission was sitting, a controversy arose over a letter from Prime Minister St. Laurent to Davidson Dunton objecting to two broadcasts on CBC radio critical of Canada's foreign policy. Critics charged that the prime minister had politically interfered in public affairs broadcasts, but St. Laurent said he had acted as a private citizen. Shortly thereafter, J.J. McCann admitted he had made "representations" to the CBC about certain programs, but refused to give details, prompting Dunton to issue a public statement that the CBC was not subject to direction from a minister of the Crown. [174]

By the time the Fowler commission reported on 15 March 1957, a federal election was nearing. St. Laurent said the outgoing government would not act on the report but, during the final days of the Liberal government, MPs continued to question the relationship between the government and the CBC.

Since 1936, the government position had always been that the CBC was not responsible to the government but merely reported to a minister for the purposes of having a spokesman in Parliament. Now, its actual practice was attacked from the left and the right. [175] Donald Fleming used the occasion to argue again for diluting the position of the CBC. "Government interference," he said, was always a danger in a situation where broadcasting was controlled by a government-appointed corporation. A Conservative government would stand for two principles: the CBC would be responsible to Parliament and there would be no government interference with the CBC. Meanwhile, John Diefenbaker referred to the CBC as a "mass propaganda agency."

A Conservative minority government, headed by Diefenbaker, was elected on 10 June 1957. The new minister of national revenue, George Nowlan, was answerable for the CBC. In view of the strong positions taken by Conservative critics during the previous ten years, supporters of public broadcasting were concerned to know what course the new government would take. In this context, the Fowler proposals appeared as a safeguard of the basic integrity of the system. The government, however, did not act on broadcasting before it went back to the people on 31 March 1958.

During the 1958 election campaign, the Conservatives promised to put into effect the type of system the private broadcasters had been demanding. In a campaign speech in Kenora, Ontario, Prime Minister Diefenbaker promised early introduction of second television stations, an independent regulatory board, and a CBC station for Kenora.[176]

Meanwhile, another attempt was being made to revive a public broadcasting lobby. Early in 1958, Graham Spry returned to Canada from England, where he was working for Saskatchewan's CCF government, in order to try to organize a group that could counteract the pressures of the commercial broadcasters.[177] On 8 April, a new Canadian Broadcasting League issued a "Memorandum on Broadcasting in Canada," stating its purpose to strive for "national agreement on a national broadcasting policy" and advocating several key measures:

1) Support the CBC – vital instrument of Canadian unity;
2) Private operation of private stations;
3) Regulation of CBC and private stations as one system;
4) A Board of Governors responsible to Parliament;
5) Adequate long-term finance for the CBC;
6) High program standards – Canadian and Imported.[178]

The "national" emphasis of the league's orientation was unmistakable. It was further highlighted on 18 July 1958, when a league delegation headed by Professor Donald Creighton met with Diefenbaker and Nowlan. The delegation was made up of national groups claiming a combined membership totalling ten million people.[179] A public statement issued in Creighton's name said:

Broadcasting, by radio or television, provides one of the greatest media ever invented for the self-expression, the self-knowledge, the self-determination of a people. It is almost impossible to exaggerate the importance of broadcasting in our Canadian national life ... It is unquestionably one of the most decisive influences on the opinions, tastes, language, and customs of Canada. It can give expression to our national character; it can give voice to our distinctive Canadian spirit. It can help us to know ourselves and to achieve our real destiny.[180]

In the speech from the throne inaugurating the largest majority government in Canadian history up to that time, the Conservatives had promised "a new agency to regulate broadcasting in Canada."[181] As though to clear the way,

CBC president Dunton resigned on 3 July, to become president of Carleton University.

## The End of the "Single System"

The new minister, George Nowlan, was a friend of the public service and early in his tenure had appeared very favourable towards the CBC in response to questioning.[182] The Cabinet, however, was said to be divided as to what course of action to take, with powerful ministers such as Davie Fulton and Donald Fleming long on record demanding more privileges for the private sector.

On 18 August 1958, Nowlan moved introduction of legislation respecting broadcasting. The government bill was in two parts: the first proposed establishment of a Board of Broadcast Governors, while the second reestablished the CBC. All of the CBC's traditional operating functions were reiterated, but the CBC was to be explicitly bound by the provisions creating the BBG.

On second reading of the bill a week later, Liberal leader Lester Pearson made a lengthy and detailed critique, introduced with these words: "In no sector of our national life more than in the field of broadcasting is there a greater and more continuing need for strong and independent public service and public control."[183] Pearson, who, like St. Laurent, had been close to the Canadian Radio League in the 1930s, noted the interesting parallel with 1932, when it had been left to a Conservative government to implement recommendations of a royal commission appointed by the Liberals.

Pearson said the opposition was concerned that the new legislation would weaken rather than strengthen the national broadcasting system. Historically, he recalled, the key feature of the system had been the predominance of the public sector and the secondary status of the private broadcasters. Over the years, we had lost sight of the importance of public control and what had at first been "a privilege for private broadcasters has gradually become a vested interest and eventually has been invoked as a right."[184]

The government claimed the bill would make only superficial changes in the framework of the system, Pearson said, but it was really "a sanctioning by law of changes which had been creeping in."[185] Here, Pearson touched on an essential aspect of the policy framework. The private sector had occupied more and more place in the system since the late 1930s. As it grew stronger it had adopted an increasingly aggressive public stance aimed at gaining legal and statutory recognition for what was already an established fact. As the Fowler commission had implied, this situation was at least partly due to the CBC's deliberately cultivated low profile and reluctance to use the power vested in it by law, a strategic practice aimed at neutralizing ideological charges of state, government, or socialistic heavy-handedness. What

Pearson did not say was that all these "creeping changes" had taken place under Liberal governments.

The leader of the opposition continued, enumerating the defects of the government's bill: "it goes a long way toward creating two national broadcasting systems ... it weakens the CBC in some undesirable ways ... [it creates an] undesirable and cumbersome administrative setup."[186]

Unlike the key Fowler recommendation, the bill not only proposed to create a Board of Broadcast Governors, but also maintained the CBC's traditional obligation of reporting to Parliament through its own minister. Thus, Pearson pointed out, the CBC would have two masters. Where Fowler had been careful to specify that it was merely shifting the CBC's regulatory function to the new board – sharing public responsibility between two related agencies – the bill would place the CBC in the same relationship to the BBG as the private sector. The CBC, Pearson feared, would have "no special position, no predominance which would enable it to discharge more effectively its national responsibility." The BBG would regulate, separately, the activities of all Canadian broadcasters as well as the relationship between them – the CBC and the private stations would appear before it as equals.

Thus, while the private broadcasters were to have disappeared under the 1932 legislation, and while their role from 1936–1958 was considered "complementary," after 1958 they would be equal to the public sector. This is what Pearson meant by the "serious weakening ... of the single national system." The new legislation was a move towards "two systems, one public and private, becoming more and more independent of each other and having equal rights and status."[187]

The Liberals were not opposed to separating the regulatory from the operating functions; this, Pearson said, would accord the private stations the fairer treatment they deserved. The proposed legislation would, however, at the same time weaken the CBC. The CBC would make its own policy through its own board of directors; but then it would have to go before the BBG to request, for example, licensing of new stations. In addition, the BBG could authorize establishment of private networks to compete with the CBC. The BBG and the CBC would report separately to Parliament, doubling the opportunity for political interference. The bill also ignored Fowler's important recommendation regarding a statutory, multiyear funding formula for the CBC, making CBC operations dependent instead on an annual appropriation and, thus, on the discretion of the minister of finance. Pearson's final word on the bill was that it was "an uneasy and uncertain compromise between two points of view," referring presumably to the Fowler report on the one hand and Cabinet hard-liners on the other. The Liberals, he said, would not support the bill.[188]

The CCF position was articulated by Douglas Fisher: "We would like to know whether this bill is designed to improve and extend the national broadcasting system, or is it designed to lead to a gradual withering away of public broadcasting and the gradual taking over of broadcasting by private broadcasters?"[189] Among other things, the bill proposed to allow up to 25 percent foreign ownership of Canadian broadcasting stations or networks (as compared to the 20 percent suggested by Fowler).

In defence of his legislation, George Nowlan said the bill simply implemented Fowler's basic recommendation and a fundamental policy of the Conservative Party, namely, "an independent regulatory board controlling regulations of both public and private stations."[190] The CBC's powers, except for the removal of regulation, were unchanged. The BBG would make regulations and the CBC board of directors would run the CBC. There was no intention to destroy the single system. In fact, Nowlan said, the CBC would be strengthened because it would not have to handle criticism on regulatory questions – the independent body would handle regulation "from both a public and private point of view."[191]

In retrospect, part of the problem lay in the formulation of the Fowler commission's proposal to create the BBG. Once one accepted the principle of separating the regulatory and operating functions of the CBC, the distinction between Fowler's and the Conservative plan was a subtle, although meaningful, one. Fowler saw the single board as strengthening the public sector and maintaining the balance in a "single system." The Conservative plan, on the other hand, was designed to strengthen the private sector and create a "dual system." It was interesting that the strong free enterprise advocates within the government stayed quiet during debate on the bill, leaving its defence to Nowlan, who was on record as being a supporter of public broadcasting. The already fuzzy distinction between Fowler's proposal and the new law was further blurred by the similar arguments of the main Liberal and Conservative spokesmen.

The important change was the one included in both the Fowler report and the legislation: the creation of a second public agency. The primary area of public intervention in broadcasting would henceforth be regulation (as in the US), with programming and operations secondary. The new regulatory process implied that "the public interest" could demand some form of mediation or arbitration between "public" and "private" broadcasters. But if the raison d'être of the BBG was to serve the public interest, what role did that leave for the CBC? Inevitably, the need to interpose a new public agency between Parliament and the CBC was interpreted as a sign that somehow the public broadcaster had got "out of hand."

Debate on third reading of the bill focused on Section 10, dealing with "objects and purposes" of the proposed BBG.[192] Earlier, Pearson had pointed out that there was no reference in the bill to "the paramount importance of the public service aspect or the purpose of broadcasting."[193] Now, Douglas Fisher moved an amendment to include the first sentence of Fowler's draft bill: "The Board is charged with supervision, regulation and control of all broadcasting in Canada in the public interest." Pearson supported the amendment, stating it was advisable to strengthen the language of the bill and maintain the explicitly "public" nature of broadcasting.

The amendment was defeated and the bill carried, with only the Liberals opposed. Although Douglas Fisher had suggested that the bill augured the victory of the private broadcasters, the CCF voted with the government, feeling that postponement would further favour the private sector. The Canadian Broadcasting League was generally satisfied with the act, except for its failure to provide statutory long-term financing for the CBC.[194] Considering the intensity of the debate that had led up to it, and the degree of change it involved for the legislative framework of the system that had been in place since 1936, the new broadcasting act[195] passed through Parliament relatively quickly and quietly.

During the next ten years the new public regulatory agency, the Board of Broadcast Governors, would reshape and restructure the system along the lines of the broad policy orientation of the government that created it. In this climate, private broadcasting would flourish. At the same time, the administrative functioning of the public broadcaster would result in an almost continuous flow of controversy surrounding CBC programming and the corporation's internal affairs.

# CHAPTER FOUR

# Commerce and Crisis (1958–68)

## INTRODUCTION

When the Conservatives came to power in the late 1950s, they took the occasion to restructure the system in the interests of the private sector. The decline of the "single broadcasting system" begun by the legislative reform of 1958 marked a major change in the sociocultural role of broadcasting in Canada. Under the Conservative government and the Board of Broadcast Governors, Canadian broadcasting ceased to be primarily an agency for political "nation building."

Between 1958 and 1963, the system was reshaped in the image of the private sector, maximizing the potential for economic profit. When the Liberals returned in 1963, on the other hand, they left private broadcasting to enjoy its new spoils and began trying to recapture the political function that the Canadian broadcasting system had been designed to serve. For the first time, a distinct strategy placed the emphasis on the central role of public broadcasting in a cultural policy designed to further the Liberal political project for Canada. It was not in innocence that the new Broadcasting Act of 1968 imposed on the CBC an explicit mandate to promote "national unity."

The tension between the economic and political purposes of broadcasting was never so evident as during these years. On the one hand, the opening up of commercial television offered unimagined possibilities for private profit; on the other, the political imperatives of the times seemed to demand firm action on the part of the state. After 1963, the national unity crisis that shook the country put politics in command.

As unrest in Quebec began to move from simmer to boil, the Pearson government mandated a Royal Commission on Bilingualism and Biculturalism[1], chaired by André Laurendeau and Davidson Dunton, to find ways to instil equality in the historic partnership between Canada's "two founding peoples." According to Bernard Ostry, the bilingualism and biculturalism commission, like the Massey commission before it, "revealed the basic connection between culture and politics and reminded Canadians that only by recognizing the centrality of this particular cultural issue to the political crisis could they preserve the national integrity of their country."[2]

But well before the bilingualism and biculturalism commission reported, the government anticipated its message and adopted a strategy for apprehending the crisis: it would use cultural policy as an instrument for keeping the country together. Under this strategy, federal cultural policy would be built around broadcasting, and the key institution to implement that policy would be the CBC.

During the 1960s, the CBC – in both French and English – would play a central role in Canada's political life and especially in the evolution of the country's national dilemma.

Traditionally, the CBC leavened Canada's cultural diet from a position to the left of political centre. Throughout its history, the parliamentary record has been littered with sporadic complaints about this or that CBC program and even accusations of Communist propaganda. A CBC radio play about US labour organizers Elizabeth Gurley Flynn and Joe Hill, aired in October 1955, was still the subject of tirades like this one by Social Credit's Solon Low nearly a full year later: "Somebody in the CBC deliberately chose that subject and wrote it up for the purpose of putting over the communist line and using the Canadian Broadcasting Corporation network to do so."[3]

Within the English network, particularly television, a critical approach to "public affairs" programming emerged during these years – an approach based implicitly on the *social* conception of the public reminiscent of the one that had inspired some of the pioneers of Canadian public broadcasting. As this approach took root at the height of the Western world's coming to grips with "the sixties," political pressure to have the CBC reflect consensus rather than conflict became intense.

In Quebec, the CBC was seen as even more closely connected with the questioning of society and was the subject of regular calls for a "clean-up job." As late as 1958, defenders of the old order such as MP Louis-Joseph Pigeon were still saying things like: "Let us throw out these people with warped ideas, leftist ideas, who grab half the television programs, such as, for example – and I have no hesitation at all in naming them – Pierre Elliott Trudeau, Gérard Pelletier, and Jean-Louis Gagnon who should be permanently kept away from the national network."[4] Not long after, these erstwhile targets of disapproval were issuing similar attacks on a new generation of social critics.

In the 1960s, the sharp challenge from Quebec to the very idea of Canada shook the foundations of the country's social life. Radio-Canada tended to view this challenge from a position of "public" rather than "national" interest

– that is, it sought to clarify and broaden the parameters of debate in the perceived interests of its constituency rather than promote a particular position. Ottawa's response was to equate more closely than ever the notions of "public" and "national" interest, and seek to correct the national/public broadcaster accordingly.

After 1968, the Liberals would see to it that the "public" broadcaster had a precise mandate to promote "national unity." At the same time, however, Quebec, under Daniel Johnson, would begin to aggressively put forward its own, alternative conception of national interest in communications, irreversibly blurring the idea of a single Canadian public.

But in 1958, the Conservatives were freshly in power in Ottawa, and their main interest in broadcasting was to see that the new structure they had created achieved the catching-up that it had been designed to achieve for private interests. In Quebec, where Duplessis was still hanging on, people were thinking about a different type of catching-up, and were beginning to take steps that mystified English Canada but did not yet concern it to the point of disrupting the national agenda.

In this context, less than sixty days after Canada's new broadcasting act was proclaimed, television producers at Radio-Canada in Montreal went on strike on 29 December 1958.

## NEW CONFLICTS IN
## BROADCASTING, 1958–59

### Nationalism and Labour Relations

The Radio-Canada producers' strike of 1958–59 was one of those events in the life of a society that, generations later, can be evoked to symbolize the meaning and feeling of a time. In Quebec, this event marked a plateau in national consciousness, the passage from the "French-Canadian" to the "Québécois" condition. Its memory encompasses other events of the period which expressed the need and desire for change that is generally referred to as the Quiet Revolution.[5]

Radio-Canada's television producers went out on strike a few days after Christmas 1958 to support their demand for the right to unionize. This was the first instance in Canadian labour history of middle-level manager-employees seeking to form a union. The producers' move was in harmony with the embryonic spirit of promotion of collective rights that would characterize the Quiet Revolution and become one of Quebec's marks of distinction from the rest of Canada. But it was totally out of sync with English-Canadian labour values of the period and, as such, was met with bemusement (if not hostility) on the part of management; it did not elicit significant support from the workers of the English-language broadcasting service either. What made things most difficult was the fact that the employer was an agency of the federal government.

At first, the government appeared to have no position on the dispute, although both Labour Minister Michael Starr and George Nowlan labelled the strike "illegal."[6] Throughout the strike, the government would maintain that it had no role to play in a dispute between the CBC and a group of individual contract employees engaged in an illegal action.

A major problem that emerged early in the dispute was that the French network executives lacked the authority to negotiate the issue of unionization with the producers.[7] Only the head office in Ottawa could move on it and, as the head office was slow to treat the matter seriously, things soon deteriorated. Radio-Canada quickly came to be seen in Quebec as a federal institution betraying its promise. Furthermore, only French Canadians were feeling the effects of the crisis. While the strike lasted, people in Quebec nurtured the idea that Ottawa really did not consider Radio-Canada an indispensable service, further evidence of the historic inequality between French and English Canada.

Deprived of indigenous television, public opinion in Quebec demanded government intervention. Quebec Liberal MPs, led by Lionel Chevrier, pressed the government to act and extracted an opinion from Solicitor General Léon Balcer to the effect that he believed the strike was not illegal.[8] In a front-page editorial in *Le Devoir* on 22 January 1959, André Laurendeau termed Radio-Canada's attitude "blindly legalistic" and called on the government to pay some attention to the dispute, lest its inaction be interpreted as support for management. In a follow-up editorial the next day, Laurendeau said the affair was making French Canadians feel that they were "abandoned, marginal, without influence on the state."[9]

The importance of the strike has to be considered in the context of the role of television in Quebec society in 1959 and in light of the fact that Radio-Canada was the only source of French-language, let alone Canadian French-language, programming.[10] One of the first English-Canadian observers to notice its impact was Douglas Fisher: "I sometimes feel there is a sweeping change taking place in French Canada ... this was the most unusual thing that ever happened; for the first time the French-Canadian intellectuals seemed to be working with the labour movement in Quebec."[11]

By February, the strike had become a "national" problem. George Nowlan blamed the situation on poor communication between CBC officials in Montreal and Ottawa and called it " the most unfortunate and unnecessary episode in labour relations in Canadian history." The minor difficulties that had led to the strike could have been dealt with in half an hour, he said.[12]

The provincial government in Quebec was delighted to see Radio-Canada off the air. The support of Duplessis's Union Nationale had been an important factor in the Conservatives' breakthrough in Quebec in 1958, and an indication of this connection came in this intervention by Conservative MP Rémi Paul (later a UN cabinet minister): "The strike ... has given the people of Quebec the impression of being rid of certain hot-headed and leftist individuals."[13]

But, of course, Quebec (and Canada) were far from rid of these individuals. Indeed, not only George Nowlan but René Lévesque as well believed the strike could have and should have been settled in half an hour.[14] Lévesque's role, as a CBC contract employee involved in the strike, is one of the legendary aspects of this story. The strike – which lasted not half an hour but sixty-eight days – was Lévesque's first public embrace of the militant nationalism that would propel him into politics. It was not settled until 7 March 1959.

The apparent indifference of English Canada, the federal government, and the broadcasting bureaucracy to the crisis deeply influenced national consciousness in Quebec. Writing in 1960, Gérard Lamarche, head of CBC French-language operations in Montreal, commented: "The affair coincided with a notorious change in tone and policy in our major French newspapers. Public participation reached an unprecedented height. No organization – federal, provincial, municipal, educational, or cultural – could thereafter escape the impact of public reaction. It is just as well that the public finally awoke. By chance, Radio-Canada was the first important experience of this kind."[15]

Yet, only a few months later, the chairman of the Board of Broadcast Governors, Andrew Stewart, felt confident to state: "It appears to me that Canadians now take the political unity of the country for granted. We no longer consider it possible that any part of the country might move to secede."[16]

Although the Radio-Canada strike has been interpreted primarily as a turning point in the emergence of a certain perception of Quebec's role in Canada, it is also interesting to consider it in light of the evolution of the social practice of Canada's public broadcaster. Labour relations became an increasingly complex question at the corporation in the 1960s and 1970s, and situated its management – both French and English – increasingly on the side of established authority, while bringing employees and contract workers into closer alignment with other groups in society involved in democratic struggles. In this respect, public broadcasting was arguably little different from broadcasting based in the private sector.

### Controversy Over "Public Affairs"

Shortly after the end of the Radio-Canada strike, Parliament appointed another Special Committee on Broadcasting. It began sitting on 12 May, with the intention of examining all aspects of Canadian broadcasting: the CBC, the BBG, and the private sector. However, by the time it reported on 10 July, it had only had time to deal with the CBC – a situation which would become a pattern in the 1960s. Increasingly, the public broadcaster would come under close parliamentary scrutiny, while the regulator and the private sector developed relatively autonomous ways of functioning.

The CBC filed with the committee a document called "Internal Rules and Regulations Governing News Policy." It emphasized that CBC news policy was based "on the primary conception that this service is in the nature of a public trust."[17] No CBC news editor would permit his personal views, whatever they may be, to influence the way he handled political copy. A section entitled "News that Might Cause Internal Friction" said news would never be presented in such a way as to encourage antagonisms which could be dangerous to national unity.[18] In a section on "International News – Propaganda," it was stated that the CBC would avoid giving statements from communist countries an authoritative ring (for example, qualifying statements through use of the adjective "communist," as in "the Communist radio in Poland says ...").

The CBC's "public trust" was considered differently when dealing with other types of programming. The corporation reiterated the policy, outlined before the Fowler commission in 1956, that general programming was to serve the entire range of Canadian interests and opinions, including "unpopular minority" ones. News, however, was clearly to serve the national interest and, above all, was not to be a divisive force. The two faces of CBC policy met uneasily in the area of "public affairs programming," where the news of the day was to be discussed and dissected from the widest possible range of positions. The nature of public affairs programming and questions of access, representation, balance, and fairness would dominate debate on the CBC, in both English and French, throughout the 1960s.

An early instance of this type of controversy took place while the parliamentary committee was sitting. On 15 June 1959, management of the CBC's English network cancelled "Preview Commentary," a daily radio public affairs program that looked at Ottawa politics. The reason given was that correspondents did not have enough time to gain perspective on the issues they were discussing. But an inquiry by the supervisor of talks and public affairs, Frank Peers, led him to conclude "that clandestine political influence had been brought to bear on CBC management."[19] Unable to gain a satisfactory explanation for the cancellation, Peers and eleven other production employees resigned.

In the House of Commons on 23 June, Lester Pearson said the event would have an "unfortunate effect on the integrity and the independence of the CBC" and would "at the very least put it in an unfavourable position with regard to private broadcasting."[20]

George Nowlan said he had not been involved in any representations to the CBC concerning programming. However, the following day, the CBC board of directors reversed the decision, reinstating the program and its officials, "in order to remove any doubt as to the independence of the corporation."[21]

The issue was aired at the parliamentary committee on 30 June. Peers testified that he had been told "[CBC acting president Ernest] Bushnell had been given two alternatives: either to take this program off the air or the corporate structure of the CBC would be endangered."[22] Peers said he had been told the statement had been made by someone with a political connection.

Peers and his colleagues considered the intervention a threat to the integrity of public affairs programming and had resigned to free themselves "to make the public aware of the issues involved." This was an important choice – the "public" over the "corporation" – and was one of the first indications that the CBC's corporate conception of the public was not the same as that of its program creators.

In its report, tabled 16 July, the parliamentary committee said there was no evidence to support the charge of "clandestine political influence" in the "Preview Commentary" affair. However, while affirming its support for the basic aims and objectives of the CBC, the committee found its administrative structure "weak and in need of a thorough revision." The CBC's recent troubles showed a "lack of clear definition of responsibilities and authority."[23]

Two days after the report was tabled, the House of Commons began its annual consideration of the CBC's operating budget. Canada's public broadcaster now evidently had *five* masters: its own board of directors, the Board of Broadcast Governors (which had not yet really begun to exercise its authority), the parliamentary committee on broadcasting, Parliament, and ultimately, the government. By 1959, along with its codified principles of public service and public trust, CBC management was necessarily guided by a finely tuned sensitivity to potential controversy and political sensibilities.

## THE RISE OF THE PRIVATE SECTOR, 1958–62

### Licensing

While the CBC made headlines, the BBG was quietly beginning to reshape the demography of Canadian broadcasting.

The BBG was set up in November 1958 with University of Alberta president Andrew Stewart as chairman. Its vice-chairmen were Roger Duhamel and Carlyle Allison, both newspaper editors with open ties to the Conservative

Party. The only member with a known sympathy towards public broadcasting was the Canadian Labour Congress's Eugene Forsey. By the mere fact of its existence, the BBG "gave the private broadcasters the recognition of their important status in the Canadian broadcasting system that they had long campaigned for."[24]

A government decision on television set the tone of the new regulatory environment. During debate on the CBC budget estimates in July 1959, George Nowlan announced in the House that the government had decided it was ready to consider applications "for additional television broadcasting stations in areas already provided with television service."[25] Nowlan lauded the salutary effect competition would have on both producers and consumers. While the broadcasting act gave the minister of transport the final word on application grants, Nowlan made it clear that the licensing of "second stations" would be done by the BBG.

The opposition linked the recent attacks on the CBC with the new policy. Lester Pearson said it was essential for the CBC to have its financial security assured if it were to be free from government pressure. The recent actions of both the government and the CBC had created "great anxiety about the future of a national broadcasting system in this country":

> [T]here seems to be developing a sudden emphasis in this country on the virtues of private broadcasting, so I ask myself, is there a concerted effort under way now to weaken and eventually destroy a publicly-owned and publicly-operated national broadcasting corporation? Is all this concerted criticism and attack preparatory to the strengthening and enlarging of the private sector in that national system at the expense of the CBC? Is it preparatory to the granting of rare and valuable public assets in second television licences in metropolitan centres? And is this to be done before the Board of Broadcast Governors has laid down conditions and standards of performance? Who are to be the favoured recipients of the potentially most profitable public franchises, perhaps, since the days, shall I say, of the East India Company?[26]

Instead of being regarded as a "gold mine," Pearson said, the available licences should be awarded "on terms that will clearly assure that abnormally large private profits will not be made, and that the maximum amount of public service will be provided from their use."[27]

Douglas Fisher was disappointed that the BBG had not enunciated "a national policy" for uniting the CBC and the private stations in one system, as the CCF had hoped. He feared the BBG would not aid the CBC to fulfil its vital function "to translate the abstract conception of nationhood into something that can be seen, heard, felt and understood."[28]

But while the function of the CBC was debated, and its performance scrutinized and criticized, the government had decided to go ahead with expanding the private sector. The government was creating an alternative to the public broadcaster in the populous, urban television markets which had heretofore been reserved for the CBC. As the opposition anxiously pointed out, this was being done in the absence of any guiding concern for what would actually transpire on the soon-to-be-licensed private stations.

The BBG held competitive application hearings for second television stations in the fall of 1959. Early in 1960, it awarded private licences for second stations in eight major urban centres. Against eight competitors, John Bassett of the strongly pro-Conservative *Telegram* won Toronto, irritating the segment of opinion opposed to interlocking media ownership. Three licences were awarded to partly foreign-owned groups: in Halifax, Montreal, and Ottawa (where it went to Ernest Bushnell, recently of the CBC).

In the House of Commons, Douglas Fisher attacked the BBG as a bunch of Conservative Party men and said that instead of awarding television licences to Tory newspaper publishers like Bassett, it should be blocking the growing corporate concentration in broadcasting. Instead of allowing the Thomson interests to acquire any available radio station, the BBG should be building a "cultural dike" against American influence. However, Fisher had no kind words for the CBC either, calling it scared and gutless with respect to public affairs programming.[29]

The BBG, meanwhile, began developing a new approach to the problem of American influence: "Canadian content." In July 1960, it announced that Canadian television operations would be expected to be at least 45 percent Canadian by 1 April 1961, with the percentage to rise to 55 percent on 1 April 1962. At regulatory hearings in November 1959, the BBG proposals had been supported by public interest advocates such as the Canadian Labour Congress and the Canadian Broadcasting League. But for the BBG, Canadian content and ownership regulations were not so much intended to serve a perceived public interest as they were designed to show that public broadcasting was not the only solution to the national interest in broadcasting.

When the newly reappointed Special Committee on Broadcasting met in February 1961, its first witness was BBG chairman Andrew Stewart, who declared that in spite of some "awkwardness" arising out of the public/private mix of the Canadian broadcasting system, "the Act is working ... it is a workable Act."[30] In Stewart's testimony it became clear that the BBG felt responsible for the private stations' financial well-being, but was reluctant to prescribe the programming activities of the private stations. The BBG did not give guidelines regarding "balance," for example, and had different expectations from a private station than from the CBC.

Thus, in 1961, the newly created public agency responsible for supervising broadcasting in Canada considered its role to protect the financial welfare of the private sector but not to orient its activities. The BBG did not appear to be concerned about the erosion of commercial revenue in the public sector, nor was it apparently concerned about the lack of reticence of the political apparatus of the state when it came to interfering in the affairs of the public broadcaster.

### New Technology

Appearing before the committee on 23 February, the private broadcasters (whose organization had reverted, by now, to calling itself the Canadian Association of Broadcasters) agreed with the BBG that the act seemed "to be working well." In a brief marked by an air of confidence, the CAB recognized that Parliament seemed to intend that the entire Canadian broadcasting system should provide an "alternative to the US radio and television signals easily available to nearly all Canadians ... Broadcasting has been selected as an instrument for furthering certain public policy objectives, especially in relation to the Canadian identity and Canadian unity."[31] The CAB patriotically pointed out that private broadcasting was prepared to do its share towards meeting these objectives at its own expense. However, there was a spectre on the horizon.

Andrew Stewart had sought to alert the parliamentarians to a new problem, unanticipated by the Broadcasting Act of 1958: the use of "community antenna television," also known as "wired systems," to improve signal delivery in areas where reception was poor. Was this a form of "broadcasting?" Present legislation did not cover it.

Now, the CAB, too, alluded to these "wired" or "cabled" systems that currently escaped regulation and risked jeopardizing the public policy objectives set forward for broadcasting. Here, the private broadcasters and their public patron, the BBG, were in agreement that a new actor was threatening the public policy objectives of the broadcasting act. The embryonic cable industry was also a financial threat to the private broadcasters, but this was not their main concern, or so it was implied.

The president of the CBC, Alphonse Ouimet, was the third party to bring up the spectre of wired systems at the 1961 committee hearings. Like the CAB, the CBC wanted the definition of broadcasting widened to include cable. In Ouimet's testimony, the classical argument for public control of broadcasting – that the "air" was a natural monopoly in the public domain – was shifted for the first time. Ouimet framed his argument in terms of "end effect" – the fact that whether messages were sent out through the air or transmitted by means of wire they were ultimately received in people's homes. Consequently, "it would be in the national interest to have the same controls over the two kinds of system." As long as they were achieving exactly the same end, the problem of controlling the means was in both cases the same.[32]

As a technical man, Ouimet understood the implications of cable's expanded carriage capacity. In 1961, most operating cable systems were basically picking up and amplifying what was already available over the air, but there was no technical reason why they could not also originate their own programming. Because the act defined broadcasting in terms of "hertzian waves," cable systems were in fact not covered. Unless the lacunae were filled in, the new systems could negate both the purpose and the effectiveness of Canadian broadcasting legislation and regulation.

In the 1960s, the cable companies would argue loudly, much as the private broadcasters had argued before them, that their services should indeed be exempt from regulation. One basis for this argument was that, unlike over-the-air broadcasting, cable was not "public" reception, as one had to subscribe and get hooked up to the service. As in the case of the private broadcasters, the state would insist on the need to regulate cable in the public interest and then proceed, through its regulatory agency, to create a context in which the main legacy of regulation was the private prosperity of the cable entrepreneurs.

There was another troubling aspect to the question of cable regulation. The wording of the act was based on the Privy Council ruling of 1932, which had awarded jurisdiction over broadcasting to Ottawa on the grounds that wireless transmissions crossed provincial boundaries. If broadcasting were now redefined in terms of "end effect" – which seemed remarkably close to saying broadcasting was to be defined in terms of its content – what was to stop the provinces from coming back with new claims that they should have control over these instruments of culture and education, especially those which could be confined to a given territory simply by establishing a wire head?

### Equal Status

Following the licensing of private stations in all of Canada's major television markets, the establishment of a private television network appeared to be a logical step. Andrew Stewart indicated just how far the BBG's *laissez-faire* attitude went: he told the parliamentary committee the board felt there was a place for a second network in Canada, but it could not force individual licensees to decide whether or not they wanted to go along. Stewart said the BBG had already given an applicant permission to launch a private network: "We have been in a sense promoting this, on the basis that it fulfils the terms of the national purposes; but if it is uneconomic and would be a burden on the individual stations, and they did not want to come into it, then we are not in a position to force it."[33]

The climate of an expanding private sector attracted a difficult line of questioning towards the CBC, and Alphonse Ouimet was obliged to justify the public broadcaster's $72 million subsidy (out of a total budget for

1961–62 of $110 million). The objectives Parliament set for national broad-
casting could not be met with a balanced budget: "You will be able to judge.
There is a second network being set up. Just see what kind of programming
they will be able to produce, how many parts of the country they will be
able to serve, at a profit."[34]

The CBC proposed to the committee that it be given a statutory grant for
five years, based on four dollars per capita the first year and rising by 5
percent each subsequent year; one-third of its revenue would come from
commercial advertising, the corporation said.

Meanwhile, the CTV Television Network, that the BBG claimed would be
a boon to Canadian programming, was created in April 1961 and was
scheduled to begin operations on 1 October. Owned by a group of nonop-
erating investors, the new network would provide commercial programs to
eight private affiliates. Although the CBC, struggling to maintain the integrity
of its own national network, did not object, the principle of a public monopoly for national network broadcasting was broken for the first time. The
implications of this were demonstrated almost immediately.

If the awarding of private stations in markets where the CBC had previously
enjoyed exclusivity could be seen as healthy competition, the formation of
a private commercial network could only weaken the CBC. This became
clear in 1961 when a controversy arose over the awarding of television rights
for Canadian professional football in eastern Canada. In a bold move, the
private Toronto station CFTO (whose owner, John Bassett, also owned the
Toronto Argonauts football club) outbid the CBC for these rights and applied
to the BBG for permission to form a network for football telecasts. The BBG
refused the request, so CFTO arranged to distribute its programs through CTV
and offer them to individual stations in other areas.

The CBC's national service already combined public and private operations: of sixty-seven television stations operating in Canada in May 1961,
fifty-nine (forty-six of them privately owned) were part of the CBC national
network. Success of the CBC network operations depended on the participation of these private "affiliates." Was the CBC now to be required to
compete with a commercial network for the loyalties of these stations? The
BBG had to clarify the role and responsibility of the second network in the
overall system.

Before the parliamentary committee, Andrew Stewart disagreed with the
CBC regarding network splitting. There was nothing wrong, he said, with
affiliates joining the second network as well, as long as it did not disrupt
their affiliation agreement with the CBC. The first interest to consider, Stewart
said, must be that of the affiliate itself. This was the first real instance of a
regulatory official placing a private commercial interest ahead of that of the
public service, and Stewart was soon called to task for it by his own board.

But first, Ouimet replied. The CBC and CTV could not be considered on a basis of competition, because they were fundamentally unequal: "The CBC is an instrument of national purpose – the CTV of commercial purpose," he wrote to the committee. The CBC's "national service" was not simply a commercial arrangement with the private affiliates, it was "the availability of instant live connection with all stations along the national networks."[35]

Although he did not put it in such terms, Ouimet was spelling out what the Conservative politicians and their appointees had forgotten in their free enterprise euphoria: that Canada's national broadcasting service had a *political* function that commercial broadcasters had no interest to fulfil. The CBC's capacity to play that role depended on such things as instantaneous access to a coast-to-coast network when necessary.

The president of the CAB, Don Jamieson, tried to justify Stewart's position. He told the committee Canada would be well served by a strong network alternative to the CBC. The broadcasting "system" was composed of public and private parts; the public element operated the national "service." A strong alternative service operated by the private element would only be good. Jamieson was careful not to suggest that the second network would be a "national" service as well. The CAB had no desire to be saddled with such responsibilities. It would be content to serve the large urban centres where the most lucrative markets existed (the first eight "second stations" already reached 70 percent of the population).[36]

The BBG evidently agreed with Ouimet. In view of the mandate imposed on the CBC by the broadcasting act, the BBG ruled that a station affiliated with one network could join a second network only with the consent of the first. On 20 June, after meeting with the BBG, Stewart reversed his previous position. The football issue highlighted the problems involved in introducing a commercial logic into the system. Private entrepreneurs would seek to maximize their profits and the public broadcaster would be obliged to meet them on their own ground in order to remain "competitive."

The debate over the role of the second network also highlighted the tension between public broadcaster and regulator that had been created by the Broadcasting Act of 1958. The act established the CBC "for the purpose of operating a national broadcasting *service*."[37] The BBG, meanwhile, was responsible for "ensuring ... a national broadcasting *system*."[38] The BBG had invoked the CBC's mandate to justify reversing Stewart's position, but what would happen when there was a more fundamental clash between the custodians of the "system" and the trustees of the "service?" And where, in all this, did the public fit in?

Having served as a forum for the BBG, the CBC, and the CAB, the parliamentary committee took no concrete steps towards resolving the major contentious issues that had been placed before it. Its only significant recommendation was to refer to the Supreme Court the question of constitutional jurisdiction over wired systems, to determine whether they were covered by "broadcasting" as defined by the act.

Meanwhile, the BBG continued to regulate the increasingly complex financial affairs of the new private stations. In the fall of 1961 it approved CFTO's request to sell 25 percent – the maximum allowed by law – to American interests. Liberal broadcasting critic J.W. Pickersgill called the proposal scandalous and blasted the agency for acting "contrary to all the principles on which all of us have believed public broadcasting stood in this country." He used the occasion to eloquently lay out the Liberal Party position that public ownership and public control are the only way to keep broadcasting Canadian: "It is precisely because we were afraid the whole market would have been taken by US interests if there had not been public participation that we have had this public participation. I have never heard any Canadian who was not a socialist defend it on any other grounds. I have never defended it on any other grounds. I think it would be far better, if we could have the assurance that the broadcasting would be Canadian, to have entirely private broadcasting."[39]

This was one of the most transparent public statements on record of the politics underlying the Canadian broadcasting compromise. Guided by this type of thinking, the Liberals would try to make broadcasting serve their conception of Canada after they returned to power in 1963.

Federal elections in 1962 returned a Conservative minority government that had little time or interest for further initiatives with respect to broadcasting, except to shift the parliamentary responsibility for the CBC and the BBG to the portfolio of the secretary of state, G.E. Halpenny.

With privatization well under way, another controversy over football telecasts made headlines in November 1962. When CTV was awarded the rights to televise the 1962 Grey Cup game, the BBG declared the game an event of public interest and instructed the CBC to broadcast it, complete with CTV's advertising, as the private network demanded. The BBG said the second network was now an "inescapable fact": "Competition for the rights to popular events is here, and the conditions of competition on a commercial basis will become nearly more equal ... even if CTV network does not yet have the same coverage as the publicly owned network, it should not for that reason be excluded from all the popular events which call for wide coverage."[40]

The "Grey Cup controversy" was the kind of conflict critics of the 1958 legislation had warned about. The BBG's handling of it highlighted the fears that the "independent" regulator was really the agent of the private sector. But the CBC struck a separate peace with the advertisers who agreed that it could carry the Grey Cup game without advertising as a public service.

The controversy was the occasion for another public manifestation of the Canadian Broadcasting League. Since adoption of the broadcasting act, the league had kept a low profile, submitting an occasional statement to the CBC and the BBG.[41] Now, it made its strongest showing since 1958, opposing the BBG order to the CBC and advocating "a mixed public-private system but with all national networks in either language operated by public authority, and the public interest in case of controversy overriding the commercial interest."[42]

But the most important influence on the changing balance of power in Canadian broadcasting during this period was the complicity of the BBG with the interests of private broadcasters. According to BBG staff members of the time, "Andrew Stewart's door was always open to the private broadcasters, and ... it was common for the permanent staff to receive instructions after such visits to the effect that some kind of relaxation of a regulation had been granted, or some new procedure was to be adopted easing some requirement."[43] Staff was rarely consulted about such changes, even when they resulted in setting new precedents.

The BBG justified its leniency towards the private sector by considering that the CBC, as a Crown corporation, already had a strong advocate in the government. But this was a convenient misinterpretation based on a superficial reading of official pronouncements.[44] Things changed when the electorate overturned the Conservative government, however, because the Liberals had their own agenda for the CBC.

### THE CRITIQUE OF BROADCASTING IN THE EARLY 1960S

By 1963, broadcasting in Canada had evolved to a point at which it was difficult, if not impossible, to characterize it in simple, schematic terms. Nevertheless, the system was subject to close scrutiny from several different directions.

A Royal Commission on Government Organization, chaired by J. Grant Glassco, had conducted a study of the CBC in 1961, and featured the case in a separate chapter of its report.[45] The Glassco commission noted that the CBC's mandate could be reduced to one simple obligation: to carry on a "national broadcasting service." While a general direction of this nature would cause no problem in a more straightforward field, its report said, "a national broadcasting service can take a hundred forms."[46]

In the absence of government or statutory guidance, the commission reported, the CBC had over the years "made its own interpretations and then proceeded to create the sort of service which it considered appropriate."[47] The commission clearly felt this was unsound. It described as "an unfortunate omission ... the lack of provision for general guidance by the government with respect to major policy decisions."[48] Although the CBC required day-to-day independence from the political process, it should not be given a blank cheque; the responsible minister should have the power of formal direction and the government should give policy guidance.

The commission found that CBC policy was not made by the corporation's board of directors, who were too remote from the centre of power, but "is largely dictated by management."[49] Sensitive to public criticism, CBC management tended to be defensive and had made "major errors of organization."[50]

Finally, the relationship between the CBC and the Board of Broadcast Governors begged for clarification: "In light, particularly, of the emergence of a private television network actively competing with the Corporation, the possible conflict between the powers of the regulatory authority and the statutory terms of reference of the Corporation is assuming serious proportions."[51] CBC policy goals would remain hazy as long as the authority and role of each body was not clearly defined, the Glassco commission concluded.

The growing contradictions between the promise and the delivery of the Canadian broadcasting system was also the subject of critique from unofficial quarters in the early 1960s. A leading contributor to the emerging critical perspective was Graham Spry – who, as we saw earlier, had returned to active involvement in policy debate with the revival of the Canadian Broadcasting League in 1958. Spry published three important articles in 1961 alone.

In "The Decline and Fall of Canadian Broadcasting,"[52] Spry argued that the system that Parliament originally intended to put into place had, in fact, not come about. The dominant structures, purposes, and programs of Canadian broadcasting were not those of the public service but had become those of the private broadcasters.

Spry was careful to state that this could not be blamed on the CBC, which had been "out-flanked, surrounded and hemmed in to a subordinate place in the structure of Canadian broadcasting."[53] Nor did he mean to attack the local private stations, for whom he recognized a legitimate role.

The private sector had become the dominant part of Canadian broadcasting. This could be shown statistically; in the number of stations (both radio and television), in time on the air, and in advertiser expenditure, private commercial broadcasting had surpassed the public service. The problem was that private broadcasting – and the commercial segment of the CBC – was "essentially a merchandizing system on the American commercial model and the Canadian audience is a minor part of the American advertising market."[54] Private stations were primarily a means of distributing the syndicated programs produced by the American entertainment industry.

This was the essence of the progressive Canadian nationalist position on broadcasting – not the narrow position of "national interest" as defined by the politicians, but the position that viewed Canadian culture as a bulwark against American domination. Spry recognized that in spite of its subsidiary condition, the CBC had done an excellent job in this regard and had been unfairly maligned by its conservative detractors.

Given the free play of the marketplace, however, the CBC was "the lesser and relatively declining sector of Canadian broadcasting."[55] If indeed the Canadian people wanted an American broadcasting system, Spry asserted, they should decide that deliberately and consciously, and not be blinded by the pressures of special interests and market forces, both Canadian and American.

A few months earlier, Spry had tackled "The Costs of Canadian Broadcasting."[56] Here, he argued that too little attention was paid to the public costs of the private sector. Spry estimated that between 1932 and 1959, individual Canadians invested about $2.5 billion in receiving sets, compared with public and private investment in broadcasting stations of $110 million; in addition, $750 million a year was spent operating sets and stations and purchasing new sets.

Each year, Canadians were spending ten times as much to receive their programs as producers were spending to make them. Canadian viewers and listeners were subsidizing American entertainment and advertising and the situation had become much worse since the introduction of television. In a single phrase that summed up the ponderous findings of the Fowler commission, Spry wrote: "Canadian broadcasting, especially at peak hours, is now a predominantly commercial system used to sell goods, most of them American goods."[57]

Also in 1961, in an article commemorating the twenty-fifth anniversary of the CBC, Spry returned to the nationalist argument, echoing the position expressed in the various statements of the Canadian Broadcasting League. National survival in an age of continentalism was at issue, he said. Canadians had to decide whether their nation was viable in the emerging world; perhaps it was not, but they had to decide: "Here, broadcasting is crucial."[58]

Spry recalled that the CBC – "an unique instrument of Canadian nationhood" – was not an inevitable creation, but a political choice. Parliament chose "a national, public service system," rather than a scattered system of local private stations, or an American-owned network, or a network based on the private sector. It was to be financed not by the taxpayer but by the audience.

But the intended system had turned into its opposite. In spite of continued political endorsement of these principles by royal commissions and parliamentary committees, the independence of the CBC had been whittled down and instead of "a system of national public ownership with supplementary

small local private stations," Canada now had a system of "predominantly
... local private stations, many of high-power, subsidized and supplemented
by the public sector."[59]

Market forces, rather than formal decisions, had been allowed to carry
the day. As a result, the Canadian system was mixed, confused, and ac-
cidental rather than designed. Instead of creating a new private television
network based on commercial criteria, Spry suggested, the key to a renewed
national broadcasting policy would be the national network of stations owned
and operated by the CBC, with reduced dependence on private stations for
the distribution of national CBC programs.

John O'Brien's 1964 thesis on the Canadian Radio League was another
contribution to critical reflection in this period. Although it was not published, it was the first major historical study related to the origins of Canadian
public broadcasting and was well circulated among interested parties.[60] To
O'Brien, the crucial consensus of the 1920s and 1930s was no longer intact.
This consensus had been based on the feeling that Canadians believed a
national broadcasting system was important to the future of Canada, and
they were prepared to pay for it. In view of recent developments, O'Brien
wrote, a new question had to be asked in the early 1960s:

> Shall the Canadian Broadcasting Corporation continue to be the national system
> of Canada, operating as a "public service," with local stations across the country
> providing a necessary but complementary service to the single national system,
> or, shall the Corporation be supplanted by a fully commercial system, operating
> as a "business," with some distinctly Canadian programs being produced and
> distributed to commercial stations by a government broadcasting agency?[61]

O'Brien's analysis indicated "that the second part of the disjunction was
unobtrusively but firmly beginning to assume the ascendancy."[62]

The questioning by official and unofficial critics during this period addressed the shortcomings of the system but still proposed that the ideals of
broadcasting could be realized if the emphasis were only shifted from the
"private" to "public" components. But the problem was far more complex,
as Alan Thomas demonstrated in a remarkable article published in 1960
under the title "Audience, Market and Public – An Evaluation of Canadian
Broadcasting."[63]

Thomas, director of the communications division of the University of
British Columbia's extension department, made one of the first attempts to
draw some theoretical conclusions from the experience of Canadian broadcasting which, he argued, had been dominated by the interaction of three
forces: audience, market, and public. These forces, he said, were in fact
"images," or interchangeable ways of describing the population when discussing broadcasting.

[T]he market carries with it characteristics of freedom of enterprise, impersonality – that is attention to things rather than people ... The Market has manifested itself in the affairs of Canadian broadcasting through the interests of "private" operators ... it is a commonplace in Canadian history that the Market is by nature continental rather than national, and its uncontrolled operations have been seen as hostile to the existence of Canada as a national entity.[64]

The public, on the other hand, is identified with activities of the state and the community. The public "as we know it and as we commonly use the word" derives its character from the influence of book and newspaper. But "there is inevitably real conflict between this notion of the public and the sort of public that seems to be growing up in a world dominated by broadcasting, about which we know very little"[65]:

[I]t is apparent that Canada's major problem has been the difficulty of maintaining a dynamic public opinion in a public whose only common bond was residence within an artificially separated territory; that is to say it has been the problem of creating a genuine public out of a set of separate and geographically determined communities ... The whole history of Canada has been a conflict between the public which is Canadian, and the market which has been predominantly American and anti-cultural in the formal sense of the word.[66]

"The audience" is something yet again. Equated to "the listening public," it tends to be defined as passive. We speak of the public being in favour of Canadian broadcasting while the audience, in the privacy of the home, turns to American channels. The audience is "wholly a creation of broadcasting ... curiously enough, [it] is basically private."[67]

Media address people not as members of a public, but as members of an audience: "The great bulk of the persuasion necessary to any society, previously identified with the dynamic public opinion of the crowd, the rally, the mass meeting, even the reader, is now concentrated on the audience."[68] But, "practices acceptable both to the Market and the Audience seem unacceptable to the Public, in the realm of politics."[69]

Thomas reviewed the history of broadcasting in Canada from this perspective of interacting forces, arguing that the various royal commissions that had examined it had been attempts to restore balance at moments when the activities of the market were outstripping those of the public. The government's handling of their recommendations tended to swing the pendulum back in favour of the market. The audience and the market tend to create a state of equilibrium, Thomas concluded, and "the role of the public ought to be to counteract these forces."[70] Having created an audience, Thomas said, we must now take steps to make it responsible and articulate. This could be done, he proposed, by promoting direct and responsible relationships between producer and audience. Instead of basing broadcasting on the assumption of one-way communication, it should be organized as a two-way passage of opinion and influence.

Programming would become "an explicit relationship" between broadcaster and audience "and the interests of the market could be both served and controlled." Information would move both ways along the national network – "the main line of communication" – "and we would come closer to the notion of direct democracy that has haunted us since the Greeks ... In this we could accept and develop the audience, and bring about the creation of a new and more active public, rather than permitting one to limit and frustrate the potentialities of the other."[71]

Thomas's article showed that in order for broadcasting to recapture the force it had once possessed, it was necessary to restore its "public" values to predominance. This implied looking beyond questions such as the institutional place to be occupied by the CBC in the evolving system, or the redefinition of national objectives in broadcasting. As Thomas suggested at the end of his article, it was necessary to explore new ways of articulating the public dimension of broadcasting.

Such thinking was ahead of its time in the early 1960s and would only attract a following later in the decade, after further exposure of the limitations of the Canadian broadcasting model.

## CULTURAL POLICY AND BROADCASTING REFORM, 1963–65

### *The Liberals' New Agenda*

Federal elections on 8 April 1963 returned the Liberal Party to power, but in spite of their vocal opposition to Conservative policies they really had no intention of dismantling the system the Conservatives had put in place.

Liberal policy on broadcasting had been established at a national party meeting in Ottawa in January 1962. A draft resolution presented to the meeting described "Canadian broadcasting with its combination of public and private stations in a single system" as a unique and valuable achievement. Delegate Pauline Jewett objected to the resolution's failure to specifically endorse the CBC and moved an amendment pledging "determined moral and financial support of the Corporation." The resolution was sent to a subcommittee for formulation. When it returned, the amendment referring to the CBC had been incorporated, but the reference to "a single system" had been dropped and replaced by a pledge that stated: "A new Liberal Government will give full scope for the parallel development of both public and private initiative in broadcasting under an independent and truly non-partisan agency of control."[72] The resolution represented the rising power of private broadcasting interests within the Liberal Party. It was incorporated in the Liberal election platform in 1962 and 1963.

With the election of the Liberals, J.W. Pickersgill became minister responsible for broadcasting (as the new secretary of state). A consummate politician, Pickersgill possessed the qualities to be described by some cabinet colleagues as "the champion of private broadcasting" while appearing in public as a friend of public broadcasting.[73] Pickersgill's first move with respect to broadcasting upon assuming office was to ask the heads of the BBG, the CBC, and the CAB to meet together and identify their points of agreement and disagreement on broadcasting policy. Their report was a year in preparation and in the interim the government held off on any major action.

The new Liberal government also had a political agenda for broadcasting and the 1963 parliamentary session saw hints of the coming storm over the CBC's role in the national question. Créditiste MP Gilles Grégoire alleged the CBC was censoring news about the Quebec separatist movement, to which Pickersgill replied that the CBC was responsible for its own decisions on programming matters.[74] Jean Chrétien introduced a private bill to change the name of the Crown corporation to Radio Canada in both languages. But when the CBC decided to change a Toronto station from English to French, Reid Scott raised the spectre of anti-French, anti-Quebec feeling that had marked the 1930s.[75]

The BBG and the broadcasters continued to fear the implications of cable systems during 1963. Reporting on BBG hearings, a Canadian Press dispatch on 5 June 1963 said public and private broadcasters had agreed "that the possible linkage of community antenna systems into what in effect would be a closed circuit national network would pose a serious threat to them."[76] The question surfaced in Parliament when Douglas Fisher of the New Democratic Party tried to amend the broadcasting act to cover "any system operated for a profit that took out of the air Hertzian waves and rebroadcast them to wired systems in homes."[77]

Pickersgill agreed that the cable systems should not be allowed to do "indirectly what we do not permit broadcasters themselves to do directly," such as bring in entire US stations. But in the absence of any regulatory mechanism, the cable companies were establishing a *fait accompli*. Already, according to Fisher, there were 332 cable systems operating in Canada, reaching 200,000 households. Having arrived unnoticed by public consciousness, technology had outpaced the legislator's capacity to control.

The government wanted community antenna systems to be subject to similar legislation as direct broadcasting but, whereas control of broadcasting depends on control of the "air," – since 1932 a recognized area of federal jurisdiction – control of cable depends on control of the land lines, and some land lines were under provincial jurisdiction. Ottawa was faced with a dilemma: how to integrate cable distribution into the domain of its regulatory apparatus without ceding at least partial jurisdiction to the provinces. Reporting in March 1964, a combined BBG and Department of Transport committee suggested that federal control could be achieved by extending the BBG's specified "objects and purposes" under the broadcasting act to include the commercial broadcasting receiving stations and land stations feeding the cable relay distribution systems. The BBG could then regulate these to ensure that they functioned in a manner "consistent with the public interest in the reception of a varied and comprehensive broadcasting service."[78]

Strangely enough, cable had first emerged to compensate for the lack of adequate broadcasting services in nonmetropolitan markets and, even more curiously, it had arrived under the sign of "community." By the early 1960s cable was recognized as a threat to the political objectives of the public sector and to the economic base of the private sector. The phenomenon soon grew to justify the fears of the established broadcasters as well as those of the regulators and the legislators. In 1968, a new broadcasting act[79] would define cable enterprises as "broadcast receiving undertakings" and place cable regulation under the jurisdiction of the regulatory authority. But meanwhile, cable television developed subject to the sole control of market forces.[80]

Pickersgill's so-called troika committee – Stewart of the BBG, Ouimet of the CBC, and Jamieson of the CAB – could not agree on much. They eventually submitted a short joint report and three lengthy individual reports, tabled in the House 25 May 1964.[81] At any rate, the government had already decided on another course of action before it had their reports in its hands.

On 6 April 1964, the new secretary of state, Maurice Lamontagne, announced in a speech to a CAB convention in Quebec City that the government would soon create a committee of inquiry on broadcasting. Lamontagne also told the private broadcasters "the government should play a greater role in the cultural affairs of our country," for which he was criticized in the House the next day by John Diefenbaker.[82]

The Advisory Committee on Broadcasting was formally created on 25 May, just as the "troika" committee's reports were tabled. The important areas of disagreement among the "troika" justified the new inquiry, which would study the broadcasting act and recommend changes, if any. The advisory committee would also reappraise the CBC in light of the Glassco commission's comments, and study "alternative" means of television services – explicitly excluding cable which had been placed under the responsibility of the minister of transport. The committee would be headed by former royal commission chairman Robert Fowler, and would include two career civil servants, Marc Lalonde and Ernest Steele. Lamontagne said the inquiry would end the existing uncertainties and lead to new legislation.

Meanwhile, on 22 July, Pickersgill (now minister of transport) stated the government's policy objectives with respect to cable. The government had two main concerns: to see that cable installations in Canada did not financially come under foreign ownership, and to ensure that they did not financially harm existing television stations.[83]

In other words, it was going to protect the Canadian cable market for Canadian capital and protect the market of Canadian private broadcasters against competition from cable. There was no mention of "public" or even "national" interest. In order to pay such close attention to the economic implications of the new technology, it had been necessary first to separate responsibility for it from the traditional "cultural" aspects of broadcasting. This would become a pattern in the next few years.

The protective role the government was proposing to play was highlighted in criticism from the free enterprise fundamentalist Liberal back-bencher Ralph Cowan, an MP who had recently called the CBC "a cancer on the body politic of Canada" and now proposed selling its assets to commercial interests.[84] But the government continued to assert belief in the importance of public broadcasting.

At the same time, there were signs of coming controversy over program content. On 26 October, John Diefenbaker called on Lamontagne to investigate an allegation by Quebec politician Bona Arsenault that the CBC's French network had been subject to "left wing communistic infiltration."[85] The same day, Conservative MP Marcel Lambert lambasted the approach of the new CBC public affairs program "This Hour Has Seven Days." Social Credit MP H.A. Olson charged that the CBC was irresponsibly spotlighting divisions between English and French Canadians by attracting attention to extremist viewpoints. The NDP's Stanley Knowles, meanwhile, congratulated the CBC for being the subject of controversy; its challenging programs were exposing us to new ideas, he said.[86]

The controversies nurtured conservative arguments that the public broadcasting service had outlived its usefulness. This position was forcefully argued by Alberta MP Hugh M. Horner, who said that a "Canadian" broadcasting system need not necessarily be a "public" one, and suggested that private industry could also provide a "Canadian" system. He proposed to sell all but the technical infrastructure of the CBC and leave programming and production to the private sector.[87] This type of argument would recur through the 1980s, but in the 1960s conventional wisdom, and government policy, still favoured major state involvement.

On 13 November 1964, Secretary of State Lamontagne made a major statement on the need for a dynamic federal cultural policy which would coordinate Canada's national cultural agencies (CBC, BBG, National Film Board, National Museum, National Gallery, National Library, and Public Archives). Canadian cultural life was anaemic, he said, and required the involvement of the state even more than did the economy: "Our poorness, and, perhaps, even more, our cultural isolation largely account for the present tension in Canada which, in many cases, is due to frustration on the part of those who are forced to live on the fringe of our society ... A cultural policy for Canada requires public cultural agencies in certain sectors where exclusive reliance on private initiative is undesirable and which fall within federal jurisdiction."[88]

Lamontagne announced that the Cabinet had established a committee on cultural matters and, for the first time, all federal cultural agencies were to be placed under one minister. Parliament would soon be asked to create a standing committee on cultural matters as well. Although he did not explicitly name the culturally rooted nationalist agitation in Quebec that had been challenging Ottawa during the previous year or so, the connection was unmistakable. Federal cultural policy was to serve a strategic political purpose in the coming struggle for Quebec.

The government intended that the leading role in this struggle be played by the CBC: "The CBC is one of Canada's most vital and essential institutions, at this crucial moment of our history. The CBC must become a living and daily testimony of the Canadian identity, a faithful reflection of our two main cultures and a powerful element of understanding, moderation and unity in our country. If it performs these national tasks with efficiency, its occasional mistakes will be easily forgiven; if it fails in that mission, its other achievements will not compensate for that failure."[89]

This was the first time since the war that the CBC's political vocation had been so sharply evoked. It was the first time the CBC's "mission" with regard to Canada's cultural and constitutional crisis was so clearly spelled out. The entire structure of Canadian broadcasting was under question. The relationship of its "public" and "private" elements was confused and increasingly troublesome, and the place of "the public" had not been widely considered in many years. However, there was a precise role to be played by a national, state-supported broadcaster, independent in its day-to-day operations but systematically guided by high government policy.

Lamontagne's speech also indicated another aspect of the cultural struggle of the 1960s: the demand for a new type of social relations. Lamontagne referred to the government's "awareness of the greater need in our complex and troubled society for greater cultural and spiritual efforts," and promised "broad popular participation" in its cultural programs.[90]

By the end of 1964, the federal government was determined to use cultural policy as a weapon to meet rising social demands. But the government's vision of the CBC saving the country did not correspond to the corporate reality of what Douglas Fisher described as "a middle-aged and rather frumpy institution which has lost a great deal of its zest."[91] By 1964, the public broadcaster's position in the overall system had been badly eroded by concessions to the private sector and bickering with the regulatory agency; its management was defensive and conservative as a result of being continuously under political attack, and, significantly, the majority of Canadians were using other broadcasting sources most of the time. It was hoped that these problems would be resolved by the wisdom of the secretary of state's special advisory committee on broadcasting.

## The Fowler Committee

The Fowler committee, it must be recalled, was not an independent inquiry like a royal commission, but an advisory committee set up by the minister. The committee never held public sessions (prompting Stanley Knowles to declare at one point that it was "a private advisory committee"[92]). However, it received briefs from fifty-five groups and individuals, in addition to submissions from the CBC and CTV networks.[93]

The committee submitted its report 1 September 1965, shortly before the federal election. The opening words indicated its tone and general attitude: "The only thing that really matters in broadcasting is programme content; all the rest is housekeeping."[94] However, most of the committee's detailed attention was paid to housekeeping aspects.

The report emphasized the crucial role of "public policy," which it characterized this way: "The State is inescapably involved in the creation of a broadcasting system ... The need for public control of the broadcasting system is, we believe, beyond question. But we must define *what* it is that is to be controlled, and *why* the control must be exercised, before the form and method of public supervision can be determined."[95]

It made a unique and important attempt to resituate the meaning of the terms "public" and "private" with respect to different aspects of the Canadian broadcasting system:

> The Canadian broadcasting system today has two main sectors – the publicly owned and supported Canadian Broadcasting Corporation, and the many private radio and television stations. The latter are "private" only in the sense that station facilities are owned by individuals or companies which operate them for profit. They are "public" in the sense that they receive the right to use public assets, are subject to public control, and have the responsibility to perform a public service. They are inextricably involved in the Canadian broadcasting system, dependent on public grants for their franchises to operate, and responsive to public direction for their performance in the use of public assets.[96]

By attributing a "public" function to the "private" stations, the Fowler committee laid the basis for reasserting that, in spite of the transformed set of ownership and regulatory relationships, Canadian broadcasting was still a single system.

Although in 1963 the total revenue of private broadcasting actually surpassed the CBC's ($112 million versus $106 million), the committee pointed out that the public sector comprised "an integrated organization with many branches and different activities subject to common direction," while the private sector had "no cohesion or unity" but consisted of independent units serving local communities. Consequently, it said, the public agency, the CBC, had "the primary responsibility and must be paramount in creating and maintaining a broadcasting system that is distinctively Canadian ... in cases of fundamental conflict between the public and private sectors the interests of the CBC must prevail ... the CBC is the *essential* element of the Canadian broadcasting system and the most important single instrument available for the development and maintenance of the unity of Canada."[97]

The committee thus reintroduced the idea of CBC supremacy which had been omitted from the legislation of 1958 and denied by the practice of the Board of Broadcast Governors. In doing so it astutely framed its argument in a combination of terms similar to those used to justify the system in the first place in the 1930s. It attributed both a "social" and a "national" purpose to public broadcasting, invoking the traditional assumption that the relationship between the two was an immutable one.

The Fowler committee proposed that the government issue a comprehensive statement of policy and create a new regulatory authority responsible for "the supervision, control, and direction of all broadcasting in Canada." Both public and private radio and television programming were lacking in balance, variety, and excellence. "Canadian content" specifications were insufficient to guarantee that Canadian broadcasting provide a "true image of Canadian life." For example, "the image of French-speaking Canada as presented to English-speaking Canada by the CBC, and vice versa, is at the present time totally inadequate."[98]

The relationship between the agencies responsible for broadcasting and Parliament had to be clarified, the committee said. The endless parliamentary questions regarding administrative and program details, and the inevitable replies that the government did not control broadcasting, were not only a waste of time and energy but also "a remarkably inefficient way to control a broadcasting system."[99] An unhappy side effect was that attention was paid exclusively to the CBC, rather than the whole system, because the CBC received parliamentary money. Clearly shifting the emphasis from where the BBG had placed it, the committee said: "We regard the public control of the privately owned broadcasters and that of the publicly owned agency as equally important."[100]

The implication was that the entire *system* was a public one, made up of a publicly financed sector and a commercial sector. The broadcasting system was marked by a "single national purpose," even if its elements were not identical. Where the royal commission of 1957 had stated the purpose of broadcasting as "to inform, enlighten, entertain and sell goods," this committee said it was "to inform, enlighten and entertain the Canadian people and promote their national unity."[101]

The committee noted that the regulatory formula proposed by the royal commission of 1957 had not been implemented and that the BBG had proven to be a weak and discordant regulator. It had not maintained an adequate dialogue "between the broadcasting system and the people it seeks to serve."[102] The agency that it now proposed should develop "a coordinated policy" and maintain a "constant flow of comment" with "interested groups" and "the public."

The committee said Parliament must define goals for the entire system; that is, it must specify both the CBC mandate and the public responsibilities of the private broadcasters. It should then delegate responsibility to public supervisory and administrative agencies and leave them free to act, subject to procedures of goal evaluation and accountability. The agencies' annual reports should go to a standing committee of Parliament; neither the government nor Parliament should be involved in "the details of administration, finance, or programming."[103]

The CBC, in particular, must have a clear mandate: "If it is to perform its function adequately and acceptably, it must be told what it is expected to do ... it should not be for the CBC to prescribe its own mandate."[104] The mandate *should* be prescribed by legislation and not be subject to the day-to-day scrutiny of members of Parliament.

The committee said CBC headquarters had become physically and emotionally inaccessible and recommended the head office be moved from Ottawa to Montreal. At present, it said, the CBC lacked cohesion, unity, and *esprit de corps*. Nevertheless, the committee awarded the CBC high marks for good programs. It said the CBC should continue to seek commercial sponsorship for programs as a way of keeping in touch with a mass audience but, as the royal commission had done in 1957, it insisted upon the need for a new basis for financing the public sector that allowed for forward planning. It recommended a statutory grant of twenty-five dollars per television household for the CBC.

Turning to the private sector, the committee noted that the complicated and financially troubled relationship between the CTV network and its member stations had turned into an "unsavory feud between private interests." It suggested that CTV be reconstituted "as a non-profit trust operating in the public interest."[105] Eventually, CTV was reorganized as a cooperative belonging to its affiliates, and the public was at least spared the intercorporate blood-letting between competing interests. But the private stations' network was never made to serve a public function.

The committee indicated an awareness that issues on the horizon would complicate the broadcasting picture in coming years: the cost of colour television (which would be introduced for Expo '67), the need to resolve the question of cable regulation, and the use of multipurpose satellites for broadcasting and nonbroadcasting communication activities. It also raised the issue of "educational broadcasting," in which a number of provincial governments had already expressed interest, and recalled that federal policy was based on C.D. Howe's 1946 statement to the effect that broadcasting was solely a federal function and no provincial agency would be awarded a licence. The broadcasting act did not address the subject, but the chairman of the BBG had reconfirmed the policy in 1962. The Fowler committee felt that while it may be sound not to grant a licence to a provincial government, educational broadcasting licences should be granted to educational institutions or corporations, even those owned by provincial governments, as long as they were independent of direct government control.

The committee thus resurrected an idea that had been dormant for a very long time: that somewhere between the "public" and "private" broadcasting models that had grown up in Canada, there was room for other forms that were neither national nor commercial.

The report of the 1965 advisory committee on broadcasting was a liberal and reflective document that legitimated several unorthodox notions about broadcasting at the same time as it underscored the overriding "national purpose" of state interest in the field. It was the starting point of three years of extensive debate which would largely put aside the committee's fresh suggestions, while enshrining the national purpose in legislation. During those three years, most of the problems indicated by the Fowler committee would deteriorate further, some of them irreversibly.

### PUBLIC BROADCASTING, AUTHORITY, AND NATIONAL CRISIS, 1966

Early in 1966, the new Parliament created a Standing Committee on Broadcasting, Films and Assistance to the Arts. Its first chairman was Gérard Pelletier.

Two days before the committee was to meet to discuss the annual CBC budget estimates, the opposition provoked an emergency debate in the House of Commons over what John Diefenbaker termed a new "crisis of uncertainty and chaos in the affairs of the Canadian Broadcasting Corporation."[106]

The crisis concerned a dispute between CBC English network management and the producers of the high-profile public affairs television program "This

Hour Has Seven Days", which had led to the recent dismissal of the program's co-hosts, Patrick Watson and Laurier LaPierre.

The issue was referred to the standing committee which met 21 April. Appearing first, the new secretary of state Judy LaMarsh recalled the recent Fowler committee's reference to "smouldering dissatisfaction" within the CBC. Now, an apparent power struggle had struck a popular program which had recently registered the highest "enjoyment index" of any program in CBC television history.[107] LaMarsh implied the present trouble was symptomatic of something more serious: "Perhaps the problem is inherent in the nature of public broadcasting."[108]

The committee's first witness was "Seven Days" producer and co-host Patrick Watson. He said he had been told by a CBC vice-president that he had a chip on his shoulder, was antimanagement, disloyal, against the corporation, and had a bad attitude towards Canada. He said he had been told: "We are afraid that you are not with us, and I do not want anyone in the CBC who is not with us," and "I do not know whether you believe in Canada or not; you have got to believe in Canada if you are going to take on such a project." The program's other regular host, Laurier LaPierre, was also said to be "not with us," and was furthermore said to "wear his feelings on his sleeve."[109]

Watson said CBC management seemed to consider public affairs programming in general as "trouble making," and was concerned to do away with "trouble makers." It was not a question of political interference, the CBC simply did not want to do controversial programming. This had been a problem since "Seven Days" first went on the air in the fall of 1964. One of the first items it had tried to program concerned Queen Elizabeth's visit to Quebec in October 1964. Regrettably, Watson said, the program had submitted to a directive ordering that there be no programming on this subject.[110]

The "Seven Days" unit had become bolder with time and experience, and had made management increasingly nervous with controversial programs that attracted criticism. Now, Watson said, "their intention is not to allow to appear on the program the things that have distressed them in the past."[111]

Watson's conception of the social and national purpose of Canadian public broadcasting turned the orthodox view neatly on its head while maintaining the basic logic of its traditional *raison d'être*. Before the parliamentary committee, he demonstrated a sophisticated feel for the power of television as a modern means of communication:

Yes, one aspect of our philosophy of public broadcasting ... is that it seems to us there is a future in having a very large number of the people of this country doing the same thing at the same time; that is, sharing an experience which then leads them, in fact, to communicate with each other. This is really quite important, in my concept of proper broadcasting; that it must be used to unite the country in that sense, not to propagandize, not to shout "Hurrah, it is a great country and we are all in it together," but rather to meet the people where they are with ideas which they can think about and use because they are moved by sharing their experiences on television. Let them go out and say to their neighbour "What is that all about?" or "I hated that ...," and in this way a dialogue will ensue, a conversation which they know is being shared across the country.[112]

The committee also heard Laurier LaPierre respond to the charge of subjectivity: "I do not think the top management can expect a citizen, whoever he may be, not to take sides in a public debate on an issue."[113] To LaPierre, "Seven Days" was "a new method of communication," mixing entertainment and public affairs in an attempt "to create a dialogue in the country between persons on important issues."[114] But in the context of the crisis of national unity, no one seemed to know what they wanted the CBC to do. In an exchange with MP David MacDonald that included some interesting insight into national unity, communication, and the CBC, LaPierre explained what he had been trying to do:

I have the feeling, sir, that we are living in 1966 and we have been engrossed in an immense national monologue. I felt that perhaps the time had come to change the monologue into a dialogue. Travelling across the country, I felt that the ignorance of the English-speaking Canadians about my province was immensely disturbing, and it was only matched by the ignorance of the French-Canadian towards English-speaking Canada. I was disturbed by that. I came to the conclusion that the means par excellence to bring about a dialogue, to bring about a confrontation, to bring about a meaningful exchange of ideas, opinions and impressions, was the CBC ...

Mr. MacDonald: Surely the assumption of the function of television, since the late '40s, was that it has been primarily a passive medium, that it is, in a way, a monologue. Are you saying that television is altogether different?

Mr. LaPierre: I would suggest "Seven Days" has demonstrated that perhaps it is completely different from that.[115]

While their theorizing about the functions of television may have appeared naïve at the dawning of the age of McLuhan, Watson and LaPierre were insisting on the right to use television as a medium of social exchange and not merely for political transmission. In this respect, they were in the tradition of Spry, Corbett, and the pioneers of the CBC "Forums." LaPierre added to the tradition a self-management impulse. In order for the CBC to exercise its public trust fully, he said, "the structure must be such that authority not only flows from above but that dialogue flows up from below."[116]

Thus it was suggested that television producers should, within the limits of policy, be free of constraints from management, just as the CBC as an institution demanded to be free of constraints imposed by government.

The parliamentary committee also heard spokesmen for CBC management. The head of English network broadcasting, vice-president and general manager H.G. Walker, told it the CBC could not have "constant challenges to basic ethics, standards, policies and all of the old-fashioned things like respect for personal privacy, good taste and integrity, and so on."[117] To CBC president Alphonse Ouimet, the issue was this: "Should the Corporation try to lead, form or direct ... public opinion or should it preserve a studious neutrality, presenting various issues as completely as possible and leaving the public to choose? It has always been the CBC policy to adopt the course of freedom of choice for the public."[118]

Of course, the question of freedom of choice was an ambiguous one. The choice of switching on or switching off to public affairs programs also had to be considered. "Seven Days" creator and executive producer Douglas Leiterman told the committee: "It was our hope that this program could bring matters of substance in public affairs to people who have never watched other kinds of public affairs programs."[119] The fact that the public, as audience, watched "Seven Days" in unprecedented numbers for a public affairs program must have indicated a choice for provocative programming over what the CBC president called "neutrality."

Aside from this question, which dealt with the broadcaster's relationship to its audience, there was also an internal issue. Walker said "Seven Days" was like "a corporation within the corporation." Ouimet referred to the "continuing challenge to management authority ... unwillingness of 'Seven Days' to function within the framework of corporate policy and operating conditions ... open defiance ... precedent for the challenge to corporate authority which we are now witnessing."[120]

"Seven Days" was thus the cutting edge of opposing conceptions of the public broadcaster's role *vis-à-vis* the public, and also the tip of the iceberg in relations between CBC management and creative staff. A similar situation existed, it turned out, in French network production as well.

The committee heard Claude Désorcy, vice-president of the French network producers' association, describe the divorce between management policy and production in public affairs as "a real malaise" based on differing interpretations of the idea of objectivity.[121] Désorcy pointed out that the French-language producers' collective agreement – the legacy of their 1959 strike – provided a grievance procedure in cases similar to that of "Seven Days"; there had been ten such grievances, he said. Not being unionized, the English-language producers had no such recourse, however. Désorcy drew an ominous link: "There is a parallel, a complete parallel between the 1959 situation and that which prevails at the present time."[122]

The general supervisor of adult education and public affairs for the French network, Marc Thibault, then indicated the scope of the problem. In a bold statement entitled "Public Affairs at the CBC," Thibault directly contradicted the president of the corporation, declaring that the role of broadcasting was to lead public opinion, as the CBC had demonstrated when it "decided to play its part as a responsible public broadcaster and contributed powerfully in bringing Quebec out of its shell" in the 1950s. Even if it did not take sides in controversial questions, the CBC did take sides in choosing which controversial questions to present: "The CBC by its very nature as a public enterprise, powerfully contributes to the shaping and influencing of public opinion, to instigate and promote far-reaching social and political changes in our milieu."[123]

The nonconformism of "Seven Days," Thibault said, was no different from the opinion leading of the Lévesques, Laurendeaus and Pelletiers in the prelude to the Quiet Revolution. There was a crisis in public affairs at the CBC, Thibault said, because of excessive "interventionist supervision" by top management.

The impasse over the conception of public affairs broadcasting and its effect on the flow of authority within the CBC was interesting in itself, but it took place in a climate of approaching crisis for the political system that the Canadian Broadcasting Corporation had been created to serve. It was thus more than a question of principle or power. As the underlying context of the affair emerged, it became clear that, once again as at every flashpoint in the history of Canadian public broadcasting, the major question was the role of the public broadcaster in the preservation of national unity.

Watson's and LaPierre's accounts of the allegations against them had indicated management nervousness about irreverent approaches to the question of Canadian nationhood. Now, questioning of Désorcy and especially Thibault by Liberal committee members from Quebec laid clear the politicians' interest in the affair. Liberal MP Marcel Prud'homme asked Désorcy whether the CBC's French network had not placed too much emphasis on the separatist movement. Désorcy replied that it had not and that, insofar as the public was interested in the subject, it had to be covered. Responding to a similar line of questioning, Thibault later said: "In my opinion, thinking about the promotion of national unity is a bad way to tackle the problems of this country. I don't believe that the CBC has the task of promoting national unity. The CBC is a public service with the task of providing a national broadcasting service to reveal the problems that exist in the whole of this country as much on the English side as on the French."[124]

Thibault was correct in stating that the CBC's only responsibility was to provide a "national broadcasting service." In 1966, the CBC's duty with respect to "national unity" was, indeed, a matter of interpretation. With the national question prominently on the country's political agenda, a serious rift had appeared between CBC top and middle management as to how to approach the question. The politicians quickly recognized the problem, which was, as Jean-Pierre Goyer put it, that the Broadcasting Act of 1958 contained "no mention of ideology or ideological orientation." Goyer candidly stated that he was troubled by Thibault's assertion that the "CBC should not be the promoter ... should not, say, create a climate of national unity." Goyer continued: "I would say that you do not have this mandate as such. But, if, say, Parliament took action – and I wonder to what extent this would be intervention in the affairs of the CBC since, while one has a country, one must believe in it – if Parliament had a statute stating that the CBC should forward the aim of national unity, would this run counter to the professional plan that you outline?"[125] Thibault took this as a hypothetical question and replied that this was for the legislator to decide.

It should be noted that middle management's position was not based on advocacy but, on the contrary, on an argument for a balanced view of the different sides to the national question rather than the one-sided flag-waving that top management felt was its duty and certain politicians felt was in their interest. Thibault explained that by doing programs that dealt with Canada's major problems, "we would achieve infinitely more for the true promotion of national unity than by following what is generally expected from the CBC in this matter."[126]

Thibault told the committee of the soul-searching that went on in Montreal over the appearance of "separatists" on the air: "We received direct and indirect hints ... that there are too many separatists taking part in our programs ... [but we concluded] that over a period of three years the expression of separatist ideas over our air waves has not been abusive ... I must say that each time we hired or invited a separatist, there was nearly always talk about it ... discussions such as these have a way of conditioning an entire personnel because with each subsequent invitation, which makes you rather queasy, you say to yourself 'the Head Office will be on our backs again'."[127]

But Marcel Prud'homme indicated the political inadequacy of this position when he asked: "According to you what are the CBC's goals? If its aim is simply to make television and radio broadcasts, do you think its existence is justified? ... There must surely be some grounds for the CBC's existence."[128]

Thibault's reply to this showed that his position was based on a different conception of public affairs and was not a political attitude with respect to the national question. Openness in public affairs, he appeared to say, could even serve the political goal of the Quebec Liberals: "The CBC's existence is justified for the excellent reason that it will keep the country together."[129]

Meanwhile, senior management's position on national unity was articulated by the vice-president and general manager of French network broadcasting, Marcel Ouimet. Denying the malaise indicated by Désorcy and

Thibault, he said there had been no orders from CBC headquarters as to how to deal with the national question. There were no written guidelines, although the subject had been discussed in internal memos and communications.

Contrary to Marc Thibault, Marcel Ouimet agreed with the government's view, but felt the CBC was well enough equipped to handle the problem. Traditionally, senior management had protected the CBC's autonomy by anticipating the politicians' will in this way. But the politicians now felt the country itself was at stake, and the crisis in authority within the CBC led them to believe that the good will of CBC senior officials was insufficient to save it.

Jean-Pierre Goyer expressed most clearly the view that the government would eventually adopt: "I find it unacceptable that persons working within the CBC, in public affairs, should make public statements favouring separatism and criticize the CBC, which frequently fosters the idea of national unity. I wonder whether the CBC should not, and whether we, Parliament, should not enact legislation to help the CBC to achieve this end." [130]

On 24 May, CBC president J. Alphonse Ouimet issued a statement maintaining the removal of Watson and LaPierre from "This Hour Has Seven Days" and evaluating its policy implications:

> It has been the considered view of management ... that Mr. LaPierre was unable to accept the principle that the CBC has no point of view on controversial matters ... [while] the decision to remove [Watson] as a host was directly related to the problem of bringing the whole Seven Days unit under the necessary degree of control ...
>
> The question of what position the CBC should take on the question of on-air "editorializing" is, by all odds, the most important that has been raised before this Committee. It is the most important in its implications for the future role of the CBC in relation to the whole process of political and social change in Canada. It is absolutely fundamental since it concerns the basic posture of the CBC in relation to the Canadian people. [131]

The public affairs people, by proposing such a departure from traditional CBC policy, had altered "the social contract between the broadcaster and his audience in the area of information and opinion," Ouimet said. The issue, he added, was who is to make editorial policy, the board of directors and management or the public affairs producers and supervisors?

Ouimet thus confused the question of authority with the substance of the policy in question. He was saying, in effect, "We have the right to make policy, they don't"; and "Our policy is correct, theirs isn't." Significantly, the implications of these two universal issues – the flow of authority and the function of public affairs broadcasting – were linked to the uniquely

Canadian issue, the role of the public broadcaster in maintaining national unity. In 1966, for the first time since R.B. Bennett first articulated the national purpose of the system, that purpose was seriously challenged from within the Canadian Broadcasting Corporation.

CBC management's conception of broadcasting in the public interest was based on the legitimacy of the dominant values of the surrounding society. But in the mid-1960s, values were in flux and the object of intense social and political struggle. The "Seven Days" affair and the debate over Quebec news coverage not only uncovered the flaws in the CBC's corporate interpretation of broadcasting in the public interest, it also undermined the legitimacy of the hierarchical administrative institution that Canadian public broadcasting had become.[132]

## FROM "PUBLIC" TO "STATE" BROADCASTING, 1966–68

### The White Paper on Broadcasting

The government was not happy with the handling of the "Seven Days" controversy. An independent inquiry ordered by Prime Minister Pearson suggested that CBC management had not followed "due process." The CBC board of directors acknowledged the criticism but said there were "cogent reasons" which justified the action nonetheless.

On 29 June 1966, the parliamentary committee tabled its report. It studiously avoided taking a position on the controversial questions that had been aired at its hearings and declined to pronounce on the dispute. The inconclusive committee report was quickly eclipsed by the tabling on 4 July of the government's White Paper on Broadcasting.[133] The white paper clearly stated the purpose of Canadian broadcasting policy: "The determination to develop and maintain a national system of radio and television broadcasting in Canada is an essential part of the continuing resolve for Canadian identity and Canadian unity."[134]

It then reiterated the traditional principles of Canadian broadcasting: that television channels and radio frequencies were public property; that the system must include public and private elements; and that, where necessary, the public element must predominate. The system must be regarded "as a single system, which should be regulated and controlled by a single independent authority."[135]

The white paper made several proposals regarding the public function of the system. Following the recommendations of the Fowler committee, it said there should be "minimum standards of public service programming" for all broadcasters, public or private. The regulatory authority should prevent any change in ownership "that is not in the public interest," and would be asked to consider creating regional broadcasting councils "to advise upon representations made by the general public with regard to programming."[136]

The white paper also showed that the government was ready to venture into new territory. In addition to calling for "collective control" by the people of Canada over "the new technologies of electronic communication,"[137] it called for "a new federal organization licensed to operate public service broadcasting facilities" for the purpose of providing educational broadcasting services to the provinces, and said that "community antenna television systems shall be treated as components of the national broadcasting system."[138] It also called for restructuring the CBC and implementing the Fowler recommendation of five-year financing.

But the white paper differed from the Fowler committee report on one important question which gave an advantage to the private sector. Fowler had proposed returning to the single system and single board concept first proposed by the royal commission of 1957. This proposal had the dubious merit of uniting the CBC and the private broadcasters against it, although it was supported by the public interest groups who supported the Canadian Broadcasting League. The white paper basically accepted the logic and rhetoric of the CBC's proposals for two boards, which conveniently dovetailed with Liberal Party policy on "parallel development" of the private and public components of the system. But it did not go as far as Alphonse Ouimet in proposing recognition of a "dual system." The regulatory mechanism it suggested was essentially the status quo.

Why did the Cabinet reject this key recommendation which would have concretely emphasized the predominantly public nature of the system? According to one observer, the answer is tied to the rise in the Liberal Party of Don Jamieson, who had been president of the Canadian Association of Broadcasters and one of the members of J.W. Pickersgill's "troika." Not only a private broadcaster but also a friend of Pickersgill, Don Jamieson was elected to Parliament in 1966 and soon replaced Robert Fowler as the Liberals' resident expert on broadcasting. The white paper "bore considerable resemblance to Jamieson's troika report."[139]

The often hair-splitting semantic debate surrounding broadcasting policy at this time characterized the important gap that had set in between officially articulated conceptions about the Canadian broadcasting system and the reality of the system. The definition of the public dimension of the system continued to be at the centre of that gap. For the rest of the 1960s the Liberal government would continue, increasingly, to reiterate the classical policy discourse of Canadian broadcasting since 1932, while the actual facts of the system would be allowed to develop in the opposite direction.

The parliamentary committee's consideration of the White Paper on Broadcasting became, in 1967, another occasion for a major airing of views and attitudes on Canadian broadcasting. The committee's first witness was Alphonse Ouimet (who had by now announced that he would step down when the new legislation came into effect).

Ouimet said the CBC agreed with the principles expressed in the white paper, but he made a stunning assessment of its claim that Canadian broadcasting was still "a single system." The single system concept had served Canada well, he said, but: "Growth has brought about two separate and highly self-sufficient operating systems – a public system and a private system ... the single system concept, which was an objective in the early days, has now been replaced in practice by two systems."[140]

Ouimet was simply saying that reality no longer corresponded to the cherished "single system" concept: "We therefore recommend recognition, acceptance and strengthening of the two-system concept within the total structure as the new foundation for the country's broadcasting policy."[141]

It was interesting that it took the president of the CBC to point out how the economic lassitude of successive governments had whittled away one of the basic precepts of Canadian broadcasting. Reality notwithstanding, the principle would not die easily, especially now that the government was determined to restore broadcasting's "national" vocation. Ouimet also pointed to a new complication that the white paper had seen as well, without recognizing its magnitude. Not only were the public and private sectors of Canadian broadcasting already in fact separate systems, but there were other distinct systems already present or soon to arrive in the environment: educational broadcasting, satellite broadcasting, and community antenna. The basic implication of Ouimet's testimony was that the Canadian way of thinking about broadcasting would have to be revised to take this into account.

The Canadian Broadcasting League, seeking "to represent the consumers' interest in broadcasting in Canada" and supported by twenty-one organizations, appeared before the committee on 17 January 1967.[142] The League expressed enthusiastic approval of the white paper, noting the predominance it gave to the "public" element.

One of the things the league read into the white paper was a "principle of independence from political control or supervision in program content." Evidently in light of the recent problems in CBC public affairs, the league promoted the notion that the regulator should be the custodian of the public interest in broadcasting. The league reasserted the "single system" view and argued that the unity of the system could be maintained by strong regulatory authority over both the CBC and the private broadcasters. It thus defended, as A.F. Laidlaw of the Co-operative Union of Canada put it, "the principle of the public sector of broadcasting and the system which we describe as the single system," and not the CBC as such.[143]

The public interest viewpoint was also presented by the Canadian Association for Adult Education, whose director was now Alan Thomas (author of the 1960 article discussed above). The CAAE introduced the idea of "public participation" to the debate, calling for a way "for the citizens of Canada to participate more intelligently, more frequently and more directly in broadcasting affairs."[144] Its brief ridiculed the existing situation, where public input took the sole form of parliamentary interventions, and supported the white paper's proposal to create regional broadcasting councils under the aegis of the regulatory authority. But in addition, the CAAE said, there should be an institutionally detached public body whose function was "comment, criticism and suggestion," directed not only towards the CBC but to all of broadcasting.

The committee also heard from the cable industry lobby, the National Community Antenna Television Association of Canada, which argued that "reception is not transmission, and in the public interest, each must be considered as separate from the other." Using a line of reasoning reminiscent of the CAB of the 1940s and 1950s, the cable companies held that it was "a dangerous concentration of authority to permit the same agency which controls transmission (broadcasting) also to control that which may be received."[145]

The cable group's argument was simultaneously based on free enterprise ideology and the market conception of the public: "The proposed regulation of CATV runs contrary to certain fundamental aspects of Canadian life ... Canada's economy has grown and flourished through competitive free enterprise. CATV is a product of our free enterprise system. It would be doing an injustice to the Canadian public to restrict the healthy growth of this public service industry."[146] At any rate, it pointed out, coming technological developments, like home video recorders and direct broadcast reception from satellites, would be impossible to regulate, so why regulate cable?

The debate over cable not only resurrected old controversies over the rights and privileges of "public" versus "private" systems of ownership, it also highlighted Alphonse Ouimet's analysis of the need to look differently at the entire question of broadcasting. Returning before the committee on 7 February 1967, Ouimet supported the white paper recommendation to integrate cable into the system, and explained that "from a purely technical standpoint, in years to come it may be very difficult to distinguish between broadcasting and other forms of communication to the public ... we simply must have a broader definition of the kind of enterprise we are engaged in."[147]

The committee's last witness was the government, represented by the secretary of state Judy LaMarsh. She reiterated the government's insistence that the structure and regulation of Canadian broadcasting be based on the premise of "a single national system made up of two components, the public and the private." [148] The government was aware of the CBC's opposition, had duly considered the corporation's views, and had rejected them.

The CBC had appeared prepared to accept the marginal, but autonomous, role that the previous Conservative government had intended for it. But the Liberal government needed the CBC, and a unified system, to fulfil its vision of Canada. The government position was based on an awareness of the shrinking position of the CBC in the broadcasting spectrum and the difficulty of integrating the private broadcasters into the national policy. It was gambling that a strongly regulated "single system" could realize broadcasting's national purpose. LaMarsh said:

[W]e have to remember that anyone who gets a licence, whether public or private, is using, in a sense, a public utility. It is not and cannot be just a money-making proposition ... up until now we have been quite prepared to let the private system feed whatever junk it wants to us. We sort of sit down in front of a television set and get mesmerized and never turn it off ... it seems to me incontrovertible that the potentially most powerful force to hold this country together or to tear it apart is in the communications field, particularly in television. [149]

The parliamentary committee report on the White Paper on Broadcasting, tabled 21 March 1967, stated: "In future, broadcasting may well be regarded as the central nervous system of Canadian nationhood." It reaffirmed the public nature of the air and the responsibility of all licensees to serve the public interest; it recalled that it was Parliament's role "to define the public interest" and "enunciate the national policy," and urged "a clear legislative declaration of the pre-eminence of the public sector" (omitted from the 1958 act), as well as recognition of the CBC as "the prime instrument of national policy in broadcasting." [150]

## The Broadcasting Act, 1968

On 17 October 1967, Judy LaMarsh introduced legislation to "establish a statutory policy for broadcasting in Canada and to assign the responsibility for interpretation and implementation of that policy to an independent public authority." [151] Speaking on second reading, she pointed out the bill's major innovation: "[It] includes, for the first time, a mandate for the national broadcasting service operated by the CBC ... The mandate set out is more than a preamble; it is an integral part of the measure, expressing the intentions of Parliament, and it will have all the force of law. Thus, the whole rest of the bill must be considered in the context of this declaration of policy." [152]

The bill sought to correct the weaknesses of the 1958 legislation: thus, "the total delegation of authority over programming," it was hoped, would end Parliament's regular involvement in broadcasting affairs; it specified the priority for the needs of the "national broadcasting service" over those of the private broadcasters; it established a firm relationship between Parliament, the CBC, and a new regulatory authority, the Canadian Radio-Television Commission (CRTC).

Essentially, the bill reaffirmed the special place of public broadcasting in the Canadian system and specified its role. The key subclause of the proposed CBC mandate, Section 2(g)iv, said that "the national broadcasting service should ... contribute to the development of national unity and provide for a continuing expression of Canadian identity."[153] This obligation, said the minister, was "perhaps the most important feature of the CBC's mandate in the new bill."[154]

It would be the CBC's responsibility to see that this obligation was carried out. Instead of complaining out of frustration, members of Parliament would have a precise statute to invoke in making demands of the public broadcaster. But, outside the government, the vagueness of the clause caused concern. On the one hand, it appeared to resolve the question of the CBC's responsibility to promote national unity; but on the other hand, it offered no clues as to what national unity meant, nor what constituted contribution to its development.

Debate in Parliament immediately focused on this contradiction. NDP critic R.W. Prittie expressed a fear: "I would not want to see a witch-hunt started because there is something in a bill saying that national unity must be promoted which would enable the government to go to anyone who was not doing exactly what was wanted and say: You are not promoting national unity; you are a separatist and therefore you are out. There is a possible danger there."[155]

The way in which the statute would be applied was indicated by Liberal MP John Munro, then a parliamentary secretary: "From now on we must hold management responsible for all phases of CBC operation ... when we criticize the French network of the corporation, Radio-Canada, for its alleged attitude in allowing too many with separatist viewpoints to express their opinions over its network, we are obviously holding management responsible."[156]

The government would no longer rely on the good will or natural affinity of CBC management. The statute would be used to assure that management maintained order over recalcitrant junior personnel. Management would henceforth enjoy the use of a powerful omnibus weapon for ideological and political control.

After second reading, the bill was referred to the parliamentary committee, where R.W. Prittie pursued the argument he had begun in the House: "National unity can, perhaps, descend to becoming national interest, and who determines what is national unity and what is national interest? I do not yet know the answer to this, but who is going to define national unity or national interest? I am rather afraid that if this is in the legislation people who are out to get those who, they think, are not contributing to national unity, or to national interest will have a stronger weapon in their hands."[157]

LaMarsh said this was the first time Parliament had tried to spell out the goals and purposes of the CBC. As she went on, the national unity mandate seemed to have become not only the institution's main purpose but, apparently, its only purpose: "[The CBC] is the instrument which Parliament has chosen with respect to broadcasting. Parliament is now, in this bill, saying to the instrument that this is one of its purposes, and as long as that purpose is there, to help weld the country together, Parliament is prepared to raise taxes from the people to keep it going."[158]

Pressed further, the secretary of state tried to give meaning to the words "national unity," and it took a Liberal back-bencher to point out the potential hazard of the government's approach:

[LaMarsh:] I suppose "national unity" is a phrase that is especially Canadian and means something to Canadians but might not mean anything to anyone coming in. Surely, it means about the same thing to all Canadians whether we are able to express it or not because it has been meaning that for, I suppose, a hundred years; certainly for the time of the CBC.

[John Reid:] Excuse me, I do not think it does. Without intending to be partisan, may I suggest that even within the same political party, the idea of national unity, for instance, in the mind of Mr. Trudeau, is quite different from that in the mind of Mr. Paul Gérin-Lajoie. It is a pious word you cannot define and you cannot define how you are going to achieve it. This is the point.[159]

National unity did not mean the same thing to all Canadians, but these undefinable words and this undefinable objective were about to become the overriding legal guideline for Canada's public broadcaster.

If parliamentarians could not agree on the meaning of national unity, as they evidently could not, why should this responsibility be placed on the broadcasters, asked Prittie. Or if it was a responsibility of broadcasting, why should it be limited to the CBC rather than binding the entire "system," public and private? LaMarsh responded eloquently about the nature of the government's commitment to public broadcasting: "I do not think there is very much more time for public broadcasting to prove itself, to prove to Canadians it is worth while spending the money on."[160] In short, if Canada had no national unity crisis, it would have no need for a public broadcaster.

Debate on the bill shifted back to the House for clause-by-clause consideration. When the "national unity" clause came up, Gérard Pelletier admitted he had doubts about it: "It is so normal to provide that a public broadcasting system will contribute to Canadian solidarity that the mere fact of mentioning it, of writing it out in full, may lead some people to believe that it is not a matter of promotion but of propaganda."[161] This was not the government's intention, he said, and perhaps the clause was superfluous. But to be sure that the CBC was not used "against the interests of Canada," the clause should be left as proposed.

The NDP proposed an amendment which would have shifted the burden of contributing to national unity to the entire system and thus include the private sector. David Lewis spoke in favour of such a sharing of "moral obligation." He asked: "Where is the moral superiority and logic in saying that anyone who wants to destroy Canada can do so if he has enough money?"[162]

Lewis tempered the notion of unity, arguing that precisely contrary to the apparent intention of the bill, the question demanded controversial treatment: "The manner of contributing to Canadian unity and building Canadian unity obviously differs in the minds of various people across this country. There are all sorts of ideas in people's minds as to what in fact contributes to Canadian unity and what in fact does not, and how a stronger Canadian unity can be built in the future. Obviously that kind of public controversy should be permitted."[163]

But the most important observation on the implications of the clause came from Conservative MP David MacDonald:

> I wonder whether the government has given sufficient thought to the insertion of this phrase in the bill because it seems to me that we have treasured in this country over the past thirty years the establishment of something that was very unique and important – a public broadcasting system, not a state broadcasting system. When we begin to move into areas such as ... national unity, we are in effect moving away from the concept of public broadcasting toward the idea of state broadcasting whereby the broadcasting system of the country becomes an extension of the state.[164]

It could be argued that this process was inherent in the political origins of Canadian public broadcasting and strengthened by its evolution. But the codification of the national purpose in these terms was a major leap in light of the division in the country over the meaning of nationhood. Unlike the previous dissenters, however, MacDonald was the only MP to see in this issue a different conception of society and of the role of the state: "While it may seem to members of the house at this time that there is nothing more important to any individual in this country than national unity, let me suggest in all humility that I think there is. I think that the individuals who make up a society are always more important. It may well be that there will be more important things in the future, even to Canadians, than national unity."[165]

While the "national unity" clause dominated the debate, it was far from the only important change in the new legislation. Indeed, in spite of LaMarsh's harsh words indicating a single purpose for public broadcasting, the legislation clearly intended to assure a prominent place for the state in every aspect of Canadian communications.

The bill proposed to return the public sector to its pre-1958 predominant position, at least nominally, by providing that "where any conflict arises between the objectives of the national broadcasting service and the interests of the private element of the Canadian broadcasting system, the objectives of the national broadcasting service must prevail." [166]

This measure elicited strong objections, across party lines, from private sector supporters such as Don Jamieson and Davie Fulton. LaMarsh described the measure as a "tilt" in favour of the public sector, but debate hinged on the definition of "public interest." In Gérard Pelletier's view there was no problem since the objectives and mandate of the CBC were being formulated "in such a way that they will coincide with the public interest in broadcasting matters." But to Conservatives like Fulton, the "public interest" and the CBC interest were not necessarily the same thing: "The public interest [should be] the arbiter of differences between the public broadcasting corporation and the private sector of the system." [167]

The Conservatives proposed amending the clause to read "the public interest must prevail." Did this mean they imagined that the interests of the private sector could be, in certain cases, even greater than the "national" interest expressed in the mandate of the CBC? The question was not put in these terms, but its implications had been the effect of their 1958 legislation. For Judy LaMarsh the key issue was "public interest" versus "private interest," but it was left to the NDP's David Lewis to interpret what that meant: "It is obvious to me that the intention of the subclause is to put the social objectives of the public broadcasting system above the company interests of the private broadcasting companies, and this should remain in the Act." [168]

The government literally lost its nerve overnight, however, and accepted a compromise amendment the following day. The act would read: "Where any conflict arises between the objectives of the national broadcasting service and the interests of the private element of the Canadian broadcasting system, it shall be resolved in the public interest but paramount consideration shall be given to the objectives of the national broadcasting service." [169]

The Broadcasting Act of 1968 also provided for the eventual regulation of cable. While "broadcasting" only referred to radiocommunication, the act invented a new term, "broadcasting undertaking," which it defined to include not only "transmitting" enterprises but "receiving" enterprises as well. [170] All broadcasting undertakings in Canada were said to constitute the Canadian broadcasting system, all aspects of which were to be supervised and regulated by the CRTC.

This new area of intervention provoked further opposition from private sector supporters in Parliament. But here, the government was on questionable legal ground as well. It would be difficult for Ottawa to claim jurisdiction except where cable lines crossed provincial boundaries. Was the inclusion of cable in the Act primarily directed at controlling the activities of the entrepreneurs or at preventing the provinces from exercising such control? Suspicion that it was the latter was fed by a further provision in the legislation for "educational broadcasting," in which several provinces, notably Quebec, had already demonstrated interest.

The act's reassertion of the central role of the state in broadcasting had to be tempered by the understanding that this was to be, once again, the federal state. State intervention was not only to be a motor of development in the public interest rather than for private profit, it was also to be a means of gaining additional leverage for the central government in the struggle that was threatening to shift power back towards the provinces after thirty-five years of virtually unchallenged federal jurisdiction.

Finally, some isolated aspects of the act indicated its overall thrust and the spirit of the government's intentions. The act made no mention of the regional broadcasting councils which had been recommended and attracted popular support. Bill C-163 had proposed a long-term financing formula for the CBC, but this did not make it into the act. A subclause making licensees responsible "for the public effects of the programs they broadcast" was amended, following Don Jamieson's objection, to remove the mention of "public effects."[171] The old act had given the BBG authority to require stations to carry specific programs in urgent situations, but the new act reserved this power to the Cabinet. As Judy LaMarsh pointed out, however, the government could already take this power if necessary by invoking the War Measures Act.[172]

The broadcasting act was passed on 7 February 1968, and became law on 1 April.[173] It did little to change the structures or relationships of Canadian broadcasting. Its main impact was ideological. While it strengthened the idea of the public as the ultimate value in broadcasting, it tied that value to a specific conception of national purpose. This link between the public dimension of broadcasting and the highly politicized struggle for national unity that was only beginning to unfold would mark Canada's broadcasting politics from 1968 until 1980.

In spite of the government's strategy to reestablish public sector supremacy in a "single system" in order to achieve its national purpose objectives, the act did not stop the pendulum from continuing to swing in favour of the private sector. It would be up to the new regulatory body, the CRTC, to determine what that meant for "the public interest."

By the time it was adopted in 1968, the new broadcasting policy was already insufficient to deal with the technological and political climate. New developments – cable, satellites, educational television – required new agencies and new policies, and meant that "broadcasting" was no longer an all-encompassing category. At the same time, new challenges and new approaches were forthcoming from the most dynamic sectors of society, which demanded a revalidation of the social functions of both broadcasting and the new technologies. In the process, new and often clashing conceptions of the public began to emerge as well, and the struggle to define the public was an integral part of the struggles of the times.

# CHAPTER FIVE

# From "Broadcasting" to "Communications" (1968–74)

## INTRODUCTION

The late 1960s was an era of unprecedented expansion of state involvement in the organization of social life, or of what Claus Offe has called the "welfare state regulatory strategies" of late capitalist societies.[1] In all the industrialized countries, contradictory pressures applied by capital and social forces resulted in a perpetual state of structural "crisis."[2] But in Canada, the structural limitations of the policy-making capacity of the state were exacerbated by the fragmented nature of state power itself. Traditionally in Canada, an initial question needs to be addressed before any new sphere of activity can be opened up to state intervention: which level of the state, federal or provincial, is to enjoy jurisdiction? This is particularly the case with respect to relations between Ottawa and Quebec.[3] It was particularly evident in the political context of 1968, and was especially acute in the area that concerns us here.

The 1960s was a crucial decade for the evolution of broadcasting ideology in Canada. Within the CBC, the classical conflicting conceptions of the public clashed as critical issues heated up in the surrounding society. The threat posed by Quebec nationalism to the national political framework itself raised the important question of the first loyalty of the public broadcaster: was it to the logic, programs, and political objectives of the state, as perceived and expressed by the government of the day, or was it to an objective, journalistic interpretation of society that might differ from the government's? Crisis after crisis led, in 1968, to the legal binding of the CBC (defined as Canada's "national" broadcasting service) to the promotion of national unity, but even the new broadcasting act did not clarify whether this was to be done by reflecting "the Canadian identity" or *la réalité canadienne*.

The constitutional crisis aside, the climate of 1968 completely changed the parameters of debate on broadcasting in Canada. The new broadcasting act confirmed that the system no longer included only "public" and "private" broadcasters, but cable undertakings and educational broadcasting as well. New actors were appearing too, and very shortly it would be virtually meaningless to talk about "broadcasting" without simultaneously talking about "communications."

Three days before the broadcasting act received royal assent, the government tabled a white paper on satellite communication.[4] It is worth noting that this policy paper was produced under the joint auspices of the Department of Industry and the Privy Council Office, by a task force of experts working discreetly without the encumbrance of public discussion. The separation of "carriage" from "content," introduced in the early 1960s when broadcasting was placed under the jurisdiction of the secretary of state while "technical" matters were left with the minister of transport, was thus reaffirmed. In 1968, while public debate had raged over the role and nature of the *content* of the Canadian broadcasting system, basic questions about the future of its form and structure were treated as technical matters that could be worked out within a government department.

A year to the day after the broadcasting act came into effect, Canada had a Department of Communications charged with developing a new technological infrastructure for telecommunication carriage.[5] The essentially economic and industrial vocation of the new department was directed towards the private sector, but it had to develop a relationship with the public as well. The DOC commissioned a vast range of studies on different aspects of the implications of the new technologies, which it promised would be the basis for a national telecommunications policy.

With the creation of the DOC, public discussion of broadcasting and communications was split between two planes. Discussion of the role of the CBC, of private versus public ownership, and of the purpose and extent of regulation, continued along established lines, although now centred around an agenda maintained by the CRTC. Meanwhile, there arose a whole range of new issues related to the possible uses of new technologies. These became the domain of the DOC.

The social context of 1968–69, characterized by the demand for participation in decision-making processes, obliged the DOC to integrate public consultation into its technological planning and development. The government's concern to provide a safety valve to contain social unrest, especially among the young, had already led to programs such as the Company of Young Canadians and would soon include Opportunities for Youth (all under the "cultural" umbrella of the secretary of state). Now, there would be demands for access to communication media – not air time on the CBC, as the public interest organizations of the 1930s, 1940s and 1950s had demanded, but autonomous, self-controlled, and interactive media. These demands would tax the recuperative talents of federal agencies like the CRTC and the DOC in the 1970s.

At the same time, the heightening challenge to Confederation coming from Quebec surpassed by far the capacity of Ottawa's traditional communication medium, the public broadcaster. Ordering the CBC to contribute to the development of national unity only highlighted the problem and created new ones, while temporarily diverting attention from Quebec's political demands for more power in communications. Not to be outdone by Ottawa, Quebec created its own Ministère des communications,[6] and the 1970s were marked by parallel development of policies, institutions, and infrastructures, as well as jurisdictional donnybrooks. The first major conflict, over educational broadcasting, surfaced even as the broadcasting act was being debated, and Ottawa eventually had to yield in this area which it had explicitly kept closed to the provinces since 1946.

Increasingly, the dramatic challenges posed to the system from Quebec persisted in revealing the limitations of the centralized vision of national broadcasting and the problem of equating "national" and "public" with respect to broadcasting. These limitations surged to the forefront again during the October Crisis of 1970. From the beginning, Quebec's claims of jurisdiction had constituted a pole of resistance to national broadcasting; in time of crisis, as it had in 1942, Ottawa's use of public broadcasting against popular aspirations in Quebec sapped its legitimacy in the eyes of an entire generation.

Thus, as the traditional scope of broadcasting widened during this period, its development would be continually marked by the increasing tension between Ottawa and Quebec.

## THE SYSTEM IN FLUX, 1968–70

### Constitutional Politics

The parliamentary debate over broadcasting and national unity had illuminated the federal government's desire to see the CBC become a strong supporter of its vision for Canada. While, superficially, the "national unity" mandate appeared to be aimed strictly at obliging Radio-Canada to correct a perceived lack of balance in its reporting on the national question, a more serious challenge from Quebec had crystallized in the form of renewed demands for constitutional powers in broadcasting.

Quebec's Liberal government of the Quiet Revolution had created a Department of Cultural Affairs but had not dealt directly with the question of broadcasting. However, in seeking increased powers and fiscal resources for Quebec in a variety of areas, the government of Jean Lesage prepared the framework through which its successors would involve the Quebec state in broadcasting and, later, communications. Quebec wanted Ottawa to refrain from intervening in areas where it felt competent to act, and to replace coast-to-coast "uniformity" in social programs with provincial determination of needs and aspirations. It was only reasonable to expect a different view from Quebec on many questions.[7]

The rapid changes of the Quiet Revolution gave way to the election in June 1966 of a revitalized Union Nationale, led by Daniel Johnson. Only a year before his election, Johnson had written that Quebec should not reject separatism as a possibly necessary solution to the constitutional struggles which had marked French-Canadian history.[8] While in power, Johnson would insist on the essential need to remake the Canadian political system on the basis of equality between two nations.

In November 1967 – while Ottawa's parliamentary committee was considering the proposed legislation on broadcasting – Johnson outlined the Quebec position at the "Confederation of Tomorrow" conference in Toronto, convened by Ontario premier John Robarts:

> Because of changes in the technical and social order, Canada today is faced with a whole series of problems which the Fathers of Confederation, however vivid their imagination, could not conceivably have foreseen. Consider, for instance, town-planning policy, regional development, economic stability, telecommunications, atomic energy, the space age, manpower policies, educational television and many other contemporary matters. Our Constitution is silent on these matters. Therefore, when a new problem arises in Canada, we are more and more likely to base each government's responsibilities for it, not on constitutional principles, but on considerations of the moment which, in turn, derive from a variety of factors such as relative capacity to act, financial resources or merely the political power wielded by a given area of government.[9]

Johnson said these problems could be divided into two categories. In "all problems which have no direct relationship with language or culture," Quebec had the same interests as the other nine provinces, but in the sociocultural area "the need for a new constitution is most pressing."[10] Here, there was a need for a basic redistribution of powers.

Two months later, in a brief prepared for the constitutional conference called by Lester Pearson, on 5–7 February 1968, Quebec reemphasized its claim to be the national homeland of French Canadians and, consequently, the need for the Quebec government to play the role of a national state in matters pertaining to language and culture. The brief cited three sectors where it was urgent to reallocate jurisdiction in Quebec's favour: social security, international relations, and radio and television.[11]

As instruments of education and culture, radio and television rightfully belong under provincial jurisdiction, the brief argued. The court interpretation of 1932 was "unacceptable" to Quebec, which should have control of radio and television stations situated on its territory. Federal agencies like the BBG and the CBC should be changed in composition to reflect the "bicultural reality" of Canada; Quebec should designate a certain number of members of the boards of these bodies. Finally, if the airwaves were in the public domain, they should in no way be in the exclusive domain of the federal government; the awarding of broadcasting frequencies could have serious cultural consequences, as could program content. Quebec could no longer tolerate being excluded from an area where its vital interests were so clear, especially considering communications in an educational perspective. [12]

Ironically, the constitutional conference met in Ottawa just as the House of Commons was in the final stages of adopting the new broadcasting legislation. In his opening remarks, Daniel Johnson based Quebec's position on the insufficiency of extending the use of French in federal institutions, the acknowledgment of the collective rights of French-speaking minorities outside Quebec, and the need to use the French-Canadian majority in Quebec to provide the appropriate organizations, institutions, and cultural environment. French Canadians could not be expected to entrust the direction of their social and cultural life to a government in which their representatives were in the minority. [13]

In discussion the following day, Johnson illustrated the problem with a hypothetical example. Under the present situation, a federal government hostile to Quebec – conceivably, one in which there were not a single francophone member – could determine, for example, the CBC's educational and cultural programming. Under the new broadcasting act, the Cabinet could even instruct the CBC regarding particular broadcasts. The solution lay in a balance of power that ensured that one culture could not dominate the other, even in time of crisis. Quebec needed more power in order to counter the potential domination of Ottawa. [14]

Johnson's illustration prompted a brief sparring match with the federal justice minister, Pierre Elliott Trudeau, who asked why Quebec should have special powers only in the cultural sphere. Trudeau argued that if Canada were to adopt Johnson's view of federalism, "we must certainly apply [it] ... to banking, to questions of taxation, tariffs and international law." Johnson replied: "If we accept the Justice Minister's argument that we must rely on federal members and ministers from Quebec to look after radio and television program contents which are closely allied – on this we all agree – with education and culture, why not extend them our confidence with respect to all matters set forth in section 92 [of the BNA Act]?" [15]

Of course, the illustration was not innocently hypothetical but carefully chosen. Parliament was twenty-four hours away from adopting broadcasting legislation not only orienting public representation of the national question in a certain way, but aimed at increasing the scope of federal powers in the new field of "educational broadcasting."

## Educational Broadcasting

Maurice Duplessis, in a statement reported in *La Presse* on 22 June 1948, had said that the centralization of broadcasting in the hands of the federal bureaucracy went against the fundamental principles of confederation "which reserved to the provinces full jurisdiction over education in all its forms." [16]

But, if the BNA Act gave the provinces clear control of education and the judicial decision of 1932 gave Ottawa exclusive jurisdiction over broadcasting, who did that place in charge of "educational broadcasting?"

The new broadcasting act simply said that "facilities should be provided within the Canadian broadcasting system for educational broadcasting." [17] As federal policy since 1946 had explicitly excluded provincial governments or their agencies from eligibility for broadcasting licences, the implication of the act was that educational broadcasting would in some way be federally sponsored. When the legislation had been introduced in October 1967, Judy LaMarsh had promised a subsequent measure to provide for educational broadcasting.

The day after the broadcasting act was adopted – the day the constitutional conference in Ottawa was coming to a close – the parliamentary committee was convened to deal with the question of educational broadcasting. The government recognized the constitutional fragility of the issue; LaMarsh said the guiding principle was "that federal policies in the field of communications, which is a federal responsibility, must not be allowed to impede, but, indeed should be directed to assisting provincial authorities in discharging their constitutional responsibilities for education." [18]

LaMarsh's proposal curiously resembled the Aird commission's recommendation for all of Canadian broadcasting. Under the umbrella of the new federal agency the government proposed to create, she said, each province would control production and programming within its own territory. The federal agency would merely provide facilities.

A Quebec Department of Education committee had been studying the question of educational broadcasting since April 1967. When the committee was created, Premier Johnson had deplored the way Quebec and Ottawa seemed locked in a perpetual foot-race to occupy new fields. At the same time, he had laid out Quebec's expectations in this area: "It would be quite unrealistic to want to set up a costly French-language radio and television organization ... I think we could agree to use what already exists, jointly controlling content when it's a question of education and culture ... Once again, I hope the federal authorities will understand that we are prepared to co-operate, but not to have educational and cultural radio and television content dictated to us."[19]

But this had been before the introduction and debate on the broadcasting act and, now, Quebec refused to appear before the parliamentary committee to state its views. All the other provinces, except Newfoundland, made submissions basically supporting the federal initiative and variously welcoming the suggestion of a provincial role (in the case of British Columbia, Alberta, New Brunswick, and Ontario) or proposing that it be handled by the CBC (Manitoba, Saskatchewan, Nova Scotia, and Prince Edward Island). Only Ontario mentioned the constitutional aspect of the question, and said it accepted the federal position in spite of the constitution. Ontario's education minister, William Davis, said Ontario would not "argue the constitutional niceties of the situation at this time, particularly when a practical solution appears to be at hand."[20]

But was there one? By this time, Quebec was already experimenting with an educational television project known as TEVEC ("té-vé-communautaire," or community television), through which broadcasts were prepared by the Department of Education and broadcast in time purchased from the CBC or private stations. Ontario had announced similar intentions, and its Department of Education would soon be broadcasting over a UHF frequency licensed to the CBC. But Ottawa's proposal to furnish an infrastructure for educational broadcasting was about to be rejected out of hand by Quebec.

Jurisdiction and political control aside, the issue of educational television raised new substantive questions about broadcasting. At the parliamentary committee hearings in February 1968, the developer of the federal plan, BBG vice-chairman and CRTC chairman-designate Pierre Juneau, spoke of the desires of educators to establish "two-way or feedback relationships" based on "reciprocal exchange" between teacher-broadcasters and students. This was clearly a new approach. Educational broadcasting, however, was strictly seen by the authorities as a kind of classroom of the air. The problem, Juneau said, was "knowing where school television ends and where public or cultural television starts."[21] Juneau made it clear that the idea was not to reproduce the American model in which "educational" and "public" television meant the same thing.[22] In the United States, Juneau noted, "'educational' is taken in the broad sense which really is not different from the general purposes of the CBC."[23] Educational television in Canada would depend on a "clearly defined public," as opposed to a general one.

Some other parties, like the Canadian Association for Adult Education, felt this could be a good occasion to recover some of the lost potential of mainstream broadcasting, and took the originality of the formula even further. Thus, the CAAE proposed to consider educational broadcasting as a general cultural and informational alternative to commercial and public service broadcasting, not limited to instructional programming. It proposed a "community-based system of control," with joint administration by federal, provincial, and local educational authorities.[24]

In this way, the debate over educational broadcasting began to broaden the terms in which broadcasting was traditionally thought about in Canada, raising new questions about new possibilities in form and content. But while these questions had been placed on the agenda, they were superseded by the federal-provincial struggle over jurisdiction.

Returning to Quebec from the constitutional conference, Daniel Johnson's government told the Quebec legislature that in the full exercise of Quebec's exclusive rights and powers in the field of education, it would be required to apply itself to the problem of radio broadcasting.[25] On 22 February 1968, Johnson declared that the government had decided to apply Duplessis's 1945 law creating Radio-Québec.[26] The law had never been put into effect because Ottawa had stated it would refuse to license broadcast operations belonging to provincial governments or their agencies. It would have to be updated, Johnson said, but the government's objective was to create an instrument to coordinate all radio and television broadcasting activities in Quebec. Radio-Québec's priority would be educational television aimed at traditional schooling at all levels, adult education, and cultural promotion "for the entire *québécois* public, francophone and anglophone."[27]

The leader of the opposition, former Liberal premier Jean Lesage (who had not included the 1945 law in the revised statutes of 1964 because, he said, it was "inoperable"), supported the principle of Quebec jurisdiction in educational and cultural broadcasting. It would be another year before Quebec updated its legislation on educational broadcasting, but the first step was enough to upset Ottawa's design. The succession to Lester Pearson and the federal elections that followed kept new measures off the agenda until a new parliamentary session convened in the fall, and by then Quebec's initiative was well advanced. The new secretary of state, Gérard Pelletier, created a task force on educational broadcasting and as late as February 1969 insisted that the CRTC would be formally instructed not to grant licences to provincial agencies.[28] On 10 March 1969, Parliament heard first reading of a bill to establish a Canadian Educational Broadcasting Agency, which would hold the broadcasting licences and provide technical services based on agreements concluded with the provinces.[29]

On 27 March 1969, Quebec premier Jean-Jacques Bertrand introduced legislation creating a Quebec Broadcasting Bureau (l'Office de radio-télédiffusion du Québec) "to establish, possess and operate a service for radio and wire broadcasting and for producing and broadcasting audio-visual material, called Radio-Québec."[30] Bertrand explained that Radio-Québec would prepare educational radio and television broadcasts and audio-visual documents, as well as coordinate audio-visual activities of government departments.[31]

On second reading, 16 May, Bertrand reviewed the history of Quebec's involvement in broadcasting recalling that "the only obstacles to Quebec's legitimate aspirations in broadcasting and telecommunications ... have come from the imperialism of federal authority."[32]

Radio-Québec had been actually operating for over a year by this time and was well into production. The law would enable it to own broadcasting facilities as well as produce programs – an important jurisdictional distinction. The purpose of Radio-Québec, Bertrand said, was not to compete with private broadcasters or even the CBC, but to provide Quebec with its own national broadcasting service.

Debate on the bill in the Quebec National Assembly took an unexpected turn. While supporting the government's claim for Quebec's constitutional right to jurisdiction over educational broadcasting, and acknowledging the historic importance of the legislation, the opposition made a vigorous and lengthy critique of the proposed composition and operation of Radio-Québec. Liberal communications critic Yves Michaud, an outspoken advocate of freedom and responsibility of the press (and, later, a leading supporter of the Parti Québécois), led the debate against the provisions, not the substance, of the bill, forcing the deliberations to carry over into the fall. The Liberals opposed the proposed close relationship between the executive authority and Radio-Québec, and called instead for an independent agency. The government maintained that it was not creating a broadcaster but, basically, an appendage to the education system.

By 1969, the Union Nationale government was perceived in liberal and progressive circles as repressive, if not reactionary, with respect to civil liberties and traditional North American notions of freedom. So while the government's constitutional position on broadcasting could be the basis of a political consensus, there was a wide divergence of opinion concerning the form of the Radio-Québec project.[33]

The Quebec situation in 1969 was rather a caricature of the Canadian one. Having built a consensus and asserted its right to national autonomy over the means of cultural production, the Quebec government viewed those means as an effective extension of itself. Outside the government, however, the issue was viewed in terms of the ideal potential of broadcasting. Although it was not articulated in the familiar language of the forty-year-old Canadian debate, the question concerned the proper relationship between media, the state, and the public, and the representatives of the Quebec state were reducing it to a question of national interest.

The law creating Radio-Québec[34] was passed on 16 October 1969, and took effect 1 November. Despite their long-winded protests, the Liberals voted with the government.

On 5 November, the federal government withdrew its bill proposing creation of a Canadian Educational Broadcasting Authority. In December,

Ottawa and the provinces settled on a definition of educational broadcasting but provincial agencies were still barred from holding licences. Ottawa was not prepared to cede any power to the provinces a moment sooner than absolutely necessary.[35]

## Satellites and New Bureaucracies

Quebec's position on broadcasting was based on the same type of sentiment that had led successive Canadian governments to seek ways to assert Canadian cultural autonomy from external threat. In a detailed statement in the legislature on the need for constitutional reform 28 March 1968, Daniel Johnson summarized the problem in a phrase that could have come from any Canadian prime minister since R.B. Bennett. Quebec's problem was how to coexist "with a group whose vast majority speaks English and lives more or less in American."[36]

This was a modern problem, unique to the age of mass communications: "Once upon a time, there was no such problem ... But the cinema, radio, and now television have caused French-Canadian culture to be in its most dangerous state since it arrived in North America ... if we are in danger, it is because we have not yet found a way to defend ourselves against this invasion ... of 'the American way of life'."[37]

Creating Radio-Québec was one attempt to counteract this influence, Johnson said, but Quebec had to consider new problems on the way. He mentioned satellite communication and the need to act in this field before the air over Quebec was saturated with the output of nonfrancophone satellites. In the absence of any assurance from the federal government in this respect, Quebec had sought help from France, which was prepared to help develop a plan to cover Quebec, Johnson announced.

The same day, in Ottawa, Industry Minister C.M. Drury published the federal position on the question, *A Domestic Satellite Communication System for Canada*.[38] In this white paper, the federal government, too, underscored the emerging new stakes of communications in Canada. It concluded "that a domestic satellite communication system is of vital importance for the growth, prosperity and unity of Canada, and should be established as a matter of priority."[39] The paper put great faith in the inherent benefit of satellite technology which, it said, "makes it possible to solve economically the unique problems created by certain physical and social characteristics of the Canadian territory."[40]

The new system would permit the introduction of telecommunication services like telephone and television to any point in Canada, thus achieving two important purposes: it would make possible the extension of the CBC's French and English services to any remote area, and it would open the Canadian North to cultural integration.

The policy indicated in the white paper blended curiously with the traditional "national" approach to broadcasting policy and an industrial strategy based on attention to private enterprise:

A domestic satellite communication system should be a national undertaking ... operating under the jurisdiction of the Government of Canada ... The satellites and earth stations together would form a single system under the control of a single management ... The organization should have a corporate form in order that it may sell its service efficiently to the common carriers and television systems; in order that it may compete effectively in those areas where competition is appropriate; and in order that it may finance its activities through a suitable combination of equity and debt capital.[41]

The thrust of government involvement in developing a satellite system was markedly different from the approach that had been taken to earlier communication technologies, like radio or cable distribution, which had been allowed to develop under private ownership before falling under the regulatory web, or, like television, which had been introduced under strict public control. Like television, a satellite system would be developed according to a coordinated plan, but private capital would have its place right from the beginning.[42]

The government proposed to create a corporation "to develop, own and operate both the satellites and the earth stations of the system." For the first time in communications, the government proposed to allow private participation in Crown activities. The actual corporate structure would emerge from discussions between the government and private industry.[43]

The parallels and divergences with the organization of Canadian broadcasting were uncanny, as though the system had been decomposed and reconstructed by a team of industrial managers. The legitimacy of government intervention was formulated in similar terms (for example, the need to serve "national interests") right down to the choice of words ("a satellite system is ... a natural monopoly"[44]). But government ownership would be limited to the extent required to maintain control and regulation. Unlike broadcasting, where there was a public sector and a private sector, there would indeed be a single satellite system wherein the public interest would depend on a partnership of government and private capital.

The growing complexity of communications pointed to the urgency of "comprehensive regulatory legislation on telecommunications," Drury's white paper had suggested. It would also require coordination of the broadening communications spectrum. To meet this urgency, the Trudeau government proposed to create a new Department of Communications as part of the reform of government organization introduced early in its administration.

Speaking on the government organization bill on 27 February 1969, the prime minister said communications in the age of satellites would require "increasing federal government involvement." In keeping with tradition, he legitimated this involvement in terms of national purpose: "In our second century they [satellites] may well prove as essential to the unity of our country as our transportation systems have been since Confederation."[45]

On 28 February, the minister-designate Eric Kierans told the House of Commons the new department would have "profound implications, social, cultural and political."[46] He explained, in the popular jargon of the day, that it would be concerned "with the medium, not with the message."[47] But the two functions – carriage and content – were interrelated and interdependent.

The DOC would be responsible for such agencies as the Canadian Overseas Telecommunications Corporation and the Canadian Transport Commission; it would administer the radio act and would be charged with setting up the domestic satellite corporation. More important, it would link these activities under a national communications policy. The centre-piece of Canadian communications was to be the new satellite corporation. Echoing Trudeau, Kierans said: "Confederation was built upon the mile upon mile of steel rails laid across this country; Confederation will be renewed ... by a communications system that meets the needs of all Canadians."[48]

The direct leap from railroads to satellites in both Trudeau's and Kierans's accounts of the evolution of Canadian communications was remarkably ahistorical in their omission of any reference to broadcasting. Responsibility for broadcasting, including the CRTC, remained with the secretary of state, but the DOC was charged with developing the policy and technology that would determine the context in which broadcasting took place. Whereas the "national broadcasting policy" had been coaxed into existence after years of public debate, less than a year after its enactment it was evidently in total eclipse by an incipient "national communications policy" in which broadcasting would be only a part. And where broadcasting was traditionally seen as a cultural tool of national purpose, "communications" had an essentially economic and industrial vocation.

This vocation was not justified ideologically in the traditional terms of free enterprise or economic liberalism, or even of social democratic economic development and management. In 1969, the ideological basis on which the Department of Communications was to be launched was technological determinism. After finishing with the national interest, Kierans went into a long philosophical discourse on communications, touching on such themes as the altering and conditioning of messages by the media through which they were communicated, the neutrality of technology, and the nonideological nature of machines.[49]

But in spite of this bias, the new minister was politically astute enough to realize that the social aspects of his portfolio would have to be reconciled with the advancing technology. To deal with this concern, Kierans announced that a task force, which he christened the "Telecommission" would examine the whole range of issues raised by a national telecommunications policy. In the meantime, it was left to the opposition to wonder what relationship there would be between culture and communications, what to do about the new provincial claims for jurisdiction, and how the proposed mixture of public and private ownership of the satellite system would protect the public interest.

The Department of Communications was created on 1 April 1969, "to promote the establishment, development and efficiency of communication systems and facilities for Canada."[50] But even before it was official, on 24 March, the government introduced legislation "to establish a Canadian corporation for telecommunication by satellite."[51] Telesat Canada would develop, own, and operate, on a commercial basis, Canada's domestic satellite communication system.

The Telesat bill proposed a unique type of ownership structure: the government would own part, the common carriers (telephone and telegraph companies) would own part, and part would be offered to "the public at large" in the form of publicly traded shares. This proposal – enthusiastically described by the new minister of communications as a "pathfinder for future government/public/private industry partnerships" – introduced a new conception of the public to the field of discourse: the stockbroker's conception of the public as shareholder. It also implied for the first time, although in a curious way, that "the government" and "the public" were not identical and might even have different interests at times.[52]

It would be necessary, Kierans told the House of Commons on second reading, to "balance the self-interest of each partner against the interest of the operation as a whole." Specific interests would have to be reconciled with the national interest, and national interest would be balanced against the need "to ensure an adequate return on investment by the shareholders of the corporation."[53]

It seemed rather cynical for Kierans, a former stock exchange president, to present the Telesat formula as one of public participation, for while a private company which begins to sell shares on the open market is commonly said to "go public," only a tiny percentage of Canadians actually participated in the stock market in 1969. Conversely, the process whereby a state-owned or Crown corporation sells off its assets in the form of shares is more accurately referred to as "privatization."

The bill was strongly opposed by the Conservatives and New Democrats. MP Heath Macquarrie referred to the government's position as "technological nationalism," and said it was basically setting up a business. Ed Schreyer described it as "a sell-out of the Canadian public interest," pointing out that only about 2–3 percent of the Canadian population would derive financial benefit from the share offering, at the expense of the general public: "It is proposed here to offer to private ownership something that should really, in the public interest, be kept under public ownership."[54]

While the Telesat bill was under debate, Quebec was also claiming a role in satellite development. With this in mind, Schreyer proposed an interesting alternative. If the government was serious about serving both the public interest and national unity, it could create a publicly owned Crown corporation in which the federal government owned a majority and the provinces owned the rest.

The bill was referred to the parliamentary committee, where Kierans reminded the NDP that Telesat was intended to be a commercial project and government ownership would be the easy way out. The tripartite arrangement, he said, would ensure "the maximum public good."[55]

The NDP persisted in committee. Max Saltsman suggested that the only reason the government was involving private companies was "that capital for the public sector is not as readily available as capital for the private sector." Kierans replied: "No. Our differences are ideological ... You feel that the government should do everything ... We feel that the government should do whatever the private sector does not or does not do very well and that is a tremendous difference."[56] This had been R.B. Bennett's basic justification for creating public broadcasting in the first place, but in 1969 the government felt the private sector was up to the task.

On 13 June 1969, the Telesat Canada Act[57] was passed, becoming law on 27 June. Canada had the Western world's first domestic satellite system. In December, this feat was recognized by the election of Eric Kierans as president of the International Telecommunications Union, the international body for regulating satellite communication.

On 28 May, the day before the Telesat bill returned to the House from committee, Yves Michaud in the Quebec National Assembly asked the government to report on its plans for satellite participation. Premier Bertrand replied that Quebec was "negotiating" with both Ottawa and France – which was developing a joint Franco-German project known as "Symphonie." Quebec would be able to receive programs from Symphonie, in French, but would not enjoy its own transmission capacity. Implicitly, Telesat would also supply French programs, via Radio-Canada. In both cases, Quebec would be frustrated by a lack of control. As long as Quebec was destined to be a receiver, the government's "negotiations" appeared to be an exercise in choosing the source of Quebec's cultural domination.[58]

Determined to match Ottawa move for move, however, the Quebec government introduced legislation on 10 December 1969, creating its own Department of Communications. "Within the scope of the jurisdiction of the province of Quebec," the Ministère des communications du Québec (MCQ) would have the function to propose and implement a communications policy for Quebec. It would oversee all of Quebec's communications networks (that is, "all means of transmitting sounds, pictures, signals or messages by wire, cable or by means of waves"), it would establish and coordinate the communication services of government departments and public agencies, mainly Radio-Québec, and it would be responsible for the provincial regulator of telephone, telegraph, railway, and other utilities, the Régie des services publics.[59]

The MCQ would be charged with promoting the internal and external interests of the Quebec state in information and communications. On second reading, Premier Bertrand explained that the department would have two main purposes: to exercise Quebec's constitutional authority, and to coordinate all the government's activities in communications. The second purpose was basically an administrative reorganization, but the first one had a clearly political design. To illustrate its role, the premier cited a recently announced CRTC decision to regulate all aspects of cable, including local programming not picked out of the air. Federal jurisdiction, Bertrand noted, was limited to over-the-air broadcasting. Closed circuit cable transmissions, like any wired transmissions by local telephone or telegraph companies, were subject to provincial regulation. Quebec was not interested in regulating content, he said, but would occupy the increasingly important field of carriage regulation. The MCQ would provide the framework for advocating Quebec's constitutional rights in this and any other area of communications.

With only a few desultory questions from the opposition, the bill passed swiftly. On 12 December 1969, Quebec became the first Canadian province to have a department of communications. The Union Nationale government that created it did not endure long enough to use it but, under Robert Bourassa's Liberals, conflict over communications between Ottawa and Quebec would reach a new height.

### Regulation and Control

The new CRTC was a busy agency, regulating not only the ownership, licensing, and programming policy of radio and television stations, as had the BBG, but cable companies as well.

On 13 May 1969, the CRTC made its first public statement on cable undertakings.[60] It described cable services as "community programming" and emphasized that they were to be complementary to, rather than competitive with, over-the-air broadcasting. The CRTC saw cable systems adding a new dimension to broadcasting by assisting in the development of community identity through locally produced programs and by helping provincial and local authorities to develop educational services.

The CRTC decision Jean-Jacques Bertrand had referred to was published 3 December 1969.[61] Following a round of public hearings, the CRTC had decided not to license cable systems that would use microwave relays to bring in distant US signals. The problem was not whether microwave technology should be used to help the development of cable, it was "to decide whether the use of additional techniques should be authorized to enlarge the coverage area of US networks and US stations and therefore their advertising markets in Canada." The spread of US television via cable "would represent the most serious threat to Canadian broadcasting since 1932 ... it could disrupt the Canadian broadcasting system within a few years."[62]

Quebec had underlined one historic aspect of Canadian communications policy emerging in the cable decision, namely the centralized domination by Ottawa of all areas of communications. The CRTC decision indicated its other historic aspect, the concern to resist US cultural influence. In these two different concerns, Ottawa had to face two different adversaries: Quebec, now increasingly using its own state power to make policy, and private industry, in this case the cable companies.

On 15 January 1970, CRTC chairman Pierre Juneau told the parliamentary committee the CRTC's position on cable was consistent with the intent of the Broadcasting Act of 1968 and, indeed, with all policy that had preceded it as far back as 1932. Cable was perhaps the most important single factor of change in the Canadian broadcasting structure, and the cable companies had to decide "whether they want to contribute to the development of a broadcasting and communications system in the country at the moment or whether they want to defend vested interest."[63] Juneau called for a concerted effort by Parliament, government, the CBC, private broadcasters, cable operators, and broadcasting unions to develop the Canadian system. For the moment, however, the only concrete expectation of the cable companies was delivery of a certain amount of local programming. Guidelines for prospective licence applicants, published in April 1970, specified that cable systems must provide at least one channel for the distribution of educational television.[64] The problem, Juneau said at a later committee appearance, was that the cable companies had been left for about fifteen years to develop outside the broadcasting act. Only now were they being brought in.

An interesting thing to emerge at the 1970 parliamentary committee was the defensive position of private broadcasters with respect to the cable companies. Private broadcasters complained about traditional problems such as the CBC's share of the advertising dollar and the lack of capital for Canadian programming.[65] Their most strenuous objection, however, was that as broadcasting transmitting undertakings, they were expected to carry the burden of meeting national objectives. This responsibility should go to the receiving undertakings – the cable companies – as well, they argued. Unlike the CRTC, with its vision of "complementarity," the private broadcasters did see the cable companies as competitors, and threatening ones at that.

Thus, by 1970, the debate on broadcasting in Canada had splintered into several parallel streams. While the basic issues remained unchanged – which level of the state was to have jurisdiction, the extent of regulation, public versus private ownership, national purpose, freedom of expression, and control – prior to 1968 they had all focused on over-the-air broadcasting, and most often on the role of the public broadcaster, the CBC. Now, new instruments beyond the traditional limits of "broadcasting" had appeared – educational television, wired systems, and space satellites – and new extensions of the federal and provincial states: not only a regulatory body, the CRTC, but cabinet-level departments of communications, and new agencies like Telesat Canada and Radio-Québec. By this time, the federal parliamentary committee that had been created in 1966 to focus and concentrate debate on broadcasting and other cultural issues was so overwhelmed by the sheer volume of material it had to deal with that it was virtually reduced to a recorder of official testimony. Stripped of its supervisory capacity, the committee was able to function a public body of inquiry only on circumstantial questions.[66] Meanwhile, the points of inquiry into communications multiplied as well, from the DOC's Telecommission which conducted more than forty studies on the present and future prospects of telecommunications in Canada,[67] to the Special Senate Committee on the Mass Media created by the inspiration of Senator Keith Davey in April 1969.[68]

But one "old" issue reappeared persistently during this period of rapid change: the question of the role of the public broadcaster, particularly with respect to Canada's developing national crisis.

With the creation of the CRTC, the CBC had to answer to a new authority. Gérard Pelletier made it clear in his first appearance before the parliamentary committee as secretary of state in the fall of 1968 that he would not be the one to "control" the CBC. But with social agitation increasing daily in Quebec, MPs continued to raise questions about alleged CBC news bias in its coverage of events like the student occupations of Quebec junior colleges, and excessive emphasis on "subversive movements." These questions were now directed towards CRTC chairman Pierre Juneau, who was asked by MP J.A. Mongrain, on 28 November 1968, whether the CRTC needed more power over the CBC. Juneau replied that the CBC's own board of directors, not the CRTC, was responsible for programs. These were "management problems," he said.[69]

The question of "separatist news bias" was exacerbated by the publication, early in 1969, of Judy LaMarsh's book, *Memoirs of a Bird in a Gilded Cage*, in which she wrote that Alphonse Ouimet had told her "that control of Radio-Canada had been completely lost and that no one responsible in Montreal would take responsibility for what was going out over the air."[70]

Although Gérard Pelletier dismissed LaMarsh's comments as "extremely vague,"[71] the parliamentary committee took the issue up with George Davidson, the new CBC president. Davidson said none of the CBC's senior officers was a separatist, and categorically repudiated the suggestion that anyone but they were in control.

Davidson passed the buck back to the MPs regarding information programming. If Parliament wanted the CBC to exercise political censorship, he said, it would have to explicitly institute it. There were certainly CBC employees who were separatists, but it was not his responsibility to get rid of them as long as they did not use their positions to "propagandize." The CBC president made it clear, however, that his own patriotism could not be questioned, characterizing separatism as "a malaise ... an illness, a disease."[72]

The MPs reacted variously to Davidson's comments. Ed Broadbent of the NDP found it peculiar, "a very undesirable extreme statement perhaps of your own position." Liberal back-bencher Harold E. Stafford, on the other hand, said that by covering separatism, the CBC was helping to spread the disease.[73]

Davidson corrected himself, to say that the malaise was in the body politic, not the people who expressed it. As for the CBC, its role was to contribute to the understanding of the Canadian people, and this meant providing balanced coverage of the political developments in Quebec.[74]

Davidson pointed out that the CBC did not pay more attention to separatism than did, say, the Toronto *Globe and Mail*. All the newspapers, as well as the CBC, had covered the recent founding of the Parti Québécois (an event, it had been suggested, that the CBC should have let pass unreported). Stafford responded, indicating a certain parliamentarian conception of the role of the public broadcaster: "The newspapers are not set up with the same aim in mind, though. Newspapers are far more free to do what they want to do than is the CBC."[75]

But for Davidson, the news had its own logic, superseding political objectives. Public broadcasting policy in news and public affairs, he said, must be based on permissiveness rather than control of political expression: "The CBC has no right to try to manipulate the news for special purposes."[76]

Davidson's three-hour appearance before the committee was followed in the coming months by continued criticism about the CBC from MPs. On 25 June 1969, Liberal André Ouellet asked Pelletier in the House of Commons if he would "at last agree that a clean-up is required at all levels of the CBC ... so that the CBC will no longer be used as a medium for separatist propaganda."[77]

A true liberal with respect to freedom of the press, Pelletier refused to engineer such a "clean-up" while he was secretary of state. Appearing in a personal capacity before the Special Senate Committee on Mass Media in

April 1970, he made a statement that unintentionally provided some interesting insight into the apparent obsession of some of his colleagues: "From now on ... a dictator in a country who would want to manipulate public opinion efficiently without becoming too odious, could very well let the free press, the printed press, operate and television would be enough to manipulate public opinion."[78]

## New Social Practices,
## New Critiques

The continuing concern over public broadcasting and the national question is interesting when seen in the light of the renewed debate and intervention on many aspects of the media, in both English Canada and Quebec, in 1969–70.

With the rise of oppositional youth and student movements in the mid-1960s, English-language "underground" newspapers aimed at this clientele had appeared in Ottawa, Vancouver, Toronto, Montreal, and other Canadian cities.[79] Very little has been written about this press, which generally conceived of its role "as an adversary one, part of a larger political and cultural program."[80]

By 1969, the notion of "underground" had expanded with the appearance of a number of periodicals that attempted to present "newsworthy" aspects of social reality ignored or underplayed by the mainstream press. In the "aboveground" media, the approach of the television program "This Hour Has Seven Days" probably corresponded the most closely to this new phenomenon, which was based on a long-range objective of informational autonomy from industrially produced media. The most important example of this was the "radical Canadian news magazine" *Last Post*, launched in November 1969 by a group of young journalists disaffected with the mainstream media in which many of them were employed. The declared purpose of *Last Post* was "to unearth and publish facts which are omitted, ignored or obscured by the commercial press." This current was eventually absorbed into the mainstream by the mid-1970s, with the legitimation of "investigative journalism."[81]

In French Quebec, alternative media were more closely tied to specific social and political movements. In 1968, the president of the Confederation of National Trade Unions, Marcel Pepin, denounced the commercial media for placing profit above the public interest, and called on the union movement and its supporters to create independent vehicles for "people's" or "popular" information. Pepin's call was followed within a year by the launching of the cooperative news weekly *Québec-Presse* and by several smaller-scale initiatives. In Quebec, the ideologies of radical nationalism, socialism, and community action were interlaced in literally dozens of media experiences, usually tied to left-wing oppositional political groups but autonomous of links to either capitalist or state interests. [82]

Public opinion in both English Canada and Quebec was also alerted to problems related to the ownership structure of media industries in the late 1960s. As early as 1961, the Royal Commission on Publications, chaired by Grattan O'Leary, had dealt with the problem of foreign periodicals in Canada and recommended the elimination of tax deductions for advertising expenses in these periodicals. [83] By 1969, the federal government was under pressure to institute such a proposal with respect to American publications that published nominal Canadian editions, like *Time* and *Reader's Digest*. (Legislation to this effect was eventually adopted in 1976.)

In Quebec, concern over the acquisition in 1967 of *La Presse* by industrialist Paul Desmarais, and other manifestations of the growing concentration of media ownership, pressured the Bertrand government to set up a special parliamentary commission on freedom of the press in the spring of 1969. The commission never published any conclusions or recommendations, in spite of hearing consistent denunciations of the danger to freedom of information posed by the free enterprise system in the newspaper sector. The commission was the catalyst, however, for creation by Quebec journalists of the Fédération professionnelle des journalistes du Québec (FPJQ), which, in the 1970s, would increasingly claim to represent the public interest in media against economic and political forces. [84] It also led to creation of the Quebec Press Council, the first in Canada, in February 1971.

In 1969–70, the focal point for most of these currents was the Special Senate Committee on Mass Media proposed and headed by Keith Davey. It was established in March 1969 to consider the ownership, control, influence, and public impact of the major Canadian media. [85]

The Davey committee brought together for the first time all the diverse experiences then taking place in both the traditional, or mainstream, media, and the new, or alternative, media in Canada. It heard submissions about such questions as the harassment of street vendors of the "underground" newspaper *Logos* in Montreal and the problems Quebec's mainstream journalists were having with the courts and police. The Davey committee's report, published in December 1970, provided one of the first official displays of legitimation for the oppositional press current of the period.

The Davey report also provided exposure to the attention that was then beginning to be paid to the utopian possibilities of the new communication technologies. It was not alone in this regard, as the technological threshold of the late 1960s was recognized as offering a potentially novel approach towards the radical social and political demands of the period.

The new technologies promised to enhance the possibility of fuller participation in public life, and the federal Department of Communications, for example, recognized early on the need to provide space in which these could be discussed. Thus, in addition to investigating questions related to hardware and regulation, the DOC's Telecommission study, launched in September 1969, organized seminars on such themes as "Telecommunications and Participation."[86]

The main social laboratory for experimenting with these possibilities in the 1970s was a communication practice that came to be known as "community broadcasting." Community broadcasting emerged with the concurrent development of relatively inexpensive light-weight video production technology and local cable distribution systems with unused channel capacity. The combination appeared to be ideally suited to decentralizing and deprofessionalizing media production, while increasing access and public participation.

Even before the first official interventions, isolated social experiments with community broadcasting had taken place in urban centres such as Vancouver, Winnipeg, Thunder Bay, and in the village of Normandin in Quebec's Lac-St-Jean region.[87]

In Quebec, community broadcasting was first introduced as part of the general approach to state intervention that characterized the Quiet Revolution. This approach was distinguished by the widespread use of community organizers (known as "social animators") to involve local communities in planning their own economic and social development.

In 1967, Quebec's Department of Education launched the community television program known as TEVEC in the region north of Quebec City. Here, social animation techniques were employed to get the community to participate in producing adult education material aired during time purchased from local television stations. Quebec went on to experiment with other methods of "de-schooling" education in the 1970s, but an important germ had been unleashed as people in Lac-St-Jean got a taste of direct, local involvement in producing television content. In 1970, the first community to become involved in cable-supported "community television" was in the small town of Normandin.

The federal program known as Challenge for Change (or Société nouvelle) was also instrumental in the origins of community media. Set up in 1967 (1969 for French-language projects), Challenge for Change was designed to use communications to promote new ideas and provoke social change in the "fight against poverty." Later community media would often be financed by short-term grants from two federal government programs set up in the early 1970s: Opportunities for Youth and Local Initiatives Projects.

The CRTC's first policy statement on cable undertakings had said that cable systems would be expected to do a minimal amount of original local programming. The Davey committee reiterated this hope, declaring that community programming distributed by cable provided the best possibility of true public access to media (it considered that the regulatory agencies had always protected private broadcasters against competition, and dismissed their association, the CAB, as "neanderthal"[88]).

In 1971, the CRTC would again emphasize the importance of community programming.[89] Nationally, one of the leading advocates of community broadcasting was CRTC chairman Pierre Juneau. In July 1972, he told the annual convention of the Canadian Cable Television Association: "The cable industry is by nature decentralized ... it recognizes that there exist decentralized communications needs. That society is fragmented, pluralistic, speaks and wants to speak and be heard in many voices ... In our mass media, this active need for authentic expression cannot be accommodated."[90]

However, while the CRTC encouraged, even urged, cable companies to provide for community programming, it did not make it obligatory. Of 387 cable companies licensed in 1972, only 139 provided some form of community programming and "very, very few of these gave open access."[91] More important, community broadcasting was not seen as a new sector to be fully developed so as to meet the needs that could not be filled by either national public broadcasting or commercial private broadcasting. The possibility of community-controlled cable *systems*, as opposed to community access channels within privately owned systems, was never seriously explored (although a working model has existed in Campbell River, B.C., since 1957[92]). The CRTC's policy of moral suasion depended entirely on the benevolence of the cable companies while resting on the paternalistic premise that local programming, unlike "national" programming, required no public resources. Only in Quebec, which operated according to its own agenda, would community broadcasting later enjoy a very limited amount of state financial support. Thus, despite some interesting alternative models provided by the community broadcasting experiences of the 1970s, the practice remained, for the most part, marginal.[93]

In fact, it can be argued that the opening up of a small space in the broadcasting environment for community broadcasting was one of the multiple steps taken in the early 1970s to contain the considerable oppositional energies that characterized youth and minority groups in this period. As community programming became the focal point of the public dimension in broadcasting, it deflected critical attention from the political reality of the Canadian broadcasting system, as well as the direction in which the system as a whole was evolving.

The importance of this deflection can be appreciated when the discourse of democratic, participatory media is considered against the backdrop of the political crisis that broke out with the kidnapping, on 5 October 1970, of the British trade commissioner in Montreal.

## BROADCASTING AND THE STRUGGLE FOR QUEBEC, 1970–71

### Political Repression

The role of the media in the October Crisis has been abundantly analyzed.[94] We should, therefore, concentrate here only on those aspects that pertain to the competing conceptions of the public that were brought into play. In the most fundamental sense, the approach of both the federal government and the Front de libération du Québec (FLQ) can be seen as an attempt to force the media to serve a political purpose. For the former, it was a matter of asserting its control over public communications while, for the latter, it was a question of establishing communications links for the first time.

The FLQ's initial strategy was to use private radio stations as conduits to the public. It sent its communiqués to two Montreal stations, CKAC and CKLM, counting on their competitiveness and drive for higher ratings to overcome any sense of patriotism. When challenged, these stations would argue that diffusing the FLQ communiqués was in the public interest.

The FLQ also made a specific demand of the federal government: that its manifesto be transmitted directly over the Radio-Canada television network. According to press reports at the time, the federal Cabinet at first refused to consider this, and Prime Minister Trudeau was so angry with the media's attitude towards the crisis that he considered imposing censorship. As late as Wednesday, 7 October, Trudeau's office directly prohibited Radio-Canada from broadcasting the manifesto, but that night it was read on the air over radio CKAC. The Montreal newspapers, which wanted to publish the document, were also applying pressure.

Finding it impossible to black out the manifesto, the government told Radio-Canada to go ahead. Gérard Pelletier was reported to have told journalists in Ottawa that the text would only serve to discredit the FLQ. On Thursday, 8 October, Radio-Canada broadcast the FLQ manifesto on television in the time usually reserved for its evening news program. The next morning it was reproduced in the press. Strangely enough, this was the only one of the FLQ's demands the government would meet.

By all contemporary accounts,[95] broadcast of the manifesto increased public sympathy and popular support for the FLQ. With the privately owned press and broadcasting outlets playing a profitably "neutral" role on reporting the events and the public broadcaster an insufficient counterweight, Ottawa brought in martial law on 16 October, which, among other things, restricted media freedom to act as a communications channel for the FLQ. In the ensuing round-up of "suspects," more than a dozen journalists were detained by police.[96]

The War Measures Act prohibited the media from publishing any news about the FLQ unless it came from official sources. They could no longer publish FLQ communiqués or even say they had received them. By achieving newsworthiness, the FLQ had taken advantage of the logic of "freedom of the press." By pressuring the government, it had even extracted a political directive giving it direct access to the public air to communicate its manifesto without institutional mediation. Now, to regain control of the political situation, the government had to first assert its authority over the media, public and private. Quebec's justice minister, Jérôme Choquette, summed it up most succinctly, when he said: "In this very special case, in the public interest, freedom of the press must be curtailed."[97]

The government's attempt to interfere with the media was denounced during parliamentary debate on the War Measures Act by MP David MacDonald: "There have been reports that not just in the private sector of broadcasting but even in the public sector unwarranted influence may have extended to the higher levels of administration in order to curb the kind of speculation and comment that the government feels would encourage the free expression of opinion that it no longer finds acceptable in that province [Quebec]."[98]

The extent of government involvement was partially indicated at the parliamentary committee meetings to consider the CBC's annual budget estimates in May 1971. CBC president George Davidson said, in response to a question, that Secretary of State Gérard Pelletier had telephoned in the early days of the crisis (before the War Measures Act had been invoked) to advise him "of the government's appraisal of the degree of seriousness of the situation," but there had been no suggestion of censorship. Pelletier said things would come to a head in a few days and left it to the CBC to act accordingly. The English network director of television information, Knowlton Nash, had happened to be in Davidson's office at the time of Pelletier's call and communicated a message, to CBC English-language newsrooms across the country, to act prudently. News programs were not restricted in any way, Davidson said, although some public affairs programs had been "cancelled, altered or postponed."[99]

After having consistently contended that the CBC's role was to maintain an even balance in its coverage of Quebec politics,[100] Davidson tried to convey the impression that all news policy decisions had been made at the proper level throughout the October Crisis. He met with only limited success, however. A dissident view was expressed by an NDP MP, Mark Rose, who said: "It seems to me, sir, that during that whole situation there was an undue effort on the part of the CBC ... to justify the government's position."[101]

The October Crisis crystallized concern for the role of media in public life, particularly within the media milieu and particularly in Quebec. As we saw earlier, this concern was already manifested by the appearance of "alternative" media to fill the political-ideological vacuum created by mainstream media, by the demand for inquiries such as the Quebec parliamentary commission on freedom of the press and the Davey committee, and by the creation of organizations such as the FPJQ. New questions concerning the role of professional journalists and "the public's right to know," and concerning access to media for marginal groups, now found their way into the debate.

As we saw earlier, the Quebec caucus of the Liberal party and Radio-Canada middle management had been in conflict since 1966 concerning the vision of Canada that should be presented on the air. The conflict was resolved in theory with the inclusion in 1968 of an explicit "national unity" clause in the CBC's mandate. The practical situation was complicated, however, by the growing demand for autonomy among unionized journalists in Quebec, and their accompanying solidarity with the nationalist and social movements of the late 1960s. With the increasing social agitation in Quebec and the growing conservative tendency of mainstream media, journalists' unions, along with the FPJQ, became the leading defenders of "the public's right to know." More so than the professional association, the unions had the means to make their presence felt directly and on a day-to-day basis.

At Radio-Canada, conflicts between journalists and management were directly related to the interpretation of the "national unity" clause.[102] On 24 June 1968, when police attacked demonstrators at the traditional Saint-Jean-Baptiste Day celebrations in Montreal, CBC cameras were ordered to remain trained on the festivities. One reporter, Claude Jean Devirieux, managed to transmit a live report about the violence and was summarily suspended for his efforts. The Radio-Canada newsroom walked out, and the federal elections the next day were covered in English only.

Early in 1970, three reporters at Radio-Canada were ordered to cease their free-lance activities with the radical, pro-independence news magazine *Point de Mire*. When one of them, Robert Mackay, refused to comply, he was fired. Testifying at a CRTC hearing eight years later, Radio-Canada news director Marc Thibault said the incident had been part of a movement among the personnel to undermine management authority. According to Thibault, the journalists in question had jeopardized their credibility.[103]

During the October Crisis, the Radio-Canada journalists' union called a press conference to denounce management interference and manipulation of the news. Among the examples they gave were: an order to play down the military intervention that had preceded the introduction of the War Measures Act; suppression of the official number of arrests under the War Measures Act; the broadcast of an unedited interview with Montreal mayor Jean Drapeau at his demand; and refusal to cover events involving groups opposed to the government's action. As a result, the two main spokesmen for the union, journalists Michel Bourdon and Denis Vincent, were fired for "insubordination."[104]

The October Crisis also had structural consequences for Radio-Canada's news operations: a new nonunionized lower-management position of "supervisor" was created, with no apparent purpose other than political surveillance. An official communiqué announcing the innovation said it was intended to see that Radio-Canada management did not abdicate its exclusive responsibility to evaluate the orientation and quality of the news it gave the public. There were to be ten supervisors for forty unionized journalists.[105]

In a book written in the wake of the October Crisis and published in 1971, Radio-Canada journalist Claude Jean Devirieux pointed to the dilemma of the "national unity" mandate. In the first place, the mandate was not even identical in English and in French: "contribute to the development of national unity and provide for a continuing expression of Canadian identity" was translated *in the act* as "contribuer au développement de l'unité nationale et d'exprimer constamment la réalité canadienne."[106] What English Canadians unproblematically considered "Canadian identity," Devirieux observed, could not be rendered into French, where the "reality" was that there is a dual Canadian identity.[107]

Furthermore, while the "development of national unity" had been elevated to a political ideology by federalist groups, led by the Trudeau government, the Canadian "reality" was that a significant and stable part of the Quebec population was in favour of independence. In this context, Devirieux argued, to place a priority on "national unity" was political propagandizing; the objective response would be to emphasize the "reality" of a country in crisis.[108]

In May 1970, the FPJQ had called on the new Liberal government in Quebec to reconvene the special parliamentary commission on freedom of the press that had died with the defeat of the Union Nationale. On 15 November, it renewed the call. The October Crisis, the FPJQ said, lent a new sense of public urgency to the question of relations between the press and the state. A few days later, Premier Robert Bourassa announced he was reconstituting the commission, but it did not meet until February 1971 in order to welcome the creation of the Quebec Press Council.

Quebec's parliamentary commission met sporadically in the coming years. Only in February 1973 did it finally consider the FPJQ brief on freedom of the press, which had by then been circulating in public for about a year. The FPJQ took the position that the traditional "freedom of the press" enjoyed by publishers should be reformulated as "the public's right to know."[109]

While its thrust was directed primarily at private enterprise and at the growing concentration of ownership in the press, the FPJQ equated for the first time the interests of the owners of capital and the state. Against the financial capacity to communicate, it placed the social responsibility of "informing the citizen." It even defined the content of this type of information: "everything a citizen needs in order to participate fully in social life."[110]

The FPJQ proposed public participation of users and journalists in the running of media enterprises as a structural means of promoting the public's right to know. It proposed that every media enterprise, private or public, be obliged by law to set up a tripartite, decision-making "news management council," made up of representatives of the owners, professionals, and the public. This formula, it said, had the advantage of taking away the absolute power to control content enjoyed by media proprietors, without upsetting the structures of ownership.

The FPJQ proposal was intended to break the link between media ownership and content by associating the public with the decision-making process. It was thus rooted in a positive view of media as a force for social change but still depended on a certain degree of state intervention: the role of the state would be to guarantee the conditions necessary for a free press to operate, such as the pluralism of sources of information. The FPJQ recognized that any state intervention in media was fraught with problems and insisted that the state should under no circumstances be a media owner itself.

The FPJQ brief raised some fundamental questions which would remain on the agenda in Quebec through the 1970s and into the 1980s, the central one of which concerned the role of the state in making media serve the public. As such, it approached the question from the dominant perspective of the Quiet Revolution, which was to seek in the state a possible solution to social problems. But it was also important from a communications perspective. Dovetailing with the other prominent Quiet Revolution view of education and participation as means of collective social development, the notion of "the public's right to know" reversed the traditional emphasis of communications policy on the "sender" of messages and placed it on the "receiver." Later a new notion would emerge, the notion of the "right to communicate," in which publics, no longer content with the right to receive, demanded equal access to the means of communication.

### Cultural Sovereignty

The army and police forces may have restored social peace, but political conflict between Quebec and Ottawa continued to mark the 1970s.

Premier Bourassa set the tone on 28 September 1970 in a speech in Chicoutimi, where he declared that the government of Quebec was the most faithful interpreter of Québécois sociocultural reality. Unveiling the banner of "cultural sovereignty," Bourassa said his government would seek to negotiate with Ottawa a strong role for Quebec in the definition of communications policy.[111]

Quebec's position was first spelled out at length in a 1971 working paper by Communications Minister Jean-Paul L'Allier, claiming Quebec's right to establish policy in communications.[112] L'Allier's paper proposed a model for cultural sovereignty that fit in with the collectivist spirit of the Quiet Revolution and the new demand for a public purpose to communications based on three general goals: "to ensure Quebec citizens' inalienable right to communication according to their cultural, social, economic and political needs ... to equip the government and its agencies with a modern communications system allowing them to fully assume their responsibilities towards the population of Quebec ... to promote and maintain a *québécois* system of communications, integrated into extraterritorial or international systems, which facilitates and contributes to meeting the objectives of Quebec."[113]

The cornerstone of Quebec's policy was to be the Régie des services publics, the regulatory board for utilities falling under provincial authority. L'Allier saw the Régie becoming a *communications* regulatory agency, extending its jurisdiction to services already under federal jurisdiction, such as cable operations. In an appendix dealing specifically with cable policy, the working paper said the cable industry must be regulated as a public service without being placed under state control. Referring to the Aird commission and the Privy Council decision of 1932, the paper recalled the historic distinction between broadcasting and transmission, and argued that the courts had given Ottawa control over carriage but not content. It said Quebec had to stop moving timidly in this field and should, therefore, claim authority over cable distribution.[114]

The Quebec paper appeared to consider all communication undertakings, regardless of ownership, as public services with common rights and obligations to be determined by policy. Consistent with the mandate which the MCQ had been created to fulfil, it lumped together communication infrastructures, public information and government publicity as different types of services to be subject to the department's policy direction.

The paper was tabled along with three bills proposing amendments to the laws governing the MCQ, Radio-Québec, and the Régie. Debating the amendments in the National Assembly, opposition members focused on the centralization of all public communication activities, from broadcasting to regulation to government information and publicity, in a single government department. PQ member Marcel Léger said Quebec was turning its department of communications into a ministry of information. Claude Ryan was quoted as having written that L'Allier's proposals were "frankly bad in their conception of state control in information and communications."[115]

Thus, while Quebec's constitutional offensive could be seen as an attempt to use the state as a liberating force, criticism within Quebec still focused on the potentially repressive aspects of state intervention. The Quebec Liberals' call for "cultural sovereignty" was an important political lever, not unlike Ottawa's appeal for "national unity." Both provided legitimacy for policies and practices geared not only towards influencing the relations between the two levels of state power, but also towards strengthening the basis of state power itself. Was Quebec's position really any more than an attempt to substitute one level of state control for another? The answer would emerge during the next decade, out of Quebec's own approach to the public dimension in broadcasting, through the experience of its own institutions such as Radio-Québec and the community broadcasters, and from the basic policy choices its governments would make. For the moment, the arrival of the Quebec state as a protagonist in communications was beginning to recall the Canadian model at which its intervention was primarily aimed.

### POLICY WARS, 1971-74

#### Regulation

Quebec's claims were introduced into an already cluttered field. By 1971, under the authority of the broadcasting act, the CRTC was ready to make policy on cable television "in the public interest." Meanwhile, beyond the question of which level of government should regulate the cable industry stood the companies themselves, also anxious to equate their interests with the public interest.

On 26 February 1971, the CRTC announced public hearings and published a statement on cable television.[116] The evolution of broadcasting since 1928 attested to a desire to maintain communications as a cohesive national force, the CRTC said. The explicit "national unity" mandate for the CBC incorporated in the Broadcasting Act of 1968 was the most recent manifestation of this. As new means of communication emerged, it was necessary to integrate them into the national system. This was what the CRTC now proposed to do with cable.

The CRTC document recognized the threat posed by the expansion of channel capacity to many Canadian television stations whose economic positions were already weak. Without directly seeking to compete with over-the-air broadcasters, the availability of new channels necessarily diminished the size of the audience of existing stations, thus deteriorating their commercial revenue base. Advertisers, both Canadian and "international," were increasingly buying time on American stations in order to reach their Canadian markets, depriving Canadian stations of an estimated $35–45 million a year. The CRTC noted that cable systems had grown more rapidly in Canada than in the US, where the Federal Communications Commission had deliberately retarded their expansion in metropolitan centres.

In raising these issues, the CRTC said it was not seeking to protect vested interests or save an outmoded technology. Its purpose, in keeping with its mandate, was to uphold the public interest and safeguard the overall system. The basic logic of the system was being undermined by the unlimited penetration of Canadian television space by cable-imported US stations; by fracturing the economic basis of the private broadcasters, cable threatened to disrupt the Canadian cultural, educational, and information imperatives of both the public and private sectors: "a solution must be found if the Canadian broadcasting system is to survive." [117]

Apparently then, by 1971, the survival of the system – in which the interests of the public sector were supposed to be "paramount" – depended on the continued economic health of the private sector. The CRTC rejected the two "extreme" solutions of no regulation or restriction of the extension of cable penetration. It proposed, instead, a policy to integrate cable into the system in such a way as to enhance the system's overall objectives. The key, it said, was to balance the notions of competition and national interest, as broadcasting policy had been seeking to do for thirty-five years. It opposed the common ownership of cable and broadcasting companies, favoured by some entrepreneurs, on the grounds that such concentration would be unhealthy and the profitable cable aspect would inevitably prevail. The CRTC suggested, instead, that cable companies and producers might work together on new types of production aimed at cable audiences. Finally, reiterating earlier statements of 1969 and 1970, it lauded the liberating possibilities of community programming for extending public access to television, especially at the local level. [118]

Community programming also offered the technical possibility for any individual to become a transmitter instead of a passive consumer. This possibility of direct participation made necessary a new approach to questions like the criteria for choosing program subjects, the use of talent, and the selection of participants. Hopefully, the CRTC said, the public hearings would clarify opinion on these types of questions.

Community programming was, at this point, something the CRTC urged but did not demand of cable companies. While it was pleased with some of the results, many cable undertakings were not engaged in it at all. The CRTC explained that it was reticent to impose rigid structures on a field where experimentation should prevail, widening the scope of broadcasting "to include those aspects of communications which allow the citizen to participate." [119] The public dimension of cable television was thus perceived in terms of the cultural enrichment and personal growth promised by community programming.

In May, soon after the CRTC cable hearings, the subject was considered by the parliamentary committee. There, the cable industry appeared to appeal to Parliament in anticipation of the forthcoming CRTC policy. The Canadian Cable Television Association contended that cable was a hybrid technology spanning both federal and provincial jurisdictions. The cable companies insisted on being recognized as representing the public and, with the different levels of government exposing the highly political nature of their interest in regulation, insisted that their position was as credible as any; as the supplier of a service "that the public obviously wants," the cable industry said it felt responsible to speak for the interests of its subscribers.[120]

The cable companies' claim to represent the public was rooted in a conception of the public as a market of consumers who had been rejected by Canadian communications policy. But their argument for autonomy also stood on the ground that their service involved no use of the public airwaves, even though cable television systems were assumed, under the Broadcasting Act of 1968, to form part of the "national broadcasting system." They could also make a new and unique claim that the multiplicity of channels they were able to offer responded to a "public demand for greater viewer choice," liberating the public from dependence on advertisers, and catering to minority audiences with special interests.

The industry brief mentioned such possibilities as multiple program scheduling, enabling the user to choose a convenient viewing time, and local program origination with community participation ("people talking with people"). Audience fragmentation was not only good for the cable companies, it could be presented as being good for democracy: cable was providing "a degree of public access that is new in the history of media," and the industry argued that it viewed the public "as the most important constituent in the broadcasting system."[121]

But the mass audience still had a role to play. It served the purpose of national unity and the interests of the over-the-air private broadcasters. The private broadcasters, through the CAB, now went on the offensive trying to carve a niche for themselves in the new broadcasting environment. Where the cable companies had appealed to the dream of technological democracy, the private broadcasters exploited the nationalist arguments that had once been used by their adversaries. The CAB brief to the parliamentary committee warned of the "dramatic invasion of the cable system by American programs" and said that "massive importation of American programs contributes to destroy the Canadian broadcasting system." Broadcasting, on the other hand, was "part of our national heritage ... control is completely in the hands of Canadian citizens." Broadcasting could ensure "the survival of the Canadian integrity."[122]

The CAB position was based on the historic Canadian need to resist the threat from abroad. In 1971, however, new phenomena like audience fragmentation were changing the context in which the national purpose had traditionally been expressed. Conservative MP W.G. Dinsdale pointed this

out in a perspicacious intervention when he said that rapidly changing technology was making it increasingly difficult to use media as a force for
national unity in Canada.[123]

But with its long experience, the CAB knew exactly which rhetorical
buttons to press. The veteran CAB spokesman T.J. Allard told the committee:
"We can let the technology rule us or we can try to shape the technology
to public policy objectives."[124]

When it came to concrete proposals, however, the CAB remained preoccupied with the traditional commercial interests of private broadcasters. In
1971 the CAB's "solution" to the threat posed by cable was that the private
broadcasters should receive the popular US station signals for rebroadcast
in Canada, with the cable companies simply carrying them on their behalf.
This, presumably, was a way to protect Canadian integrity.

In 1971, a new type of corporate enterprise appeared: the "integrated"
cable-broadcasting company. Bushnell Communications, of Ottawa, became
the first private broadcaster to apply for cable licensing. Bushnell president
Stuart W. Griffiths presented integration of broadcasting, cable, and program
production activities in a single corporate entity as the best way for a company to ensure financial survival in an evolving economic context where,
increasingly, the cable subscriber would be replacing the advertiser as the
main source of revenue.[125]

Bushnell's application was rejected by the CRTC on the grounds that too
much would then be concentrated in the company, but a few months later
the CRTC issued a policy statement in favour of integration. What appeared
on the surface as a display of regulatory vacillation, was the sign of an
emerging pattern of contradiction between the sociocultural and national
purposes of Canadian broadcasting and the financial well-being of private
broadcasters seeking to adapt to economic and technological changes.[126]

An irony that tended to be overlooked in all of this discussion was that
where the financial base of Canadian broadcasting had once been an annual
licence fee, collected by the government and used to finance the public
system, it was now increasingly a monthly rate paid to private companies
which distributed signals picked up from here and there. The public broadcaster was only one producer-programmer among many in this scheme.
While it was the only one that could be directed to act in the national interest,
the real key player was now the regulator, charged with supervising the
national system – which in 1971 mainly meant staying one step ahead of
the new dynamic force in the system, the cable industry.

As to the crucial question of content, here, too, a new framework had to
be found and the CRTC would provide its skeletal structure. Testifying before
the parliamentary committee in June 1971, Pierre Juneau criticized the CBC
for being too commercial and imprecise in its goals, especially in television.
What was needed was an overall industrial approach to production in which

the public sector would play a "relative part." The CBC would be the cornerstone of an industrial strategy, Juneau said: "but it is time to realize that we need to muster all our energies and muster the energies of private enterprise in order to compete with the rest of the world."[127]

In July 1971, the CRTC published its most comprehensive and sophisticated policy statement on cable television to date.[128] The CRTC recalled that the basis for a cable television policy was to be found in the Broadcasting Act of 1968 and did not originate with the regulatory authority. Integration of cable into the broadcasting system, it said, was a logical step in pursuit of the broadcasting act's basic policy orientation.

The problem with cable was that by taking the programs of licensed television stations off the air in one community and distributing them somewhere else, it threatened the fundamental objective that broadcasting service be relevant to the community it serves. Furthermore, the cable systems did not contribute to the cost of production of these programs which were, nonetheless, the indispensable component of their service. Television licences were thus rendered meaningless, and the public service obligations tied to them were more and more difficult to fulfil.

The CRTC cautiously stated that its intention was not to harm the cable industry but, rather, to establish a policy that would permit and support its development. However, its mandate required it to supervise the public airwaves so that the system was not disrupted "as a result of purely technological and marketing pressures which take no account of the social, cultural, economic and political objectives of the country":

> In the opinion of the Commission, there is an obvious danger that the development and even the policy of broadcasting be determined by the natural tendency of hardware, tools and machines to proliferate as a result of technological and marketing pressures. Such a proliferation can only occur if the hardware is fed with inexpensive contents. This kind of development leads to wider and wider circulation of programs without a corresponding increase in the production of messages. Messages from larger centres are spread more and more distantly. This results inevitably in a stretching process, a "more of the same" process where, in the long run, choice is reduced rather than increased and where the medium is indeed the message.[129]

The sociocultural ambiguity of cable technology was underlined by the CRTC's recognition of the possibility it offered for functions other than the retransmission of US programs. It could also provide programs from other countries via satellite, provide channels for provincial educational broadcasting, facilitate local community expression, and offer channels for various kinds of social information. In order to ensure that these aspects of cable contributed to the fundamental objectives of Canadian broadcasting, the CRTC was adopting policies establishing the basic services that a cable system must provide as well as conditions of operation.

All cable systems were to be obliged to provide certain basic priority services to their clientele: all local Canadian stations; all regional Canadian stations not part of the same network as a local station; any available distant Canadian station not part of the same network as the local and regional stations; and at least one CBC station if available. A channel had to be provided for educational broadcasting if requested by provincial authorities within the framework of cabinet guidelines. Once this basic service was provided, optional stations could be carried.

The policy recognized the responsibility to provide a local channel to take advantage of the opportunity "to enrich community life by fostering communication among individuals and community groups." This would include "community programming" defined as "a process which involves direct citizen participation in program planning and production"; "local origination programming" involving the coverage of organized local activities by cable system staff; and "informational programming" to "inform the community about matters which are of concern and interest to its citizens." The CRTC said it favoured an experimental and permissive approach to content, mixing the three forms, with priority given to community programming.[130]

Cable companies would have to make financial compensation to television stations for the programs they used. Although the cable industry argued that it was really only a common carrier selling an antenna service, "the subscribers are buying not antennas but programs," the CRTC said; the common carrier rents a communication medium to a consumer, but the cable company sells the consumer a message. This message (or program) is supplied to the cable company by a television station which ought to be compensated "to help broadcasting fulfil the ever increasing public need for Canadian programs of high standard."[131]

In order to restore "the licensing logic" of the broadcasting system, the CRTC adopted measures for the deletion of duplicated program signals on a priority basis, and for the substitution of commercials on American stations with Canadian ones. It also asked the government to amend the Income Tax Act so as to favour Canadian advertisers using Canadian stations. Cable systems would not be allowed to sell advertising themselves.

Finally, the CRTC recognized that the capacity for transmission and broadcasting in Canada had far outstripped the growth of production. Canada had to quickly develop a program production industry before Canadian broadcasting was reduced to "a technically sophisticated distribution system for imported programs." A Canadian program production industry would depend on cultural and economic initiatives, involving "government" and "industry." In the face of US influence, "the creative development and perpetuation of a Canadian program production industry is mandatory if Canada is to survive as a culturally autonomous nation."[132]

## Jurisdiction

The link between industrial and cultural considerations in CRTC cable policy illustrated the overlapping, often conflicting, and ambiguous goals of Canadian cultural and communications policy in 1971.

On the one hand, cultural policy was still intended to serve a number of traditional objectives.[133] But the DOC was more concerned with developing an industrial infrastructure. Interestingly, its activities were followed by the parliamentary Standing Committee on Transport and Communications, and not the one on Broadcasting, Films and Assistance to the Arts that had been created in 1965 to deal with "cultural" activities. The DOC's work in its first two years had been concentrated in building satellite and computer communication systems. Presenting his department's estimates in March 1971, Eric Kierans said Canada "shall become one great information system." But he made it clear that questions related to "content" were not his responsibility.[134]

The DOC was playing a dual role, however. In addition to its industrial vocation, it was acting as a think-tank charged with drawing out the theoretical potential of new communications technology. The results of the Telecommission studies were synthesized in a report tabled in April 1971, *Instant World*, that tended to refocus the idea of the public in communications on economic consumer issues.[135] Thus, for example, the public interest in telecommunications was to be protected by the regulation of rates charged to users by common carriers. Where the report dealt specifically with traditional broadcasting it again emphasized the technical aspects of regulation and description of the jurisdictional problems. It noted, for example, the problematic nature of the relationship between private broadcasters and cable television companies.

*Instant World*'s appraisal of the regulatory situation in Canada led to a suggestion that the government consider reconstituting the three existing federal regulatory agencies – the Canadian Transport Commission, responsible for the common carriers; the DOC, in charge of the technical aspects of all radio communication, including broadcasting; and the CRTC, responsible for all other aspects of broadcasting.

This recommendation would be the basis for the continuous blending, or homogenization, of broadcasting with the expanding telecommunications system through the 1970s. In the context of the attempt to rationalize the overall system, "broadcasting" was increasingly pegged as the vehicle for national expression while the public interest was redefined in strictly economic terms. In 1976, regulation of all aspects of telecommunications would finally be united under the CRTC,[136] encouraging the agency to view the public as consumer as it spent more and more of its time on economic questions.

However, *Instant World* also introduced a notion of the democratic potential of communications. In a chapter entitled "Telecommunications and People" – which had been the theme of five Telecommission seminars – the report said new telecommunications technology promised to transform broadcasting from a one-way medium "that treats viewers as largely passive homogeneous groups," into an interactive medium: "More and more people will then be able to decide for themselves what they want to watch and when they want to watch it and, still more importantly, to originate programs themselves."[137]

Recognizing the "right to communicate" as a basic human right, the report pointed to the potential of such innovations as instant feedback mechanisms for organizing public opinion referendums, and the liberating possibilities of new equipment like home video-cassette recorders and services such as multichannel cable delivery systems. But it also reported a warning made by political scientist Léon Dion, at the seminar on "Telecommunications and Participation," that information technology tended to favour "demago-technocratic type" political regimes.[138]

In 1971, then, there was a hope that communications technology might meet some of the new social demands raised by the confrontations of the 1960s, and a fear that it could enhance the authority of the established power structures. It was not entirely clear in which direction the changes in communications would lead, nor what their implications would be, but, meanwhile, the jurisdictional disputes between Ottawa and the provinces continued apace.

The question of constitutional jurisdiction over the cable industry was far from resolved. This "socio-political dimension," in Pierre Juneau's phrase, coloured the day-to-day atmosphere in which regulatory decisions had to be made. And while Ottawa and the provinces had agreed on a definition of "educational broadcasting" in December 1969, the question of provincial agencies holding broadcasting licences was equally unresolved, and as recently as 4 June 1970, a cabinet directive had reaffirmed the prohibition on CRTC licensing of provincial governments or their agents.[139] By mid-1971, not only Quebec but Ontario and Alberta as well had made loud claims for a role in these two areas.

A specific incident in June 1971 indicated the extent of this lack of clarity. When US interests in the Montreal company Cablevision nationale were forced to divest, the new owners included Quebec's Crown-owned investment fund, the Caisse de Dépôt. Conservative communications critic Patrick Nowlan saw the CRTC's approval of the transfer as a "constitutional ploy" by which Ottawa was conceding that "there may be good reasons for the province to get involved in the cablevision business, especially where the program begins and ends within provincial boundaries."[140] In Quebec, however, the opposition Parti Québécois saw the Caisse's involvement in an application to the CRTC as implied acceptance by Quebec of federal jurisdiction.

Uncertainty about the politics underlying Canada's communications policy was amplified by the resignation in April 1971 of Eric Kierans and his interim replacement by Secretary of State Gérard Pelletier, who thus became "Canada's first minister of culture and communications," as Nowlan put it. Communications and culture were indeed interrelated, Nowlan said, but there was a growing feeling that the government was making communications policy subservient to cultural criteria.[141]

In August, Robert Stanbury was named minister of communications. As secretary of state, Pelletier continued negotiating with the provinces over educational broadcasting while Stanbury took over the dossier of regulatory jurisdiction. The interconnection of "communications" and "culture" continued to be a source of confusion, however, since communications policy tended to be made with economic and industrial considerations in mind, while the lack of consensus on the national interest persistently dominated the orientation of cultural policy.

As we saw earlier, Quebec, meanwhile, had introduced legislation to give its Régie des services publics power to regulate the cable sector. Jean-Paul L'Allier's position was that nothing in the Canadian constitution, in any law or legal judgment, indicated that cable distribution was necessarily a federal jurisdiction. By subjecting the companies to double regulation, Quebec hoped to force Ottawa to open the whole field of communications to negotiation. On 23 November 1971, L'Allier told a Quebec National Assembly commission the issue was central to the whole question of jurisdiction over communications: "We are asking to review the distribution of powers so that it corresponds to reality; we are asking that the provinces, Quebec in this case, have legislative priority, be the master craftsmen of communications policy on their territory."[142]

Quebec was prepared to recognize that certain aspects could be better regulated on a uniform basis by a Canadian agency but wanted communications to develop according to its design. Communications, L'Allier said, was "absolutely indissociable from culture, education, and everything that makes up the different identity of Quebec."[143]

L'Allier was seeking the best of both worlds, not engaging in confrontational nationalism. Within the framework of Canadian national objectives, Quebec was demanding priority control over state intervention in communications. This would be an important test of the logic of the Canadian federal system and its possibility to accommodate Robert Bourassa's "cultural sovereignty."

Negotiations regarding educational broadcasting finally led to a new federal policy. On 9 December 1971, Gérard Pelletier announced that the CRTC would be authorized to license provincial agencies for educational broadcasting, provided that these were structured as independent bodies like the CBC. The CRTC would be responsible for ensuring that licensing conditions were met.[144]

Pelletier insisted that CRTC authority meant federal jurisdiction remained complete and that the provinces would have to comply with Ottawa's definition of educational broadcasting. But, in fact, it was a remarkable setback for the federal government, the first breach in Ottawa's exclusion of the provinces from broadcasting since the Privy Council decision of 1932. The new policy also meant an unprecedented broadening of the public sector, which hereafter would include provincial broadcasters as well as the CBC. "Public broadcasting" was no longer identical to "national broadcasting," except in the eyes of the federal government. One of the significant unexpected effects of this shift was to undermine the government's political will to maintain financial support for the CBC.

Jurisdictional dispute over the regulation of the cable industry continued, however. The dossier evolved slowly, largely consisting, in early 1972, of an exchange of ministerial correspondence and some contacts between civil servants. Waiting for a breakthrough, the Quebec government kept its proposed legislation before the National Assembly commission. On 22 February 1972, the Parti Québécois presented its version of a communications policy for Quebec.[145]

For the PQ, the eternal constitutional harassment between Quebec and Ottawa was proof that a rational and coherent communications policy could only be achieved in a sovereign Quebec. The purpose of such a policy – to link Quebecers in a communications system – was not only social and cultural, but also political.

The PQ saw communications as a "circuit" in which local communities were able to discuss among themselves information received from outside. "Information" would be presented in a form that permitted and encouraged the articulation of different options and solutions to social problems; the process would lead to proposals to government and resources would then flow from government back to the community. The PQ framed its approach as both a critique of the existing system and a prospective alternative: the present system provided no guarantee that media such as television would actually function as public services; there had to be a framework in which the means of "collective communications" were inserted.[146]

The PQ proposed immediate establishment of Radio-Québec (which was not yet broadcasting over the air) as a state broadcasting network to act as a social catalyst. It saw privately owned broadcasters as a guarantee of freedom of information, provided they too were considered public broadcasting enterprises and were required to serve collective cultural and educational goals. The proposed regulatory mandate of the Régie des services publics in this respect resembled that of the CRTC, with one important exception: the Régie would be charged with ensuring the participation of local populations in the effective ownership of broadcasting enterprises. Undoubtedly, the PQ said, this would imply cooperative or community ownership of media, including credit unions, labour unions, consumer groups, and the like. Such social groups would be more inclined to listen to the needs of the population than a handful of owners whose only goal was to maximize profit.[147] The process of creating community communications systems could begin with cable undertakings and the creation of community distribution networks to work with existing public agencies, the PQ said.

Quebec's proposed legislation finally returned to the National Assembly for further debate on 23 November 1972. L'Allier reported that his most recent exchanges with Ottawa indicated federal refusal of Quebec's claim to legislative priority. The PQ's Marcel Léger suggested L'Allier should recognize his failure and cross the floor, but L'Allier remained convinced that by legislating its own regulatory framework Quebec could realize a major objective: "permanent public participation in the setting and definition of communications policy."[148] The bill giving the Régie des services publics regulatory authority over cable systems was adopted unanimously, while the PQ dissented on the relatively lesser companion bills modifying the MCQ and Radio-Québec. The new measures were law before the end of the year.[149]

The sparring match between Quebec and Ottawa had continued through federal elections that returned a Liberal minority government on 30 October 1972. The new federal minister of communications, Gérard Pelletier, was determined to break the log-jam in communications once and for all. In March 1973, he published a green paper on communications policy,[150] and invited the provinces to discuss it at a federal-provincial conference in the fall.

The policy paper opened with the now standard acknowledgment of the importance of communications systems in maintaining "the existence of Canada, as a political and social entity." The most recent of these, the paper said, was the domestic satellite system. But the central component of a Canadian communications policy was still necessarily broadcasting.[151]

The paper sought to draw out the links between the technical/economic and sociocultural aspects of communications policy, and proposed that broadcasting serve as a model for shaping a set of objectives for telecommunications in Canada.[152]

One of the major problems the green paper identified was the need to harmonize federal and provincial objectives and activities in communications. To resolve the jurisdictional crisis it proposed a "two-tier system in which international and interprovincial aspects ... would be federally regulated, while all intra-provincial aspects would be subject to provincial authority." [153]

To foster Canadian social and cultural values and promote a Canadian perspective on Canada and the world, the green paper called for developing an internationally competitive Canadian alternative in mass entertainment and information. It also reflected the notion that the legislative and regulatory contexts had been bypassed by technology, and proposed to concentrate telecommunications legislation in a single law "related to clearly stated statutory national objectives." [154]

Existing legislation simply did not permit clarification of a problem like the relationship between the broadcasting and carrier functions of cable television systems and "the interest of provincial and municipal authorities in the regional and local impact of these systems." [155] The cable systems were really at the heart of the need to remake the legislative and regulatory framework, not only to take into account the constitutionally sound arguments of lower levels of government, but also to overcome the advantages that would otherwise keep accruing to the cable industry as a result of the inherent ambiguity of its technology.

Cable systems posed a regulatory problem in that they had the capacity to offer two types of services: broadcasting services, which made them subject to the CRTC, and other services similar to those of the telecommunications carriers. They were also particularly threatening to the private broadcasters, as the CRTC had already recognized. The blurred distinction between the broadcasting and carrier functions of cable systems pointed to the need for "a unified agency" having jurisdiction over both. Also, the paper warned, direct broadcast satellites providing home-reception service would further blur the distinction between broadcasting and "point-to-point" forms of telecommunications (like telephone). The as yet unregulated computer services industry also had telecommunications aspects which should not be allowed to develop uncontrolled as cable had.

Thus, it was argued, the "increasing interaction between broadcasting and other forms of telecommunications" necessitated a single regulatory agency. Furthermore, a single federal agency responsible for both the broadcasting system and federally regulated telecommunications carriers "would be in a position to give due weight to expressed provincial and local interest in the development of communications facilities." [156] Finally, a single agency would be more susceptible to dealing with the rising imbalance between the technological and the creative sides of the system.

The green paper thus recognized the gulf that had separated "communications" from "culture" in the brief period of five years since the adoption of the broadcasting act and the creation of the CRTC. Technical capacity had outstripped production capacity, hardware had taken supremacy over software, carriage had been privileged over content. The policy proposals set out to arrest and reverse that development by combining authority over the technical and cultural aspects of communications under a single regulatory agency. The chief advantage would be "the attainment of a proper balance between the social, cultural, economic and technical aspects of communications, in accordance with clearly stated national objectives."[157]

The proposals also set out to resolve the political problems that had developed in the system in the preceding five years. So, in addition to reaffirming the principles of broadcasting policy enunciated in the 1968 act; in addition to promising to ensure that new technologies like cable and satellite distribution contributed "to the capability of the Canadian broadcasting system to fulfil its responsibilities to the people of Canada"; in addition to proposing to revise and consolidate federal telecommunications legislation and combine the regulation of telecommunications and broadcasting, it set out the government's commitment to shape national communications policy objectives "in consultation with the Governments of the Provinces," and promised to develop mechanisms for "consultation and collaboration" among federal and provincial governments and regulatory bodies. Having said all this, however, the green paper closed with an insistence on a single, unitary communications policy for Canada. Far from resolving the political conflict, this simply engaged the battle with the provinces, particularly Quebec.

While overall communications policy was thus thrown open to debate for the first time, sectoral development continued to advance. As usual, policy tended to follow on the heels of technology. Thus, in April 1973, a month after tabling his green paper, Pelletier was back with a policy document on computers. The summary of policy goals in this paper was couched in familiar language that again underlined the government's determination to make the new technologies work to serve traditional "national" objectives, in spite of the industrial goals motivating their initial development.[158]

As Ottawa prepared to negotiate high policy with the provinces, the dispute with Quebec over who was to regulate the cable companies was playing itself out in practice. Operating under its new legislation, Quebec's Régie des services publics claimed the role of a licensing authority and issued policy directives to cable company operators, placing them under double regulation. Pelletier characterized this duplication of CRTC activity as "a clear attempt to superimpose provincial jurisdiction on an area of exclusive federal legislative authority," an encroachment that he said the federal government would resist "by all the means at its disposal."[159] At the parliamentary committee on transport and communications in May 1973, Pelletier was asked if the conflict with Quebec was strictly legal, or political as well. It was both, he replied.[160]

On 9 August, the Quebec National Assembly commission on education, cultural affairs, and communications convened to consider proposed regulatory guidelines on cable. This time, Jean-Paul L'Allier made it clear Quebec was after a new distribution of power with Ottawa and not a fundamental rearrangement of the structure of the system. Quebec, he said, considered cable undertakings public service but private property. Nationalization and state ownership were out of the question, although Quebec was interested in participating in ownership through its own financial institutions.[161]

Meanwhile, Marcel Léger reiterated the PQ's approach which saw cable not only as a public service, but as a service with both a "public and community character." Extending the government's arguments, he used phrases like "cultural decentralization," "public service to local communities" and "community concern as opposed to merely mercantile or commercial considerations."[162]

The commission heard broadcasting and cable industry representatives repeat the basic arguments they had been making in Ottawa, the broadcasters fearing the economic threat of cable and the cable people opposed to restrictive regulation. The industry was careful, however, not to get publicly involved in the struggle between Quebec and Ottawa.

The commission also heard from the Conseil de développement des médias communautaires du Québec, which saw Quebec's plan opening the way for the use of media as instruments of collective development. The Conseil called for the creation of "community production committees," to be financed out of cable industry revenues, and granted access to public distribution by cable on the same basis as traditional producers.[163]

The community media presentation led to a significant exchange between L'Allier and the PQ's Claude Charron. L'Allier recognized that of all existing communication technologies, cable television was probably the one that offered the greatest possibility for citizen participation. As to a decision-making mechanism such as the proposed community production committees, it all depended on how one defined community. Charron, recalling the PQ commitment to cooperative ownership and community programming and production, offered to expand on the concept: the notion of "community" encompassed those who one never sees on mainstream television, the consumers of television. They are the ones who should be the producers, creators, and directors of community television.[164]

L'Allier remained sceptical. The question of placing power in the hands of citizens "instead of technocrats or financiers" was debatable. But the question did come down to knowing just where citizens fit in, who was to represent them, and how they were to manifest themselves. The problem was that there would always be a mass of basically apolitical, poorly informed, unorganized citizens.[165]

The debate between L'Allier and the PQ was interesting in its opposition of two equally hypothetical formulas for dealing with communications in the event of achieving power. Aside from the constitutional difference – power within or outside of the Canadian Confederation – there was an even more fundamental one. In L'Allier's formulation, the state and its agencies, as the embodiment of collectivity, would speak for "community," while democracy was exercised at the level of the individual citizen. To L'Allier, as to Ottawa, the public was the state and public service served the individual and the entire collectivity. To the PQ, the idea of public service was tied to the notion of service to local communities, and the state was the agent that would make it possible. Ideologically, the Quebec government and Ottawa were not far apart in their conceptions of the public, while the PQ was apparently still very far from power in 1973.

The federal-provincial conference to discuss Ottawa's policy proposals was scheduled for the end of November 1973. The government would not consider "special status" for Quebec, Gérard Pelletier told the House of Commons 1 November. [166] Quebec was not seeking special status, however, but full autonomy over communications on the basis of a conception of Canada and "national unity" based on consent rather than coercion.

Jean-Paul L'Allier produced his own green paper for the conference, laying out a general point of view consistent with the Quebec position since 1968 and reiterating the orthodox argument that communications was one of the main guarantees of a society's specific character, its language, culture and way of life. But then it added a new dimension: communications was also an essential factor in economic development. [167]

This aspect of communications, evident in federal interventions since 1969 and explicit in the federal policy proposals, was now cited as an area of Quebec interest as well. There was little constitutional basis for this, and the Quebec paper quickly returned to more solid ground: Quebec's claim to authority in communications policy remained tied to educational and cultural criteria, and on this basis it rejected Ottawa's proposal of consolidation in favour of a new division of power.

Quebec was indignant over Ottawa's approach to formulating a "national" policy: "It would be one thing for the federal government to publish, without consulting the provinces, a document on *federal* communications policy, but it is inadmissible for the federal government, acting on its own, to publish a document on *national* or *Canadian* communications policy." [168]

This insistence on distinguishing "federal" from "national" policy not only demanded a voice for the provinces but a different way of functioning. Quebec's green paper proposed a thorough overhaul of the Canadian communications system in the direction of sovereignty over communications policy for those provinces wishing it, with certain largely residual and technical regulatory powers reserved exclusively for Ottawa.

The provinces were prepared to come to the conference agreeing to support one another's claims while not necessarily sharing a common position.

Different provinces had different priorities and different areas in which they hoped to gain jurisdiction, but the bottom line was that a province should have the right to control any but evidently "national" aspects of communications. Ontario, which had been second after Quebec to create a communications portfolio in 1971, not only shared some of Quebec's demands but fully supported Quebec's entire position.

Ontario's situation had been spelled out by Gordon Carton, minister of transportation and communications, in the provincial legislature on 17 May 1973. The constitutional argument of the 1930s in favour of federal jurisdiction was "questionable and unacceptable" with respect to cable, he said: "There is no doubt in our minds that cable television systems should be under the control and direction of the province." [169]

Carton specifically lauded his "close, constructive and rewarding working relationship" with Jean-Paul L'Allier. Quebec and Ontario had many interests in common; Ontario understood Quebec's concerns and supported its positions: "provinces must be treated as mature governments and not as just another pressure group, as is now the case in many communications matters." [170]

The federal-provincial conference took place in Ottawa on 29–30 November 1973. After the published positions of Ottawa and the provinces, especially Quebec, only one preliminary question was actually discussed. Was Ottawa prepared to open the entire sector to negotiation, L'Allier wanted to know? Only if the provinces renounced their demands and committed themselves to finding an accord, Pelletier said. The conference adjourned with all sides minimally satisfied and promising to pursue efforts at reaching agreement in 1974. But, meanwhile, communications policy was evolving under the old regime, and while Quebec maintained a firm political position, it had yet to achieve any concessions. As editorialist Laurent Laplante pointed out in Le Devoir, of all the provinces, Quebec was inherently the least likely to achieve "cultural sovereignty," even if it was the one that spoke about it the most. [171]

# CHAPTER SIX

# Policy and Politics
# (1974–80)

## INTRODUCTION

The late 1960s and early 1970s were thus, as we have just seen, a period of intense transformation in the social context of broadcasting in Canada. Technological developments made it necessary to extend any discussion of "broadcasting" to include the wider sphere of "communications." With the creation of the federal Department of Communications, and the transformation of telecommunications by the spread of satellite and computer technologies, the question of ownership and function of communications systems also spilled over the boundaries of traditional broadcasting. The DOC took charge of the new concerns, placing them in an industrial and economic perspective and left the "cultural" aspects of communications with broadcasting. The cable issue formed a bridge between broadcasting and telecommunications and was the flash-point of conflict between "public" and "private" interests while the new CRTC struggled to formulate policy in its regard.

The extension of the traditional limits of broadcasting was accompanied by a sharp challenge to exclusive federal jurisdiction by the provinces, led by Quebec. Quebec's official claims were particularly upsetting as they took place in a context of extraparliamentary social agitation that threatened to undermine the political stability of the Canadian federal state. While the broadcasting act had been intended to resolve the question of broadcasting and national unity, the question was in fact very far from settled. Quebec made broadcasting and, more broadly, communications a constitutional issue, putting forward its own state authority as a potential alternative to Ottawa's. Led by Quebec, the provinces won the power to establish "educational" broadcasting facilities and went on to demand jurisdiction over other parts of the field.

By the early 1970s, the traditional framework of broadcasting had splintered and spread in several directions. The fundamental questions remained unchanged – ownership and control, national unity, the role of the state, and the role of the public – but there were new actors (provinces, cable companies, and the DOC) and new issues (new technologies, educational broadcasting, and the demand for "participation"). There were also whole new webs of problems: federal-provincial relations, alternative and community media.

To gain an overall perspective on broadcasting, the entire constellation of issues and actors had to be taken into account. For example, while the CRTC behaved as trustee of the public interest with respect to cable policy and the CBC, the provinces, especially Quebec, claimed to represent the public interest against the central authority of Ottawa; meanwhile, autonomous public interest and community groups came increasingly to see state solutions as part of the problem and proposed and created alternatives that denied the place of state authority altogether.

Without these challenges, the road from broadcasting to communications would have been one of rapid retreat from public service to private enterprise. Against the dominant backdrop of broadcasting as a factor in public decision making was an increased tendency among political decision makers to think of the public as audience, consumer, and even stock market investor. Economistic views of the public would become more and more powerful in the coming years, even as political debate intensified.

In the second half of the 1970s, the public dimension of broadcasting continued to be hotly contested. Central state authority in communications came under constant attack from the provinces, led by Quebec, from grass-roots popular groups seeking to reinstil a classical public focus to communications, and from new social movements making new demands concerning access, regulation of image making, and power over the means of communication. In this context, the very frame of reference of "public" broadcasting was fragmented: did it refer to the national broadcaster; to the regulatory agency; to the responsibilities of all broadcasters; to the question of jurisdiction; to democratic participation? Alternative conceptions of public broadcasting would abound, but the most challenging ones remained marginal – the stakes were too high for them to be allowed to emerge.

By 1974, Canadian communications policy was seen by some people as a vehicle for cultural sovereignty vis-à-vis the United States, and by others as an obstacle to the cultural sovereignty of Quebec. Two issues dominated the agenda: Ottawa's insistence on the need to articulate a national telecommunications policy covering everything from satellites to broadcasting, in which the federal government played the dominant role, and renewed consideration of the role of the CBC with respect to Canada's internal and external national questions.

Debate exhibited a triple thrust, representing a combination of political pressures that would chip away at the traditional role of public broadcasting in Canada for the remainder of the 1970s:

1. Policy conflicts between Ottawa and Quebec continued to emphasize resistance to the federal conception of centralized state power with respect to communications
2. The developing national unity crisis continued to aggravate expectations of Canada's national public broadcaster
3. Technologically produced fragmentation of audiences continued to undermine the notion of public broadcasting based on the once-predominant "mass" audience and caused the emergence of new demands based on serving the needs of particular "publics"

The CRTC hearings on CBC licence renewals in 1974 were a watershed with regard to this latter development. For the first time, advocates of public broadcasting would sharply criticize the shortcomings of the CBC, putting forth a wide range of new possibilities in the process.

## POLICY: WHO SPEAKS FOR THE PUBLIC? 1974–76

### The CRTC versus the CBC

The CRTC had spent a good deal of its first six years wrestling with the problem cable was posing to pan-Canadian cultural sovereignty, which Pierre Juneau had described as "filling the added capacity of our distribution system with programs other than those that can be imported from other countries."[1] In 1974, the CRTC identified its fellow behemoth of Canadian cultural nationalism, the CBC, as another part of the problem.

Public hearings on the renewal of CBC licences were called for 18–21 February 1974. More than three hundred interested parties submitted briefs expressing what the CRTC considered "an attitude of proprietary interest in the CBC as the public element of the Canadian broadcasting system and a strong belief that the CBC ought to be responsive to their particular needs, whether as individuals of diverse interests and tastes, or as members of groups within the wider Canadian community."[2]

In addition to the traditional question of the need for distinctive Canadian programming, the interveners emphasized two new themes: the need for improved programming to meet specific needs (local and regional, multicultural, northern, native people, women, farmers); and the need to reduce, if not eliminate, commercial activity. Seventeen briefs singled out public affairs programming as particularly inadequate in its lack of objectivity, depth, and stimulation.[3]

The thrust of the public interventions was a remarkable contrast to the presentation of the CBC, whose president, Laurent Picard, opened the public hearings on 18 February. Picard's presentation focused on the CBC's need to maintain its audience in the face of the "brutal" impact of cable technology and its fragmenting effect. He said there were three possible models the CBC could adopt: it could become "wholly commercial," which would be unacceptable because of its public service mandate; it could be "different" and "Canadian," but aimed at a "specialized minority," which would be unacceptable because "élitist"; or it could be "different, Canadian [and] mass." This was the only acceptable strategy, he said, one conceived in terms of serving a Canadian mass audience.[4]

The distinction was important, because it established the CBC's perception of Canada as a mass society rather than a community of publics. The purpose of CBC programming would be to reach the largest possible audience, albeit with "different, Canadian" content. This was a departure from the position the CBC had taken before the Massey commission twenty-five years earlier, when it had said that it saw itself serving different segments of the society at different times.

The CBC position was a curious one in a context of audience fragmentation. One of the CRTC commissioners, Brian Land, commented that "there seems to be some conflict between this trend toward fragmentation and the future role of the CBC" as a mass audience service. Picard replied: "The greater the chance of fragmentation, the greater is the necessity for a broadcasting system which unifies the country and has a mass appeal."[5]

For three days, the CRTC heard oral interventions from groups and individuals. The ministers responsible for communications in the Maritime provinces and the Council of Maritime Premiers presented an unhappy portrait of the lack of regional input, representation and identification with the CBC. Basic service in the Maritimes was still incomplete. (New Brunswick, for example, had no English-language CBC television station.) Maritimers considered themselves poorly represented in popular CBC "national" programs; they wanted more regional programming for national distribution, to represent themselves to the rest of the country, and more local and regional programming for local and regional consumption, to represent themselves to themselves. This sentiment was later echoed by representatives of several northern and native groups as well as "ethnic" organizations who said the CBC was misinterpreting its mandate by ignoring and failing to reflect the multicultural and multilingual character of Canada in its programming. Coming after the CBC appearance, these were eloquent illustrations of the problem of a national mass audience strategy.

The British Columbia Committee on the CBC also emphasized the need for local and regional production. Its representative, Vianne Lyman, quoted from a letter the committee had received warning that it would not achieve its goals "unless the power of the Toronto-Ottawa-Montreal mafia, which dominates the CBC, is broken and the CBC transformed into a people's network that is controlled by, and operated in the interest of" the various regional groups. The committee urged the CRTC "to require the CBC to respect its mandate concerning local and regional programming as well as ... national unity."[6]

Even the CBC's private affiliates had a difficult time with the corporation's centralism. The CBC Radio Network Advisory Committee, representing fifty-five English and twenty French stations affiliated with the CBC, said the "CBC thinks in broad national terms, while the affiliates have to think in community terms." Private radio had to provide a localized service, it said.[7]

The question of financing had been a thorny one since the introduction of television necessitated a large public commitment in the late 1940s. In 1974 the CBC was still arguing, without success, for three- to five-year financial support so that it could make proper budgetary arrangements. The need to "start the fight all over again every year," in Picard's phrase, remained an important political control and another conservative influence.[8]

The Canadian Broadcasting League also addressed this question. Past president Graham Spry characterized the history of Canadian broadcasting as a series of missed opportunities in which successive governments failed to provide the means to implement the strategy repeatedly endorsed by Parliament. In the current context, the need was to resolve the "persistently inadequate" problem of CBC financing. The league proposed some form of direct audience financing or statutory grant pegged to the gross national product.[9]

The question of financing and revenue could not be separated from that of programming philosophy. A former civil servant, W.H. Bill Neville, explained that the CBC's dependence on commercial revenue for 20 percent of its overall operating budget made this the priority of CBC program policy. A short term solution would be for the CBC to receive its total operating budget from Parliament on a three- to five-year basis; then, any revenue that could be raised commercially would be returned as "a bonus back to the people," but no programming decision would have to be made on this basis. At present, Neville said, the CBC had no distinctive programming philosophy setting it apart from the other North American networks; there was no way "that you could identify it, by what you see, as the 'public' system."[10]

The Association of Canadian Television and Radio Artists (ACTRA) spoke in a similar tone. Its vice-president, Jack Gray, was concerned that commercials "represent far more than just a way of making money in broadcasting, they represent an attitude" towards broadcasting and towards the public. "We want to consider a commercial-free public system, a broad public mass system ... that is innovative and Canadian," Gray said, "in spite of the fact that ACTRA members make a lot of money in commercials." CBC withdrawal from commercials was in "the public benefit, the social benefit in the long run."[11]

Canadian advertisers did not agree. The Association of Canadian Advertisers and the Institute of Canadian Advertising said any move to reduce or eliminate advertising "would not be in the best interests of the Canadian public, the broadcasters, nor the Canadian business that uses the medium for advertising." This was the old argument that the public was a consumers' market sharing the interests of the producers of the goods it consumed. [12]

The commercial question aside, several important groups took issue with the CBC's conception of the mass audience. The Toronto-based Association of Television Producers and Directors argued that programming had to consider the viewer as an individual rather than a "faceless consumer." The association said there was a need for both "programs with wide appeal as well as programs with a more specialized or narrow focus ... as a measure of the value or the success of a program the spectrum of an audience is often just as important as the size of that audience," said association president Roy Hazzan. [13]

The Canadian Labour Congress was more direct in questioning the CBC approach. Gordon McCaffery said the CBC had reached the wrong conclusion about its programming model; it should be "a public broadcasting system which is Canadian, different and diversified," rather than orienting most of its programming towards a mass audience. By "diversified," the CLC meant: "programs which will be of interest to Canadians in all parts of the country ... but not necessarily an audience that would be called 'mass' ... it's still a 'national' audience, but it doesn't have to be 'mass'." [14]

Several groups pointed out the practical consequences of CBC philosophy. The Toronto-based Committee on Television said the question was not "high brow versus low brow programming." At present, said Abe Rotstein, "all constituencies in the country are being badly served and ought to be served better." The committee emphasized that its members were "total and unambiguous supporters of public broadcasting in this country," but they were "deeply concerned" about some aspects of the CBC's execution of its mandate, including "that public affairs programming has declined during the last several years to the point where it has become irrelevant to the country." Drama had declined to "a new level of inconsequence," the regions had been "seriously ignored," and the renaissance in film and the arts had been hardly reflected on the CBC. [15]

The Ontario Committee on the Status of Women and Women for Political Action illustrated how half the population was being misserved. Helen Lafontaine said they had decided to intervene out of "a long-standing and steadily increasing sense of outrage as each day we were assaulted and insulted by what we saw on television." Television reproduced "the age-old view of women as second-class citizens," while treating women to an "endless progression of moronic programs" during "their" part of the viewing day, the afternoon. Commercials caricaturing women were "pervasive and dangerous weapons which male society has used effectively to keep women in line." The groups presented documentation which one commissioner described as "hair-raising," showing, for example, the near-total absence of women in news programming; among its recommendations were that the CBC establish a women's television news journal, staffed by women.[16]

This type of critique led to the question of media democracy. The National Association of Broadcasting Employees and Technicians (NABET) called, among other things, for citizen participation in programming, advocating the establishment, in each region, of a representative citizens' committee to orient the direction of local programming.[17] L'Association des réalisateurs, representing all Radio-Canada and CBC producers and directors outside Toronto, said there was no such thing as a network audience, only local audiences, "and therefore, there should be more decision-making at the local level."[18]

The most eloquent argument for democracy came from two former Radio-Canada employees, Marcelle Racine and Pierre Gauvreau, who described television as "a closed system" in which the public had no means of influencing production and where the consumer's only option was to change the channel. Both private and public networks established their programming according to criteria over which the public had no influence, they said. Restrictive structures isolated the media from the public, sealing off the broadcasting system and creating a monopoly on access for a group of privileged individuals. This privilege then became entangled in a net of internal relations which transformed the messengers and their messages. Racine and Gauvreau called for democratization – turning broadcasting over to laymen – by finding a way for the public to express its creativity (for example, through public consultation with broadcasters about programming). A broadcaster should be thought of as an "agency," not an "institution."[19]

The CRTC hearing was a public forum in the tradition that had started with the Aird commission. It was not an investigation of the CBC, the CRTC insisted, yet it demonstrated the gulf that had arisen between the public broadcaster and its supporters. One aspect of this separation was the split between centre and periphery; another concerned the conception of the audience; yet a third revolved around control – was it to be bureaucratic or democratic?

On 31 March, the CRTC announced its decision on the CBC's licence renewal.[20] The problem of the audience was "the single most important and fundamental problem facing the CBC."[21] The CRTC rejected the CBC's stated objective of attracting the largest possible audience, an objective it attributed to the infiltration of a commercial mentality at the corporation. The "constraints of the marketing environment" had drawn the CBC "into a mode of operation increasingly based on mass appeal." Key personnel had become biased towards "highly commercial mass concepts," resulting in the erosion of "the original public interest purposes of the organization."[22]

In order to fulfil its mandate, the CBC had to take the initiative in changing its own commercial policy in spite of the commercial climate of the overall broadcasting environment: "Despite the need for the CBC to continue to provide a 'popular' broadcasting service ... the CBC, as a public service institution, should guard strongly against considering itself as a 'mass-medium' and particularly against considering its audience as a 'mass'."[23] The CBC should treat its audience instead "as an active community of people, with real and varying communication needs."[24]

The CBC's national unity mandate, the CRTC said, had historically attracted more attention than any other. Confusion could be avoided if there were agreement as to what the mandate did not mean. It did not mean favouring a particular attitude towards federal-provincial disputes, suppressing the views of those who questioned proposed constitutional arrangements, or consistently ignoring Quebec separatists, artists with extreme political views, or proponents of Canada's integration with the United States.[25]

However, the CRTC's bottom line was unequivocal towards the CBC's fundamental role regarding Canada's internal and external national questions: "There should be no disagreement about the fact that the phrase does mean being consciously partial to the success of Canada as a united country with its own national objectives, independent from those of other countries."[26]

Next, the CRTC dealt with the commercial question, reiterating that the CBC's traditional role "is especially threatened if the criteria of the marketplace are permitted to predominate."[27] Following an announced intention by the CBC, the CRTC attached a condition to the corporation's licence requiring it to eliminate commercials entirely from CBC radio and from CBC children's television programs.

Describing the CBC as "the nation's most powerful public platform," the CRTC supported the right of CBC journalists "to inquire freely into and expose [the] issues, problems and conflicts [affecting contemporary society] and to investigate abuses or threats to freedom wherever they occur." It insisted, however, that this right had to be exercised according to internal rules and professional discipline that guaranteed fairness and balance.

Many Canadians, the CRTC said, felt that the CBC was closed to new ideas, slow in responding to public needs, ponderous in making decisions, "and tends to operate as if it were a private vested interest."[28] The CBC had to guard against a programming philosophy "which reflects less the needs of the public and the challenges of the mandate than the need for institutional survival." For example, the CRTC referred to "the protracted process by which an idea becomes a program at the CBC" as "surely inimical to a free flow of ideas especially for those geographically removed from production centres, or unable to lobby from a position of strength within the Corporation."[29]

The report reiterated its earlier warnings that increased cable penetration created a threatening imbalance between distribution and production, and indicated that the extension of CBC services would be part of the solution to this problem. It applauded the CBC's "accelerated coverage plan" for extending basic radio and television service in English and French to every community of five hundred or more people, and the Northern Broadcasting Plan that proposed to extend national service to even smaller communities in the north and develop special services designed to meet northern broadcasting needs. But the obvious need to spend great sums on "transmission" or "hardware" should not obscure the need to adequately support broadcasting "programming" or "software," the CRTC said. The only possible way this could be done was through additional public funds for program services.[30]

In sum, the CRTC's 1974 decision appeared to mediate between public opinion, as expressed in the submissions it had received, and the CBC's perception of itself. The CRTC saw the CBC's shortcomings coming from two sources: a kind of internal sclerosis, brought on by corporate self-interest and integration to the dominant marketing mentality of North American broadcasting, and the government's political reluctance to provide it with adequate, autonomous financing. On the whole, the CRTC's view of the public interest in broadcasting was a fair synthesis of the interventions that had been made during the public consultation. The hearings had revealed the extent to which public expectations of the CBC exceeded the requirements stated in the broadcasting act. While the CBC had come under strong criticism, the concept of public broadcasting had been broadly, and virtually unanimously, supported. As for the CRTC, it appeared, for once, to be playing the role expected of a regulatory agency.[31]

## Redefining the CRTC

The CRTC's strong position regarding the CBC and the high profile surrounding the 1974 licence renewal hearings obscured another major aspect of the agency's activities during the early 1970s: just as the BBG had done before it, the CRTC was overseeing the gradual extension of the private sector in broadcasting, at the expense of the public. The problems the CRTC had so eloquently identified with respect to the CBC could not be resolved without clear political commitment to the public sector *as public sector*. This was not on the agenda in the 1970s, and the CRTC played an important part in keeping it that way.

In July 1972, the CRTC awarded a licence to Global Communications for a new regional commercial television network in southern Ontario. This extension of the system on the private side was carried out in the guise of stimulating Canadian production; at no time was any serious consideration given to facing the problem by expanding the system on the public side instead.[32]

Following the Global decision, the CRTC held hearings around the country for similar regional licences. Between June 1973 and April 1975, "third station" licences were awarded for Edmonton, Montreal, Quebec City, Winnipeg, and Vancouver, despite organized public opposition in all of these centres. When the Global licensee ran into serious financial problems and faced liquidation in 1974, the CRTC chaperoned a bail-out operation to keep it alive.[33]

The CRTC effectively enshrined the private property rights of commercial broadcasters by refusing to delve into the "managerial prerogatives" of their financial affairs, even where these might have had bearing on fulfilment of licence requirements. The CRTC habitually granted automatic licence renewals, refused to allow competitive applications, tolerated a *de facto* traffic in licences between buyers and sellers of broadcasting enterprises, and would not enforce licence conditions. In spite of the explicit wording of the broadcasting act, the CRTC protected the interests and guaranteed the profitability of the broadcasting industry – a particularly contradictory attitude when seen in light of the CRTC's approach to the CBC.[34]

At this crucial juncture, the agency charged with supervising Canada's national objectives in broadcasting placed its stake on expanding the private sector which had historically demonstrated its incapacity to meet these objectives. Frustration with the CBC's failure to perform was one side of the problem. Determination to keep the public sector centred in a single national institution was the other and, perhaps, more important side. Thus, in the 1970s, the commercial forces in broadcasting continued their advance while the public dimension was increasingly hemmed in to the confines of a national broadcaster under siege.

After the federal elections of July 1974 returned a Liberal majority, the government moved to rationalize the communications sector by unifying everything related to telecommunications under a single agency. In October, legislation was introduced proposing to combine the functions of the CRTC with those of the telecommunications committee of the Canadian Transport Commission (CTC), which up until then regulated the common carriers under federal jurisdiction.[35]

In the House of Commons on 4 March 1975, Communications Minister Gérard Pelletier explained that the government attached significance to both aspects of telecommunications: broadcasting and transmission.[36] Thus, "carriage" and "content" were to be joined; this new approach had been made necessary because of the advent of cable television, which was neither broadcasting nor telecommunications but contained characteristics of both.

Pelletier had indicated the context of the latest policy thrust in an October 1974 appearance before the Standing Committee on Transport and Communications. There, he evoked the problem posed to Canada's national integrity by the north-south pull of new technologies like "teleprocessing" and the increasing importance of communications generally for cultural, social, economic, and scientific development.[37]

Pelletier had also, at that time, summed up the situation in federal-provincial relations in communications. The federal government and the CRTC had been closely scrutinizing provincial interventions that might be in violation of federal jurisdiction, and Ottawa was involved in a court battle with Quebec over a cable licence granted by Quebec's Régie des services publics. But by March 1975 Pelletier was saying that the government would seek provincial collaboration in the new regulatory process on the basis of the position outlined in his 1973 green paper.[38]

The role of the provinces was unclear, however, especially in the ongoing state of conflict over jurisdiction. The Conservatives leapt on this contradiction. MP Jim Balfour said provincial participation should be the cornerstone of federal communications policy, for example, by replacing the CRTC with a commission made up of federal and provincial nominees, and by encouraging public bodies at all levels to participate in broadcasting endeavours with a minimum of federal control. The proposed legislation, on the other hand, masked the policy that lay beneath its surface, Balfour said; it was "another step toward solidifying the federal government's position vis-à-vis the provinces without their consent or consultation."[39]

Quebec Conservatives saw the bill contributing to the divisiveness brought on by the Liberals' national unity policy. "If Canada was built, linked and united by railways ... paradoxically it is now divided on the matter of communications," Claude Wagner said.[40] The question of jurisdiction was a political, not a legal one, and should be resolved by dialogue and negotiation, not the courts. Roch LaSalle said all talk of national unity was not serious if the government did not give up its centralizing policies; national harmony was a more viable goal than national unity.[41]

The NDP saw the issue in different terms. Cyril Symes described the danger in creating a "superregulatory agency": "The large agency tends to be subservient to the communications corporation interest ... they tend to allow vertical integration and strengthening of the monopoly of a few key industries in the communications system ... [to have a] fixation on technology."[42]

Symes hoped the philosophy of the CRTC, which had been more attentive to individuals and consumer groups, would prevail over that of the CTC, which had listened more carefully to the large corporations. But even the CRTC had not had the resources to back up its decisions.

The bill was referred to the parliamentary committee on broadcasting, and returned to the House on 21 April. For the Conservatives, Patrick Nowlan said there was clearly no national consensus on broadcasting and communications policy, which, he recalled, had not been seriously debated since 1968: "We really do not know who is calling the shots in respect of communications in this land."[43] Cyril Symes reiterated his earlier argument, adding that there was a need for "some provision for consumer advocacy in the field of broadcasting and telecommunications."[44] But the NDP supported the bill as it passed third reading. The Act to Establish the Canadian Radio-Television and Telecommunications Commission[45] received royal assent on 19 June 1975, and took effect on 1 April 1976, making the CRTC the leading agency of Canadian communications.

The debate on the CRTC act provided a snapshot of the various national parties' positions on policy issues in the mid-1970s. The government's concern was to rationalize the regulatory process in a framework it saw corresponding to the new technological context. Coming in the midst of negotiations with the provinces, the move underlined federal determination to retain mastery over the direction of change as well as power. The Conservatives, politically less inclined towards centralization, supported the provinces, their small Quebec caucus endorsing the Quebec government's nationalist claims. As for the NDP, it provided a social-democratic critique of the situation, but true to its traditional orientation, supported the centralist position nonetheless.

### Ottawa versus Quebec

Meanwhile, Quebec pursued its own communications policy. In marginal areas of no apparent interest to Ottawa, such as community media, it moved on its own. In 1973, the MCQ began providing regular funding to community radio, television, and newspapers through a special program of aid to community media (PAMEC), with an initial overall grant of $200,000. Thus, in an attempt to recapture some broadcasting space unoccupied by Ottawa, Quebec began to support a unique form of media fraught with all the contradictions of dependency on state control of the purse-strings.[46]

In many cases, despite these constraints, community media were working models of democratic communication. In the original Normandin experiment, 150 villagers had taken part in choosing themes, researching, interviewing, editing, and otherwise manipulating technical equipment during three hours of nightly television distributed by cable through five towns in the region.[47] The experience led to the creation of Quebec's first community broadcasting council, in which representatives of about fifty community associations and individual members participated regularly. Now, as community television took hold and spread, similar councils were formed in other regions of Quebec.[48] At the same time, as the result of a 1973 CRTC policy proposal for FM radio,[49] community radio became a legally viable communication form. Within a year, community radio stations took root in

Vancouver, Kitchener, Chicoutimi, and Montreal. But in community radio, too, only the Quebec government was willing to systematically provide funding, albeit in a limited way, and aside from college campuses and northern native communities in the rest of Canada, community radio took hold largely only in Quebec. In the 1970s, Quebec community broadcasting thus developed and spread as an associative form of communication made possible by provincial state subsidies and federal regulatory provisions.

Quebec also concentrated on developing and expanding the services of Radio-Québec. Ottawa and the provinces had agreed on a definition of "educational broadcasting" in 1969. Since 1972, Radio-Québec had been diffusing programs over closed-circuit cable systems, but was not yet an actual broadcasting network. After the CRTC approved Radio-Québec applications for broadcasting transmitters in Montreal and Quebec City in April 1974, Jean-Paul L'Allier announced that 1974–75 would mark Quebec's entry into the world of mass media.[50] To achieve this, Quebec proposed to spend $12.3 million. Radio-Québec was not to be another elitist medium, L'Allier promised, it would not become an ivory tower, producing programs that had only to be transmitted to an acquiescent public.[51]

However, this did not mean it was to be a "community" network. Educational and cultural television, L'Allier said, would be more than a mere means of intellectual exchange put at the disposal of the people. Mechanisms ensuring public participation would have to be worked out.

But even at this early stage, a gap was appearing between the promise of Radio-Québec and its reality. The agency was paralysed by a four-month labour conflict in 1973–74. A document produced by the CNTU-affiliated employees' union (Syndicat général des employés de Radio-Québec) painted a dismal picture of self-censorship, bureaucracy, a hierarchy impervious to communication, and a feeling of powerlessness among the personnel.[52]

Radio-Québec began broadcasting on its own UHF frequency in January 1975. In March, the Quebec Broadcasting Bureau (l'Office de radio-télé-diffusion du Québec), the Ontario Educational Communication Authority, and the Alberta Communication Corporation created the Canadian Educational Television Agency. But Radio-Québec was under fire as public expectations for a truly different television arose. Between April and October 1975, the ORTQ held public hearings on programming and development around Quebec. The hearings demonstrated a strong public demand for a democratic, decentralized educational network based in Quebec's regions.[53]

At the same time, the cable issue was coming to a head. Since 1973, the roughly 160 cable companies operating in Quebec were subject to regulation by the Régie des services publics as well as the CRTC. It took until November 1974 for a conflict to occur, when the two agencies awarded licences to different applicants for a cable concession in the lower St Lawrence region near Rimouski. The Dionne-d'Auteuil case would eventually be decided by the Supreme Court of Canada, in a decision as full of political implications as the Privy Council ruling of 1932.

The uniting of regulatory responsibility for broadcasting and telecommunications was an important step in Ottawa's consolidation of communications activities under the authority of the DOC. The secretary of state (now Hugh Faulkner) no longer had anything to do with broadcasting. Anything specific to the CBC or private broadcasting was dealt with directly by the CRTC (although, with the commission's new responsibilities in telecommunications, there was some concern over the amount of attention that broadcasting would continue to attract). But overall political orientation came increasingly from the minister of communications, the main spokesman for federal policy.

Having unified the regulatory mechanism, Pelletier's priority in April 1975 was to produce a national policy reflecting the consolidation of broadcasting and telecommunications. In order to do this, it was necessary to bring the provinces to heel. On 24 April 1975, Pelletier told the parliamentary committee on broadcasting (which now took over communications from the committee on transport and communications):

Our difficulties with some provinces are that it is difficult to make them realize that we are not attached to our jurisdiction, it is not power for power. We think there is a national broadcasting system, a Canadian system, which includes a private and public sector, and we think it is very important that this system not be balkanized in any way. That is why we say that the decisions of tribunals all over the country were very wise, because they always sustained the federal jurisdiction over broadcasting. [54]

Also in April 1975, Pelletier published a major policy paper. [55] The government's primary concern, the paper said, was to ensure that the development and use of new technology in communications "shall be the subject of a conscious choice which establishes a proper balance between the economical employment of scarce resources and the development of effective service to the public over as wide a range as possible." [56]

The ongoing conflict with the provinces dominated the tone of the paper as it set out the logic of the federal position that had governed the distribution of jurisdiction since 1932. The components of a Canadian system amounted to more than the sum of ten provincial systems, and the federal government's responsibility was to avoid fragmentation and to achieve a harmonization of goals with the provinces in a "cooperative spirit." It cited as priorities the provision of efficient, economical consumer services; the preservation and strengthening of the economic, social, cultural, and political fabric of Canada; the establishment of strong communication links within and between all parts of Canada; and the "free flow of information between all Canadians." Separate mention was made of the government's concern to maintain the traditional objectives of the national broadcasting system and, particularly, the traditional role of the Canadian Broadcasting Corporation.

The paper proposed setting up a "Committee for Communications Policy" made up of federal and provincial ministers. It offered to seek provincial concurrence in the nomination of part-time members of the CRTC (the first official proposal of this sort since the report of the Aird commission). But it insisted on exclusive federal jurisdiction over the broadcasting aspect of cable systems, although recognizing the potential use of these systems for other services which could come under provincial jurisdiction.

The federal government was willing to allow provinces a greater share of the licensing and regulatory process, in exchange for an agreement "explicitly accepting federal authority to impose criteria or conditions on any undertaking offering any form of 'programming' for distribution on coaxial-cable systems"; subject to such a guarantee, the government was prepared to negotiate other uses for cable.

Aside from the aspect of federal-provincial jurisdiction, the paper said there was a need for "complete revision of existing statutes" to establish "a coherent body of federal law on communications" following the CRTC reform, clarifying the respective roles of the government and the regulatory body. The government "should be authorized to give formal directions to the Commission on the interpretation of statutory objectives and the means for their implementation." In short, the government was to have more power.[57] Despite several efforts by Pelletier's successors, this "second stage" of the legislative reform had still not been realized by 1988.

The second federal-provincial conference of communications ministers was not convened until May 1975. This time the provinces presented a joint position stating that policy had to be made by eleven governments, not one in consultation with the others as Ottawa proposed. Ottawa's position had hardened considerably since November 1973. Gérard Pelletier now claimed he was only authorized to discuss administrative arrangements and not anything implying a possible constitutional change, which only the first ministers could resolve. Pelletier proposed creation of a consultative federal-provincial committee on communications policy and the conference adjourned to mid-July.

When it reconvened, Ottawa demanded that the provinces recognize its jurisdiction prior to joining the consultative committee, a position unacceptable to Quebec. Quebec withdrew from the conference, stating: "The case is closed."[58] Ottawa would not negotiate its exclusive jurisdiction over broadcasting, including cable. It was willing, however, to give the provinces more regulatory authority over telephone systems, and on this basis eight provinces agreed to participate in the proposed "council of communications ministers." Only British Columbia's NDP government shared Quebec's indignation.[59]

At any rate, the aborted conference marked the end of serious negotiations over a new sharing of powers in communications, to the humiliation of the provinces. This was the last area where Quebec had maintained an aggressive constitutional stance, and the Parti Québécois opposition declared the failure of Bourassa's "cultural sovereignty" policy along with the demise of the interprovincial common front.[60] René Lévesque publicly invited Jean-Paul L'Allier to join the PQ, but L'Allier retreated into the cocoon of government, reemerging as minister of cultural affairs in an August 1975 cabinet shuffle that moved a far more conventional minister, Denis Hardy, into the communications portfolio.

In Ottawa, Gérard Pelletier also resigned in August 1975 to become Canada's ambassador to France. His replacement as minister of communications, Pierre Juneau, failed to win a seat in a Montreal by-election and was obliged to resign in October. Jeanne Sauvé was named federal communications minister in December. By June 1976, Hardy and Sauvé had agreed to negotiate specific issues and leave the broader question of power in abeyance.

### Cable

After completing its major intervention on the CBC, the CRTC had returned its energies to establishing a framework for cable undertakings. On 17 February 1975, it announced a series of regulations, specifying the required and permissible range of services a cable undertaking could, or must, offer. Every cable operation would be required to provide certain services, such as a community channel (which they had only been "encouraged" to offer previously). Licensees would be required to devote at least 10 percent of gross annual subscription revenue to operating the community channel.[61]

There were over four hundred licensed cable systems in Canada by the end of 1974, with the capacity to reach 80 percent of all households. Thirty-eight percent of households already subscribed to cable service and revenue from cable operations totalled about 50 percent of television revenues and was growing at a faster rate.

The CRTC deplored the attitude of traditional broadcasters towards the cable industry and said its duty was not to protect any particular sector but to promote an economic strategy for the entire broadcasting system. For example, the cable industry had to be involved in finding solutions to the problems of Canadian program production. Cable had to take its responsibility as "a technologically and financially mature member of the Canadian broadcasting system."[62]

With the cable question as focal point, the CRTC was developing a discourse similar to the one that had once characterized the public authorities' approach towards private broadcasting. Invoking a consumers' protection perspective, the CRTC said: "Persons licensed in the public interest should hardly need to be reminded of their obligations to the public they are licensed to serve."[63] Not all licensees needed such a reminder, the CRTC added; many had understood the importance of their role as part of the overall system and had explored innovative ways of contributing to it.

There was, however, a remarkable difference with traditional broadcasting which no one had yet mentioned. While cable, like radio and television, was subject to public policy and regulation, it was exclusively in the private sector of the economy. In spite of the CRTC's claim to implement public policy objectives with regard to its operations, all cable undertakings in Canada were to be governed by the logic of the marketplace.

After holding public hearings in June 1975, the CRTC published a further policy statement on cable television in December.[64] It was now specified that cable licensees should "make a contribution to the quality and diversity of the Canadian broadcasting and program production industries; assume an increasing responsibility to contribute to the strength of the total broadcasting system; contribute a unique social service in the form of a community programming channel; improve the quality of cable television service and the relations between the cable television industry and the public it serves."[65]

Cable was expected to provide superior service, based on ever-expanding choice to its subscriber-public, without threatening "free" over-the-air broadcasting, which, as "the only service available to many Canadians ... must remain the primary element of the Canadian broadcasting system."[66]

Meanwhile, the expansion of cable was not aiding the need to develop program production. On the contrary, the cable distribution system was better oriented towards the promotion of American programming than to the creation and evolution of Canadian work.

The CRTC still held out high hope for the role that could be played by community programming, most significantly "its ability to turn the passive viewer of television into an active participant."[67] But it was not prepared to oblige the cable entrepreneurs to support community programming with their profits: It now retreated from its February position, deciding not to adopt a 10 percent minimum allocation. Instead, the CRTC announced it would "expect licensees to allocate a reasonable percentage of their gross subscriber revenue for the ongoing operation of the community channel."[68]

Finally, regarding pay-television, the CRTC found little public enthusiasm; only the cable companies appeared to favour it. Pay-television would cause increased audience fragmentation and further dilution of the "Canadian" aspects of the system; it would siphon away yet more of the audience of the over-the-air broadcasters; it would not likely bring much benefit to Canadian producers; yet, the CRTC said it was "highly probable in the future."[69] The CRTC position on pay-television begged the question: Why did Canadian authorities repeatedly permit the introduction of conceptually foreign technological innovations which they knew would weaken the indigenous elements of the system and make its objectives more unlikely?

On the whole, the CRTC's 1975 cable policy was a classic example of regulatory ambivalence. Despite its own rhetoric, not to mention the strongly articulated views of the various publics whose interest it was supposed to represent, the CRTC was becoming increasingly a captive of the industries it regulated. The complicity between the industry and the agency was particularly well illustrated by the candid testimony at the June 1975 hearings of D.R. Graham, representing the Canadian Cable Television Association: "Your problem, one of your problems, is to give the outward appearance of satisfying the public that their interests have been looked after and you don't like perhaps to say to the public that we are perhaps more competent to make this evaluation than you, an average citizen."[70] The spectre of the phantom public formed a bonding link between the cable industry and the CRTC.

### Managing Diversity

In addition to the cultural problems posed by the need to develop a cable policy suitable to the system's entrepreneurs, the political problem with the provinces persisted in 1976. Communications Minister Jeanne Sauvé told the parliamentary committee the situation had been at an impasse since the July 1975 federal-provincial conference, which, she said, had resolved nothing. In spite of appearances, Sauvé said, the provinces' concerns, Quebec's included, were really economic rather than cultural, and related to the need to plan the orderly development of the telecommunications system.[71]

Sauvé said she would not compromise the federal jurisdiction and expected the provinces to come around to the federal position as they realized the importance of protecting the telecommunications industry from fragmentation. This was an interesting characterization of the federal-provincial dispute, which was beginning to appear as one in which opposing "national" discourses were in fact covering up economic concerns.

A strong indication of the scope of the problem by the mid-1970s had come earlier in 1976, during CRTC hearings for cable licences in Saskatchewan. There, the provincial government put forward the view that broadcasting "should be employed as a conscious instrument of social policy": "It is regrettable that existing federal broadcasting legislation fails to recognize the potential contribution of broadcasting to regional development in Canada. Surely the national objectives found in the Broadcasting Act pertaining to Canadian identity and national unity are only meaningful if they are based on strong regional cornerstones in communications."[72]

Unlike Quebec, which had traditionally demystified Canadian broadcasting policy from the perspective of an alternative nationalism, Saskatchewan highlighted the negative aspects of national broadcasting for Canada's regional communities. It proposed that the CRTC recognize the need for "a meaningful cross-fertilization between locally-owned, autonomous, broadly-based community controlled undertakings and regional and national programming networks and agencies." Specifically, it called for Crown monopoly ownership of cable hardware and support for nonprofit programming cooperatives as "appropriate means of achieving community relevance in broadcasting."[73]

The CRTC rejected Saskatchewan's attempt to use cable as a technological resource for social and economic development, approving the traditional private sector model in its place. But in November 1976, the federal government signed an agreement with the province of Manitoba allowing the provincially Crown-owned Manitoba Tel to own cable distribution hardware while Ottawa retained jurisdiction over broadcast-related services. The Manitoba scheme was much less socially far-reaching than Saskatchewan's, which contained a strong public component. Both were far less threatening than the intentions of Quebec. But the Canada-Manitoba agreement added a rift between the government and the CRTC to the growing list of entanglements in the communications sector in the late 1970s.[74]

Another provincial initiative which, if heeded, would have drastically transformed the nature of the Canadian broadcasting system took the form of an Ontario government Royal Commission on Violence in the Communications Industry, chaired by the former federal secretary of state, Judy LaMarsh. With a mandate "to report upon matters relating to the possible harm to the public interest of the increasing exploitation of violence in the communications industry," it reported in 1976.[75]

The LaMarsh report concluded that there was no way to deal with the problem of violence in communications without calling into question the structures of Canadian television. Citing as alternative models the German, British, and Dutch systems, the commission recommended "a radically altered national television system, more sensitive to the needs of the public."[76] The new system would eliminate existing Canadian broadcasting structures and place all television programming "under public control of an organization to be called Television Canada to serve all Canadians with a multi-channel, publicly directed cable system to include US and other imported programs, but with a stricter control of violent content."[77]

Television Canada would be financed by advertising and user fees, established along the lines of existing cable fees, and would not require a parliamentary subsidy. All programs other than news would be purchased from independent producers. Television Canada would be "completely independent and answerable only to Parliament"[78] through a minister who would be required to make public any advice he or she gave the public body. Television delivery systems (cable, public and private stations, and networks) would be combined under a second corporation of mixed public and private ownership, called Tele-Distribution Canada.[79] The existing facility owners would be shareholders of Tele-Distribution Canada, which would distribute the programs of the public programmer, Television Canada.

Having clearly implied that the Canadian broadcasting system was insensitive to the needs of the public, and after making proposals bordering on nationalization of the private broadcasters and cable companies, the Ontario royal commission then went on to make recommendations that would result in the radical democratization of the system: "To decentralize control and make such a system more responsive to viewers and their real social imperatives – such as what models for behaviour are being shown – there [would] be regional councils of volunteer listeners and viewers, for each official language, made up of nominees from interested groups. Each regional council would make nominations to Television Canada's Board of Directors, with such members to elect the chairman of the board."[80]

This "council broadcasting" was reminiscent of the advisory councils operated by the CBC during the "Forum" era and recalled the 1950 recommendations of the Quebec Catholic labour unions to the Massey commission; the electoral procedure was similar to the plan of the Alberta farm and labour groups for their abortive cooperative station in 1946; on the whole, the proposal was as far-reaching as those made previously by organizations such as the Fédération professionnelle des journalistes du Québec, while going far beyond anything proposed up to that point by official agencies such as the CRTC.

Finally, it called for a new broadcasting act "to redefine the primary purpose of Canadian television as an independent service in the enlightened public interest and to provide for a better balance in all program categories, truly reflecting not only high ethical standards but also the cultural and regional diversity of Canada."[81]

But the thrust of federal communications policy was in a different direction by 1976. It was becoming essentially economic, and there were already indications of where it was headed. For example, Telesat Canada, the domestic satellite corporation created in 1969, was operating domestically as a commercial service and working on developing technology that Canada could sell abroad. Telesat was owned 50 percent by the federal government and 50 percent by its customer common carriers. This was certainly a unique corporate structure, Telesat president D.A. Golden told the parliamentary committee, but he hoped to see it become more unique still by entertaining Eric Kierans's idea of "going public," which had never been put into effect.[82]

On 25 May 1976, the new chairman of the reconstituted CRTC, former CBC broadcaster and department head, Harry J. Boyle, told the parliamentary committee that the CRTC's concern was to develop an understanding of broadcasting and telecommunications that could be translated into policies and objectives consistent with its mandate. One of the CRTC's priorities was still the rationalization of off-air broadcasting. Cable, Boyle said, had evolved out of "the public will," the will "to be a completely open society and to have as much of the good things as possible, irrespective of the cost."

Local programming could be an antidote to audience fragmentation, but national programming was more problematic – there was not enough of an audience base to support the creative and production resources of the country.[83]

This problem – the problem of the broadcasting *market* – had, of course, been identified by the Aird commission and had convinced R.B. Bennett that only a public system could assure Canada of national broadcasting. Now, the chairman of the national agency charged with overseeing the Canadian system added that only an overall cultural policy could deal with this problem; broadcasting alone could not. Liberal MP John Roberts supported Boyle's view of broadcasting as the core of a cultural strategy, taking it a step further. Canada's strategy for culture, he told Boyle, must be based on "the shoring up of the Canadian identity which is an obligation both on you and on the CBC."[84]

By mid-1976, the Canadian communications system was thus increasingly complex and multitentacled, and its situation was complicated by the fact that the economic and political needs it was designed to meet did not perfectly overlap. It had to reconcile such diverse elements as the pressures from the provinces, the question of public service, and the federal government's national unity strategy. Within the government, the minister of communications was charged with developing the industrial base of communications, while the secretary of state had to consider cultural objectives. The CRTC, for example, had as its new mandate to regulate the rates of the telecommunications common carriers in the public (that is, consumers') interest, to manage the climate in which commercial broadcasters and cable company operators had to function, and to ensure that broadcasting served to maintain and strengthen the country's national objectives (the first of which was to remain a country). The CBC was torn in several directions at once, expected to serve the cultural and political objective of nation building without impeding the economic development which called for reducing public commitments and building up private enterprise.

The election in Quebec of the Parti Québécois in November 1976 temporarily ordered the priorities.

## POLITICS: WHO SPEAKS FOR CANADA? 1976–80

### The CBC and the National Question

The 1974 CRTC hearings had shaken the CBC's image of itself, and the public image of the CBC. On 1 August 1975, the corporation got a new president, A.W. Johnson, a senior civil servant. A strong nationalist, Johnson adopted a strategy of emphasizing the CBC's historic importance as an instrument of Canadian nationhood and the continuing need for a strong CBC.

In his first major public intervention after taking office, Johnson told members of the Canadian Club in Toronto that the Canadian Club and the CBC shared "the same essential objective: the preservation and enrichment of Canadianism."[85] "Canadianism," to Johnson, was what one felt when looking beyond one's local community. It was difficult to imagine "Canada," he said, without the CBC to reflect "*Canadian* values, *Canadian* attitudes and perceptions, and *Canadian* institutions and history."[86]

In the present context of expanded television choice, Johnson estimated Canadians were spending less than one-third of their three hours of television viewing time per day watching Canadian programs. Canadians were watching American programs, "absorbing American interpretations of events ... soaking up the value system of American society ... coming to expect Canadian traditions and institutions to look and behave as if they were American traditions and institutions."[87] Things appeared to be as bad as they had been before Parliament created a national broadcasting service. The only solution was to produce Canadian programs that people would choose to watch.

Johnson said he was impatient with the "populist versus élitist" programming dichotomy. Canadian programming, whether diverting or more discriminating, must be "distinctive"; distinctiveness would be its mark. Distinctiveness was a matter of knowing one was tuned to CBC; CBC radio was distinctive, "a Canadian thing, something that you can identify with because you recognize it as having identified something that is part of you, that belongs to you." CBC radio had developed "its own Canadian brand of broadcasting professionalism ... which our listeners recognize as being distinctively Canadian." In television, creative people were under pressure to match the American brand of professionalism so that Canadian programs tended to look like American ones.[88]

Being Canadian had a price, and Parliament had to be prepared to come up with funds. The Canadian people had to realize, too, that their cultural survival was at stake and that this was more important than arguments about regionalism or the style of programming.

On 4 May 1976, Johnson made his first appearance before the parliamentary committee on broadcasting. The CBC was seeking $415 million from Parliament for 1976–77, and Johnson recalled its purpose as an instrument of nationhood. Conservative MP Gordon Fairweather wondered if the constant search for Canadian nationalism had not become counterproductive. Johnson said he took it as a premise that the CBC's first objective was "the unity of the country and the reflection of one part of the country to the other."[89]

The committee hearings gave the impression that a separation of discourse from reality was setting in. While "national unity" remained the *raison d'être* of the CBC, the crisis in broadcasting was reflected in new concerns. John Roberts said "the crunch is here"; decisions had to be made about pay-television, about cable systems, about the degree of foreign penetration to allow, about the role of provinces – "a whole variety of decisions are going to be taken which have enormous implications."[90]

As the Quebec election approached, MPs from Quebec expressed concern about the CBC and its shortcomings as a vehicle for national unity. On 26 October 1976, Liberal back-bencher Hal Herbert attacked the "so-called independence" of the CBC, accusing Radio-Canada of having insulted Robert Bourassa by refusing to transmit his videotape announcing the election call. Jacques Guilbault, parliamentary secretary to the secretary of state, intimated the government's attitude in a comment about television personality Lise Payette's decision to run for the Parti Québécois: "Given the mandate of the CBC which is to promote national unity and reinforce the Canadian cultural fabric as espoused in the Broadcasting Act, it would be difficult to envisage the possible return of Lise Payette to CBC employment."[91]

At the parliamentary committee on 2 December, the recently named secretary of state, John Roberts, reiterated what he had said to Harry Boyle in May: "the obligation placed upon [the CBC] is to assist and to strengthen national unity within the country" but he did not want to be "a kind of minister of information whose function is to tell the CBC what it should be doing in its attempt to fulfil its mandate."[92]

But the pressure continued from Quebec-based Liberals, including ministers like Jean Chrétien and André Ouellet. On 18 February 1977, former NDP leader T.C. Douglas asked for clarification of government allegations that the CBC was "not giving a fair and balanced view ... of the debate between federalism and separatism."[93] The senior government member present, Finance Minister Donald Macdonald, said: "There is a feeling I think among many federalists from the province of Quebec that Radio-Canada is not discharging its mandate above all to work for the unity of Canada."[94]

Douglas asked whether the government was not equating itself with unity and "criticizing the CBC more for the fact that it is not willing to be the slave of the Liberal party rather than that it is not supporting federalism?" Gordon Fairweather added: "Is jumping on the CBC to be a substitute or an excuse for a government that seems unable to reconcile the strains of Confederation?"[95]

On 25 February, Prime Minister Trudeau told the House the government was "very concerned about the possibility of CBC Radio-Canada propagandizing separatism."[96] The problem was how to reconcile freedom of speech with the CBC's duty to promote Canadian unity, he said. Former opposition leader Robert Stanfield said the government's charges reminded him of its attitude during the October Crisis when all sorts of unsubstantiated allegations had been made. The prime minister should launch an inquiry, Stanfield said.

Trudeau said he liked the suggestion. Everyone knew "that the overwhelming majority of employees in the CBC are of separatist leaning"; CBC management, he said, was asking itself "what can we do about it without infringing freedom of speech." Trudeau hinted that if the issue were not resolved, financial sanctions could be taken against Radio-Canada.[97]

On 4 March 1977, Trudeau wrote to the chairman of the CRTC: "Doubts have been expressed as to whether the English and French television networks of the Corporation generally, and in particular their public affairs, information and news programming, are fulfilling the mandate of the Corporation. This merits examination by a body with the expertise available to make as objective a determination as possible concerning them. Accordingly, I am writing to invite the Commission to establish an inquiry into the matter."[98]

On 8 March, opposition leader Joe Clark asked Trudeau to make his charges specific, noting that the attacks on the CBC had come essentially from cabinet members and other prominent Liberals. Trudeau said he had simply "invited" the CRTC to make an inquiry, and the agency was free to act upon the invitation or not. However, he said: "Anyone who has had the advantage of living in the province of Quebec and talking to the people would know that there is a loud, continuing and even agonized cry about the CBC destroying the unity of this country."[99]

On 14 March, the CRTC established a committee of inquiry to look into the government's allegations. The CRTC inquiry was the crowning attempt by the government to bring the CBC to heel on the national question. Public attacks on Radio-Canada and less publicized attempts to influence its information programming had been the order of the day throughout the Trudeau era. Radio-Canada management, while resisting the government charges, was anxious to avoid giving them any credence. Soon after the 1976 Quebec elections, Radio-Canada had hired Trudeau's former press secretary, Pierre O'Neil, to head its television public affairs programming. In Quebec, Radio-Canada appeared to be in the government's pocket.[100]

On 14 June 1977, in light of the CRTC inquiry, CBC president A.W. Johnson issued a major statement, *Touchstone for the CBC*,[101] articulating a program philosophy and plan of action. Successive governments and their agencies had failed to provide the policies and the funding necessary "to safeguard our Canadianism and our culture through broadcasting," especially in English Canada, and the CBC had failed to be sufficiently forceful in dramatizing the need for these. Consequently, the CBC had failed to play a proper leadership role "in the national battle for Canadianism – for our national heritage." Johnson astutely identified the dual nature of the Canadian dilemma: "the combination of national life-threatening arguments about our nationhood and the relentless American cultural penetration."[102]

A shift in emphasis and a change in direction was indicated to reinforce

Canadian nationhood by passionate development of Canadian culture and public broadcasting. The challenge to safeguard Canada from foreign cultural domination was less dramatic than the challenge of national unity, Johnson said. But in spite of the CBC's specific mandate to contribute to national unity, it had to provide balance.

If Canadians wanted the CBC to carry the message of Canadianism, Johnson said, they had to be prepared to pay for it. The only valid question was how to increase the range, quality, and viewing of Canadian programming. Debates with the provinces over jurisdiction, or with the private sector about their operations and practices, had to be directed with this overriding objective in mind.

Canada was the only country in the world that allowed "the massive intrusion of a foreign culture." Canada was "a global aberration," its governments failing to take action "with tragic myopia."[103] The "brutality of the glutted marketplace" was going to get worse with the technological explosion of television viewing options. In the face of the need to "Canadianize" programming and reflect English and French Canada to one another, the CBC now proposed "to lead a resurgence of truly Canadian broadcasting as a cornerstone of Canadian culture, identity and nationhood."[104] This proposal was put in the form of a plan of action, based on the "Canadianization" of English television to enhance Canadian identity, and the "broadening" of French television so that it reflected "the full diversity of the nation" and not only Quebec: "The vibrant political, social and economic dynamism of contemporary Canada must be reflected in our programming on both networks in the same way."[105]

Johnson's strategy for increasing the viewing of Canadian programs included the introduction of a second service, in both French and English (CBC-2/Télé-2), which would offer "distinctive, thoughtful, alternative programming," commercial-free on cable. CBC-2 would selectively repeat successful productions of the main CBC networks as well as produce new specialized programs. In addition, Johnson promised "a visibly open and responsive CBC" that provided greater and more direct participation for the public and a greater role in planning and development for creative personnel.[106] This would include setting up a number of "advisory councils" in specific program areas, a "broadcast complaints commission," and the holding of public forums. CBC services would be asked to maintain contact with community groups at national and regional levels.

In sum, *Touchstone for the CBC* dealt boldly with the overall problem of providing a comprehensive "Canadian" broadcasting service and the need to pay for it with public funds. It did not address the immediate question of concern to the politicians, that of the perceived shortcomings of CBC's coverage of the national unity crisis. But if Johnson was correct that "television is the single most powerful instrument for strengthening Canadian nationhood," then his strategy would serve the purpose. That was the gamble: by building up the CBC, by increasing Canadian television viewing, and by reflecting both Canadas to one another and to themselves, the country would be saved.

The CRTC reported on its inquiry into the CBC on 20 July 1977. In a letter to the prime minister accompanying the inquiry report, CRTC chairman Harry Boyle reaffirmed the CRTC's commitment to a "national broadcasting service" and said it was evident that "the Canadian public wants the CBC and feels a need for it." The CRTC felt the CBC had fulfilled some of its mandatory obligations, but it cited three areas of deficiency: overcentralization of production and programming in Toronto and Montreal; separation of French and English networks into two distinct and isolated services; and excessive reliance on American programming. These deficiencies were at the root of the CBC's failure to contribute to the development of national unity.[107]

The CRTC questioned whether there was any real desire to change the situation. It felt a full-scale inquiry like a royal commission would be inappropriate and counterproductive in the absence of a political will to implement the type of changes that might emerge. Instead, the CRTC said it would pursue the contentious issues when the CBC's licences came up for renewal in 1978–79.

The CRTC found sources of discontent with the CBC that could not be blamed on "separatist bias": complaints that it did not reflect regional issues, that it was too centralized, too influenced by commercial pressure, too expensive.

But Canada was "a marginal society" alongside its gigantic neighbour, the US, and the CBC was one of a series of innovations developed since Confederation to preserve a distinct Canadian identity. In 1977, the effort needed to keep Canada together was at least as great as it had been in 1867; the Canadian media had a grave role to play in this. The CRTC summed up the situation with an astute justification of the need for a CBC that, paradoxically, opened the door to arguing for smaller-scale alternatives as well: "In the modern world, political and economic developments tend to centralize; cultural developments, on the other hand, tend to be regional, arising in much more sharply delimited areas. But radio and television represent both a cultural development and a powerful economic and political force. Private broadcasting tends to fall in with economic developments only; a public broadcasting system is needed which will counteract this."[108]

The report continued in the tone of the CRTC's 1974 licence renewal announcement, but in stronger, more free-wheeling and more analytical terms. It was quite critical of the CBC's response to the evolution of broadcasting in recent years: the French services had become parochial and inward-looking, while the English tended to imitate a foreign model. Like the CBC's *Touchstone* document, its focus was significantly broader than the prime minister's question: "The CBC, the English network particularly, seems to have fallen between its mandate of being an instrument of Canadian public interest, and a more or less deliberate self-imprisonment in the North American television mould of entertainment and commercial sponsorship."[109]

The CRTC was making a liberal interpretation of the CBC's mandate here; in fact, the broadcasting act did not mention "public interest" when discussing the "national broadcasting service." The CRTC's view of the CBC's role seemed rather to be based on a certain reading of Canada's broadcasting history and the attitude towards mass programming that the CBC had taken once upon a time; the CBC had retreated a long way from the close involvement with its public that had marked the radio days of the "Forum" era. It had to recognize that it could never win the ratings game and would not consistently have a mass audience in the foreseeable future. The CBC standard ought to be qualitative: "It is not the number of people watching a program that matters, but the importance of the program, and the cultural situation of the people who are watching it."[110]

This was an unorthodox notion. Not only had a program to be judged by its "quality" – already a vague and subjective category – but the "cultural situation" of the audience had to be taken into account. The CRTC was saying it was legitimate to make a program with a specific, even marginal public in mind, provided it could be shown that the program was important to that public.

The CRTC approached the CBC's shortcomings in contributing to national unity as a structural problem – English and French services presented different views of the country, nurturing instead of bridging the communications gap. A content analysis of French and English television news done for the inquiry[111] indicated that newscasts played a very small role in shaping common values and norms; on the contrary, they tended to reinforce value differences along linguistic lines. "In this sense," the study concluded, "the news content patterns can be seen as not contributing in any significant way to a shared sense of Canadian identity." The problem was not what the news included, but what it left out.[112]

Only about 15 percent of French and English newscasts covered the same ground, the study found; the most striking difference was that the main thrust of the French newscasts was Quebec (about 50 percent of newscast time). Another study[113] showed that the CBC did not allow for the fact that Canadians tended to view things from a regional perspective and were most concerned about regional and local issues. Yet, nearly three-quarters of all news items originated in one of four cities: Ottawa, Toronto, Quebec City, or Montreal.[114]

The CRTC made a damning indictment of CBC news policy on the basis of these findings. The CBC tended to characterize the current political situation "as a more or less routine federal-provincial constitutional argument." But the statistics showed that CBC newscasts, both English and French, "are biased to the point of subversiveness. They are biased because, so far as they are able, they prevent Canadians from getting enough balanced information about Canada to make informed decisions regarding the country's future. They are biased by their assumptions about what is newsworthy and what their audiences want to hear." [115]

The audience, on the other hand, was more sophisticated. A survey done for the inquiry showed 60 percent of Canadians felt the CBC was contributing to Canadian identity and unity (although English-speaking Quebecers particularly disagreed); 66 percent of anglophones and 44 percent of francophones thought the CBC should promote the cause of federalism, but 75–80 percent of both groups disapproved of any restriction on freedom of expression or government control of information even in time of crisis. [116]

The most important conclusion the CRTC drew from the different studies done for the inquiry was that the notion that "Canada is in a state of deep schizophrenia" was a creation of the media, while the Canadian public's "interest, attitudes, and sense of priorities about the news are much the same whether they speak English or French, or live near the Atlantic or the Pacific." [117] Where the media presented "two solitudes," the public saw "one community": while all the media were delinquent in this respect, only the CBC had the specific mandate to work against such representation.

Here, at last, was a new conception of Canada's national crisis and of the national unity function of the public broadcaster. The CRTC appeared to be saying the question was not one nation or two, the forces of fragmentation were not along the lines of the traditional ethnolinguistic dualism, the issue was not a power struggle between Ottawa and Quebec. The Canadian public, said the CRTC, "has clearly recognized and accepted the fact that the expression of diversity is an essential part of the mandate of unity ... The mandate of unity has nothing to do with managing or distorting news, or inserting pro-federalist editorializings into the news ... CBC television will do most for the unity of the country, not by editorially supporting federalism, but by regaining the presence in Canadian life that CBC radio had a generation ago, and to a considerable extent still has." [118]

On the one hand, the CRTC was addressing the CBC and its shortcomings in this statement, but it was also telling the government it was pointless to build a political strategy on the editorial support of the national broadcaster. More sophisticated than the government, the regulatory agency believed that "state" broadcasting would not in fact serve the "national" interest. The CRTC called instead for renewing the relationship between the CBC and its public, but it did not elaborate on the form that a renewed relationship between broadcaster and public could take. Ultimately, the CRTC, too, failed to appreciate the inherent limitation of "national" broadcasting in a society like Canada's, a limitation indicated by Thelma McCormack when she wrote, in a paper that appeared as an appendix to the survey done for the inquiry, that the crux of the issue was not "whether the media are now interpreting Quebec sentiment fully and fairly for the public. It is whether there is a public, or whether we have become a society so stratified by conflicting and diverse interests that the national media are speaking to everyone and communicating with no one."[119]

## Mandates and Agendas

The events of 1977 demonstrated the extent to which political expectations of the CBC did not mesh with either a truly "national" broadcasting service or a service conceived with the "public" in mind. The government appeared to recognize this when it created a new agency, the Canadian Unity Information Office, at the year's end.

The national question remained high on Ottawa's agenda in 1978. A travelling Task Force on Canadian Unity, chaired by Jean-Luc Pepin and John Robarts, kept the question in the spotlight. CBC president A.W. Johnson appeared before it to discuss the CBC's role in "the public debate of the national unity issue currently confronting Canadians, the debate about the political and constitutional future of the country."[120]

Agonizing over the CBC's choices, Johnson exposed the vastness of the public broadcaster's dilemma. The CBC operated on the premise that Canadian society was a community based on freedom of speech, opinion, and expression. Its function was to facilitate the exercise of these freedoms "by communicating to the public the information and ideas which are the ingredients of free discussion and debate." The CBC's current affairs programs had to "fully reflect the debate about Canada's future ... the case for Canada as a nation, whatever its form of federalism – the social and economic, the cultural and political benefits of nationhood to individual Canadians." At the same time, however, they had to reflect "the tensions of Canadian society, and the arguments for changes in the political and constitutional arrangements designed to reduce those tensions," including "the arguments against nationhood as we know it – the arguments, for example, in favour of the independence of Quebec, with or without economic association with the rest of Canada":

For Canada's public broadcasting system even to air such arguments against nationhood is distasteful to some Canadians. But if we are to exemplify and to respect the freedom of speech and discussion upon which Canada is founded, we must accord "freedom for the thought you hate," as an internationally renowned jurist once put it. To give expression to this freedom is not in any way to tolerate a bias against nationhood; any such bias would be quite unacceptable to the CBC. Rather it is a matter of respecting, as we say, the basic tenet of freedom of expression and debate. The very credibility of the CBC as a service to the people of Canada depends upon taking this posture. Put another way, it is not for the CBC to suppress any particular point of view: only the community of Canada, through its Parliament, has the power to do so, to declare subversive, and thus to suppress, any particular point of view. [121]

The CBC's role was to ensure that the choices being put to the Canadian people were reported fully, fairly, responsibly, and in a balanced manner, according to "the principles on which the best journalism is based." The CBC would contribute to the development of national unity by objectively reporting on the crisis ... in a context of "freedom for the thought you hate."

Earlier, on 26 January 1978, the CRTC had announced that it would hold a public hearing to consider CBC licence renewals later in the year. The CBC made public its brief on its own behalf in May. [122] It was closely based on the "Canadianization" spirit of the *Touchstone* statement, [123] referring back to the statement's emphasis on the development of a more open and responsive CBC with more direct public and creative community participation. Yet it took a strong centralist position: "The CBC is really all about the creation of a national consciousness ... In a country like Canada, broadcasting has always been, must always be, a central concern of national policy." [124]

There were few new proposals in the submission, but a stern warning: "As a nation, we can still make sure that new technological innovations in broadcasting, such as pay-television and fibre optics, are introduced *only* if they are likely to lead to an increase in the availability of Canadian programming – and *only* if they are likely to lead to an increase in the viewing of Canadian programming. We should learn a lesson from our experience with cable." [125] There was also a suggestion for a basic principle: "*Any* change that tends to make the Canadian broadcasting system less Canadian is not likely to be in the best interests of Canada." [126]

The CBC's 1978 submission to the CRTC included an important chapter on "CBC Journalism and the Public's Right to be Informed." [127] Journalistic programming was the most important service the CBC provided, it said. The whole notion of democratic society was based "on a rational dialogue of an informed public"; only the media could provide the information base for that rational dialogue. The journalist, the brief said, was an "agent" for the citizen in the quest for knowledge. There were few higher public services in a free society than serving the citizens' need and right to be informed.

Journalism was necessarily pluralistic and decentralized, the brief said. Constant intervention was an impossible form of editorial control. At the CBC, policy directives constituted the framework for journalistic programming; responsible control was exercised by making certain that journalists worked within this framework. The process took the form of a "natural circular flow," from establishment of policy by the board of directors through the recruitment and training of staff, the articulation and application of policy, evaluation, policy review, and recommendations for change.[128]

Inevitably, the discussion of CBC journalism returned to the question of national unity. As in its submission to the Task Force on Canadian Unity earlier in the year, the CBC again argued reassuringly for a cool, professional approach to the crisis.

At the public hearings in October, oral testimony by the heads of English- and French-language television information programming underscored how the national unity crisis represented a different challenge for the respective linguistic divisions. Knowlton Nash, director of television news and current affairs on the English side, was able to spend his time soberly showing how the CBC had responded to the criticisms aired at the CRTC's 1974 hearings, and spoke expansively about "socially responsible journalism" and the public's right to be informed. Meanwhile, his counterpart, French services news director Marc Thibault, had to justify a news service under siege.

Unlike other news undertakings in Quebec, Thibault said, Radio-Canada was not and could not be *engagé*. When a journalist came to work there, he or she had to understand that they would not be able to promote their opinions as they might do in another media. There was no question about it, journalists were constrained by the institutions in which they worked.

In other words, if Nash's journalism had a certain universal quality to it, Thibault's was coloured by the role of the institution. "Involved" journalism was all right in an involved medium; it was unacceptable at the CBC. The unstated aspect of this assumption was this: perhaps the CBC was, indeed, not impartial, as Thibault claimed, but in fact partial in another direction. About Radio-Canada's referendum coverage, he said: "We must get organized and mobilized to face up to the most awesome challenge in news programming in the history of the corporation."[129] Radio-Canada would make a special effort to become aware, and make its public aware, of the feelings of English Canada. This was the opposite of the CBC, which would cover the referendum with the normal detachment accorded a major news event.

The CRTC decision on the CBC's licence renewal was announced on 30 April 1979.[130] It declared the emergence of a continental broadcasting system: "The Canadian broadcasting system, especially in English-speaking Canada, has become the northern exposure of the US commercial television system. This transformation has deepened the contradictions that exist in the Canadian broadcasting system."[131]

As in 1974, the CRTC said the CBC was hampered from fulfilling its mandate by excessive allegiance to North American marketing and mass programming practices. But in 1979, the CRTC necessarily addressed the question of "national unity and Canadian identity" in a separate section of its decision:

"The *identity-unity* mandate is the raison d'être of the national broadcasting service. Accordingly, one can only measure the success or failure of this service in relation to the fulfillment of this double objective."[132]

This was a startlingly transparent statement of the CRTC's own bias: since 1974, the CRTC had been developing and articulating a critique of the CBC, which, it now seemed to say, should be seen as its own interpretation of the "identity-unity" mandate. The decision expanded further on this.

Both English- and French-language network television could be said to express Canadian identity, to varying degrees; the French network, it was generally admitted, was far more "Canadian" than the English. But, the CRTC said, while English television suffered from "Americanization," French television, in news and public affairs, "has restricted itself to a uni-dimensional regionalism" – it was centred on Quebec. Consequently, in different ways, both networks were failing to fulfil the second part of the mandate, to contribute to national unity.[133]

The CRTC expressed surprise that the CBC had not made greater progress in reflecting the two main linguistic groups to one another, and attributed this to the fact that the networks "functioned in isolation and without the benefit of a common policy." The French network still functioned "as a regional enterprise, not attuned to the realities and needs of all of Franco-phone Canada," while the English network was mainly preoccupied with its competition with American-dominated private stations. The problem was not a new one, the CRTC said, but had become increasingly serious because of "the Canadian crisis."

Indeed, the problem was not new but neither was the crisis. As we saw earlier, the structure and functioning of the CBC was a historically rooted reflection of the chronic national dilemma. The national broadcasting service had been split like an ovum, in pre-embryo stage, because "the nation" could not tolerate a single service. The twins, nonidentical at birth, were further distinguished by the environments in which they evolved. Radio-Canada emerged as a pole of resistance to cultural domination, just as the alternative national construct "Quebec" emerged in resistance to political domination. It was precisely those aspects of the French network that were absent from the English one that gave Radio-Canada a subversive edge: the failure to express Canadian identity in English undermined national unity by increasing the centripetal pull of the United States; successfully express-ing it in French, which meant centring on Quebec, undermined national unity by tending to fragment the Canadian nation.

The French network had often been held up as a model of indigenous expression for the English network to follow; now it was told by the CRTC to start behaving more like a national network than a regional service. But the French network had significantly fewer resources available to it than the English, especially outside its major production centre, Montreal. The CRTC suggested that the key was "greater cooperation between the two services" – sharing facilities, correspondents, and programs.

There was no suggestion that this be done on the basis of budgetary parity with the English network, however. The CRTC wanted the French network to give top priority to offering the same type of service as the English network, despite its lesser resources. The centuries-old Canadian question of equality between peoples, one a majority and the other a minority, remained unstated but had been effectively posed.

The CRTC inquiry into the CBC's handling of the national unity crisis had launched a general discussion on information programming which the CBC had taken up in its 1978 submissions to the Task Force on Canadian Unity and the CRTC. In its 1979 decision, the CRTC basically adopted the CBC's position on "the public's right to be informed," tempering the CBC's theory with commentary that had been made during the public hearings in October. There was a link to be made between the CBC's commitments to high professional journalistic standards and to a more open and responsive service.

Specifically, the CRTC approved of the CBC's intention to create "advisory councils" in different programming areas. Earlier in the decision, it had suggested that the CBC create an advisory committee to deal with services to official language minorities as well.

In sum, the 1979 CBC licence renewal process reemphasized the situation the CRTC had identified in 1974, intensifying it with the sense of urgency brought on by the national unity "crisis." The CRTC had now twice identified the problem of the CBC and articulated a critique, but it apparently would take more than a critique to resolve the problem.

### Communications and the Parti Québécois

While the question of the CBC's role *vis-à-vis* national unity remained preeminent in the late 1970s, federal-provincial conflict over communications continued to demonstrate the problem of disunity. Ottawa's solution, ever-increasing centralization, was itself problematic and less and less able to encourage a consensus.

On 22 March 1977, Jeanne Sauvé introduced a bill intended to combine all legislation "respecting telecommunications in Canada" under a single act. The telecommunications act[134] would have replaced the broadcasting act, the radio act, the telegraphs act and the CRTC act. It would have given the federal communications minister power to make agreements with the provinces or delegate powers to them, as well as to provide general policy guidelines to the CRTC. Bill C-43's line on policy was that "efficient telecommunications systems are essential to the sovereignty and integrity of Canada,"[135] but it never got past first reading.

The Parti Québécois government did not actively engage Ottawa over communications policy. Quebec did not, for example, participate in the March 1977 meeting of the "council of communications ministers" that had emerged from the 1975 federal-provincial conference.

Under the PQ, Jean-Paul L'Allier's green paper[136] continued to stand as government policy. Even the terminology remained the same. Thus, when Quebec opposed Bill C-43, it was on the grounds of "the need for Quebec to be master craftsman of communications on its territory."[137] On 3 May 1977, Quebec's National Assembly commission adopted a motion by PQ back-bencher Jean-François Bertrand asking Ottawa to withdraw Bill C-43 and recognize Quebec's legislative predominance in broadcasting, telecommunications, and cable distribution.[138] This rather feeble appeal underlined Quebec's lack of power over communications under the existing political system. Communications Minister Louis O'Neill said Quebec would be its own "master craftsman" when it finally became a sovereign country: that was the only real solution to Quebec's communication problems.[139]

On 30 November 1977, the Supreme Court of Canada ruled on the Dionne-d'Auteuil case, judging that Ottawa had exclusive jurisdiction over cable distribution.[140] The ruling essentially brought the 1932 jurisprudence up to date, and quashed Quebec's hope of circumventing the federal government's absolute refusal to negotiate a new arrangement. The three Quebec justices on the highest court dissented from the majority judgment, which was taken in Quebec as another important example of Ottawa's insensitivity to Quebec attempts to control its own means of cultural development.[141] But communications was coming to be seen increasingly in economic terms in Quebec as well by the late 1970s.

In its early years, the PQ government considered communications a branch of cultural development, but attached a lot less importance to its cultural implications than had previous Quebec governments since 1968. Communications occupied only a chapter in Camille Laurin's important white paper on cultural development.[142] The chapter added little new, drawing largely for inspiration on the free press debate of the early 1970s and the Bourassa government's policy struggle with Ottawa. It enunciated a number of general principles as guidelines for state intervention, which it said should be "sober but sufficient." All communications media had a community service function to perform, but "public" media had even greater responsibilities.

The Quebec Charter of Human Rights guaranteed the right to information, but in order for this to be effective, the means of communication had to be relatively decentralized. The problem, the paper went on, was that the Quebec state did not enjoy the power to put these principles into practice. Quebec needed power to control, supervise, and regulate the activities of cable companies, telecommunications companies, private radio and television companies operating on its territory, as well as a say on CBC development in Quebec.

Under the existing system, Quebec wanted to work out an agreement with Ottawa to enable it to be involved in dealing with day-to-day problems. For example, Quebec suffered from an unequal distribution of communication services among regions, and in spite of the Supreme Court ruling, it could take part in trying to rectify this. The white paper suggested, for example, that profitable cable operations in urban centres be obliged to subsidize services for less profitable regions. But the PQ's communications program from its opposition days was toned down somewhat, the more radical proposals now reformulated as questions like: "Would the collective ownership of cable distribution be more likely to encourage local participation?"[143]

The PQ in power was continuing programs and policies begun by Union Nationale and Liberal governments, such as Radio-Québec, now a full-fledged broadcaster, and support for community media. It had new problems to deal with regarding these indigenous media: programming and regionalization policies for Radio-Québec to oversee; the question of the appropriate degree of financial and political state involvement in community media.

The debate surrounding "regionalization" of Radio-Québec well illustrated official Quebec's traditional approach to communications. The question of regionalization had arisen during public hearings on the development of Radio-Québec in 1975, and had led to the creation of consultative committees around Quebec. In November 1977, the committees submitted a joint proposal to Radio-Québec calling for a reorganization of operations in which they would have an active programming role. The committees' vision was that of a decentralized television service emanating from the regions and based on community participation. But Radio-Québec was already well embarked on replicating the centralized, administrative, "national" public broadcasting model at the level of Quebec. In 1978, a seven-month labour conflict further complicated the issue.[144]

Since its creation, Radio-Québec had been an important beach-head in Quebec's attempts to occupy the field of communications. But by the late 1970s public expectations were not synchronized with this grand policy objective. The PQ's policy towards Radio-Québec reflected the tension between state objectives and popular demands. In 1979, the government amended the legislation governing Radio-Québec to institutionalize the regional committees,[145] and put through a new law broadly defining "educational programming" and placing it under the jurisdiction of the Régie des services publics.[146]

Henceforth, Radio-Québec programming and policy decisions would be made – in theory at least – by nine regional committees composed of community representatives, and the network's board of directors was expanded from seven to twenty-one members to include regional representation.

In January 1978, federal Communications Minister Jeanne Sauvé again presented legislation intended to complete the unification of telecommunications activity under a single act.[147] Bill C-24 was "designed to rationalize federal communications regulation, to make it more responsive to technological change and to allow better coordination of telecommunications policies between the federal and provincial governments."[148] But the telecommunications legislation again failed to become law. It was reintroduced once more in November 1978,[149] only to die a third time when elections were called.

Also in 1978, the DOC had set up a "consultative committee," under the direction of J.V. Clyne, to recommend a strategy for restructuring the Canadian telecommunications system "to contribute more effectively to the safeguarding of Canadian sovereignty."[150] The Clyne committee reported in March 1979 that the situation was "perilous," and urged the government to act immediately to establish "a rational structure for telecommunications in Canada as a defence against further loss of sovereignty in all its economic, social, cultural and political aspects."[151] It concluded that Canadian sovereignty could be best served by supporting the CBC, recognizing the provincial broadcasting agencies of Quebec, Ontario, and Alberta as full-fledged public broadcasters, and pursuing superior quality programming; it found no evidence to warrant early introduction of pay-television. None of these recommendations was heeded.

### Interregnum

The Conservative minority government led by Joe Clark that came to power in May 1979 combined responsibility for culture and communications by naming a single minister, David MacDonald, both secretary of state and minister of communications. MacDonald was genuinely inclined towards democratic reform, but he had to live with the situation he had inherited.[152]

On 7 November 1979, MacDonald announced creation of an advisory committee, headed by Louis Applebaum, composer and executive director of the Ontario Arts Council, to look into means of coordinating the various activities of the federal government in the cultural sphere. The next day, before the parliamentary committee, MacDonald said the advisory committee's work would be followed by a major public policy review, "a kind of update" of the Massey commission.[153] The process was intended to bring policy making out of its bureaucratic confines to ensure that "through Parliament the Canadian public should be more directly involved in the development of a cultural policy and over-all framework."[154]

The arrival of the Clark government meant a thaw in the intensity of federal-provincial relations. MacDonald told the parliamentary committee the government's priority would be federal-provincial cooperation and regional input to national policies. In October 1979 he had told a federal-provincial conference of communications ministers he agreed with the intention of recognizing provincial powers and responsibility in communications: "The time is long past when a federal government could say we alone will make decisions with respect to broadcasting, we alone will make decisions with respect to telecommunications policy."[155]

MacDonald's priorities as minister thus combined aspects of the responsibilities of both his portfolios. At the same time as initiating the cultural policy review and the new attitude towards the allocation of state jurisdiction, MacDonald emphasized the growing interconnection of "cultural" and "communications" questions – his even-handed reference to broadcasting and telecommunications reflected this connection, which had been recognized in the CRTC Act of 1976, and which had, in fact, been inevitable ever since the creation of the Department of Communications in 1969. On 27 November 1979, the link was further solidified with a change in the name of the parliamentary committee that had dealt with broadcasting, film, and the arts since 1965 (and with communications since 1975), to the Standing Committee on Communications and Culture.

Two days later, MacDonald appeared before the committee to report on the "communications" side of his double portfolio. The shores were awash with new technologies – satellites, fibre optics, pay-television, interactive television, computer communications – and one of his priorities would be "to find the appropriate vehicles to generate greater public awareness of the issues."[156]

MacDonald emphasized the importance of the recently recognized ties between communications and culture. The new technological changes in communications had cultural implications, making it necessary to coordinate cultural and communications policy developments, particularly concerning broadcasting. As an example of this twin concern, the DOC was proceeding with the development of "a comprehensive policy for television in the 1980s, a policy which which would take full advantage of new technology, such as satellites to distribute a variety of program fare and to introduce pay-tv to Canada."[157]

Until very recently, the major debates over Canadian broadcasting had been "couched in terms unsuited to the distribution technologies of the 1970s and 1980s." Legislation, including the Broadcasting Act of 1968, was geared to managing "a scarce publicly-owned natural resource, the radio frequency spectrum"; the very concept of off-air broadcasting had been eroded by newer technologies, like cable and satellites, with their greater carriage and coverage capacities. Coming developments in fibre optics and direct broadcast communications would further extend distribution capacity. These would "effectively remove the constraints which have traditionally limited access to the system by both viewers and programmers, and offer innumerable possibilities for the nation-wide distribution of varied and comprehensive programming."[158]

The new technologies held out a democratic promise, but an important question remained unposed: did the erosion of the place occupied by traditional broadcasting also imply the erosion of the principle on which it had been based, that of public service? MacDonald would not be minister long enough to come to grips with this question, which soon forced its way on to the agenda. The scarcity of the radio frequency spectrum had justified placing it in the public domain. Now, in the new context of distribution abundance, public ownership seemed less important. A public trust had been required to regulate broadcasting in conditions of scarcity, but like other abundant commodities in Western society, the new broadcasting media, beginning with cable, would be left in the marketplace.

### *"The Problem of Canada Itself"*

David MacDonald's views on Liberal "national unity" policy were on the record. In 1968 he had been the only MP to deplore inclusion of the CBC's "national unity" mandate in the law on the grounds that it symbolized the passage from "public" to "state" broadcasting. As minister, he told the parliamentary committee: "I still remain strongly convinced that ad hoc 'national unity' programs are no substitute for a strong federal commitment to mutual understanding among Canadians which is based on the expression and appreciation of our diverse cultural identity."[159]

In the context of the upcoming referendum in Quebec, this position was certainly more in touch with that of the CBC than the Trudeau government's had been. The committee, however, was interested to hear from the CBC about the role it intended to play. The CBC spelled out its position in a paper prepared for the committee by A.W. Johnson.[160] The vital role of the CBC in this critical period, Johnson said, was in

communicating to Canadians generally and to Quebecers in particular the information, the ideas and the arguments which they will need, and will want to consider, in settling upon the course of Canada for the future ... The CBC will be looked to by Canadians to present in fairness and with integrity the information they will require and the arguments they will have to hear in order to settle this question of Canadian nationhood ... Canadians will want a CBC which they can trust – a CBC with utter integrity and credibility.[161]

Johnson recalled the conflicting aspects of the CBC's mandate – to contribute to the development of national unity, while at the same time providing a reasonable, balanced opportunity for expressing their views "to those who are bent upon dividing the country." The solution he proposed was the same one he had twice put to the CRTC[162] and to the Task Force on Canadian Unity[163]: strict standards of professional journalism.[164] The CBC was a "public trust"; its job was not to influence the outcome of any public discussion or debate, but to enlarge the powers of others to do so – to enhance the abilities and capacities of the Canadian people to decide and shape their own destinies.[165]

Since the Trudeau government had accused the CBC of bias towards "those bent on destroying the country," Johnson had evidently done an impressive job of selling the merits of objective journalism as a political strategy to the nation's political élite. Now, the Liberal critic on the parliamentary committee, former communications minister Jeanne Sauvé (herself a former journalist), approved the CBC's proposed code of conduct:

National unity will be best served if both options for Canada are thoroughly aired via the CBC and the various interveners feel completely free to express their views on the issue. It would be illusory to even think that national unity could survive any attempt to tamper with the media or tip the scales by not reflecting the whole reality, or by favouring one option over the other. I think we have to remain confident that after an exhaustive examination of the issue, federalism will win over independence.[166]

Ultimately, the referendum campaign was covered by CBC television, and the media generally, as a straight news event, journalists and commentators reporting on the activities of partisans of the two sides. How can this new consensus on the role of state television on the eve of a referendum on the future of the nation be explained? It has been written that the questions surrounding the referendum had been part of the Québécois political discourse for years. They had been debated in books and pamphlets, editorials, and discussions among friends. The referendum had already been constituted "as a sociopolitical phenomenon" well before the official campaign began.[167]

Part of this aspect of the referendum consisted of the fact that its unfolding could be followed daily, at times hourly, on radio and television. For the public, the referendum campaign was a spectacle, no more or less a part of everyday life than any other television fare. Television did not explore the possibilities of either outcome, nor the cultural phenomenon of the referendum campaign itself.[168] The political decision to "cover" the campaign according to scrupulous journalistic norms, rather than be involved in it was based on an assessment of the potential role of television. As both the CBC and the politicians' statements make clear, the dispassionate approach was perceived as more likely to favour the cause of federalism. A modern political undertaking *par excellence*, the referendum campaign was based, for both sides, on discovering what people were thinking and feeling and constructing a political discourse wherein "Yes" or "No" coincided with the public mood. Both sides attempted to maximize their constituencies through advertising and propaganda campaigns addressed to the population directly. The Liberal government that was returned on 8 February 1980 made use of the institutions it had especially created for the purpose, such as the Canadian Unity Information Office, and the direct interventions of federal politicians, gambling that its cause would be inherently served by media allowed to run their normal course. This would appear to have been an astute assessment of the situation, since the media almost "naturally" characterized the federalist option as the path of sobriety and the *souverainiste* option as a wild adventure. [169]

In short, in 1980 it was no longer a question of using the public media as an extension of state power. The liberal rationale for this merely covered up a new reality: the CBC was no longer perceived to be the crucial agent of influencing public opinion. [170]

The reliance by the federal government on means other than its traditional public broadcaster eventually had major implications for the historic role of public broadcasting in Canada. The CBC's Johnson later wrote that during the pre-referendum debate "the government's National Unity office was allocated a very substantial budget to produce and to televise commercials designed to heighten the attachment of Canadians to their country, and to increase their interest in constitutional change." According to Johnson, "it was not a failure to perceive the potential of television to contribute to the national identity which influenced the nation's political leaders to attach such a low priority to television. Rather it was the perception, shared by certain of them, that this potential was not being used in the proper way, as they saw it, to promote national unity. It was this that led to their failure to support a higher priority for broadcasting." [171]

At the height of the debate, in 1979, one of Johnson's predecessors, Alphonse Ouimet, had remarked that it was not surprising to find the CBC at the centre of the national soul-searching: "CBC is Canada's alter ego. Being unsatisfied with ourselves as a nation, or as two, it is perhaps only natural that we should blame our alter ego for our own failure ... it is the problem of Canada itself." [172]

After May 1980, with "the problem of Canada" apparently resolved, what further need would there be for a national public broadcaster?

Throughout the 1970s, Canadian broadcasting policy had sought to put the economy in command. Industrial strategy, in which private enterprise would play a leading role, came to take precedence over cultural goals necessarily dependent on a strong public sector. This strategy had to settle into place slowly, against the objections of a vocal Canadian nationalist lobby in English Canada, and against the threat posed by the increasingly troublesome Québécois nationalist movement in Quebec.

Meanwhile, a new liberal consensus on the role of state television had emerged as the Quebec referendum on sovereignty-association approached. The CBC announced it would adhere strictly to a policy of journalistic objectivity in the referendum campaign, and the politicians appeared to accept it. Beneath the principle lay a new political strategy, articulated by media-astute people like CRTC chairman Harry Boyle, CBC president A.W. Johnson, and Communications Minister Jeanne Sauvé. Basically, it went like this: The public broadcaster could do far more to aid the cause of national unity by performing a ritual function than by transmitting government propaganda which the public had become too sophisticated to accept. The communications spectrum was brimming with messages and could no longer really be controlled, and the part that could be directly controlled (the CBC) represented only a small slice anyway. Audience fragmentation meant the end of potential state monopoly, the lack of monopoly made propaganda absurd, and the political cost of tampering with the public media could be high as well as inexpedient.

So, with the victory of the federalist position in the referendum, the stage was set for a fundamentally different policy approach to broadcasting and communications in general, to the role of the state and public broadcasting in particular. After 1980, the balance shifted definitively with removal of one of the principal arguments in favour of a strong, national "public" broadcasting policy.

# CHAPTER SEVEN

# The Eclipse of Public Broadcasting (1980–88)

## INTRODUCTION

The federalist victory in the Quebec referendum created a new context for public broadcasting in Canada by removing the strongest basis of its political legitimation. Whatever was said about cultural sovereignty and Canadian identity, these would never be political priorities on the same level as the need for national unity. Through the 1970s, the national unity crisis had allowed the public cost of the CBC to grow in spite of the unanswered criticism and dissatisfaction in its regard – both conservative proponents of a privatized broadcasting sector and advocates of a renewed public sector had been frustrated.

In the 1970s, while "the public" had remained that in the name of which the state intervened, the fragmentation of the broadcasting audience into a multiplicity of "publics" had created another type of legitimation crisis for the state. As the public came to be defined as the broadcasting audience, audience fragmentation meant the public broadcaster no longer addressed more than a fraction of the political constituency of the state.[1] With the national unity crisis out of the way, how could the state logically justify a policy based on the national public broadcaster as "cornerstone?"

Thus, the broadcasting environment was subjected to new scrutiny and federal policy began a process of transformation in which the public sector would be increasingly marginalized and reduced in function and importance. To the extent that it would be maintained, it was as a pacifier to the cultural nationalist constituency in English Canada, and as a safety valve, an avenue of last resort for the government to speak to at least a fraction of the nation (as, for example, when Prime Minister Trudeau decided to use the CBC to talk to Canadians about the economy in November 1982).

With the federal cultural policy review of 1982 and the policy initiatives of the DOC under Francis Fox, the role of the public authorities began to be redefined to encompass regulation (CRTC), planning (DOC), and patronage (Telefilm Canada) rather than programming and production. The latter would be considered more and more as belonging to the private sector, and the CBC appeared headed towards a reduced role as carrier of particular messages, purveyor of particular policies of the state, and caterer to the needs of various cultural minorities.

One of the problems marking the early 1980s was the lack of a central focus for public policy making in broadcasting. The broad objectives of Canadian broadcasting remained those specified in the 1968 legislation but the major actors tended to interpret these objectives differently. The public broadcaster, the CBC, and the regulatory agency, the CRTC, had different interpretations of the national objectives of broadcasting (and their own respective roles), and each was subject to particular pressures. The CRTC's stewardship over the entire system implied maintenance of the financial well-being of the private sector, while the CBC had to deal with a shrinking political commitment to public funding. The government, meanwhile, viewed the national objectives of broadcasting increasingly in terms of industrial development, and the Department of Communications was charged with carrying out this essentially economic function.

The contradictions were clearest in the successive debates over the introduction and insertion of new services to the system. First with respect to pay-television, then on the question of "specialty" services, the discussion followed the traditional patterns: Did Canada need these new services, or was it responding to the inevitability of technology? How could such services be introduced without leading to the further "Americanization" of Canadian broadcasting? How could they be made to reflect and serve Canada's cultural and linguistic duality? What was to be the relationship between public and private ownership and purpose? While there was no shortage of principled answers and alternative proposals put forward, each of these issues was resolved in historically predictable ways.

In 1984, riding a worldwide wave of ideological conservatism in the industrial countries, a new government was elected on a general platform that did not bode well for the classical conception of public broadcasting. Brian Mulroney's Conservatives undertook a full-dress review of the objectives and the mechanics of Canadian broadcasting policy. But a sweeping study by a ministerial task force, followed by the exhaustive investigation of a parliamentary committee and detailed debate over a wholly rewritten Broadcasting Act, provided many surprises. Not the least of these was the resolve of public interest organizations and groups emerging from social movements to keep Canadian broadcasting in the public sphere, despite the powerfully supported pressures of technology and economics. By the end of the Mulroney government's first term, however, the tentative legacy of the process was the serious institutional problem it pointed to: how to make broadcasting policy begin to approach the hopes, aspirations, and *fundamental rights* of the community of publics that it is deemed to serve.

In this respect, the 1980s had to be seen as a decade of steep decline. Already by the summer of 1980, as the new dominant perspective was just beginning to emerge, the different sectors of Canadian cultural power were vigorously jockeying to consolidate their positions.

## CANADIAN BROADCASTING IN THE 1980S

### *Policy Making After the Referendum*

The Liberals had been reelected in February 1980, and Francis Fox was the new secretary of state and minister of communications. Fox was an economistic minister, in the tradition of Eric Kierans. His major concern, he told the parliamentary committee in June, was to assure the orderly development of the new technologies, to ensure "balanced development of hardware and software, a balanced increase in productivity and a humane approach to the dislocations it could produce." Equally important was to prepare for the impact of these technologies "on our social and cultural life in the broadest sense." The new technologies offered "considerable opportunities and potential benefits to Canadian manufacturers, to operators of our communications systems and services and to the public."[2]

From this first intervention, Fox gave signs that the debate of the 1980s would be similar in tone to those of the 1950s and 1960s. NDP critic Simon De Jong suggested the new government was repeating a past pattern of letting technology overtake policy and legislation. Was the government not concerned that the new technologies be publicly controlled, he asked? Fox replied: "What you are suggesting is that there be public ownership of the communications area in general. Our feeling has always been that there is room for public ownership but there is also indeed room for private enterprise."[3] Not only was there room for private ownership, said Fox, but even for private monopoly, subject to regulation. This, in fact, described the situation of cable distribution. De Jong persisted:

[Mr. De Jong:] Would you not agree that the carrier, that the hardware, should be publicly owned?

[Mr. Fox:] What do you mean by publicly owned? Is Bell Canada publicly owned? Are you really talking about a government-owned operation when you say publicly owned?

[Mr. de Jong:] Yes, I would suggest that it be publicly owned and that ownership through Bell Telephone does not necessarily guarantee public ownership. Bell is a regulated industry, it is not a public industry.

[Mr. Fox:] If you are suggesting that companies like Bell Canada and the cable companies should all be publicly owned, I would beg to differ with you.[4]

Fox was asked to elaborate on the social and cultural aspects of his portfolio and, particularly, on the differences in function between the federal secretary of state and the provincial ministers responsible for cultural affairs. The federal minister's main role, he said, was "to enhance the feeling of belonging to Canada as a whole," as opposed to "the feeling of belonging to the different communities and enhancing the feeling of distinctiveness."[5]

The Conservative government of 1979–80 had described Canada as a "community of communities." But, here, Fox reasserted the Liberals' unitary approach to cultural affairs. Especially now that the Quebec referendum was past, the development of an industrial, as opposed to a political, approach to culture and communications could be accelerated. In July 1980, the arts and culture branch of the secretary of state's department and ministerial responsibility for the cultural sphere were transferred to the Department of Communications. Fox told the parliamentary committee that the diffusion of culture would depend increasingly on an industrial base and the DOC would, therefore, be increasingly concerned with the growth of the cultural industries.[6]

This new notion – "cultural industries" – would upset the balance between culture and communications and offset the centre of gravity of Canadian cultural policy from the political and ideological sphere of the secretary of state to the industrial and economic sphere of the Department of Communications.

Meanwhile, Fox lauded the work of Louis Applebaum's advisory committee created by David MacDonald to review federal cultural policy. On 28 August Fox transformed it into the Federal Cultural Policy Review Committee and named Jacques Hébert, a civil libertarian writer and publisher and one of Prime Minister Trudeau's oldest friends, as co-chairman.

### The Further Decline of the CBC

In Canadian nationalist circles, public broadcasting was still seen as a vehicle of resistance against American domination. This view continued to be reflected in the official interventions of CBC president A.W. Johnson. In 1979, Johnson had told the parliamentary committee that 75 percent of English Canadian and 42 percent of French Canadian television viewing time was spent watching foreign programs; among young people the figures were 83 percent and 56 percent respectively.

The CBC's operating budget for 1979–80 was $604 million, of which $477 million came from Parliament and $97 million from commercial revenue (the other $30 million was listed as "depreciation"). Programming constituted $412 million, or 68 percent of total expenses, Johnson told the committee. He proposed to make the CBC "the unique and distinctive Canadian network," increasing Canadian programming to 80–85 percent of the schedule, but this would require significantly more money.[7]

For Johnson, the problem confronting broadcasting had not really changed since the 1920s. Increased importation of foreign channels via cable and preponderant scheduling of American programs by private television broadcasters were its contemporary manifestations. On 30 October 1980, Johnson told the parliamentary committee he foresaw the CBC attacking these overall aspects of the problem: "I have sought to define the role of the CBC ... in respect of its contributions to the Canadianization of television ... I have sought to determine how we might best work with other elements in the broadcasting system to realize the broad objectives of Canadianization."[8]

In a sense, Johnson was trying to recapture the CBC president's erstwhile role as leading statesman of Canadian broadcasting, a role last played by Davidson Dunton prior to the reform of 1958. "Canadianization" was the key to that role. Ever since Alphonse Ouimet declared the end of the single system in 1962, CBC presidents had concentrated on the corporation. Now, just as the CBC faced a diminishing role in the system, Johnson was boldly reclaiming a pivotal position. The CBC's submission to the Applebaum-Hébert committee, for example, was expansive in scope and perfectly inscribed in the historic tradition begun by the Aird commission, linking the fate of nationhood to that of the public dimension of broadcasting: "The future of our cultural industries, and especially the future of our broadcasting industry, does not depend on a choice between public and private. It does depend on the realization that in Canada market forces alone cannot provide the quantity or the quality of indigenous cultural products necessary to ensure our survival as a separate and distinct nation."[9]

But the CBC was going through hard times. In Quebec, a crippling journalists' strike paralysed French network and English regional news for eight months beginning in the fall of 1980, evoking parallels with the producers' strike of 1959. The journalists' union framed the issue in terms of a conflict between "the public's right to know" and "management's right to manage." Johnson's statesmanship was unable to resolve the dispute, reviving the old feeling of two solitudes within the CBC.[10]

When the CBC appeared before the parliamentary committee in May 1981, there was evidence of a certain fragmentation of issues facing the corporation. The traditional imbalance between English and French services was one. Referring to the CBC's internal regime as one of "sovereignty-association," Quebec MP Dennis Dawson said: "It seems that there are two policies at CBC: one budget, two policies."[11] Johnson denied the allegation and said the CBC had only one policy in areas such as journalism and labour relations.

Meanwhile, MPs appeared dissatisfied with the CBC's contribution to issues such as multiculturalism and the fight against western separatism. The notion of a homogeneous public interest, long a fixture of the policy-making firmament, appeared to be exploding in favour of the emergence of "micro-publics." It was becoming increasingly difficult to satisfy MPs who, like Aideen Nicholson, wanted "to try to get some kind of a picture from the officials of the place of a public broadcasting service in protecting and enhancing Canada's cultural life."[12] Johnson's answer was that only the public broadcaster would do whatever had to be done to reflect the linguistic, regional, and cultural communities of the country, no matter how unprofitable that was.

However, on the same day that Johnson appeared before the parliamentary committee, the CRTC denied the CBC's application for CBC-2/Télé-2,[13] the two-channel noncommercial satellite-to-cable service first proposed in *Touchstone for the CBC*.[14] With this rejection, an essential part of the CBC's strategy for "returning Canadian audiences to Canadian programs"[15] fell by the boards. The government had not been prepared to make the relatively small financial commitment (an estimated $30 million) necessary to enhance the channel space occupied by Canadian public television, and the CRTC opted for another solution that some saw as a sinecure for the problems in the system: pay-television.

## *The CRTC and Pay-television*

No episode better illustrates the decline of the public dimension of broadcasting by the early 1980s than that of pay-television. In the unfolding of this issue, the policy apparatus and the regulatory agency demonstrated one of the classical syndromes of Canadian broadcasting: the tendency to expand the capacity of the system by introducing a new technology according to criteria which have everything to do with private interests and nothing to do with public needs.

Experiments with closed-circuit point-to-point telecasts had taken place as early as 1937 in the US and 1960 in Canada. Hotels in both countries were offering pay-television services to their customers by the early 1970s. In September 1975, the first mass-marketable project appeared in the US, when the American company Home Box Office (HBO) began delivering programs directly to subscribers via domestic satellite. Canadian entrepreneurs were already lobbying for introduction of a similar model to Canada.[16]

The CRTC had been sporadically concerned with pay-television since 1970, but held its first hearings on the subject in June 1975. Of forty submissions received, fourteen were from cable company operators favourable to immediate introduction of pay-television. Six were from broadcasters who suggested that pay-television would be harmful to their interests; seven were from program production interests who said that any move towards pay-television should be made in a way that would provide maximum benefits for the Canadian production industry; and thirteen briefs from outside the industry illustrated to the CRTC "that little public enthusiasm was evident for, the introduction of a Canadian pay-television service."[17]

In December 1975, the CRTC issued a policy statement opposing the introduction of pay-television because of the potential disruption it would have caused to the system at that time, but encouraging interested parties to continue developing the idea.[18] The context was reminiscent of the situation at the time of the introduction of television in the late 1940s – public policy was resisting the pressure of Canadian entrepreneurs for rapid introduction of a new technology along the lines of a commercial model developed in the United States, in the absence of either clear public demand in Canada or clear Canadian policy goals. But with television, there had at least been an effort to introduce an important variation to the model by emphasizing the public sector in developing Canadian television. With pay-television, the only Canadian element would be the rhetoric.

The cable industry stepped up its pressure during 1976. US pay-television was apparently a financial success. A few isolated closed-circuit operations in Canada were threatening to spread and undermine the cable industry's product. The industry was experiencing a decreasing growth rate and unused distribution capacity. The cable companies saw pay-television as an important source of new and additional revenues.

On 2 June 1976, Communications Minister Jeanne Sauvé called for reconsideration of pay-television. Developed to ensure maximum benefit for Canadian program production, pay-television would be a "watershed in broadcasting," she said. All groups interested in broadcasting – "private and public broadcasters, cable operators, program producers" – could gain from pay-television, whether it was organized as a private, public, or mixed service. Sauvé's important statement of the government view was made before a meeting of the Canadian Cable Television Association, the cable industry lobby.[19]

The chairman of the CRTC, Harry Boyle, followed suit with a similar statement, characterizing pay-television as not simply a broadening of television choice, but the first step in a "national policy of cultural security for Canada," an opportunity to repossess Canadian broadcasting and "convert technical systems to a national purpose."[20] On 30 June, the CRTC called for submissions and proposals on the question of pay-television. It was not satisfied with the quality of the 105 submissions received and called for revisions and new submissions. The two rounds combined yielded a total of 140 submissions which were the subject of public hearings convened on 13 June 1977.

According to the CRTC report on the 1977 hearings, a majority of submissions in which an opinion was expressed indicated strong opposition to pay-television. Support was concentrated in the cable industry, while opposition was centred among broadcasters and public interest groups (who felt that pay-television would not contribute to meeting the objectives of the broadcasting act). Following the hearings, the CRTC conducted a public opinion survey and found that there was no compelling demand for pay-television, nor was it considered essential by Canadians. In addition, the CRTC felt that "no single proposal achieved an acceptable level of commitment to present broadcasting policy objectives and requirements."[21] Again, it declined to recommend pay-television.

But the CRTC report made it clear that this was only a temporary denial and went on to propose a pay-television policy for Canada. The proposal made transparent the CRTC's perception of its role: faced with a dilemma between public opposition and industry pressure, it would opt for the industry. Canada, the CRTC said, could put the technological and industrial inevitability of pay-television to the service of its national concerns through a national policy that ensured conformity to the objectives of the broadcasting act. Pay-television must provide "a predominantly Canadian programming service of high quality"; it must "maximize both the exhibition opportunities for Canadian programs and the proportion of pay-television revenue available to acquire and invest in Canadian programs"; it must provide programming "in Canada's two official languages"; and it must be "a national service with its extension throughout the country being consistent with its ability to remain predominantly Canadian."[22]

The CRTC had accepted to study proposals for pay-television services "by individual licensed operators" who could be existing cable licence-holders or new licensees, and who would compete locally for the discretionary television dollars of the communities they served. But in its view, the national objectives could only be achieved by "a single national pay-television network." This proposal, and the underlying logic justifying it, was consistent with federal government thinking on communications in the 1970s, but the CRTC extended that logic to a new extreme in its discussion of the corporate form the new agency could take.

There were three possibilities: a Crown corporation (like the CBC); a mixed corporation "combining private and government interests" (the CRTC specifically mentioned Telesat Canada as the model for this); or a private company. In the CRTC's view, a private company would be the most suitable. The interveners who had suggested a Crown agency, the CRTC said, had not demonstrated "that there is any unique co-relation between government control or ownership and the significant achievement of national objectives."[23]

It had also been suggested that the board of directors of any pay-television agency be representative "of all potential interests," including broadcasters, cable operators, producers, and the public. The CRTC, on the other hand, felt "that the Board of Directors should in fact represent the shareholders," and it was understandable that these private interests would require that protection of their investments be ensured by majority representation on the board. "It does not follow, however, that in a private incorporation the concern for this private investment will prejudice the company's overall commitment to pay-television objectives."[24]

Now, nothing in the history of Canadian broadcasting up to that time justified such an incredible assertion of confidence in the patriotic impulses of Canada's private broadcasting entrepreneurs. To the contrary, every official statement on the subject since 1928, including prior statements from the CRTC, had concluded the opposite: that only the public sector could ensure the meeting of national objectives in broadcasting. The CRTC experience in the 1970s, however, was marked by an incapacity to force either the public or the private sector to comply with these objectives and it had always come down to a question of money. With pay-television, the CRTC floated the curious idea that commercial success was the path to achieving what fifty years of public and private broadcasting had failed. This was the diametrical opposite of the Aird report: a call for a private, national monopoly to operate on the front line of technological advance.

The report on pay-television was the first major CRTC statement under the chairmanship of Pierre Camu, the former president of the Canadian Association of Broadcasters who had succeeded Harry Boyle on 1 October 1977.[25] A staunch federalist francophone Quebecer and friend of Liberal insiders like Pierre Juneau and Maurice Sauvé, Camu had "the right obsessions" for the CRTC job. According to Herschel Hardin, "it provided him with the means, he said, to respond to the Quebec threat to national unity."[26] Heading the CRTC was, for Camu, a way of "contributing to the debate, the big debate as we call it,"[27] but it had an interesting fringe benefit for the private sector of broadcasting. The pay-television report was a clear manifestation of the CRTC's pro-industry bias.

Late in 1979, Communications Minister David MacDonald reopened the question of pay-television, as part of a package to deal with the problems of northern communications. Delay in extending mainstream broadcasting services to the north had led to a proliferation of unlicensed satellite dishes. The spectre of Canadians evading the regulatory process to receive American signals directly (including American pay-television) haunted DOC officials and concerned MacDonald. MacDonald was also confident that properly set up, a pay-television system could have a beneficial effect on Canadian production. In November 1979, he asked the CRTC to report on these questions.[28]

In January 1980, the CRTC, now headed by John Meisel, a distinguished political scientist from Queen's University, set up a committee on the extension of services to northern and remote communities. After receiving close to four hundred submissions and holding public hearings, the committee reported in July 1980.[29] It was split on the question of pay-television, but the majority recommended introduction. Although the Clyne committee on the future of Canadian telecommunications had recently reiterated the lack of public demand for pay-television in Canada,[30] the service was continuing to grow in the US. Pay-television was "a new and unique opportunity to foster the beneficial development of the Canadian film and program production industries while supporting and complementing the Canadian broadcasting system and catering to the needs of Canadian viewers," the committee, presided by CRTC vice-chairman Réal Therrien, reported.[31] However, it opposed the idea of a single national agency and proposed provincial involvement, while insisting that pay-television should be a lower priority than the extension of more basic services to unserved areas. A minority on the committee felt that no significant benefits would accrue to the Canadian broadcasting system from pay-television, which, it felt, would increase the volume of US programming available in Canada.

On 21 April 1981, after another opinion survey showed that 14 percent of Canadians would potentially subscribe to pay-television, the CRTC called for applications for national, regional, and local pay-television licences. Twenty-seven applicants were heard in three weeks of hearings held in the fall. Guided by the Therrien committee's recommendation that pay-television must "make a significant and positive contribution to broadcasting in Canada, make effective use of Canadian resources, and that a significant amount of the revenues flow to the Canadian program production industry,"[32] the CRTC announced the successful supplicants on 18 March 1982.[33] It awarded national general-interest licences in French and English (First Choice Canadian/Premier choix), a national specialty licence for performing arts (C Channel), regional licences for general-interest services in Alberta, Ontario, and the Atlantic provinces (Super Channel), and a regional multilingual service in British Columbia. Later, a regional licence (TVEC) was added for Quebec. *Maclean's* magazine described the licensees as "the new purveyors of national culture," and CRTC chairman John Meisel was quoted as saying: "It's our last chance to get Canadian content right."[34]

Pay-television went on the air in Canada on 1 February 1983. The arts licensee, C Channel, went bankrupt less than five months later. Premier choix and the regional Quebec licensee, TVEC, had to amalgamate and be refloated with provincial government aid. First Choice only survived thanks to an eleventh-hour bail-out arrangement enabled by the CRTC. As for pay-television's contribution to Canadian program production, the tone was set from the start by First Choice and Super Channel, which greeted their publics on opening day with the American film *Star Wars*. Canadian pay-television was another boon to the American export market, so obviously that a First Choice vice-president was able to tell a Hollywood trade publication in late 1982: "We're giving out money – would you like some of it? It's not, let's go to Canada and save money. It's let's go to Canada and make much more money." [35] Pay-television turned out to be "a straightforward, prosaic, altogether predictable, mercantile, high-cost extension of the American distribution system in Canada." [36]

Reading the literature produced by the CRTC, one gets the impression that it could only have turned out this way. However, this is not the case. There were at least two alternative paths for development placed on the discussion table in the late 1970s and early 1980s.

The first was the CBC's plan for additional, noncommercial services in English and French, CBC-2/Télé-2, first proposed in 1977. [37] This proposal for a satellite-to-cable channel took a public service approach to increasing the available space for Canadian production. It would have been provided at relatively little public cost (estimated at $30 million) and at no direct cost to subscribers. It was, in a certain sense, a public service version of the pay-television idea. But the climate in which it was proposed was clearly unfavourable to the CBC. The government was not willing to provide additional funding to an already strapped CBC, possibly out of vindictiveness for the CBC's perceived role in Quebec. The CRTC, already critical of the CBC's shortcomings in carrying out its mandate, said it could not justify approving a new service when the CBC was not adequately carrying out its other ones. On 27 May 1981 – only one month after calling for applications for pay-television licences – the CRTC denied the CBC's second network application while seeing "much merit" in the concept and considering it within the objectives of the broadcasting act. [38] Speaking to the parliamentary committee in April 1982, John Meisel said the CRTC had rejected CBC-2 "because we did not think it was good enough," but accepted pay-television in the hope that it would evolve into something better than what was being licensed. [39] Thus, on a gamble and within the period of a few months, the CRTC approved one plan that enhanced the private sector of broadcasting and rejected another that would have expanded the public sector. Both decisions were made in the name of Canadian broadcasting goals.

More directly tied to the pay-television decision was the CRTC's refusal to consider alternative proposals for the organization of pay-television. In 1977, 1980, and 1981 the CRTC heard various proposals for "universal" pay-television schemes which met its stated objectives and may have been more appropriate for the Canadian context, but did not fulfil the unstated criterion of cable industry profitability. Theoretically, universal pay-television meant directly associating cable subscribers with Canadian production through a mandatory additional charge collected by the cable companies but earmarked for a special service to be programmed by a separate licensee. A major submission to the 1977 CRTC hearings from the Council of Canadian Film Makers called for adoption of the universal pay model as the system that would produce the largest possible revenue for Canadian production at the lowest cost to the subscriber; it would organize the Canadian market on the basis of maximum efficiency for a small market, instead of the American model which could only work in a larger market. The CRTC's 1978 report said the CCFM submission was a "compelling contribution" and "established significant standards for future policy commitments." However, it rejected the idea of a "universal" model because of the implied "mandatory tax on all cable subscribers which is not sanctioned by legislation."[40]

In 1980, a similar proposal was made to the Therrien committee by a Joint Action Committee on Pay-Television and Satellite Policy representing eleven organizations of union, cultural, and public interest groups.[41] Their proposal called for a Crown corporation, TeleCanada, that would provide and market a complete, eleven-channel Canadian broadcasting satellite service. TeleCanada's board of directors would be made up of representatives of private and public broadcasting interests, the provinces, and the public; the revenues generated by the service would go into purchasing or subsidizing Canadian program production. The Therrien committee simply acknowledged this proposal, along with others.[42]

The TeleCanada concept was repackaged for the 1981 pay-television application hearings as a noncommercial private venture to be governed by a membership of twenty-five "broadly representative people" (including the now former minister of communications, David MacDonald). Its application was denied, but the CRTC decision called for a future hearing into the question of universal pay-television.[43] Meanwhile, a licence to serve remote communities was awarded in April 1981 to Canadian Satellite Communications Inc. (Cancom), a consortium of private broadcasters who had also made a submission to the Therrien committee in 1980. Instead of the diversified package proposed by TeleCanada, northern Canadians would receive an assortment of private broadcast signals supplied by members of the consortium. When John Meisel resigned as chairman of the CRTC in November 1983, he was replaced by André Bureau, a business executive who, until that time, had been the president of Cancom.

Pay-television was a microcosm of the problem of Canadian broadcasting in the 1980s. It was the most striking example since commercial radio of Canadian assimilation of a broadcasting technology developed in the United States and introduced into Canada on behalf of Canadian entrepreneurs. But unlike the 1920s, there was now a regulatory agency and it heard alternatives to the American commercial model *before* the new innovation was introduced; with radio, the public alternative only emerged after the fact and the vestiges of private broadcasting were able to grow and develop into the dominant sector. In the case of television, industry pressure had at least been resisted sufficiently to allow establishment of a public presence before the profit taking began. Cable distribution, like radio, had established itself by the time policy makers became aware of its implications. With commercial pay-television, however, the facts were known before any determining move was made; it only remained to say "no," and that was not done. In the 1980s neither the government nor its regulatory agency was willing to resist a new American commercial model. Incredibly, American-style pay-television was adopted amid waves of rhetoric about serving Canadian national objectives. The long-shot possibility that pay-television might bring some benefit to the struggling Canadian production industry was allowed to justify introducing a new service whose only sure effect was to enrich a few cable companies. Another historic opportunity to expand the public dimension was missed although, as usual, the trade-off was made in the name of the public. But the public's only role with respect to pay-television was in its decision to hook up or switch off.

### New Disputes: Who's in Charge?

As the pay-television scenario illustrated, the early 1980s was the period for the proponents of cultural industry to build on ground broken in the late 1970s but frozen while political priorities were elsewhere. Now, with industrial objectives on the rise, the question of authority over the entire system was at stake as well.

A DOC perspective on the issue of control had been presented to an international conference in 1976 by a senior department official (later deputy minister), Robert Rabinovitch. The DOC was an essentially hardware-oriented department, he said, only recently beginning to add to its mandate certain responsibilities in broadcasting policy. But new legislation was about to be introduced that would "reinforce the role of the government in the development of specific broadcast policy." Ottawa had established "a very powerful regulator," the CRTC, to compensate for its earlier involvement in broadcasting policy, and now it was attempting "to redress the balance between the two."[44]

In the crisis atmosphere of the late 1970s, the legislation Rabinovitch referred to never became law, although it had been introduced three times by Jeanne Sauvé alone. The "problem" of the government's relationship to the CRTC carried over into the 1980s. In a sense, the CRTC's steam-rolling of pay-television in 1981–82 could be seen as an attempt by the regulatory agency to assert its own position in the system.

Under John Meisel, the CRTC was concerned to maintain its independence from government. At the parliamentary committee on 15 July 1980, Meisel voiced this concern, tempering it with the view that legislators should make clear policy decisions and then leave the regulator to carry them out.[45] Meisel also sought to strengthen the CRTC's legitimacy by broadening the base of responsibility for resolving the problems of Canadian broadcasting. On 19 May 1981, he told the parliamentary committee: "No one agency or no one broadcaster, or one media can do it ... it will have to follow from a very conscious effort on the part of all elements in the broadcasting industry, private as well as public, the media, Canadian citizens, the government."[46]

This was in keeping with the CRTC's traditional claim to the mantle of leadership that had resulted, since 1974, in a state of perpetual tension bordering on rivalry between the regulator and the CBC. The broadcasting act gave the CBC special status in its relationship to the CRTC, which could neither revoke nor suspend its licence and, thus, could not enforce conditions imposed on the CBC. The CRTC argued that it should have the same power over the CBC as it had over the private sector. Indeed, the often conflict-ridden relationship between the CRTC and the CBC begged the question of who was representing the real public interest: the public broadcaster or the regulatory agency? The CRTC decision regarding CBC-2 and, in its own curious way, its treatment of pay-television as a bold gamble, were part of the struggle to answer this question. But the question was becoming an academic one.

On 28 May 1981, the day after the CRTC's CBC-2 decision, Fox told the parliamentary committee about the "increasingly tight relationship between culture and communications" since the transfer of responsibilities for arts and culture from the secretary of state to the Department of Communications nearly a year before. Thanks to this administrative "marriage of communications and culture," communications policy was henceforth being made with regard to both cultural messages and the impact of technology on culture. Fox was asked why the government would not increase support to the CBC (whose parliamentary grant was now up to $650 million, but subject to restraints on expansion). He replied that while the CBC was "a very important part of the Canadian broadcasting system" because of its role in increasing Canadian content and developing a Canadian program production industry, the Cabinet now wanted to look at "all the players in the system" (radio, television, and cable) with a view to establishing their respective roles. The public sector was not the only element involved.[47]

Fox said Canada needed a new, overall broadcasting strategy to take account of this new conception of the role of the CBC: "It was decided long ago that it was far preferable for Canada to have a single, Canadian network. At the time, the CBC was really the focal point of the whole broadcasting system. The technology has changed, but the problems have not. If we take other issues, such as national unity, we can look at the speeches made in 1867 and those made today, and we find that the problems have not changed."[48]

In short, Fox was saying, if the CBC was no longer the focal point of the Canadian broadcasting system, it was because of "technology." The problems of Canada, national unity for example, remained unchanged. Strategy for dealing with those problems had to be adapted to fit the new technological context.

The Quebec referendum not only marked a major transition in federal political strategy regarding communications, it also changed the nature of the jurisdictional conflict between Quebec and Ottawa.[49] Unlike in Ottawa's case, communications was not a major strategic front for Quebec during the Parti Québécois's first mandate and the period leading up to the referendum. This was especially paradoxical in light of the Bourassa government's approach which had made communications the main battleground of Quebec's attempt to assert its "cultural sovereignty." The PQ, on the other hand, initiated no new major project in communications and even maintained the constitutional battle at a minimal level.

In April 1981, the PQ was reelected, and during its second mandate communications regained a certain prominence. But, again paradoxically, Quebec would now place an even greater priority than Ottawa on the economic aspects of communications. In the new political climate created by the result of the referendum, Quebec appeared to lose interest in the socio-cultural side of communications in favour of developing its own industrial capacity in the sector. In terms of Quebec-Ottawa relations, communications switched from a field of political conflict to one of economic competition.

Quebec's new communications minister, Jean-François Bertrand, signalled the new situation in June 1981: far from being uninterested in communications, the PQ believed that communications must be part of an overall sociopolitical project.[50] The PQ, Bertrand said, had concentrated on consolidating Quebec's own communications structures, such as community media and Radio-Québec, rather than pursuing the constitutional battle. The major themes that had been articulated in 1972–73 were still valid, he said, and were inscribed in the current of social change unleashed by the Quiet Revolution.

Every one of the concrete steps taken by Quebec to assert itself in communications had been made in the context of fierce competition between federal and provincial governments each seeking to assert its control of the situation. Every Quebec government since 1929 had intervened in communications and, now, Bertrand outlined what the PQ intended to do: to add to the cultural dimension an economic dimension. PQ communications policy would be based on economic development and not on making demands of Ottawa.[51]

The new approach was part of the PQ's overall move away from Quebec's traditional political and cultural concerns after the referendum. Quebec under the PQ seemed determined to outpace Ottawa in shifting the accent in communications from the cultural and political to the industrial and economic spheres.[52] In cultural terms, Quebec seemed to be saying: "We don't need English Canada to show us how to become Americans; we're quite able to do that on our own." Politically, this new focus of Quebec's relationship with Ottawa underlined something else: there was only a relative advantage to be expected from substituting the Quebec state for the Canadian one.

In Ottawa, meanwhile, the new consciousness of the limited effectiveness of a state propaganda vehicle and the release of tension following the Quebec referendum was also bringing about a restructuring of Canadian communications policy away from a cultural and towards an industrial orientation. However, in view of the historic tradition, it was convenient, perhaps essential, to frame this restructuring in traditional ideological terms.[53] On 20 April 1982, Francis Fox told the parliamentary committee that the relationship of culture and communications was most apparent in broadcasting. Challenged by new technologies and public expectations of greater program choice (the public as audience), the Canadian broadcasting system faced an "increasingly competitive environment." Broadcasting strategy would have to be an integral part of a national cultural policy.

On 1 August 1982, A.W. Johnson was replaced as president of the CBC by Pierre Juneau (who had been deputy minister of communications since 1976). Juneau was soon under fire for granting three evenings of prime time broadcasting to his old friend, the prime minister. This raised the hackles of the CBC's own journalists, and was satirized in an exceptional broadcast on the CBC's flagship current affairs television program, "The Journal," while CBC executives issued scholastic statements distinguishing between the corporation's "journalistic" mandate to report on events and its "institutional" function to transmit government messages.[54] This old-fashioned CBC controversy was eclipsed only by the publication of the report of the Federal Cultural Policy Review Committee and its drastic recommendations concerning the CBC.[55] When Juneau made his first appearance as CBC president before the parliamentary committee on 3 December 1982, NDP member Mark Rose told him: "I suppose you are the closest thing we have to a cultural tsar, and you know what happened to the tsar."[56]

### PATHWAYS TO PRIVATIZATION

#### The Applebaum-Hébert Review

The Federal Cultural Policy Review Committee chaired by Louis Applebaum and Jacques Hébert reported on 16 November 1982. In many spheres of cultural life, it invited involvement from provincial and municipal governments but broadcasting policy and regulation had to remain under exclusive federal jurisdiction.

The Applebaum-Hébert report necessarily returned to basics: "One of the elements of the philosophy of Canadian broadcasting regulation that is still with us today is the view that there is a 'single national system' in which privately owned broadcasting is supposed to cooperate or at least co-exist with the state-owned network."[57]

Apart from hinting that the "philosophy" of Canadian broadcasting was beginning to smell of mothballs, this statement was remarkable as a rare official characterization of the CBC as a "state-owned" rather than a public network. The report quickly reverted to referring to the "publicly owned" network, but the momentary lack of concern for precision indicated the emerging new attitude towards the public dimension of broadcasting. Applebaum-Hébert leaned heavily on the broadcasting act's insistence that the entire system must offer "balanced" programming. In the overall package, "what Canadians need from the CBC is an alternative to private broadcasting."[58]

This was to become the new basis of legitimation for public broadcasting: to ensure "balance" in the system by satisfying consumer interests and national objectives which private broadcasting could not supply. The unstated implication of labelling the CBC as the "alternative" was that private broadcasting was now the dominant sector.

The report recapitulated the various objectives of the broadcasting act and came to a severe conclusion: it was difficult to determine the extent to which they had been achieved, because the objectives themselves were "vague ... largely unmeasurable, and ... inconsistent."[59] The system "probably serves industrial and economic objectives fairly well," but the same could not be said for its cultural objectives. The rest of the report's chapter on broadcasting appeared to suggest that the system should stick to what it did well.

The report identified two problems which had reduced the CBC's ability to devise programming "that truly fulfils its role and objectives as a public broadcaster": reliance on advertising revenue (the problem already identified by the CRTC in 1974) and the extensive use of in-house production.[60]

Concerning the CRTC, the report considered that its main instrument for implementing cultural objectives, Canadian content requirements, had not worked. The CRTC (like the BBG before it, and the CBC before it) had been reluctant to use its power to make and enforce strong regulations because of their possible impact on the economic viability of private broadcasters. "The inherent conflict here, as in many other areas of cultural policy, is between an industrial and a cultural strategy," and here too, industrial strategy seemed to have the upper hand.[61]

The report dealt rapidly with the problems posed by private broadcasters and cable and satellite systems, concluding that restriction of these elements of the private sector was not the solution. If cable television had posed a threat to Canadian broadcasting, "it is sobering to contemplate what the impact will be when a host of US services can be received via satellite anywhere in Canada." Auguring an era of open skies, the report said no government or regulatory agency could, or should, "prevent the public from obtaining access to the foreign programs and services it wants." The only way for Canada to retain a strong programming presence in its own broadcasting environment was to "use all its technological and creative resources to provide Canadian programs and services that Canadians want to see and hear, programs that are competitive in quality with those from other countries."[62] The review committee's contribution to the "philosophy" of Canadian broadcasting was to see this new energy coming from the private sector.

The Applebaum-Hébert report recognized the role of the CBC as "the voice of the public's interests, the expression of Canada's multifaceted reality." The key element in the system was the public broadcaster: "to provide original and stimulating programs that private broadcasters will not provide because they may not be profitable; to ensure that Canada's artists and producers are encouraged to develop new ideas, new forms of entertainment, new program concepts; to be involved with developing technologies and engaged in video and audio experimentation. We need a public broadcaster free to reach audiences, in Canada and elsewhere, through all possible means. In short, we need a better, more vital, more courageous CBC."[63]

The report then proposed changes that would enable the CBC to recapture its lost position as Canada's leading broadcaster. The CBC should "concentrate all its energies on building programs in response to public needs."[64] It should abandon the commercial field by eliminating advertising from television and ceasing its affiliation arrangement with private stations. It should phase out local programming and, then, it should get out of all television production, except for news, "in favour of acquiring its television program materials from independent producers."[65]

The CBC would become "the public programmer," thus clarifying its purpose and direction. The privatization of program production, the report insisted, did not mean a transfer of the CBC to the private sector, nor even a relinquishing of control over programs to the independent producers, whose material would be commissioned according to public policy objectives. While the stated objective of this recommendation was to make the CBC "a public television corporation that is an alternative to private broadcasting," the push for industrial development was not far beneath the surface. For example, the report stated, it would be a good thing if production and production-oriented service companies began to acquire studio and other technical facilities released by the CBC – or in other words, even if the CBC were to continue to play a central role, the production services that it had traditionally provided and the assets used to provide them should be privatized.[66]

The Applebaum-Hébert committee recognized that its recommendations meant reconsidering the mandate of the CBC. To mark such reconsideration unequivocally, it proposed that a new broadcasting act be introduced. The *status quo* could not go on, the report said: "Too many Canadians are beginning to question the very need for a public broadcaster such as the CBC."[67]

The proposed new broadcasting act should "give clear authority to the CRTC in matters related to the CBC"; at the same time, the CRTC should be stricter in its efforts to enforce the licence conditions of private broadcasters; the need to protect their business concerns was "not as important as the need for new Canadian program production."[68]

The new act should also modify the government's relationship to the CRTC. Under the *status quo*, the Cabinet could overrule individual licence decisions but had no authority to give the CRTC policy direction. The report proposed reversing the situation by having the act "confirm the total independence of the CRTC from political intrusion in matters relating to licensing, but permit direction by the minister on matters of general policy, under certain specified conditions."[69] This was one recommendation the government would quickly try to implement in its determination to reassert communications policy leadership.

The Applebaum-Hébert report's chapter on broadcasting generally confirmed the transfer of emphasis away from the public dimension and towards a new double focus: industrial development through privatization and political control in the interests of expediency. But buried within its pages were a handful of discordant proposals that reintroduced a long-dormant subject to the broadcasting agenda: democratization.

Early on, the report had insisted that broadcasting regulation remain exclusively in the hands of a single, federal agency, the CRTC, which "should continue to license provincially and municipally based broadcasting undertakings."[70] But the report also saw the CRTC as the ultimate guardian of the public interest in broadcasting. Thus, in addition to regulation, it proposed that the CRTC set up "advisory committees" in each province "to assist in performance evaluation of licensees and to provide advice and reaction from a local perspective on all broadcast activities."[71]

Elsewhere, the report resurrected an old CRTC recommendation that cable television operators be required to allocate "a significant percentage" of gross revenue towards facilities and programming of community channels. Wherever there were community channels, the CRTC should then encourage establishment of "Local Programming Leagues ... nonprofit organizations composed of representative groups and citizens within each community ... In the community channel operations, direct participation by members of the community in all aspects of programming is not only possible but the norm."[72] Local programming by cable, "attuned to a remarkable degree to specific local needs and aspirations," could provide "a better broadcasting service in line with the interests of local residents, more opportunities for performers and producers to test themselves and to grow, and more involvement by citizens in ensuring television's usefulness in their lives."[73]

Free of industrial considerations, these few recommendations recalled some of the social objectives of broadcasting.

## The DOC's Proposals

The Applebaum-Hébert committee's report was addressed first of all "to the Minister of Communications and his colleagues in the federal government."[74] The minister had little difficulty integrating its approach to his policy orientation. Two weeks after the report was published, Francis Fox told the parliamentary committee his forthcoming policy document would take the position that the challenge in broadcasting had to be met "by greater use of the private sector."[75]

This was official confirmation of the reversal of the traditional position that only the public sector could assure the national purpose of broadcasting. Originally, it had been believed that a public system of program production and distribution was needed in order to guarantee "Canadian" broadcasting. Now, the minister said the challenge of building infrastructures and distribution had been met, and the remaining challenge, that of programming, would rely increasingly on the private sector.

Fox's strategy paper, *Towards a New National Broadcasting Policy*, was published on 1 March 1983. Its orientation was described in the subtitle: "New policies and initiatives to provide Canadians with greater program choice and make the Canadian broadcasting industry more competitive: A response to new technologies and a changing environment."[76]

The objectives of the broadcasting act of 1968 were still valid, the paper said, but technological innovations had given rise to new challenges and opportunities, promising benefits on the one hand but also threatening to "undermine the present Canadian broadcasting system and weaken our cultural integrity as a nation."[77] To maximize the benefits and minimize the threat, the broadcasting strategy had three goals:

> To maintain the Canadian broadcasting system as an effective vehicle of social and cultural policy in light of a renewed commitment to the spirit of the broadcasting objectives set out in the 1968 Broadcasting Act.
>
> To make available to all Canadians a solid core of attractive Canadian programming in all program categories, through the development of strong Canadian broadcast and program production industries.
>
> To provide a significantly increased choice of programming of all kinds in both official languages in all parts of Canada.[78]

At the heart of the strategy were four new policy initiatives. The first called for expanding the choice of available programming to Canadians, through the cable system, "the most cost-effective means of significantly expanding the viewing choice of most Canadians, while at the same time ensuring that the broadcasting system remains identifiably Canadian." New Canadian and foreign programming and nonprogramming services would be made available as cable becomes "a major vehicle for delivering the 'information revolution' to Canadian homes." Canadian high-technology industries would benefit directly from this "revolution": Cable companies would require new hardware, from earth stations to scrambling and descrambling devices, and Canadian high-technology industries would benefit directly. Not insignificantly, "jobs should be created as a result."[79]

The second policy initiative called for strengthening Canadian programming. The crisis in Canadian program production was both economic and cultural, the government said. Its solution was to establish a Canadian Broadcast Program Development Fund "to assist private production companies and independent producers." The "hunger for new content" in a global broadcasting environment marked by a multiplicity of channels was a tremendous opportunity for Canadian program producers. The fund would provide the resources with which Canadian producers could compete effectively in these new markets and in the domestic market, helping them produce "Canadian programming that people will choose to watch."[80]

The third policy initiative concerned the government's intention to acquire the power to direct the CRTC on policy matters. The government proposed to amend the broadcasting act to allow Cabinet to issue broad policy directives to the CRTC, "subject to appropriate safeguards and procedures." The CRTC would continue to establish regulations and issue licences, but fundamental policy making belonged with the government and Parliament: "In a rapidly changing technological environment ... the Government [must] have the ability to adjust broadcasting policy quickly to meet new challenges and opportunities."[81]

The fourth policy initiative called for abolishing satellite dish licensing requirements for individuals and certain commercial establishments in order to redress the imbalance in program accessibility for people living in areas unserved by cable. The new policy acknowledged "a fundamental truth of the new broadcasting environment – that satellites are rapidly emerging as the preferred medium for delivery of distant programming signals to cable systems and to areas unserved by cable."[82]

Taken together, the four new policy initiatives clearly indicated the orientation and preoccupations of the Department of Communications. The "cultural" and "national" objectives of broadcasting received only cursory lip-service as justification for the proposals. The technological context and economic imperatives were the new vehicles of legitimation for industrial development and consolidation of political control. The new broadcasting system would be based on a publicly regulated but privately owned network of cable distribution operations, providing the widest possible range of services, including Canadian programming provided increasingly by state-subsidized private production companies. The guardian of Canadian content and the public interest would continue to be the CRTC, but the government would hold the steering wheel, via a new power to issue directives. Finally, the government promised to protect its preferred agent, the cable companies, from the competition of the new technology, direct broadcast satellites – just as it had once upon a time protected broadcasting from cable systems. Once again, the government was basing its strategy on protecting a familiar technology from a new one, but it had intimated that this attitude could change once it figured out how to bring the new technology under control.

The four policy initiatives covered the government's most pressing priorities in March 1983. At the same time, the paper indicated eight general areas where further consideration was necessary before firm policies could be established:

1. The private broadcasting sector had to be strengthened and encouraged to play a greater role in Canadian programming
2. French-language broadcasting and programming services in Quebec and across Canada should be enhanced, possibly by establishing a second private French-language television network
3. A framework for the international marketing of Canadian television programs had to be created
4. Services had to be equalized throughout the country by employing distribution technologies such as those made available by Cancom
5. A new northern broadcasting policy was needed to respond to the specific needs of native people
6. The regulatory environment had to be made more flexible, especially with respect to the introduction of new services
7. The legislative framework had to be revised, redefining broadcasting in light of the new technologies and realigning Parliament's statutory objectives for broadcasting in light of technological changes
8. "The strengthened performance of the public broadcasting system as a crucial component of an identifiably Canadian broadcasting system" had to be assured; to this end, there would be "a fundamental review of the role of the CBC to ensure that it provides programming appropriate to the new broadcasting environment"[83]

Aside from the question of northern policy, which the document simply left undeveloped, this last point was the only one that was not strictly industrially oriented but focused on the public dimension of broadcasting. It was left open for the time being, pending a new policy framework for the CBC alone, which would be published seven months later.

### Some Responses

In the spring of 1983, the parliamentary committee on communications and culture heard submissions respecting the report of the Federal Cultural Policy Review Committee. At the first session on 17 March, Louis Applebaum said the policy review had taken "a long view of culture," proposing fundamental principles on which future governments could base decisions. Applebaum felt the government's new broadcasting strategy was "in line with the direction that we are endorsing," but did not deal adequately with the interrelationships between different elements of the system.[84]

The key, Applebaum said, was to clarify the roles of the different actors. For example, the CBC's priority must be programming, even to the exclusion of everything else. Local broadcasting, on the other hand, had to be based on "direct response to local needs as voiced by the local community." The CBC should concentrate on the national interest and leave local interests to "alternative systems."[85]

Here, much more clearly than in his committee's formal report, Applebaum laid out a new organizational vision of Canadian broadcasting, where the CBC was responsible for national and regional programming and "local" broadcasting took on a new public character. But he did not elaborate as to the mechanism through which this could take place. Paradoxically, "national" broadcasting would continue to be publicly funded but hierarchically structured and bureaucratically organized, while "local" broadcasting would be democratically organized and funded some other way.

One of the witnesses the committee heard was Paul Audley of the Canadian Institute for Economic Policy, who had been involved in the TeleCanada pay-television proposal.[86] He said the existing mechanisms for developing and implementing public policy did not permit an effective integration of communications and cultural concerns: "The ultimate purpose of policies affecting the cultural industries should be social and cultural and not economic."[87] Industrial development should be designed to further social and cultural ends, Audley said. This was difficult because the overall structure of Canadian cultural industries was built around "the activity of providing foreign content to Canadians." Thus, he implied, industrial development could be said to be in inherent conflict with cultural policy goals. The Applebaum-Hébert committee's recommendations, not to speak of Fox's policy, could actually lead to a decline in Canadian programming.

It was not enough to produce programs, Audley said, a market had to be developed for those programs. Past policies – the capital cost allowance for investment in Canadian film productions, pay-television, and now the program development fund – did not do that. Audley said public opinion surveys showed "that there really is tremendous public support for a good deal stronger approach than the government has been taking." The problem was not so much with the public; it was with the private interests: "We really have it backwards. We keep trying to make the whole thing work by pushing it at the production end with absolutely no attention being paid to having some kind of pull there in the marketplace."[88]

CBC president Pierre Juneau told the committee the CBC agreed with the spirit of the Applebaum-Hébert report's outline of the goals of public broadcasting in Canada. The CBC was willing to get out of local programming but opposed the report's recommendation about production, which Juneau described as "Americanizing" the system. Juneau believed the CBC would continue to hold its current share of the television audience – about 44 percent of French-language and 22 percent of English-language viewers. The CBC, he said, "is not a selective service for a small group. It is a popular, democratic kind of service."[89]

The committee also heard from two associations representing CBC English television producers and directors from Toronto and the regions. Their spokesmen, Marvin Terhoch and Arnold Amber, emphasized the need for more democracy in public broadcasting both within the CBC and in its relations with the public. Corporate objectives, Terhoch said, could be "top down" but programming objectives had to come "bottom up." Amber said the CBC had fallen away from its cultural mandate and the communities that supported it over the years. It had to reconnect "with people who are involved, as people might be helpful in making programs and watching programs. The public nature of the corporation ... means we have to go back and talk to the public as well ... if we are going to talk about public broadcasting, we have to set in place some mechanisms that allow public broadcasting to happen."[90]

So, a number of cracks in the policy that arose out of the Applebaum-Hébert review had been identified. Fox's piecemeal, industrial approach was designed to solve the economic problems of a national broadcasting system, but it barely attacked the cultural aspects. It did not even seem to recognize the existence of a social purpose to broadcasting which, still, in 1983, could only be realized by emphasizing the public dimension.

### Resituating the CBC

The recommendations of the Federal Cultural Policy Review Committee had initiated wide public debate on the future of the CBC, at least among the cultural, intellectual, and media élite of English Canada. The hearings and recommendations of the parliamentary committee on communications and culture had furthered that debate. In addition, at the request of the minister of communications, the CBC's board of directors submitted policy proposals[91] to the Department of Communications, which then conducted its own "comprehensive review."[92]

A comprehensive Canadian broadcasting strategy would be incomplete without a new policy for the CBC, the DOC said. But it indicated that the main enduring value of the CBC to the new strategy was historic and traditional. The CBC's strength was "that of a national institution which has woven itself into the very fabric of our national consciousness over the last 50 years."[93]

The DOC paper lauded the CBC's role in creating "our electronic heritage, a shared audio-visual record of what it has meant to be a Canadian over the past 50 years," and presented the CBC as "an essential instrument of Canadian cultural development" charged with "a massive task." It emphasized the need for this task to be performed "as efficiently as possible with adequate accountability to the Government of Canada, Parliament and, through them, to the Canadian people."[94]

For nearly fifty years the CBC had "interpreted us to ourselves and helped us to define the meaning of our involvement in the scattered and diverse national community that is this country."[95] But the present "technological revolution" had changed the context of which it was a part.

The broadcasting act mandated the CBC to provide "a balanced service of information, enlightenment and entertainment for people of different ages, interests and tastes covering the whole range of programming in fair proportion." Given the expansion of private broadcasting, provincial broadcasters, cable services, and videocassettes, "there is now less need for the CBC to provide such a comprehensive programming service."[96]

The broadcasting environment was in the process of being even further modified by new services available by satellite. These included the Cancom network delivering a full package to remote communities formerly served only by CBC; pay-television; a wide range of US services technically available, if yet unauthorized, in Canada; and, soon, inexpensive direct broadcast reception: "In this new multi-channel environment ... it has become ever more imperative that the CBC find a new and more relevant role – one which provides programming distinctive from the kind already so abundantly available from other domestic and foreign programming services."[97]

The specific new role envisaged for the CBC was complementary to that foreseen for the private production sector in the policy that created the Canadian Broadcast Program Development Fund (Telefilm Canada, which began functioning on 1 July 1983).[98] As "the publicly owned provider of our national broadcasting service," the CBC would ensure a strong Canadian programming presence in the new environment. As a programmer (the role proposed by the Applebaum-Hébert committee[99]), the CBC would participate in developing a strong Canadian (privately owned) production industry and would provide a program outlet (domestic market) for its products. The task was beyond the capabilities of either public or private broadcasting sectors acting alone; their roles had to be complementary in order to fulfil the system's cultural objectives.[100]

The new technology, with its power "to abolish distance and ignore national boundaries," recreated the cultural crisis that previous broadcasting policies had been intended to meet. The "new cultural challenge" would have to be met by a new type of collaboration between the public and private sectors. Canada seemed to be moving back to the "single system," but with completely redefined roles for the system's intermeshing parts.

The CBC's mandate would be redefined by an amendment to the broadcasting act requiring it to provide "a distinctive and predominantly Canadian service," while the system as a whole would be required to be "balanced and comprehensive." But the CBC would still be expected to "remain a popular service ... appealing to all Canadians," and not become "a northern version of the US Public Broadcasting System with its narrow public following." The CBC would be expected to increase its Canadian content level to 80 percent and seek to attract new audiences. At the same time, the policy called for continued reliance on television advertising revenue (contrary to CRTC and Applebaum-Hébert recommendations). While CBC policy would be expected to ensure the primacy of programming objectives over commercial objectives, there was an evident contradiction: the CBC would have to purchase or produce "distinctive" Canadian programs able to compete for large audiences and advertising dollars in a shrinking market.

In addition, the CBC was expected to play an important role in developing the independent production industry. It would have to increase to 50 percent the proportion of national network programming produced outside and lease production facilities to independent producers. The CBC had expensive production facilities which most independent producers would not wish to own, the paper said, because of the costs of maintaining and operating them.

The paper also talked about "more cost-effective distribution of programming," aggressive commercial merchandising of CBC products from programs to consulting services, and improved financial efficiency and accountability. There was no indication of increased funding for the CBC in the near future. It would be expected to find additional resources through improved efficiency and internal reallocation and would benefit indirectly from the new program development fund.

The paper paid almost no attention to the CBC's national unity role. Somewhat lethargically improvising a pastiche of recent interpretations, it said: "The phrase in the CBC mandate, 'contribute to the development of national unity' is deemed to mean being 'consciously partial to the success of Canada as a united country with its own national objectives, independent from those of other countries', while maintaining the highest standards of professional journalism."[101] The government appeared to have lost interest in the question of national unity, expressing confidence in the wisdom of relying on high professional standards and complete autonomy. However, the paper reiterated a number of standard wishes: the CBC should have more regional programming on its national networks; there should be more collaboration between French and English services; news and public affairs programming in both English and French should reflect national issues. Finally, it claimed that the major new measures, like Canadianization of the CBC schedule and increased use of independent producers, would help, but it did not specify how.

## Final Liberal Thrusts

The legislative structure of communications in Canada had not been touched since Gérard Pelletier added telecommunications to the CRTC's responsibilities in 1976.[102] Broadcasting was still legally constituted under the Broadcasting Act of 1968.[103]

Pelletier had said the CRTC Act of 1976 was only the first stage of a reform. Jeanne Sauvé had tried three times to bring in communications legislation, but none of her efforts got past first reading. David MacDonald had promised the same, but he was not in office long enough to introduce legislation.

Francis Fox's turn came on 8 February 1984, with Bill C-20, an omnibus bill amending the basic legislation to accommodate the DOC's recent policy proposals.[104] The CRTC act would be amended to enable the government to issue directives to the CRTC on any matter under its jurisdiction, with the exception of specific broadcasting licences. Where "matters of public interest" were concerned, however, a cabinet directive affecting specific licensees would be permissible. The broadcasting act, meanwhile, would be amended to state that "the Canadian broadcasting system should provide a balanced service of information, enlightenment and entertainment for people of different ages, interests and tastes, covering the whole range of programming," while the CBC was redefined as "a distinctive service of information, enlightenment and entertainment within the Canadian broadcasting system."[105] Bill C-20 would have given the government of the day the power to direct the CRTC regarding "the overall architecture" of the Canadian broadcasting system, in Fox's words. But it died on the order paper.

Fox made one more major intervention. In May 1984, he published a national film and video policy, completing the series of DOC initiatives taken while he was minister.[106] This paper sought to synchronize film and broadcasting policy to take account of the increasing overlap between the two technologies. Once again, Fox framed the overall policy in terms of "a public sector thrust intended to assure a more focused and more effective cultural and social role for the public sector [that is, the National Film Board] ... and a private sector thrust intended to assure the economic development of a strong private Canadian film and video industry."[107]

After sixteen years as leader of the Liberal Party of Canada, Pierre Trudeau retired and was replaced in June 1984 by John Turner. Turner automatically became prime minister and formed a new government in which the industrial and cultural aspects of the Department of Communications were divided along lines which resembled the situation prior to 1980. The new minister of communications, Ed Lumley, was to be responsible for hardware while the secretary of state, Serge Joyal, inherited software. However, they both lost their jobs on 5 September 1984, in the Conservative election sweep that reminded Canada of the Diefenbaker victory of 1958. Not only in politics, but in broadcasting and communications policy, it would be 1958 again.

## CONSERVATIVES IN POWER, 1984–88

### Transition and Intentions

Late in 1984, on the cusp between two political eras, Canadian cultural and communications policy seemed to be a victim of determinism, always dealing with a crisis caused by yesterday's technology. As distribution technology – cable today, satellites tomorrow – moved further and further away from classical "broadcasting," the new spaces it opened tended to be occupied by private, corporate, albeit Canadian, capital. The notion of a dominant public sector – let alone a public system or a system where the public played the dominant part – had been replaced by a new perspective where the role of the public sector was restricted to providing the framework in which the private sector was the dynamic force.

The broadcasting system the Liberals left behind was increasingly organized according to capitalist market criteria, with their attendant disastrous effects on the cultural ecology. The policy arm of the state could insist on the system's need to serve national cultural objectives but, in the absence of a political crisis with cultural implications, the available space for culture would continue to shrink and be marginalized. The federal government would see to it that an identifiable, "distinctive" Canadian presence was maintained at least in some corner of the "multi-channel environment," for without it "Canada" would collapse like a house of cards. But with this proviso, broadcasting continued to evolve like any other sector of the industrial economy.

As they had done in 1958, the Conservatives were determined to radically restructure the framework of Canadian broadcasting in line with their own image. They had a full mandate ahead of them in which to go through the due process of white papers, parliamentary hearings, and legislative debates. Unfettered by Liberal ideology, the Conservatives were well-placed to complete the industrialization of broadcasting.

Brian Mulroney's government quickly committed itself to reversing some of the basic tenets of Liberal economic policy, telling potential American investors that Canada was open for business again.[108] It was not difficult to assume that broadcasting was one of the areas they were thinking of. In November 1984, the finance minister, Michael Wilson, announced economic austerity measures in public spending and ordered the CBC to cut $75 million from its operating budget.[109] In December, the minister of communications, Marcel Masse, announced that the government would undertake yet another full-scale broadcasting policy review.

The focusing of public attention, especially in English Canada, on the CBC's budget cutbacks, highlighted only one – albeit crucial – aspect of the problem, the role of the national public broadcaster. But the minister of communications himself was the first to admit that the CBC's fiscal crisis was only the tip of the iceberg. The entire *system* was being rethought and would be reorganized on the basis of a new consensus (to emerge from where, it was not yet clear). The government appeared determined, at least, to reduce the role of the federal state in the broadcasting business and would strive to create a broadcasting environment in which private enterprise could flourish.

The Conservative policy thrust in communications was, of course, part of a process that was neither specific to that party nor, indeed, to Canada. The new government rode a global wave of general conservatism which was marked by the redefinition of the role of the state in all aspects of public life. "Deregulation," "privatization," and reduced budgets for public services were all manifestations of this general shift. That these manifestations happened to coincide with the general ideological orientation of the Conservative Party may have been coincidence, or it may have been the reason the Tories were in power; whatever the case, a fundamental change was taking place in the system over which the government presided.

As Conservative intentions in broadcasting and communications began to crystallize, Marcel Masse appeared to be the man of the hour. Once again, the architect of Canadian communications policy was a politician from Quebec, an enigmatic figure whose policy approach was based on three principles: reduced public spending, expanded private development, and – a new wild card – a greater role for provincial governments and agencies. In his speeches, Masse took to quoting R.B. Bennett, especially passages which showed Bennett advocating a public broadcasting system as a transitional measure in anticipation of future improvements in economic and technological conditions.[110] To Masse, the future was now and he seemed to be everywhere at once, reintroducing the Liberals' fallen telecommunications legislation one day,[111] signing the first federal-provincial communications accord with Quebec the next.[112]

The appointment of Masse to the reunified portfolio of communications-cum-culture brought credit to Brian Mulroney's reputation for political astuteness. Masse was not only a dyed-in-the-wool Tory, but a Quebec nationalist who had earned his stripes with the Union Nationale government of the late 1960s in its battles against federal centralism in communications and for more provincial cultural power via agencies like the provincial broadcasting network. Considered an "ultranationalist" member of Daniel Johnson's government, Masse served as minister of state for education and, later, under Jean-Jacques Bertrand, as minister of intergovernmental affairs. He was thus close to one of the stormiest dossiers in federal-provincial relations of that era, educational broadcasting, and was part of the government that created Radio-Québec. His appointment was not a naïve one, as he would have come to the direct attention of the new prime minister at least as far back as 1968, when Mulroney worked closely with the Union Nationale in planning Conservative electoral strategy for Quebec in that year's federal election.[113]

Masse was, thus, just the man to apply the axe to the CBC when Michael Wilson ordered him to find savings in November 1984. Only vaguely committed to a public broadcasting system, both in principle and as a vehicle for promoting national unity, the Tories traditionally had little care for the CBC. On the other hand, in tendering the olive branch to the provinces, particularly Quebec, as Masse began doing, the government quickly made significant political capital, while the increased space opened up for private sector expansion by a diminishing CBC met the expectations of the Tories' traditional clientele, particularly the private entrepreneurs of Canadian culture.

Better than anyone else, Masse could "denationalize" the public dimension of Canadian broadcasting – that is, to separate, in a way no Liberal or Canadian nationalist could ever do, its "national" purpose from the direct responsibility of the state. His approach was laid out in an interview published in *Le Devoir* on 20 December 1984, in which he made it clear that the era of massive state involvement in defining Canadian culture was a thing of the past:

> The Conservative Party applies its theories in every sector, in communications as elsewhere ... the state is an important tool in economic affairs as in cultural affairs, but we are not about to have a culture of the state ... we are going to have a culture of Canadians. We have insisted, to the exclusion of everything else, that the defence of Canadian culture was the CBC's responsibility. We have insisted on this until everyone else wound up believing they had no responsibility. Perhaps it is time to redress the balance. Canadian culture belongs to the Canadian people, and it is up to them, through all their institutions, to see that it flourishes.[114]

Masse went on to reiterate the importance of viewing the private sector as *equal* in importance to the public sector – a point that had been fundamental to the Tory reform of 1958 and that had marked its departure from previous policy: "The independent broadcasters are part of the Canadian experience. They should not be perceived by the CBC, nor by the Canadian government, as secondary vehicles."[115]

The Tory policy was also one of "denationalization" in the sense that it saw a major role for what the Liberals, ever insistent on a centralized vision of national unity, only accepted begrudgingly: an important role for the "other" public broadcasters, the provincial television networks. In effect, this was a farming out by Ottawa of public service responsibilities. Masse told *Le Devoir* he saw provincial broadcasters as positive instruments for regional cultural development which should no longer be viewed as invaders of federal territory.

The inclusion of the provinces in the strategy for extricating the federal government from state responsibility augured a tripartite approach to national policy (Ottawa-provinces-private sector) which Quebec found particularly attractive. In addition to the government, a certain segment of Quebec nationalist opinion considered that the prospect of a new distribution of resources in communications outweighed the negative effects of federal policy on traditional public services. In an editorial on 23 March 1985, *Le Devoir*'s Lise Bissonnette called the pro-CBC campaign of the artistic and cultural community of English Canada "unacceptable and dangerous" for Quebec because of its centralizing tendencies. She asked: "Are we prepared, in Quebec, to accept being enclosed in the obscure concept of 'Canadian culture'?" From Quebec's point of view, she said, there was cause to applaud the move away from the massive federal involvement in cultural affairs that characterized the Trudeau regime. [116] This critical view was consistent with the long line of Quebec dissidence from an otherwise "national" consensus on broadcasting since the Taschereau government and the Dominion argued the question of jurisdiction before the Supreme Court in 1931 and the Privy Council in London in 1932.

Part of the problem in the crisis of 1984–85 clearly lay with the public itself. Referring to the ease with which the government put the axe to the CBC budget, Peter Desbarats commented in the *Financial Post* on 29 December 1984:

> Not since the controversy over the political independence of "This Hour has Seven Days" in the 1960s had Ottawa dared to establish such a direct link between the cabinet and CBC management. In contrast with the events of two decades ago, the CBC appeared to accept this emasculation without any public signs of outrage. Its apathy was matched only by the public's apparent lack of concern, a sad commentary on the corporation's loss of contact and identification with its audience, particularly its television audience. [117]

In the months following that article, there was a significant public response to the CBC cutbacks. [118] But in several other areas where the government anticipated its own new policy there was no public intervention. While public debate and media attention focused on the attempt to rationalize public spending on broadcasting by cutting CBC budgets, and the legitimate critique that this would have a disastrous effect on the cultural production community, a much more insidious and far-reaching set of problems remained obscured.

However we care to criticize it, the CRTC has the merit of being, in theory at least, an independent agency through which the public interest can and should be represented. By the early 1980s, the CRTC and the DOC – an arm of government, not an independent public agency – were locked in a power struggle bordering on impasse. The Liberal government's Bill C-20[119] had tried to bring the CRTC under ministerial control, but the bill never made it into law and fell with the Liberal government. The Conservatives reintroduced it on 20 December 1984. [120] With attention massively focused on the CBC cutbacks it went relatively unnoticed – except in Quebec, where public interest groups tend to be sensitive towards government attempts to assert political control. Indeed, only the most persevering followers of policy developments seemed bothered by it, yet Bill C-20 had long-range implications which made the CBC cutbacks pale in comparison.

The new version of the bill seemed to anticipate the charge of political interference. It no longer referred to special measures which might be necessary in the "public interest." Speaking in the House on second reading 31 January 1985, Masse emphasized the "guarantees" that protected the public against abuse by the bill: (1) the Canadian charter of rights, which protects freedom of expression; (2) the exclusion of directives involving particular licensees; (3) a new provision requiring the minister to consult with the CRTC before issuing a directive; and (4) a thirty-day delay during which the directive would be referred to a parliamentary committee (also in the Liberal version). [121]

At the same time, Masse presented the bill as a major element of the new edge the government was putting on communications policy. He presented the new Tory gospel of Canadian communications history, lauding Canada's telecommunications and broadcasting systems as concrete realizations of the prophetic dreams of men like John A. Macdonald and R.B. Bennett – and as the result of dynamic cooperation between the private and public sectors.

Bill C-20, the minister said, was intended to clarify and establish a new equilibrium in the distribution of powers between the government and the regulatory agency. It would close the gap between communications legislation and the cultural possibilities of the new technologies which existing legislation did not foresee. Quoting Montesquieu and Cardinal Richelieu on the role of the state, Masse said it may be in the public interest to deregulate certain telecommunication services. The telecommunications industry would flourish in the marketplace provided public regulatory intervention were kept to a minimum, and Bill C-20 aimed to facilitate this. It was time to review telecommunications and broadcasting policy, Masse said, and this bill was somehow related to that review, but in just what way he did not make clear. [122]

Another telling move about the government's attitude towards broadcasting came in a discreet move made in May 1985, when the Cabinet abrogated a Liberal directive to the CRTC limiting cross-ownership of different media in a single market.[123] In July 1982, in the wake of the Royal Commission on Newspapers' conclusions about concentration of ownership in the Canadian newspaper industry, the Liberal government of the day moved to limit further concentration by instructing the CRTC not to grant or renew radio or television licences to companies owning newspapers in the same market. Between 1982 and 1985, the CRTC, nonetheless, granted seven requests of this type.[124]

As Denise Faille pointed out in the Quebec federation of journalists' periodical, *Le 30*, the CRTC had always exhibited a wide gap between principle and action on this matter; as early as 1974, and again in 1979, the CRTC had come out in favour of the separation of press and broadcast ownership, especially in the same markets. One month before the Cabinet's reversal of the 1982 directive, CRTC chairman André Bureau told a Montreal business group: "The CRTC attaches such great importance to the financial solvency of an undertaking that we are now disposed to foresee loosening the rules that limit mixed property, in cases where such a structure is indispensable to the strength and viability of the enterprise."[125]

The Cabinet's decision opened the way for a bid by Power Corporation, the conglomerate owner of four Quebec daily newspapers including Montreal's *La Presse*, to purchase Télé-Métropole, Quebec's most lucrative privately owned television station. Public interest groups in Quebec opposed the sale on the grounds that it presented a dangerous concentration of ownership, but the CRTC rejected Power's bid in April 1986 on other grounds, considering that Power did not "satisfactorily demonstrate that any significant and unequivocal benefits would flow from the proposed transaction to the communities served, the broadcasting system in general and the public at large."[126] The CRTC's attitude towards concentration was made clear when it awarded Télé-Métropole less than a year later to the Quebec cable giant, Vidéotron.

## The Cultural Sovereignty Debate

As the Liberals had done when they returned to office in 1963, the Conservatives decided to begin their policy review with an advisory committee to the minister. On 9 April 1985, Masse announced creation of a task force to be chaired by Gerald Caplan, a former national secretary of the NDP, and Florian Sauvageau, a Laval University communications professor. The task force was mandated to make recommendations "on an industrial and cultural strategy to govern the future evolution of the Canadian broadcasting system through the remainder of this century":

> The strategy will take full account of the overall social and economic goals of the government, of government policies and priorities, including the need for fiscal

restraint, increased reliance on private sector initiatives and federal-provincial co-operation, and of the policies of the government in other related economic and cultural sectors. It will also take full account of the challenges and opportunities in the increasingly competitive broadcasting environment presented by ongoing technological developments.[127]

It would be a challenge to the imagination to introduce a public dimension to a strategy based on such considerations but the Caplan-Sauvageau task force took the terms of its mandate with a grain of salt, reaching out to the public in spite of the minister's stated desire for an expeditious resolution of the problem of broadcasting. Masse's directive had specifically excluded public hearings, but the task force responded to public pressure and held a series of public meetings across the country at which anyone could come and present their views. These were not formal hearings, however, and were supplementary to the more substantial private meetings the task force held with interested groups. The public manifestations in themselves illustrated an important aspect of the problem at hand: unlike the earlier era of broad consensus on the role and nature of a public broadcasting system (at least in English Canada), in 1985 nearly all groups to appear before the federal task force did so with some special interest to promote. Perhaps characteristic of this, the task force was swamped with demands from various disparate interest groups, while there seemed to be a remarkable shortage of overall vision of what a public broadcasting system should be. While the debate surrounding the task force's work focused on the national issue of cultural sovereignty and the industrial problems of Canadian broadcasting, the extent to which the Canadian public, or publics, found themselves excluded from effective participation in the system, except as taxpayers and individual consumers of services, was submerged. Instead of being asked to imagine a new definition of broadcasting as public service, the task force was expected to navigate an unmarked course across a sea of competing private or special interests.

These interests were not equal in nature and could be schematically divided into two broad categories: the cultural *communities* (national and regional groups, ethnic and social minorities) and the cultural *industries* (private sector, public sector, creators and producers). In a system based on public service, it should have been self-evident that the purpose of policy was to ensure that the latter were enabled to fulfil the needs of the former. However, the debate was not so clearly focused. The argument in favour of "Canadian" broadcasting came mostly from the cultural and artistic milieux with a direct work-related interest, and there was a grand defence of national/public broadcasting organized in and around the CBC. But there was little positive discussion about what else besides "Canadian" Canadian broadcasting should be, and there was no critical questioning of what national public broadcasting in Canada had become.

The deliberations of the task force took place in the context of a broader debate on the Mulroney government's key objective of liberalizing trade arrangements with the United States. The government's commitment to "free trade" created a paradoxical situation for Canada's so-called cultural industries. Unlike other sectors, these industries were not seeking access to US markets but protection against US incursions.

The issue was important enough to the captains of Canadian cultural industry to have them set up a high-power, high-profile "strategy committee" to lobby the government against selling out Canada's cultural sovereignty. The committee included the president of Maclean-Hunter, one of Canada's leading publishers of commercial periodicals and also a cable company proprietor; the president of Télémédia, the largest chain of private radio stations in Quebec; the chief executive of Toronto's CFTO-TV, the oldest and most profitable private television station in Canada and flagship of the CTV network; the president of the private Ontario regional network, Global television; and the president of the CBC. Their purpose was to convince the government that Canadian industries should be protected in any free trade negotiations with the US.[128]

This was not the only cultural sovereignty lobby. Organizations representing artists and other cultural workers, such as the Canadian Conference of the Arts, actively waved the banners of nationalism and protectionism. Communications Minister Masse endeared himself to this constituency when he announced in September 1985 that Canada would not compromise its cultural sovereignty in free trade negotiations with the US. Canadian culture would not be placed on the bargaining table, he told a federal-provincial meeting of cultural affairs ministers in Halifax.[129]

According to *Saturday Night* magazine editor Robert Fulford – a man with impeccable cultural nationalist credentials – the effect of the cultural sovereignty issue was "to obscure other issues, and to create a distorted impression of what Canadian culture is and why it deserves protection."[130] Cultural sovereignty was a foil, masking private sector ambitions and plans and protecting the valid but corporatist interests of the cultural production milieu. Most important, it did not pose the taboo question: what is Canadian culture, anyway?

The historic importance of cultural protectionism in Canada, and the possibility that free trade would eliminate it, mobilized the artistic and cultural circles and forged a solidarity of common interest between the entrepreneurs and the creators of Canadian cultural industry. In the process, as Fulford noted, the minister of communications went through a metamorphosis from a budget-cutting villain to a far-sighted nationalist hero.

The real issue obscured by the cultural sovereignty debate concerned the progressive withdrawal of the state from social and financial responsibility in the cultural sphere. The cultural columnist for the periodical *This Magazine*, Susan Crean, wrote in April 1986: "I think what may be happening is simply that a class of cultural capitalists now exists in Canada which has learned, over the years, how to make a fancy buck out of trafficking in American (or imitation, made-in-Canada, American) culture, and they now have high stakes in the status quo ... For the artistic community, I think cultural sovereignty is a slyly laid trap."[131]

Crean was right about the cultural capitalists' stakes in the *status quo*, especially in broadcasting where the government was eager to support the increased ascendancy of the private side of the system. It was assisted in this by the CRTC which, in spite of lip-service antagonism towards the government, continued to make decisions strengthening the private and diminishing the public interest. The CRTC in 1985–86 authorized new commercial services, such as the addition of seventeen new specialized subscriber services on Canadian cable systems, and a new private French-language television station in the important Montreal market; it renewed CBC broadcasting licences without public hearings and proposed to allow telecommunications carriers to raise their rates automatically, bypassing public hearings there as well.[132]

The issue of cultural sovereignty and the thrust to develop the private sector overlapped curiously with the government's apparent intention to move towards greater collaboration with the provinces. Almost immediately upon assuming office in 1984, the Conservatives had made a number of important gestures to indicate the arrival of a new era in federal-provincial relations, especially with respect to Quebec and especially regarding communications, which had been a notable area of discord.

On 1 February 1985, Ottawa and Quebec signed an agreement on communications enterprises development, the first intergovernmental communications accord between them since establishing their respective communications ministries a few months apart in 1969. Under the accord, the two governments would provide $40 million to stimulate investment and job creation in the communications sector, as well as encourage research and technical innovation and support the production, development, and marketing of communications goods and services, especially in export markets.[133]

In May 1985, the fruits of federal-provincial collaboration yielded a major report on "The Future of French-Language Television."[134] A joint committee, chaired by the deputy ministers of communications of both Ottawa and Quebec, had been formed soon after the 1984 elections to examine the particular question of French-language broadcasting. This was the first time the question had been considered in a context stripped of political or constitutional implications.

The report enumerated the achievements of French-language television in Canada: in the private sector, it was well-developed, profitable, and enjoyed high ratings; the Canadian public network was diversified, of high quality, and reached a large audience. In both sectors, a large proportion of French-Canadian productions could be found consistently at the top of the ratings. There was a growing and healthy competition between the two, and the provincial educational broadcaster, Radio-Québec, was also building a following by offering more "cultural content" than the others. Finally, the report noted an active group of community television organizations in Quebec "concerned with meeting local needs that the major networks are largely unable to satisfy."[135]

The report noted the following problems, however: erosion of the French-language audience by English television (accounting for 20 percent of viewing time of French Canadians); the possibility of further erosion due to new English services; the inability of the French market to support audience fragmentation for cabled specialty services; the reluctance of governments to augment public television spending; limited access of the independent production industry to the television market; and the lack of French services outside Quebec and in small communities in Quebec. It made one recommendation which, if heeded, would change the future course of Canadian broadcasting evolution: "that the special nature of the French-language television system be recognized within the Canadian broadcasting system, and that government policies and regulations be adapted accordingly."[136]

This would mean, for example, that Radio-Canada "should be allowed to evolve separately from the CBC" – a major departure from the historic approach of "two services, one policy." There would be a need for ongoing consultation between Ottawa and Quebec regarding the roles of public and private sectors in the evolution of the French system (traditionally, Ottawa had insisted on exclusive jurisdiction over policy and regulation, while Quebec had fought to occupy space on the line of Ottawa's weakest resistance).

The bulk of the proposals, however, indicated the importance of private economic development in the joint committee's scheme of things. Thus, cable policy should favour French services over English ones (a kind of protectionism for Québécois entrepreneurs as well as a measure of cultural self-defence); there should be more investment in French programming by private broadcasters, more public support for independent production, and collaboration between private and public networks to maximize audience penetration and minimize the effects of fragmentation; finally, French signals should be delivered to underserved areas (and if the pan-Canadian model for service to remote areas was followed, this would mean a consortium of private broadcasters piggy-backing on public satellite resources).

The "separate evolution" proposal was not only important for its rupture with traditional federally centred policy. The context affecting French television in Canada imposed problems that were different and required their own solutions. For example, as the report brought to light: only 48 percent of Quebec households subscribed to cable versus 64 percent in the rest of Canada; thus, one would expect that Quebec television viewers were less exposed to American television fare and, indeed, that hypothesis was borne out by viewing time statistics. In 1983, 45 percent of Quebec viewing time was devoted to foreign production, as opposed to over 50 percent in English Canada. Finally, the report's breakdown of the dollars and cents of Canadian French-language television clearly indicated where the priorities lay. In 1984–85, Radio-Canada spent $236 million on French television, Radio-Québec had a total budget of $57 million, and Quebec's ministry of communications gave out about $600,000 in subsidies to community television. The private sector, meanwhile, made $32 million profit on $181 million revenue.[137]

The new climate of Ottawa-Quebec "collaboration" was temporarily dampened by the provincial election that returned the Liberals to power in Quebec in December 1985, but the honeymoon in communications still appeared to be on. During the provincial election campaign, the Quebec Liberal Party had promised to freeze Radio-Québec's budget at its existing level, pending debate in Quebec's parliamentary commission on culture, on the mandate, orientations, and objectives of Radio-Québec.[138] In January 1986, just more than a month after taking office, Quebec Communications Minister Richard French proposed to make Radio-Québec the centre-piece of a national (Canadian) French-language educational network.[139]

Two days later, Marcel Masse voiced his approval of the idea. On 14 February, Masse and French signed a new four year agreement on federal-provincial cooperation aimed at "harmonizing" French-language television policies in areas such as the new international francophone satellite station, TV5. Quebec now enjoyed an official role in determining federal policy, Masse announced.[140] The joint ministerial statement declared the extension of Radio-Québec to English Canada to be a priority. Richard French referred to it as the "export" of Quebec's educational programs.

But in March, Quebec announced an $8 million budget cut to Radio-Québec (about 14 percent) in spite of the Liberals' election promise and the expansions planned by French and Masse. It was soon revealed that the cuts would be effected largely by shutting most, if not all, of Radio-Québec's nine "regional" offices – which had grown out of the reform of the educational broadcaster's structure and programming in the late 1970s. Union and public interest groups opposed the plan on the grounds that it disposed of Radio-Québec's specific vocation in the Quebec televisual galaxy, and would turn the province's *autre télévision* into *une télévision comme les autres*.[141]

At a high-profile Ottawa conference organized by the Canadian Conference of the Arts in October 1985, the past president of the CBC, A.W. Johnson, said Canadian broadcasting had been "Americanized" by three sets of policy decisions: importation (licensed importing by cable of whole us systems), privatization, and fiscal deprivation.[142]

As the thrust of Johnson's talk indicated, most of the rekindled public debate surrounding broadcasting focused on the "national" aspects and the national public broadcaster, the CBC. Aside from the vague notion of national purpose – which often tended to express itself as undisguised corporate self-interest – there was an absence of overriding direction in most interventions and especially of efforts to define and express the public interest in broadcasting. In the rush to protect Canada's cultural "industries," it appeared to be remarkably difficult to speak cohesively for Canada's cultural "communities."

The exceptions to this rule provided the most interesting perspectives. One of the most important interventions to the Caplan-Sauvageau task force on behalf of the public interest came from the Institut canadien d'éducation des adultes (ICEA), the Quebec-based adult education organization with a thirty year history of intervening on broadcasting policy. The key to the ICEA position was the need to place a priority on sociocultural objectives over economic ones – simple enough, and obvious enough, but exactly contrary to the government directive defining the terms of reference of the task force.

The ICEA brief to the task force[143] called for a new complicity between creators and the public. Canadian culture was not only threatened by American incursion but also by itself, the brief said, by the constant degradation of Canadian programming. The problem, the ICEA pointed out, was that the "quantitative" (ratings-based) approach relied too strongly on the private sector, while the "quality" expected of the public sector was only addressed to a cultivated élite. In other words, the current approach demanded that the industry be profitable while giving the élite the signs of cultural standing that it craved.

Such a strategy implied a total reversal of the basic principles having guided the development of the system up to now. With a "dual" as opposed to a "single" system, television, "instead of being a factor of democratization, becomes an instrument for the spread of inequality."[144] The challenge facing the task force was to get past the corporatist interests of the cultural industries and make proposals designed to meet broader social objectives.[145]

The ICEA's concern for "democratization" of media dated to its earliest interventions of the 1950s and 1960s. However, it was inscribed in a current of increasing, if as yet marginal, importance. The problems of Canadian broadcasting for the ICEA were fourfold: the invasion of new foreign services and programming; concentration of ownership; the tendency towards uniform content and imbalance in information; and absence of the public at the major points of decision making.[146] The ICEA's first recommendation was therefore: "That Canadian broadcasting's public service status remain the central point of broadcasting policy, implying the maintenance of the present definition of the system as a single system, made up of public and private sectors." [147]

In English Canada, the issue of public broadcasting tended to focus on "defence of the CBC." In Canada, according to Toronto publisher John Macfarlane of the Friends of Public Broadcasting, "public broadcasting is cultural national defence." [148] But that, clearly, was only part of the issue. Public broadcasting, according to Gene Lawrence of TV Ontario, was "that in which the production and the scheduling of programming are not controlled by the source of the funding." [149] By that definition, one would probably have had to conclude that there was no public broadcasting in Canada by 1985.

### Report of the Task Force on Broadcasting Policy (1985–86)

The Task Force on Broadcasting Policy submitted its report [150] in June 1986, just as the prime minister was preparing a cabinet shuffle that would move Marcel Masse out of communications and replace him with Flora Mac-Donald. It was reported that Masse took the only copy of the report with him when he left office and, apocryphal as the story may be, the report was not released until late September.

The report underscored the historic dilemma of Canadian broadcasting and its obsession with "national" considerations. It contained a number of interesting elements that reaffirmed and broadened the notion of a public sphere where broadcasting played a central role, while submerging these elements in a wave of rhetoric whose key word was "Canadianization." Characteristically, the nationalist aspects of the report eclipsed its social aspects in the public eye, obscuring some very important considerations which, if translated into policy, would have marked a historic shift in Canadian broadcasting.

The report debunked the myth that Canada's broadcasting interests could only be promoted by omnipotent, central agencies under the exclusive control of the federal government. On the contrary, it insisted that the social and cultural objectives of Canadian broadcasting could and must be met by a multiplicity of agents, and that these objectives must themselves be enlarged to meet the needs of the communicationally disenfranchised of Canada, not only those of the élite.

It recognized the legitimacy of hitherto marginal forms of broadcasting in Canada, notably provincial, native, community, and minority broadcasting. While it never really tied these together, an important new idea emerged between the lines of the report: that of a diversified public sector comprised of not only federal agencies such as the CBC, Telefilm Canada, and the National Film Board, but also the newer, less-centralized forms of public broadcasting. It further proposed that new public services be established outside the institutional framework of existing central agencies.

While the task force did not couch its proposals in a framework of democratization *per se*, that would have been the effect of broadening the public sector – increasing public access by multiplying the number of entry points to the system and the control points at which participation in its different components becomes possible. But at the same time, the task force proposed to perpetuate the dominance of central elements of the system and it accepted the prevailing logic of the need to develop Canadian "cultural industries" as an intrinsic good in the national interest, regardless of their impact on the social objectives attributed to broadcasting. [151]

Indeed, the tragic flaw in the task force report was that it did not make the revalidation of the public sphere an *explicit* objective of its reform package but had it appear as a fringe benefit. [152]

The task force tried to introduce the notion of "quality" to the definition of what constituted Canadian programming but had to recognize that any attempt to define "high standards" in programming would be élitist and antidemocratic. Audience measurement thus remained the only "yardstick of success," even though it could not tell anyone whether people really liked what they were watching; Canadian content measurement, specifically, favoured the broadcasters, not the audience. Furthermore, program choice was unequally distributed in the Canadian system, depending on such factors as region of residence, linguistic group, and whether or not one had access to cable.

The task force recognized that the expanding importance of cable distribution brought with it a new set of privileges, because not all Canadians, for economic or geographic reasons, enjoyed access to cable and others might not want it. Yet, the spread of cable was the central consideration to the development of a strategy that would ensure the economic well-being of the entire broadcasting industry. [153]

As the spread of video-cassette recorders was beginning to show at the time of the task force's deliberations, each new level of technology brings with it new problems of privilege and élitism, as it limits, at least for a time, access to the full range of available services and poses the problem of regulation. Just as Canada was achieving universal access to television, the issues had already shifted to other areas: new distribution systems that were not public property and that aimed for subscribers had increased choice for some but abandoned others. Increasingly, the policy objective of "balance" was being interpreted to mean balance within the entire system, including specialized subscriber services not universally available, let alone accessible. As the task force stated: "A new class division has appeared between the information rich and the information poor."[154]

In spite of prevailing conventional wisdom, the task force reported that no one, least of all the private sector, had petitioned for an end to regulation.[155] On the contrary, private broadcasters wanted the maintenance of measures such as the 1976 legislation providing tax write-offs for advertising on Canadian stations, and the CRTC's rules for simultaneous substitution of Canadian signals for US ones on cable systems. According to the task force, these two measures were worth about $90–95 million a year in additional revenue to Canadian broadcasters, yet did "not necessarily do anything for Canadian programming."[156] Indeed, Bill C-58 encouraged broadcasters to go after the most popular American programs, while the simultaneous substitution rules incited them to schedule these programs during the same prime time viewing hours as the US networks. So, here were two measures that favoured Canadian broadcasters economically while disfavouring Canadian cultural policy objectives. The Canadian audience was created by American television but delivered to Canadian advertisers by Canadian cable systems, to the profit of Canadian broadcasters, thanks to Canadian legislation and regulation, and without any benefit to Canadian programming or production.

In general, the task force found, the most profitable sectors of Canadian broadcasting (for example, Canadian independent stations) contributed least to Canadian programming, production, and diversity. The very profitable cable industry was, indeed, part of the problem rather than the solution; cabled households had a lower proportion of Canadian programming available and consumed more US programs.[157]

The task force recognized the severe limitations of the regulatory process, however, particularly the capacity of public interest groups and individuals to intervene effectively before the CRTC. It therefore recommended appointment of a "public advocate" in each region to receive complaints and "to oversee public participation and represent the public interest at licence renewal hearings."[158] Canadians want to participate in the system, the task force reported, and in order for them to be able to do so, government support should be made available to help interested citizens' groups get organized and monitor broadcasting activities effectively. Documents should be more accessible, more easily available, and more informative – for example, in the case of broadcasters' financial reports; the process should be opened up by allowing cross-examination at licence hearings.

The task force made an important breach with traditional policy in calling for treatment of "the federal and provincial governments and local communities as partners in broadcasting, all with roles to play and the right to participate in the formulation of broadcasting policy."[159] This went against the grain of the history of Canadian broadcasting policy, as well as against a specific recommendation of the Applebaum-Hébert report, but it was consistent with the Conservative government's overtures to Quebec and its general move to shift the burden of state responsibility to other levels.

With respect to the historic one-dimensional approach to national broadcasting policy, it proposed a significant departure (which the federal-provincial committee had already recognized), recommending "that the distinctive character of Quebec broadcasting be recognized both in itself and as the nucleus of French-language broadcasting throughout Canada."[160] The task force further proposed to recognize "the autonomy of French-language services within the CBC" and to allow them to develop distinctly from the English-language CBC: "The two sectors, serving distinct societies, should be allowed to take different approaches to meeting the objectives assigned to public broadcasting."[161] A radical restructuring of the CBC hierarchy in 1983 had concentrated powers previously exercised by the two networks in the CBC's Ottawa head office, and the task force noted: "Decisions made in Ottawa are often English-network-oriented."[162] Budgetary disparities between the two networks had to be corrected, especially in public affairs programming (but a key task force proposal, to create a CBC English-language all-news channel, perpetuated the problem of inequality[163]). Finally, the task force said, the CBC's national unity mandate "seems to us inappropriate for any broadcaster, public or private"; the task force proposed the CBC be obliged to contribute to the development of national consciousness instead.[164]

On another plane, the task force called for replacing the traditional "single system" concept with a new notion of a "composite system," attributing a specific role to all of the multiple agents of Canadian broadcasting as well as the traditional private and public sectors.[165] For example, in a key section on "access," it spoke of the need to provide "an equitable place for everyone in the broadcasting system."[166] The task force had been struck by the number of groups who stated in their consultations "that they had little or no access to the system"[167]: "Although Canadians have access to innumerable radio and television programs, comparatively few Canadians manage to express themselves through radio and television ... The introduction of a new multichannel environment increases the number of doorways but does not necessarily open them."[168]

The solution it proposed was to recognize community broadcasting in the act "as a distinct sector in the system, on an equal footing with the public and private sectors which it complements."[169] Community broadcasting "must be seen as an essential third sector of broadcasting ... community broadcasting goes beyond what is possible in a commercial or fully professional system ... In an era when the 'global village' has become a cliche in communications, community broadcasting is at the other end of the scale from the world-spanning vision of communications the phrase implies. We might see it as a form of appropriate technology for the world of broadcasting, providing an antidote to the 'production values' of American broadcasting."[170]

A related question concerned the need for regional broadcasting: "We came away from our consultations convinced that finding an appropriate role for regional television broadcasting is the most vexing single question in the current debate on the role of the CBC. It is also one of the most important."[171] The CBC was under severe pressure, however, and while seeking ways to enhance its regional performance, the task force came up with an alternative: "Canadians who live outside the central regions want desperately to have their lives reflected in our national broadcasting media. This will be no easy chore. But its achievement cannot even be contemplated without the participation of provincial broadcasters."[172]

There was a leitmotif here: the CBC was overburdened and, aside from serving a "national" purpose, other vehicles had to be created, other solutions had to be found. Thus, in a major proposal, the task force called for creation of a new, noncommercial, satellite-to-cable public service in English and French, TV Canada/Télé-Canada, "to contribute substantially to redressing the present imbalance that favours foreign programs on Canada's television broadcasting system."[173] Elsewhere, the task force's attitude was typified by its endorsement of a proposal by the Inuit Broadcasting Corporation, insisting that independent native broadcasters be considered an integral part of the public system and not an appendage to the CBC's northern service.[174] Thus, the task force's calls for "a substantially expanded public sector in broadcasting" situated the CBC as a major component of public broadcasting, but not the only one.[175]

The task force evidently had some trouble tying together its proposals, however, and the result was a string of new contradictions which were easily exploited and turned against themselves in the subsequent period. For example, the emphasis on community broadcasting as the entry point to the system tended to obscure the extent to which the Canadian public lacked access to the mainstream public and private sectors, for which it was paying, in the mid-1980s, about $2 billion a year in parliamentary grants and advertising. The task force proposal that community broadcasting be financially self-reliant – an elegant way of saying it would not cost the public purse anything – was cynically used by the government of Quebec in 1986 to justify drastic reductions in support that the community sector had come to depend upon.[176] In a similar vein, the task force openness towards provincial broadcasting could justify the deflection of federal fiscal responsibility for regional broadcasting to the provinces. This was already evident in 1986 when the CBC cut back on regional production after Ottawa demanded that it trim its budget.

A single proposal – for a CBC English-language satellite-to-cable all-news channel[177] – embraced virtually the entire range of contradictions and stood as a negative example of the type of policy motivation the task force denounced elsewhere in its report. It was inspired strictly by a perceived need to provide a Canadian alternative to an American commercial service (Ted Turner's Cable News Network, CNN); proposed as an English service only (because the need was not perceived to exist in French), it would extend the recognized disparity between available English- and French-language services; like TV Canada, it would be available only to cable subscribers; it would extend the responsibilities of an already over-extended CBC. This proposal became a haunting reminder of policy pitfalls when the CRTC approved such a service in late 1987 to a wave of protest and, eventually, government intervention.

In sum, the problem with the task force proposals lay in the way in which they remained rooted in a framework that made a fetish of "Canadianization." The task force recognized this in an ironic aside that well summed up the problem: "This Task Force has had fun with the problems of being Canadian. How Canadian do we wish our broadcasting system to be? As Canadian as possible – under the circumstances. How public must our broadcasting system be to be as Canadian as possible? As public as possible – under the circumstances."[178] Thus, while the task force reflected the continued stability of the basic sixty-year-old consensus in favour of "Canadian" broadcasting, it did not so much refocus debate as it highlighted the contradictory nature of the problems of broadcasting policy in Canada in the 1980s.

### A New Approach to Regulation

First, as the task force struggled with its mandate and, then, as its report began to gather dust on the shelf, there was no moratorium on evolution in the Canadian broadcasting system. Prodded by both the government and the CRTC, the system continued to move farther and farther away from one with a primarily public focus.

In 1986–87, the CRTC completed the restructuring of the regulatory framework for broadcasting, after two and a-half years of consultation on new regulations for cable, radio, and television.[179] The key to the reform was a new "supervisory" function for the CRTC, a "shift away from a detailed and rigid regulatory approach," towards "self-regulation," or what the CRTC described as industry recognition of its responsibilities to the Canadian public[180]: "The CRTC has made a conscious effort to reduce its involvement in detailed regulation particularly in areas that readily lend themselves to self-regulation by the industry concerned."[181]

One such area concerned the question of sex-role stereotyping, an issue that had generated an unprecedented volume of public interest in the 1970s and 1980s. The CRTC had experimented with industry self-regulation since 1979 and reported that it "had been only partially successful in improving the portrayal and participation of women in the Canadian broadcasting industry."[182] At public hearings in April 1986, women's groups produced statistics showing that a news item dealing with a women's issue or an event organized by women had one chance in twenty-five of being mentioned on prime time television. On television news, 88 percent of experts interviewed, 83 percent of eyewitnesses, and 70 percent of "people in the street" were men.[183] In December 1986, the CRTC announced a policy "designed to ensure a more realistic portrayal of the significance and diversity of roles played by women in our society."[184] It said it would include in all future licence renewals a condition of licence "requiring adherence to a code developed by the Canadian Association of Broadcasters and accepted by the Commission."[185] Progress would be measured in 1988. But this begged the question: if self-regulation had not worked in the years since 1979, what would make it work now?

The "more supervisory approach" the CRTC planned to take towards regulation would be especially aimed at advertising. In radio, the CRTC removed restrictions on AM advertising, and exempted certain FM program formats from commercial limitations, as incentives to increase Canadian programming. In response to industry pressure, it also reduced the minimum French-language requirements from 65 percent to 55 percent on French-language stations.[186] In television, the new regulations eliminated "outdated ... or unnecessary" restrictions in such areas as advertising during newscasts and subliminal advertising, "in the expectation that the industry would develop suitable codes to govern those areas"[187]; after opposition at public hearings held in 1986, the CRTC withdrew its proposal to reduce Canadian content requirements from 60 percent to 50 percent during daytime hours. In cable, the CRTC declared that "a more flexible regulatory environment will offer the cable industry the ability to compete effectively while better meeting consumers' demands by offering improved and expanded services."[188]

The CRTC also reduced Canadian content requirements for "discretionary" (pay-television) services, stating that "none of the licensees have realized the subscriber penetration levels projected in their initial licensing proposals."[189] The movie channels operated by First Choice, Allarcom, and Premier choix had their requirements reduced to 30 percent Canadian content in prime time and 20 percent the rest of the day, with 20 percent of gross revenue to be spent on Canadian programming – the original licences had called for 50 percent Canadian programming, with 45 percent of gross revenue to be spent on Canadian programming. With renewal applications for this first generation of pay-television services scheduled for the spring of 1988, the CRTC announced hearings on the awarding of new specialty services for the summer of 1987.[190]

Meanwhile, in 1986–87, the CRTC held a series of licence renewal hearings for the major television networks. In the case of the CBC, the first hearings since 1979 lasted eight days and led to the formulation by the CRTC of nineteen "expectations" and four conditions of licence. Among the long-term objectives mentioned by the CRTC were 90 percent Canadian content, including twenty-five hours per week in prime time of which ten hours must be Canadian drama; "fair and equitable balance between regional and network production and a reasonable level of program exchange between the English and French networks"; acquisition of 50 percent of all programming other than news, sports, and public affairs from Canadian independent producers (an Applebaum-Hébert proposal); representation of native Canadians in mainstream programming that reflects their just place in Canadian society; better, more balanced representation of multicultural minorities; more relevant services for French Canadians outside Quebec; a complete closed-captioned schedule; and a representative number of broadcast performances by Canadian performing artists. In short, the CRTC's demands were unrealistically out of sync with government orientation *vis-à-vis* the CBC, and were symptomatic of the CRTC's imposition of conditions that the CBC could not meet and that it could not enforce.[191]

The CRTC also renewed the licence of the CTV network, noting that "its success enabies its affiliates to rank among the largest, most profitable of Canada's television stations." Given this, the CRTC required "that the CTV contribute substantially more to the broadcasting system," and imposed conditions of licence regarding expenditures and broadcast time for Canadian programming, including drama and children's shows. CTV promised to increase spending to $403 million over five years, or 75 percent more than it spent the previous five years.[192]

But the clearest example of the CRTC's continued invention of the future according to its own industrial design was to be seen in its awarding, in January 1987, of the transfer of French Canada's most important private television station, Télé-Métropole Inc., to the owner of Quebec's main cable company, Le Groupe Vidéotron Ltée. The transaction created a new model of corporate concentration – the fully integrated video supermarket – in the hope of launching a Canadian enterprise into the big leagues of transnational television.[193]

As the task force on broadcasting had noted with pique, the CRTC had no policy on concentration of ownership, on cross-media ownership in single markets, or on vertical integration. Where private ownership transactions

were concerned, it judged every case on its merits, leaving important precedents in its wake.

Less than a year earlier, the CRTC had rejected a similar bid for Télé-
Métropole by Power Corporation on the basis of Power's flimsy promise of
performance, although organizations in Quebec had called for the rejection
because the Power group already owned the Montreal daily newspaper
*La Presse*.[194] (Some cynics in Quebec saw the CRTC's rejection of Power
as the final act of a personal drama involving CRTC chairman André Bureau
and Power CEO Paul Desmarais, who had fired Bureau from one of his
subsidiaries fifteen years before.)

The main beneficiaries of the hiatus were Télé-Métropole's owners, who
watched their property's selling price rise by 35 percent in a period of nine
months, from $98 million to $134 million, between the two bids. The CRTC
decision shocked the critics of media ownership concentration who thought
they had successfully opposed Power's bid, only to have the CRTC approve
a much more onerous form of concentration.

Télé-Métropole's CFTM-TV, or "Channel 10" as it is known in Montreal,
is the proverbial little company that grew.[195] Founded in 1961 by J.A.
Desève, it was Quebec's first French-language private sector television station. The foundation set up to manage Desève's estate after his death was
not particularly interested in television. It began ploughing its profits back
into resource exploration ventures – a typically Canadian approach, but not
quite what the broadcasting act had in mind as preserving the country's
cultural fabric. The Desève heirs had been ready for some time to take their
leave of the television business, but they were hemmed in by the founder's
will which specified that Télé-Métropole could only be sold to Québécois
interests.

Channel 10 was not only Quebec's most profitable private station, but
was also the flagship and principal shareholder of its major private network,
TVA. Through TVA, the station supplied about 70 percent of the programming
seen on French-language private television in Quebec, contributing considerably to Télé-Métropole's 1986 revenue of about $100 million. There were
not many pools of Québécois capital that could easily buy up such a property.
On that basis alone, Power Corporation apparently felt its proposal could
not be turned down. Power offered a mere $1 million a year in additional
money for programming and no guarantees that Télé-Métropole's news
operations would be insulated from those of Power's other media interests.
The CRTC judged the proposal inadequate and told Télé-Métropole to come
back with another buyer.

Vidéotron learned from the Power experience and seduced the CRTC with
a more substantial plan that pushed all the right nationalist buttons. It promised a range of new programming initiatives worth $30 million over five
years. As the company had not been previously active in traditional information (that is, news) marketing, the proposed transaction did not raise the

same degree of public concern. The Fédération professionnelle des journalistes du Québec, for example, which had vocally opposed the Power
Corporation project, was acquiescent towards Vidéotron. The CRTC award
to Vidéotron was, however, far more insidious in its implications for democratic communications.[196]

Founded by André Chagnon, a cable company engineer who put together
enough capital to buy out his employer in 1981, Vidéotron is another example
of a little company that grew. Through a series of acquisitions and innovative
use of research and technology, Vidéotron rode the expanding wave of cable
subscription and new pay services of the early 1980s. In 1986, before
acquiring Télé-Métropole, it reported revenue of $130 million; that figure
had grown to $306 million by 1988.[197]

Vidéotron is literally a household name in Quebec. In 1988, the company
controlled about 56 percent of the Quebec cable market, with 800,000
subscribers in 150 municipalities including Quebec City and the eastern half
of Montreal island.[198] In all of Canada, only Rogers Cablesystems is bigger,
but Rogers is relatively less monopolistic as its interests are diffused from
coast to coast for control of about one-quarter of the total Canadian market.[199] Rogers has no interests in Quebec, but Vidéotron acquired an Alberta
cable company, QCTV, in 1986, adding another 120,000 subscribers to its
clientele.

That is only part of the story, however. As new technical possibilities
and consumer habits present themselves, Vidéotron has been building on
its initial foundation to become a producer and provider of diversified
television-based services. In the Montreal area it currently programs eleven
nonbroadcast channels, and is developing an interactive system (Videoway)
for telemarketing which, among other things, will enable users to buy a
range of goods and services from their homes. In November 1986, Vidéotron
concluded an agreement with the Steinberg supermarket chain to promote
Steinberg's weekly specials on one of its nonbroadcast channels. Within a
few years, Vidéotron announced at the time, nonbroadcast television advertising would be a more important source of revenue for the company
than cable subscriptions.

In addition to cable distribution and telemarketing services, Vidéotron
also operates a production facility, a subsidiary that sells and services con-
verters, and a research and development company. By purchasing Télé-
Métropole, it acquired, along with Channel 10, a television station in Chicoutimi, a major advertising agency, another production house, a post-
production and subtitling company, Télé-Métropole's interest in TVA and a
smaller regional network, as well as the Desève group's oil and gas interests
(which it promptly sold off).

Its major scheme, however, was to expand into overseas markets, particularly in France, and to do this it had to have Télé-Métropole. In 1983
Vidéotron entered into an agreement to supply technical expertise to La

Compagnie générale des eaux, a private French company involved in cabling several dozen major urban centres in France. In November 1986, Vidéotron acquired 10 percent of the C.G.E. subsidiary that was doing the cabling. Through Télé-Métropole, it intended to participate in the world's first privatization of a national public broadcaster, France's TF 1, which the Chirac government put on the trading block in 1986. Arrangements for Vidéotron's participation in the TF 1 privatization were made public in November and were contingent on CRTC approval of the Télé-Métropole takeover. Soon after, however, Vidéotron renounced the plan and settled for a piece of the much smaller Canal Cinq, France's equivalent to pay-television. In 1988, it was involved in negotiations with British media tycoon Robert Maxwell about participating in the cabling of the British Isles, and was part of a group that was setting up the Arab world's first private television enterprise in Morocco.[200]

The internationalization of Vidéotron/Télé-Métropole was not only an important element of André Chagnon's grand design in itself, it was essential to making this unprecedented degree of concentration and vertical integration palatable. In his presentation to the CRTC in December 1986, Chagnon spelled it out:

> Only a major enterprise can hope to carve a choice place for Quebec in the world of audio-visual titans taking shape on the horizon ... Vidéotron believes that the present international evolution of broadcasting towards giant corporations like those of Berlusconi, Murdoch, Maxwell, Viacom, Hersant-Hachette-RTL, demands that Quebec's principal television station make alliances. Refusal to take our place among these audio-visual giants will sooner or later mean the domination of their products in our markets.[201]

By framing its project this way, Vidéotron appealed to the view that Canadians must be prepared to place industrial considerations ahead of sociocultural ones, in this case sacrifice the possibility of pluralism in broadcasting for a piece of the global communications pie.

The acquisition of Télé-Métropole made Vidéotron "the most important broadcasting system in Quebec," the CRTC said announcing the decision.[202] The eclipse of the public sector by the private was henceforth total – and quintessentially Canadian. If telecommunications were, indeed, to the twentieth century what railroads were to the nineteenth, then Vidéotron was as Canadian as the CPR.

As the 1980s began to recede, the best illustration of the policy deformation process was to be seen in the struggle surrounding the awarding of licences for new "specialty" cable-delivered television services. The struggle involved Ottawa, Quebec, the private sector, the CBC, and the CRTC; only the public was absent from the jockeying taking place to determine the shape of this crucial new sector.

On 29 January 1987, Parliament referred the Caplan-Sauvageau report to the Standing Committee on Communications and Culture, instructing it to report "on all matters relevant to the development of broadcasting legislation" no later than 15 April. [203]

Now, aside from the gargantuan, if not impossible, task that this implied, there were further constraints. Normally, the standing committee would have been the forum for a full public discussion of the report and its proposals, but the time frame drastically limited that prospect. At the same time, the CRTC was proceeding with a call for applications for new so-called specialty services – really, a whole new generation of satellite-to-cable services: the cutting edge of the new technology, where all the theoretical and rhetorical questions relating to cultural sovereignty, the relationship of public to private sectors, and the future make-up of the "package" to be available to individual consumers, were being played out. Because of the CRTC's accelerated agenda, the parliamentary committee felt it had to accord priority to the question of specialty services, although its mandate was to examine all aspects of broadcasting.

The question of specialty services struck at the heart of the task force proposal to create a new noncommercial public agency independent of the CBC, TV Canada, to help redress the imbalance between Canadian and foreign programs available under the existing system. In 1986–87, the proposal migrated through several versions. The minister of communications, for example, said she favoured a mixed, public-private, consortium, while Quebec's Department of Communications said the emphasis should be placed on private specialized services. [204]

Opinions expressed to the parliamentary committee varied, predictably, according to the interests of the parties expressing their views. Provincial broadcasters, for example, preferred to see new federal funds put into supporting provincial broadcasting initiatives. The Canadian Cable Television Association told the committee: "We are not persuaded the description of this channel given by the task force would be a palatable or attractive service to our subscribers at the price proposed." [205] The Satellite Communications Association of Canada took another approach. It felt the proposed new services represented excellent opportunities for developing Canadian broadcasting and should be given priority.

Here, a certain historic pattern was being played out: an established sector of private broadcasting enterprise (cable) opposed introduction of a new public service, while a new emerging sector that stood to benefit from expansion of the system (satellite communication) supported it. Citing the past record of introduction of new services, such as pay-television, the parliamentary committee reported: "The most serious danger in the coming hearing on applications for specialty services is that decisions will be made based on a series of unrealistic promises from the applicants about what they are going to do for Canadian programming." [206] It further noted, with remarkable self-restraint: "That there is no consensus yet on the creation of these services is not particularly surprising, given that they remain very general concepts and that they affect different interests in different ways."[207]

Finally, the parliamentary committee proposed that the minister of communications take the lead in convening all parties to consider establishment of new noncommercial services, and expressed the wish that the CRTC not foreclose on such a possibility. The CRTC meanwhile announced that it would award licences for specialty services on the basis of hearings to be held in July.

The underlying question – did Canada need such new services at all? – was not posed before the CRTC which dealt, first of all, with the generic nature of the new services to be created and, then, with the specific types from among a range of proposals. Would all the new services be offered universally to all cable subscribers? Or would they be optional and subscriber-based, as the range of services licensed as pay-television five years earlier? What role would the cable companies play, other than distribution? Would the new services be public, private, or a combination of both?

The issue was not without paradox – especially since there was no demonstrable public demand for new cable-delivered services of any kind. The way in which the issue had forced its way onto the national agenda illustrated instead, once again, the way in which broadcasting and communications policy comes about in Canada:

1. A new technology is developed and placed on the commercial market in the United States
2. Canadian industry pressures for rapid introduction of a Canadian model on the Canadian market
3. The Canadian public authorities inquire into the possible impact of the new technology
4. An operational model is proposed, reflecting the historic compromise between sociocultural and economic-industrial objectives

Pay-television had been the most recent example of this phenomenon. Despite the fact that all studies showed there to be almost no public interest in the service, pay-television was introduced in 1982 under circumstances virtually guaranteed to ensure that it could not meet its ascribed cultural objectives. Almost immediately, industry began clamouring for yet more services; in its call for applications on 4 May 1983, the CRTC made this clear.[208]

But in October of that year, the CRTC had to publicly recognize the general paucity of the forty-one applications it had received, and announced that it would license non-Canadian services instead, in order to add diversity and make marketing of pay-television services easier for the cable companies and the licence-holders involved. Cable companies would be authorized to distribute up to five non-Canadian services, to be selected from a list of seventeen established by the CRTC and "tiered," or offered along with available Canadian services.

At that point, the Task Force on Broadcasting Policy reported in 1986, the CRTC had three choices: it could authorize the wholesale importing of American signals into Canada (which was already being done by pirate satellite dishes); it could authorize Canadian licence-holders to put together packages of Canadian and American services (as broadcasters did, for example); or it could authorize creation of new Canadian public services to produce Canadian programs (the only way to serve the stated objectives of the system).[209] The CRTC chose the second scenario, the standard Canadian hybrid approach.

In April 1984, following public hearings where it again had to recognize the deficiency of most of the requests it had received, the CRTC awarded two licences for new Canadian services (sports and music) and authorized a range of American services for cable companies to import. A company formed by Toronto broadcasters CHUM Ltd and CITY-TV was awarded a licence to operate a rock video service, MuchMusic, and a subsidiary of the John Labatt Ltd brewery was granted a licence for The Sports Network (TSN). These two Canadian-*owned* services were obliged to provide 10 percent and 18 percent Canadian content respectively. At the same time, the CRTC authorized cable companies to bring in seventeen American services, including CNN. The cable companies were to be the key players in assembling the new "packages" of first generation pay-television, new Canadian, and American services. It is to be noted that no new French-language service was added to the televisual landscape as a result of this new wave of licensing. Between 1984 and 1986, the CRTC eventually authorized more Canadian services: a health service, Life Channel, which lasted only a year (1985–86); two ethnic services, Telelatino and Chinavision; and a French-language rock video service, Musique Plus, run by the owners of MuchMusic.[210]

Thus, after 1984, pay-television and specialty services were offered in combined packages put together by the cable companies according to a formula authorized by the CRTC. According to a 1987 DOC study, the most successful optional services were reaching 13 percent (movie channel), 15 percent (music channel), and 16 percent (sports channel) of the Canadian audience. However, actual use of these services still represented only 2 percent of total viewing time in 1987 (as compared to 6 percent in the US).[211]

As the Task Force on Broadcasting Policy stated: "The satellite networks reproduce the issues and options tackled earlier by broadcasting policy in the conventional Canadian television services. In the new struggle to create strong Canadian satellite networks, as in the old struggle for Canadian TV programming, there are two principal objectives: to make sure Canadian services exist and to provide a balance of Canadian and non-Canadian programs."[212]

The parliamentary committee on communications and culture, on the other hand, reported on 16 April 1987 that the various US services the CRTC authorized for import were quickly becoming established as part of the Canadian system, to the point of compromising potential development of equivalent Canadian ones.[213]

According to figures supplied to the committee, three of the US services, including CNN, were already being received in more than 400,000 Canadian households. To the committee, the question of specialty services was a major challenge and it warned against the danger that the CRTC might award licences for new Canadian services on the basis of unrealistic promises.

It was in this context that the CRTC called once again, on 13 August 1986, for offers to provide new Canadian specialty services. In July 1987 it heard twenty-one requests and received over 1,800 interventions in the longest round of public hearings ever held. A wide range of public and private enterprises were represented among the applicants, including the CBC, the NFB, TV5, private broadcasters, cable companies, and pay-television operators. Many of the thematic issues prevailing in Canadian broadcasting were present and, once again, in passing judgment on the various projects, the CRTC got to cast its early vote on the reshaping of the Canadian broadcasting system.

On 30 November 1987, the CRTC issued a lengthy decision awarding licences for eleven new specialty services and rejecting ten other applications. Among those rejected was the request sponsored by the National Film Board which closely resembled the task force's TV Canada proposal. The CRTC moved existing sports and music services from the "optional" to the "basic" cable band and approved new services ranging from the weather to TV5. Among those approved was the CBC application for a twenty-four hour English-language all-news service.[214]

The new services were to be financed by incremental increases in cable subscription charges; individual cable operators would decide which new services, if any, to offer, but for the subscriber it would be "take it or leave it"; anyone subscribing to basic cable service would have to buy the new specialty channels offered in their area, whether they were interested in them or not. This posed a consumers' rights problem, and the Consumers' Association of Canada appealed to the Cabinet to overturn the CRTC decision. It was not alone – a defeated applicant for the all-news channel awarded to the CBC, the pay-television operator Allarcom Ltd of Edmonton, appealed as well. To ensure access for French-language services, the CRTC obliged cable operators in francophone markets to take all or none of the new French services, while anglophone services could be added à la carte. Thus, among the many potential absurdities of the situation was the spectre of the "two solitudes" in, say, Montreal, where citizens could have found themselves electing residence in the east or west sectors of the island according to the choices offered by cable companies. When the new services came into effect in September 1988, an unforeseen problem surfaced right away: cable distributors outside Quebec refused to offer TV5. The government and the CRTC had to intervene to persuade and compensate the cable companies before the already- underserved francophone minorities outside Quebec could gain access to this innovative service.[215]

Even before the new licences took effect, a major political storm broke over the proposed CBC all-news channel. While the private broadcasting lobby and the Tory caucus of western MPs rallied around the Allarcom appeal, francophone public opinion was outraged at the CBC's proposal to create a new "national" service in English only (a problem that had eluded the Caplan-Sauvageau task force and had hardly raised an eyebrow at the CRTC public hearings).[216] While the CRTC and the CBC squirmed with egg on their faces, the government scored points all around by advising the CBC to reconsider its position before using its licence. In a letter to Pierre Juneau in January 1988, Flora MacDonald suggested the CBC find a private sector partner for its project and broaden it to include French-language service as well.[217]

Many sectors of the informed public spoke out against this government intervention in broadcasting,[218] but the CBC accepted the government's terms. In October 1988, Pierre Juneau advised Flora MacDonald that the CBC was prepared to accept "significant private sector involvement in distribution and marketing" of the all-news channel, and that a proposal would be made to the CRTC to create an equivalent service in French. The government happily accepted the proposal.[219] Twenty-five percent of all-news programming would be purchased from the private sector or produced by nonbroadcast media like the *Globe and Mail* and the *Financial Times*. The all-news service would be distributed to cable companies exclusively by the private satellite service, Cancom. It would be governed by "a mixed public-private sector board of management."[220]

As for the French-language service, its nature remained to be seen. The CBC proposed to finance the service out of the fees cable companies would be charging to their English subscribers, auguring problems like the ones provoked by the distribution of TV5. Meanwhile, in Quebec, commentators questioned the anomaly of creating new services to compete with existing ones whose budgets were being cut.[221] Similar criticism had been made of the initial project in English Canada when the government first intervened.[222]

In short, the specialty services dossier laid bare the major inadequacies of the system in 1988: the insensitivity and moral ambivalence of the CBC, the insouciance and industrial bias of the CRTC, the accumulating power of the cable industry, and the government's determination to control and politicize the policy agenda.[223]

### THE MULRONEY GOVERNMENT'S
### BROADCASTING POLICY,
### 1988

Flora MacDonald's first year as minister of communications was, in public, essentially one of reaction to circumstances such as publication of the Caplan-Sauvageau report and the CRTC decision on specialty services. Behind the scenes, however, it was marked by the preparation by DOC officials of a new broadcasting policy. According to former CRTC chairman John Meisel, "The DOC came to believe ... that the task force, in devising a broadcast scenario, had basically failed to take into account existing and evolving conditions."[224] To buy time, MacDonald referred the report to the Standing Committee on Communications and Culture, while setting up an internal "broadcasting policy working group" within the DOC. At the same time, research was commissioned and private consultations were conducted throughout the broadcasting milieu, with a general view towards producing a policy that would be more in tune with the government's orientation than the Caplan-Sauvageau report.

MacDonald's background, politics, and personal style placed her in a completely different position in Cabinet from that which Masse had occupied. She was a Conservative Party stalwart, but not a Mulroney crony, and a "red Tory" Canadian nationalist, not a social conservative from Quebec. Less flamboyant than Masse in public, she was able to inspire fierce loyalty in an important group of civil servants at the DOC, gain the necessary support for her approach from the other federal departments concerned, and commit the other members of Cabinet to approve the broadcasting policy drafted under her stewardship.[225]

However, before things reached this stage, the standing committee became a fly in the ointment. It took its mandate very seriously indeed, and its hearings in 1987 and 1988 became yet another public forum for debate on broadcasting policy, enriched this time by the specific proposals of the Caplan-Sauvageau report.

*The Standing Committee on Communications*
*and Culture, 1987–88*

The committee hearings were the most thorough and extensive yet. Aided by several hundred public interventions, the committee reviewed the entire range of Caplan-Sauvageau proposals, and also had lengthy exchanges with the minister, the chairman of the CRTC, and Caplan and Sauvageau themselves.

The Standing Committee on Communications and Culture tabled its final report on 9 June 1988.[226] It was a politically nonpartisan, if cautious document. Milder in many respects than the Caplan-Sauvageau report, it was nonetheless more difficult to set aside as it was, after all, the product of a committee dominated by a Conservative majority.

The report broadly reiterated the general view of the task force, reaffirming the basic principles on which Canadian broadcasting had been built: "We believe this is the kind of broadcasting system Canadians want in spite of – or perhaps because of – the major cultural, social, economic and technological developments of the intervening years."[227]

In its report, the committee indicated its dissatisfaction with the minister's attitude towards its work. After asking the committee to adhere to a tight timetable and report on specific urgent aspects awaiting policy decisions (for example, the power of direction to the CRTC, new specialty services, and new legislation), "the government decided to delay any substantial action until it had a full grasp of the overall policy picture, an approach that differed from its earlier plans and from the expectations of the committee."[228]

In fact, one of the interesting aspects of the committee's work was its ongoing dialogue with the minister over questions such as the appropriate parameters of activities to be covered by broadcasting legislation and regulated by the CRTC. The committee endorsed the Caplan-Sauvageau recommendations to define "broadcasting" and "programming" in such a way as to include cable, satellite-to-cable, and direct broadcast satellite program delivery, and to clarify the distinction between programming and nonprogramming services. The minister, in her response, questioned whether the committee's proposals might encompass too much.

The committee report reaffirmed that "broadcasting policy is Canada's premier cultural policy"[229] and fleshed this out in terms that addressed the historic as well as contemporary issue of Canadianization:

Owing to Canada's vulnerability to inundation by programming from the United States, the first objective of freedom of broadcasting in Canada is to maintain Canadian control of a broadcasting system that is regulated and supervised by a single agency. The second goal is to make this system responsive to the broadcasting needs of Canadians without intruding on their rights.[230]

The report pointed out that new legislation should provide guarantees that cable and other distribution undertakings contribute to Canadian programming, as the 1968 act theoretically did for over-the-air broadcasters. It recalled that the system had created a public element ("the Canadian Broadcasting Corporation, joined in more recent years by a number of provincial educational broadcasting authorities"[231]) and a private sector ("by far the largest provider of programming"[232]). New legislation, it said, echoing Caplan-Sauvageau, should recognize the community sector "as a component of the general system."[233]

A new broadcasting act, in the committee's view, should be user-driven, spelling out broadcasting objectives more extensively than in the past, and giving broadcasters "a clear understanding of what Canadians expect from the system."[234] The central issue it had to address concerned "what programming the system ought to make available to Canadians."

> In broad terms that act should state that the system should encourage the development of Canadian expression, providing a wide range of programming that reflects Canadian attitudes, opinions, ideas, values and artistic creativity, displaying Canadian talent in entertainment programming, and offering information and analysis concerning Canada and other countries from a Canadian point of view.[235]

Canadian broadcasting should "stimulate Canadian consciousness and serve the special needs of each region and both official language groups, providing exchanges between both regions and language communities."[236] It should respect the equality provisions of the Canadian Charter of Rights and Freedoms, and provide in its programming a balanced representation of Canadian society. It should provide freedom of expression and the right to receive, implementing the latter "by means of concerted action by the public sector" if necessary.[237] "In a simpler world, the fact that Canadians want to have Canadian broadcasting services and Canadian programming should in itself ensure that they would be available ... However, the reality of broadcasting is such that there are other factors which also help to determine what will be offered to Canadians." Essentially economic realities, the report stated, "have created the need for deliberate and coherent public policies for broadcasting."[238]

One area in which the committee indicated public policy was needed was that of property ownership. According to the committee, the CRTC had become softer in the 1980s in allowing transactions leading to increased concentration.

It cited the following examples of recent CRTC decisions allowing enhanced concentration in the interest of "financial viability":

1. Licensing Irving interests for a CBC television affiliate with retransmitters covering the entire province in New Brunswick and a second network to cover Nova Scotia and New Brunswick
2. Licensing CFCF, owner of a CTV affiliate, cable company, and production company in Montreal, to start Quebec's second French-language private network, Télévision Quatre Saisons
3. Authorizing Vidéotron to take over Télé-Métropole, flagship of the TVA network and owner of a major program production company
4. Authorizing take over of Ottawa CTV station CJOH by Baton Broadcasting Inc., owner of CTV flagship CFTO, two CTV stations in Saskatchewan, and a major production company

5. Authorizing take over of independent television station CKVU in Vancouver by CanWest Broadcasting, owner of stations in Winnipeg, Regina, and Saskatoon as well as a share of Global Broadcasting

> While the new acquisitions authorized for these important broadcasting enterprises are still competitive, these CRTC decisions do provide examples of the different kinds of concentration that have caused concern in the past: horizontal integration, cross-media ownership, vertical integration and ownership of media by non-media conglomerates.[239]

The problem, according to the committee, was that "there is really no guideline on the issue of how much competition is enough, or how much concentration is too much ... The haphazard development of CRTC ownership decisions over the years to cope with various situations has left the Commission virtually bereft of clear or discernible policies in this area."[240] But the context made it "imperative that clearer policies be established."[241]

The committee went further than the task force, which had recommended a CRTC policy review of the question. First, it said, a research program should be conducted and its results published. Then, after the public has been made aware of the issue, public hearings should be held, if necessary under the auspices of a special committee. It was more critical of the situation created under the stewardship of the CRTC and more sceptical about the economic benefits and necessity of concentration. But, like the task force before it, it took no position, thus paving the way for the minister to remain mute on the question in her policy statement and proposed legislation.[242]

### The Minister's Policy Statement

The parliamentary committee's report was followed within days by Flora MacDonald's policy statement[243] and the simultaneous tabling of Bill C-136,[244] on 23 June 1988.

Actually, the policy and draft legislation had been approved by Cabinet in April, and were only delayed in order to follow the committee's report.[245] The result was a policy package which was, in many respects, remarkable in light of the public debate of the previous years.

The policy paper's basic assumption was that "some key ingredients are missing" from the Canadian broadcasting system, and it set out to provide them, "to ensure that Canadians have a real choice of quality Canadian programs to watch and listen to, including the kinds of programs that are currently lacking."[246] In doing so, it recognized that "the problems and challenges for English-language broadcasting and French-language broadcasting are not the same," thus echoing the general policy thrust reflected in the Caplan-Sauvageau report, the parliamentary committee report, and the Conservative government's approach to broadcasting duality in general.

The policy statement distinguished three major areas of policy issues. The first had to do with programming. Here, it identified the need to increase the Canadian presence in drama and variety on prime time English-language television; to help French-language programming remain qualitatively competitive; and to provide alternative programming "to meet needs not addressed by mass-audience broadcasting."[247] Measures proposed included additional funding to the CBC and Telefilm Canada, a new "performance incentive" system to help the CRTC enforce its conditions of licence ("without necessitating excessively intrusive procedures"), and "a new national alternative television programming service."[248]

The second set of issues dealt with "fairness and access," recognizing "the different cultural and economic characteristics of the French and English broadcasting environments"[249] and further responding to recent social and political changes "by requiring that, in both its operations and its programming, the entire broadcasting system should be reflective not only of Canada's linguistic duality but also of our multicultural nature, and the special role of aboriginal persons."[250] It recognized the rights of disabled persons, extension of services to underserved areas, and the dignity and equality of all men and women.

The third set of issues concerned technology. Recognizing that broadcasting goes beyond traditional over-the-air technologies, Canadian broadcasting policy would henceforth be "technology neutral," that is, based on a definition of broadcasting in terms of its content rather than means of distribution. Referring obliquely to the difficulties of controlling the cable industry under the 1968 legislation, the statement said the new policy would thus "be better able to adapt to changing technologies without risking erosion of federal regulatory jurisdiction."[251] But it would clearly be industry-oriented, allowing for "the optimum use of new technology without predetermining a legislative or regulatory bias for or against a particular technology."[252] "The 1988 Broadcasting Bill is technology neutral. It distinguishes among activities as opposed to technologies."[253] Broadcasting would no longer refer strictly to a set of activities conducted by means of a specific technology and, conversely, broadcasting technologies could also be developed for nonbroadcasting (and therefore, nonregulated) activities.

The policy also proposed changes to the CBC and the CRTC, but underplayed these by presenting them as essentially "administrative." In the case of the CBC, this was largely the case. For the umpteenth time in the corporation's history, dissatisfaction with the way the corporation was being run was addressed by a structural reform at the top. At the end of Pierre Juneau's term, the position of president would be split in two, providing for a chairman of the board responsible for policy execution and a chief executive officer responsible for operations. The *de facto* distinction between French- and English-language services, as well as the new official policy stance, would be reflected in two top-level standing committees of the CBC board, one for each set of language services.

With respect to the CRTC, nothing could be less merely administrative and further from controversy than the "power of direction" that the new policy proposed. Successive governments had tried, without success, since 1976 to introduce such a mechanism, which would allow the Cabinet to issue policy directives to the CRTC. The CRTC's runaway authority as a power impossible to check had led to an essential consensus that some means of intervention was necessary to ensure that the CRTC was actually carrying out the letter and spirit of Canadian broadcasting policy. Caplan and Sauvageau had recommended either a power of direction or the existing appeal to Cabinet of CRTC decisions, but not both. The standing committee had proposed a limited power of review. Now, the new policy and the bill proposed both, a power of direction and the right to overturn CRTC decisions. This was to be one of the most highly contested sections of the bill.[254]

## The Broadcasting Act, 1988 (Bill C-136)

The new legislation basically followed the structure of the existing broadcasting act, concentrating policy provisions in Article 3. At the level of rhetoric, it made some important concessions to the progressive sentiment expressed in the public debate of the preceding few years. In many cases, however, the regressive aspects of the legislation emerged when one did a close, parallel reading of the bill and the minister's policy statement.

The policy clause recognized the Canadian broadcasting system as "a public service essential to the maintaining and enhancement of national identity and cultural sovereignty."[255] It should "strive, through its operations and programming, to reflect the circumstances and aspirations of Canadian men and women, including the linguistic duality and multicultural nature of Canadian society and the special place of aboriginal people within that society."[256] The CBC's national unity mandate was replaced by a stipulation that the corporation "contribute to shared national consciousness and identity."[257] The bill reaffirmed that Canadian broadcasting was a "single system" whose objectives could best be met by providing for the regulation and supervision of an independent public agency.

Bill C-136 specified, vaguely, the expectations of both public and private broadcasters: "Each element of the Canadian broadcasting system shall contribute in an appropriate manner to the creation and presentation of Canadian programming, making maximum use of Canadian creative and other resources."[258] The CBC would be "predominantly and distinctively Canadian," seeking large audiences with commissioned, independently produced entertainment programming. This implied "change in the way the CBC addresses its mandate," although it did not "reduce the basic importance of Canada having a strong national public broadcaster."[259] The CBC, the policy stated, "can best serve Canadians by providing quality Canadian programming, aimed at large audiences, especially in peak viewing hours, and enabling Canadians in all regions to contribute to both national and regional programming."[260] To do this, the CBC's parliamentary appropriation would be increased by a specifically earmarked $35 million ($20 million for English and $15 million for French programming). In addition, $18 million would be added to the budget of Telefilm Canada (allocated evenly between English and French).

Private undertakings would be expected to contribute to Canadian programming "to an extent consistent with the financial and other resources available to them."[261] In addition to the existing CRTC powers, the policy proposed a new approach, a "performance incentive," by which each station's Canadian programming requirements would be tied to advertising revenues, and on the other side of the ledger, the amount of actual Canadian programming would lead to either a financial reward or a penalty, depending on the initial assessment.

Meanwhile, the government recognized the insufficiency of existing services to meet the overall objectives of the system. It, therefore, proposed a new "complementary" television programming service to "cater to tastes and interests not adequately provided for by the programming provided for mass audiences."[262] This was yet another new version of the old CBC-2 project, initially revived by the Caplan-Sauvageau report as TV Canada. But in the spirit of MacDonald's policy statement, it was neither the CBC nor necessarily the public sector which would sponsor the new service. According to the government guidelines, the CRTC would be asked to define the new service and then invite licence applications.

The alternative programming service, according to the policy statement, was urgently required in English but not in French, where audiences "already receive special-interest programming from Radio-Canada and, in Quebec, from Radio-Québec ... In English, the need is greater, especially as the CBC is largely dedicated to mass audience programming."[263] This was a paradoxical way to act on the provision of the new act that "English and French language broadcasting, while sharing common aspects, operate under different conditions and may have different requirements."[264] In light of the controversy over the CBC's English-only all-news project, it fanned the sparks of protest from francophone groups.[265]

The "technology neutral" policy would allow cable companies to participate in programming activities, overriding the better judgment of the task force and parliamentary committee which had warned against possible conflict of interest arising from excessive concentration of activity in the hands of "hybrid" programming and distribution undertakings. The bill was less generous towards other types of activity. It recognized in a phrase that the system should include "educational programs" (without legitimating the existing educational "services" or "stations") and made no mention at all of community broadcasting, encompassing this in a catch-all subclause stating that "the programming provided by the Canadian broadcasting system should ... be drawn from local, regional, national and international sources."[266] All these provisions were justified in the name of limiting legislative restriction and maximizing broadcaster efficiency.

In sum, the policy and the bill were notable for updating the human rights provisions of broadcasting policy and for reaffirming and somewhat enhancing the status of the CBC. These attributes were more than offset, however, by their failure to operationalize the newly decreed specificity of francophone broadcasting (and, in fact, by implanting a new inequality in proposing a new alternative programming service in English only); their handing unprecedented power to the cable industry, under the guise of technological neutrality; their mealy-mouthed approach to provincial and community broadcasters; their desultory approach to the CRTC; and their silence on the question of private property concentration of ownership.

Most of these questions would be raised during yet another, and final, round of parliamentary committee hearings on the draft bill that occupied interested parties during the summer of 1988 – and that led to an unusual set of amendments.

### Amending Bill C-136

Reaction to Bill C-136 from the groups that had participated in the policy consultation process and lobbied for the previous three years was almost universally negative, varying only by degree and, significantly, according to the area of greatest disaffection.

One of the "most spectacular and vociferous"[267] groups was the Friends of Canadian Broadcasting, a latter-day incarnation of the Canadian Radio League that had successfully used direct mail campaigns and full-page newspaper advertisements to be able to claim some 17,000 members by 1988. Led by broadcasting activists such as former task force co-chair Gerald Caplan, ACTRA president Paul Siren, and Canadian Association for Adult Education president Ian Morrison, and supported by media personalities such as Adrienne Clarkson and Pierre Berton, the Friends represented mainstream English-Canadian nationalist opinion. Initially known as the Friends of Public Broadcasting, the group changed its name in the spring of 1988 after a market study showed greater public response to fund-raising requests under the "Canadian" label.

According to Meisel,[268] the group was "considered important enough to merit at least two encounters with senior DOC officials" and the minister herself, in the period leading up to Bill C-136. But while they generally welcomed the "constructive principles" contained in the bill, the Friends criticized its failure to provide mechanisms for implementing them, especially with respect to provisions on Canadian programming. The Friends were far less critical of the bill's other shortcomings and, with respect to directing the activity of the CRTC, seemed to feel the government was not going far enough: "For two decades, Canadians have witnessed a CRTC unable or unwilling to enforce existing broadcasting legislation ... In view of this performance record, why does the government place so much confidence in the CRTC to create as well as implement broadcasting policy?"[269]

The Institut canadien d'éducation des adultes welcomed the reaffirmed public character of the system and the enhanced role envisaged for the CBC, but was fiercely critical about the lack of enforcement of the role of private broadcasters, the pandering to cable companies, the absence of protection from the effects of the Canada-US free trade agreement, and, especially, the power of direction over the CRTC, which it saw as instituting a threat of political control over broadcasting.[270] The ICEA position, published in *Le Devoir* on 16 July 1988, was read into Hansard virtually in *toto* by Liberal broadcasting critic Sheila Finestone three days later.[271]

The bill was referred to a legislative committee of the House of Commons that conducted further consultations with the minister and more than fifty groups. The legislative committee and the minister between them generated ninety-two amendments to Bill C-136 that were published at the end of the summer, but the debate did not end there. When the bill returned to the House on 14 September, opposition critics took to the floor and introduced further amendments. Astonishingly, in view of all that had gone before, the national media paid nearly no attention to the final stages of the broadcasting policy debate.[272] But when one compared the initial copy of the bill, the amendments, the Hansard version of the debate, and the final version of the bill as adopted at third reading, one learned some startling things.

Right at the beginning was a new addition to the "interpretation" section of the bill[273] stating that the act "shall be construed and applied in a manner consistent with the freedom of expression and journalistic, creative and programming independence enjoyed by broadcasting undertakings." A similar provision was added to the Canadianization clause of the policy section, which now read that the Canadian broadcasting system should "encourage the development of Canadian expression, providing a wide range of programming that reflects Canadian attitudes, opinions, ideas, values and artistic creativity, displaying Canadian talent in entertainment programming, and offering information and analysis concerning Canada and other countries from a Canadian point of view."[274]

The human rights provision was strengthened, adding explicit references to employment opportunities, needs and interests, and equal rights to a

subclause which now specified that the system should, "through its programming and the employment opportunities arising in its operations, serve
the needs and interests, and reflect the circumstances and aspirations, of
Canadian men, women and children, including equal rights, the linguistic
duality and multicultural nature of Canadian society and the special place
of aboriginal peoples within that society."[275]

The system was now expected to include "educational and community"
programs. Programming was to aim at "men and women," rather than
"people," of all ages, interests and tastes. CBC programming was expected
to "enlighten," as well as "inform" and "entertain" (enlightenment had
lapsed from the historic mandate of broadcasting in the original version of
the bill). For the first time, it was specified that the CBC must "strive to be
of equivalent quality in English and French," and the corporation's mandate
to serve the regions was made explicit. Clauses were added recognizing the
claims of aboriginal and disabled people for broadcasting resources that
would meet their respective specific needs.[276]

All of these examples found their way into Bill C-136 as amendments
inspired by the insistence of public interest lobby groups. They were semantic
distinctions, perhaps, but essential and revealing ones in light of the nature
of public discussion over Bill C-136.

Equally important were the softening-up provisions to the part of the
legislation concerning the CRTC. The Cabinet's power to issue "policy directions" to the CRTC became "directions of general application on broad
policy matters," attenuating the uneasiness about possible government interference in individual licensing matters. The minister would be required
to consult with the CRTC before any cabinet directive. A proposed power
for Cabinet to exempt some members of a given class of broadcasters from
a directive applying to that class, was dropped. The Cabinet's power to set
aside a CRTC decision was maintained, but reasons would have to be supplied.

At this point, a certain segment of public opinion turned around and a
new consensus seemed to form regarding the bill, which, as amended, was
now supported by many earlier critics. Former task force co-chair Florian
Sauvageau, for example, stated that the amended Bill C-136, while far from
perfect, was preferable to the *status quo* and should be adopted.[277] *Le Devoir*
editor-in-chief Paul-André Comeau echoed Sauvageau's call, adding that it
would undoubtedly be seen as "the Conservatives' only concrete achievement in the area of cultural sovereignty."[278]

However, the parliamentary opposition continued to fight the bill, partly
in the spirit of pre-election fever, but also because of its remaining flaws.
During the nine days of debate on third reading in the House of Commons,
critics of the bill argued, for example, that it did not provide adequate
protection against the future (and as yet unclear) implications of the free

trade deal for the broadcasting sector. Also, the highly contested provision which would allow the government to "direct" the CRTC on matters of policy, was only partially modified in the final version.

According to NDP broadcasting critic Lynn McDonald, native people, educational broadcasters, and women's groups were still unhappy with the bill, despite the improvements.[279] (A former deputy minister of communications, TV Ontario chairman Bernard Ostry, recalled that both the task force and the standing committee had recommended recognizing educational broadcasting as an integral part of the system: "Yet, to my surprise, Bill C-136 does not offer any regard for ... the distinctively unique energy educational broadcasters infuse into the system. Instead, Bill C-136 glances over our very existence and says only that 'educational and community programs' should be among those provided by the system. Anyone might do that."[280])

Also, the debate could not be separated from the leading political issue of the day, free trade. "The government has reneged," Lynn McDonald said: "The Americanized Conservative government wants continentalization."[281] She read into the record a Canadian Association of Broadcasters statement that "a post-free trade environment will undoubtedly generate increased pressure for access to the Canadian market for a wide variety of United States broadcasting and programming services,"[282] and agreed with the CAB's assessment that Bill C-136 provided no defense against that pressure: "I hope the free trade deal, which is at the bottom of all that is wrong with this particular Bill, will be stopped."[283]

On 28 September 1988, Bill C-136 was adopted by the House of Commons with the Liberals and New Democrats voting against it. It was immediately sent to the Senate, where Conservative senator Jean Bazin, a Mulroney appointee, made an eloquent and well-prepared presentation. Bazin concluded: "Inevitably, with any legislation of this scope and complexity affecting an industry with so many different sectors, there are many competing interests to be balanced. This bill goes a long way towards achieving a balance among those interests ... This bill represents as much of a consensus as it is ever possible to achieve in an area where so many competing viewpoints must co-exist."[284]

The Liberals refused to let the bill go through, however. The following day, 30 September, Liberal senator Royce Frith announced that his party supported "the principle" of the bill, but wanted to study it in committee. The "four pillars of Canadian broadcasting" – the CBC, the CRTC, the private broadcasters, and the cable industry – were all opposed to it, he said, and the Senate should look into why. (After a lunch-hour break, Frith candidly corrected himself – he announced that he had spoken with cable lobbyist Michael Hind-Smith during lunch to discover that the cable industry actually wanted the bill passed.) On Frith's insistence, the bill was referred to the

Standing Senate Committee on Transport and Communications. A few hours later, Brian Mulroney asked the governor-general to call an election, and along with Canada's thirty-third Parliament, Bill C-136 passed into history.

Was it a cynical electoral balloon that the government was just as happy to see pop, or a real consensus turned into a partisan football by a hungry opposition? Bill C-136 was probably part of both. The elements of consensus that forced their way into the bill would only have done so in a pre-election context. (How else can one explain the sudden concession of things as niggardly but long denied as the mere mention of equal rights, or community broadcasting?) In this respect, Bill C-136 represented the reward of years of effort for recognition and *inclusion* in the Canadian broadcasting system by women's groups, native people, community and educational broadcasters, independent producers, and the panoply of cultural groups that make up Canada as we know it. Many of these groups remained dissatisfied with the legislation and were not prepared to endorse its adoption; others were prepared to see it adopted on strictly strategic grounds.

Then there was free trade. According to Article 2005 of the Canada-United States Free Trade Agreement of 1988,[285] "cultural industries," such as broadcasting, are exempt, except for certain specific provisions to change existing situations which the US side considered non-negotiable impediments.[286]

As promised, no changes were made to Canadian ownership provisions, the status of Canadian crown corporations, or programs designed to promote Canadian culture or make Canadian products more competitive in the marketplace. However, a "notwithstanding" clause was placed like a sword of Damocles over the head of the entire cultural sector. In general, either side was allowed to retaliate with "measures of equivalent effect in response to actions that would have been inconsistent with this agreement but for (the exemption)."[287] Under this provision, *every* Canadian cultural policy, program, or mechanism, existing or future, could be subject to retaliation. Thus, for example, if the Americans were to consider that Parliament's annual $1 billion grant to the CBC discriminated against the US broadcast production industry, they could take action covering an equivalent sum in, say, steel or lumber products. This was the threat to Canada's existing cultural policy programs. As for new initiatives, it would take a measure of boldness Canada has never seen to move against the grain of an integrated economy and the sociocultural base that this implied.[288]

The worst part about this was that, as a generic syndrome, none of it was really new. The gap between broadcasting policy and practice in Canada had been widening for sixty years, ever since Sir John Aird and his colleagues proposed a blueprint that was promptly mashed out of shape and has since been misquoted, perverted for political purposes, and otherwise ignored. Indeed, the report of the Royal Commission on Radio Broadcasting and its destiny have remained the model for Canadian broadcasting policy making down through the years.

In 1988, there was a consensus on at least one important point: new legislation was long overdue. But broadcasting legislation is always long overdue in Canada, a result of the difficulty of reconciling sociocultural objectives of mythical stature, a historically deep-rooted vision of "Canada" as a place to do business, and a stubborn public that insists on aggravating the due process of technocracy by repeatedly calling up the contradictions between rhetoric and reality.

If there is one thing the history of Canada's broadcasting policy demonstrates, it is that the policy-making process is inevitably highly politicized. In a democracy, it goes (or should go) without saying that any activity as political as this requires constant, direct, and, above all, meaningful input from the people. But in Canada, at the dawning of the 1990s and presumably for some time to come, the broadcasting policy framework operated according to its own arcane rules and the mechanics of influencing and making decisions were increasingly inaccessible to ordinary people. The choices waiting to be made, meanwhile, had never been so clear.

# Conclusion

## POLICY, THE PUBLIC, AND THE STATE – LEARNING FROM THE CANADIAN EXPERIENCE

As this was being written, Canada was in the throes of yet another wrenching debate on the future of its broadcasting system. Other Western societies were going through similar debates generally set, as in Canada, in an often ahistorical and timeless framework of technological and sociopolitical urgency.

The type of questions raised in this book, while present on the intellectual and territorial margins, were not at the centre of the debate. Basically, the stakes of broadcasting in 1989 were being played out around the future of traditional state-based national, publicly owned broadcasting systems versus the place to be accorded the economic development of essentially private-sector-based communications industries. In this struggle, the overwhelmingly dominant response of progressive circles was retrenchment in defence of the traditional "public service" institutions.[1]

In Canada and elsewhere, this defence tends to be framed in terms of cultural sovereignty rather than social or public service objectives. The result is perpetuation of the type of problem that was identified above: strategic retreat from criticism of the limits of administrative broadcasting, blindness to the repressive potential of broadcasting when used as a national policy instrument, and co-optation by entrepreneurs of positive sentiment towards local cultures. This continues to inhibit the emergence of alternatives to both state and market conceptions of a "mass" public, alternatives that could be the basis for democratic uses of broadcasting and communications.

Throughout the twentieth century, it has been necessary, in all the Western countries, to "defend" the very idea of public life against the advancing ideology of the marketplace.[2] The emergence of public broadcasting systems in the 1920s and 1930s was, along with the introduction of social welfare measures, a manifestation of an expanding state as well as an issue of principle.

The historic importance of the state as a patron, organizer, and enabler of both the cultural and the technological aspects of communications systems in Canada is self-evident. State intervention has been a means to guarantee Canada's national sovereignty, a secure capital base for its entrepreneurs and financiers, and free expression and access to communications for various interest groups.[3]

This multiple role has been made possible by an identification of the political function of the state with the "defense of the public interest." As the state – if not the government of the day – is perceived as the institutional embodiment of the public interest, its interventions are made in the name of public interest. Conversely, criticism of government/state interventions tend to be made by putting forward alternative representations of the public interest at any point in time. This process tends to obscure the actual role of the state, as the promoter of particular *private* interests, and obscures the fact that as a pivotal social institution, the modern state has its own particular private interest.[4]

In general in the advanced, industrial West, the state interest includes (1) the need to maintain and promote a sound national economy based on the expansion of capital and the furnishing of a minimal social welfare net; (2) the need to maintain social peace by minimizing class conflict and cross-cultural, interregional harmony; (3) the need to negotiate a favourable position for the national entity it represents on the global, geopolitical scale; and (4) the need to maintain its own legitimacy above and beyond question.

In the specific case of Canada, the state has had three principal tasks: (1) to protect the integrity of the national entity from the centripetal pull of the imperial neighbour to the south; (2) to protect the internal cohesion of the national entity from the threat of fragmentation posed by Canada's particular "national unity" crisis; and (3) to protect the market environment for the commercial prosperity of Canadian entrepreneurs. Until recently, a strong, central communications and broadcasting system was perceived as fundamental to all of these tasks, and federal policy flowed from that perception. This basic assumption has now changed.

Since the 1920s, broadcasting has been one of the central arenas of the public sphere in Western society. In the 1980s, with the ideological winds prevailing towards notions such as "privatization" and "deregulation," the public function of broadcasting has been rolled back. In response, critics of the shortcomings of the classical public broadcasting tradition have necessarily begun to rethink the idea of the public with respect to broadcasting.[5] At the same time, in all Western countries, policy making goes on.

This rethinking and repositioning of the role of the state is by no means limited to the communications sector. In all Western countries, governments themselves propose to renegotiate the state's functions and responsibilities, seeking to maximize its political position and minimize its financial burden. In this process, the *social* function that the state has largely exercised for the past sixty years is shuffled around the bargaining table as the piece of the puzzle that refuses to fit. There is no shortage of entrepreneurial energy ready to occupy the economic spaces being evacuated by the state. But who will fill the social spaces, and in what way? For the past sixty years, for better and for worse, the dominant alternative to letting the market economy determine social relations has been a managerial, bureaucratic form of state intervention, to such an extent that even disinterested representatives of the public interest are often hard pressed to imagine any other possible alternative. Indeed, the problem is not only the way the state has intervened but also the lack of durability of prominent alternative strategies for social change.

The case of Canadian broadcasting is revealing in this respect. For example, by the time television was being introduced to Canada in the 1950s, the contradictions in the system had become blurred to the point that "public broadcasting" had little ideological connotation *per se*, and was simply a generic synonym for the CBC. Government policy continued to see public broadcasting as the vehicle for meeting national objectives, and social groups continued to see it as a space in which they could democratically advance their interests, but public discussion was essentially reduced to the question of defending the CBC or promoting private enterprise in broadcasting.

Later, while broadcasting – especially in the framework of Liberal national unity policy – continued to play a political role, "communications" in the broader sense was conceived and established along industrial, economic development lines. In this context, the "public" role remained the traditional one of providing costly infrastructures and support services, regulating competition, and legitimating the expansion of indigenous capitalism.[6]

During the 1970s, the question of the public was diffuse. Public broadcasting was seen as a particular form of activity with two possible purposes: to foster broad government policy or to address the burning social issues of the day. But broadcasting as a whole was still seen as a public activity and was, thus, regulated by a public agency, the CRTC. The CRTC clashed with the CBC, both clashed with the government, and neither the CBC, the CRTC, nor the government were able to satisfy the proliferation of social demands with respect to broadcasting.

Meanwhile, the Department of Communications charted a course of industrial development far from concern over public purpose and often even far from public eyes. As long as the government had political designs on the public broadcaster, a certain balance was maintained between the cultural and economic objectives of communications. But by the late 1970s the political and financial costs of using the CBC as a vehicle for promoting national unity outweighed the benefits, and when the national unity crisis diminished after the Quebec referendum of 1980, the Canadian context irreversibly changed. The indication of this change was the wholesale transfer of the entire cultural sector, including broadcasting, from the responsibility of the secretary of state to that of the minister of communications in 1980. Thereafter, public broadcasting would be a clearly marginal enterprise among the myriad of activities that take place under the rubric of communications. The era of cultural industry had arrived.

So, whereas the rationale of Canada's cultural policy in the 1960s and 1970s was political, in the 1980s it was economic. The immediate implication of this was hard times for traditional Canadian public broadcasting, and the natural response of the traditional cultural lobby was to use the political argument that had served past Liberal governments in defence of the public broadcaster. In the process, however, a host of important questions went not only unanswered but even unasked. Important proposals went unconsidered, and there was a virtual taboo on any discussion that did not address the bottom-line of "Canadian" broadcasting.

The September 1986 Report of the Task Force on Broadcasting Policy underscored this dilemma. It contained a number of important elements which reaffirmed and broadened the notion of public service broadcasting, but submerged them in a wave of rhetoric whose key word was "Canadianization." At the same time, the task force accepted the prevailing logic of the need to develop Canadian "cultural industries" as an intrinsic good in the national interest, regardless of their impact on the social objectives attributed to broadcasting. The subsequent report of the parliamentary committee on communications and culture and the ensuing debate over Flora MacDonald's proposed new broadcasting act followed much along similar lines.

During the four years of the Mulroney government's first term, the public discussion of broadcasting generated tens of thousands of pages of official documents and consumed several million dollars in public funds. Yet, as of the federal election of 1988, the public debate had yet to translate into anything as concrete, albeit general, as a piece of legislation reflecting the points of consensus that had emerged.[7]

Dozens of organizations and hundreds of serious individuals had invested thousands of hours and unquantifiable volumes of energy in the policy-making process during these years. Important victories were won but they were mainly at the level of general principle. Anyone reading the policy documents could easily come away with the impression that the battle for an expanded, revitalized, more liberal, more humane, and human-serving public broadcasting system had been won. But in the real world of broadcasting industry – as opposed to the make-believe one of policy proposals – this is what actually happened:

While the policy debate droned on, the Canadian broadcasting system continued to evolve without any of the necessary new checks required by the new context. The CRTC completely rewrote its radio, television, and cable regulations, and declared it would henceforth take a "supervisory" approach to its task, relying on industry to adopt measures of "self-regulation." Public broadcasting continued to suffer budgetary constraints, not only nationally but among provincial and community broadcasters as well. In the private sector, the concentration of ownership among a shrinking handful of giant corporations rose to a new height in the name of the need to be competitive on a global scale. New "specialty" television services were licensed for cable distribution, amid waves of controversy surrounding the proposed funding and programming formulas. All the while, the Americanization of Canadian broadcasting continued apace.

These developments in themselves provided good grounds for arguing the need to recentre broadcasting decision making in the public sphere. But it was even more important to keep sight of the reason for maintaining a strong public presence in broadcasting in the first place.

In the late 1980s, conventional wisdom held that the Canadian broadcasting system was "in crisis." Moments of crisis often have the salutary effect of permitting the emergence of hitherto unimagined social possibilities. It would, indeed, be a richly ironic paradox if in response to the apparent threat to the traditional public role for broadcasting in Canada, new approaches emerged that moved it closer to its unrealized democratic potential.

FROM "NATIONAL" MEDIA TO "PUBLIC" MEDIA

In 1938, the Canadian scholar Harold Innis identified "the weakening of nationalism, the strengthening of regionalism, and the stress on imperialism" in Canada as the weak link in the continental political economy of North America.[8] This perceptive observation was important to recall in light of the Canadian government's attempt to negotiate a "free trade" agreement with the US, while insisting that Canada's "cultural sovereignty" was not for sale. Historically, as we have seen, the principal Canadian policy issue has always been how to deal with American cultural domination, and it may be time to consider whether that emphasis does not obscure more than it reveals about the real nature of Canadian media. The emphasis on national considerations has only been maintained at the cost of subsuming the other major tensions in Canadian broadcasting: between public and private ownership, between different jurisdictional models, between different structural

approaches. By persistently camouflaging these issues, the cultural sovereignty argument has prevented the extension of the public dimension of
broadcasting in Canada. In fact, if one were inclined to see things this way,
one could argue that the thwarting of the democratic potential of media in
Canada in the name of a national interest actually serves American interests
in the long run. Perhaps that's what Innis was getting at.

In a general overview of Canadian communications issues published in
1977, Patricia Hindley, Gail Martin, and Jean McNulty raised the crucial
question: "If Canada is so intent on resisting American domination, what
are we resisting it *for*?"[9] This is really the fundamental question in Canadian
communications and, not surprisingly, it originated in British Columbia, a
region that has produced the most trenchant critiques of communications in
English Canada, in the work of people like Dallas Smythe, Herschel Hardin,
George Woodcock, and Liora Salter.[10] Indeed, part of the problem lies in
the fact that in anglophone central Canada it is virtually impossible to raise
such questions. For Hindley et al., it is necessary "to dig deeply into the
core of the Canadian experience, where we come face to face with the
critical tensions: between provincial and federal, regional and national,
periphery and centre."[11]

This is where, in practice, an institution like the CBC has been deficient,
partly due to the political and economic pressures placed upon it by successive governments, and partly due to its own administrative logic. This
logic is not contested in most of the eloquent pleas in support of an un-
specified "Canadian" broadcasting that characterize central Canadian policy
interventions.[12] It does not address the basic problem with the Canadian
formula which, according to Hindley et al., is the relationship of the parts
to the whole:

> In communications terms, what happens to the provinces and the regions in policy
> and practice is that they become the spokes of a wheel of which Ottawa, Toronto
> or Montreal is the hub. Communications among the members of the periphery is
> encouraged *only* if it passes *through* the hub ... Ultimately, of course, the struggle
> to reorganize the communications patterns of the country becomes a struggle for
> power. The one-way, central Canada-dominated communications pattern is the
> counterpart to the political and economic structure of the country.[13]

The critique of "national" broadcasting in Canada points to, but does not
yet name, the most important social aspect of the system – its profoundly
undemocratic nature. Most of the time, in its most important manifestations,
Canadian broadcasting exhibits the characteristics of what C. Wright Mills
called "mass," as opposed to "public" media.[14] But within the system,
there is a "hinterland dynamic" at play, to use Liora Salter's term for the
responses from the territorial and intellectual margins that emerge in the

form of critical journalism and autonomous media. In her view: "Some news and public affairs programming on CBC radio is public; a small proportion of CBC television or commercial media production is public as well. Also there are journalists who can be said to act within the public domain, although they write for commercial media. Those who work in community radio and cable systems and edit or publish small journals work in public media." [15]

Thus, in spite of the tendency of media to extend the reaches of empire and create monopolies of knowledge that rob the public of legitimacy in the interpretation of its own experience (an idea attributed to Innis), they also have the capacity to develop at the periphery of empire and serve as vehicles of resistance, decentralizing information and, hence, diffusing power. This phenomenon, evident for example in the experience of Quebec within the Canadian media context, is what Hans Magnus Enzensberger termed, in an important essay first published in 1970, the relationship between the "emancipatory" and "repressive" aspects of media. [16]

With mainstream critical concern tending to focus massively on the "national" problems of the Canadian broadcasting system, few voices have been raised to deal with its "social" problems. An important exception was the 1981 public appeal by the former federal minister of communications David MacDonald, calling for media democratization. [17] Reform of the media, making them publicly accountable and giving the citizen power to do more than consume, was the key to a more democratic political system and would regenerate political life, MacDonald wrote. "Democratization" of media would mean structural safeguards to prevent favouritism towards or discrimination against particular groups or individuals; expanded contact between decision makers and a diverse public; increased public participation in decision making; and raised critical awareness of and responsibility for the operation of media institutions.

This clearly implied a complete transformation of the relationship between people and the media. In place of the free flow of information, MacDonald called for a *fair* flow, "based on the rights of recipients as well as originators, on a more even two-way exchange, and on the principle of public accountability." [18]

Reframing the fundamental issues in Canadian broadcasting in terms of democratization rather than national purpose would make it possible to deal with them from a public media perspective. The issue encompasses and goes beyond cultural sovereignty and allows us to distinguish particular, private interests from social, or public interests. Democratization is the necessary pathway from the present media system to a system that would be "public" in the classical sense. [19]

In the present situation, the only way we can speak about public media is in tandem with a program for democratization. The constituent elements of a democratic, public media system exist, in the historic experience, concrete examples, and proposals that have been made in the context of Canadian broadcasting. They have only to be ordered and put into practice. As we have seen, there has been a continuous historic demand for socially involved broadcasting in Canada, expressed variously throughout the years in calls for a less centralized and less commercial CBC, for grassroots, autonomous or community media, and for access to media. These demands are still present today, even if they often appear to be eclipsed by the dominant critical positions.

## PATHWAYS TO DEMOCRATIZATION
## – SOME ALTERNATIVE NOTIONS

### Public Service Media

In Britain, as Tom Burns's study of the BBC[20] has shown, the practice of public service broadcasting became defined by a certain standard of "professional excellence." Particularly after the introduction of commercial television, public broadcasting in practice was the result of a negotiation between the government, representing the national interest, and the professionalism of the broadcasting organization. The result was, by definition, the public good.

In this type of situation, state-dependent public service broadcasting contains the seeds of its own undoing. The vested interests of the broadcasting organization do not long remain unnoticed by the publics they are supposed to serve, and as soon as these interests no longer coincide with those of their publics, the struggle between broadcasters and government takes place in the absence of any base of support. Great Britain's Committee on the Future of Broadcasting (the Annan committee) recognized as much when it reported, in 1977: "We do not consider ... that the relations between the broadcasters and the public are satisfactory ... The most voluminous evidence we received was from those who wanted more public scrutiny of broadcasting ... there must be some change in the structure of broadcasting, so that the public and the interest groups are better able to put their views directly to the broadcasting organisations."[21]

In Canada, an important attempt to deal with the relationship between media professionals and their publics has been made by the collective associations of CBC English-language television producers (described in Chapter seven above). The producers' critique was particularly interesting in light of what is known about CBC production practices. This area of knowledge has been well-protected from independent scrutiny and has only been penetrated by the most persistent researchers. For example, when Peter Bruck was trying to set up the field work for his doctoral dissertation, he was told at one point by the assistant-director of CBC English radio current affairs:

"You see, the people who work here work for a public corporation, that's true, but everybody wants also to keep his privacy, a privacy about his doing his job ... I want my privacy. And I think we have a right to it, we work for a public corporation, but we have our private ways of doing it."[22]

As Bruck showed, what the news worker considered his legitimate "privacy" was merely a superficial manifestation of the considerable power embedded in professional news work. The power arrangements in and through which news is produced have a specific influence on what enters the public sphere as "knowledge of the world," making news "one of those cultural practices where power and knowledge cross."[23] The power attached to media work is all the more important at an institution like the CBC, which is deemed to represent the public interest. Thus, it is all the more important that any plan for democratic media reform take the producer/consumer relationship into account.

The existing situation, on the other hand, contributes to the alienation of the audience from the producers, product, and most important, the substance of the product. According to Ian Taylor, CBC production practices bring about the sublimation of politics from the Canadian sociocultural experience.[24] Taylor argues that the CBC's high-profile nightly television news program "The Journal" depoliticizes the day's events by constructing its audience as voyeur and denying the idea of a public politics. This critique is similar to that of many classical news analysis studies,[25] but Taylor points out the interesting distinction between the origins of "The Journal" as part of a senior management strategy to reestablish a strong CBC presence in current affairs, and that of "This Hour Has Seven Days", which was initiated by relatively junior personnel critical of the CBC's corporate practices.

In the late 1980s debate on the future of Canadian broadcasting, "The Journal's" executive producer, Mark Starowicz, made several well-publicized interventions in defence of the corporation, equating CBC interests with those of the Canadian public or, indeed, the nation.[26] Totally different in tone and approach from those of the producers' associations, for example, these interventions could be read as an expression in promotion of professional power, and they indicated the problem inherent in the automatic and uncritical defence of existing public service institutions.

### Autonomous Media

Raymond Williams has described the emergence of "alternative" and "oppositional" cultural practices on the margins of dominant cultural forms.[27] In light of the transformations taking place in the political economy of communications, and especially the accelerated withdrawal of the state from broadcasting, other critics are beginning to speak of the emergence of new public spaces between the state and private capital.[28] In countries such as

France, Belgium, and Italy, the recent experience of the *radios libres*[29] has provided a concrete basis for reflection on the pertinence and effectiveness of alternative broadcast media. Graham Murdock, for example, asks: "[Can alternative media be] strengthened and linked together to create a genuinely popular public sphere that would break with the populism of the market and the paternalism of the existing public institutions, to develop a new kind of communications system?"[30]

The Canadian alternative known as "community broadcasting" has been described in Chapters five and six above.[31] The experience of northern broadcasting in Canada provides another example of an attempt to create autonomous public media.

The CBC began operating a northern service in 1958 and, according to Lorna Roth, policy in this area evolved on a *post hoc* basis "in response to a technological policy determined to make Canada internationally competitive in the aerospace industry."[32] It was a policy based strictly on objectives formulated from a "southern" perspective – technological extension, industrial development, protection of national sovereignty, cultural integration – until the northern population organized itself into lobby groups in 1974 to promote its regional and cultural interests with respect to an "Accelerated Coverage Plan" announced by the CBC.

Inuit pressure for a native-managed, organized, and maintained communications system led to self-initiated Inuit media projects aimed at developing pertinent uses of broadcasting technology and encouraging participation in community development. These projects included field tests to explore forms of communication suited to the north (for example, interactive audio, local film and video production centres, interactive video/audio satellite links between villages); projects to counter the effects of southern program influence (for example, film production workshops organized with the National Film Board and community television); and projects using community media for collective organization and community development.

By 1980 the Inuit projects had become "a viable means of challenging the federal government to define the parameters of its Northern communication policies."[33] Inuit efforts by this time had led to acceptance of the position that any new television channels in Inuit communities would be controlled by the community through "local broadcasting societies," and any revenue generated would be allocated to the community broadcasting society for production of Inuit programs.

In 1980, the CRTC set up a special committee to study the extension of services to northern and remote communities. One Inuk representative was invited to serve on the committee, which became a public forum exploring the television program options of northern groups.

The Inuit Taparisat of Canada proposed establishment of an Inuit broadcasting corporation to do programming, distribute its own production, provide transmitter access, transmit educational and community development video, and ensure community control of additional channels as they were made available by satellite. In addition, it called for reducing the CBC northern service to ten to twelve hours per day, freeing four to six hours on the national northern network for Inuit broadcasts. Satellite time for the northern channel would thus be shared by the CBC and Inuit broadcasters, on the premise that the CBC by itself had been unable to meet Inuit needs.

In July 1980, the CRTC committee published its report, providing the first real framework describing the planning assumptions of Canada's northern broadcasting policy.[34] The report recommended the licensing of commercial satellite services to the north (a proposal which led to the creation in 1981 of the private consortium Cancom); the interim delivery by the federal government of "one composite public service channel of alternative entertainment programming"; the extension of basic services; provision for native cultural opportunities; a separate parliamentary appropriation for native broadcasting; and the introduction of pay-television to Canada.

The Inuit organization applied for a network television licence and proposed that the CBC lease a northern channel on satellite to share with it. The licence was awarded in July 1981, along with $3.9 million as an operating advance against pending land claims settlements. The Inuit Broadcasting Corporation began broadcasting in January 1982.

Despite the need to remain constantly mobilized and vigilant to protect their initiative from the continued imposition of a policy logic rooted in the south, the northern experience is a good example of community organization and mobilization to oblige the policy apparatus to respond to sociocultural needs.[35]

## Struggling for the Public Interest

Broadcasting in Canada was originally shaped by the influence of a strong and well-organized national lobby, the Canadian Radio League. The original league has never really been equalled in influence, energy, or prestige, although analogous groups have reappeared at critical junctures in the evolution of broadcasting.

As the public interest has been redefined in other than traditional national terms, non-national organizations have emerged to try to articulate a general public broadcasting perspective. Two major organizations of this type have been the Association for Public Broadcasting in British Columbia (APBBC) and the Quebec-based Institut canadien d'éducation des adultes (ICEA).

The APBBC was founded in 1972 "to block the projected licensing of new commercial television stations in western Canada and to put forward a public, noncommercial alternative."[36] By 1973 it had official support from environmental, consumer, artistic, and labour groups, and was vigorously lobbying the CRTC. Its argument was: "Public broadcasting should be the norm for Canada, not the exception. The licence structure should be expanded on the public, noncommercial side."[37] Its strategic aim was the creation of a new public network anchored in the west, to counter the power of the Toronto-centred CBC.

The first APBBC plan called for the sharing of cable revenue between the existing distributors and the new public broadcasting organization. In place of advertising, the public broadcaster would carry public service information. When the CRTC rejected this proposal, the APBBC recommended reallocating cable licences to nonprofit, viewer-owned cooperatives, as licence terms expired. When this plan was turned down too, the APBBC decided to stay in business as a vehicle of public education and a public broadcasting advocate.

During the 1970s, the APBBC kept issues of a broad public broadcasting nature on the agenda, even if its concrete successes were limited. Its interventions included objecting to "advocacy advertising" by large corporations, lobbying for a broader mandate for provincial broadcasters, calling for headquartering the proposed CBC-2 network in western Canada, and pursuing its attempt to build a new noncommercial programming sector by applying for individual cable licences as they came due. The group's 1976 campaign in Victoria made competitive licence renewals a Canada-wide issue.

One of the main sites of critical analysis, research, and intervention on communications in Quebec, the ICEA grew out of the pan-Canadian adult education movement and was founded as a separate body in 1956. During the 1950s and 1960s, it became the principal French-Canadian social (as opposed to nationalist) lobby in communications, as well as an agent of social development and popular education.

Since then, the ICEA has been active in every public discussion on broadcasting in Canada and Quebec. It has regularly organized study sessions and other forms of public exchange on mass communications media.[38] In 1963 it undertook the first critical study of television program content done in Quebec,[39] and the following year produced a major document on the history of broadcasting in Canada which still stands as a key reference source.[40] Beginning with a *colloque* held in 1965, it has maintained a concern for the quality of media news and information programming.[41]

In the 1970s, the ICEA broadened its role to begin acting as a catalyst for collective action on communications questions in Quebec, spearheading a common front of social groups that became the main public voice in the decisive debates surrounding the structure and orientation of the educational television network, Radio-Québec.[42] Since 1979, the ICEA has brought together a communications action-research group made up of representatives of the major Quebec labour federations and voluntary associations, communications workers' and artisans' unions and collective associations, and communications researchers. This group provides resources and expertise for the ICEA's interventions, while also acting as a clearing-house of ideas and, most important, as a meeting-place where the full range of progressive organizations in Quebec come together to deal with communications issues. This has resulted in important publications, public manifestations, and countless common interventions on pressing questions.[43] In 1985, the focal point of its presentation to the federal task force on broadcasting policy was the need for democratization of the Canadian broadcasting system – the legal provision of entry points for grassroots public participation in policy making, regulation, and programming.[44]

As models of critical reflection and action around media, the APBBC and the ICEA are excellent examples of public interest intervention. Typically, they come from the periphery of mainstream Canada.

### Decentralized Broadcasting

As we have seen, one of the characteristics of Canadian broadcasting has been an unresolved conflict between the popular desire for public broadcasting on a less-than-national scale and the centralization that resulted from the political demands of Canada's national broadcasting objectives. The federal government, through most of the history of Canadian broadcasting, has fiercely resisted attempts to create public broadcasting at "lesser" levels of jurisdiction. The establishment of provincial educational television in the 1970s was the major breakthrough in this respect, and has been described above.

Abstracting from the specific Canadian context, there is a strong argument to be made for the advantages of a decentralized broadcasting system. In most Western countries, including Canada, the "national" solution to the problem of broadcasting has been thought to be the development of domestic industries capable of mass production. As Italian researcher Giuseppe Richeri has pointed out, this is insufficient:

> Alongside the mass production it is necessary to be able to develop a local production (regional or provincial) which is "low cost" and which can circulate throughout the country ... If each television station as well as being a program *diffusion* and *viewing* point also became a *production* centre of programs which can then circulate to other stations, this would mean a true multiplication of the *sources* and a widening of the *production base* of the different kinds of program ... This is, on the other hand, the only way to definitely consolidate the decentralization of the television system which represents the inevitable step towards making television a democratic instrument.[45]

To the contrary, the Canadian experience has been to experiment and move timidly towards such a system, then away from it boldly in time of economic or political retrenchment. But as Rowland Lorimer and Jean McNulty have argued, the elements of decentralized broadcasting are already present, although scattered throughout the Canadian system. CBC's regional production centres, the provincial educational broadcasters, the local community broadcasters, and local and regional commercial broadcasters, are all engaged in "non-national" broadcasting, but their impact is reduced by a splintering of resources and an unclear overall policy framework.[46] Restructuring the system to bring these diverse elements in touch with each other, as Lorimer and McNulty suggest, would be a serious move towards decentralization. Measures could include, for example, direct federal funding of regional production that does not go through the CBC; wider access to public funding for independent noncommercial production; statutory resources for community broadcasting; an expanded role for provincial broadcasters; and a public mandate for local and regional private sector broadcasters. As described above, many of the recommendations of the Task Force on Broadcasting Policy pointed in this direction. But such a move would imply a devolution of power that the federal government and its agencies have so far been reluctant to grant.

The prospect of alternatives was also broached by Frank Spiller and Kim Smiley, in a background paper prepared for the Canadian Conference of the Arts symposium on broadcasting in October 1985: "There are alternative structures if we dare to imagine them and have the courage, tenacity, and political will to allow people with new ideas a chance to implement them," they wrote,[47] suggesting the Australian model of public broadcasting as one on which to build Canadian noncommercial regional television services. Australian public radio, they pointed out, comes in an assorted variety of actually-existing forms: community-owned and -operated; cooperative; educational-institutional; local government-owned; corporate-sustained; government-sustained; and those operated by statutory authority.[48]

For such a system to be instituted in Canada, it would be necessary to break with more traditions than the one of federal absolutism over provincial fiefs. It would be necessary, for example, to begin thinking in terms such as the suggestion of John Macfarlane of the Friends of Public Broadcasting, for a tax to be levied on the profits of private broadcasters and earmarked for the operations of public services.[49] Macfarlane politely referred to his proposal as a "rental fee" for using the air, and noted that in recompense private broadcasters could be relieved of the cultural obligations now gently demanded of them by the CRTC. But the private sector and its political supporters are not likely to be fooled by such euphemisms.

### New Models

On the edges of the grand debates of the 1980s, a number of thoughtful proposals were made which, if heeded, would have drastically transformed the nature of the Canadian broadcasting system. The more official of these have already been dealt with above.

One perceptive contribution from an unlikely source that is worth noting was that made by the past president of the CBC, Alphonse Ouimet, in 1979. Defining the key "moment of flux" that accompanies the implementation of new technologies, Ouimet suggested that the proliferation of easy access to multiplied channel choice provided the occasion for introducing a new intermediary structure between program producers and content carriers, which he described as a broadcasting "programming undertaking." Rather than allow the cable companies to play the role of programmer that they were demanding for themselves, a new type of agency should be created, Ouimet argued.

Ouimet's "programming undertakings" would involve groups or corporations responsible for programming one or more channels; that is, for selecting, packaging, and scheduling a particular channel in line with the needs of the particular audience that it was supposed to serve. The resulting complementary programming, he wrote, would provide television's chance "to serve at the same time all tastes and needs and not just those of some artificial mass, [with] channels deliberately specialized so as to appeal to the many different interests in our pluralistic society."[50] This recognition of the key question of programming in a multichannel environment added a new element to the familiar ones dealing with control of the system and national origin of program content, but in Ouimet's scheme it was still unclear who would control the programmers.

In 1983, Paul Audley presented a model for restructuring the basic twelve-channel cable television service.[51] He would remove US channels from the basic service and provide foreign content through Canadian commercial services; decommercialize CBC services and allow the present CBC affiliates and independent private broadcasters to develop a second private English-language national network; and introduce new satellite-to-cable services along the lines of the proposed publicly funded CBC-2 service and nonprofit pay-television.

Audley's most interesting proposal was for a nonprofit corporation (possibly a joint venture between the private broadcasters and the CBC) to acquire foreign programming and sell it to Canadian public and private broadcasters; it could also program unpurchased foreign programming on its own nonprofit channel. This system would restrict foreign programming to one channel instead of the present three or four, would ensure a higher quality, and would generate revenue that could be used to support Canadian production. Consumers who still wished to acquire American signals could do so via the augmented cable converter service.

Audley estimated that this plan would increase the amount of funds available for Canadian production by 80 percent, of which only 30 percent would have to come from public funds. Obviously, this assumed that the currently constituted private sector, particularly the cable companies, should be obliged to see a large part of its profits ploughed back into Canadian production. On the other hand, it would create more space in the system for Canadian entrepreneurs, particularly producers and broadcasters. This basically nationalist model thus included a creative effort to integrate a private enterprise element into a public service-oriented system – while recognizing that this could only come about by enhancing the public sector. The decision to finance such a transition, Audley insisted, was the critical element that would permit all the other changes.

The great limitation of this model, from our perspective, is that it is still of a bureaucratic "administrative" type, and restricts the definition of "public" interest to an equation with national purpose. It could usefully be adapted, however. For example, a cable-distributed system based on a full range of public television services might look like this:

*National services*

1. Two channels of mainstream service, one English and one French, operated by national public corporations and programmed by democratically selected citizens' boards
2. One channel providing specific minority services, operated by a separate national public corporation which would develop and program projects proposed by minority groups
3. Two channels offering foreign programming, in English and French, operated by a separate national public corporation and programmed by a representative citizens' board

*Provincial/regional services*

1. One channel of mainstream service in each designated "region" of Canada, each operated by a public corporation set up according to the same principle as the national mainstream service
2. One channel to provide service to the cultural/linguistic minorities within each region, structured according to the same principle as the national minority service

*Local/community services*

1. Separate for each territory covered by a cable licensee, one or more channels as necessary to provide locally determined services not available via other channels, to be acquired or produced out of cable company revenues and programmed by local/community boards

Remaining frequencies could be conditionally licensed to "private" broadcasters, subject to competitive renewal procedures; remaining positions on the basic cable service could be filled by the local/community programming board from a range of available services; available services deemed lower priority would be programmed on higher tiers, providing additional revenue for the system without attaching discriminatory user fees to services that were considered socially important.[52]

However, proposals like the ones outlined here have been more than offset by those made by professional policy advisers impregnated with the ideology of neo-liberalism, who see the role of the public as that of supplier of finance capital for private industry. In the 1980s, arguments which advocate dismantling the public sector in favour of private enterprise were at the cutting edge of the debate on the future of Canadian broadcasting; if they were to have their way, "fashioning Canadian investment to create a viable private sector [would] be established as the priority."[53]

The alternative would be to redesign our public institutions and, indeed, arrive at a new consensus on what we mean by public.[54] In this project, there would be an important cross-fertilization to be carried out between different national experiences. In both Great Britain and Australia, for example, popular dissatisfaction with traditional "public" and "private" television has led, in the past decade, to the state-sanctioned creation of new, noncommercial complementary services – the independent Channel Four, in the case of Britain,[55] and the multicultural Special Broadcasting Service in Australia.[56] The interesting thing about both these initiatives is that they are clearly in the public domain but outside of the corporate structures of the established national public broadcasters. In Canada, comparable initiatives were the CBC-2 project and the Task Force on Broadcasting Policy's proposal for TV Canada. However, neither got off the ground, the first aborted by the CRTC precisely because it appeared to be an attempt to expand the responsibilities of an already over-extended national public broadcaster, and the second because the political will to create it simply was not there.

Examples of alternative structures for a mainstream public broadcaster are to be found in countries like Sweden and Holland, where broadcasting was initially organized along relatively more democratic lines. The Swedish broadcasting system, for example, was set up with a structure of public ownership by representative socioeconomic groups, thus short-circuiting the problem of political dependency on the state.[57] The Dutch system, meanwhile, has been cited as a model of pluralism in broadcasting because of its basis on open access to the air for divergent political and religious groups.[58] As we saw very briefly in the introduction, West Germany provides a bold contrast with Canada in that jurisdiction is essentially vested in *Lander*, or states, equivalent to the Canadian provinces.[59] Even in the United States of America it was necessary to create a form of independent public broadcasting to blunt the effects of an otherwise completely commercial system.[60]

It is important to bear in mind that none of these models fell from the sky, but that each one emerged out of conflicts specific to its own political context. Furthermore, it would be foolish to suggest that any of these examples is beyond criticism and, indeed, each one tends to pose its own new problems, as the literature cited here shows. They are important to note, however, as concrete evidence of alternative modes of organization and, especially, as proof that different paths can be taken.

### RECONSTITUTING THE PUBLIC – ELEMENTS OF DEMOCRATIC PUBLIC BROADCASTING

The problem of the public is still very much on the agenda in the West in 1989, since being able to invoke its support remains the most powerful vehicle of legitimation in our type of society. The stakes involved in controlling the definition of what is public opinion, the public interest, and the public domain are high. In this sense, things have not changed much since the early days of broadcasting or, indeed, not since long before.

The technological threshold on which we are living brings an additional sense of urgency to the question. In all the major industrial countries, governments are trying to roll over technological innovation into economic prosperity and are doing so in the name of the public. Governments are themselves pioneering new conceptions of the public as they seek to justify their policies with regard to new communication technologies. The different micropublics that make up society must do the same if they do not want to lose the right to speak for themselves.

We live in an era of unprecedented availability of information. Increasingly, power will depend on people's ability to use information to promote their own social objectives. The question of "access" is thus a qualitative question, not a quantitative one. Communications systems reflect the nature of the societies in which they operate, and the unequal relationships built into the major communications systems in the world today pose a fundamental problem for democracy, as the report of the International Commission for the Study of Communication Problems (the MacBride report) emphasized in 1980:

> One barrier [to the democratization of communication] that exists almost everywhere is the structure of vertical communication, where the flow runs from top to bottom, where the few talk to the many about the needs and problems of the many from the standpoint of the few ... [This is] particularly the case in developing countries, but also true for social and cultural minorities in both industrialized and developing countries ... Pluralism suffers through the concentration of power over communication, whether in the hands of state authority or of private interests.[61]

The starting point for dealing with the democratization of communications is to clarify the place of communications in democratic public life. The most radical demand one can make regarding media at the present time is for their universally public character to be recognized (as the character of our society's education and health care systems were recognized, following lengthy struggles).

In light of the dramatic changes that took place in European broadcasting systems in the late 1980s, some important new theoretical contributions to this issue began to be made. The most interesting of these tended to see the repositioning of "information" or "cultural" industries as a stake in the restructuring of capitalism as well as the formulation of strategies of resistance. In this perspective, media are not seen as instruments of power but as sites for constituting power, as social spaces with their own contradictions and possibilities.[62]

In Europe, public broadcasting occupied, until recently, a strategic place as, what Armand Mattelart has called, "an activity escaping from the logic of profit, a non-capitalist space within capitalism itself."[63] In the case of Canada, one must point out, public broadcasting was the major cultural agent for building and maintaining a national political consensus and, yet, it was never entirely isolated from the logic of profit as in Europe. Instead, it evolved by meandering between the European notion of public service and the American market approach. The historic, as well as current, confusion surrounding the Canadian system is rooted in this hybrid situation, while in Europe the market function is only beginning to supersede the social function of broadcasting.

The current experience of certain western European countries is revealing in this respect, particularly insofar as some of them are repeating, with painful results, the mistakes made by Canadian policy makers thirty and more years ago. In Italy, for example, commercial television, introduced in 1976, has been characterized by the rapid emergence of a small number of dominant stations and chains, relying almost exclusively on cheap imports in a quest for maximum audience numbers. But aside from the cultural and economic effect of this reliance on imported programs, the new context has transformed the public service, Radiotelevisione Italiana (RAI), which at first tried to remain aloof from it. Stunned by the erosion of its audience (54 percent in 1982), there has been, according to Richeri, a "progressive sliding of the RAI from the role of a public service towards that of a commercial logic in programme planning and thus in buying and production."[64] The main beneficiary of this "demonopolization" of European broadcasting is transnational capital, and what remains of public broadcasting is becoming increasingly commercial in form and "non-national" in content.[65] This is not news to Canadians.

On the other hand, some European writers, especially in France which had, up until 1981, the archetypical state broadcasting system, see the dismantling of public monopolies as a positive development, and they put forward a neo-liberal analysis of the role of the state and the public in broadcasting. Jean-Louis Missika and Dominique Wolton, for example, see the introduction of private broadcasting as the advent of pluralism, and the marketplace as the arbiter of democracy.[66] The market, not the state, incarnates the will of the public, they say, opposing what they call a new *télévision de société* to the old *télévision d'Etat*. This type of thinking is possible only in a society which, up until very recently, knew only the most stringent form of state monopoly in broadcasting. It will be interesting to see if they change their tune after a few years of exposure to the benefits of the marketplace.

But in a political and ideological context favourable to "privatization," a real problem for proponents of public broadcasting is the search for new alternatives. In this respect, it is disappointing to note the extent to which the dominant alternative to "private" broadcasting continues to be the traditional national broadcasters. Nicholas Garnham has referred to this as "a crisis of the imagination – an inability to conceive of an alternative to broadcasting controlled by profit-seeking private capital other than as centralised, bureaucratic, inefficient, arrogantly insensitive to people's needs, politically subservient to the holders of state power and so on."[67]

What this usually means is a difficulty to mobilize popular support for public broadcasting, as the "public" that the traditional public broadcasters have been deemed to serve retreat into cynicism, if not despair. As this type of argument penetrates the consciousness of broadcasting critics, it begins to generate new critical approaches to the problem.

As Garnham points out, the crisis facing public broadcasting "is part of a wider political crisis, namely a profound shift in people's attitudes to the State and to the State's proper role in social life."[68] Putting the problem in more programmatic terms, Mattelart writes: "Projected into a situation where they are forced to assume responsibility for themselves when the state abandons its responsibilities towards them, groups which struggle against these anti-democratic measures can hardly avoid an analysis of the necessary articulation between their demand for the 'democratisation' of the state and the search for new forms of solidarity and a decentralisation which means a real redistribution of power and responsibility."[69]

The project of redefining democracy "is linked to the emergence of new democratic actors who seek new inter-personal relations and a new group identity, no longer only a class identity."[70] Can this "new identity" be a *public* one?

Even in Canada, this type of analysis is – very slowly and tentatively – beginning to penetrate the debate, as some of the alternative discourses mentioned earlier indicate. This is an encouraging sign, but in order to move beyond the rhetoric of cultural sovereignty it is necessary to acquire a new understanding of the social structures of broadcasting and persist in transferring the debate to another plane.

## OPPORTUNITIES TO SEIZE

In Canada, these are the various actors we came across in the course of this study: the Canadian government, the federal Department of Communications, the regulatory agency, provincial governments and their agencies, the national public broadcaster, the public treasury, the private broadcasting production and distribution sectors, domestic business, foreign interests, the various professionally interested groups, organized public interest and cultural nationalist lobbies, collective associations, and the voting/taxpaying/media-consuming citizen.

The politics of broadcasting is a struggle for control between these competing interests. The issue surrounding the transformation of traditional forms of public control is this: is control to be transferred to a narrower set of economically motivated private interests, or extended by multiplying the points of popular decision making? In this sense, the fundamental question of democracy is at the centre of debates surrounding broadcasting and, in a broader sense, all cultural and communications policy.[71]

At one level, Canada's broadcasting policy debate provides some indication of the issues at stake and the choices available in broadcasting, not only in Canada but in advanced societies in general. But it is possible that the most interesting aspect of the debate lies in what it reveals about the policy-making process. Policy making in Canada has never been as political as it is today, and there has never been a greater need to bring the process closer to the people. The choices are basic to democracy, yet they are made mainly by functionaries in the interests of business. There is, increasingly, a gap between the stated objectives of Canadian broadcasting and the concrete measures taken to carry them out.

Broadcasting can become an instrument of democratic social development only if its public dimension is fully realized. For this to happen in Canada, a number of critical areas must be transformed.

1. First, there is the question of jurisdiction. This must be reorganized to include not only the federal and provincial governments but other levels of political jurisdiction as well, such as municipalities, regional governments, and future institutions of popular control which do not yet exist.

2. The question of cultural sovereignty must be framed in a manner that reflects the diverse reality of the Canadian sociopolitical context, which is more than a "national" or "Canadian" one.

3. The place of private capital and cultural industries must be clearly specified as subsidiary to the objectives of public service and the needs of communities. The "arm's length" relationship of government to cultural

agencies must be not only maintained but enhanced, so that no future "national crisis" leads to a repeat performance of attempts by the federal government to control the CBC. As a corollary to these, the regulatory agency, the CRTC, must act on behalf of the public and not on behalf of any private interest.

4. A significant space in the system must be opened up to accommodate and encourage socially justified autonomous media, regardless of their economic viability or political expediency.

5. Finally, public participation must be widely extended and clearly defined in each of the following spheres:

(a) Policy making, where there must be a mechanism for direct public participation at every stage of the policy formation and evaluation process

(b) Regulation, where there must be a reform of the nomination process of members of the regulatory authority as well as a restructuring of the formal mechanisms of public participation which will increase their effectiveness

(c) Programming, where representative citizens' councils could easily be involved in nontechnical decisions at national, regional, and local levels of both publicly and privately owned broadcasters and distribution systems

(d) Access, as consumers, to a healthy and balanced product; as communicating citizens, to the message making and distribution systems; and as potential producers, to autonomous means of production for those who wish it.

Public broadcasting needs more than a national focus; cultural sovereignty or other national(ist) objectives in broadcasting should be a catalyst for achieving the public interest, not a smoke-screen for camouflaging and helping to repress it. If there is "a" public interest, it is in seeking to achieve a context for the just and equitable coexistence of different, distinct, and often conflicting publics. The role of the state may be to mediate, but it is not to impose, and the only way the state can possibly play a neutral role is if there are effective (that is, democratic) and meaningful (that is, determining) public controls.

But in 1989, the debate on the future of Canadian broadcasting was pegged in different terms, such as these: What steps are necessary to promote maximum Canadian participation in the production and consumption of broadcasting? What is the appropriate relationship between the public and private sectors in broadcasting, that is to say, between the state and private capital? How much public funds are we prepared to commit to broadcasting and how are they to be distributed? What steps are necessary to promote and develop Canadian broadcasting industries and make them competitive in domestic and world markets? How can jurisdiction be reorganized to better reflect the political structure of the Canadian nation-state?

The terms in which the debate was *not* posed, except on the margins, were these: How can the broadcasting system be restructured to better fulfil its public service function? How can broadcasting be reorganized to aid in the enhancement of the democratic quality of public life? How can the technology of broadcasting be put to social use, to meet the different needs of particular communities as well as the general interest? What kind of programming, regardless of national origin, would respond to these questions? How can we assure a more democratic process of decision making regarding programming?

In Canada we need to stop talking about public broadcasting and start acting on it. We need to create these spaces in which the different constituent elements of the public can articulate their needs and entertain a reasonable expectation of obtaining meaningful results. This will come about only with increased public presence in the decision-making centres of broadcasting, and only if we reverse the present unequal relationship between a dispersed array of public interest groups and the very effective industry lobbies. We need to establish a new basis for complicity between the public *as social entity* and the producers, programmers, and policy makers. In short, the ways and means of guaranteeing real public control over the system should be the central element of broadcasting development strategy.

Once upon a time, yet not so long ago, an astute observer of the human condition by the name of Bertolt Brecht proposed that broadcasting be considered as a means of communication rather than distribution. Anticipating his detractors, he then added: "If you should think this is Utopian, then I would ask you to consider why it is Utopian."[72]

# *Notes*

The following abbreviations have been used in the notes to direct the reader to the appropriate entry in the bibliography:

| | |
|---|---|
| CBC | Canadian Broadcasting Corporation |
| CRTC | Canadian Radio-Television Commission and, after 1976, Canadian Radio-Television and Telecommunications Commission |
| DOC | Canada, Department of Communications |
| FPJQ | Fédération professionelle des journalistes du Québec |
| HOC | Canada, Parliament, House of Commons |
| ICEA | Institut canadien d'éducation des adultes |
| *Minutes* | *Minutes of Proceedings and Evidence* |
| NAC | National Archives of Canada |

## PREFACE

1 All sources have, of course, been systematically credited at the appropriate places in the text. Particular mention must be made, however, of the pathbreaking work of Frank W. Peers, whose two-volume history of Canadian broadcasting up to 1968 is the standard general source on the subject (Peers, *The Politics of Canadian Broadcasting 1920–1951* and *The Public Eye*).
2 See Dallas Smythe, "New Directions for Critical Communications Research."

## INTRODUCTION

1 Fisher, *Broadcasting in Ireland.*
2 Briggs, *The History of Broadcasting in the United Kingdom*; and Barnouw, *Tube of Plenty.*

3 Lippmann, *Public Opinion*. In the US, Lippmann's thesis was contested directly by John Dewey and indirectly by Robert E. Park, both of whom saw media contributing to the empowerment of people by acting as a forum and catalyst of public debate. See Dewey, *The Public and its Problems*, and the relevant essays by Park collected in *Society*. The opposing views of the public reflected in the polemic between Lippmann and Dewey derive from the theories of such authors as Gustave Le Bon and Gabriel Tarde, discussed in Park, *The Crowd and the Public*. In a phrase, the issue turns about the capacity of a collective body to act in a rational way, and the role of media in contributing to or detracting from public rationality. The historical development of this question is presented in Part I of the author's unpublished doctoral dissertation, "Broadcasting and the Idea of the Public."

4 Burnham, *The Managerial Revolution*.

5 Great Britain, Broadcasting Committee, *Report*, 6.

6 See Burns, *The BBC*.

7 Quoted in Smith, *The Shadow in the Cave*, 187.

8 Quoted in Friendly, *Due to Circumstances Beyond Our Control...*, 291.

9 See Lazarsfeld, "An Episode in the History of Social Research."

10 See Mackinnon, *On the Rise, Progress and Present State of Public Opinion in Great Britain and Other Parts of the World*.

11 See Bernays, *Public Relations*.

12 See Raboy, "Broadcasting and the Idea of the Public."

13 Canada, Royal Commission on Radio Broadcasting, *Report*.

14 Ibid., appendix.

15 Ibid., 12.

16 See Canada, Royal Commission on National Development in the Arts, Letters and Sciences, *Report*.

17 See, for example, HOC, *Debates* (1964–65), 10080–4.

18 Laurin-Frenette, *Production de l'Etat et formes de la nation*, 60.

19 Quoted in Burns, *The BBC*, 9–10.

20 Canada, Statutes and Bills, The Canadian Radio Broadcasting Act.

21 Canada, Statutes and Bills, The Canadian Broadcasting Act.

22 Iseppi, "The Case of RAI," 350.

23 See Smith, *The Shadow in the Cave*.

24 See Raboy, "Media and Politics in Socialist France."

25 Hodgetts, "Administration and Politics," 459.

26 Ibid., 460. Emphasis added.

27 Ibid., 465.

28 Ibid.

29 Falkenberg, "No Future?"

30 Ibid., 236.

31 Ibid.

32 Canada, Statutes and Bills, Broadcasting Act (1958).

33 Canada, Statutes and Bills, Broadcasting Act (1967–68).

34 Salter, "'Public' and Mass Media in Canada."

35 See Raboy, "Radical Radio."

36 See Engelman, "From Ford to Carnegie."

37 See, for example, Althusser, "Ideology and Ideological State Apparatuses."

38 See, for example, Negt, "Mass Media"; and Kluge, "Film and the Public Sphere." An English version of Habermas's classic work, *Strukturwandel der Öffentlichkeit*, was published in 1989 (Habermas, *Structural Transformation of the Public Sphere*). See also Enzensberger, "Constituents of a Theory of the Media."

39 See, for example, Sénécal, "Médias communautaires."

40 See, for example, CRTC, *Radio Frequencies are Public Property*.

41 CRTC, Committee of Inquiry into the National Broadcasting Service, *Report*.

42 CRTC, "Community Antenna Television"; CRTC, "The Improvement and Development of Canadian Broadcasting and the Extension of US Television Coverage in Canada by CATV"; CRTC, *Cable Television in Canada*; CRTC, *The Integration of Cable Television in the Canadian Broadcasting System*; and CRTC, *Canadian Broadcasting – "A Single System."*

43 CRTC, *More Canadian Programming Choices*.

44 Richeri, "Television from Service to Business." For case-oriented accounts of recent developments in various west European countries, see two theme issues of *Media Culture and Society*: "Public Service Broadcasting – The End?" and "West European Broadcasting"; theme issue of *Dossiers de l'audiovisuel*: "L'Europe des télévisions privées"; Kuhn, *The Politics of Broadcasting*; and Kleinsteuber et al., *Electronic Media and Politics in Western Europe*.

45 Murdock, "The 'Privatization' of British Communications," 265. The Thatcher government's intention to bring British broadcast legislation into line with its overall orientation was announced in a white paper, *Broadcasting in the '90s*.

46 Smith, "Deregulation, New Technology, Public Service," 4.

47 Ibid., 5. See also, Smythe, "Radio Deregulation and the Relation of the Private and Public Sectors"; and Tunstall, *Communications Deregulation*.

48 Richeri, "Television from Service to Business."

49 Smith, "Deregulation, New Technology, Public Service."

50 See, dossiers in *Politique d'aujourd'hui*, "Médias"; and *Médiaspouvoirs*, "Moins d'Etat dans la communication?" For a summary account of the evolution of the French situation, see theme issue of *Dossiers de l'audiovisuel*, "L'esprit des lois ou comment réformer l'audiovisuel."

51 For example, Keane, *Public Life and Late Capitalism*; Garnham, "The Media and the Public Sphere"; and Mattelart and Mattelart, *Penser les médias*.

52 See discussion in chapter seven. For an embryonic critical analysis of this debate see the relevant chapters of Lorimer and Wilson, *Communication*

*Canada*. The role and influence of different social actors in broadcasting policy making in Canada is being explored by the author and associates in an ongoing research project at Laval University and will be discussed in forthcoming publications.

CHAPTER ONE

1 See, for example, Gagné, "Technology and Canadian Politics."
2 Hardin, *A Nation Unaware*.
3 Ibid., 55.
4 Vipond, "The Nationalist Network," 4.
5 Ibid., 46.
6 See Faris, *The Passionate Educators*.
7 Ibid., 19.
8 See, for example, one of the earliest French-Canadian texts on broadcasting, a brief, unsigned note entitled "La radiodiffusion," in the nationalist monthly *L'Action canadienne-française* (December 1928): 375.
9 This section is based on Weir, *The Struggle for National Broadcasting in Canada*; Peers, *The Politics of Canadian Broadcasting, 1920–1951*; Toogood, *Broadcasting in Canada*; Lavoie, "L'évolution de la radio au Canada français avant 1940"; Montigny, "Les débuts de la radio à Montréal et le poste CKAC"; and Smythe, *Dependency Road*.
10 Canada, Statutes and Bills, Wireless Telegraph Act.
11 Canada, Statutes and Bills, Radiotelegraph Act.
12 Canada, Royal Commission on Broadcasting, *Report*, 297.
13 Lavoie, "L'évolution de la radio au Canada français avant 1940."
14 HOC, *Debates* (1928), 1951.
15 Ibid., 3621–2.
16 Ibid., 3662, 3708.
17 Canada, Royal Commission on Radio Broadcasting, *Report*, 1.
18 For example, Ottawa *Citizen*, 21 March 1928.
19 Bowman, quoted in O'Brien, "A History of the Canadian Radio League, 1930–36," 45.
20 Bowman, *Ottawa Editor*, 124.
21 Ibid.
22 Bowman, quoted in O'Brien, "A History of the Canadian Radio League, 1930–36," 46.
23 Canada, Royal Commission on Radio Broadcasting, *Report*, appendix.
24 Ibid., 24–5.
25 Ibid.
26 "M. Taschereau et le [*sic*] radio de la province," *Le Devoir*, 20 March 1929.
27 Ibid.

28 Quebec, Statutes, Loi concernant la radiodiffusion dans cette province.

29 Montigny, "Les débuts de la radio à Montréal et le poste CKAC."

30 NAC, Files of the Royal Commission on Radio Broadcasting, RG 42.

31 Canada, Royal Commission on Radio Broadcasting, *Report*, 6.

32 NAC, Files of the Department of Marine and Fisheries, vol. 1076: 105–1–1.

33 Quebec, Legislative Assembly, *Journaux* (1929), 295.

34 NAC, Files of the Royal Commission on Radio Broadcasting, vol. 1:227–10–1.

35 Ibid., 227–10–5.

36 NAC, Files of the Department of Marine and Fisheries, vol. 1076:227–6–3.

37 Ibid.

38 Ibid.

39 NAC, Files of the Royal Commission on Radio Broadcasting, vol. 1:227–9–9/10.

40 Ibid.

41 Ibid.

42 See, for example, letter to the commission from the Association d'éducation des canadiens-français du Manitoba, NAC, Files of the Department of Marine and Fisheries, vol. 1076:227–8–3.

43 NAC, Files of the Royal Commission on Radio Broadcasting, vol. 1:227–10–5.

44 Bowman, *Ottawa Editor*.

45 "Memorandum prepared by Augustin Frigon in Connection with the Work of the Royal Commission on Radio Broadcasting," and "Royal Commission on Radio Broadcasting – Report by Charles A. Bowman," NAC, Charles Bowman Papers, reel no. M–826.

46 Ibid.

47 NAC, Files of the Royal Commission on Radio Broadcasting, vol. 2:227–14–1.

48 Ibid.

49 Ibid.

50 Canada, Royal Commission on Radio Broadcasting, *Report*, 6.

51 Ibid.

52 Ibid., 5.

53 Ibid., 6.

54 Ibid.

55 Ibid., 10.

56 Ibid., 12.

57 Bowman, *Ottawa Editor*, 131.

58 See "Highlights of Editorial Comment," Memo from Donald Manson to Sir John Aird, 31 March 1930, NAC, Files of the Department of Marine and Fisheries, vol. 1076:109–1–1.

59 Ibid., 105–1–1.

60 Ibid., 109–1–1.
61 "Aird Project Menaces the Trade and Commerce of Radio"/"Le projet Aird menace l'industrie et le commerce de la radio," NAC, Files of the Department of Marine and Fisheries, vol. 1076:105–1–1.
62 "Radio Public Service for Canada," NAC, Files of the Department of Marine and Fisheries, vol. 1076:105–1–1.
63 Frigon, "The Organization of Radio Broadcasting in Canada," 409.
64 NAC, Files of the Royal Commission on Radio Broadcasting, vol. 3:227–5–1.
65 See HOC, *Debates* (1930, 1st sess.), 30, 45, 1356, 2918.
66 "Explanatory Remarks re BILL An Act to incorporate the Canadian Radio Broadcasting Company," NAC, Files of the Royal Commission on Radio Broadcasting, vol. 2:227–14–1/2/3. Emphasis in original.
67 For example, O'Brien, "A History of the Canadian Radio League, 1930–36"; Prang, "The Origins of Public Broadcasting in Canada"; and Peers, *The Politics of Canadian Broadcasting, 1920–1951*.
68 Vipond, "The Nationalist Network," 39.
69 O'Brien, "A History of the Canadian Radio League, 1930–36," 33.
70 Quoted in O'Brien, "A History of the Canadian Radio League, 1930–36," 75.
71 O'Brien, "A History of the Canadian Radio League, 1930–36."
72 Corbett, who was involved at the time with the University of Alberta's radio station CKUA, later described how this worked: "I became the western representative of the Radio League, and everywhere I went I carried copies of the Aird Report, propaganda literature released by the Ottawa office of the Radio League, and whenever there was an opportunity I attempted to get formal resolutions passed by responsible organizations supporting the recommendations of the Aird Report. In less than a year some fifty resolutions from farm organizations, women's institutions, boards of trade, church societies, etc., were sent from Alberta to the office of the Radio League in Ottawa as evidence of the interest already existing among western people regarding the future of broadcasting in Canada" (Corbett, *We Have With Us Tonight*, 56–7).
73 O'Brien, "A History of the Canadian Radio League, 1930–36," 141.
74 NAC, Brooke Claxton papers, MG 32, B 5, vol. 5.
75 Ibid.
76 Weir, *The Struggle for National Broadcasting in Canada*, 114. An anecdote related by Charles Bowman indicates how the private sector lobby worked: "Soon after the Conservatives took office, private interests were busy lobbying on Parliament Hill, against the Aird report on radio policy. Sir Edward Beatty, president of the Canadian Pacific Railway, invited me to meet him at the Chateau Laurier. He wanted me to consider the possibilities of one national broadcasting corporation, privately owned and operated ... rather than public ownership, or a multiplicity of private stations ... As I gathered from

my confidential interview, it would only require me to reverse my position on public ownership, to produce results of benefit to myself as well as to the community in general. I failed to appreciate the alluring prospects of this proposal" (Bowman, *Ottawa Editor*, 134–5).

77 See, for example, Spry, "The Canadian Broadcasting Issue."

78 "Government vs. Private Ownership of Canadian Radio," NAC, Files of the Department of Marine and Fisheries, vol. 1076:105–1–1.

79 Quebec, Statutes, Loi modifiant la Loi concernant la radiodiffusion dans cette province.

80 Quebec, Statutes, Loi concernant la radio.

81 Quebec, Statutes, Loi concernant la responsabilité civile en matière de radiodiffusion.

82 NAC, Files of the Department of Marine and Fisheries, vol. 1076:104–1–2.

83 "Broadcasting Systems – Different Methods Considered," NAC, Files of the Department of Marine and Fisheries, vol. 1076:104–1–2.

84 See *Dominion Law Reports* (1931), vol. 4:865–94; and Claxton, "Legislative Control of Radio in Canada."

85 Prang, "The Origins of Public Broadcasting in Canada."

86 Plaunt, quoted in O'Brien, "A History of the Canadian Radio League, 1930–36," 219.

87 NAC, Brooke Claxton papers, MG 32, B 5, vol. 17.

88 *Dominion Law Reports* (1931), vol. 4:865–94.

89 Claxton, "Legislative Control of Radio in Canada," 454.

90 NAC, Brooke Claxton papers, MG 32, B 5, vol. 5.

91 Prang, "The Origins of Public Broadcasting in Canada."

92 Claxton, "Broadcasting in Canada."

93 *Dominion Law Reports* (1932), vol. 2:81–8.

94 See Rémillard, "Le fédéralisme canadien," 309–43. Rémillard was later Quebec's minister of intergovernmental affairs after Robert Bourassa returned to power in 1985.

95 O'Brien, "A History of the Canadian Radio League, 1930–36"; and Prang, "The Origins of Public Broadcasting in Canada."

96 Spry, "The Canadian Radio Situation," quoted in O'Brien, "A History of the Canadian Radio League, 1930–36," 227–8.

97 Spry, "A Case for Nationalized Broadcasting," 153.

98 Ibid., 169.

99 Spry, "The Origins of Public Broadcasting in Canada," 136–9.

100 Spry, "Radio Broadcasting and Aspects of Canadian-American Relations," 107.

101 Ibid., 108n.

102 Ibid., 114.

103 Ibid., 116–7.

104 Rickwood, "Canadian Broadcasting Policy and the Private Broadcasters," 80.

105  HOC, *Debates* (1932), 236.
106  HOC, Special Committee on Radio Broadcasting, *Minutes* (1932), 42.
107  Ibid.
108  Ibid., 45–6.
109  Ibid.
110  Ibid.
111  Ibid., 97.
112  Ibid., 521.
113  See, for example, this exchange:
> "Hon. Mr. Cardin: Is it not a fact that the main desire of the Province of Quebec is to exercise a control of what is broadcasted in the Province of Quebec?
> "M. Geoffrion: That is one thing, but I believe the Province of Quebec is afraid of granting absolute mastery of the biggest influence conceivable to the Dominion of Canada" (Ibid.).
114  Ibid., 391.
115  Ibid., 124.
116  Ibid., 271.
117  Ibid., 718.
118  Ibid., 662.
119  Ibid., 667.
120  Ibid., appendix 38:289–93.
121  Ibid., 544–5.
122  Ibid., 545–6.
123  Ibid., 564–5.
124  Ibid., 571.
125  Ibid., 575.
126  Ibid., 651.
127  Ibid., 729.
128  Ibid., 731.
129  Peers, *The Politics of Canadian Broadcasting, 1920–1951*, 105; and O'Brien, "A History of the Canadian Radio League, 1930–36," 296.
130  HOC, *Debates* (1932), 3035.
131  Ibid., 3036.
132  Ibid., 3037.
133  Canada, Statutes and Bills, The Canadian Radio Broadcasting Act.
134  O'Brien, "A History of the Canadian Radio League, 1930–36."
135  Quoted in Peers, *The Politics of Canadian Broadcasting, 1920–1951*, 106.
136  According to Weir, the Canadian Radio Broadcasting Act "was easily the most significant and far-reaching accomplishment of Bennett's five years in office ... his endorsement of nationalized radio has been an embarrassment to reactionary members of his party" (Weir, *The Struggle for National Broadcasting in Canada*, 135).

CHAPTER TWO

1 Hardin, *A Nation Unaware*, 294.
2 Canada, Royal Commission on Broadcasting, *Report*, 304.
3 See, for example, Dennison, "Radio in Canada"; and Spry, "Radio Broadcasting and Aspects of Canadian-American Relations."
4 King's concept of nationalism at this time and its cultural implications are well documented in Nelson, *The Colonized Eye*, chapter three.
5 Canada, Statutes and Bills, The Canadian Broadcasting Act.
6 For example, Joyce Nelson has written with respect to the emergence of Canada's National Film Board that its founder, John Grierson, was motivated by the goal of "increasing mass allegiance to authoritarian power structures in order to ensure the better management of society" (Nelson, *The Colonized Eye*, 100).
7 For example, Burnham, *The Managerial Revolution*.
8 Charlesworth, *I'm Telling You*, 54. According to Charlesworth, "nationalized radio had been brought into being largely by the Prime Minister's personal initiative, against a cabinet, partly hostile and partly indifferent, and a caucus somewhat of the same frame of mind ... few comprehended what radio really signified at all" (54).
9 See Peers, *The Politics of Canadian Broadcasting, 1920–1951*, 136.
10 Quoted in O'Brien, "A History of the Canadian Radio League, 1930–36," 316.
11 Weir, *The Struggle for National Broadcasting in Canada*, 149.
12 Ibid., 151.
13 Corbett, "Planned Broadcasting for Canada," 22.
14 Weir, *The Struggle for National Broadcasting in Canada*, 150–2.
15 Charlesworth, *I'm Telling You*, 99.
16 Charlesworth later wrote about this problem as well: "Throughout my term as Chairman I could have wished that some of our English-speaking politicians were as tolerant as their French-Canadian compatriots. If there is a separatist feeling in Quebec it has been provoked in no small degree by the narrow-minded hostility of certain groups of English-speaking Canadians" (Ibid., 98–9).
17 Richer, "Le ministère Bennett et les canadiens-français."
18 Peers, *The Politics of Canadian Broadcasting, 1920–1951*, 136, 159.
19 Some thirty years later, in a brief to the Royal Commission on Bilingualism and Biculturalism, the Canadian Broadcasting Corporation reflected (without elaborating on the circumstances) on this aspect of its pre-history, and the origins of its "equal partnership" practice. See CBC, *Submission to the Royal Commission on Bilingualism and Biculturalism*, 5–6.
20 HOC, Special Committee on the Operations of the Commission under the Canadian Radio Broadcasting Act (1932), *Minutes*, 24.

21 Ibid., 426.

22 Ibid., 401.

23 Ibid., 299, 500, 503.

24 Ibid., 584.

25 O'Brien, "A History of the Canadian Radio League, 1930–36."

26 See Peers, *The Politics of Canadian Broadcasting, 1920–1951*, 156.

27 Ibid., 158.

28 The commentator for *L'Action nationale*, "H.B.," wrote in November 1933: "We, the uninitiated, are asking ourselves more and more often: What is the purpose of the CRBC? Lord knows the daily program fare is not getting any better. The same screaming music, the same shameless massacre of the French language, the same stumbling, bumbling announcers. At the price we're paying for the Commission and the commissioners, we could have hoped for more. If the Commission has no role to play, no authority, no responsibility, why was it set up in the first place?" (H.B., "A quoi ça sert?" 193 [trans. M.R.].)

29 Laurendeau "La radio," 130, 134 (trans. M.R.). See also, Laurendeau, "La radio (Suite et fin)."

30 O'Brien, "A History of the Canadian Radio League, 1930–36."

31 Spry, "Radio Broadcasting and Aspects of Canadian-American Relations," 115, 117–18.

32 O'Brien, "A History of the Canadian Radio League, 1930–36," 346.

33 Quoted in O'Brien, "A History of the Canadian Radio League, 1930–36," 351.

34 HOC, Special Committee on the Canadian Radio Commission, *Minutes*, 21.

35 HOC, *Debates* (1936), 1234–5.

36 HOC, Special Committee on the Canadian Radio Commission, *Minutes*.

37 "Proposals of the Canadian Radio League for the Organization of Broadcasting in Canada," HOC, Special Committee on the Canadian Radio Commission, *Minutes*, appendix 3.

38 Ibid.

39 Ibid.

40 Ibid.

41 Ibid., 350.

42 Ibid., 361–2.

43 Ibid., 371.

44 Ibid., 556.

45 Ibid., appendix 3.

46 Quoted in Weir, *The Struggle for National Broadcasting in Canada*, 204.

47 Charlesworth, *I'm Telling You*, 39.

48 HOC, Special Committee on the Canadian Radio Commission, *Minutes*, 784–5.

49 HOC, *Debates* (1936), 3709.

50 Ibid., 3710.

51 Ibid.

52 Quoted in O'Brien, "A History of the Canadian Radio League, 1930–36," 365.

53 Ibid.

54 See correspondence quoted in Peers, *The Politics of Canadian Broadcasting, 1920–1951*, 204–6.

55 HOC, *Debates* (1938), 249.

56 See Weir, *The Struggle for National Broadcasting in Canada*, 228–9.

57 HOC, Standing Committee on Radio Broadcasting, *Minutes*, 195.

58 HOC, *Debates* (1938), 2781–2.

59 See Peers, *The Politics of Canadian Broadcasting, 1920–1951*.

60 Quoted in HOC, *Debates* (1939, 1st sess.), 12.

61 Ibid.

62 HOC, Special Committee on Radio Broadcasting, *Minutes* (1939), 34.

63 Ibid., 341.

64 Ibid., 225.

65 Ibid., 91, 254.

66 Canada, Statutes and Bills, The Radio Act, s. 3(1)d.

67 HOC, *Debates* (1938), 2753.

68 HOC, Special Committee on Radio Broadcasting, *Minutes* (1939), 184.

69 Ibid.

70 HOC, *Debates* (1940, 2d sess.), 1584.

71 Peers, *The Politics of Canadian Broadcasting, 1920–1951*.

72 Ibid.

73 Quoted in HOC, *Debates* (1941–42), 64.

74 Ibid., 225.

75 The CBC was supported in this by a Department of Justice ruling treating it as a government department for the purposes of labour relations. In a memo to staff early in 1939, Murray had said the government would frown upon any attempts by CBC employees to unionize. See HOC, Special Committee on Radio Broadcasting, *Minutes* (1942), 151.

76 HOC, *Debates* (1941–42), 3781.

77 See HOC, Special Committee on Radio Broadcasting, *Minutes* (1939), 248.

78 HOC, *Debates* (1941–42), 385.

79 *L'Action nationale* 17, no. 6 (June 1941): 507 (trans. M.R.).

80 See Lamarche, "Radio-Canada et sa mission française."

81 For example, French network programming continued to be subject to approval from Toronto after the war. At the parliamentary committee of 1946, French network director Jean-Marie Beaudet testified: "Nothing is done on the French network without prior consultation with the national program office ... [English and French networks] follow the same policies, although programs must be adapted and suited to French listeners' tastes" (HOC, Special Committee on Radio Broadcasting, *Minutes* [1946], 534, 545).

82 See Legris, *Propagande de guerre et nationalismes dans le radio-feuilleton (1939–1955)*.
83 Ibid., 21.
84 Kerr, "Skirting the Minefield," 46.
85 Ibid.
86 *L'Action nationale* 14, no. 1 (September 1939): 3.
87 *L'Action nationale* 14, no. 2 (October 1939): 125.
88 Kerr, "Skirting the Minefield."
89 See "Suggestions re Opinion in Canada," unsigned document, dated 29 May 1942, NAC, Brooke Claxton papers, MG 32, B 5, v. 137.
90 See Laurendeau, *La Crise de la conscription*, 104.
91 Quoted in Laurendeau, *La Crise de la conscription*, 105 (trans. M.R.).
92 Laurendeau, *La Crise de la conscription*, 106.
93 Quoted in Laurendeau, *La Crise de la conscription*, 108 (trans. M.R.).
94 "Les partisans du 'NON' ne pourront utiliser la radio d'Etat," *Le Devoir*, 10 April 1942.
95 "Le plébiscite: MM. King et Cardin demandent de faire confiance au gouvernement; M. Duplessis déclare qu'il votera 'non'," *Le Devoir*, 25 April 1942.
96 HOC, Special Committee on Radio Broadcasting, *Minutes* (1946), 796.
97 HOC, Special Committee on Radio Broadcasting, *Minutes* (1942), 96.
98 Ibid., 299.
99 Ibid., 299–300. The word "not" was added to the transcript in a correction on page 681 of the document.
100 As the CBC's "Farm Forum" series was already doing in agriculture.
101 HOC, Special Committee on Radio Broadcasting, *Minutes*, (1942), 346.
102 Ibid., 699.
103 Ibid., 984.
104 Ibid., 1088.
105 See Weir, *The Struggle for National Broadcasting in Canada*, 234.
106 See Faris, *The Passionate Educators*.
107 Corbett, *We Have With Us Tonight*, 141.
108 Ibid., 143.
109 Nicol et al., *Canada's Farm Radio Forum*. Even today, the CBC's farm programming is studied as a model for use of radio in Third World rural development. See World Conference on Community-Oriented Radio Broadcasting, *Community-Oriented Radio Broadcasting Throughout the World*.
110 Corbett, *We Have With Us Tonight*, 149–50.
111 See Faris, *The Passionate Educators*.
112 Corbett, *We Have With Us Tonight*, 171.
113 Claxton wrote to Winnipeg *Free Press* editor John Dafoe: "The CCF are ingenious and persistent in discovering means to put the radio to political use in their interest. How the thing can be regulated so that there can be honest

discussion without too much partisanship is a problem that has me stumped"
(Quoted in Peers, *The Politics of Canadian Broadcasting, 1920–1951*, 339,
n. 42). But in a memo to the prime minister, Claxton spelled out the problem in far more explicit political terms: "The program is of the utmost political importance. It will be concerned with a field which the CCF has made
peculiarly its own and in which the Liberals have said little. Phrases in the
titles like 'new hopes,' 'longing for a better world,' and 'full employment'
use the jargon which the CCF has succeeded in appropriating ... The program
must be fundamentally changed ... so as to give adequate representation to
the centre position ... This whole incident points to the necessity of reorganizing the CBC and of the government coming out with a strong reconstruction
policy ... This is a subject of paramount importance and we are handing it to
the CCF" (Quoted in Faris, *The Passionate Educators*, 105).
As an MP from Montreal, Claxton had also been actively involved in the
conscription plebiscite campaign.

114 Faris, *The Passionate Educators*.

115 Faris attributes this to the decline of Canadian social movements after the
war and to the fact that unlike the "Farm Forum," the "Citizens' Forum"
did not encourage listener "action projects": "Since political and economic
constraints on both sponsoring organizations [CAAE and CBC] prevented the
development of clearly radical programming or associated action projects, no
possibility of sustaining a social movement existed. Thus, the forum was
viewed not as a goad to group social action but, rather, as a means of personal enlightenment which might or might not lead to personal action"
(Ibid., 110).

116 Ibid., 111.

117 At time of writing, the CBC had French and English advisory councils in
three areas: agricultural, religious, and scientific programming.

118 HOC, Special Committee on Radio Broadcasting, *Minutes* (1943), 124–5.

119 Ibid., 125.

120 Ibid., 199.

121 Ibid., 259.

122 HOC, *Debates* (1944), 865.

123 HOC, Special Committee on Radio Broadcasting, *Minutes* (1944).

124 Ibid., 263.

125 Ibid., 412–13.

126 Ibid., 537.

127 Ibid.

128 Ibid., 556.

129 Quebec, Statutes, Loi autorisant la création d'un service de radiodiffusion
provinciale.

130 "Le débat sur le bill de la radio provinciale est engagé," *Le Devoir*, 14
March 1945.

131 Ibid.
132 Quebec, Statutes, Loi autorisant la création d'un service de radiodiffusion provinciale, s. 5.
133 HOC, *Debates* (1946), 1167.
134 See Atkey, "The Provincial Interest in Broadcasting Under the Canadian Constitution"; and Zolf, "Educational Broadcasting."
135 HOC, Special Committee on Radio Broadcasting, *Minutes* (1946), 17.
136 Ibid., 685.
137 See Canada, Royal Commission on Broadcasting, *Report*, appendix 2.
138 See Legris, *Progagande de guerre et nationalismes dans le radio-feuilleton (1939–1955)*.
139 HOC, Special Committee on Radio Broadcasting, *Minutes* (1946), 272.
140 "In the Canadian scene, a community consists of a centre with its surrounding satellite communities and its adjacent rural territory" (Ibid.).
141 See Rickwood, "Canadian Broadcasting Policy and the Private Broadcasters."
142 HOC, Special Committee on Radio Broadcasting, *Minutes* (1946), 578.
143 Ibid., 581.
144 Ibid., 736.
145 By 1946, the problems inherent in the organization and control of Canadian broadcasting were sufficiently pronounced to make the CBC the subject of a case study on the relationship between administration and politics by political scientist J.E. Hodgetts, who wrote: "Even though civil servants may take the lead in fostering a program in the public interest ... there is the possibility that they will come to retain a vested interest in their own definitions of the public welfare which may be difficult to shake when conditions change" (Hodgetts, "Administration and Politics," 462–3).
146 HOC, Special Committee on Radio Broadcasting, *Minutes* (1946), 846.
147 HOC, *Debates* (1946), 5288, 5296.
148 HOC, Special Committee on Radio Broadcasting, *Minutes* (1947), 132.
149 Ibid., 148.
150 Ibid., 472.
151 Ibid., 624.
152 HOC, *Debates* (1947), 5614.
153 "Statement on Television by the Board of Governors, Canadian Broadcasting Corporation, Montreal, May 17, 1948," in NAC, Briefs and Transcripts of the Public Hearings, Royal Commission on National Development in the Arts, Letters and Sciences, 1949–50.
154 Ibid., 3.
155 "Statement on Television ... Ottawa, November 3, 1948," in NAC, Briefs and Transcripts of the Public Hearings, Royal Commission on National Development in the Arts, Letters and Sciences, 1949–50.
156 Ibid., 1.
157 Ibid., 2.
158 Ibid.

159 "Canadian Broadcasting Corporation – Television," in NAC, Briefs and Transcripts of the Public Hearings, Royal Commission on National Development in the Arts, Letters and Sciences, 1949–50.

160 "Confidential – Television," in NAC, Briefs and Transcripts of the Public Hearings, Royal Commission on National Development in the Arts, Letters and Sciences, 1949–50.

161 Ibid., 1–2.

162 Ibid., 3.

163 Ibid., 6.

164 Ibid., 7.

165 "Television – Statement of Government Policy," HOC, *Debates* (1949, 1st sess.), 2050–2.

166 Ibid., 2050–1.

167 Ibid., 2051.

168 Ibid.

169 Canada, Royal Commission on National Development in the Arts, Letters and Sciences, *Report*, xvii.

CHAPTER THREE

1 Barnouw, *Tube of Plenty*, 99.

2 Ibid., 100.

3 Canada, Royal Commission on National Development in the Arts, Letters and Sciences, *Report*.

4 See Smythe, *Dependency Road*, 176–9.

5 Lower, "The Question of Private TV," 173.

6 Canada, Royal Commission on Broadcasting, *Report*, 44.

7 In NAC, Briefs and Transcripts of the Public Hearings, Royal Commission on National Development in the Arts, Letters and Sciences, 1949–50, RG 33/28.

8 Ibid., 6 September 1949, Transcript, 1.

9 Ibid., 4.

10 Ibid., 5.

11 See ibid., "Summary" of CBC brief:1, microfilm reel 5.

12 Ibid., 15.

13 Ibid., 6 September 1949, Transcript, 49.

14 Ibid., 13 March 1950, Transcript, 4–5.

15 Ibid., 6.

16 Ibid.

17 Ibid., "A Report on Private Radio in Canada," reel 5.

18 Ibid., "Memorandum," 16 August 1949, 4 (filed with CAB brief, reel 5).

19 Ibid., untitled, undated document.

20 Ibid., 8 September 1949, Transcript, 16–17.

21 Ibid., CAB supplementary brief, 12 April 1950, 6, reel 5.

22 Ibid., 33.

23 Ibid., 9 January 1950, Transcript, 3. Emphasis in original.

24 Ibid., "Brief on National Radio":1, reel 7.

25 Ibid., 4.

26 Ibid., reel 1.

27 Ibid., reel 5.

28 Ibid., reel 14. In 1947–48, 23,000 members of this "people's university of the air" had met in 1,351 groups.

29 Ibid., reel 11.

30 Ibid., reel 1.

31 Ibid., reel 7.

32 Ibid., reel 17.

33 Ibid., reel 11. The full mandate of the Elliott-Haynes survey was:
"1. To measure the trend of Canadian public opinion on the general question of socialism vs. private enterprise
2. To chart public thinking in relation to the socialization of specific businesses and industries
3. To measure public regard towards representative Canadian corporations and
4. To furnish a labour-management relations barometer on such questions as public appraisal of the reasons for the increased cost of living, opinion as to the manufacturer's profit, attitude towards labor unions, strikes, picketing, the closed shop, union membership, profit sharing and other such issues"
(NAC, Briefs and Transcripts of the Public Hearings, Royal Commission on National Development in the Arts, Letters and Sciences, "A Continuing Study of Public Attitudes Towards Canadian Business and Industry," RG 33/28, microfilm reel 11).
The results of the survey can be summarized as follows:

[Table 1]

| General question of private vs. government ownership | 1944 | 1949 |
| --- | --- | --- |
| Favour private ownership | 45% | 62% |
| Favour government ownership | 37% | 23% |
| Favour dual system | 10% | 6% |

| Specific question of ownership of radio broadcasting industry | 1944 | 1949 |
| --- | --- | --- |
| Favour private ownership | 48% | 58% |
| Favour government ownership | 31% | 20% |
| Favour dual system | 15% | 16% |

34 Ibid., reel 10.

35 Ibid., reel 11.

36 Ibid., reel 18.

37 Ibid.

38 Ibid., reel 12.

39 Ibid., untitled brief:12, reel 13.

40 Ibid., 13 (trans. M.R.).

41 HOC, *Debates* (1950, 1st sess.).

42 Ibid., 1455.

43 Ibid., 1458.

44 HOC, *Debates* (1951, 1st sess.), 4279, 4918.

45 Canada, Royal Commission on National Development in the Arts, Letters and Sciences, *Report*, 27.

46 Ibid., 28.

47 Ibid., 35–6.

48 Ibid., 34.

49 Ibid., 42.

50 Dallas Smythe has argued that if Canada had been serious about resisting cultural domination, drastic measures would have (and could have) been taken at this point. The Massey commission, according to Smythe, "totally misread the lessons of broadcasting history," and stuck to platitudes while the public service aspects of the Canadian broadcasting system were steadily deteriorating (Smythe, *Dependency Road*, 178).

51 Canada, Royal Commission on National Development in the Arts, Letters and Sciences, *Report*, 276.

52 Ibid., 281.

53 Ibid., 283–4.

54 Ibid., 285.

55 Ibid., 287.

56 Ibid., 294.

57 Ibid., 384–408.

58 Ibid., 399.

59 For an overall critique of the legacy of the Massey commission, see Woodcock, *Strange Bedfellows*. On the broad context of Canada's cultural politics, see Ostry, *The Cultural Connection*, and Mitchell, "Culture as Political Discourse in Canada."

60 HOC, *Debates* (1951, 2d sess.), 868.

61 Ibid., 1204–6, 1844–1913.

62 HOC, Special Committee on Radio Broadcasting, *Minutes* (1951), appendix, 150–227. The CAB was thus claiming that the sum of individual opinions represented by the opinion poll was more pertinent than the opinions of organized groups. This position would be more and more widely taken by conservative social bodies with the spread of opinion research.

63 Ibid., 471.

64 Ibid., 473.

65 Liberal MP Pierre Gauthier, in HOC, Special Committee on Radio Broadcasting, *Minutes* (1951), 17.

66 Ibid., 472. To the minister responsible for broadcasting, J.J. McCann, IS was Canada's contribution to "the free world's position in the current struggle for the minds of men" (HOC *Debates* [1952], 4247).

67 *Relations*, "Le Rapport de la Commission Massey," 169.

68 See, for example, Canada, Royal Commission on National Development in the Arts, Letters and Sciences, *Report*, 297, where the need for greater equality between English and French broadcasting services is recognized.

69 Laurendeau, "Tant de clairvoyance et tant d'aveuglement" (trans. M.R.). Emphasis in original.

70 Ibid. (trans. M.R.)

71 HOC, *Debates* (1952), 4247.

72 Ibid.

73 Rickwood, "Canadian Broadcasting Policy and the Private Broadcasters," 362, 365.

74 HOC, *Debates* (1952–53), 72.

75 Ibid., 74.

76 Ibid., 116–17.

77 Ibid., 409.

78 Ibid., 410. In passing, he described a recent CBC program dealing with extramarital pregnancy as disgraceful and filthy, and asked the minister what he intended to do about it. The government did not propose to take any action, McCann said, as the CBC had full responsibility for all programming matters.

79 Ibid., 1360. Fleming also cited a new Elliott-Haynes survey which showed Toronto television viewers preferred US stations to the CBC by about three to one, and a Gallup poll for November 1952 in which 53 percent supported private stations and 24 percent the CBC.

80 Ibid., 2133.

81 Ibid., 4723.

82 Ibid., 3007–8.

83 Ibid., 3012.

84 Ibid., 3022.

85 Ibid., 3077.

86 Ibid., 3393.

87 HOC, Special Committee on Broadcasting, *Minutes* (1953), 257.

88 HOC, Special Committee on Broadcasting, *Minutes* (1953).

89 Ibid., 216, 220.

90 Ibid., 449.

91 Ibid.

92 HOC, *Debates* (1952–53), 5417.

93 HOC, *Debates* (1953–54), 345–6.

94 Ibid., 4093.

95 Ibid., 5514.

96 Ibid., 5515.

97 See, for example, HOC, *Debates* (1955), 651. In reply to the throne speech, Montreal Liberal MP Guy Rouleau said the CBC should not control private stations: "We would prefer that it be treated on an equal footing, or nearly so, with stations belonging to private enterprise. Such a practice would be more consistent with the democratic principles of liberalism."

98 HOC, *Debates* (1955), 2564.

99 Ibid., 1805.

100 HOC, Special Committee on Broadcasting, *Minutes* (1955), 13.

101 Ibid., 10.

102 The Chamber of Commerce was more directly active in broadcasting during this period through its participation on the CBC's "Citizens' Forum" advisory committee along with other groups, including the Canadian Federation of Agriculture, the Canadian Home and School Federation, the Canadian Congress of Labour, the Canadian Council of Churches, the National Council of Women, the Canadian Manufacturers' Association, the Trades and Labour Congress, the United Nations Association, the Canadian Association of Consumers, the Canadian Institute of International Affairs, the Canadian Citizenship Council, and the Canadian Association for Adult Education. Of these, only the Canadian Manufacturers' Association was sympathetic to the argument for a separate regulatory body.

103 HOC, Special Committee on Broadcasting, *Minutes* (1955), 808.

104 Ibid., 814.

105 Lower, "The Question of Private TV."

106 Ibid., 177.

107 Ibid., 178.

108 Rickwood, "Canadian Broadcasting Policy and the Private Broadcasters," 462.

109 See, for example, Laurence, "Le début des affaires publiques à la télévision québécoise"; and Pelletier, *Les années d'impatience (1950–1960)*.

110 Laurence, "Le début des affaires publiques à la télévision québécoise," 219. In more general terms, Bernard Ostry notes that radio and television "made Quebec more self-consciously French and all other regions correspondingly more self-absorbed." When the CBC launched Canadian television with separate programming in English and French in 1952, "While broadcasting in both languages was inevitable and necessary, the resulting creation of two solitudes in production was not" (Ostry, *The Cultural Connection*, 98).

111 Order in Council (P.C.) 1955–1796, in Canada, Royal Commission on Broadcasting, *Report*, appendix 1.

112 See NAC, Briefs presented to the Royal Commission on Broadcasting and transcripts of the public hearings, 1955–56, RG 33/36.

113 HOC, *Debates* (1956), 2498.

114 Letter dated 29 March 1956:i, in NAC, Briefs presented to the Royal Commission on Broadcasting and transcripts of the public hearings, 1955–56, RG 33/36, Exhibit 1.

115 NAC, Briefs presented to the Royal Commission on Broadcasting and transcripts of the public hearings, 1955–56, RG 33/36, Exhibit 1, 66.

116 Ibid., 16.

117 Ibid., Exhibit 14, 1–3.

118 Ibid., 47.

119 Ibid., 384.

120 Ibid., Exhibit 16.

121 Ibid., Exhibit 313, 2.

122 Ibid., 5.

123 Ibid., Exhibit 316.

124 Ibid., 493.

125 Ibid., 534.

126 Ibid., 694.

127 In addition to the organizations mentioned here, these included educational groups (Association canadienne des éducateurs de langue française, Canadian Association of University Teachers), farm groups (Canadian Federation of Agriculture, Alberta Federation of Agriculture, Manitoba Farmers' Union), cooperative groups (Saskatchewan Wheat Pool, Manitoba Federation of Agriculture and Cooperation), radio and television employees (National Association of Broadcast Employees and Technicians), and a group of Regina housewives.

128 NAC, Briefs presented to the Royal Commission on Broadcasting and transcripts of the public hearings, 1955–56, RG 33/36, Exhibit 306, 4.

129 Ibid., 14.

130 Ibid., Exhibit 213, 3.

131 Ibid., Exhibit 194.

132 Ibid., Exhibit 184. In addition to the party's main presentation, five regional committees of the LPP (for Saskatchewan, Alberta, Manitoba, north-west Ontario, and the Windsor-Essex area), as well as its Quebec-based equivalent, the Parti ouvrier canadien, came before the commission in different parts of the country. In Saskatchewan, the LPP's provincial committee proposed extending forum-style programs to the community level through televising local public meetings and the like.

133 Ibid., Exhibit 37.

134 See also the CBC's document on "National Program Service" cited above, in NAC, Briefs presented to the Royal Commission on Broadcasting and transcripts of the public hearings, 1955–56, RG 33/36, Exhibit 14, 51–3.

135 NAC, Briefs presented to the Royal Commission on Broadcasting and tran-

scripts of the public hearings, 1955–56, RG 33/36, Exhibit 193.

136 Ibid., Transcript, 4478, 4518.

137 Ibid., Exhibit 169. See, for example: "Of all the services set up by the federal government, Radio-Canada has the distinction of being the only one to have constantly taken into account the presence of French Canadians as a distinct collectivity. This institutional recognition of the French fact in Canada was actually imposed on the state radio, which was not at liberty to ignore the ideals, needs, and demands of French Canadians as an organized and homogeneous minority, distinct from the anglophone majority. The so-called bilingual stations of the early days of radio and television were short-lived. The peoples' ethnic and cultural dualism necessitated the organization of French-Canadian networks. It was necessary to take into account the sociological reality and renounce the unitary policy that usually prevails in federal agencies" (Ibid., Exhibit 169, 16–17 [trans. M.R.]).

138 Ibid., Exhibit 80, 1.

139 Ibid., Exhibit 170.

140 Ibid., 2800, 2811.

141 Ibid., 2921, 2928.

142 Rickwood, "Canadian Broadcasting Policy and the Private Broadcasters."

143 O'Brien, "A History of the Canadian Radio League, 1930–36," 376.

144 Reproduced in NAC, Briefs presented to the Royal Commission on Broadcasting and transcripts of the public hearings, 1955–56, RG 33/36, Exhibit 316.

145 At Fowler's insistence, according to Rickwood ("Canadian Broadcasting Policy and the Private Broadcasters").

146 NAC, Briefs presented to the Royal Commission on Broadcasting and transcripts of the public hearings, 1955–56, RG 33/36, Exhibit 249, 1.

147 Ibid.

148 Ibid.

149 Ibid., 2–3.

150 Ibid., 6–7.

151 Ibid., 9.

152 Ibid., Exhibit 314, 3.

153 Ibid., 9.

154 Assessments of the effect of Canadian Radio and Television League intervention vary. According to Rickwood, the league served its purpose, resurrecting the old public interest coalition in order to help the CBC resist the attacks of the private sector (Rickwood, "Canadian Broadcasting Policy and the Private Broadcasters," 471). O'Brien is more severe, concluding that the organization "was unable to influence broadcasting policy in any apparent way" (O'Brien, "A History of the Canadian Radio League, 1930–36," 443).

155 Scott, "La guerre des ondes."

156 Laurendeau, "La télévision et la culture au Canada français" (trans. M.R.).

157 Institut social populaire, *Influence de la presse, du cinéma, de la radio et de la télévision*.

158 ICEA, *Le public canadien et la télévision*.

159 Canada, Royal Commission on Broadcasting, *Report*, 13.

160 Canada, Royal Commission on Radio Broadcasting, *Report*, 6.

161 Canada, Royal Commission on National Development in the Arts, Letters and Sciences, *Report*, 299.

162 Canada, Royal Commission on Broadcasting, *Report*, 85.

163 Ibid., 91.

164 Ibid., 139.

165 Ibid., 144–5.

166 Ibid., 159.

167 Ibid.

168 Ibid., 160.

169 Ibid., 250.

170 Ibid., 242.

171 Ibid., 243.

172 Ibid.

173 HOC, *Debates* (1956), 6625–6.

174 HOC, *Debates* (1957).

175 See, for example, this comment from the CCF's Stanley Knowles: "It seems to us that if we have freedom of discussion on the CBC in this country it is due to belief in that principle by Mr. Dunton and those around him rather than to sufficient belief in that principle on the part of the government" (HOC, *Debates* [1957], 2821).

176 Weir, *The Struggle for National Broadcasting in Canada*, 352; and Rickwood, "Canadian Broadcasting Policy and the Private Broadcasters," 560.

177 O'Brien, "A History of the Canadian Radio League, 1930–36," 378–9; Rickwood, "Canadian Broadcasting Policy and the Private Broadcasters"; and Peers, *The Public Eye*.

178 Quoted in O'Brien, "A History of the Canadian Radio League, 1930–36," 379–80.

179 Peers, *The Public Eye*, 138.

180 Quoted in O'Brien, "A History of the Canadian Radio League, 1930–36," 380, 385.

181 HOC, *Debates* (1958), 6.

182 Ibid., 812.

183 HOC, *Debates* (1958), 4048.

184 Ibid., 4049.

185 Ibid., 4050.

186 Ibid.

187 Ibid., 4051.

188 Ibid., 4054. Pearson later wrote in his memoirs: "My general view was that broadcasting should be treated as education and that there should be the greatest possible public control; that the emphasis should be on the public system and private broadcasting should be very much a subsidiary" (Pearson, *Mike*, vol. 3:189).

189 HOC, *Debates* (1958), 4055.

190 Ibid., 4073.

191 Ibid., 4077.

192 "The Board shall, for the purpose of ensuring the continued existence and efficient operation of a national broadcasting system and the provision of a varied and comprehensive broadcasting service of a high standard that is basically Canadian in content and character, regulate the establishment and operation of networks of broadcasting stations, the activities of public and private broadcasting stations in Canada and the relationship between them and provide for the final determination of all matters and questions in relation thereto" (Canada, Statutes and Bills, Broadcasting Act (1958), s. 10).

193 HOC, *Debates* (1958), 4078.

194 O'Brien, "A History of the Canadian Radio League, 1930–36."

195 Canada, Statutes and Bills, Broadcasting Act (1958).

CHAPTER FOUR

1 Canada, Royal Commission on Bilingualism and Biculturalism, *Report.*

2 Ostry, *The Cultural Connection*, 108.

3 HOC, *Debates* (1956), 7567.

4 HOC, *Debates* (1958), 2228.

5 The details of the strike and the sociopolitical context in which it took place have been written about at length. See, for example, Roy, "La grève des réalisateurs de Radio-Canada"; Roux, "Radio-Canada, 1959"; and Pelletier, *Les années d'impatience (1950–1960).*

6 See, for example, HOC, *Debates* (1959), 9.

7 See Pelletier, *Les années d'impatience (1950–1960).*

8 HOC, *Debates* (1959), 308.

9 Laurendeau, "Ottawa va-t-il laisser Radio-Canada saborder son réseau français?" and "Avons-nous des députés à Ottawa?" (trans. M.R.).

10 See, for example, Desaulniers, "Television and Nationalism."

11 HOC, *Debates* (1959), 442.

12 Ibid., 776.

13 HOC, *Debates* (1958), 916.

14 According to Pelletier, *Les années d'impatience (1950–1960).*

15 Lamarche, "Radio-Canada et sa mission française," 11 (trans. M.R.). According to Pelletier (*Les années d'impatience (1950–1960)*, Lamarche had tried in vain to get Ottawa to deal seriously with the producers to avert a strike.

16 Stewart, "Broadcasting in Canada," 36.

17 HOC, Special Committee on Broadcasting, *Minutes* (1959), 139.

18 It cited as examples antagonisms such as English versus French, gentile versus Jew, native versus foreign-born, employee versus employer, east versus west (Ibid.).

19 Quoted in HOC, *Debates* (1959), 5035. Frank W. Peers later wrote a two-volume history of Canadian broadcasting up to 1968 (Peers, *The Politics of Canadian Broadcasting, 1920–1951*, and *The Public Eye*).

20 Ibid., 5036.

21 Quoted in HOC, *Debates* (1959), 5199.

22 HOC, Special Committee on Broadcasting, *Minutes* (1959), 523.

23 Ibid., 808–9.

24 Rickwood, "Canadian Broadcasting Policy and the Private Broadcasters," 587.

25 HOC, *Debates* (1959), 6300.

26 Ibid., 6301, 6306.

27 Ibid., 6306.

28 Ibid., 6307.

29 HOC, *Debates* (1960), 5196.

30 HOC, Special Committee on Broadcasting, *Minutes* (1960–61), 10.

31 Ibid., 92–3.

32 Ibid., 149–51.

33 Ibid., 300.

34 Ibid., 566–7.

35 Quoted in HOC, Special Committee on Broadcasting, *Minutes* (1960–61), 981–4.

36 See also Jamieson, "A National Broadcasting Policy," and *The Troubled Air*.

37 Canada, Statutes and Bills, Broadcasting Act (1958), s. 29. Emphasis added.

38 Ibid., s. 10. Emphasis added.

39 HOC, *Debates* (1960–61), 8754.

40 Quoted in HOC, *Debates* (1962–63), 1507–8.

41 O'Brien, "A History of the Canadian Radio League, 1930–36," 386–7.

42 Quoted in O'Brien, "A History of the Canadian Radio League, 1930–36," 389–90.

43 Nichols, "Interest Groups and the Canadian Broadcasting System," 82.

44 Nichols relates the following anecdote: "During the 1963 election, when I was a radio producer for the CBC, a Cabinet minister who had come to the studio to be recorded became quite irate in giving me his views on radio commentators. His words were roughly that they had to be shut up. He said that although George Nowlan supported the CBC, none of the other ministers did" (Ibid., 33, n. 43).

45 Canada, Royal Commission on Government Organization, *Report*, vol. 4, c. 19. The study concentrated on three areas: the relationship between the CBC,

the government and Parliament; the relationship between the CBC's board of directors, the government, and CBC management; and the suitability of the CBC's type of management and organization.

46 Ibid., 25.
47 Ibid.
48 Ibid., 27.
49 Ibid., 29.
50 Ibid., 50.
51 Ibid., 32.
52 Spry, "The Decline and Fall of Canadian Broadcasting."
53 Ibid., 213.
54 Ibid., 216.
55 Ibid., 219.
56 Spry, "The Costs of Canadian Broadcasting."
57 Ibid., 512.
58 Spry, "The Canadian Broadcasting Corporation, 1936–61," 14.
59 Ibid., 16.
60 See, for example, Spry, "The Origins of Public Broadcasting in Canada."
61 O'Brien, "A History of the Canadian Radio League, 1930–36," 445–6.
62 Ibid., 446.
63 Thomas, "Audience, Market and Public – An Evaluation of Canadian Broadcasting."
64 Ibid., 22.
65 Ibid., 23.
66 Ibid., 24.
67 Ibid., 25.
68 Ibid.
69 Ibid., 26.
70 Ibid., 43.
71 Ibid., 46.
72 Quoted in Trotter, "Canadian Broadcasting Act IV, Scene '67 or Double Talk and the Single System," 468. According to Rickwood ("Canadian Broadcasting Policy and the Private Broadcasters"), this important modification was the result of a manoeuver in committee by delegate Keith Davey. As Peers (*The Public Eye*) points out, Davey, as a Young Liberal in the 1950s, had been a mover of the resolution asking the Liberal government of the day to introduce a separate regulatory agency.
73 Rickwood, "Canadian Broadcasting Policy and the Private Broadcasters," 654.
74 HOC, *Debates* (1963), 4356.
75 Ibid., 6341.
76 Quoted in HOC, *Debates* (1963), 5277–8.
77 Ibid., 5278.
78 HOC, *Debates* (1964–65), appendix, 1278–9.

79 Canada, Statutes and Bills, Broadcasting Act (1968).

80 See Smythe, *Dependency Road*, 183.

81 Ouimet later told Frank W. Peers that the group's discussions had been "an exercise in futility" (Peers, *The Public Eye*, 275).

82 HOC, *Debates* (1964–65), 1846.

83 Ibid., 5799.

84 HOC, *Debates* (1963), 6341.

85 HOC, *Debates* (1964–65), 9414.

86 Ibid., 9420–55.

87 Ibid., 9533.

88 Ibid., 10080–1.

89 Ibid., 10084.

90 Ibid., 10086.

91 Ibid., 10437.

92 Ibid., 9436.

93 Submissions received by the Advisory Committee on Broadcasting included briefs from the Canadian Federation of Agriculture, Farmers' Union of Alberta, Communist Party of Canada, Canadian Teachers Federation, Canadian Broadcasting League, Institut canadien d'éducation des adultes, Canadian Labour Congress, Canadian Association of University Teachers, several groups representing broadcasting industry workers and private interests, and a number of prominent individuals such as professors A.R.M. Lower and Marshall McLuhan (Canada, Advisory Committee on Broadcasting, *Report*, appendix).

94 Canada, Advisory Committee on Broadcasting, *Report*, 3.

95 Ibid., 5–6. Emphasis in original.

96 Ibid., 8.

97 Ibid., 12. Emphasis in original.

98 Ibid., 65.

99 Ibid., 89.

100 Ibid., 91.

101 Ibid., 96.

102 Ibid., 100.

103 Ibid., 94.

104 Ibid., 123, 125.

105 Ibid., 238.

106 HOC, *Debates* (1966–67), 3977.

107 "Enjoyment index": A measurement developed by CBC research services to add a qualitative dimension to audience ratings. See Payette, "Etude d'un conflit de travail entre cadres à Radio-Canada."

108 HOC, Standing Committee on Broadcasting, Films and Assistance to the Arts, *Minutes* (1966–67), 18.

109 Ibid., 36.

110  Ibid., 66.
111  Ibid., 68.
112  Ibid., 127–8.
113  Ibid., 142.
114  Ibid., 161.
115  Ibid., 186–7.
116  Ibid., 189.
117  Ibid., 497.
118  Ibid., 605.
119  Ibid., 336.
120  Ibid., 611.
121  Ibid., 749.
122  Ibid., 770.
123  Ibid., 789.
124  Ibid., 846–7.
125  Ibid., 888.
126  Ibid., 896–7.
127  Ibid., 898–9.
128  Ibid., 905–6.
129  Ibid., 906.
130  Ibid., 954.
131  Quoted in HOC, Standing Committee on Broadcasting, Films and Assistance to the Arts, *Minutes* (1966–67), 1004–6.
132  Helen Carscallen ("Control in a Broadcasting System") has demonstrated the link between the breakdown in the normal "hierarchical bureaucratic" functioning of the CBC and the conflicting conceptions of the public interest in broadcasting that the breakdown revealed. From its first telecast in October 1964, she wrote, "'Seven Days' caused misgivings at the senior management level concerning the program's interpretation of what content is in the public interest" (11). As long as public interest programs only attracted minority audiences, they were tolerated within the mandate of the CBC; but once they became attractive to a majority audience "the content and package must be stringently standardized and controlled" (13). In March 1966, the CBC's own audience research showed 3.2 million people watching "Seven Days." It was precisely this mass popularity, the nonmarginality of "Seven Days," that provoked management to bring it into line; the value gap separating the program's producers from CBC senior management became threatening just as "Seven Days" began to make public interest programming competitive in marketing terms. According to Carscallen: "It may well be that 'Seven Days' served to articulate and highlight changing values in Canadian society unrecognized by a management which conceived of its function as an ideological bureaucracy, to follow rather than lead public opinion" (18). See also Koch, *Inside Seven Days*.

133 Canada, Secretary of State, *White Paper on Broadcasting*.

134 Ibid., 5.

135 Ibid., 8.

136 Ibid.

137 Ibid., 5.

138 Ibid., 13.

139 Rickwood, "Canadian Broadcasting Policy and the Private Broadcasters," 701.

140 HOC, Standing Committee on Broadcasting, Films and Assistance to the Arts, *Minutes* (1966–67), 1348.

141 Ibid. Some observers had noted this as early as 1962. See, for example, Hull, "The Public Control of Broadcasting."

142 HOC, Standing Committee on Broadcasting, Films and Assistance to the Arts, *Minutes* (1966–67), 1566. The supporting groups were the Association of Radio and Television Employees and General Workers; Association of Canadian Television and Radio Artists; Canadian Brotherhood of Railway, Transport and General Workers; Canadian Co-operative Implements Ltd; Canadian Federation of Agriculture; Canadian Jewish Congress; Canadian Labour Congress; Catholic Women's League of Canada; Consumers' Association of Canada; Co-operative Insurance Services Ltd; Co-operative Union of Canada; Farmers' Union of Alberta; Federated Women's Institutes of Canada; International Alliance of Theatrical Stage Employees and Moving Picture Machine Operators of the United States and Canada; Maritime Co-operative Services; Maritime Federation of Agriculture; Prairie Agencies; Saskatchewan Wheat Pool; United Automobile, Aerospace, and Agricultural Implement Workers of America; Union des Artistes; United Farmers of Alberta Co-operative Ltd.

143 Ibid., 1611.

144 Ibid., 1940.

145 Ibid., 1621.

146 Ibid., 1625–6. With 360,000 subscribers, cable at this time was reaching into some 8 percent of Canadian television homes.

147 Ibid., 1910.

148 Ibid., 2036.

149 Ibid., 2040, 2045, 2057.

150 HOC, Standing Committee on Broadcasting, Films and Assistance to the Arts, *Minutes* (1966–67), appendix, 1–16.

151 HOC, *Debates* (1967–68), 3174.

152 Ibid., 3747.

153 Canada, Statutes and Bills, Broadcasting Act (1968).

154 HOC, *Debates* (1967–68), 3754.

155 Ibid., 3762.

156 Ibid., 3875.

157 HOC, Standing Committee on Broadcasting, Films and Assistance to the Arts, *Minutes* (1967–68), 12.

158 Ibid., 13.

159 Ibid., 19.

160 Ibid., 64.

161 HOC, *Debates* (1967–68), 6017. This is precisely what the Task Force on Broadcasting Policy would conclude in 1986, when it recommended altogether removing the "national unity" mandate from the act. See Canada, Task Force on Broadcasting, *Report*.

162 Ibid., 6018.

163 Ibid.

164 Ibid., 6025.

165 Ibid.

166 Canada, Statutes and Bills, Broadcasting Act, Bill C-163 (1967–68), s. 2 (h).

167 HOC, *Debates* (1967–68), 6177, 6182.

168 Ibid., 6184.

169 Canada, Statutes and Bills, Broadcasting Act (1968), s. 2 (h).

170 Ibid., s. 3 (d).

171 Ibid., s. 2 (c).

172 HOC, Standing Committee on Broadcasting, Films and Assistance to the Arts, *Minutes* (1967–68), 23.

173 Canada, Statutes and Bills, Broadcasting Act (1968). Lester Pearson later wrote: "I was quite pleased about the way it worked out" (Pearson, *Mike*, vol. 3:190).

CHAPTER FIVE

1 Offe, *Contradictions of the Welfare State*, 35.

2 See O'Connor, *The Fiscal Crisis of the State*.

3 See, for example, McRoberts and Posgate, *Quebec*, 8.

4 Canada, Minister of Industry/Privy Council Office, *A Domestic Satellite Communication System for Canada*.

5 Canada, Statutes and Bills, Government Organization Act, ss. 7–12.

6 Quebec, Statutes, Loi du Ministère des communications.

7 This position was outlined by Jean Lesage in a speech to the Victoria, B.C., Canadian Club on 23 September 1965, quoted in Quebec, Ministère des communications, *Le Québec, Maître d'oeuvre de la politique des communications sur son territoire*, 14–15.

8 Johnson, *Egalité ou Indépendance*, 105.

9 "Government of Quebec, Preliminary Statement, Confederation of Tomorrow Conference, Toronto, Nov 27–30 1967," in Ontario, The Confederation of Tomorrow Conference, *Proceedings*, appendix B, 8 (official translation).

10 Ontario, The Confederation of Tomorrow Conference, *Proceedings*, 10–11.

11 Quebec, "Ce que veut le Québec."

12 Ibid., 81.

13 Canada, Constitutional Conference, first meeting, Ottawa, 5–7 February 1968, *Proceedings*, 61.

14 Ibid., 219.

15 Ibid., 229, 239.

16 Quoted in Quebec, Ministère des communications, *Le Québec, Maître d'oeuvre de la politique des communications sur son territoire*, 13.

17 Canada, Statutes and Bills, Broadcasting Act (1968), s. 2 (i).

18 HOC, Standing Committee on Broadcasting, Films and Assistance to the Arts, *Minutes* (1968–69), 170.

19 Quebec, Legislative Assembly, *Journal des débats* (1966–67), 2187 (trans. M.R.).

20 HOC, Standing Committee on Broadcasting, Films and Assistance to the Arts, *Minutes* (1968–69), appendix M, 430.

21 HOC, Standing Committee on Broadcasting, Films and Assistance to the Arts, *Minutes* (1968–69), 175.

22 See, for example, Carnegie Commission on Educational Television, *Public Television*.

23 HOC, Standing Committee on Broadcasting, Films and Assistance to the Arts, *Minutes* (1968–69), 177.

24 Ibid., appendix BB.

25 Speech from the throne, in Quebec, Legislative Assembly, *Journal des débats* (1968), 3.

26 Quebec, Statutes, Loi autorisant la création d'un service de radiodiffusion provinciale.

27 Quebec, Legislative Assembly, *Journal des débats* (1968), 38 (trans. M.R.).

28 HOC, *Debates* (1968–69), 6008.

29 Canada, Unpassed Bills, Canadian Educational Broadcasting Agency Act, Bill C-179 (1968–69); and HOC, *Debates* (1968–69), 6378.

30 Quebec, Statutes, Loi de l'Office de radio-télédiffusion du Quebec, s. 21.

31 Quebec, National Assembly, *Journal des débats* (1969), 639.

32 Ibid., 1722 (trans. M.R.).

33 For example, Claude Ryan wrote in an editorial in *Le Devoir*: "The idea of a new law is excellent. But the project that has been made public unfortunately does not contain the essential guarantees of objectivity and autonomy that one can rightfully expect of Quebec's broadcasting agency" (Ryan, "Veut-on faire de Radio-Québec une créature servile de l'exécutif?" [trans. M.R.]).

34 Quebec, Statutes, Loi de l'Office de radio-télédiffusion du Québec. The new law repealed Quebec's broadcasting legislation of 1929 and replaced the 1945 act to authorize the creation of a provincial broadcasting service that Daniel Johnson had finally implemented in 1968.

35 See Atkey, "The Provincial Interest in Broadcasting Under the Canadian Constitution."
36 Quebec, Legislative Assembly, *Journal des débats* (1968), 974 (trans. M.R.).
37 Ibid., 974–5 (trans. M.R.).
38 Canada, Minister of Industry/Privy Council Office, *A Domestic Satellite Communication System for Canada*.
39 Ibid., 8.
40 Ibid., 32.
41 Ibid., 45–6.
42 Ibid., 46, 50.
43 Ibid., 50.
44 Ibid., 58.
45 HOC, *Debates* (1968–69), 6016.
46 Ibid., 6076.
47 Ibid., 6077.
48 Ibid., 6079.
49 For example: "Without accepting uncritically the dictum that the medium is the message, it is obvious that the former affects the latter and that any message is altered and conditioned by the medium through which it is communicated ... Communications constitutes the most important single element in the technological revolution that has overtaken us and which is carrying us along ... toward a kind of society which we can as yet only dimly perceive ... technology is altering our political system, and specifically ... technology is drawing the ideological content, the traditional ideological content, from our political wars. A machine is non-political, neither Liberal nor Conservative nor New Democrat nor Créditiste. Nor for that matter is it a capitalist machine or a communist machine. No matter who designs it or where it is designed, a machine is a machine" (HOC, *Debates* [1968–69], 6080–1).
50 Canada, Statutes and Bills, Government Organization Act, ss. 7–12.
51 Canada, Statutes and Bills, Telesat Canada Act.
52 HOC, *Debates* (1968–69), 7492.
53 Ibid., 7492, 7497.
54 Ibid., 7505.
55 HOC, Standing Committee on Broadcasting, Films and Assistance to the Arts, *Minutes* (1968–69), 1475.
56 Ibid., 2134.
57 Canada, Statutes and Bills, Telesat Canada Act. The act left it to the Cabinet to determine the actual proportion of shares and directorships to be held by each category, but limited government investment to $30 million, plus $40 million in loans. It restricted foreign ownership to 20 percent of the "public" shares, and placed a ceiling of 2.5 percent ownership for any person or Canadian province.

58 Quebec, National Assembly, *Journal des débats* (1969), 2105–21.

59 Quebec, Statutes, Loi du Ministère des communications.

60 CRTC, "Community Antenna Television."

61 CRTC, "The Improvement and Development of Canadian Broadcasting and the Extension of US Television Coverage in Canada by CATV."

62 Quoted in CRTC, *Cable Television in Canada*, 14.

63 HOC, Standing Committee on Broadcasting, Films and Assistance to the Arts, *Minutes* (1969–70), 17/27.

64 CRTC, *Cable Television in Canada*, 17–20.

65 HOC, Standing Committee on Broadcasting, Films and Assistance to the Arts, *Minutes* (1969–70), 20/50–20/114, 21/79–21/87.

66 For example, its investigation of the City of Montreal's charges that the Company of Young Canadians was a hotbed of foreign-backed subversive activities, which occupied the committee from October–December 1969.

67 See DOC, *Instant World*.

68 See Canada, Special Committee of the Senate on Mass Media, *Report*.

69 HOC, Standing Committee on Broadcasting, Films and Assistance to the Arts, *Minutes* (1968–69), 462–3.

70 LaMarsh, *Memoirs of a Bird in a Gilded Cage*, 271.

71 HOC, *Debates* (1968–69), 4485.

72 HOC, Standing Committee on Broadcasting, Films and Assistance to the Arts, *Minutes* (1968–69), 541.

73 Ibid., 548.

74 Ibid., 550.

75 Ibid., 551.

76 Ibid.

77 HOC, *Debates* (1968–69), 10609.

78 Canada, Special Committee of the Senate on Mass Media, *Report*, 43/12.

79 See Woodsworth, *The 'Alternative' Press in Canada*.

80 Levy, "The Styles and Motives of Alternative Media," 22. According to Levy: "The underground press in Canada ... derived much of its political and cultural meaning from its role in 'the Movement', a heterogeneous ideological opposition to what was perceived as *technocracy* or the 'American' system ... Much of the energies of the Canadian underground were devoted to the issue of nationalism and the overall consequences for Canadians of the multinational corporations ... the Canadian papers tended to articulate the sort of regional preoccupation found in the mainstream Canadian press as well" (Levy, "The Styles and Motives of Alternate Media," 22–3).

81 See Raboy, "Investigative Journalism in Canada."

82 See Raboy, *Movements and Messages*.

83 Canada, Royal Commission on Publications, *Report*.

84 See Raboy, *Movements and Messages*.

85 Canada, Special Committee of the Senate on Mass Media, *Report*, vol. 1:v.

86 See DOC, *Instant World*.

87 See CRTC, *A Resource for the Active Community*; Berrigan, *Access*; McNulty, *Other Voices in Broadcasting*; and Girard, *Les télévisions communautaires au Québec*.

88 Canada, Special Report of the Senate on Mass Media, *Report*, vol. 1:204.

89 CRTC, *The Integration of Cable Television in the Canadian Broadcasting System*.

90 Juneau, "Local Cablecasting," 119.

91 Berrigan, *Access*, 87.

92 Berrigan, *Access*; and Hardin, *Closed Circuits*.

93 See Barbier-Bouvet et al., *Communication et pouvoir*; Salter, "Two Directions on a One Way Street"; and Sénécal, "Médias communautaires."

94 For example, in *Last Post*, "October 1970: The Plot Against Quebec"; "B.R.," "Une information 'totalitaire,' prise à son propre piège"; Siegel, "Canadian Newspaper Coverage of the FLQ Crisis"; Latouche, "Mass Media and Communication in a Canadian Political Crisis"; Robinson, "The Politics of Information and Culture During Canada's October Crisis"; and Raboy, *Movements and Messages*. Except where otherwise indicated, description of the October Crisis is based on Raboy, *Movements and Messages*, 64–71.

95 For example, Pelletier, *La Crise d'octobre*.

96 FPJQ, *Dossier sommaire sur les interventions de l'administration de la police et de la justice dans le travail des journalistes (Dossier Z)*.

97 Quoted in Raboy, *Movements and Messages*, 69.

98 HOC, *Debates* (1970–72), 250.

99 HOC, Standing Committee on Broadcasting, Films and Assistance to the Arts, *Minutes* (1970–71), 6/7.

100 For example, in HOC, Standing Committee on Broadcasting, Films and Assistance to the Arts, *Minutes* (1969–70), 28/98.

101 HOC, Standing Committee on Broadcasting, Films and Assistance to the Arts, *Minutes* (1970–71), 6/18–19.

102 See Raboy, "La tour infernale."

103 CBC, *CBC Information Programming/L'information à Radio-Canada*.

104 FPJQ, *Dossier sommaire sur les interventions de l'administration de la police et de la justice dans le travail des journalistes (Dossier Z)*.

105 Quoted in Agence de press libre du Québec, "Le manifeste pour la liberté de l'information ... censuré."

106 Canada, Statutes and Bills, Broadcasting Act (1968), s. 2.g.iv.

107 Devirieux, *Manifeste pour la liberté de l'information*, 60.

108 This was in fact not far from the official position of the CBC. Nonetheless, when, upon request, Devirieux submitted his manuscript to a CBC vice-president for approval, he was asked (and agreed) to amputate several passages, including reference to the firing of Bourdon and Vincent (Agence de presse libre du Québec, "Le manifeste pour la liberté de l'information ... censuré").

109 FPJQ, *Mémoire sur la liberté de presse au Québec*, 18.

110 Ibid., 21 (trans. M.R.).
111 Quoted in Quebec, National Assembly, *Journal des débats* (1971), B–298, and (1972), 2945.
112 Quebec, Ministère des communications, *Pour une politique québécoise des communications.*
113 Ibid., 5–7 (trans. M.R.).
114 Ibid., appendix 8.
115 Quoted in Quebec, National Assembly, *Journal des débats* (1971), 4374 (trans. M.R.).
116 CRTC, *The Integration of Cable Television in the Canadian Broadcasting System.*
117 Ibid., 5–6.
118 "A community, whether it be the local community, regional community, or the national community, speaks with many voices. Much of the Canadian identity is in fact defined by its diversity: cultural diversity, provincial policies, regional character. Community programming can personify this variety at the community level. It has the time. Cable television can seek out minority audiences. It can serve groups which, because of ethnic affinities or by virtue of economic circumstances, tend to occupy a particular part of the community; and 'communities of interest,' people with similar interests who may be located throughout the total population but who come together as a result of their viewing pattern" (Ibid., 26).
119 Ibid., 30.
120 HOC, Standing Committee on Broadcasting, Films and Assistance to the Arts, *Minutes* (1970–71), appendix A, 8/80, 8/82.
121 Ibid., 8/90.
122 Ibid., appendix D, 13/49.
123 Ibid., 13/22.
124 Ibid.
125 Ibid., appendix E, 14/44–5.
126 See, for example, Pierre Juneau, "Canadian Broadcasting, 1970–1," in which he states that the fundamental transformation brought about by cable technology was a greater threat to private broadcasting operations than to the basic objectives of Canadian broadcasting (Ibid., appendix F, 15/57–69).
127 Ibid., 15/41–2.
128 CRTC, *Canadian Broadcasting – "A Single System."*
129 Ibid., 10–11.
130 Ibid., 16–17.
131 Ibid., 22.
132 Ibid., 38, 41.
133 In March 1971, the parliamentary committee had been given the following breakdown of the elements of federal cultural policy: "(1) to improve the quality of the individual and collective lives of Canadians; (2) to strengthen

the Canadian personality; (3) to promote solidarity among Canadians in order to achieve national unity; (4) to expand and reinforce the Government's language policy; (5) to stimulate the culture of the two main language groups and to encourage contributions reflecting the originality of the other cultures; (6) to give a more democratic dimension to our cultural lives; (7) to give the artist and the researcher the means to enrich Canada's cultural heritage; and (8) to cooperate closely with the provinces and with other countries on all cultural matters" (HOC, Standing Committee on Broadcasting, Films and Assistance to the Arts, *Minutes* [1970–71], 2/7).

134 HOC, Standing Committee on Transport and Communications, *Minutes* (1970–1), 5/6.

135 DOC, *Instant World*.

136 Canada, Statutes and Bills, Canadian Radio-Television and Telecommunications Commission Act.

137 DOC, *Instant World*, 28.

138 Ibid.

139 See HOC, Standing Committee on Broadcasting, Films and Assistance to the Arts, *Minutes* (1970–71), 15/68–9.

140 HOC, *Debates* (1970–72), 7459.

141 Ibid.

142 Quebec, National Assembly, *Journal des débats* (1971), B-5230 (trans. M.R.).

143 Ibid. (trans. M.R.)

144 HOC, *Debates* (1970–72), 10302.

145 "Pour une politique globale des communications au Québec," in Quebec, National Assembly, *Journal des débats* (1972), annexe, B-195–9.

146 Ibid., B-196–7.

147 Ibid., B-198.

148 Quebec, National Assembly, *Journal des débats* (1972), 2949 (trans. M.R.).

149 Quebec, Statutes, Loi modifiant la Loi de la Régie des services publics; Loi modifiant la Loi du Ministère des communications et d'autres dispositions législatives; and Loi modifiant la Loi de l'Office de radio-télédiffusion du Québec (1972).

150 DOC, *Proposals for a Communications Policy for Canada*.

151 Ibid., 3.

152 Ibid., 5.

153 Ibid., 8.

154 Ibid., 13.

155 Ibid., 18.

156 Ibid., 21.

157 Ibid., 23.

158 DOC, *Computer/Communications Policy*. For example, "It is important that computer communications, as they affect both existing services and lead to

the development of new ones, be oriented in such a way as to emphasize the national identity, the achievement of major economic and social aims, both national and regional, and the maximization of Canadian influences and control over the key activities and services" (DOC, *Computer/Communications Policy*, 3).

159 HOC, *Debates* (1973–74), 3909.
160 HOC, Standing Committee on Transport and Communications, *Minutes* (1973), 10/6.
161 Quebec, National Assembly, *Journal des débats* (1973), B-4055.
162 Ibid., B-4059.
163 Ibid., B-4284.
164 Ibid., B-4290, B-4299–300.
165 Ibid., B-4307–8.
166 HOC, *Debates* (1973–74), 7425.
167 Quebec, Ministère des communications, *Le Québec, Maître d'oeuvre de la politique des communications sur son territoire.*
168 Ibid., 20 (trans., M.R.). Emphasis in original.
169 Ontario, Legislative Assembly, *Debates* (1973), 2299.
170 Ibid.
171 Laplante, "Cette douteuse souveraineté culturelle."

CHAPTER SIX

1 HOC, Standing Committee on Broadcasting, Films and Assistance to the Arts, *Minutes* (1972), 4/7.
2 CRTC, *Radio Frequencies are Public Property* ("Decision"), 1.
3 CRTC, *Radio Frequencies are Public Property* ("Report").
4 Ibid., 5.
5 Ibid., 11.
6 Ibid., 70, 72.
7 Ibid., 87.
8 Ibid., 6.
9 Ibid., 25–6.
10 Ibid., 107.
11 Ibid., 36–7.
12 Ibid., 34.
13 Ibid., 43.
14 Ibid., 113.
15 Ibid., 54.
16 Ibid., 75–6.
17 Ibid., 30.
18 Ibid., 86.

19 Ibid., 83.
20 CRTC, *Radio Frequencies are Public Property* ("Decision").
21 Ibid., 7.
22 Ibid., 10.
23 Ibid., 11.
24 Ibid.
25 Ibid., 24. The decision quoted CRTC commissioner Northrop Frye's interpretation of the problem, originally made in *The Bush Garden* (Toronto: House of Anansi, 1971), ii: "When the CBC is instructed by Parliament to do what it can to promote Canadian unity and identity, it is not always realized that unity and identity are quite different things to be promoting and that in Canada they are perhaps more different than they are anywhere else. Identity is local and regional, rooted in the imagination and in works of culture; unity is national in reference, international in perspective, and rooted in a political feeling ... Assimilating identity to unity produces the empty gestures of cultural nationalism; assimilating unity to identity produces the kind of provincial isolation which is now called separatism."
26 Ibid.
27 Ibid., 35.
28 Ibid., 53.
29 Ibid., 54.
30 Ibid., 74.
31 The 1974 CRTC hearings were the focus of a Ph.D thesis on management decision making in CBC English television by R. Bruce McKay (McKay, "The CBC and the Public"). According to McKay: "The balancing process in the CBC was clearly significantly more complex than in any other broadcasting service in North America, if not in the world" (198). The CBC needed to balance the uniquely Canadian dimensions of regional and cultural difference, its own combination of public service and commercial activities, and the imbalance between its commitments and resources. The CRTC, the "structural centerpiece" of Canadian broadcasting, mystified the problem. Its approach to cable was typical in this respect: the CRTC itself was caught up in the North American market system, whose dangers it appeared to denounce.

McKay argued that organizational decision making in CBC English television in 1974 was significantly shaped by the relationship between the CBC and the three structures acting on behalf of "the public at the national level" – the CRTC, Parliament, and the government. The nature of that relationship was illustrated by the fact that the basis for the 1974 public discussion about the future of the public broadcaster was a secret cabinet document. According to McKay, the CRTC had set out the framework for the licence renewal hearings in a set of notes prepared for the Cabinet in 1971. The CRTC had informed the CBC of this, but McKay was denied access to this document in

1975 because "it was the policy of the government not to release, at that time, memoranda to Cabinet dated 1971" (118–19).

The evident dependency of the CBC on the government for annual funding, rather than the commercial imperative cited by the CRTC, was the main cause of CBC defensiveness and conservatism, according to McKay. The Association of Television Producers and Directors had told the 1974 hearings: "The environment in which we work is one of managerial anxiety – a sensitivity to pressure of almost any kind" (254). McKay commented: "The Corporation appeared to be continually under pressure not to disturb vested interests ... The formal structural arrangements did not clearly establish boundaries of jurisdiction and responsibility for the Government, the regulatory agency, and the national broadcasting service; in practice, the policy development and interpretation process was uncoordinated" (255, 262).

In its arguments with the CRTC, the CBC was reflecting the position of the government "which – unlike the CRTC – was paying its bills" (262). The structural arrangement for broadcasting in Canada seemed to give creative control of the system to the CRTC and financial control of the CBC to the government. The problem of "control", McKay noted, had plagued Canadian public broadcasting since its inception. The result of the existing control and support structure was that the CBC ended up publicly defending the policies of the government of the day. The way out was for the CBC to develop a meaningful relationship with its public and thereby establish the basis for independence: "The linkage between the CBC and the public – through Parliament, the Government, and the CRTC – didn't work ... What seems required is a coordinated mechanism for public broadcasting policy development which operates openly in public and clearly in the public interest" (270).

The CBC as a corporate entity had to become more open with the Canadian people. Management and decision making must cease to be invisible; there was a need for something other than "the outward radiation of programming from a central source"; there was a need to decentralize responsibility for control; broadcasters had to yield control over certain parts of their transmitter time; public accountability must be extended to enable groups and individuals with an interest in overall broadcasting policies to take part in broadcasting management in a practical way: "The Broadcasting Act doesn't label the CBC as Canada's 'public' broadcasting service. Perhaps it should, if only as a semantic reminder to national institutions that the most important relationship in public broadcasting in Canada must be between the CBC and the public" (331).

32 Herschel Hardin, who was involved at the time in a popular movement to promote a "public, noncommercial alternative" to new commercial licences in western Canada, later wrote: "The licensing of Global cut another deep wound in the Canadian broadcasting tradition ... [it] opened the structure wide on the commercial side ... Why did the CRTC license Global when ex-

isting CTV commercial operators had so freely abandoned original promises of performance?" (Hardin, *Closed Circuits*, 47, 50.)

33 Babe, *Canadian Television Broadcasting Structure, Performance and Regulation*; and Hardin, *Closed Circuits*.

34 Robert E. Babe writes: "In view of the fact that the CRTC was created precisely for the purpose of changing the behaviour of private broadcasters so that the cultural objectives would be followed, it is indeed ironic that the CRTC has placed so much of its regulatory powers in support of broadcasting as high finance" (Babe, *Canadian Television Broadcasting Structure, Performance and Regulation*, 230).

35 HOC, *Debates* (1974–76), 28.

36 Ibid., 3760.

37 HOC, Standing Committee on Transport and Communications, *Minutes* (1974–76), 3/21.

38 DOC, *Proposals for a Communications Policy for Canada*.

39 HOC, *Debates* (1974–76), 3762.

40 Ibid., 3768.

41 Ibid., 3781.

42 Ibid., 3772.

43 Ibid., 5037.

44 Ibid., 5043.

45 Canada, Statutes and Bills, Canadian Radio-Television and Telecommunications Commission Act.

46 See Conseil de développement des médias communautaires du Québec, "Community Media and the Ideology of Participation"; Barbier-Bouvet et al., *Communication et pouvoir*; and Sénécal, "Médias communautaires."

47 See Girard, "Les télévisions communautaires au Québec."

48 See CRTC, *A Resource for the Active Community*.

49 See CRTC, *FM Radio in Canada*.

50 Quebec, National Assembly, *Journal des débats* (1974), B-2171.

51 Ibid., B-2220.

52 Quoted in Quebec, National Assembly, *Journal des débats* (1974), B-2222.

53 See ICEA, *Radio-Québec pour qui?*, and *Le défi de Radio-Québec*. The ICEA, Quebec's leading adult education organization, wrote: "One thing justifies Radio-Québec's existence: It must be an instrument serving collectivities and controlled by them, so that television can play a true social role. Radio-Québec must do more than bring élite culture into people's homes. it must become a way for local communities to express themselves, a collective promotional instrument for the popular majority" (ICEA, *Radio-Québec pour qui?* [trans., M.R.]).

54 HOC, Standing Committee on Broadcasting, Films and Assistance to the Arts, *Minutes* (1974–76), 18/29.

55  DOC, *Communications – Some Federal Proposals*.

56  Ibid., 3.

57  Ibid., 11.

58  "L'impasse des communications: C'est un dossier clos, dit Jean-Paul L'Allier," *Le Devoir*, 16 July 1975.

59  "Le contentieux des communications: Huit provinces acceptent une trêve," *Le Devoir*, 17 July 1975.

60  "Après l'échec de L'Allier: Trois mythes qui se dégonflent, dit le PQ," *Le Devoir*, 18 July 1975.

61  CRTC, *Policy Announcement on Cable Television*.

62  Ibid., 10.

63  Ibid., 12.

64  CRTC, *Policies Respecting Broadcasting Receiving Undertakings (Cable Television)*.

65  Ibid., 1.

66  Ibid., 2.

67  Ibid., 5.

68  Ibid., 14.

69  Ibid., 10.

70  Quoted in Babe, "Regulation of Private Television Broadcasting by the Canadian Radio-Television Commission," 46.

71  HOC, Standing Committee on Broadcasting, Films and Assistance to the Arts, *Minutes* (1974–76), 52/13.

72  Saskatchewan, *Cable Television in Saskatchewan*, 2.

73  Ibid., 5.

74  See Woodrow et al., *Conflict Over Communications Policy*, 44.

75  Ontario, Royal Commission on Violence in the Communications Industry, *Report*, terms of reference.

76  Ibid., recommendation 3.

77  Ibid.

78  Ibid., recommendation 6.

79  Ibid., recommendation 5.

80  Ibid., recommendation 9.

81  Ibid., recommendation 10.

82  HOC, Standing Committee on Broadcasting, Films and Assistance to the Arts, *Minutes* (1974–76), 51/6.

83  Ibid., 54/12. For an extended view of Boyle's perspective on broadcasting, see Boyle, "Responsibility in Broadcasting."

84  Ibid., 54/36.

85  CBC, *The CBC and Canadianism*, 1.

86  Ibid., 3. Emphasis in original.

87  Ibid., 11.

88  Ibid., 13.

89 HOC, Standing Committee on Broadcasting, Films and Assistance to the Arts, *Minutes* (1974–76), 48/28.

90 Ibid., 49/5.

91 HOC, *Debates* (1976–77), 497.

92 HOC, Standing Committee on Broadcasting, Films and Assistance to the Arts, *Minutes* (1976–77), 2/27, 2/35.

93 HOC, *Debates* (1976–77), 3188.

94 Ibid., 3189.

95 Ibid.

96 Ibid., 3420.

97 Ibid., 3425.

98 Quoted in CRTC, Committee of Inquiry into the National Broadcasting Service, *Report*, v.

99 HOC, *Debates* (1976–77), 3747.

100 See Vincent, "A Radio-Canada, ça fait 10 ans qu'on menace de mettre la clé dans la porte"; and Fournier, "S'ils veulent nous violer, eh bien, crions très fort!"

101 CBC, *Touchstone for the CBC*.

102 Ibid., 2.

103 Ibid., 21.

104 Ibid., 45.

105 Ibid., 52.

106 Ibid., 63.

107 CRTC, Committee of Inquiry into the National Broadcasting Service, *Report*, x.

108 Ibid., 9.

109 Ibid., 11.

110 Ibid., 14.

111 Siegel, *A Content Analysis, the CBC*.

112 Ibid., 42.

113 Osler, *No One is Listening*.

114 Siegel, *A Content Analysis, the CBC*.

115 Ibid., 30.

116 English and French-speaking viewers had a similar evaluation of news coverage: there was enough coverage of national and international events, Ontario and Quebec news, labour disputes and urban problems, Quebec separatism, and Canadian unity; there was not enough coverage of other regions, ethnic minorities, rural problems, and the "other" linguistic groups (Centre de recherches sur l'opinion publique, *An Appraisal by Canadians of Information Broadcasting by the Canadian Broadcasting Corporation*).

117 CRTC, Committee of Inquiry into the National Broadcasting Service, *Report*, 62–3.

118 Ibid., 61–2.

119 McCormack, "Revolution, Communication, and the Sense of History," 201.

120 CBC, *The CBC – A Perspective*, 371.

121 Ibid., 371–2.

122 CBC, *The CBC – A Perspective*.

123 CBC, *Touchstone for the CBC*.

124 CBC, *The CBC – A Perspective*, 1, 3.

125 Ibid., 62. Emphasis in original.

126 Ibid. Emphasis in original.

127 Ibid., 377–424.

128 Ibid., 416–17.

129 CBC, *CBC Information Programming/L'information à Radio-Canada*, 18.

130 CRTC, *Decision: Renewal of the CBC's Television and Radio Network Licences*.

131 Ibid., 3.

132 Ibid., 13. Emphasis in original.

133 Ibid., 14.

134 Canada, Unpassed Bills, Telecommunications Act, Bill C-43 (1976–77).

135 Ibid., s. 3.a.

136 Quebec, Ministère des communications, *Le Québec, Maître d'oeuvre de la politique des communications sur son territoire*.

137 Quebec, National Assembly, *Journal des débats* (1977), B-1744.

138 Ibid.

139 Ibid., B-2095.

140 Canada, Supreme Court, *Supreme Court Reports* (1978), vol. 2:191–210.

141 See Rémillard, *Le fédéralisme canadien*.

142 Quebec, Ministère d'Etat au Développement culturel, *La politique québécoise du développement culturel*, 225–42.

143 Ibid., 235.

144 See Syndicat général des employés de Radio-Québec (SGERQ), *Radio-Québec* in Quebec, National Assembly, *Journal des débats* (1978), 2892–900.

145 Quebec, Statutes, Loi modifiant la Loi de l'Office de radio-télédiffusion du Québec (1979).

146 Quebec, Statutes, Loi sur la programmation éducative.

147 Canada, Unpassed Bills, Telecommunications Act, Bill C-24 (1977–78).

148 HOC, Standing Committee on Broadcasting, Films and Assistance to the Arts, *Minutes* (1977–78), 16/6.

149 Canada, Unpassed Bills, Telecommunications Act, Bill C-16 (1978–79).

150 DOC, Consultative Committee on the Implications of Telecommunications for Canadian Sovereignty, *Telecommunications and Canada*.

151 Ibid., 76.

152 One critic, Herschel Hardin, later wrote of him: "MacDonald was known for his strong social conscience and for his impassioned support of cultural development. He was a man who had the courage of his convictions, and was

a cultural nationalist. He was also jocosely referred to in industrial circles as a dolphin among a school of sharks" (Hardin, *Closed Circuits*, 300).

153 HOC, Standing Committee on Communications and Culture, *Minutes* (1979), 1/41.

154 Ibid., 1/20.

155 Ibid., appendix 1, 1A/9.

156 Ibid., appendix CC-6, 6A/4.

157 Ibid., 6A/6.

158 Ibid., 6A/7.

159 Ibid., appendix 1, 1A/14–5.

160 CBC, *The Canadian Broadcasting Corporation and the Referendum Debate*, in HOC, Standing Committee on Communications and Culture, *Minutes* (1979), appendix BR-3, 4A/28–43.

161 Ibid., 2, 5 (4A/29, 4A/32).

162 CBC, *Touchstone for the CBC* and *The CBC – A Perspective*.

163 CBC, *The CBC – A Perspective*, 363–75.

164 For example, "The essence of the CBC's role in the referendum debate, it seems to us, is clearly defined by the premise which underlies the very existence of the Canadian community: that it is a community based upon freedom of speech and opinion and expression. And the function of the media in such a society is to facilitate the exercise of this freedom of speech and debate by communicating to the public the information and the ideas which are the ingredients of free discussion and debate. Only if the Parliament of Canada were for some reason to decide that this freedom should be curtailed could it be otherwise" (CBC, *The Canadian Broadcasting Corporation and the Referendum Debate*, 7 [4A/34]).

165 Ibid., 9 (4A/36).

166 HOC, Standing Committee on Communications and Culture, *Minutes* (1979), 4/11.

167 See Attallah, "Axes d'une recherche sur le référendum."

168 See Desaulniers, "Television and Nationalism."

169 Attallah, "Axes d'une recherche sur le référendum."

170 The extent of this "alternative" approach on Ottawa's part has been indicated by Frank Stark: "On May 14, 1980, in the build-up to the Quebec referendum, the federal government had 11 advertisements on the TVA network in Montreal. On the 15th, 16 were shown, by May 16 and 17, the federal government showed 23 advertisements each day. On Sunday May 18 there were 29 – all underlining federal government services and subsidies, ending with the word 'Canada' flashing on the screen. The federal government spent undisclosed millions on this 1980 referendum" (Stark, "Persuasion, Propaganda, and Public Policy," 23–4).

171 Johnson, "The Re-Canadianization of Broadcasting," 10.

172 Ouimet, "The Communications Revolution and Canadian Sovereignty," 149.

CHAPTER SEVEN

1 According to Pierre Juneau, the CBC's audience share in 1988–89 was "about 20 percent" in English and "almost a third" in French (CBC, "Introductory Remarks by Pierre Juneau, President of the CBC," 2).

2 HOC, Standing Committee on Communications and Culture, *Minutes* (1980–83), 1/12.

3 Ibid., 1/22.

4 Ibid.

5 Ibid., 1/28.

6 Ibid., 2/9.

7 CBC, *The Canadian Broadcasting System*, in HOC, Standing Committee on Communications and Culture, *Minutes* (1979), appendix 2, 4A/1–27.

8 HOC, Standing Committee on Communications and Culture, *Minutes* (1980–83), 5/19.

9 CBC, *Culture, Broadcasting and the Canadian Identity*, 22.

10 See Raboy, "La tour infernale."

11 HOC, Standing Committee on Communications and Culture, *Minutes* (1980–83), 15/18.

12 Ibid., 16/16.

13 CRTC, "Decision CRTC 81–353: Canadian Broadcasting Corporation."

14 CBC, *Touchstone for the CBC*.

15 CBC, *The Canadian Broadcasting System*, 19 (4A/19).

16 CRTC, *A Report on Pay-Television*.

17 Ibid., 9.

18 See CRTC, *Policies Respecting Broadcasting Receiving Undertakings (Cable Television)*.

19 Quoted in CRTC, *A Report on Pay-Television*, 10.

20 Quoted in CRTC, *A Report on Pay-Television*, 12.

21 CRTC, *A Report on Pay-Television*, 36.

22 Ibid., 37–8.

23 Ibid., 40.

24 Ibid.

25 Herschel Hardin claims Boyle was forced to resign after his inquiry into the CBC's national news services dismissed Prime Minister Trudeau's allegations of "separatist bias" at Radio-Canada. See Hardin, *Closed Circuits*.

26 Hardin, *Closed Circuits*, 171.

27 Quoted in Hardin, *Closed Circuits*, 171–2.

28 See CRTC, Committee on Extension of Service to Northern and Remote Communities, *The 1980s*, appendix B, 84–5.

29 CRTC, Committee on Extension of Service to Northern and Remote Communities, *The 1980s*.

30 DOC, Consultative Committee on the Implications of Telecommunications for Canadian Sovereignty, *Telecommunications and Canada*.

31 CRTC, Committee on Extension of Service to Northern and Remote Communities, *The 1980s*, 58.

32 Ibid., 59.

33 CRTC, "Decision CRTC 82–240: Pay-Television."

34 Both quoted in Hardin, *Closed Circuits*, 305.

35 Quoted in Hardin, *Closed Circuits*, 310.

36 Hardin, *Closed Circuits*, 311.

37 CBC, *Touchstone for the CBC*.

38 CRTC, "Decision CRTC 81–353: Canadian Broadcasting Corporation." The CRTC feared the service might cost more than the projected $30 million, and would have a negative impact on existing CBC operations; it would have limited reach and inadequate production funds.

39 HOC, Standing Committee on Communications and Culture, *Minutes* (1980–83), 27/10.

40 CRTC, *A Report on Pay-Television*, 36.

41 ACTRA, NABET, the Directors' Guild of Canada, the Syndicat général du cinéma et de la télévision, the Canadian Council of Film Makers, the Canadian Conference of the Arts, the Canadian Labour Congress, the council of Canadian Union of Public Employees broadcasting bargaining units, the Inuit Taparisat of Canada, the Canadian Broadcasting League, and the Regulated Industries Program of the Consumers' Association of Canada.

42 CRTC, Committee on Extension of Service to Northern and Remote Communities, *The 1980s*.

43 CRTC, "Decision CRTC 82–240: Pay-Television."

44 Rabinovitch, "Communication Policy and Planning in Canada," 238.

45 HOC, Standing Committee on Communications and Culture, *Minutes* (1980–83), 3/5.

46 Ibid., 13/13.

47 Ibid., 17/20.

48 Ibid., 17/24.

49 See Tremblay, "La politique québécoise en matière de communication (1966–1986)."

50 Quebec, National Assembly, *Journal des débats* (1981), B-326–7.

51 Ibid., B-329.

52 See, for example, Quebec, Ministère des communications, *Bâtir l'avenir* and *Le Québec et les communications*.

53 For example, this statement by Francis Fox: "The Government of Canada and the Department of Communications consider the Canadian cultural industries critical. They are strategically important in the larger goal of maintaining our nation as a nation" (HOC, Standing Committee on Communications and Culture, *Minutes* [1980–83], 26/6).

54 See, for example, "Tandis que Juneau défend son intégrité: Trudeau promet de ne pas être partisan," *Le Devoir*, 19 October 1982; "Timing of PM's speeches causes five-day tempest for the CBC," *The Globe and Mail*, 20 Oc-

tober 1982; and "CBC newsmen sign petition protesting lack of in-depth coverage of PM's talks," *The Gazette*, 22 October 1982.

55 Canada, Federal Cultural Policy Review Committee, *Report*.

56 HOC, Standing Committee on Communications and Culture, *Minutes* (1980–83), 38/14.

57 Canada, Federal Cultural Policy Review Committee, *Report*, 273.

58 Ibid.

59 Ibid., 275.

60 Ibid., 279.

61 Ibid., 286.

62 Ibid., 285.

63 Ibid., 288.

64 Ibid., 291.

65 Ibid., 292.

66 Ibid., 293.

67 Ibid., 298.

68 Ibid., 306.

69 Ibid., 307.

70 Ibid., 308.

71 Ibid., 310.

72 Ibid., 304.

73 Ibid., 305.

74 Ibid., 12.

75 HOC, Standing Committee on Communications and Culture, *Minutes* (1980–83), 37/5.

76 DOC, *Towards a New National Broadcasting Policy*, 1.

77 Ibid., 2.

78 Ibid., 5.

79 Ibid., 6–7.

80 Ibid., 7.

81 Ibid., 10–11.

82 Ibid., 11.

83 Ibid., 20.

84 HOC, Standing Committee on Communications and Culture, *Minutes* (1980–83), 48/8–9.

85 Ibid., 48/10.

86 Audley later published a book, *Canada's Cultural Industries*, and in 1984 was one of three advisors named by Conservative Communications Minister Marcel Masse to oversee emergency CBC budget cuts. In 1985–86 he was executive director of the federal Task Force on Broadcasting Policy, and in 1987–88 was director of research for the Standing Committee on Communications and Culture. For this insider's view of the policy-making process, see Audley, "The Agenda for Broadcasting Policy."

87 HOC, Standing Committee on Communications and Culture, *Minutes* (1980–83), 50/4.
88 Ibid., 50/13–14.
89 Ibid., 53/13.
90 Ibid., 61/32–3. In their brief, *A New Beginning*, the producers took a highly critical view of the way the CBC had fulfilled its public service mandate and proposed radical changes in programming and production decision making. They argued against the CBC approach of attempting "to beat the Americans at their own game" with big-budget national productions, which, they said, "results in fewer resources available for diverse programming or experimental programming in the context of local needs and individual area interests" (Canadian Television Producers and Directors Association/Association of Television Producers and Directors [Toronto], *A New Beginning*, 44, n. 24). The pooling of funds for network production eroded the capacity of Canadian producers to develop "distinctive, responsive programming" where it was most important, in the regions, the producers said. Coming from the centre of the system, this was a strong indictment.

The producers proposed a programming procedure whereby objectives would be determined in the regions and then made public before being discussed at the national level. Public response could then influence programming decisions, which would be made "in a competitive forum" involving regional producers and management of the different program areas. The setting of clear and publicly known regional and network objectives would provide a framework for considering specific program proposals from in-house or independent producers. Decision making would be "zero-based," that is, every program would need to be proposed and justified annually. While admittedly awkward and difficult, the producers said such a process was "essential to the foundation and maintenance of a responsive television service which meets public needs and aspirations." It would require a fundamental organizational restructuring of the CBC. (Regarding CBC production practices, see Bruck, "Power Format Radio.")
91 CBC, *The Strategy of the CBC*.
92 DOC, *Building for the Future*. The subtitle announced: "New policies and initiatives to assure the strengthened performance and improved accountability of the national broadcasting service as a crucial component of an identifi-, ably Canadian broadcasting system and as an essential instrument of Canadian cultural development."
93 Ibid., 3.
94 Ibid., 4–5.
95 Ibid., 6.
96 Ibid., 7.
97 Ibid., 8.
98 DOC, *Towards a New National Broadcasting Policy*.

99 Canada, Federal Cultural Policy Review Committee, *Report*.

100 DOC, *Building for the Future*, 9.

101 Ibid., 16. In this statement, the CBC mandate is taken from the broadcasting act (Canada, Statutes and Bills, Broadcasting Act (1968), s. 2.g.iv); the interpretation of its meaning is taken from the CRTC's 1974 decision renewing CBC licences (CRTC, *Radio Frequencies are Public Property*); and the reference to high standards is from the CBC's proposed code of conduct enunciated at the time of the 1980 Quebec referendum (CBC, *The Canadian Broadcasting Corporation and the Referendum Debate*).

102 Canada, Statutes and Bills, Canadian Radio-Television and Telecommunications Commission Act.

103 Canada, Statutes and Bills, Broadcasting Act (1968).

104 Canada, Unpassed Bills, Bell Canada Reorganization Act, Bill C-20.

105 Ibid., s. 3.c.1, s. 3.g.1.

106 DOC, *The National Film and Video Policy*.

107 Ibid., 8.

108 See, for example, "Welcome mat is out again for foreign investors," *Toronto Star*, 26 September 1984.

109 "Network gets budget cut of $85 million [sic]," *Toronto Star*, 9 November 1984.

110 For example, Masse, "La radiodiffusion canadienne."

111 Canada, Unpassed Bills, An Act to Amend the CRTC Act, the Broadcasting Act and the Radio Act, Bill C-20.

112 Canada/Quebec, *Canada-Quebec Subsidiary Agreement on Communications Enterprises Development 1984–1990*.

113 See Godin, *Daniel Johnson*, vol. 2.

114 "Marcel Masse: Radio-Canada prend trop de place dans le budget culturel," *Le Devoir*, 20 December 1984 (trans. M.R.).

115 Ibid. (trans. M.R.)

116 Bissonnette, "L'envers du décor" (trans. M.R.).

117 Desbarats, "Tories put the squeeze on the message and the media."

118 See, for example, the two-page advertisement in the Toronto *Globe and Mail*, 13 February 1985, signed by 1,200 "Friends of Public Broadcasting." The *ad hoc* "Friends," whose public voices included such figures as Pierre Berton, A.W. Johnson, and Frank W. Peers, was reminiscent of the old Canadian Radio League coalition and would continue to intervene in the debate of the late 1980s.

119 Canada, Unpassed Bills, Bell Canada Reorganization Act, Bill C-20.

120 Canada, Unpassed Bills, An Act to Amend the CRTC Act, the Broadcasting Act and the Radio Act, Bill C-20.

121 HOC, *Debates* (1984–86), 1845–8.

122 Ibid.

123 Order in Council (P.C.) 1985–1737.
124 See Faille, "Le CRTC et la concentration." Cases noted include Maclean-Hunter/CFCN; *London Free Press*/CFPL; *London Free Press*/CKNX; Southam and Selkirk/broadcasters in Lethbridge, Calgary and Niagara; *The Intelligencer*/Belleville-Trenton cable; *Regina Leader-Post*/Armdale Broadcasting; Irving family/New Brunswick Broadcasting.
125 Quoted in Faille, "Le CRTC et la concentration," 18 (trans. M.R.).
126 CRTC, *Annual Report* (1986–87), 47.
127 DOC, "Review of the Canadian Broadcasting System."
128 "L'opposition au libre-échange s'organise," *Le Devoir*, 15 February 1986.
129 "Masse: Le Canada devra vivifier son économie sans compromettre sa souveraineté culturelle," *Le Devoir*, 25 September 1985.
130 Fulford, "Blaming the Yanks," 7–9.
131 Crean, "Cultural Sovereignty," 25.
132 See CRTC, *Annual Report* (1985–86).
133 Canada/Quebec, *Canada-Quebec Subsidiary Agreement on Communications Enterprises Development 1984–1990.* See also, "Masse et Bertrand signent une entente de $40 millions pour développer l'industrie des communications au Québec," *Le Devoir*, 2 February 1985.
134 Canada/Quebec, *The Future of French-Language Television.*
135 Ibid., 1.
136 Ibid., 2.
137 Ibid.
138 Quebec Liberal Party, *La politique culturelle du Parti libéral du Québec.*
139 "Radio-Québec pourrait devenir la cheville d'un réseau national de télévision éducative en français," *Le Devoir*, 8 January 1986.
140 "Masse d'accord avec un réseau national français," *La Presse*, 10 January 1986; "Communications: Masse et French signent la paix," *Le Devoir*, 14 February 1986.
141 Bissonnette, "L'appareil s'ajuste."
142 Johnson, "Canadian Broadcasting and the National Dream."
143 ICEA, *La radiodiffusion au Canada.*
144 Ibid., v (trans., M.R.).
145 Ibid.
146 Ibid., 29.
147 Ibid., 41.
148 Macfarlane, "Presentation to the Conference on the Future of the Canadian Broadcasting System."
149 Lawrence, "Remarks on Producing, Programming, and Financing Canadian Productions for Television."
150 Canada, Task Force on Broadcasting Policy, *Report.*

151 An example of the task force's thinking in this regard: "The key regulatory issue in Canada is where the balance is to be struck between the business-like decision and the public's right to a return in Canadian programming for the private broadcasters' use of public frequencies and protection from undue competition under the licensing process" (Ibid., 443).

152 For development of this point, see Raboy, "No Canadianization without Democratization."

153 See, for example, Canada, Task Force on Broadcasting Policy, *Report*, 71: "As cable displaces over-the-air, we see the introduction of a new balance of financial support between revenues from taxes, advertising, and users, together with uneven coverage." Sixty-five percent of Canadian households were cabled in 1986.

154 Ibid., 154.

155 Ibid., 38.

156 Ibid., 459–60.

157 Ibid., 104.

158 Ibid., 180.

159 Ibid., 75–6.

160 Ibid., 223.

161 Ibid., 217.

162 Ibid.

163 Ibid., 283.

164 Ibid., 285.

165 Ibid., 148.

166 Ibid., 153.

167 Ibid.

168 Ibid., 152–3.

169 Ibid., 153.

170 Ibid., 491, 492, 506.

171 Ibid., 304.

172 Ibid., 337. See also, ibid., 340: "We believe provincial government broadcasting operations make a significant contribution to the Canadian broadcasting system, both in developing and encouraging regional production and in reflecting Canada's regions, and that contribution may well be more general than simply educational programming, however it is defined."

173 Ibid., 353.

174 Ibid., 520.

175 See, for example, ibid., 265.

176 "Les Télés communautaires en peril," *Le Devoir*, 1 October 1986.

177 Canada, Task Force on Broadcasting Policy, *Report*, 301–4.

178 Ibid., 265.

179 See CRTC, *Cable Television Regulations*; CRTC, *Regulations Respecting Radio Broadcasting*; and CRTC, *Regulations Respecting Television Broadcasting*.

180 See CRTC, *Annual Report* (1986–87), 39.
181 CRTC, *Regulations Respecting Television Broadcasting.*
182 CRTC, *Annual Report* (1986–87), 55.
183 In briefs presented by FRAPPE (Femmes regroupées pour l'accessibilité au pouvoir politique et économique) and MediaWatch, quoted in Beauchamp, *Le Silence des médias*, 181–2, nn. 1–2. See also the report of the task force on sex-role stereotyping in the broadcast media: CRTC, *Images of Women.*
184 CRTC, *Annual Report* (1986–87), 55.
185 Ibid. See also Sanderson and Potvin, *Adjusting the Image.*
186 CRTC, *Annual Report* (1986–87), 40.
187 Ibid., 48.
188 Ibid., 50.
189 Ibid., 51.
190 Ibid., 52–3. See also Public Notice CRTC 1986–199, "Call for Applications for Network Licences to Offer Canadian Specialty Program Services."
191 CRTC, *Annual Report* (1986–87), 44–5. See also CRTC, "Decision 87–140: Current Realities: Future Challenges."
192 CRTC, *Annual Report* (1986–87), 45. See also CRTC, "Decision 87–200: CTV Television Network Limited."
193 CRTC, "Decision CRTC 87–62: Applications for authority to transfer effective control of Télé-Métropole to Le Groupe Vidéotron Ltée." See also Raboy, "Tele-Monopoly Capital," on which the following section is based.
194 See, for example, FPJQ, *Mémoire de la Fédération professionelle des journalistes du Québec aux audiences du CRTC sur l'achat de Télé-Métropole inc.*
195 According to the Bureau of Broadcast Measurement, CFTM had 26 percent of the audience share of the Montreal market in the fall of 1985, as compared, for example, to CFTO's 19 percent in Toronto (quoted in Canada, Task Force on Broadcasting Policy, *Report*, 628).
196 See ICEA, *Vidéotron/Télé-Métropole.*
197 *The Financial Post 500* (Summer 1989): 102.
198 *Info Presse Canada* (July-August 1988): 20.
199 Canada, Task Force on Broadcasting Policy, *Report*, 636.
200 See "Vidéotron veut s'attaquer à la câblodistribution en Angleterre," *Les Affaires*, 30 January 1988; and "Vidéotron investit $3 millions dans une station marocaine," *Le Devoir*, 14 September 1988.
201 Chagnon, "Vidéotron/Télé-Métropole," 33 (trans. M.R.).
202 CRTC, "Le CRTC approuve la transaction Télé-Métropole/Vidéotron," 32–3 (trans. M.R.). The sentence with this phrase does not appear in the English version of the same press release.
203 HOC, Standing Committee on Communications and Culture, *Interim Report on the Recommendations of the Task Force on Broadcasting Policy.*
204 Communications Canada, "Notes for a Statement on Broadcasting Policy by

the Honourable Flora Macdonald, M.P. for Kingston and the Islands, Minister of Communications, to the Standing Committee on Communications and Culture"; and Quebec, Ministère des communications, *Les réactions du MCQ au rapport Sauvageau-Caplan.*

205 Quoted in HOC, Standing Committee on Communications and Culture, *Interim Report on the Recommendations of the Task Force on Broadcasting Policy,* 32.

206 HOC, Standing Committee on Communications and Culture, *Interim Report on the Recommendations of the Task Force on Broadcasting Policy,* 24.

207 Ibid., 32.

208 See CRTC, Public Notice 1983–93: "Call for New Specialty Programming Services," 4. The CRTC defined "specialty services" this way: "By a specialty programming service, the Commission means narrow-cast television programming designed to reflect the particular interests and needs of different age, language, cultural, geographic, or other groups."

209 Canada, Task Force on Broadcasting Policy, *Report,* 476.

210 Ibid., 477–9.

211 DOC, *Vital Links.*

212 Canada, Task Force on Broadcasting Policy, *Report,* 484.

213 HOC, Standing Committee on Communications and Culture, *Interim Report on the Recommendations of the Task Force on Broadcasting Policy.*

214 CRTC, *More Canadian Programming Choices.* The new services created by this decision were the following:

[Table 2]

| Service | Language of Broadcast | Owners | % of share held | Monthly cost to subscriber |
|---|---|---|---|---|
| All-news | E | CBC | 100% | $0.40 |
| The Sports Network | E | John Labatt Ltd | 100% | $0.80 |
| MuchMusic | E | CHUM Ltd | 100% | $0.06 |
| Vision TV | E | Canadian Interfaith Network | 100% | Free |
| YTV | E | CUC Ltd | 25.4% | |
| | | Rogers Broadcasting Ltd | 25.4% | |
| | | Appletree Television Productions | 12.2% | |
| | | Jon Slan Enterprises Ltd | 7.3% | |
| | | Canamedia Productions Inc. | 5.3% | |
| | | Decima Research Ltd | 5.3% | |
| | | Cablecasting Ltd | 5.3% | |
| | | Others | 13.7% | $0.30 |

| | | | | |
|---|---|---|---|---|
| TV5 | F | Consortium comprised of:<br>Radio-Canada<br>Radio-Québec<br>TV Ontario<br>Télé-Métropole<br>Cogéco<br>Quatre-Saisons<br>National Film Board<br>Film Sat | 100% | $0.27 |
| Réseau des sports | F | Télémédia Communications Inc.<br>The Sports Network | 50%<br>50% | $1.00 |
| Musique Plus | F | CHUM Ltd<br>Radiomutuel Ltée | 50%<br>50% | $0.10 |
| Canal Famille | F | First Choice<br>Télévision de l'est du<br>Canada TVEC<br>Cogéco and SODICC<br>Public | 39.9%<br><br>12.3%<br>8.6%<br>35.8% | $0.50 |
| MétéoMedia/<br>MeteoMedia | F/E | Lavalin<br>The Weather Channel (US) | 80%<br>20% | $0.20 |

For a more detailed analysis, see Raboy, "New Television Services and Cultural Identity in Canada."

215 See "TV5 ne peut sortir du Québec," *Le Devoir*, 21 September 1988; "'TV5, c'est excellent, nous allons l'étendre partout,' dit Mulroney," *Le Devoir*, 22 September 1988; "Le CRTC doit intervenir," *Le Devoir*, 24 September 1988; "Must carry new French station, English cable TV firms warned," *The Globe and Mail*, 29 September 1988; and "TV5 gratuit hors Québec," *La Presse*, 30 September 1988.

216 See, for example, Désilets, "Le canal d'information unilingue anglais."

217 DOC "Flora MacDonald Announces Government's Stance on Appeals on CRTC Specialty Services Decisions."

218 See, for example, Comeau, "Les pouvoirs usurpés"; and Trudel, "La liberté d'information est menacée."

219 DOC, "Government Pleased CBC Has Changed Its All-news Plans."

220 Ibid.

221 "Quand Radio-Canada concurrence Radio-Canada," *Le Devoir*, 19 October 1988; Comeau, "Multiplication des pains."

222 McGillivray, "PCS' Manoeuvering on CBC Channel is for the Best"; and Winsor, "Fuss Over CBC's News service Masks a More Important Issue."

223 See Comeau, "Une décision à revoir"; and ICEA, *Les canaux spécialisés en français*.

224 Meisel, "Near Hit," 8. See also, Meisel, "Flora and Fauna on the Rideau."

225 Meisel ("Near Hit") provides an intriguing account of this process.

226 HOC, Standing Committee on Communications and Culture, *A Broadcasting Policy for Canada.*

227 Ibid., 3.

228 Ibid., 4–5.

229 Ibid., 11.

230 Ibid., 14.

231 Ibid.

232 Ibid., 14–15.

233 Ibid., 15.

234 Ibid., 16.

235 Ibid.

236 Ibid., 17.

237 Ibid., 18.

238 Ibid., 22.

239 Ibid., 321.

240 Ibid., 326, 329.

241 Ibid.

242 For a rare statement illuminating the CRTC's position on concentration, see Bureau, "La radiodiffusion et la concentration de la propriété." Here, Bureau justified the CRTC's recent refusal of a takeover bid by the Quebec media conglomerate Cogéco of an FM radio station in Trois-Rivières, where Cogéco already owned two television stations. Concentration was more acceptable and justifiable at the national level, where it posed less of a threat to the diversity of information and offered the positive benefit of forming strong units capable of high quality production and international competition. On the scale of the Cogéco bid in Trois-Rivières, there was the danger of reducing diversity in a local market without offering any advantages (other than the obvious ones to Cogéco). The case confirmed Bureau's conviction that it was neither useful nor realistic to have a national policy regarding concentration, but preferable to study each case for its merits.

243 DOC, *Canadian Voices Canadian Choices.*

244 Canada, Unpassed Bills, Broadcasting Act, Bill C-136, first reading.

245 Meisel, "Near Hit," 21.

246 DOC, *Canadian Voices Canadian Choices*, 6.

247 Ibid., 7.

248 Ibid., 8.

249 Ibid.

250 Ibid., 9.

251 Ibid.

252 Ibid.

253 Ibid., 52.

254 See, for example, Adam, "Ce bill qui inquiète." According to Meisel ("Near Hit"), it was the CRTC's handling of the all-news application that determined

the minister and the DOC to push for a heavy "power of direction" clause in the new legislation.

255 Canada, Unpassed Bills, Broadcasting Act, Bill C-136, first reading, s. 3.1.a.

256 Ibid., s. 3.1.c.iii.

257 Ibid., s. 3.1.n.iv.

258 Ibid., s. 3.1.d.

259 Ibid., s. 3.1.n.i.; DOC, *Canadian Voices Canadian Choices*, 23.

260 Ibid., 24.

261 Canada, Unpassed Bills, Broadcasting Act, Bill C-136, first reading, s. 3.1.p.i.

262 Ibid., s. 3.1.j.ii.

263 DOC, *Canadian Voices Canadian Choices*, 34.

264 Canada, Unpassed Bills, Broadcasting Act, Bill C-136, first reading, s. 3.1.b.

265 See, for example, Désilets, "Les zones d'ombre du projet de loi sur les ondes."

266 Canada, Unpassed Bills, Broadcasting Act, Bill C-136, first reading, s. 3.1.g.ii and iii.

267 Meisel, "Near Hit," n.35.

268 Ibid.

269 Friends of Canadian Broadcasting, *Brief to House of Commons Legislative Committee re: Bill C-136*, 9.

270 Désilets, "Les zones d'ombre du projet de loi sur les ondes."

271 HOC, *Debates* (1988), 17749–51.

272 A singular exception was *Montreal Gazette* columnist William Johnson, who wrote a series of columns opposing the bill while it was being debated in the House. To Johnson, Bill C-136 was an "ideological" law designed to further the "Meeching" of Canada (a reference to the Mulroney government's constitutional position). By reflecting "the view that Quebec is a distinct society," the bill would "break the national coherence of the CBC and prepare the way for a future government to demand control" (Johnson, "'Meeching' of Canada Takes Another Step Forward"). In partially regionalizing the CRTC's activities, the bill "threatens the unity of Canada as a community of communications. It contains within the seeds of fragmentation" (Johnson, "Coherence of Nation-wide Broadcasting is Put at Risk"). In general, by imposing obligations on broadcasters, the bill "violates the Canadian people's freedom of expression" (Johnson, "Freedom of Expression is Under Attack"). Johnson's columns were abundantly quoted by Liberal Senator Royce Frith in his filibuster which marked the death knell of the bill in the Senate a week later.

273 Canada, Unpassed Bills, Broadcasting Act, Bill C-136, third reading, s. 2.

274 Ibid., s. 3.1.c.ii.

275 Ibid., s. 3.1.c.iv.m.

276 Ibid., s. 3.1.k.iv.

277 Sauvageau, "De l'urgence d'une réforme en radiodiffusion."

278 Comeau, "La radio des anges."

279 HOC, *Debates* (1988), 19743.

280 Letter to Senator Royce Frith, cited in Canada, Senate, *Debates* (1988), 4554.

281 HOC, *Debates* (1988), 19741.

282 Cited in HOC, *Debates* (1988), 19742.

283 Ibid., 19743.

284 Canada, Senate, *Debates* (1988), 4529.

285 Canada, Department of External Affairs, Canada-US Free Trade Agreement, *Trade: Securing Canada's Future.*

286 Under the accord, tariffs on audio and video recordings and commercial printed material were lifted; the privileged tax treatment of advertising placed in Canadian magazines (Bill C-58) was repealed – but maintained for radio and television; and Canadian cable distributors were required to pay for re-broadcast rights of signals from American stations. This last point has implications for broadcasting which are as yet impossible to ascertain.

287 Ibid., Article 2005.2.

288 See Nelson, "Losing it in the Lobby"; Crean, "Reading Between the Lies – Culture and the Free Trade Agreement"; Fairbairn, "The Implications of Canada-United States Free Trade for the Canadian Broadcasting Industry"; "Les artistes se mobilisent contre le libre-échange," *Le Devoir*, 26 October 1988; and Patrick, "Global Economy, Global Communications." For an official portrait of the context of Canada's cultural industries in the era of free trade, see DOC, *Vital Links*; and for a critical assessment, see Lacroix and Lévesque, "Industries culturelles canadiennes et libre-échange avec les États-Unis."

## CONCLUSION

1 On this point, see the critique of Nicholas Garnham, "Public Service Versus the Market."

2 See, for example, Keane, *Public Life and Late Capitalism.*

3 See Hardin, *A Nation Unaware.*

4 The classic theoretical work on this question is Jürgen Habermas's *Structural Transformation of the Public Sphere.* For its pertinence to broadcasting, see Garnham, "The Media and the Public Sphere."

5 See, for example, Mattelart, Delcourt, and Mattelart, *International Image Markets*; Robins and Webster, "Broadcasting Politics"; and Salter, "The New Communications Environment" and "Reconceptualizing the Public in Public Broadcasting."

6 See Lacroix and Lévesque, "Les Libéraux et la culture."

7 See Raboy "Two Steps Forward, Three Steps Back."

8 Innis, "Economic Trends in Canadian-American Relations," 238.

9 Hindley et al., *The Tangled Net*, 166. Emphasis in original.

10 See, for example, Smythe, *Dependency Road*; Hardin, *A Nation Unaware*, *Closed Circuits*, "Pushing Public Broadcasting Forward"; Woodcock, *Strange Bedfellows*; and Salter, "Two Directions on a One Way Street," "'Public' and Mass Media in Canada," "The New Communications Environment," "Reconceptualizing the Public in Public Broadcasting."

11 Hindley et al., *The Tangled Net*, 166.

12 See, for example, A.W. Johnson, "The Re-Canadianization of Broadcasting." As shown above, the 1985–86 Task Force on Broadcasting Policy took a nuanced approach to the question, but this was often buried in its own rhetoric and did not easily emerge in the public debate.

13 Hindley et al., *The Tangled Net*, 167–8. Emphasis in original.

14 Mills, *The Power Elite*, 303–4.

15 Salter, "'Public' and Mass Media in Canada," 202. See also, Salter, "The New Communications Environment" and "Reconceptualizing the Public in Public Broadcasting."

16 Enzensberger, "Constituents of a Theory of Media."

17 MacDonald, "Prime Time Democracy."

18 Ibid., 26.

19 See Raboy, "No Canadianization Without Democratization."

20 Burns, *The BBC*.

21 Great Britain, Committee on the Future of Broadcasting, *Report*, 53–4. See also, Annan, "Public Service Broadcasting – The Debate in Britain."

22 Bruck, "Power Format Radio," 90.

23 Ibid., 109.

24 Taylor, "Depoliticizing Current Affairs Television."

25 For example, Tuchman, *Making News*.

26 See, for example, Starowicz, "Slow Dissolve" and "Citizens of Video-America."

27 Williams, "Base and Superstructure in Marxist Cultural Theory."

28 See, for example, Mattelart and Mattelart, *Penser les médias*.

29 See Raboy, "Media and Politics in Socialist France" and "Radical Radio."

30 Murdock, "The 'Privatization' of British Communications," 288.

31 See also, Canada, Task Force on Broadcasting Policy, *Report*, 491–507.

32 Roth, "Inuit Media Projects and Northern Communication Policy," 43.

33 Ibid., 46.

34 CRTC, Committee on Extension of Service to Northern and Remote Communities, *The 1980s*.

35 See also Canada, Task Force on Broadcasting Policy, *Report*, 515–25; European Joint Study on the Role of Communication in the Cultural Development

of Rural Areas, *Native Broadcasting in the North of Canada*; and Roth and Valaskakis, "Aboriginal Broadcasting in Canada.".

36  Hardin, *Closed Circuits*, 53.

37  Ibid., 55.

38  ICEA, *Le public canadien et la télévision*; *La parole, ça se prend*; *Les médias*; *Actes des Etats-généraux populaires sur les communications, 21–22 janvier 1984*; and *Rapport sur le débat national sur le rapport Sauvageau-Caplan*.

39  ICEA, *Une semaine de télévision – Etude comparative*.

40  ICEA, *La radiodiffusion au Canada depuis ses origines jusqu'à nos jours*.

41  ICEA, *L'information à la presse, à la radio et à la télévision* and *La conquête des ondes en information*.

42  ICEA, *Radio-Québec pour qui?* and *Le défi de Radio-Québec*.

43  For an exhaustive bibliography of ICEA documents, see Réseau québécois d'information sur la communication, *L'Institut canadien d'éducation des adultes et les communications, 1956–1987*.

44  ICEA, *La radiodiffusion au Canada*.

45  Richeri, "Television from Service to Business," 29–30. Emphasis in original.

46  Lorimer and McNulty, "The Case for and Structuring of Regional, Local and Educational Community Broadcasting."

47  Spiller and Smiley, "Reflections on the Role and the Future of Broadcasting in the Canadian Society."

48  Ibid., based on Lewis, *Media for People in Cities*.

49  Macfarlane, untitled presentation to the Conference on the Future of the Canadian Broadcasting System.

50  Ouimet, "The Communications Revolution and Canadian Sovereignty," 140.

51  Audley, *Canada's Cultural Industries*, 306–15.

52  Such a system was in fact suggested by the author in a letter to the Task Force on Broadcasting Policy in 1985 (Raboy, "Possible range of publicly-programmed television services").

53  Lyman, *Canada's Video Revolution*, 159. Earlier, Lyman writes: "When Canada had few of the necessary ingredients in investment capital and private-sector entrepreneurship in cultural activities there was more reason to favour the public-enterprise emphasis. Now however, Canada appears to have the resources necessary to make a strategy that puts more emphasis on the private sector work. Cultural industries are highly complex and too much influenced by technological change to operate largely under the aegis of Crown corporations as they have done in the past. Public institutions are not designed to respond rapidly to technological change. As well, public institutions are bound by specific mandates that cannot adequately cope with shifting cultural-industry boundaries" (156).

54  See, for example, Salter, "Reconceptualizing the Public in Public Broadcasting."

55  See Lambert, *Channel Four*.

56 See Australia, Special Broadcasting Service, *Annual Report 1984–85*.
57 See Ortmark, "Sweden."
58 See Wigbold, "Holland."
59 See Falkenberg, "No Future?"
60 See Carnegie Commission on Educational Television, *Public Television*; Carnegie Commission on the Future of Public Broadcasting, *A Public Trust*; and Engelman, "From Ford to Carnegie."
61 UNESCO, International Commission for the Study of Communication Problems, *Many Voices One World*, 167–8. There is a burgeoning literature on the questions raised by this analysis; see, for example, Mosco and Wasko, *The Political Economy of Information*; Raboy and Bruck, *Communication For and Against Democracy*; and Wasko and Mosco, *Democratic Communications in the Information Age*.
62 This notion is much beholden to the work of Armand Mattelart. See, for example, Mattelart, "For a Class and Group Analysis of Popular Communication Struggles" and "Communications in Socialist France."
63 Mattelart, "For a Class and Group Analysis of Popular Communication Struggles," 52.
64 Richeri, "Television from Service to Business," 34.
65 See European Television Task Force, *Europe 2000*.
66 Missika and Wolton, *La Folle du logis*.
67 Garnham, "Public Service Versus the Market," 21.
68 Ibid., 20.
69 Mattelart, "For a Class and Group Analysis of Popular Communication Struggles," 64.
70 Ibid., 65.
71 This theme is explored from various international vantage points in the essays collected in Raboy and Bruck, *Communication For and Against Democracy*.
72 Brecht, "Radio as a Means of Communication," 26.

# Bibliographic Note

The present study provides a new reading of the history of Canadian broadcasting policy but it is indebted to previous scholarship that covered parts of the same terrain.

Frank W. Peers's two volumes are the benchmark by which the historical literature must be read. Peers was the first to review the vast public record produced by several royal commissions, annual parliamentary committees, and public and private interest groups, placing it in a political context. Austin Weir's book, often mentioned in the same breath as Peers's, is far less exhaustive, although the author's long personal involvement with the subject provides additional material and unique insights. Neither of these works goes beyond 1968, however.

In the 1920s and 1930s, writing on broadcasting in Canada was largely confined to people actively involved in the debate, such as Augustin Frigon, Brooke Claxton, and especially Graham Spry. One of the earliest scholarly articles on broadcasting was J.E. Hodgetts's study of the CBC from a management perspective. Historian A.R.M. Lower examined "the question of private television" in 1953. Alan M. Thomas's consideration of "audience, market and public" was a fresh attempt to understand broadcasting ideology that is still highly relevant today.

In Quebec, a number of articles and brief pieces in *L'Action canadienne-française* and *L'Action nationale*, along with two articles by Arthur Laurendeau, are the main evidence of intellectual production on broadcasting prior to about 1950. Florent Forget marked "the coming of television" in a journal article in 1952, and in 1956 the journal *Cité libre* published an entire issue on radio and television. Also in 1956, André Laurendeau published a series of articles on television and French Canada in *Le Devoir*. In 1957, the Institut social populaire published a collection of papers from a conference on the influence of press, radio, cinema, and television. In 1959, the Institut canadien d'éducation des adultes (ICEA) published its first broadcasting-related study.

Scholarly writing on broadcasting has proliferated since the 1960s. Among the existing studies on particular aspects of Canadian broadcasting history of interest here are John O'Brien's thesis on the Canadian Radio League; Margaret Prang's and Kenneth Dewar's articles on the origins of Canadian public broadcasting; Elzéar Lavoie's article on French-Canadian radio prior to 1940; Ron Faris's monograph on the struggle for adult educational radio broadcasting in English Canada; Renée Legris's study of wartime propaganda in the Québécois radio serial; and articles by Gérard Laurence on Radio-Canada television in the 1950s and by Jean-Pierre Desaulniers on the relationship between television and nationalism in Quebec. The historical record is enriched and enlivened by a number of memoirs from active participants. These include books by Hector Charlesworth, E.A. Corbett, André Laurendeau, Charles Bowman, Judy LaMarsh, and Gérard Pelletier.

In the policy area, an early Ph.D thesis by Alexander Toogood studied the entire field, and another by Roger Rickwood examined policy and the private broadcasters. Helen Carscallen and Robert Nichols examined particular policy issues of the 1960s, respectively dealing with the "Seven Days" crisis and with interest group pressure leading up to the policy reform of 1968. Robert Babe published two important studies of the regulatory process, the first dealing with cable and telecommunications and the second with the entire broadcasting structure. A significant contribution to the problem under consideration here was Bruce McKay's Ph.D thesis on "the CBC and the public." For the most recent period, two articles by John Meisel on the process leading up to Bill C-136 are highly pertinent. In Quebec, Gaëtan Tremblay has analysed the evolution of Quebec communication policy from a historical perspective.

Finally, a major contribution has been made by a relatively small group of studies that seek to place broadcasting in a wider critical framework. These include Dallas Smythe's *Dependency Road*, which in fact deals not only with broadcasting but with all of Canadian "consciousness industry"; Herschel Hardin's *A Nation Unaware*, which explores the Canadian "public economic culture", and *Closed Circuits*, examining the CRTC; Liora Salter's articles on community media, "public and mass media," and the need to rethink public broadcasting; and several articles interpreting Canadian communications policy from a Quebec perspective, by Jean-Guy Lacroix and Benoît Lévesque. Still in the field of critical studies, the ICEA in Quebec has published several books and reports based on its own action-research.

The most important documentary source for this study was the public record. Official Canadian government mandates, from the Royal Commission on Radio Broadcasting to the Task Force on Broadcasting Policy, left behind not only their reports but archival collections of briefs and public hearing transcripts. As well, parliamentary debates and committees meeting nearly every year have provided thousands upon thousands of pages of proceedings, often supplemented by appended documents from interveners. Records of the CBC, the BBG, the CRTC, and the Department of Communications provide further evidence. Less voluminous but equally pertinent material is available at the provincial level, in legislative debates, parliamentary commission hearings, and particular studies.

This material provided the research base for the book. The House of Commons *Debates* from 1928–88 were systematically checked for all discussion of broadcasting (and after 1968, communications). The *Minutes of Proceedings and Evidence* of all parliamentary committees dealing with broadcasting from 1932–88, and appended documents, were read through. The journals of the Quebec legislature were consulted for debate on the Quebec broadcasting legislation of 1929, 1931, and 1945, and the *Journaux des débats* which Quebec began to publish in 1964 were systematically reviewed through 1988 for relevant debate in the National Assembly and its commissions.

Official documents, reports, and regulatory decisions of the CBC, the BBG, and the CRTC were examined, along with submissions made to them in the course of regulatory hearings. Numerous circumstantial documents, reports, and research studies done on behalf of these agencies were reviewed, as were similar documents produced in the name of the Department of Communications, Quebec's Ministère des communications, and other federal and provincial agencies.

Special federal bodies set up to investigate broadcasting whose work was reviewed include the Royal Commission on Radio Broadcasting, the Royal Commission on National Development in the Arts, Letters and Sciences, the Royal Commission on Broadcasting, the secretary of state's Advisory Committee on Broadcasting, the Federal Cultural Policy Review Committee, and the Task Force on Broadcasting Policy. In the case of the three royal commissions, briefs and hearing transcripts available in the National Archives of Canada were consulted, along with material in the NAC files on the Department of Marine and Fisheries and the personal papers of Charles Bowman and Brooke Claxton.

In addition, other pertinent reports that were consulted include those of the Royal Commission on Dominion-Provincial Relations, Quebec's Commission royale d'enquête sur les problèmes constitutionnels, the Royal Commission on Publications, the Royal Commission on Government Organization, the Royal Commission on Bilingualism and Biculturalism, the Special Committee of the Senate on Mass Media, Ontario's Royal Commission on Violence in the Communications Industry, the Royal Commission on Corporate Concentration, the Task Force on Canadian Unity, the Royal Commission on Newspapers, the Royal Commission on the Economic Union and Development of Prospects for Canada, and the Task Force on Program Review.

# Bibliography

Adam, Marcel. "Ce bill qui inquiète." Editorial, *La Presse*, 27 August 1988.

Agence de presse libre du Québec (APLQ). "Le manifeste pour la liberté de l'information … censuré." *Bulletin* 32 (22–28 October 1971).

Allard, Thomas J. *Straight Up: Private Broadcasting in Canada, 1918–58*. Ottawa: Canadian Communications Foundation, 1979.

Althusser, Louis. "Ideology and Ideological State Apparatuses (Notes towards an Investigation)" [1969]. In *Lenin and Philosophy and other essays*. New York: Monthly Review Press, 1971.

Annan, The Lord. "Public Service Broadcasting – The Debate in Britain." *Studies of Broadcasting* 25 (March 1989): 144–64.

Atkey, Ronald G. "The Provincial Interest in Broadcasting Under the Canadian Constitution." *Canadian Communications Law Review* 1 (December 1969): 212–74.

Attallah, Paul. "Axes d'une recherche sur le référendum." *Communication Information* 5, nos. 2–3 (Winter-Summer 1983): 65–106.

Audley, Paul. *Canada's Cultural Industries: Broadcasting, Publishing, Records and Film*. Toronto: James Lorimer, 1983.

– "The Agenda for Broadcasting Policy: Reflections on the Caplan-Sauvageau Task Force." In *Communication Canada: Issues in Broadcasting and New Technologies*, edited by Rowland Lorimer and Donald Wilson, 199–213. Toronto: Kagan and Woo, 1988.

Australia. Special Broadcasting Service. *Annual Report, 1984–85*. Sydney: Commonwealth of Australia, 1985.

Babe, Robert E. *Cable Television and Telecommunication in Canada (An Economic Analysis)*. East Lansing, Mich.: Michigan State University Press, 1975.

– "Regulation of Private Television Broadcasting by the Canadian Radio-Television Commission: A Critique of Ends and Means." In *The Crisis in Canadian Broadcasting*, edited by the Canadian Broadcasting League. Ottawa: Canadian Broadcasting League, 1976.

– *Canadian Television Broadcasting Structure, Performance and Regulation*. A study prepared for the Economic Council of Canada. Ottawa: Minister of Supply and Services Canada, 1979.

Barbier-Bouvet, Jean-François, Paul Beaud, and Patrice Flichy. *Communication et pouvoir: Mass médias et médias communautaires au Québec*. Paris: Anthropos, 1979.

Barnouw, Erik. *Tube of Plenty: The Evolution of American Television*. New York: Oxford University Press, 1975.

Beauchamp, Colette. *Le Silence des médias*. Montreal: Editions du remue-ménage, 1987.

Bernays, Edward L. *Public Relations*. Norman, Okla.: University of Oklahoma Press, 1952.

Berrigan, Frances, ed. *Access: Some Western Models of Community Media*. Paris: UNESCO, 1977.

Bissonnette, Lise. "L'envers du décor." Editorial, *Le Devoir*, 23 March 1985.

– "L'appareil s'ajuste." Column, *Le Devoir*, 26 April 1986.

Black, Edwin R. "Canadian Public Policy and the Mass Media." *Canadian Journal of Economics* 1, no. 2 (1968): 368–79.

Bowman, Charles A. *Ottawa Editor*. Sidney, B.C.: Gray's, 1966.

Boyle, Harry J. "Responsibility in Broadcasting." *Canadian Communications Law Review* 2 (December 1970): 191–215.

'B.R.', journaliste. "Une information 'totalitaire', prise à son propre piège." In *Québec-occupé*, edited by Jean-Marc Piotte, 179–216. Montreal: Parti pris, 1971.

Brecht, Bertolt. "Radio as a Means of Communication: A Talk on the Function of Radio," trans. Stuart Hood. *Screen* 20, no. 3/4 (Winter 1979–80): 24–28. (First published as "Radio theorie." In *Schriften zur Literatur und Kunst* [*Gesammelte Werke* 18, Suhrkamp Verlag, 1967.])

Bréniel, Pascal. "Les radios communautaires, coincés entre la communauté et la rentabilité?" *Le 30* 11, no. 2 (February 1987): 16–18.

Briggs, Asa. *The History of Broadcasting in the United Kingdom*. London: Oxford University Press, 1961.

Brooks, Stephen. *Public Policy in Canada: An Introduction*. Toronto: McClelland and Stewart, 1989.

Bruck, Peter A. "Power Format Radio." Ph.D. diss., McGill University, 1984.

Bureau, André. "La radiodiffusion et la concentration de la propriété." *Le Devoir*, 28 September 1988.

Burnham, James. *The Managerial Revolution*. 1941. Reprint. Bloomington, Ind.: Indiana University Press, 1960.

Burns, Tom. *The BBC: Public Institution and Private World*. London: Macmillan, 1977.

Canada. Royal Commission on Radio Broadcasting. *Report*. Commission chairman was Sir John Aird. Ottawa: King's Printer, 1929.

– Royal Commission on Dominion-Provincial Relations. *Report*. Commission chairmen were N.W. Rowell and Joseph Sirois. Ottawa: King's Printer, 1937.

– Royal Commission on National Development in the Arts, Letters and Sciences. *Report*. Commission chairman was Vincent Massey. Ottawa: King's Printer, 1951.
– Royal Commission on Broadcasting. *Report*. Commission chairman was Robert Fowler. Ottawa: Queen's Printer, 1957.
– Royal Commission on Publications. *Report*. Commission chairman was Grattan O'Leary. Ottawa: Queen's Printer, 1961.
– Royal Commission on Government Organization. *Report*. Commission chairman was J. Grant Glassco. Ottawa: Queen's Printer, 1963.
– Advisory Committee on Broadcasting. *Report*. Committee chairman was Robert Fowler. Ottawa: Queen's Printer, 1965.
– Secretary of State. *White Paper on Broadcasting*. Prepared by Judy LaMarsh. Ottawa: Queen's Printer, 1966.
– Constitutional Conference, first meeting, Ottawa, 5–7 February 1968. *Proceedings*. Ottawa: Queen's Printer, 1968.
– Minister of Industry/Privy Council Office. *A Domestic Satellite Communication System for Canada*. Prepared by C.M. Drury. Ottawa: Queen's Printer, 1968.
– Royal Commission on Bilingualism and Biculturalism. *Report*. Commission co-chairmen were André Laurendeau and Davidson Dunton. Ottawa: Queen's Printer, 1969.
– Special Committee of the Senate on Mass Media. *Report*. Committee chairman was Keith Davey. Ottawa: Information Canada, 1970.
– Royal Commission on Corporate Concentration. *Report*. Commission chairman was Robert B. Bryce. Ottawa: Minister of Supply and Services Canada, 1978.
– Task Force on Canadian Unity. *Report*. Task Force co-chairmen were Jean-Luc Pepin and John Robarts. Ottawa: Minister of Supply and Services Canada, 1979.
– Royal Commission on Newspapers. *Report*. Commission chairman was Tom Kent. Ottawa: Minister of Supply and Services Canada, 1981.
– Federal Cultural Policy Review Committee. *Report*. Committee co-chairmen were Louis Applebaum and Jacques Hébert. Ottawa: Minister of Supply and Services Canada, 1982.
– Royal Commission on the Economic Union and Development Prospects for Canada. *Report*. Commission chairman was Donald Macdonald. Ottawa: Minister of Supply and Services Canada, 1985.
– Task Force on Broadcasting Policy. *Report*. Task Force co-chairmen were Gerald Caplan and Florian Sauvageau. Ottawa: Minister of Supply and Services Canada, 1986.
– Task Force on Program Review. *An Introduction to the Process of Program Review*. Task Force chairman was Erik Nielsen. Ottawa: Minister of Supply and Services Canada, 1986.
Canada, Department of Communications (DOC). *Instant World: A Report on Telecommunications in Canada*. Ottawa: Information Canada, 1971.
– *Proposals for a Communications Policy for Canada: A Position Paper of the Government of Canada*. Prepared by Gérard Pelletier. Ottawa: Information Canada, March 1973.

– *Computer/Communications Policy: A Position Statement by the Government of Canada*. Prepared by Gérard Pelletier. Ottawa: Information Canada, April 1973.

– *Communications – Some Federal Proposals*. Prepared by Gérard Pelletier. Ottawa: Information Canada, 1975.

– Consultative Committee on the Implications of Telecommunications for Canadian Sovereignty. *Telecommunications and Canada*. Committee chairman was J.V. Clyne. Ottawa: Minister of Supply and Services Canada, 1979.

– *The Information Revolution and its Implications for Canada*. Prepared by Shirley Serafini and Michel Andrieu. Ottawa: Minister of Supply and Services Canada, 1980.

– *Towards a New National Broadcasting Policy*. Prepared by Francis Fox. Ottawa: Minister of Supply and Services Canada, March 1983.

– *Building for the Future: Towards a Distinctive CBC*. Prepared by Francis Fox. Ottawa: Minister of Supply and Services Canada, October 1983.

– *The National Film and Video Policy*. Prepared by Francis Fox. Ottawa: Minister of Supply and Services Canada, 1984.

– "Review of the Canadian Broadcasting System: Terms of Reference for the Task Force." Ottawa: DOC Information Services, 9 April 1985.

– *Vital Links: Canadian Cultural Industries*. Ottawa: Minister of Supply and Services Canada, 1987.

– *Communications for the Twenty-first Century: Media and Messages in the Information Age*. Ottawa: Minister of Supply and Services Canada, 1987.

– "Notes for a Statement on Broadcasting Policy by The Honourable Flora MacDonald, MP for Kingston and the Islands, Minister of Communications, to the Standing Committee on Communications and Culture." Ottawa: Communications Canada Information Services, 5 February 1987.

– *Canadian Voices Canadian Choices: A New Broadcasting Policy for Canada*. Ottawa: Minister of Supply and Services Canada, 1988.

– "Flora MacDonald Announces Government's Stance on Appeals on CRTC Specialty Services Decisions" [press release]. Ottawa: Communications Canada Information Services, 27 January 1988.

– "Government Pleased CBC Has Changed its All-news Plans" [press release]. Ottawa: Communications Canada Information Services, 17 October 1988.

Canada, Department of External Affairs. The Canada-U.S. Free Trade Agreement, *Trade: Securing Canada's Future*. Ottawa: Minister of Supply and Services Canada, 1988.

Canada, Parliament, House of Commons. *Debates*, 1928 through 1988.

– Special Committee on Radio Broadcasting. *Minutes of Proceedings and Evidence*, 1932, 1939, 1942, 1943, 1944, 1946, 1947, 1950, 1951.

– Special Committee on the Operations of the Commission under the Canadian Radio Broadcasting Act (1932). *Minutes of Proceedings and Evidence*, 1934.

– Special Committee on the Canadian Radio Commission. *Minutes of Proceedings and Evidence*, 1936.
– Standing Committee on Radio Broadcasting. *Minutes of Proceedings and Evidence*, 1938.
– Special Committee on Broadcasting. *Minutes of Proceedings and Evidence*, 1953, 1955, 1959, 1960–61.
– Standing Committee on Broadcasting, Films and Assistance to the Arts. *Minutes of Proceedings and Evidence*, 1966–67, 1967–68, 1968–69, 1969–70, 1970–71, 1972, 1973, 1974, 1974–76, 1976–77, 1977–78, 1978–79.
– Standing Committee on Transport and Communications. *Minutes of Proceedings and Evidence*, 1970–71, 1973, 1974–76.
– Standing Committee on Communications and Culture. *Minutes of Proceedings and Evidence*, 1979, 1980–83, 1984–86, 1986–88.
– Standing Committee on Communications and Culture. *Interim Report on the Recommendations of the Task Force on Broadcasting Policy: Specialty Services and Some Proposed Legislative Amendments*, 16 April 1987.
– Standing Committee on Communications and Culture. *A Broadcasting Policy for Canada (Report)*. Ottawa: Minister of Supply and Services Canada, 1988.
Canada, Parliament, Senate. *Debates*, 1988.
Canada, Statutes and Bills. Wireless Telegraph Act. *Statutes of Canada* 1905, c. 49.
– Radiotelegraph Act. *Statutes of Canada* 1913, c. 43.
– The Canadian Radio Broadcasting Act. *Statutes of Canada* 1932, c. 51.
– The Canadian Broadcasting Act. *Statutes of Canada* 1936, c. 24.
– The Radio Act. *Statutes of Canada* 1938, c. 50.
– Broadcasting Act. *Statutes of Canada* 1958, c. 22.
– Broadcasting Act, Bill C-163, First Reading, 17 October 1967 (27th Parl., 2d sess., 1967–68).
– Broadcasting Act. *Statutes of Canada* 1967–68, c. 25.
– Government Organization Act. *Statutes of Canada* 1968–69, c. 28.
– Telesat Canada Act. *Statutes of Canada* 1968–69, c. 51.
– Canadian Radio-Television and Telecommunications Commission Act. *Statutes of Canada* 1974–76, c. 49.
Canada, Supreme Court. *Supreme Court Reports*. Ottawa: Queen's Printer, 1978.
Canada, Unpassed Bills. Canadian Educational Broadcasting Agency Act, Bill C-179, First Reading, 10 March 1969 (28th Parl., 1st sess., 1968–69).
– Telecommunications Act, Bill C-43, First Reading, 22 March 1977 (30th Parl., 2d sess., 1976–77).
– Telecommunications Act, Bill C-24, First Reading, 26 January 1978 (30th Parl., 3d sess., 1977–78).
– Telecommunications Act, Bill C-16, First Reading, 9 November 1978 (30th Parl., 4th sess., 1978–79).

– Bell Canada Reorganization Act, Bill C-20, First Reading, 8 February 1984 (32d Parl., 2d sess., 1983–84).
– An Act to Amend the CRTC Act, the Broadcasting Act and the Radio Act, Bill C-20, First Reading, 20 December 1984 (33d Parl., 1st sess., 1984–86).
– Broadcasting Act, Bill C-136, First Reading, 23 June 1988 (33rd Parl., 2d sess., 1986–88).
– Broadcasting Act, Bill C-136, Third Reading, 28 September 1988 (33rd Parl., 2d sess., 1986–88).
Canada/Quebec. *The Future of French-Language Television*. Report of the Federal-Provincial Committee. Ottawa and Quebec: Government of Canada/Gouvernement du Québec, 1985.
– *Canada-Quebec Subsidiary Agreement on Communications Enterprises Development 1984–1990*. Ottawa and Quebec: Government of Canada/Gouvernement du Québec, 1985.
Canadian Broadcasting Corporation (CBC). *Submission to the Royal Commission on Bilingualism and Biculturalism*. Ottawa: CBC, 1964.
– *The CBC and Canadianism*. Address by A.W. Johnson to the Canadian Club, Toronto, 12 April 1976. Ottawa: CBC, 1976.
– *Touchstone for the CBC*. Statement by A.W. Johnson, June 1977. Ottawa: CBC, 1977.
– *The CBC – A Perspective*. Submission to the CRTC in support of application for renewal of network licences, May 1978. Includes submission to the Task Force on Canadian Unity, Ottawa, 27 February 1978. Ottawa: CBC, 1979.
– *CBC Information Programming/L'information à Radio-Canada*. Testimony by Knowlton Nash and Marc Thibault to the CRTC hearings on CBC licence renewals, Ottawa, October 1978. Ottawa: CBC Documents, 1979.
– *The Canadian Broadcasting System: The Context of Today – The Challenge of the 80s*. Statement by A.W. Johnson to the House of Commons Standing Committee on Communications and Culture, Ottawa, 22 November 1979. Ottawa: CBC, 1979.
– *The Canadian Broadcasting Corporation and the Referendum Debate*. Statement by A.W. Johnson to the House of Commons Standing Committee on Communications and Culture, Ottawa, 23 November 1979. Ottawa: CBC, 1979.
– *Culture, Broadcasting and the Canadian Identity*. Brief to the Federal Cultural Policy Review Committee, March 1981. Ottawa: CBC, 1981.
– *The Strategy of the CBC*. Broadcasting policy plans submitted in response to the request of the Minister of Communications. Ottawa: CBC, 1983.
– *Let's Do It! A Vision of Canadian Broadcasting*. Proposals to the Task Force on Broadcasting Policy. Ottawa: CBC, 1985.
– *Journalistic Policy/Politique journalistique*. 1982. Revised Edition. Montreal: CBC Enterprises/Les Entreprises Radio-Canada, 1988.
– "Introductory Remarks by Pierre Juneau, President of the CBC." House of Commons Standing Committee on Communications, Culture, Citizenship and Multiculturalism, 24 May 1989.

Canadian Radio-Television Commission (CRTC). "Community Antenna Television." Public announcement, 13 May 1969. In *Cable Television in Canada*, 11–13. Ottawa: Information Canada, 1971.

– "The Improvement and Development of Canadian Broadcasting and the Extension of US Television Coverage in Canada by CATV." Public announcement, 3 December 1969. In *Cable Television in Canada*, 15–17. Ottawa: Information Canada, 1971.

– *Cable Television in Canada*. Ottawa: Information Canada, 1971.

– *The Integration of Cable Television in the Canadian Broadcasting System*. Public announcement: Statement in preparation for public hearings, 26 February 1971. Ottawa: CRTC, 1971.

– *Canadian Broadcasting – "A Single System."* Policy statement on cable television, 16 July 1971. Ottawa: CRTC, 1971.

– *Radio Frequencies are Public Property*. Public announcement and decision on CBC licence renewals, and report on the public hearing, 31 March 1974. Ottawa: CRTC, 1974.

– *A Resource for the Active Community*. Ottawa: Information Canada, 1974.

– *FM Radio in Canada: A Policy to Ensure a Varied and Comprehensive Radio Service*. Ottawa: CRTC, 1975.

– *Policy Announcement on Cable Television*. Public announcement, 17 February 1975. Ottawa: CRTC, 1975.

– *Policies Respecting Broadcasting Receiving Undertakings (Cable Television)*. Public announcement, 16 December 1975. Ottawa: CRTC, 1975.

Canadian Radio-Television and Telecommunications Commission (CRTC). Committee of Inquiry into the National Broadcasting Service. *Report*. Ottawa: CRTC, 1977.

– *A Report on Pay-Television*. Ottawa: CRTC, 1978.

– *Decision: Renewal of the CBC's Television and Radio Network Licences*. CRTC Decision 79–320, 30 April 1979. Ottawa: CRTC, 1979.

– Committee on Extension of Service to Northern and Remote Communities. *The 1980s: A Decade of Diversity (Broadcasting, Satellites and Pay-TV)*. Ottawa: Minister of Supply and Services Canada, 1980.

– "Decision CRTC 81–353: Canadian Broadcasting Corporation" (27 May 1981). In CRTC, *Decisions* 7:72–6. Ottawa: Minister of Supply and Services Canada, 1981–82.

– "Decision CRTC 82–240: Pay-Television" (18 March 1982). In CRTC, *Decisions* 7:630–69. Ottawa: Minister of Supply and Services Canada, 1981–82.

– *Images of Women*. Report of the Task Force on Sex-Role Stereotyping in the Broadcast Media. Ottawa: Minister of Supply and Services Canada, 1982.

– "Call for New Specialty Programming Services." Public Notice CRTC 1983–93, 4 May 1983. Ottawa: CRTC, 1983.

– *Cable Television Regulations*. Public Notice CRTC 1986–182, 1 August 1986. Ottawa: CRTC, 1986.

– "Call for Applications for Network Licences to Offer Canadian Specialty Programming Services." Public Notice CRTC 1986–199, 13 August 1986. Ottawa: CRTC, 1986.

– *Regulations Respecting Radio Broadcasting.* Public Notice CRTC 1986–248, 19 September 1986. Ottawa: CRTC, 1986.

– *Regulations Respecting Television Broadcasting.* Public Notice CRTC 1987–8, 9 January 1987. Ottawa: CRTC, 1987.

– "Decision CRTC 87–62: Applications for authority to transfer effective control of Télé-Métropole to Le Groupe Vidéotron Ltée" (27 January 1987). Ottawa: CRTC, 1987.

– "Le CRTC approuve la transaction Télé-Métropole/Vidéotron" [press release]. Ottawa: CRTC, 27 January 1987.

– "Decision CRTC 87–140: Current Realities: Future Challenges – renewing CBC television network licences" (23 February 1987). Ottawa: CRTC, 1987.

– "Decision CRTC 87–200: CTV Television Network Limited" (24 March 1987). Ottawa: CRTC, 1987.

– *Annual Report,* 1986–87. Ottawa: Minister of Supply and Services Canada, 1987.

– *Annual Report,* 1985–86 and 1986–87. Ottawa: Minister of Supply and Services Canada, 1986 and 1987.

– *More Canadian Programming Choices.* Ottawa: CRTC, 1987.

Canadian Television Producers and Directors Association/Association of Television Producers and Directors (Toronto). *A New Beginning: A Proposal for Transformation of CBC's English Language Television Service.* Toronto: CTPDA/ATPD, 1983.

Carnegie Commission on Educational Television. *Public Television: A Program for Action.* New York: Harper and Row, 1967.

Carnegie Commission on the Future of Public Broadcasting. *A Public Trust.* New York: Bantam Books, 1979.

Carscallen, Helen. "Control in a Broadcasting System." Master's thesis, University of Toronto, 1966.

Centre de recherches sur l'opinion publique (CROP). *An Appraisal by Canadians of Information Broadcasting by the Canadian Broadcasting Corporation.* Background research paper to the *Report of the Committee of Inquiry into the National Broadcasting Service.* Ottawa: CRTC, 1977.

Chagnon, André. "Vidéotron/Télé-Métropole." Notes for oral presentation to the CRTC, 1 December 1986.

Charlesworth, Hector. *I'm Telling You.* Toronto: Macmillan, 1937.

*Cité libre* 15 (August 1956). Theme issue. "Radio et télévision."

Claxton, Brooke. "Legislative Control of Radio in Canada." *Air Law Review* 2, no. 4 (November 1931): 439–54.

– "Broadcasting in Canada." *Air Law Review* 4, no. 1 (January 1933): 17–31.

Comeau, Paul-André. "Des pouvoirs usurpés." Editorial, *Le Devoir,* 30 January 1988.

– "Une décision à revoir." Editorial, *Le Devoir*, 16 April 1988.
– "La radio des anges." Editorial, *Le Devoir*, 20 September 1988.
– "Multiplication des pains: L'utopie d'un canal francophone d'informations continues." Editorial, *Le Devoir*, 24 October 1988.
Conseil de développement des médias communautaires du Québec (CDMC). "Community Media and the Ideology of Participation" [1977]. In *Communication and Class Struggle*. Vol. 2, edited by Armand Mattelart and Seth Siegelaub, 393–401. New York: International General, 1983.
Corbett, E.A. "Planned Broadcasting for Canada." In *Education on the Air*, edited by Josephine H. Maclatchy, 19–29. Fifth yearbook of the Institute for Education by Radio. Columbus, Ohio: Ohio State University Press, 1934.
– *We Have With Us Tonight*. Toronto: Ryerson Press, 1957.
Crean, Susan. "Cultural Sovereignty: Negotiating the Non-Negotiable." *This Magazine*, April 1986, 22–5.
– "Reading Between the Lies – Culture and the Free Trade Agreement." *This Magazine*, May 1988, 29–33.
Dennison, Merrill. "Radio in Canada." *Annals of the American Academy of Political and Social Science* 177 (1935): 49–54.
Desaulniers, Jean-Pierre. *La télévision en vrac (Essai sur le triste spectacle)*. Montreal: Albert Saint-Martin, 1982.
– "Television and Nationalism: From Culture to Communication." In *Television in Transition*, edited by Phillip Drummond and Richard Paterson, 112–22. London: BFI Books, 1986.
Desbarats, Peter. "Tories Put the Squeeze on the Message and the Media." *Financial Post*, 29 December 1984.
Désilets, Esther. "Le canal d'information unilingue anglais: Les francophones s'avoueraient-ils vaincus?" *Le Devoir*, 7 January 1988.
– "Les zones d'ombre du projet de loi sur les ondes." *Le Devoir*, 16 July 1988.
Devirieux, Claude Jean. *Manifeste pour la liberté de l'information*. Montreal: Editions du Jour, 1971.
Dewar, Kenneth C. "The Origins of Public Broadcasting in Canada in Comparative Perspective." *Canadian Journal of Communication* 8, no. 2 (January 1982): 26–45.
Dewey, John. *The Public and its Problems*. New York: Henry Holt, 1927.
Doern, Bruce G., and Richard W. Phidd. *Canadian Public Policy: Ideas, Structures, Process*. Toronto: Methuen, 1983.
*Dominion Law Reports*. Toronto: Canada Law Book Co. Ltd, 1931 and 1932.
*Dossiers de l'audiovisuel*, no. 20 (July-August 1988). Theme issue. "L'esprit des lois ou comment reformer l'audiovisuel."
*Dossiers de l'audiovisuel*, no. 21 (September-October 1988). Theme issue. "L'Europe des télévisions privées."
Ellis, David. *Evolution of the Canadian Broadcasting System: Objectives and Realities, 1928–68*. Ottawa: DOC, 1979.

Engelman, Ralph. "From Ford to Carnegie: The Private Foundation and the Rise of Public Television." In *Studies in Communication*. Vol. 3, edited by Sari Thomas, 233–42. Norwood, N.J.: Ablex, 1987.

Enzensberger, Hans Magnus. "Constituents of a Theory of the Media" [1970]. In *The Consciousness Industry*, 95–128. New York: Seabury Press, 1974.

European Joint Study on The Role of Communication in the Cultural Development of Rural Areas. *Native Broadcasting in the North of Canada: A New and Potent Force*. Ottawa: Canadian Commission for UNESCO, 1988.

European Television Task Force. *Europe 2000: What Kind of Television?* (Report). Manchester, UK: European Institute for the Media, 1988.

Faille, Denise. "Le CRTC et la concentration: Une position de principe claire, des gestes confus." *Le 30* 9, no. 9 (November 1985): 18.

Fairbairn, Barbara. "The Implications of Canada-United States Free Trade for the Canadian Broadcasting Industry: A Survey of the Issues as they Relate Specifically to Television Broadcasting." Ottawa: CBC Research, 1988.

Falkenberg, Hans-Geert. "No Future? A Few Thoughts on Public Broadcasting in the Federal Republic of Germany, Spring 1983." *Media, Culture and Society* 5, nos. 3–4 (July-October 1983): 235–45.

Faris, Ron. *The Passionate Educators: Voluntary Associations and the Struggle for Control of Adult Educational Broadcasting in Canada, 1919–1952*. Toronto: Peter Martin Associates, 1975.

Fédération professionnelle des journalistes du Québec (FPJQ). *Dossier sommaire sur les interventions de l'administration de la police et de la justice dans le travail des journalistes (Dossier Z)*. Montreal: FPJQ, 1971.

– *Mémoire sur la liberté de presse au Québec*. Brief to the National Assembly commission on freedom of the press, February 1972. Montreal: FPJQ, 1972.

– *Mémoire de la Fédération professionnelle des journalistes du Québec aux audiences du CRTC sur l'achat de Télé-Métropole Inc.*. Brief to the CRTC, February 1986. Montreal: FPJQ, 1986.

*Financial Post 500*, Summer 1989.

Fisher, Desmond. *Broadcasting in Ireland*. London: Routledge and Kegan Paul, 1978.

Fletcher, Martha, and Frederick J. Fletcher. "Communications and Confederation: Jurisdiction and Beyond." In *Canada Challenged: The Viability of Confederation*, edited by R.B. Byers and Robert W. Reford, 158–87. Toronto: Canadian Institute of International Affairs, 1979.

Forget, Florent. "L'avènement de la télévision au Canada." *Revue trimestrielle canadienne* 38, no. 149 (Spring 1952): 38–57.

Fournier, Louis. "S'ils veulent nous violer, eh bien, crions très fort!" *Le 30* 1, no. 7 (Summer 1977).

French, Richard D. "The Francophone Summit." *Canadian Journal of Communication*, special issue (December 1987): 47–53.

Friendly, Fred W. *Due to Circumstances Beyond our Control*. New York: Vintage Books, 1967.

Friends of Canadian Broadcasting. *Brief to House of Commons Legislative Committee re: Bill C-136*. Toronto: Friends of Canadian Broadcasting, 1988.

Frigon, Augustin. "The Organization of Radio Broadcasting in Canada." *Revue trimestrielle canadienne* 15, no. 4 (December 1929): 395–410.

Fulford, Robert. "Blaming the Yanks." *Saturday Night*, March 1986, 7–9.

Gagné, Wallace. "Technology and Canadian Politics." In *Nationalism, Technology and the Future of Canada*, edited by Wallace Gagné, 9–51. Toronto: Macmillan, 1976.

Garnham, Nicholas. "Public Service Versus the Market." *Screen* 24, no. 1 (January-February 1983): 6–27.

– "The Media and the Public Sphere." In *Communicating Politics: Mass Communications and the Political Process*, edited by Peter Golding, Graham Murdock, and Philip Schlesinger, 37–53. Leicester, UK: Leicester University Press, 1986.

Girard, Anne. *Les télévisions communautaires au Québec: D'hier à demain*. Quebec: Ministère des communications, 1985.

Godin, Pierre. *Daniel Johnson*. Vol. 2. Montreal: Editions de l'Homme, 1980.

Great Britain. Broadcasting Committee. *Report*. Committee chairman was Sir Frederick Sykes. London: King's Printer, 1923.

– Committee on the Future of Broadcasting. *Report*. Committee chairman was Lord Annan. London: Queen's Printer, 1977.

Great Britain, Secretary of State for the Home Department. *Broadcasting in the '90s: Competition, Choice and Quality. The Government's Plans for Broadcasting Legislation*. London: HMSO, 1988.

Habermas, Jürgen. *Structural Transformation of the Public Sphere: An Inquiry into a Category of Bourgeois Society* (*Strukturwandel der Öffentlichkeit*, 1962, trans. Thomas Burger with the assistance of Frederick Lawrence). Cambridge, Mass.: MIT Press, 1989.

Hardin, Herschel. *A Nation Unaware: The Canadian Economic Culture*. North Vancouver: J.J. Douglas, 1974.

– *Closed Circuits: The Sellout of Canadian Television*. Vancouver: Douglas and McIntyre, 1985.

– "Pushing Public Broadcasting Forward: Advances and Evasions." In *Communication Canada: Issues in Broadcasting and New Technologies*, edited by Rowland Lorimer and Donald Wilson, 214–31. Toronto: Kagan and Woo, 1988.

'H.B.' "A quoi ça sert?" *L'Action nationale* 2, no. 3 (November 1933): 193.

Hindley, Patricia, Gail M. Martin, and Jean McNulty. *The Tangled Net: Basic Issues in Canadian Communications*. Vancouver: Douglas and McIntyre, 1977.

Hodgetts, J.E. "Administration and Politics: The Case of the Canadian Broadcasting Corporation." *Canadian Journal of Economics and Political Science* 12, no. 4 (November 1946): 454–69.

Hull, W.H.N. "The Public Control of Broadcasting: The Canadian and Australian Experiences." *Canadian Journal of Economics and Political Science* 28, no. 1 (February 1962): 114–26.

*Info Presse Canada*, July-August 1988.

Innis, Harold A. "Economic Trends in Canadian-American Relations." Address to the Conference on Educational Problems in Canadian-American Relations, University of Maine, 21–23 June 1938. In *Essays in Canadian Economic History*, 233–41. Toronto: University of Toronto Press, 1956.

Institut canadien d'éducation des adultes (ICEA). *Le public canadien et la télévision – Rapport d'une enquête et journée d'étude*. Montreal: ICEA, 1959.

– *Une semaine de télévision – Étude comparative*. Montreal: ICEA, 1963.

– *La radiodiffusion au Canada depuis ses origines jusqu'à nos jours*. Montreal: ICEA, 1964.

– *L'information à la presse, à la radio et à la télévision: Rapport d'un colloque*. Montreal: ICEA, 1965.

– *Radio-Québec pour qui?* Montreal: ICEA, 1974.

– *Le défi de Radio-Québec: Démocratiser la télévision*. Brief to the public hearings on the orientation of Radio-Québec, October 1975. Montreal: ICEA, 1975.

– *La parole, ça se prend*. Montreal: CEQ/ICEA, 1979.

– *Les médias: Une école insoupçonnée*. Montreal: ICEA, 1980.

– *Actes des Etats-généraux populaires sur les communications, 21–22 janvier 1984*. Montreal: ICEA, 1984.

– *La radiodiffusion au Canada: Un service public*. Brief to the Task Force on Broadcasting Policy. Montreal: ICEA, 1985.

– *Vidéotron/Télé-Métropole: Une super-concentration insoupçonnée*. Brief to the CRTC, 12 November 1986. Montreal: ICEA, 1986.

– *Rapport sur le débat national sur le rapport Sauvageau-Caplan*. Montreal: ICEA, 1987.

– *Les canaux spécialisés en français: Un meilleur choix s'impose*. Montreal: ICEA, 1988.

– *La conquête des ondes en information: Un enjeu important pour les francophones*. Brief to the CRTC regarding CBC application for French-language all-news channel, 7 June 1989. Montreal: ICEA, 1989.

Institut social populaire. *Influence de la presse, du cinéma, de la radio et de la télévision*. Proceedings of the Semaines sociales du Canada, 34th sess., Montreal, 1957. Montreal: ISP, 1957.

Iseppi, Franco. "The Case of RAI." *Media, Culture and Society* 2, no. 4 (October 1980): 339–50.

Jamieson, Don. "A National Broadcasting Policy." *Canadian Communications* 2, no. 2 (1962): 11–18.

– *The Troubled Air*. Fredericton: Brunswick Press, 1966.

Johnson, A.W. "The Re-Canadianization of Broadcasting." *Policy Options* 4, no. 2 (March 1983): 6–12.

– "Canadian Broadcasting and the National Dream." Conference on the Future of the Canadian Broadcasting System, Canadian Conference of the Arts, Ottawa, October 1985.

Johnson, Daniel. *Egalité ou Indépendance*. Ottawa: Editions Renaissance, 1965.

Johnson, William. "'Meeching' of Canada takes another step forward." Column, *Montreal Gazette*, 21 September 1988.

– "Coherence of nation-wide broadcasting is put at risk." Column, *Montreal Gazette*, 22 September 1988.

– "Freedom of expression is under attack." Column, *Montreal Gazette*, 28 September 1988.

Juneau, Pierre. "Local Cablecasting: The Barefoot Media." Address to the Canadian Cable Television Association, 6 July 1972. In *Canadian Communications Law Review* 4 (December 1972): 116–29.

Keane, John. *Public Life and Late Capitalism: Toward a Socialist Theory of Democracy*. Cambridge: Cambridge University Press, 1984.

Kerr, George D. "Skirting the Minefield: Press Censorship, Politics and French Canada, 1940." *Canadian Journal of Communication* 8, no. 2 (January 1982): 46–64.

Kleinsteuber, Hans J., Denis McQuail, and Karen Siune, eds. *Electronic Media and Politics in Western Europe*. Frankfurt and New York: Campous Verlag, 1986.

Kluge, Alexander. "Film and the Public Sphere." *New German Critique* 24–25 (Fall-Winter 1981–82): 206–20.

Koch, Eric. *Inside Seven Days*. Scarborough: Prentice-Hall, 1986.

Kuhn, Raymond, ed. *The Politics of Broadcasting*. New York: St. Martin's Press, 1985.

Lacroix, Jean-Guy and Benoît Lévesque. "L'unification et la fragmentation des appareils idéologiques au Canada et au Québec: le cas de la radio-télévision." *Les Cahiers du socialisme* 5 (Spring 1980): 106–35.

– "Les industries culturelles au Québec: un enjeu vital." *Cahiers de recherche sociologique* 4, no. 2 (Autumn 1986): 129–68.

– "Industries culturelles canadiennes et libre-échange avec les Etats-Unis." In *Un marché, deux sociétés?*, edited by Pierre-J. Hamel, 212–42. Montreal: Cahiers scientifiques (ACFAS) 51, 1987.

– "Les Libéraux et la culture: de l'unité nationale à la marchandisation de la culture (1963–1984)." In *L'ère des Libéraux: Le pouvoir fédéral de 1963 à 1984*, edited by Yves Bélanger, Dorval Brunelle, et al., 405–41. Sillery, P.Q.: Presses de l'Université du Québec, 1988.

*L'Action canadienne-française* 20 (December 1928): 375. "La radiodiffusion."

*L'Action nationale* 14, no. 1 (September 1939): 3. Untitled editorial note.

*L'Action nationale* 14, no. 2 (October 1939): 125. Untitled editorial note.

*L'Action nationale* 17, no. 6 (June 1941): 507. "La litanie de l'unité nationale."

Lamarche, Gérard. "Radio-Canada et sa mission française." *Canadian Communications* 1, no. 1 (Summer 1960): 6–15.

LaMarsh, Judy. *Memoirs of a Bird in a Gilded Cage*. Toronto: McClelland and Stewart, 1969.

Lambert, Stephen. *Channel Four: Television with a Difference?* London: BFI Books, 1982.

Laplante, Laurent. "Cette douteuse souveraineté culturelle." Editorial, *Le Devoir*, 30 November 1973.

*Last Post* 1, no. 5 (no date). "October 1970: The Plot Against Quebec."

Latouche, Daniel. "Mass Media and Communication in a Canadian Political Crisis." In *Communications in Canadian Society*, edited by Benjamin Singer, 374–85. Toronto: Copp Clark, 1975.

Laurence, Gérard. "Le début des affaires publiques à la télévision québécoise." *Revue d'histoire de l'Amérique française* 36, no. 2 (September 1982): 215–39.

Laurendeau, André. "Tant de clairvoyance et tant d'aveuglement." Editorial, *Le Devoir*, 6 July 1951.

– "La télévision et la culture au Canada français." Address to the Humanities Association of Canada, Montreal, 7 June 1956. Published as "Sur la télévision et les canadiens-français" in *Le Devoir*, 13–15 June 1956.

– "Ottawa va-t-il laisser Radio-Canada saborder son réseau français?" Editorial, *Le Devoir*, 22 January 1959.

– "Avons-nous des députés à Ottawa?" Editorial, *Le Devoir*, 23 January 1959.

– *La Crise de la conscription*. Montreal: Editions du Jour, 1962.

Laurendeau, Arthur. "La radio." *L'Action nationale* 4, no. 2 (October 1934): 117–34.

– "La radio (Suite et fin)." *L'Action nationale* 4, no. 3 (November 1934): 211–12.

Laurin-Frenette, Nicole. *Production de l'Etat et formes de la nation*. Montreal: Nouvelle optique, 1978.

Lavoie, Elzéar. "L'évolution de la radio au Canada français avant 1940." *Recherches sociographiques* 12, no. 1 (January 1971): 17–49.

Lawrence, Gene. "Remarks on Producing, Programming, and Financing Canadian Productions for Television; and the Future of Public Television in Canada." Conference on the Future of the Canadian Broadcasting System, Canadian Conference of the Arts, Ottawa, 15–18 October 1985.

Lazarsfeld, Paul. "An Episode in the History of Social Research: A Memoir." In *The Intellectual Migration: Europe and America, 1920–1960*, edited by Donald Fleming and Bernard Bailyn, 270–337. Cambridge, Mass.: Harvard University Press, 1969.

Le Bon, Gustave. *The Crowd* (translation of *Psychologie des foules*, 1895). Harmondsworth, UK: Penguin Books, 1960.

Legris, Renée. *Propagande de guerre et nationalismes dans le radio-feuilleton (1939–1955)*. Montreal: Fides, 1981.

Levy, David. "The Styles and Motives of Alternate Media." Basic Issues in Canadian Mass Communication Series. Montreal: Graduate Program in Communications, McGill University, no date.

Lewis, Peter, ed. *Media for People in Cities*. Paris: UNESCO, 1984.

Lippmann, Walter. *Public Opinion*. 1922. Reprint. New York: Macmillan, 1957.

Lorimer, Rowland, and Jean McNulty. "The Case for and Structuring of Regional, Local and Educational Community Broadcasting." In *Canadian Broadcasting: The Challenge of Change*, edited by Colin Hoskins and Stuart McFadyen, 31–9. Edmonton: University of Alberta, no date.

Lorimer, Rowland, and Donald Wilson, eds. *Communication Canada: Issues in Broadcasting and New Technologies*. Toronto: Kagan and Woo, 1988.

Lower, A.R.M. "The Question of Private TV." *Queen's Quarterly* 60, no. 2 (Summer 1953): 170–80.

Lyman, Peter. *Canada's Video Revolution: Pay-TV, Home Video and Beyond*. Toronto: James Lorimer, 1983.

MacDonald, David. "Prime Time Democracy." *Policy Options* 2, no. 4 (September-October 1981): 25–8.

Macfarlane, John. Untitled presentation to the Conference on the Future of the Canadian Broadcasting System, Canadian Conference of the Arts, Ottawa, 15–18 October 1985.

Mackinnon, William A. *On the Rise, Progress and Present State of Public Opinion in Great Britain and Other Parts of the World*. London: Saunders and Otley, 1828; Reprint. Shannon: Irish University Press, 1971.

Masse, Marcel. "La radiodiffusion canadienne – un nouveau climat de confiance." Notes for a speech to the Fédération professionnelle des journalistes du Québec, Montreal, 10 December 1984. Ottawa: DOC Information Services, 1984.

Mattelart, Armand. "For a Class and Group Analysis of Popular Communication Struggles." Introduction to *Communication and Class Struggle*. Vol. 2, edited by Armand Mattelart and Seth Siegelaub, 17–67. New York: International General, 1983.

– "Communications in Socialist France: The Difficulty of Matching Technology with Democracy." In *Marxism and the Interpretation of Culture*, edited by Cary Nelson and Lawrence Grossberg, 581–606. Urbana and Chicago: University of Illinois Press, 1988.

Mattelart, Armand, Xavier Delcourt, and Michèle Mattelart. *International Image Markets: In Search of an Alternative Perspective* (translation of *La culture contre la démocratie?*). London: Comedia, 1984.

Mattelart, Armand, and Michèle Mattelart. *Penser les médias*. Paris: La Découverte, 1986.

McCormack, Thelma. "Revolution, Communication, and the Sense of History." Appendix to *An Appraisal by Canadians of Information Broadcasting by the Canadian Broadcasting Corporation*, prepared by the Centre de recherches sur l'opinion publique, 199–227. Background research paper to the *Report of the Committee of Inquiry into the National Broadcasting Service*. Ottawa: CRTC, 1977.

McGillivray, Don. "PCS' manoeuvering on CBC channel is for the best." Column, *Montreal Gazette*, 28 January 1988.

McKay, R. Bruce. "The CBC and the Public: Management Decision-making in the English Television Service of the Canadian Broadcasting Corporation, 1970–1974." Ph.D. diss., Stanford University, 1976.

McNulty, Jean. *Other Voices in Broadcasting: The Evolution of New Forms of Local Programming in Canada.* Ottawa: DOC, 1979.

– "Technology and Nation-Building in Canadian Broadcasting." In *Communication Canada: Issues in Broadcasting and New Technologies*, edited by Rowland Lorimer and Donald Wilson, 176–198. Toronto: Kagan and Woo, 1988.

McRoberts, Kenneth, and Dale Posgate. *Quebec: Social Change and Political Crisis.* Toronto: McClelland and Stewart, 1980.

*Media, Culture and Society* 5, nos. 3–4 (July-October 1983). Theme issue. "Public Service Broadcasting – The End?"

*Media, Culture and Society* 11, no. 1 (January 1989). Theme issue. "West European Broadcasting."

*Médiaspouvoirs*, no. 2 (March 1986): 59–123. Dossier. "Moins d'Etat dans la communication?"

Meisel, John. "Flora and Fauna on the Rideau: The Making of Cultural Policy." In *How Ottawa Spends: The Conservatives Heading Into the Stretch*, edited by K.A. Graham, 49–80. Ottawa: Carleton University Press, 1988.

– "Near Hit: The Parturition of a Broadcasting Policy." Typescript, to be published in *How Ottawa Spends: 1989/90*, edited by K.A. Graham. Ottawa: Carleton University Press, forthcoming.

Mills, C. Wright. *The Power Elite.* 1956. Reprint. New York: Oxford University Press, 1959.

Missika, Jean-Louis, and Dominique Wolton. *La Folle du logis: La télévision dans les sociétés démocratiques.* Paris: Gallimard, 1983.

Mitchell, David. "Culture as Political Discourse in Canada." In *Communication Canada: Issues in Broadcasting and New Technologies*, edited by Rowland Lorimer and Donald Wilson, 157–74. Toronto: Kagan and Woo, 1988.

Montigny, Bernard. "Les débuts de la radio à Montréal et le poste CKAC." Master's thesis, Université de Montréal, 1979.

Mosco, Vincent. *The Pay-per Society: Computers and Communication in the Information Age.* Toronto: Garamond Press, 1989.

Mosco, Vincent, and Janet Wasko, eds. *The Political Economy of Information.* Madison, Wis.: University of Wisconsin Press, 1988.

Murdock, Graham. "The 'Privatization' of British Communications." In *The Critical Communications Review.* Vol. 2, edited by Vincent Mosco and Janet Wasko, 265–90. Norwood, N.J.: Ablex, 1984.

National Archives of Canada (NAC). Charles Bowman papers. Manuscripts Section, MG 30, D79. Partially on microfilm, reel no. M-826.

– Brooke Claxton papers. Manuscripts Section, MG 32, B 5, vols. 5, 17, 137.

– Files of the Royal Commission on Radio Broadcasting, 1929. Public Records Section, RG 33/14, vols. 1–5.

– Briefs and Transcripts of the Public Hearings, Royal Commission on National Development in the Arts, Letters and Sciences, 1949–50. Public Records Section, RG 33/28. On microfilm, 24 reels (Toronto: Micromedia, 1972).

– Briefs presented to the Royal Commission on Broadcasting and transcripts of the public hearings, 1955–56. Public Records Section, RG 33/36. On microfilm, 10 reels (Toronto: Micromedia, 1974).

– Files of the Department of Marine and Fisheries. Public Records Section, RG 42, vols. 1076–7.

Negt, Oskar. "Mass Media: Tools of Domination or Instruments of Liberation? Aspects of the Frankfurt School's Communications Analysis." *New German Critique* 14 (Spring 1978): 61–80.

Nelson, Joyce. "Losing it in the Lobby." *This Magazine*, October-November 1986, 14–23.

– *The Colonized Eye: Rethinking the Grierson Legend*. Toronto: Between The Lines, 1988.

Nichols, Robert W. "Interest Groups and the Canadian Broadcasting System." Master's thesis, Carleton University, 1970.

Nicol, John, Albert A. Shea, and G. J. P. Simmins. *Canada's Farm Radio Forum*. Paris: UNESCO, 1954.

O'Brien, John E. "A History of the Canadian Radio League, 1930–36." Ph.D. diss., University of Southern California, Los Angeles, 1964.

O'Connor, James. *The Fiscal Crisis of the State*. New York: St. Martin's Press, 1973.

Offe, Claus. *Contradictions of the Welfare State*. Cambridge, Mass.: MIT Press, 1984.

Ontario. The Confederation of Tomorrow Conference, Toronto, 27–30 November 1967. *Proceedings*. Toronto: Queen's Printer, 1968.

– Legislative Assembly. *Debates*, 17 May 1973.

– Royal Commission on Violence in the Communications Industry. *Report*. Commission chairman was Judy LaMarsh. Toronto: Queen's Printer, 1976.

Ortmark, Åke. "Sweden: Freedom's Boundaries." In *Television and Political Life: Studies in Six European Countries*, edited by Anthony Smith, 142–90. London: Macmillan, 1979.

Osler, Andrew. *No One is Listening: Media Voices from the Regions of Canada*. Background research paper to the *Report of the Committee of Inquiry into the National Broadcasting Service*. Ottawa: CRTC, 1977.

Ostry, Bernard. *The Cultural Connection*. Toronto: McClelland and Stewart, 1978.

Ouimet, Alphonse. "The Communications Revolution and Canadian Sovereignty." In *Gutenberg Two: The New Electronics and Social Change*, edited by David Godfrey and Douglas Parkhill, 131–50. Toronto: Press Porcépic, 1979.

Park, Robert E. *The Crowd and the Public* (translation of *Masse und Publikum*, 1904). In *The Crowd and the Public and Other Essays*, edited by Henry Elsner Jr, 1–81. Chicago: University of Chicago Press, 1972.

– "Natural History of the Newspaper" [1923]; "News as a Form of Knowledge" [1940]; "News and the Power of the Press" [1941]. In *Society*, 89–104; 71–88; 115–25. Glencoe, Ill.: The Free Press, 1955.

Patrick, Lanie. "Global Economy, Global Communications: The Canada-US Free Trade Agreement." In *Communication For and Against Democracy*, edited by Marc Raboy and Peter A. Bruck, 95–108. Montreal: Black Rose Books, 1989.

Payette, Jean. "Etude d'un conflit de travail entre cadres à Radio-Canada." Master's thesis, Université de Montréal, 1967.

Pearson, Lester B. *Mike: The Memoirs of the Right Honourable Lester B. Pearson.* Vol. 3, edited by John A. Munro and Alex I. Inglis. Toronto: University of Toronto Press, 1975.

Peers, Frank W. *The Politics of Canadian Broadcasting, 1920–1951.* Toronto: University of Toronto Press, 1969.

– *The Public Eye: Television and the Politics of Canadian Broadcasting, 1952–1968.* Toronto: University of Toronto Press, 1979.

Pelletier, Gérard. *La Crise d'octobre*. Montreal: Editions du Jour, 1971.

– *Les années d'impatience (1950–1960)*. Montreal: Stanké, 1983.

*Politique Aujourd'hui* New series 7, (November-December 1984): 44–62. Dossier. "Médias: La fin du service public?"

Prang, Margaret. "The Origins of Public Broadcasting in Canada." *Canadian Historical Review* 46, no. 1 (March 1965): 1–31.

Quebec. Commission royale d'enquête sur les problèmes constitutionnels. *Rapport.* Commission chairman was Thomas Tremblay. Quebec City: Province du Québec, 1956.

– "Ce que veut le Québec." Brief submitted by Daniel Johnson to the Constitutional Conference, first meeting, Ottawa, 5–7 February 1968. In *Le gouvernement du Québec et la constitution*, 66–98. Quebec City: Office d'information et de publicité, 1968.

Quebec, Legislative Assembly. *Journaux*, 1929, 1930–31, 1945.

– *Journal des débats*, 1964 through 1968.

Quebec, Ministère des affaires culturelles (MAC). *Pour l'évolution de la politique culturelle*. Prepared by Jean-Paul L'Allier. Quebec City: MAC, 1976.

Quebec, Ministère des communications (MCQ). *Pour une politique québécoise des communications*. Prepared by Jean-Paul L'Allier. Quebec City: MCQ, 1971.

– *Le Québec, Maître d'oeuvre de la politique des communications sur son territoire.* Prepared by Jean-Paul L'Allier. Quebec City: Editeur officiel, 1973.

– *Politique de développement des médias communautaires*. Quebec City: MCQ, 1979.

– *Bâtir l'avenir*. Quebec City: Gouvernement du Québec, 1982.

– *Le Québec et les communications: Un futur simple?* Quebec City: Gouvernement du Québec, 1983.

– *Rapport annuel, 1984–85*. Quebec City: Gouvernement du Québec, 1985.

– *Les réactions du MCQ au rapport Sauvageau-Caplan*. Quebec City: MCQ, 13 April 1987.

Quebec, Ministère d'Etat au Développement culturel. *La politique québécoise du développement culturel.* Prepared by Camille Laurin. Quebec City: Editeur officiel, 1978.

Quebec, National Assembly. *Journal des débats,* 1969 through 1988.

Quebec, Statutes. Loi concernant la radiodiffusion dans cette province. *Statuts du Québec* 1929, c. 31.

- Loi modifiant la Loi concernant la radiodiffusion dans cette province. *Statuts du Québec* 1930–31, c. 35.

- Loi concernant la radio. *Statuts du Québec* 1930–31, c. 36.

- Loi concernant la responsabilité civile en matière de radiodiffusion. *Statuts du Québec* 1930–31, c. 105.

- Loi autorisant la création d'un service de radiodiffusion provinciale. *Statuts du Québec* 1945, c. 56.

- Loi de la Régie des services publics. *Statuts refondus du Québec* 1964, c. 229.

- Loi de l'Office de radio-télédiffusion du Québec. *Statuts du Québec* 1969, c. 17.

- Loi du Ministère des communications. *Statuts du Québec* 1969, c. 65.

- Loi modifiant la Loi de la Régie des services publics. *Statuts du Québec* 1972, c. 56.

- Loi modifiant la Loi du Ministère des communications et d'autres dispositions législatives. *Statuts du Québec* 1972, c. 57.

- Loi modifiant la Loi de l'Office de radio-télédiffusion du Québec. *Statuts du Québec* 1972, c. 58.

- Loi modifiant la Loi de l'Office de radio-télédiffusion du Québec. *Statuts du Québec* 1979, c. 11.

- Loi sur la programmation éducative. *Statuts du Québec* 1979, c. 52.

Quebec Liberal Party. *La politique culturelle du Parti libéral du Québec: Un outil de développement économique et social.* Quebec City: QLP, 1985.

Rabinovitch, Robert. "Communication Policy and Planning in Canada" [1976]. In *Perspectives in Communication Policy and Planning,* edited by Syed A. Rahim and John Middleton, 235–43. Honolulu: East-West Center, 1977.

Raboy, Marc. "La tour infernale: La petite histoire de l'information à Radio-Canada." *Le Temps fou,* April 1981, 18–22.

- "Investigative Journalism in Canada." Unpublished paper, Graduate Program in Communications, McGill University, 1982.

- "Media and Politics in Socialist France." *Media, Culture and Society* 5, nos. 3–4 (July-October 1983): 303–20.

- *Movements and Messages: Media and Radical Politics in Quebec.* Toronto: Between The Lines, 1984.

- "Radical Radio: An Emancipatory Cultural Practice." *Border/lines* 1 (Fall 1984): 28–31.

- "Marcel Masse et le sens de l'histoire." *Le Devoir,* 22 December 1984.

- "Broadcasting Policy and the Public." *Border/lines* 3 (Fall 1985): 14–17.

- "Vers une nouvelle appréciation du public dans le domaine des médias." *Possibles* 9, no. 4 (Summer 1985): 125–32.

- "Possible Range of Publicly-programmed Television Services." Appendix to letter to the Task Force on Broadcasting Policy, 25 October 1985.

– "Public Television, the National Question, and the Preservation of the Canadian State." In *Television in Transition*, edited by Phillip Drummond and Richard Paterson, 64–86. London: BFI Books, 1986.

– "The Public Dimension of Broadcasting: Learning from the Canadian Experience." Paper to the Second International Television Studies Conference, London, UK, 1986.

– "Broadcasting and the Idea of the Public: Learning from the Canadian Experience." Ph.D. diss., McGill University, 1986.

– "Tele-Monopoly Capital: Now Playing in Quebec." *Border/lines* 7–8 (Spring-Summer 1987): 6–7.

– "No Canadianization Without Democratization: The Contradictions of National Policy-Making in the Shadow of the American Empire." Paper to the Canadian Communication Association/International Communication Association joint meetings, Montreal, 1987.

– "Public Broadcasting and the Public Sphere." *Studies in Communication and Information Technology*. Working Paper no. 14, Queen's University, 1987.

– "New Television Services and Cultural Identity in Canada: Two Solitudes in the Era of Multiple Choice." Paper to the 16th congress of the International Association for Mass Communication Research, Barcelona, 1988.

– "Canada's Broadcasting Policy Debate." *Canadian Issues/Thèmes canadiens* 10, no. 6 (1988): 41–54.

– "Two Steps Forward, Three Steps Back: Canadian Broadcasting Policy from Caplan-Sauvageau to Bill C-136." *Canadian Journal of Communication* 14, no. 1 (1989): 70–5.

Raboy, Marc, and Peter A. Bruck, eds. *Communication For and Against Democracy*. Montreal: Black Rose Books, 1989.

*Relations*. "Le Rapport de la Commission Massey." Editorial, July 1951, 169–70.

Rémillard, Gil. *Le fédéralisme canadien: Eléments constitutionnels de formation et d'évolution*. Montreal: Québec-Amérique, 1980.

Réseau québécois d'information sur la communication. *L'Institut canadien d'éducation des adultes et les communications, 1956–1987: bibliographie analytique*. Sainte-Foy, P.Q.: Laval University, 1988.

Richer, Léopold. "Le ministère Bennett et les canadiens-français." *L'Action nationale* 6, no. 1 (September 1935): 42–51.

Richeri, Giuseppe. "Television from Service to Business: European Tendencies and the Italian Case." In *Television in Transition*, edited by Phillip Drummond and Richard Paterson, 21–35. London: BFI Books, 1986.

Rickwood, Roger R. "Canadian Broadcasting Policy and the Private Broadcasters: 1936–1968." Ph.D. diss., University of Toronto, 1976.

Robins, Kevin, and Frank Webster. "Broadcasting Politics: Communications and Consumption." *Screen* 27, nos. 3–4 (May-August 1986): 30–44.

Robinson, Gertrude J. "The Politics of Information and Culture During Canada's

October Crisis." In *Studies in Canadian Communications*, edited by Gertrude J. Robinson and Donald F. Theall. Montreal: Graduate Program in Communications, McGill University, 1975.

Roth, Lorna. "Inuit Media Projects and Northern Communication Policy." In *Communications and the Canadian North*, 42–66. Montreal: Department of Communication Studies, Concordia University, 1983.

Roth, Lorna, and Gail Guthrie Valaskakis. "Aboriginal Broadcasting in Canada: A Case Study in Democratization." In *Communication For and Against Democracy*, edited by Marc Raboy and Peter A. Bruck, 221–34. Montreal: Black Rose Books, 1989.

Roux, Jean-Louis. "Radio-Canada, 1959." In *En grève!* (Coll.), 179–280. Montreal: Editions du Jour, 1963.

Roy, Michel. "La grève des réalisateurs de Radio-Canada." *Relations industrielles* 14, no. 2 (April 1959): 265–76.

Ryan, Claude. "Veut-on faire de Radio-Québec une créature servile de l'exécutif?" Editorial, *Le Devoir*, 12 April 1969.

– "Bouder ou s'accommoder?" Editorial, *Le Devoir*, 17 July 1975.

Salter, Liora. "Two Directions on a One Way Street: Old and New Approaches in Media Analysis in Two Decades." Unpublished paper, Department of Communication, Simon Fraser University, 1979.

– "'Public' and Mass Media in Canada: Dialectics in Innis' Communication Analysis." In *Culture, Communication and Dependency: The Tradition of H. A. Innis*, edited by William H. Melody, Liora Salter and Paul Heyer, 193–207. Norwood, N.J.: Ablex, 1981.

– "The New Communications Environment: A View from Canada." *International Journal* 42 (Spring 1987): 364–94.

– "Reconceptualizing the Public in Public Broadcasting." In *Communication Canada: Issues in Broadcasting and New Technologies*, edited by Rowland Lorimer and Donald Wilson, 232–48. Toronto: Kagan and Woo, 1988.

Salter, Liora, and Peter S. Anderson. *Responsive Broadcasting: A Report on the Mechanisms to Handle Complaints About the Content of Broadcast Programs*. Study prepared for the Department of Communications, Ottawa, 1985.

Sanderson, Samantha, and Rose Potvin. *Adjusting the Image: Women and Canadian Broadcasting*. Report of a National Conference on Canadian Broadcasting Policy, Ottawa, 20–22 March 1987. Vancouver: MediaWatch, 1987.

Saskatchewan. *Cable Television in Saskatchewan*. Presentation to the CRTC, Regina, 9 February 1976. Regina: Queen's Printer, 1976.

Sauvageau, Florian. "De l'urgence d'une réforme en radiodiffusion." *Le Devoir*, 20 September 1988.

Scott, F.R. "La guerre des ondes." *Cité libre* 15 (August 1956): 44–9.

Sénécal, Michel. "Médias communautaires: Etat de marginalité ou marginalité d'Etat?" *Revue internationale d'action communautaire* 6, no. 46 (Fall 1981): 29–42.

Shea, Albert A. *Broadcasting the Canadian Way*. Montreal: Harvest House, 1963.

Siegel, Arthur. "Canadian Newspaper Coverage of the FLQ Crisis: A Study of the Impact of the Press on Politics." Ph.D. diss., McGill University, 1974.

– *A Content Analysis, the CBC: Similarities and Differences in French and English News*. Background research paper to the *Report of the Committee of Inquiry into the National Broadcasting Service*. Ottawa: CRTC, 1977.

Smith, Anthony. *The Shadow in the Cave: The Broadcaster, His Audience and the State*. Urbana, Ill.: University of Illinois Press, 1973.

– "Deregulation, New Technology, Public Service: Vision versus Rhetoric." *Canadian Journal of Communication* 10, no. 4 (Autumn 1984): 1–15.

Smythe, Dallas W. *Dependency Road: Communications, Capitalism, Consciousness, and Canada*. Norwood, N.J.: Ablex, 1981.

– "Radio Deregulation and the Relation of the Private and Public Sectors." *Journal of Communication* 32, no. 1 (Winter 1982): 192–200.

– "New Directions for Critical Communications Research." *Media, Culture and Society* 6, no. 3 (July 1984): 205–17.

Société de radio-télédiffusion du Québec (SRTQ). *Radio-Québec Maintenant*. Montreal: SRTQ, 1985.

Spiller, Frank, and Kim Smiley. "Reflections on the Role and the Future of Broadcasting in the Canadian Society." Background paper prepared for the Conference on the Future of the Canadian Broadcasting System, Canadian Conference of the Arts, Ottawa, 15–18 October 1985.

Spry, Graham. "The Canadian Broadcasting Issue." *Canadian Forum*, April 1931, 246–9.

– "A Case for Nationalized Broadcasting." *Queen's Quarterly* 38 (Winter 1931): 151–69.

– "The Canadian Radio Situation." In *Education on the Air*, edited by Josephine H. Maclatchy. Second yearbook of the Institute for Education by Radio. Columbus, Ohio: Ohio State University Press, 1931.

– "Radio Broadcasting and Aspects of Canadian-American Relations." In *Proceedings of the Conference on Canadian- American Affairs Held at St. Lawrence University, 17–22 July 1935*, edited by Walter W. McLaren, Albert B. Corey, and Reginald G. Trotter, 106–19. Boston: Ginn and Co., 1936.

– "The Canadian Broadcasting Corporation 1936–61." *Canadian Communications* 2, no. 1 (1961): 13–25.

– "The Costs of Canadian Broadcasting." *Queen's Quarterly* 67, no. 4 (Winter 1961): 503–13.

– "The Decline and Fall of Canadian Broadcasting." *Queen's Quarterly* 68, no. 2 (Summer 1961): 213–25.

– "The Origins of Public Broadcasting in Canada: A Comment." *Canadian Historical Review* 46, no. 2 (June 1965): 134–41.

Stark, Frank. "Persuasion, Propaganda, and Public Policy." Paper to the Fourth Annual Conference of the Canadian Communication Association, Vancouver, June 1983.

Starowicz, Mark. "Slow Dissolve: The End of Public Broadcasting." *This Magazine*, April 1985, 4–8 and 32–33.
– "Citizens of Video-America: What Happened to Canadian Television in the Satellite Age?" Paper to a symposium on Television, Entertainment and National Culture: The Canada-US. Dilemma in a Broader Perspective, Quebec City, 1989.
Stewart, Andrew. "Broadcasting in Canada." *Canadian Communications* 1, no. 3 (Winter 1960): 27–37.
Syndicat général des employés de Radio-Québec (SGERQ). *Radio-Québec: Une télévision éducative à réinventer.* Brief to the Quebec National Assembly commission on communications, 12 May 1978. Montreal: SGERQ, 1978.
Tarde, Gabriel. *The Public and the Crowd* (translation of *Le public et la foule*, 1901). In *On Communication and Social Influence*, edited by Terry N. Clark, 277–94. Chicago: University of Chicago Press, 1969.
Taylor, Ian. "Depoliticizing Current Affairs Television: The Nightly Project of *The Journal.*" *Border/lines* 5 (Summer 1986): 14–18.
Thomas, Alan M. "Audience, Market and Public – An Evaluation of Canadian Broadcasting." *Canadian Communications* 1, no. 1 (Summer 1960): 16–47.
Toogood, Alexander F. *Broadcasting in Canada: Aspects of Regulation and Control.* Ottawa: Canadian Association of Broadcasters, 1969.
Tremblay, Gaëtan. "La politique québécoise en matière de communication (1966–1986): 'De l'affirmation autonomiste à la coopération fédérale-provinciale'." *Communication* 9, no. 3 (Summer 1988): 57–87.
Trotter, Bernard. "Canadian Broadcasting Act IV, Scene '67 or Double Talk and the Single System." *Queen's Quarterly* 73, no. 4 (Winter 1966): 461–82.
Trudel, Pierre. "La liberté d'information est menacée." *Le Devoir*, 4 February 1988.
Tuchman, Gaye. *Making News: A Study in the Construction of Reality.* New York: Free Press, 1978.
Tunstall, Jeremy. *Communications Deregulation: The Unleashing of America's Communications Industry.* Oxford: Basil Blackwell, 1986.
UNESCO. International Commission for the Study of Communication Problems. *Many Voices One World.* Commission chairman was Sean MacBride. London: Kogan Page, 1980.
Vincent, Denis. "A Radio-Canada, ça fait 10 ans qu'on menace de mettre la clé dans la porte." *Le 30* 1, no. 4 (March 1977).
Vipond, Mary. "The Nationalist Network: English Canada's Intellectuals and Artists in the 1920s." *Canadian Review of Studies in Nationalism* 7, no. 1 (Spring 1980): 32–52.
Wasko, Janet, and Vincent Mosco, eds. *Democratic Communications in the Information Age.* Toronto: Garamond Press, forthcoming.
Weir, E. Austin. *The Struggle for National Broadcasting in Canada.* Toronto: McClelland and Stewart, 1965.
Wigbold, Herman. "Holland: The Shaky Pillars of Hilversum." In *Television and Political Life: Studies in Six European Countries*, edited by Anthony Smith, 191–231. London: Macmillan, 1979.

Williams, Raymond. "Base and Superstructure in Marxist Cultural Theory." *New Left Review* 82 (November-December 1973): 3–16.

Winsor, Hugh. "Fuss over CBC's news service masks a more important issue." Column, *Globe and Mail*, 1 February 1988.

Woodcock, George. *Strange Bedfellows: The State and the Arts in Canada*. Vancouver: Douglas and McIntyre, 1985.

Woodrow, R. Brian, Kenneth Woodside, Henry Wiseman, and John B. Black. *Conflict over Communications Policy: A Study of Federal-Provincial Relations and Public Policy*. Montreal: C.D. Howe Institute, 1980.

Woodsworth, Anne. *The "Alternative" Press in Canada: A Checklist*. Toronto: University of Toronto Press, 1972.

World Conference on Community-Oriented Radio Broadcasting. *Community-Oriented Radio Broadcasting Throughout the World: Preliminary Appraisal*. Montreal: WCCORB, 1983.

Zolf, Dorothy. "Educational Broadcasting: A Problem of Divided Jurisdiction." *Canadian Journal of Communication* 12, no. 2 (Winter 1987): 21–49.

# Index